I0754465

AGRICULTURE IN THE OLDEN TIME.

[Santa Barbara Mission, Established A. D. 1786.]

THE

PATRONS OF HUSBANDRY

ON THE

PACIFIC COAST.

BEING A COMPLETE HISTORY OF THE ORIGIN, CONDITION AND PROGRESS OF AGRICULTURE IN DIFFERENT PARTS OF THE WORLD; OF THE ORIGIN AND GROWTH OF THE ORDER OF PATRONS, WITH A GENERAL AND SPECIAL GRANGE DIRECTORY, AND FULL LIST OF CHARTER MEMBERS OF THE SUBORDINATE GRANGES OF CALIFORNIA.

ALSO, OF THE FOES OF THE FARMERS, OR MONOPOLIES OF LAND, WATER, TRANSPORTATION AND EDUCATION; OF A PROTECTIVE TARIFF, CURRENCY AND BANKING.

BY

EZRA S. CARR, M. D., LL. D.,

Late Professor of Agriculture in the University of California, and Past Master of Temescal Grange.

SAN FRANCISCO:

A. L. BANCROFT AND COMPANY,

PUBLISHERS, BOOKSELLERS AND STATIONERS.

1875.

TO THE

HUSBANDMEN, MATRONS AND TEACHERS

OF THE

PACIFIC COAST,

AND ALL WHO CO-OPERATE WITH THEM IN ITS INDUSTRIAL, SOCIAL AND INTELLECTUAL DEVELOPMENT,

THIS VOLUME IS RESPECTFULLY DEDICATED.

PREFACE.

To present in a compact and readily accessible form the annals of the farmers' movement in California, with a summary of the advantages thus far secured by combination and coöperation, was the primary object of this work. In addition, I have thought it desirable to show the general relations of agriculture to human progress; to give the results of recent official investigations into railroad affairs, and to treat of some other questions of general public interest, by summarizing important and recent reports not generally accessible to Patrons.

Again, I know of no single work in which the statistical information which farmers so often need for reference can be obtained. I have endeavored to meet this want, in the discussions of the various subjects to which such information appropriately belongs.

As the work grew upon my hands, I have found that the presentation of my subject involved a constant reference to authorities. As far as possible, therefore, I have allowed each witness to speak for himself, to the exclusion of all claims to originality on my own part. I am greatly indebted to able writers, Professor Perry, President Anderson, Henry George, Hon. M. M. Estee and others, who have placed their valuable papers at my disposal, and I only regret that want of space has made it necessary for me to exclude any portion of them.

The second chapter, defining the "office of Agriculture in the Social Economy," is a condensation of the instruction in Political Economy, given more than twenty years ago, to college classes, by the late John H. Lathrop, LL. D., first President of the Universities of Missouri and Wisconsin. In the chapter on "Agriculture in the Public Schools," it will be observed that the agitation of this question is not a recent thing in agricultural bodies. The Grange has done little more than to organize the public sentiment of farmers for the effective exercise of their legitimate powers. Its progress is no marvel to those who have been in sympathy with the working classes of the country, who understand their needs, and are ready to lend a hand in removing their burdens.

Great care has been taken to insure correctness in the statistical part of the work, and to omit nothing of importance in the documentary history of the State Grange. The names of the charter members, having been copied from the original dispensations, where the signatures are not unfrequently nearly illegible, it has been impossible to entirely avoid orthographical mistakes. The attempt to preserve a complete record of the founders of Subordinate Granges, will, we trust, excuse a few unavoidable errors in its execution.

Valuable assistance has been rendered by the officers of the State Grange, and especially by W. H. Baxter, its Worthy Secretary; also by the officers and agents of the various business associations. To Mr. Edward Vischer, of San Francisco, who has kindly furnished the rural illustrations from his own admirable sketches of California life and scenery; to the editors of the "Rural Press," and other agricultural and local journals, I am under many obligations.

E. S. C.

OAKLAND, August 1st, 1875.

CONTENTS.

PART FIRST.

Relation of Agriculture to Progress.

CHAPTER I.

ORGANIZATION OF LABOR.

PAGE.

CHAPTER II.

THE OFFICE OF AGRICULTURE IN THE SOCIAL ECONOMY.

CHAPTER III.

AGRICULTURE IN THE ANCIENT WORLD.

CHAPTER IV.

AGRICULTURE IN MODERN EUROPE.

PAGE.

CHAPTER XXIII.

MANAGEMENT OF RAILROADS IN OPERATION.

CHAPTER XXIV.

RAILROADS IN CALIFORNIA.

CHAPTER XXV.

AGRICULTURAL EDUCATION IN THE PUBLIC SCHOOLS.

CHAPTER XXVI.

HIGHER AGRICULTURAL EDUCATION.

CHAPTER XXVII.

THE INDUSTRIAL EDUCATION OF WOMEN.

CHAPTER XXVIII.

PAPER MONEY AND A PROTECTIVE TARIFF.

AUTHORS QUOTED.

Adams, D. W., W. M. National Grange.
Alexander, Gen. B.
Anderson, Hon. M. W.
Anderson, J. A., President Kansas Agricultural College.
Arnold, L. D., American Dairyman's Association.

Bidwell, Hon. John.
Brereton, Hon. R. M.

Carpenter, S. H., Professor Wisconsin University.
Carr, Dr. E. S.
Carr, Mrs. Jeanne C.
Cole, Hon. Cornelius.

Davidson, Professor George, United States Irrigation Commissioner.
Dodge, J. R., United States Statistician, Department of Agriculture.
Dewey, A. T., Pacific Rural Press.

Eaton, Gen. John, United States Bureau of Education.
Estee, Hon. M. M.
Emerson, Ralph Waldo.

Felton, C. C., President Harvard College.
Flint, Chas. L., Secretary Massachusetts Agricultural Society.
Flagg, W. C. President Illinois Farmers' Association.

Garretson, N. W., General Deputy, National Grange.
George, Henry, Editor of San Francisco Evening Post.

Hallett, Hon. Edwin.
Hamilton, J. M., W. M. California State Grange.
Hoyt, J. W., United States Commissioner to Paris and Vienna Expositions.
Higby, Hon. A., Chairman of Legislative Committee on Education in California.
Hittell, Hon. John S.
Hyatt, Hon. T. Hart.

Lathrop, J. H., "Chancellor" University of Wisconsin.

McKune, Hon. J.
Mendell, Col. G. H., United States Irrigation Commissioner.
Moore, Mrs. J. P.
Mill, J. Stuart.

Nordhoff, Charles, Author of "Communistic Societies in U. S.," etc., etc.
Northrup, Hon. B. G., Superintendent of Schools, Connecticut.

PART FIRST.

RELATION OF AGRICULTURE TO PROGRESS.

CHAPTER I.

ORGANIZATION OF LABOR.

"Order is the condition of all progress; progress is the object of order. It is rational to look at the evolution of society from a historical stand-point."—*Auguste Comte.*

THE MASONIC FRATERNITY—GUILDS—MOVEMENTS OF LABOR IN THE PRESENT CENTURY—THE SPIRIT OF INDUSTRY CONSTRUCTIVE—WHAT EQUALITY IS—HOW EDUCATION PROMOTES EQUALITY—SELF LOVE VS. SOCIAL FEELING—MR. SEWARD'S OPINION—ALL GREAT MOVEMENTS HISTORICAL AS WELL AS PROGRESSIVE.

THE history of the Masonic Fraternity is that of the first attempt of labor to elevate itself by organization. Originally consisting of a simple association of practical builders, who traveled from place to place in pursuance of their calling; they gave the name of lodges to their temporary camps, and bound themselves by the solemnities of an oath and ritual to coöperation and fellowship. The advantages thus gained for defense were equally powerful for improvement—the skill of each became a tangible benefit to all; the offices were elective, and conferred honor upon the most skillful and capable. From this simple beginning, a purely industrial and social order was not only enabled to maintain and extend itself through the most turbulent periods of European history, but to become a teacher of democratic and religious principles, and to exercise in many cases a controlling influence upon the policy of governments. In process of time, actual participation in a particular calling was no longer required, a symbolic representation of the underlying truths and principles of the order, sufficing to preserve its unity and usefulness.

During the middle ages, other classes of laborers organized into *guilds*, and wrought out their emancipation from the condition of serfs to that of freemen. In all these movements, those mechanic arts which were nearest to the necessities imposed by war, took precedence. Next in order were those which ministered most directly to the luxury and vanity of kings and nobles. It was reserved for the latest and most Christian era to witness the uprising of the agricultural class to a true understanding of its office in the social economy, of its disabilities, and their proper remedy.

The movement which has been so nearly simultaneous in England and America, finds its explanation in conditions and dangers almost identical in their nature and effects, though differing in many important particulars. In England, for instance, a *monopoly of land*, without suffrage, has degraded the farm laborer to a state of helplessness, for which emigration seems the only remedy. In America, though land is abundant and cheap, and suffrage universal, the centralization of the power of capital has created other monopolies, which, having obtained a controlling influence in the government, are equally subversive of the interests of the people. The English farm laborer tills another man's land at starvation wages; the American farmer tills his own at starvation prices, while the rich are growing richer, and the poor poorer, and the separation of society into antagonistic classes, is becoming more and more complete.

No single individual, or class of mankind, has intentionally set itself to construct an oppressive system; these are evil growths in the rank soil of human selfishness. The responsibility of their existence should be shared even by those who suffer from them, lacking the individuality and self-respect to maintain the position of freemen. It is probably not more just to blame capital for the exclusive attention it pays to its own interests, than to blame labor for neglecting to claim the consideration that is due to its influence upon the public welfare.

During all the vicissitudes through which industry has passed, there have been reasons why the masses of the people could not look upon the accumulation of capital as the first step in its own progress. They had too often experienced its oppressive power to appreciate its constructive value; they have not always remembered that a large capital has the same inviolable character as a small one; that the banker's millions (if they are savings), are as sacred as the peasant's cow and miner's pick. Edward About, in his admirable papers to workingmen, says: "To lay violent hands upon capital is to attack the incarnation of labor, and it is as monstrous to strip a man of his savings as to reduce him to slavery. Slavery is the confiscation of potential labor, the other crime would confiscate labor performed."

This whole subject may be put in a nutshell. All men set out in life with more or less capital, the gift of nature. To that is added, in proportions not more varied than are the natural faculties of men, a share in the savings of those who have gone before. Capital, therefore, as we stand related to it to-day, is the saving of either the product of nature or of labor.

Education, which adds so much to every man's natural capital of intellectual faculty, and gives him the power to call it into service at any time, also enables him to take a greater share in the accumulation of others. It is the great equalizer of human conditions. It is both a power and a preparation for the exercise of power. The ignorance, the partial and defective education of laboring men, whether farmers or mechanics, is the most serious drawback to their progress; and from whatever monopolies they suffer, that of education is the worst.

Hitherto, the superior training and culture of the aristocratic and professional classes have given them preponderance in government; they have, naturally enough, made laws to suit their own interests.

It makes little difference whether we live under a tyranny which denies us rights, or one which monopolizes privilege. The division of men into classes has been maintained by the inequalties of intellectual condition. They must necessarily disappear; an equal and just distribution of the good things created by labor, must necessarily arise whenever labor is intelligent enough to create its own safeguards.

Self-love is still so much stronger than social feeling in the human breast, that no man can safely entrust the irresponsible guardianship of his well-being to another. This is as true of classes as of individuals. Social progress, therefore, depends upon a true equality; a true reciprocity.

Said William H. Seward: "Free labor has at last apprehended

its rights, its interests, its powers and its destiny, and is learning how to organize itself in America." The final organization is far in the future; the germ of it lay far back in the past. No great constructive movement can originate which is not historical as well as progressive in its spirit; it must otherwise limit itself to temporary conditions, and a few generations. In order that we may rightly understand the work of our noble order, the Patrons of Husbandry, we need to examine the economy of civilized society, and the relations of agriculture to civilization.

CHAPTER II.

THE OFFICE OF AGRICULTURE IN THE SOCIAL ECONOMY.

"The hand is almost valueless at one end of the arm if there be not a brain at the other end."—*Horace Mann.*

Man and Nature—Agriculture the Foundation of Industry—Raw Materials—First steps toward Manufactures—Civilization regards all the Processes of Equal Value—The Social Body, its Different Parts and Functions—How Division of Labor Increases Production—How it Begets Exchange or Commerce—Commerce a Charge upon Agriculture; Magnitude of the Tax—How this Enriches the Farmer—Money as a Commercial Agent—Office of the Railroad and of Money to Cheapen Exchange—Relations of Agriculture to the Professions: To the Growth of Towns: To Science.

In the beginning, man was alone with nature. Without arts, without capital, without implements, he took his sustenance from the bosom of the earth, as the common mother of the race. It was his destiny not only to share the spontaneous productions of nature with his fellow animals, but to search out the physical elements and determine their capabilities; to make the needful combinations—to bring into action their productive powers; not only to supply the animal wants, and minister to the pleasure of his organic nature, but to render them tributary to his intellectual, moral and social development, and his ultimate spiritual elevation and well being.

In the discharge of this great duty, every avocation of man has its work to perform. It is the province of agriculture to begin the process by the tilling of the ground, as the term imports, by stimulating and guiding the productive energies of the physical elements to results infinitely transcending, in quantity and quality, the yield of the same elements, unaided by human agency.

The gross results of agriculture constitute what is called Raw Material, because, with the exception of fruits and green vegetables, material products do not come from the hand of the agriculturist prepared for human use. They are gross and incomplete; the proper material which the arts are to take and fashion into forms of utility and beauty, adapted to the satisfaction of the physical wants, and the gratification of the tastes of men.

In the three great classes of our physical wants,—food, clothing and shelter,—how few are the commodities which come from the agriculturist ready for the consumer. Men want not wheat, but bread; therefore the crop, as raw material, must be subjected to the manufacturing processes of the miller and baker. Men want not wool, but clothes; therefore the fleece must undergo successive changes in the hands of the carder, the spinner, the weaver, the fuller and the dyer, before it reappears in the form of cloth. And what does the cloth avail, till the tailor, with his divine art, finishes—the man? So men want not timber and stone, but houses, barns, ships, temples of education and temples of religion; and here again the raw material must be subjected to numberless changes to fit it for the purposes of masonry and architecture. It is obvious, therefore, that there is nothing in the hands of the artisan, the merchant or the manufacturer, that has not previously been in the hands of the farmer. Agriculture thus lies at the foundation of the economical structure of society.

But too much of relative dignity and importance must not be assumed by agriculture in consequence of this distinction. To him who enjoys the final product, the initial, the medial, and the finishing process, are all equally important. It is true, that without the raw material furnished by the agriculturist, the occupation of the artisan, merchant and manufacturer is gone forever. But without the labors of these, what would be the value of the raw material? Would it be produced at all? It is true, that the industrial structure rests upon agriculture, as the foundation. But what is the value of a foundation, and would it be laid at all, if no superstructure were to be built upon it?

It is no disparagement to agriculture that it cannot say to manufacture, "I have no need of thee," or to the mechanic arts, "I have no need of thee." It is no disparagement to all or any of these that they cannot say to commerce, "we have no need of you." It ennobles all these, that none of them any more than the professions, can say to education "we have no need of thee." As in the natural body, there is a divine harmony running through the whole structure of the body economical. One member cannot suffer without all the other members suffer with it.

In all civilized countries the *division of labor and of employments* corresponds to the degree of civilization which there prevails. In the production of material wealth in its thousand departments, agriculture, mechanic arts and manufactures, this division of labor results in a vast increase of every kind of production, through time and labor saved, and the means furnished for intellectual, moral, and social improvement.

But again, the division further begets the need of Exchange, and of an extended system of exchanges, for the mutual benefit of the producers; and owing to the different and sometimes distant localities of production, transportation is also necessary. To effect the latter with economy and dispatch, the accumulation and combination of capital has been required.

The true principle of the division of labor is, that inasmuch as all produced values are the results of agriculture and manufactures, commerce ought to take to itself whatever share is on an average a fair remuneration for its service, leaving in the hands of producers a balance far exceeding in amount and value their whole production, providing they were obliged to effect transportion and exchanges themselves. Although the setting up of the mercantile class, reacts upon production, enlarging its volume, and enriching the producers themselves; still, it is an ultimate and fixed fact, which ought to be distinctly understood, that commerce is a charge upon agriculture and manufacture—that the whole cost of commercial machinery must withdraw just so much of the gross value produced, from the hands of the producer. If the process be clumsily and expensively performed, he suffers, and is less prosperous. The farmer, therefore, is interested in every improvement of the commercial process which will diminish the expenses of transportation and exchange, as truly as in the improvements in manufacture or in implements, which will diminish the cost of production.

When we look at the vastness and complication of the machinery of commerce, by land and by sea; and the enormous expense of maintaining it, we may well wonder at the miracle, that the shoulders of agriculture and manufacture are broad enough to sustain, uncrushed and unbent, the whole burden of the charge.

And yet they do sustain it. Not a dollar goes into the treasury of these improvements which is not taken from the produced values of those who are ultimately the mutual parties interested in the exchange, and in the consumption of the commodities transported. The gross values of the producer are diminished, aye, taxed, if you please, to this amount,—and the farmer pays his portion of the tax. But is he oppressed by it? Not unless the process has been fraudulent, because:

1st. In consequence of a reduction in the cost of exchange which commerce secures, his produce is worth more on his farm.

2d. The merchandise which he needs costs less for the same reason.

3d. Because the commercial agency takes away a smaller portion of his produced values, leaving a larger balance in his hands; he is affected precisely as if his land had become more productive; therefore his real estate rises in value.

We will now look at *money as a commercial agent.* Gold and silver coin, embodying the two qualities of universal receivability and divisibility at will, has been adopted by common consent and the action of civil governments as the money of the commercial world, and is as distinctly a part of the machinery of commerce, as the railroad or steamboat.

It is the office of the railroad to facilitate and cheapen transportation, and this constitutes its whole value as a railroad; so it is the office of coined money to facilitate and cheapen exchanges, and this constitutes its whole value as money.

Were barter entirely convenient and economical, money would have no office to perform,—no necessity would have suggested its creation—its presence in the business of the world would be without meaning; it would never have been thought of.

When we consider what an enormous sum of money the exchanges of this country require; that the annual charge for this expensive commercial agent is the yearly interest of this sum, with the addition of the annual cost of the coinage, the loss by the wear and tear, by shipwreck and otherwise, we wonder again, are the shoulders of agriculture and manufacture broad enough to sustain the burden of this charge?

They do sustain it, with incalculable advantage and profit to the producer. For the simple reason that money, although itself an expensive agent, so facilitates and cheapens exchanges, as to relieve agriculture and manufacture from the far greater cost of making these same exchanges by the time and labor consuming processes of barter.

We have seen that *agriculture is interested in the prosperity and improvement of all mechanical and manufacturing interests; that agriculture in common with the arts is interested in the prosperity of commerce.*

Agriculture, in common with manufacture and commerce, is interested in the prosperity of the professions. Without the agency of these; without the sound social conditions of HEALTH, ORDER and MORALITY, production would be at an end. So much for the economic argument. Above all, it is interested in that agency which terminates not on the physical products, nor yet directly on social conditions, but on the *man* himself. The raw material of the educator is the young mind, the unformed intellect of the community. This resulting product is the finished man, prepared by varied knowledge and discipline, and by special training, to act well his part as agriculturist, artisan, merchant, capitalist, physician, lawyer, or teacher; useful in the civil state, and in those more exalted relations which concern him as a member of the human family, and a subject of the universal empire of God.

The educator, whether of the school or the press, stands at the point of power, and applies the moving force to the mechanism of human society. His is the highest office in the social economy.

Agriculture is interested in the prosperity and growth of large towns. A town or city is a part of the business machinery of the country. In some agricultural communities there has sprung up a narrow jealousy of the town, grudging its prosperity, tainting legislation by unequal taxation, and a denial of the facilities necessary to healthy development. In the large town the principle of competition is the most active, and furnishes the best check upon monopoly. The interests of town and country are mutual and harmonious.

Lastly, agriculture is interested in the improvement and perfection *of its own processes, in the discoveries of science and their applications,* in that close union of the intellect of the state with its productive arm, which will finally do away with social distinctions, and leave each individual to stand on his personal merit as a part of the social system.

CHAPTER III.

AGRICULTURE IN THE ANCIENT WORLD.

"It began to be a question whether Egypt was going to live much longer, when she paid more attention to embalming her grandfathers than she did to inspiring her children."

Civilization a Relative Term—Wealth—Wild Wheat and Wild Rice—The Date—Millet—Egyptian Agriculture and Horticulture—Flax Culture—Granaries Models of our Elevators—Condition of the People—China—Confucius a Teacher of Agricultural Thrift—How Silk Culture has been Promoted—Implements—Size of Farms—Wages—Japan compared with Great Britain—Wheat Culture—Rural Life in Greece—Xenophon a Farmer—Hesiod's "Works and Days"—Public Gardens—Decay—Aristotle the Father of a Rational Polity—Slavery—Rome—Patricians and Plebeians—Size of Farms—Common Pasture—Tenants—Cato's Description of a Steward—The Rome of To-Day.

A complete history of agriculture has yet to be written. From the traditions of different nations, their works of art, and their literatures, we find abundant evidence that, however splendid the superstructure, the civilization of every nation has rested where it does to-day, upon the toil of millions for their daily bread—the satisfaction of the common wants of humanity.

Whatever may afterward be added to improve, adorn and elevate the social or spiritual condition of man, his relation to the soil remains unchanged; there is the basis of his prosperity. It was given to him "for usufruct alone," not for consumption, and still less for profligate waste. Wherever the obligation to maintain the harmonious balance between organic and inorganic nature has been met, there we find the oldest and most permanent civilizations. Wherever the selfish pursuit of profit, the vile principle "After us the Deluge," has been the ruling motive, the deluge has followed, leaving in its wake a human deterioration which corresponds with the destruction of virgin lands. From the old center and cradle of the race we may trace man as he flies from the arena of his own actions, in Palestine, in Greece, in Italy, in the north of Africa and Spain, leaving behind him soils rendered infertile through the demolition of forests, "thorns and thistles," or the depauperated forms of once noble races of plants. Having reached the western limit, the tide of emigration must ere long return upon its course, to restore and recover the wastes it has created. Indigenous species of animals and plants needlessly extirpated, must be replaced by alien forms, and the balance re-adjusted as far as a better knowledge of the laws of animal and vegetable life will make such readjustment possible.

Civilization is a relative term. It does not consist in the multiplication or modes of supply of the artificial wants of mankind; it is the development of social order in place of individual independence and savage lawlessness. It is the improvement of the mass through the perfection of its units. This is a common sense view of the subject, and common sense, as Mr. Guizot says, "is the genius of mankind."

Civilization, therefore, determined by the character of the units of the social order, is susceptible of continual progress, and the highest perfection. But it is dependent upon physical agents, chiefly upon climate and soil, which determine the most important conditions of human welfare.

The first step of progress is the *accumulation of wealth*, which in all regions of the earth is created by labor. The moment man produces more than he consumes, the law of distribution comes into play and we see a movement toward an organization of industry. It does not depend upon race. The same Mongolian and Tartar tribes which, wandering over the steppes and barren lands of Central Asia, never emerge from the rudest condition of pastoral life, because they never accumulate; have risen to the highest civilization whenever they have broken through the mountain ranges and descended into more fertile regions. The wild Arab, whom we know best as the Bedouin of the desert, transplanted to Persia or Spain, left noble architectures behind him, and made valuable contributions to literature and science.

Even the Indian races of the new world, wherever nature permitted the accumulation of the wealth derived from a genial climate and fertile soil, have left, as in Mexico and in Peru, splendid monuments of their advancement in the arts of life. Everywhere the basis is the same; it was rice and wheat culture on one continent, maize on the other.

How many ages were consumed in impressing the stamp of utility upon the products of wild nature it is impossible to tell. Some of the most useful food plants are found in a wild state. Wheat in upper Egypt and the hill country of India; rice of excellent quality, though not identical in species, abounds in the North American lakes.

But the wild wheat is a thin and comparatively miserable

seed, unfit for bread, and the wild rice, though productive, is black and coarse compared with its cultivated kindred. The notable proportion of flesh-producing material contained in wheat represents to us the flesh and blood of thousands of generations who have persisted in bringing it to its present perfection.

As with wheat and rice, so all the varied products of our gardens and fields are trophies of man's conquest over wild nature, for to whatever he bring his intelligence, he seems to impart an added beauty and utility. A wild plant or animal is only such in its relations to him, its separation, so to speak, from his uses; and the nearer animal life approaches to man in the scale of power and intelligence, the more capable it seems of entering into his service.

This process of assimilation began in the morning of time, and has left no trace of its earlier steps. The oldest agricultural records are seen upon the Egyptian monuments, where we find the foodful date tree everywhere represented. The banks of the Tigris, Euphrates and the Nile were doubtless the scene of the earliest attempts at agricultural labors in propagating and increasing the fertility of this tree, upon which both men and animals depended for sustenance. It is a singular fact that the date requires artificial impregnation. This fact was early discovered, and led to a simple festival known to this day as the marriage of the palm, in which not only the peasants, but camels, asses, and even fowls and dogs participate. The exuberance of vegetable life in the valley of the Nile, where a favorable temperature is constant, and where inexhaustible fertility is maintained by the periodical distribution of new materials, accounts for the speed with which wealth was created and population increased. Four hundred date palms may be grown on one and three quarters acres of land, each bearing a hundred pounds of fruit. From the rich soil of the river the lotus furnished a nourishing seed or bean, from which the bread of the common people was made. Later the dhourra, or millet, which now yields to the labor of upper Egypt a return of two hundred and forty fold, served the same purpose. All these plants and their modes of culture are described in pictures and hieroglyphics which seem to defy the effacing finger of time.

We also find upon the Egyptian monuments the earliest records of the application of machinery to the cultivation of the soil. We see the plow represented, with handles to guide it, yoked oxen harrowing in the grain, laborers hackling it upon an implement set with sharp teeth, and herdsmen, distinguished from other laborers by their dress, bringing in sheep and wool. In the tomb of Menophres at Saccara, two bulls are represented. The symbolic worship of the bull gave a peculiar sanctity to bovine animals.

Not only does picture-writing reveal the condition of the art of agriculture, but it gives us a glimpse of the social state. In a tomb at Erlethya we see a proprietor inspecting his farm. Before him goes a writer with implements; obsequious servants follow with stool and slippers, his bow and quiver. His dress shows what manner of man he was; he wears a collar and robe, and holds in his hand both scepter and staff. Two herdsmen bring in cattle, one prostrates himself, while the other is in the attitude of a person reporting the condition of the flocks. Upon the tablet is written, "cattle, 122; rams, 300; goats, 1,300; swine, 1,500." On another tomb 944 sheep are mentioned as the property of the occupant.

In the Scriptures we find an account of the first *grain monopoly*, viz: that of Joseph, who, with Pharaoh, created a corner in wheat.

Horticulture in all its departments was also carried to great perfection; the variety of gourds, cucumbers, melons, fruits and vines which added to the luxury of a vast population, is most surprising. Flax was grown in abundance, and the modes of its preparation for the spinner were identical with those now used. Their granaries, of which millions lined the banks of the Nile, are the models of the grain elevators of our own time.

But in all this creation of utilities man himself was left out of the account. What remain to us as monuments of a civilization, falsely so called, are but stupendous and convincing proofs of a revolting despotism, based upon cruelty and upheld by superstition. "The very resources which the people had created were turned against themselves." The condition of the captive Israelites was that of the toiling millions upon both hemispheres, where the accumulation of wealth without its dispersion secured to the upper classes a monopoly of the very sources of power. National improvements were made which are the wonder of modern times, but the masses of the people received no benefit from them. The reckless prodigality with which labor was expended in works of doubtful utility showed the esteem in which it was held. A man was of as little account to the builders of the Pyramids as is the reef-making polyp to the inhabitant of the coral islands.

What was true of Egypt was equally true of India, of Mexico and Peru; wherever the separation of a nation into castes divided society against itself, and planted the seeds of its dissolution in the ignorance of the masses of the people.

The notable exception which China furnishes to other ancient nations, is due to the fact that centuries ago she began to organize and practically develop the national intellect. She has thus, to a considerable degree, obviated the evils of caste, created a motive for industry and thrift, and maintained herself in permanent prosperity, while other nationalities have melted away.

China owes her immense population and wealth to the most thrifty and skillful agriculture practiced on the face of the earth, except in Japan and Holland. Shoo-Ming, the primeval farmer, who first substituted grain for raw meat, and the Emperor Wanti, who took the plow into his own hand and originated one of the great festivals of the nation, are more highly honored than those monarchs who aggrandized the Empire by the conquest of new peoples. One of their Sagas, "Keep your lands clean, manure them richly, make your fields resemble a garden," though it has a modern sound to us, is of great antiquity. Scarcely any other country exhibits such practical obedience to the teachings of its prophets as China gives to those of Confucius, whose laws regulating labor are still carried into effect by the government. As the government, *i. e.*, the Emperor, is the universal owner of land, the only security the laborer enjoys with respect to its possession is the perfection of its culture; for, though the law allows him to be dispossessed at pleasure, custom continues it in the same family for many generations.

There is sound statesmanship in the proclamation of Wan Choo Tung, Commissioner of Revenue of the Nan Kiang provinces, in the year 1845, who desired to introduce the silk culture into his district. After a somewhat exhaustive lecture on the advantages of this industry, he commands "all our officers to assemble the village gentry and elders, and let them admonish the people and lay down the best rules, and let the same be published with descriptive plates. Let the father instruct his child, the husband his wife, then shall we see men at the plow, and women at the loom; no laborer will be unemployed, and no resource of the soil be lost." Still higher patronage is given to this culture by the Imperial example. The Empress must make silk-weaving one of her occupations, and to her is committed the homage due to the god of the silk-worm.

Long before the era of European civilization, China appears to have understood the true relations of agriculture and the mechanic arts. The division of labor led to wonderful results in the perfection of manufactures and the extension of commerce.

Marco Polo tells us that the Chinese have used paper money since the year 119 B. C. We know they had established banks, and conducted financial operations by promissory notes and bills of exchange, at an early period.

Every practicable spot in China is devoted to tillage, which is mostly accomplished by hand labor. Implements are few, light and simple in construction. The *le* or plow is of wood, with an iron point, and is drawn by a single buffalo. Only the edge of the hoe is of iron; the harrow has teeth thickly set, and ten inches long, an excellent pulverizer. The bamboo rake, used for harvesting, gleaning, gathering scraps of manure, may be said never to leave the hands of the Chinese farmer. The bill hook or leen is another instrument, serving all the purposes of pruning-knife, scythe and sickle.

Six or eight acres is a large farm. Divided by belts or lines of carefully tended grass, instead of fences, these garden farms present a finished picture of the highest cultivation. Two and even four crops are obtained yearly from the same ground by alternating grain and vegetables. Liquid manure is freely used; ashes, oil cake, night soil, lime from bones and oyster shells, even human hair from the barbers is carefully saved.

The wages of the lowest description of laborers averages about sixty cash, (30 cents) per month, and the cost of maintenance is from a dollar to a dollar and a half. Artisans, such as carpenters and blacksmiths, receive five dollars a month, with a corresponding increase in the cost of maintenance.

In the year of 1013 of our era, Tchin-Tsoung published the census of the industrial population, and reported 21,966,965 engaged in agricultural pursuits, not including women or young people under twenty-one years of age. In the year 1732 the imperial taxes were removed from the tenants of farms and placed upon the larger proprietors; and for the further encouragement of a class of such vital importance to the empire, it was decreed that the governor of every city or village of a certain number of inhabitants should send to the court the name of the most successful farmer, distinguished for good conduct and the good will of his neighbors, for frugality, and freedom from excesses.

This wise and diligent agriculturist was thereupon raised to the dignity of a mandarin of the eighth order by letters patent. He might visit the governor, sit down in his presence and drink tea with him. Respected for the remainder of his days, he should receive the honorable funeral of a mandarin on his decease; and while his name was written on the tablets of his ancestors, it would be cherished by the government as of one who had rendered the highest service to his country.

Of all countries, Japan is the most remarkable for the development of her agricultural resources. There the agricultural interest has been protected by the most enlightened conduct toward the producing classes, who stand next in rank to the defenders of the State. A very interesting paper on this subject, contributed by Hon. Horace Capron to the report of the Department of Agriculture for 1873, shows that even in wheat culture we have much to learn from the large experience of this thrifty and intelligent people. The well-known practice of the Japanese and Chinese in dwarfing plants, throwing their strength into fruit or flowers, at the expense of wood or leaves, is applied to wheat, thus shortening and thickening the straw, increasing the size of the heads, and rendering it less liable to lodge.

Japan is far too tempting a subject to be more than touched upon here. If "China is old, and immovably conservative," Japan, not younger in years, but in the spirit which welcomes new truths in science and new applications of these to the arts of life, is vigorous with an eternal youth.

In Japan we have a stable civilization based upon absolutism, imperiled by the existence of caste, isolated for unknown centuries from intercourse with other countries, yet maintaining itself within narrow limits by an almost universal, practical education, and the dignity accorded to the pursuit of agriculture. The organization of the national intellect is as complete, and far more rational than that of China. That government may be considered as having builded "better than it knew" which discriminated in favor of the agriculturists in respect to educational privileges; for these classes are necessarily the most averse to changes in government. Political disturbances and agitations, like war, are a constant threat to the prosperity of the farmer, and to him, sooner than the representative of any other class, may new ideas be intrusted with safety to the nation.

Japan gives us the highest example of national thrift, if the density of population in proportion to extent and original excellence of territory is the test. The surface is broken by ranges of mountains, the coast by bays and inlets which render navigation dangerous, and the variations of temperature are excessive. Yet she feeds, clothes, shelters and instructs a larger population than that of Great Britain. The perfection of culture which has enabled her to accomplish this, unassisted by foreign commerce, must be studied in detail to be understood. She has done it mainly by the most wonderful economy of fertilizing materials, and the preservation of her forests.

Rural life in Greece is presented in a charming book which has woven the facts of the nation's life into a prose poem. President Felton says: "If the Greeks were preëminently a nation of poets and artists, they were no less preëminently a nation of farmers." Here for the first time we find the rural home. The pictures which Homer gives of the scenes of rustic toil are fresh and enchanting as those in the pages of Whittier. Nor were the Hellenes unlike our New England forefathers in the virtues of thrift and temperance, in their proverbial philosophy, the wit which goes "like bullet to its mark," or their weather-wisdom. Like the American Indian, they knew the time of day by the turning of leaves and the opening and shutting of flowers. The charm of Homer to the English mind is in the familiarity of scenes which are depicted in his immortal lines. The Greek mind absorbed beauty as the Greek body took in health and wholeness (another word for holiness) from the earth it loved. "The love of rural life was one of the deepest passions of the Grecian heart, beyond the realm of Arcadia, real or ideal." Through the whole compass of Greek literature the sights and sounds of the country—the murmuring of the bees, the rising sun smiting the earth with his shafts, the rich meadows, the cattle feeding in the pastures—furnish images on which the city poets delight to dwell, and share with the sea the thoughts that move harmonious numbers. The plains of Attica were covered with rural homes; the country was full of little sanctuaries for the rural deities, nymphs, and others who frequented them.

In the Greek classics we not only find how much they knew of agriculture, but how little we have improved upon their knowledge. They knew the virtues of guano, fish and sea-weed in the corn fields; that land recovered its strength by lying fallow; that hay ricks might become heated and burn up. Though the grain was trodden out by cattle or horses on the threshing floor, they had invented the flail, and a winnowing machine; and well they knew the value of the potent juice of those golden or purple clusters which grew on every tree and sunny wall. They trained their grapes from tree to tree, making lofty arches, beneath which the breezes could freely play, abundant currents of pure air being regarded as no less essential to the perfect maturing of the grape than constant sunshine. The art of preserving the grape itself for the use of the table, either in a fresh state, or as raisins, was everywhere practiced.

The richest agricultural and horticultural contributions have come down to us from the master minds of Greece. They drew their inspiration directly from nature herself, and not from what some earlier writer had said about nature. The pupil of Socrates, the leader of the immortal retreat of the ten thousand, wrote from his farm at Elis: "Agriculture, for an honorable and high-minded man, is the best of all occupations and arts, by which men procure a living. For it is a pursuit that is most easy to learn and most pleasant to practice; it puts the bodies of men in the fairest and most vigorous condition, and is far from giving such constant occupation to their minds, as to prevent them from attending to the interests of their friends or their country. A man's home and fireside are the sweetest of all possessions."

Hesiod's "Works and Days" are devoted to the rustic lore which embodied the experience then attained. Nor can we fail to see how apt those Yankees of the Orient were to snatch every improvement, every new culture from the nations they conquered, as we read Homer's description of the gardens of Alcinous, where flourished

> High and broad fruit-trees that pomegranates bore;
> Sweet figs, pears, olives and a number more
> Most useful plants did there produce their store,
> Whose fruits their hardest winters could not kill;
> Nor hottest summer wither; there was still
> Fruit in his proper season; all the year
> Sweet zephyr breathed upon them, blasts that were
> Of varied tempers, these he made to bear
> Ripe fruits, these blossoms, pear succeeded pear,
> Apple grew after apple, grape the grape,
> Fig after fig; time made never rape
> Of any dainty there.

In Greece, also, we have the first example of public gardens created by the magistrates for the use of the citizens; and history takes account of the botanic garden founded by Theophrastus, at Athens. Another was created by Mithridates, King of Pontus, 135 years before Christ.

It is very pertinent to our subject to inquire how all this came to be changed—to find a reason for the Greece of to-day.* Mr. Felton ascribes it to the lack of a common central government; to the seeds of division planted by the predominance of the city over the country; to extensive migrations, and the formation of rival confederacies. All these were, doubtless, modifying causes, but we must look upon the Greek experiment at civilization in a broader light—as one of many great experiments necessary to precede a conception of society in which the quality of the units should be of the first importance.

Plato looked with distrust upon popular governments. He considered the people little better than a mob, and would have subjected the individual entirely to the State. Not so Aristotle, the father of a rational polity. He maintains that the legitimate object of government is not to increase the wealth of the few, nor to favor the poor at the expense of the rich, nor to encourage mere equality, nor to promote trade and commerce only, but to make good and virtuous citizens, and to promote hap-

*"Of Athens there remains only a small castle, a hamlet, undefended from foxes and wild beasts. Its people, once free, are now under the yoke of slavery to the cruelest brutes,"—*Nicholas Goibel, a writer of the 16th century.*

piness. Those, therefore, who can contribute most to these results have the best title to a share in the government. He proceeds to show that the middle, *i. e.*, the producing classes, who are exempt alike from the temptations of poverty and riches, are most likely to be governed by reason. Nor was this great practical philosopher a mere utilitarian. "The most necessary and useful things," he said, "are undertaken for the sake of leading toward the most beautiful."

The military arm was only valuable in preserving peace. Labor was valuable in securing leisure for the highest enjoyments.

The decay of Greece began in the degradation of labor, through the introduction of slavery and the growth of luxury. Education, at first exceedingly practical, aiming at bodily and moral, as well as intellectual perfection, grew more and more one-sided, and ended in speculations upon philosophical subjects, mental gymnastics, as profitless in their relations to popular welfare as the theological dogmas have been which have divided the world. Agriculture became more and more subordinated to trade and commerce. The mines were all worked by slaves. The ratio of the free to the slave population brought from the shores of Asia, became as one to three; and as almost every eminent citizen was owner of from fifty to one thousand slaves, we can understand the rapidity with which the thousand years of Grecian civilization drew to its close.

Having shown that in the free States of Greece we find the elements of all that is best in society, and a philosophical recognition of the true relations of man and land, we will turn to Rome, where civilization presents the same phenomena of progress and decay. As in Greece, we here find the supreme power of the State derived from laws made by common consent of the people, and that the division of land was made according to families, reserving a portion for common use. The early Romans had only two arts—war and agriculture. Every husbandman was also a soldier; and as the laws forbade him to sell or alienate his land, the growth of population naturally led to the establishment of a patrician class. The whole policy of Roman war and conquest rested on the desire to extend their territory, and with it the freehold system, of such vital consequence to the State. The Roman government never lost a foot of land;

every vanquished nation was compelled to merge itself into the yeomanry of Rome, or to cede a third part of its domain, which was thereupon converted into Roman farms. It has been well said, that many nations have gained victories and conquests as the Romans did; but none have equaled them in securing to the plowshare what was won by the sword.

The extent of a middle sized Roman farm was about twelve and a half acres, the chief crops wheat, and spelt, which is even better adapted than wheat to primitive cultivation. Peas, beans, and a great variety of vegetables were diligently cultivated. The rearing of cattle for milk or meat does not appear to have been practiced until later times. From the Greeks they borrowed the culture of the olive, fig and vine. The farmer and his sons guided the plow, which was drawn by the ox or cow; horses, asses and mules being used only as beasts of burden. The cattle, geese and swine were kept in the *agrarium* or common pasture.

So perfectly was the plowing performed, and so closely were the furrows laid that harrowing was dispensed with altogether. The farmer had many holidays—going weekly to market and keeping zealously all the religious and family festivals. After the winter sowing, a whole month was considered a holiday.

At a very early period there seems to have been no distinction made between the rights of the large or small land-holder in the common pasture, which was the property of the State, and not of the community. Day laborers were common, but there were few slaves, and as these were of the same blood and race, captives from Etrurian or Volscian neighbors, they were permitted and doubtless encouraged to work out their freedom.

A careful reading of Roman history, especially that part of it which relates to the division of society into two great classes, patricians and plebeians, the differences that arose about the use of the common pasture, the concentration of land and capital into fewer hands, dispossessing the small farmers and cultivating estates with rural slaves, is necessary to a right understanding of the agricultural condition of modern Europe.

In the sixth century, (Roman era,) Roman husbandry consisted in the management either of the large estates of the aristocracy, or of the pasturage, *i. e.*, the public or common lands, or in the tillage of petty holdings. Mommsen says "the whole system was pervaded by the unscrupulousness characteristic of the power of capital. Slaves and cattle were now placed on the same level; they were fed as long as they could work as a matter of economy, and sold when they were worn out, as a matter of economy also." One of Cato's maxims was that a slave must either work or sleep, and no attempt was ever made to attach the slaves to their estate or to their master by any bond of human sympathy. The abject position of the practical husbandman, not enslaved, is further shown in Cato's description of what a *steward* ought to be.

"He is the first to rise and the last to go to bed; he is strict in dealing with himself as well as with those under him, especially his stewardess; he is careful of his slaves and oxen; is always at home; never borrows nor lends; makes no visits and gives no entertainments; troubles himself about no worship, save of the gods of the hearth and field; leaves all dealings with the gods and with men to his master; he modestly meets that master faithfully and simply, and conforms to his instructions." By this time, such of the yeomanry as were not swallowed up by capital, held small parcels of land, and were generally so poor that the hoe was substituted for the plow in their labors. The farmers were irretrievably ruined, and the more so that they gradually lost the moral tone and frugal habits of the earlier ages of the republic. The other branches of industrial arts were undeveloped, the force and energy of the population being consumed in war and commerce.

From the third to the fifth century of the Roman era, capital had waged its warfare against labor by withdrawing the revenues of the soil from the working farmers, in the form of interest on debt, and transferring the capital thence derived to the field of mercantile activity opened up by the commerce of the Mediterranean. There was no longer an agricultural class among the citizens; and although a high and even an improved culture was maintained, it was simply the application of the capitalist system to the produce of the soil. Cato, who regarded himself as a reformer, and had declared that farmers made the bravest men and the best soldiers, states that Italy at the end of the sixth (Roman) century, was far weaker in population than at the end of the fifth, and no longer able to furnish its former war levies.

The half savage herdsman who confronts the traveler in the Roman Campagna, is an unconscious witness of the estimation which noble and aristocratic Rome placed upon her citizen farmers while the nation was shaping itself. "She did not exactly desire their destruction, but allowed it to run its course, and so desolation advanced with gigantic steps over the flourishing land of Italy, where countless numbers of free men had lately rejoiced in well earned prosperity."

CHAPTER IV.

AGRICULTURE IN MODERN EUROPE.

GERMANY AND ENGLAND—RANKS—FOLKS LAND AND RENTS—DEGRADATION OF THE BRITISH LABORER—ALLOWANCE OF FOOD—ELEVATION OF THE MECHANICAL CLASS—PROPORTION OF LAND OWNERS TO POPULATION—VARIATIONS IN CONDITION—WAGES OF LABORERS—HOW ENGLAND IS FED—SCOTLAND A WHEAT GROWING COUNTRY—AMELIORATION OF CLIMATE THROUGH AGRICULTURE—PEDIGREE CATTLE AND SHEEP—FRANCE—SMALL FARMING AND POPULATION—GREAT PRODUCTION OF WHEAT—THE LATE WAR—HOLLAND AND THE LOW COUNTRIES—A MODEL FOR CALIFORNIA—DEEP TILLAGE—DIVERSITY OF CROPS—USE OF MACHINERY—NIGHT SOIL AND MANURES—ROTATION—MODERN GERMANY—BEET CULTURE—MAIZE CULTURE IN AUSTRIA—RUSSIA OUR RIVAL IN WHEAT—CONCLUSION.

THE orderly development of agriculture among the Germans was retarded by the military spirit which distinguished them, and by a policy exactly the reverse of that pursued by the Romans. The Germans returned the lands to the people they conquered, on condition of receiving military assistance, and required of their tributaries that one half of the population should alternately fight and till the soil. The feudal system arose in their dislike of agricultural pursuits, and was entirely subversive of the freehold or allodial rights essential to their successful prosecution; and although these rights were preserved in some parts of Germany and France, the tendency to vassalage was almost irresistible. Indeed, there was no other security in those distracted times, either for life or property, and the oath of fealty exacted from the peasant by the lord, was required of the lord himself to the next higher in authority, and so on until it rested at the throne; thus diminishing in all classes the sense of degradation.

In the long procession of nobility, first came the Earls Palatine, then simple Earls, then Companions in Germany, corresponding to the Thanes of England, then the *Ceorls* or tenants, and lastly the slaves or villains who tilled the soil. These aristocratic distinctions were engrafted upon Great Britain, with other Teutonic customs, during the Saxon ascendency.

Agriculture was introduced into Britain by the Gauls, one hundred years before the Roman invasion. The division of land followed the Roman custom, *i. e.*, it was divided into "hides," a hide being about as much as could be cultivated with a single plow, or from sixty to one hundred and twenty acres. No man was allowed to guide a plow who could not construct one. To reclaim land gave the use of it for five years. Just at this period the Saxon distinction between "folks land," or the property belonging to the State and the people at large, and bocland, or private property, begins distinctly to appear, as also the system of rentals. According to the law of Ina, king of the West Saxons in the eighth century, a hide of plow land paid the following rent, viz: Ten casks of honey; three hundred loaves of bread; twelve casks of strong ale; thirty casks of small ale; two oxen; ten wedders; ten geese; twenty hens; ten cheeses; one cask of butter; five salmon; twenty loads of forage, and one hundred eels.

In the time of Alfred the Great, we hear complaints that arable lands were exhausted of their natural fertility, and three fourths of that which was susceptible of cultivation was devoted to pasturage.

The English farmer earned his black and bitter bread during the Middle Ages, known as a "churl" or hind, with little motive for self-improvement or that of his lands. The plowman, shepherd and swineherd belonged to the soil, and fishermen were rented and sold with the fisheries where they were employed. The cottager's house was a thatch-covered hut, chinked with mud or clay, without chimney, window or floor. A hide, dressed with the hair on, swung like a hammock, served him for a bed; there were no mills except those operated by hand. He was his own tailor, tanner and clothier. The kit of a blacksmith consisted of four pieces; a carpenter's of six. There was no division of labor. The plow, a pick, a clod-breaker, spades, sickles and baskets for winnowing grain comprised the list of agricultural implements.

The allowance of the laborer was two herrings a day, a loaf of wheat or barley bread, and milk from the manor house, with which to make his cheese.

Twenty years after the accession of William the Conquerer, nearly the whole territory of England had been wrested from its original proprietors and given away, making the condition of the agricultural population even worse than before. Still the art of agriculture progressed, thanks to the monks, and the proportion of freemen increased in consequence of the necessity for handicrafts which required intelligence and skill. By the year 1367, forty-eight "mysteries of labor," as the various employments of saddlers, brewers, masons, etc., were called, had been established in London and were strongly organized into guilds and fraternities. But the laws strictly forbade the teaching of any mystery to a husbandman or son of a husbandman. The mechanics having achieved an acknowledged political position as free subjects of the crown, the agricultural serfs showed signs of following their example. A statute of the First Richard (1377), is made "at the grievous complaint of the Lords and Commons of the realm, that in many parts the villains who owe services and customs to said lords have of late and do daily withdraw their services, and affirm them to be utterly discharged of all manner servage, due as well of their body as of their said tenures, and will not suffer any distress or other justice to be made upon them, and which more is, gather themselves in great routs, and agree by such confederacy that every one shall aid the other to resist their lords with the strong hand."

The memorable request of such a "confederacy," headed by Wat Tyler, "for the abolition of slavery for themselves and their children forever; for the reduction of rent, and the privilege of buying like other men in fairs and markets," resulted in the addition of insult to the injuries of this long-suffering class. "Rustics ye have been, and are," the king told them, "and in bondage ye shall yet remain—not such as ye have heretofore known, but in a condition incomparably more vile." From that time it was enacted that all persons who had been employed in any labor or service of husbandry until the age of twelve should from thenceforth abide at the same labor, and be forever incapable of being put to any other business. The evil effects of this irrational discrimination exercised toward agricultural industry, were not confined to the farming class, nor to England alone. Tenancy at will and tenant rights are more serious matters for English statesmanship to deal with now than they were before the Great Charter secured personal rights and a trial by jury to every freeman born upon English soil.

At the time of the Norman conquest the population of England was supposed to be a million and a half, and the roll of *land owners* numbered over 45,000. In 1861, with a population of 20,000,000, the number of land owners is reduced to 30,000, and every twentieth man is a pauper. In Ireland, just before the famine, the rural population amounted to twenty-five for every hundred acres; in France, at the same period, to sixteen; in England to twelve, and in the Scotch Lowlands to five. *Land monopoly* has driven two millions of agricultural laborers out of Great Britain. The English farm laborer has been cheated of his manhood; first, by a *monopoly of government*, which, by withholding the ballot, kept him in a servile condition; second, by *monopoly of land*, which destroyed the highest motive for industry, viz: the improvement of his condition, and the attainment of a permanent home; and third, a *monopoly of education*.

In 1848 an English statesman was asked if something could not be done to check the stream of emigration setting from Ireland toward America. "Not while middlemen hold all the land as agents of the aristocracy, and get all the profits," was the significant reply.

Professor J. Thorold Rogers has given us a history of British agriculture from 1259 to 1793. He shows, from carefully collected data, how gradually the emancipation of the agricultural classes took place; how the aristocracy were eating each other up with expensive wars and the extravagance of courts; how the yeomanry lost ground during the reformation; what was their Golden Age, and that the English peasant is again becoming a serf, and the yeomanry disappearing in the absorption of nearly all the land by a small number of great proprietors.

If the end of labor, and of wealth created by labor, is man himself, the civilization of England finds a parallel in that of Rome, and for the same reasons. Its agriculture, successful and wonderful in its results during the last century and a half, is an exhibition of the power of capital applied to land. The development of agricultural wealth and of civilization in the United States and in Australia is an exhibition of the power of manhood similarly applied.

The advance in the price of agricultural labor in England has been slower than in other countries. In 1273 the hay maker got 2½d. an acre; 2¼d. in 1400, with board; women laborers 8d. and fed themselves. The price for washing and shearing sheep was a penny a score; in twenty years sixteen were sheared for a penny, then ten, and finally eight. We read of one farmer at about the year 1500 who gave his women shearers 1½d. a day and fed them. And yet Joseph Arch tells us that agricultural labor, all things considered, fared better then than now.

The price of meat and dairy products in England makes cattle raising more profitable than grain. Some one has said, and it is very near the truth, that a failure of the turnip crop for two years would bankrupt England. Agriculture is therefore growing in importance hourly, and so are all questions involved in the feeding of that vast and rapidly increasing population. England is increasing her acreage as fast as she can, by reclamation, and reducing her pasturage. The culture of sainfoin, a crop good for six or seven years, has proved advantageous, also of buckwheat for fodder.

In 1789, 9,000,000 acres were cultivated; in 1869, 36,100,153; in 1870, 46,177,370, of which 11,755,053 acres were devoted to wheat culture. How far that goes in feeding the English millions is best seen by a statement of the imports of wheat and flour from the United States for fifteen years.

Year.	Cwt. Wheat.	Cwt. Flour.
1856	5,542,983	2,892,518
1857	2,819,934	1,464,867
1858	2,576,791	1,764,795
1859	159,926	216,462
1860	6,479,339	2,254,322
1861	10,866,891	3,794,865
1862	16,140,670	4,449,534
1863	8,704,401	2,531,822
1864	7,895,015	1,745,933
1865	1,177,618	256,769
1866	635,239	280,792
1867	4,188,013	722,976
1868	5,908,149	676,192
1869	13,181,507	1,711,000
1870	12,372,176	2,154,751

England cannot afford to raise her breadstuffs. She is compelled to make meat, hence the great preponderance of her agricultural work must be in the direction of hay and root crops. In these she is eminently successful.

Of Scotch farming, it may be said that it has made great

advances in the last century, chiefly from the superior education of the agricultural class. So great have been the agricultural improvements that the climate is already perceptibly ameliorated, the winters commencing a month later, and the snow disappearing a month earlier. Yet until the breaking up of the clans and the large consequent emigration of the Highlanders to Canada, there was no husbandry in Scotland worthy of the name. It now produces the finest wheat in the United Kingdom. The farms range from fifty to a thousand acres; the latter, however, is exceptionally large. One fifth of the cereal crops are oats. The breeding of pedigree cattle and sheep commands the attention of the best Scotch farmers. The condition of farm laborers is far superior to that in England, and rural economy is better understood.

Mr. W. Little, in a treatise on the technical education of farmers, says: "The success to which British farming has arrived is owing to mechanical rather than scientific causes. Drainage, steam culture, and a liberal use of capital we have tried; but now chemistry in its application to artificial manures is taking such a prominent position, it is of the first importance that our farmers should be educated, should have such a general knowledge of science as will serve them in their labors."

Great attention has been paid to the production of timber in Scotland; and the results of her experiments show that no crop pays better in the end, than *trees.* Larch and pine are the chief varieties of timber produced.

French agriculture, like that of England, proves that industry requires freedom for its success. In lectures upon special cultures I have given the history of several movements, experimental and educational, which have been of immense importance to this nation; but the *want of land* is the great want of the French farmer. Small farming in the department of the Nord is carried on to excess, "even to misfortune," according to French authorities. In spite of the developments of manufactures, the population is in the proportion of one to two and a half acres, or greater than in any country except China. France produces almost as much wheat as the United States, upon a territory not larger than Texas. She has, through her work of acclimatization, done more than any other nation to improve the breeds of animals, changing the Spanish merino sheep into the superior French variety. She has also made great advances in veterinary science. She has made herself rich and great by the persistent development, side by side, of all the branches of agriculture and manufactures.

The rapidity with which France has recovered from the effects of the late war, is due to the prosperity and hoarded wealth of the small land-holders, whose savings were laid upon the altar of patriotism; a good augury, we feel, for the ultimate success of the republic.

It is in Holland, that country "redeemed by weeds from the dominion of the sea," that we find the laborer and the land enjoying the highest prosperity. There is no waste land in the Low countries, and no waste of human power. Recreation with this frugal people is not so much rest as a change of occupation; and while neither art nor any higher culture is neglected, there is no subordination of the useful to these ends.

Deep tillage is the characteristic of husbandry in the Low countries, and the most perfect adjustment of the system of rotation to the special conditions of the soil. "No manure, no coin; no coin, no commerce," has been on the lips of the Fleming for generations. The following table shows the diversity of products which would be obtained from one thousand acres:

Cereals and farm crops	387.34
Alimentary roots	50.66
Manufacturing plants	25.22
Legumes, pears, beans, vetches, etc	26.38
Fodder plants	59.83
Prairie land	139.19
Fallow	31.08
Gardens	19.17
Wood	186.58
Waste (at rest or periodically cultivated)	124.55
Total	1,000.00

A great deal of machinery is used by the large farmers. Tanks for the collection of night soil are seen along the roadsides; parings of turf and animal droppings are carefully gathered and composted. Liquid manure is preferred on account of its freedom from weeds. An hectare is frequently treated with 50–100 hectolitres, especially for tobacco. We cannot wonder at the enormous crops which are obtained. Dung pits are made for the excrements of cattle. Ammoniacal fertilizers are so perfectly saved that the stables are fresh and sweet as a Flemish kitchen; and besides all these natural resources, manure is manufactured in great quantities. The commonest way is to add sulphate of iron to animal manures at the rate of one kilo of the sulphate dissolved in twenty pints of water, to the manure of twenty head of cattle. Cattle abound. The introduction of Durham cattle added one third to the value of this kind of stock; but other breeds are used.

The rotation practiced in Flemish husbandry is as follows: First, potatoes; second, rye, with carrots; third, flax; fourth, rye; fifth, turnips; sixth, oats. This is for a poor, sandy soil. For the best soils: first, tobacco; second, colza; third, wheat, with clover; fourth, clover; fifth, rye; sixth, oats; seventh, flax; eighth, turnips. We have here the great principles of successful farming admirably illustrated—*rotation, fine tillage, high manuring*. Even flax growing, which is considered in England an exhausting crop, is made beneficial to the soil of Flanders, and gives an average crop of thirty-three or thirty-four hundred weight to the acre. Between Ghent and Antwerp a cow is kept for every three acres of land. The beet-root is of immense value to Holland, and also to France and Germany, in supporting their cattle and in giving additional value to the manure.

Throughout Modern Germany, from the Baltic Sea to the borders of Italy and Turkey, the resources of science and education are fully utilized in the development of agriculture. The beet sugar culture, in which not less than one hundred and fifty colleges are giving practical instruction, is but one of many examples of the earnestness of government in this direction. Austria is giving great attention to the culture of maize, and the utilization of the whole plant, leaves, stalks, and grain.

But it is in Russia, the great rival of the Pacific Coast in the production of cereals, that we find the most remarkable improvements. She is already in a position, through the unexampled development of her agricultural and manufacturing resources, to be the dictator of all Europe, because she can consume more of all that they produce, and can produce more of all that they consume. Her trade is worth nearly or quite 600,000,000 of rubles. Great Britain and the other European countries devoured over 100,000,000 rubles worth of her wheat in 1867; and she has been increasing her export at the rate of 20,000,000 rubles per annum. She has been exporting flax, and flax seed, tallow, raw wool, honey, wax and hemp, in a steady stream for years; while the unspent forces of a new and rising population are applied every year, to the land. Her marvelous advances in industrial education will be spoken of in another connection.

The study of the details of experimental farming in France, Germany, Austria and now in Russia, should be a part of the training of every American farmer. In no European country can the time-honored privileges of class give way to the necessities and claims of agricultural labor without a conflict; while in America, free lands, liberty of conscience and free education offer to it a prospect as boundless as it is inspiring. As every narrow sentiment of nationality is here becoming lost and merged in the more exalted sense of humanity, so the distinctions of class and the jealousies between capital and labor will lose themselves in an equality of education, and the application of science to the laws of individual, social, and national life.

CHAPTER V.

AGRICULTURE IN THE UNITED STATES.

"The provision in the Mosaic code, (Leviticus, xxvi, 35,) that the Israelites should abstain from agriculture every seventh year, was probably intended to prevent the soil from being exhausted by excessive cultivation."

American Independence due to the Farmers--The South Atlantic States—Want of System—Cotton and Tobacco—Gov. Hammond on South Carolina Agriculture—Georgia Silk Culture—Gov. Collier on the Wants of Alabama—The Old Dominion and the Old Commonwealth Contrasted—Emigration—First Agricultural Societies and Journals were Established in the South—Diversified Industry would have Secured Emancipation—Louisiana—Texas.

The history of agriculture in the United States covers a brief period as compared with that of other nations, yet perhaps on no other part of the earth's surface has the lesson of man's true relation to the land been more impressively written. Our historians have scarcely deigned to notice any of the important facts concerning it; among the storied names of eminent men, we find soldiers, sailors, authors and inventors, while those of the benefactors of agriculture have no place. Yet it was to this class that America owes her independence. Tories swarmed in the cities; and it was commonly stated in England that the Revolution was one of "yeoman, who left their plows in their furrows, to aid the farmer of Mount Vernon," in unyoking their land from tyranny. Three illustrious farmers, George Washington, John Adams, and Thomas Jefferson, did not obey the injunction to "let politics alone," and are therefore less known than they deserve to be as Patrons of Husbandry. They were not only practical but scientific cultivators. Jefferson devoted much time to improvements in plows, and Washington kept himself fully informed by maps and weekly reports of the exact condition of his crops, when absent on his campaigns. But the rank and file do not seem to have profited by these illustrious examples. We have at least a hint of the reason in a letter from Sir William Berkeley, Governor of Virginia, in 1641, to the home government. "But I thank God," he says, "there are no free schools or printing, for learning has brought disobedience and heresy and sects into the world, and printing has divulged them, and libels against the best government. God keep us from both."

At first, the virgin soil amply repaid the labors of the husbandman. The lighter and poorer lands first brought under tillage were soonest exhausted of their fertility; there was little attempt at systematic rotation in the Northern, and still less in the Southern States, where cotton and tobacco formed the surplus crops, and found the readiest market abroad. These staples were cultivated without manure, and the result proved how fatal to the prosperity of a country the exclusive production and monopoly of any great staple may become, even where there is a regular, extensive and profitable demand for it.

Notwithstanding the encouragement given to silk and other cultures, by the British government, cotton and tobacco received more and more attention; as the land gave out, population pushed backward, the cost of transportation to the seaboard in a country whose resources are undeveloped, being usually considered less than the cost of reclaiming lower and richer lands.

Thus emigration peopled Tennessee, Kentucky, and the Gulf States, where the exceeding fertility of the river bottoms offers some exceptional features to the inevitable results of exclusive cropping. The bottoms of the Mississippi, Yazoo, Red, Arkansas, and Big Black Rivers, are unrivalled for the production of cotton and sugar-cane, but the carefully kept statistics of the years of French domination, now in possession of that government, show that those surpassingly fertile regions are by no means inexhaustible. Texas, an empire in the extent of her territory and her boundless prospective wealth, will do well to heed the warning voices of her elder sisters.

Among the original thirteen States, South Carolina took the lead in the initiation of new cultures. Her most eminent family possessed in Eliza Lucas Pinckney, a gentlewoman, fitter than almost any other to have reigned over the Republican Court, or to be the Ceres of a national grange, a matron profoundly interested in the development of the State. She introduced the culture of rice and indigo into Carolina. She made silk culture the fashion, and carried to England sufficient spun silk, grown and manufactured by herself, to make three dresses, "remarkable for beauty, fineness and strength." One of these gowns was presented to the Princess Dowager, another to Lord Chesterfield, and the third was handed down in the Pinckney family for many generations.

In an address before the South Carolina Institute, in 1849, Gov. Hammond said: "But a small portion of the land of this State will now produce two thousand pounds of ginned cotton to the hand. It is thought our average production cannot exceed twelve hundred pounds, and a great many planters do not grow over a thousand, that is about two per cent. in cash on the capital invested, after paying current plantation expenses. Our State must soon become utterly impoverished, and in consequence wholly degraded. Depopulation to the utmost possible extent must take place rapidly. This process has been going on year by year, at first hardly noticed, but illustrated so constantly now as to be within the knowledge of every one of us. The most fatal loss which exemplifies the decline of our agriculture and the decay of our slave system, has been owing to emigration. No war, famine or pestilence has checked the natural increase of population, but our census shows that it is diminishing at the rate of eight thousand per annum, our slaves being carried off by their owners from a soil that has yielded twelve hundred pounds to one that will produce eighteen hundred. While the fertile regions of the south-west are open to cotton planters, it is in vain to expect any improvement. If a people would flourish, their industrial system must embrace not only agriculture but manufactures and commerce, and cherish each in due proportion."

During the same year Gov. Collier, of Alabama, in his address before the Legislature, said: "We are exhausting our lands without an effort to reclaim them. Alabama grows cotton in abundance, at a profit below the statute rate of interest, while she yields to the manufacturer in Europe or New England, exclusive of the cost of transporting the raw material, a profit exceeding her own of at least two hundred per cent. The Northern States are growing richer, while Alabama, with her delightful climate and her varied resources, is growing poorer; because, instead of bringing the loom to the cotton, we are sending our cotton to the loom. It is a mistake to suppose that the white man is disinclined to labor at the South, on account of the climate, or among a different and subordinate class of laborers; the trouble is that labor is not remunerative or sufficiently diversified."

An address to the planters of Georgia, by one of her patriots, sets forth the same facts in even stronger terms: "If we intend to recover our former prosperity, and preserve even the present value of our lands, we must not only understand our present condition, but what it is likely to be in the future. The lands of the Southern States, taken as a whole, including that portion of the Mississippi valley, properly southern, when first settled were more valuable, considering climate, soil, their extent, and that of their sea-coast, than those of any other country. To speak within bounds, they would produce, (with bad tillage,) thirty bushels of Indian corn, and eight or ten hundred pounds of seed cotton to the acre; less than half a century has reduced their productiveness, in the older states, to twelve bushels of corn, and three or four hundred pounds of cotton. Continue the same destructive system, judge of the future by the effects of the past, and our progress to ruin will be accelerated, until we are compelled to abandon the country. But it may be said, and is said by the planter, 'I will continue to make cotton, I will move to Arkansas or Texas.' Shall we delude ourselves by resorting to this merely temporary expedient? For in truth it is no remedy; it increases for a time the productiveness of cotton, and by so much the quantity of worn-out lands. Its temporary benefits to the emigrant are at the expense of the Old State. The time is coming with alarming rapidity when we can neither raise corn nor cotton."

Upon the settlement of Georgia the culture of silk was contemplated as a principal object of attention. Lands were granted on condition that one hundred mulberry trees should be planted for every ten acres cleared. Had this industry been persistently fostered, Georgia might have become to America what Lyons is to France, for the quality of the product was unrivaled. A package of raw silk weighing two hundred pounds, exported in 1790, brought the highest price in the foreign market. It is interesting to contrast the policy of the Old Dominion with that of the Old Commonwealth. Massachusetts, keeping the factory and the farm in close contact, though sorely crippled at times by a policy thrust upon her by the South, has, during all that period, "against even the laws of nature," drawn the cotton of other States to her looms, the iron of other States to her anvils, the wool of other States to her factories, their leather to her lapstones, until the value of her soil, per foot, has exceeded the value of the same per acre in States which set out with her in the race.

It was humiliating to the statesmen of Virginia, remembering that she was among the first to call attention to agricultural improvements in the structure of implements, in the qualities of domestic animals, and to the importance of diffusing agricultural information, to feel herself thus distanced. Her eastern shore seemed to invite a direct emigration from Europe, and was cut with natural canals offering the cheapest transportation; yet, ten or twelve years before the civil war, her most enlightened and patriotic citizens were endeavoring, through her agricultural societies, to do something for "the depressed and wretched condition of the farming interests throughout the State." In most of the counties of the tide-water region there was a great extent of waste land, impoverished by the injudicious culture of corn and tobacco. In the year 1845, a hundred and twenty families from the Northern States settled in Fairfax county, and purchased 24,000 acres of land, at a cost of about $180,000. These settlers, by their industry and skill, not only fertilized and beautified their own estates, but imparted to their neighbors a part of their own indomitable energy. In a very few years the advance in the price of land averaged fifty per cent. Col. John Taylor, of Caroline, said "he was satisfied that wheat would not pay (grown by slave labor), when the product fell below ten bushels to the acre." The average product was then eight bushels! It is seven at the present time!

As early as 1816, Mr. Jefferson had said: "We must now place the manufacturer alongside of the agriculturist."

It must not be supposed that we would undervalue the capacity or the patriotism of the Southern land-holders. In no part of our country has there appeared a more genuine attachment to the land, or a more earnest desire for improvement. The first agricultural associations were formed in the South; that of South Carolina was started in 1784, and is still in existence. The Philadelphia society, in 1785; that of New York City, in 1791; the "Massachusetts society for promoting agriculture," in 1792. The first Agricultural Exhibition was held in Pittsfield, Mass., May 10, 1810.

The South also took the lead in the importation of valuable stock. Maryland was the first to establish agricultural journals, and to ask the aid of government in behalf of agricultural education. In fact, Maryland ranks next to Massachusetts in the traits which are required by a progressive agriculture. The zeal and earnestness with which her noble sons—her Calverts, Caprons and others, addressed themselves to this work, is beyond all praise. In 1824, John S. Skinner, who had in 1819 commenced the publication of the American Farmer, distributed in Maryland a new and till then unknown fertilizer, in the shape of two bushels of guano, received directly from the Pacific, and accompanied it with translations from Humboldt and Ulloa concerning its nature and uses.

Nor was the sunny-land wanting in model plantations, homes and farms, adorned with everything which art and luxury can add to the charms of rural life. Her temptation and her trial lay in a direction better understood now than it was before the war, in the distance of her market, and the cost of transportation. Increase in the value of land, increase in population, diversity of employments, tend toward freedom as certainly as matter obeys the law of gravitation. In a Southern journal of 1850, we read: "If a demand for labor existed in the slave States, consequent upon making a market on the land for its products, the necessity for emigration would pass away, and immigration would begin. The people of the South would not then desire *to go to California,* nor would those of the North deem it necessary to pass laws to prevent them from so doing. All the discord between the different portions of the Union results from a system which tends continually to depreciate the value of the laborer and the land. For, with increase in value, division of the land naturally follows. Great plantations would become small ones, each of which would yield more than is now yielded by the whole. Small farms would come, cultivated by negro tenants, who step by step are becoming free, while their masters are becoming rich."

But this peaceful solution was not to be. To the blighting effects of a mistaken policy, was added the scourge and desolation of war! All honor to the noble spirits, north and south, who labored with their might to hold a united country to the pursuits of peace; and, failing in this, waited for the cloud to pass, ready to rebuild the waste places, and lay the foundations of an everlasting commonwealth. In this glorious work *the Grange* is to-day the most efficient helper. The South is of vast extent and resources. Hard as it is to restore land without animals, and hard as it is to obtain forage upon land that is thin and poor, "there is life in the old land yet;" its hills are seamed with iron and coal; it has gold and lead, limestone and salt. Above all it has children, than whom none are more noble; with great memories of a brilliant past, and everything to hope for in the future.

Louisiana, whose sugar industry was her strength, who has suffered so much from the war, is still enduring an almost total eclipse of productive energy. The want of capital, and the want of confidence, are serious obstacles, to which the want of labor may be added. Her late slave population forsook the country for the towns and cities; the planters were forced to employ imported Chinese laborers in their place. Add to this the wasteful system of manufacture of the cane sugar—which M. Boucherau believes to result in the actual burning up of a hundred millions of sugar annually,—and we can realize the relations of social order to progress, in any direction. The acreage of sugar production is now small—not more than one hundred and fifty thousand acres; Louisiana might supply the whole United States. Her condition is one which every State in the Union is interested in improving, especially those to whom she offers facilities for building up a vast interior commerce.

Texas, the largest State in area, is yet small enough in population to offer a camping-ground for half the discontented nations of Europe. Lands as good as the sun shines upon may be had for twenty to forty cents an acre. She raises the finest corn and cotton; her flocks abound; she needs only wisdom in her councils, to make herself the seat of a great southern civilization.

CHAPTER VI.

AGRICULTURE IN THE EASTERN AND MIDDLE STATES.

——— "The country's flinty face
Like wax their fashioning skill betrays,
To fill the hollows, sink the hills,
Bridge gulfs, drain swamps, build dams and mills,
And fit the bleak and howling place
For gardens of a finer race "—*R. W. Emerson.*

VALUE OF STATISTICAL REPORTS—HIGHEST AVERAGE YIELD OF WHEAT IN MASSACHUSETTS—A SOUTHERN VIEW OF NEW ENGLAND—VALUE OF HAY-CROP—VERMONT AND THE WOOL INTEREST—WHAT THE NEW ENGLAND STATES RAISE AND WHAT THEY EAT—THE EMPIRE STATE—GENESEE WHEAT—THE WEEVIL—FISH AND FUR CULTURE—PROFITS OF CHEESE AND BUTTER FACTORIES—MR. ARNOLD ON THE FUTURE OF DAIRYING—PENNSYLVANIA AND HER COLONIES—NEW JERSEY A MARKET GARDEN—CRANBERRY CULTURE—PEACH CULTURE IN DELAWARE AND MARYLAND.

COMPARISONS are odious; but it is only by their constant use that we are able to form correct estimates either of our standing or of our progress. The reader will find appended at the close of Part First several tables made up from the reports of the Agricultural Department at Washington, which will enable him to estimate the great value of such information. He will observe that the average yield of wheat per acre is larger in Massachusetts than in any State except Oregon; while that of tobacco is greater by two thirds than in any of the so-called tobacco States. However small the acreage may be, the increase in the average productiveness, year by year, is a test of successful agriculture. With the poorest soil and most trying climate, New England has contrived her remarkable success, "spinning her improvements out of her own bowels, as a spider spins its web." She has done this mainly by the application of brains to her affairs. The results tersely described in a Southern journal of the year 1848, are far more marked at the present time.

"The seven wonders of New England," in the eyes of a Southern traveler:

1. Every man is living in a bran, span new house, or one

that looks as if it had been painted as white as snow within the past week.

2. All the houses are of wood, while all the fences are of stone, which in some places lie so thick as to require to be removed at the rate of a ton from six feet square.

3. Wood for house and kitchen all sawed and split up into one uniform length and size, and snugly piled away under cover of an open shed, so that the work of house and kitchen may suffer the least possible interruption; in a word, a place for everything and everything in its place.

4. The care obviously bestowed in the saving and preparation of manure by accumulation and composting.

5. Universal attention to a bountiful supply of vegetables and fruit adapted to the climate.

6. Not a poor or superfluous ox, cow, horse, hog, or sheep; the proportion of the short-lived, expensive horse, being, on the farm, wisely and economically small.

7. The seventh wonder is, after a day's ride in stages at seven and a half miles an hour, or on railroads at thirty, where are these people's staple crops? What do they make for sale? Where are their stack-yards of wheat, straw and fodder? Where their tobacco-houses and gin-houses; their great herds of cattle and swine, rooting in the swamps, browsing in the fields, or reposing in the shade? How do they contrive to keep out of debt, and never repudiate? How do they go on improving their rocky farms, carrying *stun* from their hills to under-drain their meadows, building school-houses within sight of each other, and expending millions on education, while, buying for themselves, one a little bank stock, another a little railroad stock, or that of a neighboring factory, where he sells his milk, apples, poultry and potatoes; once in a while adding to his farm by paying one hundred dollars an acre for some smaller parcel in the neighborhood. The key to the riddle is, diversity of industries in general, and of agriculture in particular."

The same writer speaks of the eighth wonder, viz., that one county in Massachusetts, to which was apportioned two thousand dollars of the surplus money distributed by the general government, "to be loaned on good security to the farmers of said county," could not find a farmer who wanted to borrow money. This, it must be confessed, was more than thirty years ago, before the era of bonds and subsidies.

This flattering picture shows what energy and economy of time and labor may accomplish with indifferent materials. The records of the State Agricultural Society, and Legislature of Massachusetts prove with what zeal she has set herself to correct her own mistakes. A committee on "exhausted pastures" issues a circular inquiring of the owners of pasture lands if they are exhausted in any degree; what amount of stock they will carry; what amount they carried ten, twenty, and even forty years ago; what have been the results of sheep pasturage, and other questions, the replies to which, published and widely circulated, make every reading farmer understand how much of his land is taken away in milk; why his cows gnaw at old bones, and what must be done to keep them from gnawing. A recent lecture by Prof. Stockbridge, of the Agricultural College, before the State Board of Agriculture, illustrates the usefulness of such investigations so well that no apology is needed for quoting it here:

I find we have said to each other, and to the world, that the hay crop is the most valuable of any single crop cultivated; that the hay and grass crop combined is worth in the aggregate, in the United States, somewhere between five and six hundred millions of dollars. This is its money value; and, more than all that, we have said to the farmers of the country, that its value in dollars and cents is as nothing compared with its indirect value, in the influence it has in preserving the fertility of our farms, as being the great source of manurial supply. We have said that no farm can be kept in a high state of fertility, or do otherwise than depreciate, if in its ordinary management, we sell the hay produced upon it; and no man's farm is supporting itself or him, where the grass crop is depreciating. So great is the value of the grass crop of the country, that we can afford to take our best soils up, and to bring our poorer soils to the highest degree of fertility for the production of feed. Now in regard to our pasture lands. The Board of Agriculture have agreed unanimously to this: that there has been a great deterioration in the producing power of our pastures for the last fifty or one hundred years; that the time was when our hill-sides yielded an abundance of sweet, nutritious grasses, which made milk, butter, cheese and beef of splendid quality. Our pastures do this no longer, and the brambles and briars growing in the place of those sweet, natural grasses, do not do it. The cause of the deterioration is apparent; it is because we have been building up animal structures or manufacturing cattle products which have been taken away from the fields which produced them, never to return; that when all the products have not been transported to the market, we have taken the milk for the manufacture of butter and cheese; and the manurial qualities that were contained in the milk left at home, have been given to other fields, instead of being carried back to the pastures which produced them; and that we have thus been sending away hundreds of tons annually from those New England pastures in the form of phosphates and sulphates in the bones of animals, and nitrogen in their muscles and tissues.

Again, we have said to the world, that from one third to one fourth of all these pasture lands should never have been deprived of their original forest covering. We cannot keep the soil in place in pasture or in cultivation. Our mountains and hill-sides should not only be allowed to go back again to forests; this should be assisted by systematic effort. The effect of this would be to shelter our cultivated lands, to make our climate more equable, and to give us a more equal distribution of rain, instead of having alternate seasons of drought and floods.

Of the Agricultural College of Massachusetts, and her large contributions to agricultural knowledge, mention will be made in another connection. She leads all the States in respect to an enlightened, agricultural economy, and is the pattern followed by the rest of New England.

Vermont, making her maple woods more than supply her own sugar, has always been sufficient for herself. She has played an important part in developing the wool interest of the whole country. The Spanish and French merino sheep, introduced by Consul Jarvis, of Weathersfield, have been improved by late importations, until the Vermont flocks have become standards of excellence. Her Morgan, Black Hawk and Hambletonian horses have enjoyed an equally high reputation.

Of the six States east of the Hudson, Vermont comes nearest to raising its own bread, producing 454,000 bushels of wheat in 1869, or a bushel and a peck to each inhabitant; taking the army ration of twenty-two ounces of flour per day as a basis for computing the consumption of bread, it follows that Vermont raises bread enough to supply the people of the State thirty-seven days, and that to make up the deficiency, they are obliged to purchase 3,836,000 bushels per annum.

Maine makes the next best showing in the cultivation of wheat, producing in 1869, 278,000 bushels, sufficient to last eleven days, and purchasing 8,500,000 bushels. New Hampshire, with a decreasing population, was a trifle behind Maine, producing 193,000 bushels, a little more than half a bushel to each inhabitant—and purchasing 4,360,000 bushels, or ten day's supply.

Connecticut makes a much poorer show than New Hampshire, producing 38,000 bushels, enough to supply the people with bread for ten days, and purchasing 7,518,000 bushels. Massachusetts, though having a larger area than Connecticut, raised only 34,000 bushels, which, ground to powder, was sufficient to give the inhabitants of the State bread enough for breakfast and dinner, but not enough for supper.

The people of this commonwealth purchase 20,300,000 bushels of wheat. Rhode Island raised 733 bushels of wheat in 1869, and purchased about 3,000,000 per annum. The six New England States together purchase in round numbers, from 40,000,000 to 50,000,000 bushels of wheat, and quite as much of the other grains, or in round numbers 100,000,000 bushels of grain.

The early farming of the Hudson and Mohawk valleys owed much to the Dutch element which preponderated in the population. Neat stone walls, clean fields, well built houses for families, and substantial barns for stock, were common before the Revolution. Wheat and all the cereal crops gave abundant returns; orchards throve, and flocks and herds multiplied, while the climate permitted the culture of more delicate fruits than that of New England. As cultivation progressed in a westerly direction, the growth of wheat became more and more profitable; this again received an immense stimulus from the opening of cheap water communication between the great lakes and the Atlantic. Genesee wheat and the flour of the Rochester mills, became a synonym for perfection of breadstuffs. The great Genesee valley, and countless less noted spots along the head waters of the Delaware and Susquehanna, poured a flood of plenty toward the sea-board.

Manufactures flourished, as also inland commerce; while the system of internal improvements consumed the labors of a vast army of foreign emigrants. The forests disappeared before the greedy locomotives, or were wasted by accidental fires. The averages of cereal crops perceptibly diminished. The weevil appeared, at first in isolated and limited districts, but ere long it became impossible to grow wheat with profit between Lake Ontario and the southern line. The southern counties resorted to dairying and stock farming; those nearest the metropolis, to market gardening to a considerable extent; until gradually all the benefits of a diversified industry were fully manifested. Cattle breeding has received a large share of attention. The memorable cattle sale at which the eighth

"Duchess of Geneva" brought the sum of $30,000, shows the high estimate placed upon Short-horns.

The present condition of agriculture in the Empire State is most flattering. Her scientists have diffused so much information respecting the laws of forestry, that the State is moving with unanimity to preserve a large part of the Adirondack mountain region, the forest feeder of her noble rivers, from further devastation. The preservation of natural pasturage will follow.

Among other recent industries, fish culture and fur culture deserve attention; the one for its novelty, the other for its immense importance. Trout raising has been made as certain and profitable as that of chickens and turkeys. The fur bearing animals have retired before civilization to such an extent that their extermination has been looked upon as probable. In 1867, Mr. Rassigue, of Oneida County, New York, commenced the rearing of minks, which can be done anywhere, all that is needed being a constantly flowing spring, and a small plot of ground. They breed rapidly, are subject to no diseases, and are worth from five to eight dollars a head, when grown.

The development of the dairying interest in the United States would require a volume for its full explanation. Mr. X. A. Willard, to whom it owes so much, stated, little more than a year ago, that American dairying represents a capital of more than $1,000,000,000.

The cheese product in 1872 sold for $30,000,000, and the butter product for $200,000,000.

Nine years ago, the first cheese factory was established in Oswego county; now, there are fifty. In one town are five factories, which work the milk of 2,200 cows. One of them made over 200,000 pounds of cheese. The number of cows in the county has increased from 10,000 to 30,000, under the stimulus of coöperation and association; each cow representing *in herself*, including land for keeping, factories, implements, and fixtures for marketing, a capital of $300, making a total investment of $9,000,000 in the dairy agriculture of the county. The average product of cheese per cow does not exceed 350 pounds in a season. Many dairies make an average of fifty pounds of butter per cow, also. Two hundred pounds of butter per cow is considered a good yield for butter dairies. Mr. L. D. Arnold, before the New York Dairymen's Association, thus states his views upon the future of dairy husbandry:

"At the present rate of increase of population in the United States, the year 1900 will find us with 100,000,000 of inhabitants. If we continue to consume cheese at no greater rate than at present, it will require two and a half times the quantity that we now consume; or 450,000,000 to supply the annual home consumption. The shipping demand must also increase. Nothing but a war with England can prevent it. The English are a cheese-eating people, and are now using twice as much per head as we do. Nor is that rate of consumption likely to be abated. It is the readiest and cheapest way to supply the laboring man with animal food, as it contains twice as much nutrition, pound for pound, as meat; while more pounds of cheese than meat can be produced from a given quantity of feed. The population of England is increasing, while her cheese-producing capacity is not. Germany supplies her with what we do not; and, as no other European country produces any quantity for export, the increasing wants of England must be supplied from the United States. If we continue to consume cheese at the present rate, and England also, the increase of population will require for the year 1900, not less than a *billion pounds!*"

Then there is the butter interest, larger still. We export but little butter, but we consume three and a half times as much as we do of cheese, varying from thirteen to seventeen pounds per head per annum. I have often heard dairymen predict a high reward for dairy products in the future, especially for cheese, because the demand was so rapidly exceeding the limited capacity of the dairy districts of the country. The State of New York is more exclusively devoted to dairying than any other State in the Union, but only a small portion of the State is accredited as being good dairy land.

Pennsylvania has so nearly the same natural advantages and manufacturing interests as the State of New York, that her agriculture has developed in a similar manner, though without as many vicissitudes. The Keystone of the "Old Thirteen," Pennsylvania has been the mother of the States upon her western boundary; she attracted the first, and has been the theatre of the most successful attempts at foreign colonization. The Friends, the Swedes, the Moravians, the Mennonites, and various other religious sects, have assisted in giving a peculiar character to her institutions, while the superiority of her soil, and the industries growing out of her mineral wealth, have maintained the balance of power most certain to secure prosperity.

New Jersey is the market garden of two great thriving cities, and fruit and vegetable-growing has there attained the greatest perfection. A blackberry grower, in West New Jersey, with seventy-five acres in cultivation, realized therefrom a net profit of $14,000. The cranberry has proved one of the most profitable crops. Sixty acres, in bearing, have netted over $13,000. Cranberry lands have brought $1,000 per acre. The agriculture of New Jersey has been created by facilities of transportation; waste lands are being rapidly reclaimed, and her growth is steady and continuous. Sixty-six per cent. of all the land in New Jersey is improved in farms, whose average value per acre is $86 14; the largest of any State in the Union.

Delaware and Maryland deserve more extended notice than our brief limits will allow. They are fast coming to be the garden spots of America. The peach crop of these States is immense—the average net profit of the crop of 1871, was seventy-five cents per basket. A peach farmer of Middletown, Delaware, cleared $38,000 from four hundred acres. The "Peach Blossom Farm," in Kent County, Maryland, contained six hundred acres of trees just coming into bearing, and was sold in winter for $31,500. The same year the purchaser sold peaches enough from it to amount to $52,000. One canning establishment in Dover, Delaware, consumed in 1873, of peaches, 18,000 bushels; of pears, 2,000 bushels; of tomatoes, 480 tons; of strawberries, 30,000 quarts; of cherries, 30,000 pounds.

In all these States, the advancing condition of agriculture is largely due to the influence of education and the press. The most influential journals—and those not especially devoted to this subject—maintain an extensive correspondence, and give considerable space to the treatment of matters of agricultural interest, at home and abroad.

CHAPTER VII.

FARMING IN THE WESTERN STATES.

"Consumption is the crown of production, and the wealth of a nation is only to be estimated by what it consumes."—*John Ruskin.*

THE WORLD'S GRANARY—RELATIVE VALUE OF CORN AND WHEAT—STOCK FARMING VS. WHEAT FARMING—IMPROVED IMPLEMENTS: TRIAL OF AMERICAN MACHINES—MISSOURI, TENNESSEE AND KENTUCKY—CALIFORNIA AND OREGON—AGRICULTURE OF THE CATHOLIC MISSIONS—JOHN GILROY AND HIS NEIGHBORS—LARGE WHEAT FIELDS—ENORMOUS CROP OF 1872—MARKET FOR CALIFORNIA WHEAT—FARMERS NOT ENRICHED BY THIS STREAM OF WEALTH—TONNAGE: PRICES—CALIFORNIA THE CENTER OF WINE AND WOOL PRODUCTION.

PASSING the great lakes, the emigrant farmer found a country awaiting him, where Providence, in the abounding conditions of prosperity, to use the language of one of their number, had not only "smiled, but laughed outright." A sea of verdure richer and more luxuriant than the meadow lands of the Connecticut or Genesee, dotted here and there with park-like, natural plantations of oaks, indicated lands for the plow, and sites for the homestead. Priceless in prospective value, it came almost without price into the hands of the settler. A season's labor in breaking the strong sod of the prairie, made it ready for wheat, secured him against want, and in the possessory right to the soil. The winters were not more severe, though a little more open than those of the northern sea-board. The northern belt of States, Michigan, Wisconsin and Iowa, soon poured a silver stream of wheat into the granaries of the world; Ohio, Illinois, Indiana and Missouri, also wheat growers to a considerable extent, contributed a golden stream of corn, the noblest product of the new world. Up to the year 1800, the export of American corn had only exceeded, by a trifling amount, two million bushels. This crop is first set down in the census of 1840, at three hundred and seventy-seven million five hundred and thirty-one thousand eight hundred and seventy-five bushels; in 1850, it covered thirty-one million of acres, and yielded six hundred million bushels; in 1860, it amounted to eight hundred and thirty-eight million seven hundred and ninety-two thousand seven hundred and forty-two bushels, the export being worth ten million dollars.

The ease and certainty with which the farmer may provide

for his live stock in winter, through the great productiveness of maize, has made *pork raising* one of the most important features of western agriculture. The State of Iowa reports many fields which produce as high as one hundred and five bushels of Indian corn to the acre. In the year 1872, over two and a half millions of acres were devoted to this crop, which covered one fourth of all the land in cultivation, and the supply was so greatly in excess of the demand, that large quantities of it were used as fuel; corn at eighteen cents a bushel being cheaper than wood at eight dollars and fifty cents per cord. In the year 1872, Illinois raised the enormous quantity of two hundred and seventeen million, six hundred and twenty-eight thousand bushels of corn. It is very important that the farmer should understand the relative value of corn and wheat, and how a surplus of either affects the market. The increase in the production of corn always brings a proportionate increase in live stock, fed and fattened with it, and thus the productiveness of the soil is maintained by corn culture to a far greater degree than by wheat. The agricultural prosperity of what are now called the States of the Interior, is due far more to corn than to wheat and wool.

Wheat culture in those States, though developed to an enormous magnitude, has had the same history and results that have been sufficiently dwelt upon in describing exclusive production on the Atlantic coast. "If wheat growing was the only branch of western husbandry, the country would soon be poverty-stricken. They cannot compete with the newer lands of California and Oregon," says the President of the Michigan State Agricultural Society. "Our old agriculture, to save itself from ruin, must turn to new sources of wealth, must seek new branches of husbandry, and learn lessons of political economy from her immediate and older neighbors, Ohio, Indiana and Illinois. All those have relinquished wheat growing, because it became necessary to do so, and have turned their attention to stock. The products of her dairies, her beef and pork, are worth more than her wheat ever was, when the land no longer refused to yield wheat."

The process of soil deterioration from continuous wheat culture, was far more rapid west of the great lakes than it had been at the East, in the days of the sickle and the scythe. The invention of improved implements has saved millions of dollars a year in the cost of teams and wages, thus increasing the aggregate of production, and of consequent exhaustion, by millions of bushels. Not only have improved plows, harrows, and cultivators led to this, but also threshers, mowers, reapers and headers, saving waste in harvesting, until we feel that only the more economical use of the steam plow is needed, to diminish the amount of manual labor to its minimum quantity. At the international exhibition, at Paris, in 1855, American machines, though comparatively imperfect at that time, were brought into competition with the world. The trial was made about forty miles from Paris, on a level piece of oats, with machines which cut and reaped at the same time. The American machines were successful; the judges could hardly restrain their enthusiasm, but cried: "Good! good!" "Well done;" while the excitable people shouted for the American Reaper: "That's the machine!" The report said: "All the laurels have been gloriously won by Americans; and this achievement cannot be looked upon with indifference, as it plainly foreshadows the ultimate destiny of the New World."

Three States, lying in the heart of the continent, rich in forests, in mineral wealth, and in navigable streams, seem to have been designed by nature for the most successful and varied industrial development. Missouri, Kentucky, and Tennessee, have a climate which enables them to grow fruits and vines, as well as cotton and corn, fine horses and mules. Their best lands are yet unwasted and unworn; the energies of the people, paralyzed during the civil war, are now bent toward improvements in agriculture and in education.

To the Catholic missionaries, who, from the spacious harbor of San Diego to Mendocino Bay, prospected the grandest field for a successful agriculture to be found on the surface of our planet, belongs the credit of being the pioneer agriculturists of the Pacific Coast. It must also be confessed that they were the first labor monopolists; the whole race of aborigines were compelled to work without recompense, for the benefit of the Church, though the Fathers exacted no more than they cheerfully rendered in their own persons. All the improvements, the vineyards and orchards, the countless herds and flocks added nothing to the wealth of the ignorant natives who produced them. The missions were the centers of a stock-raising experiment on a vast scale, without which the subsequent history of California would have been impossible; the trade in hides and tallow having brought in the settlers by whom the gold discovery was made.

The accumulation of wealth by the fathers was enormous. According to Rev. Walter Colton, chaplain of the U. S. ship *Congress*, the first Protestant clergyman that resided in California, in 1825, the Mission of San Francisco owned 76,000 head of cattle; 950 tame horses; 2,000 breeding mares; 84 stud of choice breed; 820 mules; 79,000 sheep; 2,000 hogs, and 456 yoke of working oxen.

The Santa Clara Mission had 74,280 cattle; 407 yoke of working oxen; 82,540 sheep; 1,890 horses, broken to saddle; 4,235 breeding mares; 725 mules, and 1,000 hogs. This mission, in the year 1823, branded 22,400 calves, as the increase of that year.

The Mission of San José had 62,000 cattle; 840 broken horses; 1,500 mares; 420 mules; 310 yoke of working oxen, and 62,000 sheep.

The Mission of San Juan Bautista, as early as 1820, owned 43,870 cattle; 1,360 tame horses; 4,870 mares and colts, and 96,500 sheep.

The San Carlos Mission, in 1825, had 84,600 cattle; 1,800 horses and mares; 365 yoke of working oxen, and 7,500 sheep.

The Soledad Mission, in 1826, owned 36,000 head of cattle; a larger number of horses and mares than any other mission; 70,000 sheep, and 300 yoke of oxen.

The Mission of San Antonio, in 1822, had 52,800 head of cattle; 1,800 tame horses; 3,000 mares; 500 yoke of oxen; 600 mules; 48,000 sheep, and 1,000 hogs.

The San Miguel Mission, in 1821, had 91,000 cattle; 1,100 tame horses; 3,000 mares; 2,000 mules; 170 yoke of oxen, and 74,000 sheep.

The Mission of San Luis Obispo had 84,000 cattle; 2,000 tame horses; 3,500 mares; 3,700 mules; and 72,000 sheep. One of the fathers of this mission took one hundred thousand dollars with him when he left for Spain, in 1828.

All the other missions were equally rich in stock; while the specie in the coffers of the fathers, and the value of the gold and silver ornaments of the churches, exceeded half a million of dollars.

When John Gilroy, the first permanent home-maker, settled

in the Santa Clara valley, (1814,). his nearest neighbors on the North were the Russians, at Bodega. Eight large ranches covered the land lying between San Jose and Los Angeles. There was not a flour mill or a wheeled vehicle on the coast. The people lived on wheat, cracked in mortars, maize, beef, fish and game. One thousand bushels of wheat, the first cargo I have seen mentioned, was shipped from Monterey to South America, prior to 1820. The product of 1874 reached twenty-eight millions seven hundred and eighty-four thousand five hundred and seventy-one bushels.

California, as we see, is not alone in this wonderful development of her resources. Oregon has some advantages over her for wheat and stock raising, and has improved them well. Both these young States are the reservoirs and sources of a river of breadstuffs which is flowing to the markets of the world in a stream of unequaled magnitude, commensurate with the scale of operations which have produced them. As we need to see the mammoth trees, not once, but many times, before the mind takes in the grandeur of their dimensions, so one must grow into a realization of the proportions of our agricultural industry and its requirements. From 1848 to 1862 California obtained her flour from Chili and the East. In 1856 and 1857 she imported one hundred and twenty thousand barrels from Oregon, and thirty thousand from the Atlantic States. These importations did not cease entirely, though they were diminished for two or three years, when the two years drought again raised them to seventy-two thousand nine hundred and thirty-six barrels from Eastern ports, forty-three thousand three hundred and forty-seven from Chili, and nineteen thousand five hundred and twenty-nine from Oregon. From that time the tide began to set in the other direction.

Some remarkable facts stand out prominently in connection with the Pacific slope States and Territories. First of all, it appears that the population increased, between 1850 and 1870, no less than three hundred and eighty-seven per cent., or nearly quintupled. The increase during the latter ten years was not at as high a rate as during the former, but still it mounts to the very respectable figure of fifty-seven per cent. Between 1850 and 1860 the number of improved acres increased more than nine-fold; between 1860 and 1870 the increase was equal to almost one hundred and fifteen per cent.; and the number in

1870, as compared with 1850, was nearly twenty times as large. In the cash value of farms the increase shown is in a nearly similar ratio, the figures being almost thirteen times as large for 1870 as for 1860. The increase in the extent of wheat cultivation is yet more striking. There was over fourteen times as much wheat raised in 1860 as in 1850; nearly three times as much in 1870 as in 1860, and more than thirty-eight times as much in 1870 as in 1850. As to all kinds of cereals, there was over fifteen times as much produced in 1860 as in 1850, nearly two and one half times as much in 1870 as 1860, and nearly thirty-six times as much in 1870 as in 1850. The amount of cereals produced per head increased nearly seven-fold in the twenty years ending in 1870. The increase in the value of manufactured products during the same period was considerably more than five-fold. It is hardly necessary to say that no other group of States in the Union makes such an exhibit as this in reference to its agriculture.

In California we have the *largest wheat field in the world.* On one side of the San Joaquin river it extends for thirty miles, on the other about fifty, with an average width of eighty miles; six hundred and seventy-two square miles, or four hundred and thirty thousand and eighty acres. With the average yield, in good years, of sixteen bushels to the acre, this field will produce one hundred and six thousand four hundred and thirty-eight tons, and would require a train of cars nearly two hundred miles long to move it away. It is owned and worked by different parties, but is only broken by the river which flows through it.

The Livermore and San Joaquin valleys raised over twelve million bushels in the year 1872. Three wheat farms in the San Joaquin, with areas respectively of thirty-six thousand, twenty-three thousand, and seventeen thousand acres, averaged nearly forty bushels to the acre, some portions running up to sixty bushels.

The years 1870 and 1871 had been dry years, and nature had thus provided the wheat lands with a partial Sabbath. In 1872 an unusual breadth of land was seeded, but as the season advanced the estimates rose to ten, twelve, and finally to twenty millions of centals.

How could such a crop be disposed of? A prominent grain firm in San Francisco had already some sixteen warehouses in different parts of the State, which would contain from five hundred to ten thousand tons each. Once in the warehouse, the farmer who is out of debt can afford to bide his time, and the advance in prices. If he is in debt, warehouse expenses only sink him deeper. One large commission house, that of Isaac Friedlander, was at this time buying three fourths of the grain exported, having agents scattered throughout the State, making estimates of the crop and the supply of tonnage required to move it, the rates at which it could be bought, etc., etc. All the wheat sent to England is purchased prior to arrival. Houses dealing in wheat here make known to the grain brokers in Liverpool all these facts, who, on behalf of the grain merchant there, contract with our merchants for the purchase and delivery of grain in that city; which, from the year 1869 to 1872, had taken twenty-four million centals. During this period, the Eastern States had taken of us about two million five hundred thousand centals. Australia, two thirds as much; China, about seven hundred thousand; Peru, two hundred thousand; the balance went to various points of the southern coast and islands. The flour export was also considerable; taken together, up to July, 1872, it had been thirty-seven million five hundred and fifty-nine thousand six hundred and twenty-seven centals, of a value of upwards of seventy-one million dollars. *How much of this went to the farmer?*

Few were prepared to answer this question. Many could say, that, practicing all reasonable economy, they could not make days' wages by raising wheat on their own lands, while the parties handling the wheat were becoming rich. Knowing these facts, they began to look into the reasons. The first thing they learned was, that the whole business of marketing had been taken out of their hands; that they were ignorant of a great many questions that affect legitimate trade; while to cope with speculative trade, they were utterly incompetent. The agents of production, commerce, and transportation, had got the upper hand, and were likely to hold it, unless they could free themselves by coöperation.

Finding that England was likely to be their principal market for many years, the wheat growers set themselves to learn something about ocean transportation. They found that in 1866, one hundred and twelve vessels carried off the crop; fifty-two were bound for Liverpool; twenty-four for Australia; twenty for eastern ports, and sixteen for China. The next year almost doubled the number; two hundred and twenty-three ships left the port of San Francisco laden with wheat. The crop of 1872 required three hundred and eighty-three vessels; the freight of which would go far to provide a mercantile marine for this coast. In July of that year, the rate of tonnage to Liverpool was £4 15s. per ton, or $1 14 per cental; the average for twelve years was about £2 11s. per ton, or a little more than sixty-one cents per cental.

The highest prices ever reached were in the years 1858, when it brought $6 75 per cental, and 1865, when it brought $5 30 per cental. The lowest price was in November, 1860, when distilling wheat was sold in San Francisco for $1 00 per cental. The farmers found that inland transportation was effected by rail, steamboat, and barge. The crop of 1872 was sufficient to load sixty-five thousand railroad cars; or about one thousand three hundred and forty average sized barges. The railroad freight rate from Merced, one of the great centers, was thirteen cents per cental; from Butte, by barge, $6 00 per ton; from Chico, $6 00; from Merced county, $4 20, and from Monterey, by steamer, $5 00. The handling, re-loading, etc., of this great crop would require the labor of several hundred persons.

Not only the cereal crops, but the other great staples of wine and wool were concerned in this question of transportation.

The wool interest has yielded the highest average profit. Indeed, California is the banner State in the quantity of the staple produced, the size of her flocks and the average weight of her fleeces. The climate is very favorable; and when wool-growing becomes essentially an agricultural business, from the necessary restrictions of the pasturage system, alfalfa promises to take the place occupied by grass and clover crops in the east, and to keep the proportionate advantages in our favor. But it is to the fruit and vine cultures that we may look for the most distinguishing features of our husbandry. As our wines grow in the world's esteem; as our raisins find their way into the world's markets; as our choice and luscious fruits, without loss of flavor, variously prepared for export, become indispensable luxuries, and bring remunerative prices, small farms will exceed in profit the large ranches of the present day; and California will more and more resemble the belt of fruit-growing States on the Atlantic Coast.

The following table shows the shipment of wine and wool to New York, *via* Panama, from January 1, 1874, to October 31, 1874:

Month.	Wine.		Wool, Raw.	
	Gallons.	Value.	Pounds.	Value.
January, February, March	113,088	$ 75,626	434,339	$ 78,248
April, May, June	172,629	109,702	286,679	70,467
July, August, September	150,813	92,212	338,985	69,598
October	64,837	44,224	800,194	136,753
Totals	501,367	$321,764	1,860,197	$355,066

SAN FRANCISCO.

The receipts and shipments by sea of flour and wheat for seventeen harvest-years, each closing June 30, were as follows:

Years.	Flour.		Wheat.		Total Wheat*	
	Receipts.	Shipments.	Receipts.	Shipments.	Receipts.	Shipments.
	Barrels.	*Barrels.*	*Bushels.*	*Bushels.*	*Bushels.*	*Bushels.*
1857	38,127	36,541	566,716	37,095	757,351	219,800
1858	35,456	5,387	405,086	6,335	582,366	33.270
1859	68.500	20.577	721,670	205	1,063,170	103,080
1860	91,400	58,926	1,641,710	636,880	2,138,710	931,510
1861	122,809	197,181	3,607,200	2,549,873	4,221,245	3,535,778
1862	111.269	101,652	2,419.110	1,419,740	2,975,455	1,928,000
1863	149,825	144,883	3,151.295	1,789,420	3,900,420	2,461,835
1864	99,208	152,633	3,073,066	1,785,486	3,569,556	1,548,651
1865	61,670	91,479	848,605	42,281	1,156,955	500,676
1866	166,843	279,554	3,570,653	1,732,525	4,404.868	3,130,295
1867	300,397	465,337	8,697,560	6,060,306	10,199.145	8,386,891
1868	206,176	423,189	8,401,990	6,339,630	11,599,851	8,515,625
1869	207,980	453,920	10,558,971	7,230,873	11,603,871	9,560,473
1870	171,108	352,962	10,941,776	8,106,485	11,797,316	9,871,295
1871	120,913	196,219	7,967,090	5,953,073	8,571,655	6,934 168
1872	146,749	270,079	3,908,350	2,340,636	4,642,095	3,691,031
1873	328,990	263,645	18,580,830	16,371,146	19.725,780	17,488,371

*Including flour reduced to wheat-bushels.

The receipts and shipments of the first six months of the harvest-year, closing December 31, 1873, were as follows: Flour, receipts, 262,068 barrels; shipments, 328,031; wheat, receipts, 9,614,186 bushels; shipments, 7,844,861 bushels; total wheat and flour reduced to wheat-bushels, receipts, 10,244,526 bushels; shipments, 9,485,016 bushels.

The flour-barrel in the above table contains 200 pounds; wheat is estimated at 60 pounds per bushel. The manufactures by the city mills during the last four calendar years were as follows: 1870, 250,000 barrels; 1871, 240,000 barrels; 1872, 310,000 barrels; 1873, 250,000 barrels. Of the exports of 1873, nearly all the wheat and the largest part of the flour were sent to the United Kingdom. This flour export, however, was an exceptional trade resulting from the failure of European wheat-crops. In the previous years the flour export to the British islands was comparatively small.

The receipts of corn, rye, oats, and barley for eight harvest-years were as follows:

Years.	Corn.	Rye.	Oats.	Barley.
	Bushels.	*Bushels.*	*Bushels.*	*Bushels.*
1865–66	76,071	4,107	891,025	2,080,675
1866–67	44,285	12,142	910,983	1,605,550
1867–68	54,821	10,000	936,602	1,462,718
1868–69	100,800	7,857	790,000	1,305,917
1869–70	119,100	8,035	883,111	1,573,668
1870–71	149,107	15,170	881,944	1,585,325
1871–72	67,678	15,890	1,066,902	1,655,610
1872–73	214,285	19,642	659,580	2,281,893

Corn and rye are to a very small extent exported, the small supply being required mostly for city consumption. During 1873 the export of oats amounted to 9,541 bushels, against 16,950 bushels in 1872. The exports of barley in 1873 were 434,816 bushels, against 293,588 bushels in 1872 and 20,618 bushels in 1871.

TABLE

SHOWING THE AVERAGE YIELD PER ACRE AND PRICE PER BUSHEL, POUND, OR TON OF FARM PRODUCTS FOR THE YEAR 1873.

[From the Report of the Agricultural Department.]

States.	CORN.		WHEAT.		RYE.		OATS.		BARLEY.		BUCKWHEAT.		POTATOES.		TOBACCO.		HAY.	
	Bushels.	Price per bushel.	Bushels.	Price per bushel.	Bushels.	Price per bushel.	Bushels.	Price per bushel.	Bushels.	Price per bushel.	Bushels.	Price per bushel.	Bushels.	Price per bushel.	Pounds.	Price per pound.	Tons.	Price per ton.
Maine	24	$0 91	11	$1 90	14.5	$1 15	21	$0 58	16.7	$0 91	17.4	$0 72	117	$0 52	......	......	.93	$12 20
New Hampshire	37.5	92	15	1 88	17.2	1 10		55	20	1 00	18.7	75	150	48	1,285	$0 15	1.05	15 00
Vermont	31	85	16	1 67	16.1	95	32.6	49	23.8	86	20.5	72	140	44	1,272	20	1.10	13 38
Massachusetts	35	84	19	1 66	17	1 04	33.3	59	22	1 03	15.6	86	125	70	1,459	17	1.04	25 10
Rhode Island	28.7	92	......	......	16.2	97	31.3	61	25.5	1 15	......	......	96	81	......	......	.95	37 50
Connecticut	30	94	18	1 65	16	1 06	32	60	23.5	1 10	18.2	98	97	83	1,647	23	1.09	25 00
New York	31	70	13.5	1 60	14	86	31	43	21.2	1 10	19.7	77	103	54	1,000	11	1.02	18 00
New Jersey	36	62	16.2	1 65	14.1	85	26.5	49	24	1 10	16.5	96	90	67	......	......	1.03	24 50
Pennsylvania	35.1	60	14.2	1 50	14.5	81	30.2	43	20.6	1 05	19.5	81	96	65	1,186	12.3	1.15	17 80
Delaware	19	53	11	1 68	11	87	19.3	46	17	90	23	70	97	78	......	......	.81	26 00
Maryland	21.4	68	11.3	1 54	12.5	80	18.8	44	18	85	17	75	80	70	877	7.7	1.00	19 00
Virginia	19	59	7.5	1 45	9.7	78	16.3	44	18.5	70	17.9	70	70	71	608	9.2	1.00	17 20
North Carolina	14.2	64	6.2	1 55	8.1	85	16.3	56	16.6	66	16.6	65	94	69	591	9	1.20	13 00
South Carolina	9.5	94	5.5	2 25	7	1 60	14	85	20	2 00	......	......	70	1 10	545	10	1.10	27 00
Georgia	12.3	82	7	1 75	6	1 64	13.4	75	13.2	1 20	......	......	78	1 15	750	20.7	1.05	20 50
Florida	10.4	1 11	......	......	......	......	13	1 02	......	......	......	......	......	......	601	33	......	......
Alabama	14.5	84	7.3	1 70	9.4	1 56	15.5	78	......	......	......	......	80	1 20	727	15	1.20	18 50
Mississippi	15.5	85	9.6	1 75	10	1 60	14.4	86	......	......	......	......	87	1 20	739	17	1 27	20 25
Louisiana	16.5	90	......	......	......	......	16.3	84	......	......	......	......	60	1 05	777	18	1.20	17 50
Texas	19	80	17	1 40	17	1 10	30	82	30	1 04	......	......	90	1 65	833	26.2	1.50	12 75
Arkansas	23.5	80	10	1 50	12.8	1 50	23.4	70	......	......	......	......	80	1 00	650	15.2	1.18	16 00
Tennessee	22.5	58	7.2	1 33	9	90	20.6	41	19.2	85	10.5	95	75	66	675	6	1.25	15 50
West Virginia	29	54	9.6	1 43	12.8	84	27	38	24	92	17.1	81	70	70	775	9.3	1.10	14 00
Kentucky	29.5	44	9	1 21	8.5	77	24	36	20	1 00	15.3	86	55	62	734	7.2	1.23	13 00
Ohio	35	42	12	1 31	11	75	27	35	21.8	98	11.4	99	85	88	1,181	5.5	1.05	14 61
Michigan	31	47	12.2	1 35	13.5	72	30.2	34	18	91	14.3	78	75	76	......	......	1.15	14 00
Indiana	25.6	40	11.2	1 22	14.2	71	20	32	22.2	1 06	12.1	88	56	35	800	6	1.25	11 50
Illinois	21	32	13.5	1 10	15.5	58	30	28	23	95	8.5	99	40	1 12	850	9	1.25	8 75
Wisconsin	30	44	16.5	97	15.7	62	35	33	26.6	1 08	11	92	71	80	1,050	6	1.30	9 50
Minnesota	31.5	41	18.3	80	20.2	51	36.1	33	26.6	77	12.7	82	99	63	......	......	1.38	5 60
Iowa	29	31	13	79	18	48	33	27	19	73	10.5	95	44	88	......	......	1.25	6 25
Missouri	23.5	38	12.8	1 13	14.5	64	28	30	21	86	12.5	77	38	87	800	8.8	1.25	9 50
Kansas	39.1	31	14	1 00	11	56	33	23	27.5	70	12.5	80	100	94	611	10	1.50	3 90
Nebraska	35	28	15.5	75	16	53	30	26	30	82	14.5	67	28	98	......	......	1.40	4 50
California	41	73	13.5	1 32	20	90	30	84	26.5	85	23.5	1 20	110	85	......	......	1 37	16 00
Oregon	30	60	19	90	25	82	37.5	42	28	52	20.3	1 20	130	56	......	......	1.40	10 50
Nevada	30	1 60	20	1 75	......	......	33	1 00	28	1 65	......	......	110	2 20	......	......	1.30	20 00
The Territories	28.5	97	23	98	23.5	90	35.1	70	32	80	......	......	120	71	......	......	1.40	13 00

Value of Farms and Farm Property throughout the United States.

[From the Report of the Agricultural Department for 1873.]

States and Territories.	Value of Farms.	Value of Farm Implements.	Value of Live-Stock.	Total Value.	Value Per Capita.	
					Of population.	Of persons engaged in agriculture.
United States.....	$9,262,803,861	$336,878,429	$1,525,276,457	$11,124,958,747	$285 80	$1,878
Maine............	102,961,951	4,809,113	23,357,129	131,128,193	209 16	1,599
New Hampshire..	80,589,313	3,459,943	15,246,545	99,295,801	311 96	2,132
Vermont.........	139.367,075	5,250,279	23,888,835	168,506,189	530 77	2.911
Massachusetts ..	116,432,784	5,000,879	17,049,228	138,482.891	95 02	1,902
Rhode Island.....	21,574,968	786,246	3,135,132	25,496,346	117 80	2,164
Connecticut......	124,241,382	3,246,599	17,545,038	145,033,019	269 85	3,322
New York.......	1,272,857,766	45,997,712	175,882,712	1,494,738,190	341 05	3,993
New Jersey.	257,523,376	7,887.991	21,443,463	286,854,830	316 58	4,544
Pennsylvania	1,043.481,582	35,658,196	115,647,075	1,194,786,853	339 24	4,594
Delaware	46,712,870	1,201,644	4,257,323	52.171,837	417 32	3,267
Maryland	170,369,684	5,268,676	18,433,698	194,072,[illegible]58	248 50	2,412
Virginia	213.020,845	4,924,036	28,187,669	246,132,550	200 90	1,006
North Carolina..	78.211,083	4,082,111	21,993,967	104,287,161	97 53	387
South Carolina..	44.808,763	2,282,946	12,443,510	59,535,219	84 37	288
Georgia.........	94,559,468	4,614,701	30,156,317	129,330,486	109 22	385
Florida	9,947 9[illegible]0	505,074	5,212,157	15,664,521	83 43	369
Alabama........	67,730,036	3,286,924	26,690,095	97,716 055	98 01	335
Mississippi	81,716,576	4,456,633	29,940,238	116,113.447	140 24	448
Louisiana.......	68,215,421	7,159,333	15,929,188	91,303,942	125 74	615
Texas	60.149,950	3,396,793	37,425,194	100,971,937	123 50	605
Arkansas.......	40,029,698	2,237,409	17,222,506	59.489,613	122 79	544
Tennessee	218,743 747	8,199,487	55,084,075	282.027,309	224 09	1,056
West Virginia .	101,604.381	2,112,937	17,175,420	120,892.738	273 50	1,634
Kentucky ...	311,238,916	8,572,896	66,287,343	383,099,155	290 00	1,467
Ohio............	1,054,465,226	25,692,787	120,300,528	1,200,458,541	450 41	3,023
Michigan	393,240,578	13,711,979	49,809,869	461.762,426	389 98	2,406
Indiana.........	634,804,189	17,676,591	83,776,782	736,257,562	438 08	2,760
Illinois	920,50[illegible],346	34,576,587	149,756,698	1,104,839,631	395 62	2,935
Wisconsin	300,414,064	14,239,364	45,310,882	359,964,310	341 31	2,254
Minnesota	97,847,442	6,721,120	20,118,841	124,687.403	283 57	1,659
Iowa............	392,662,441	20,509,582	82,987,133	496,150,156	415 53	2,300
Missouri.........	392.908,047	15,596,426	84,285,273	492,789,746	286 29	1,867
Kansas..........	90,327,040	4,053.312	23,173,185	117,553,537	322 50	1,605
Nebraska	30,242,186	1,549,716	6,551,185	38,343,187	311 75	1,659
California........	141,210.028	5,316,690	37,964,752	184,521,470	329 36	3,855
Oregon	22,352,989	1,293,717	6,828,675	30,475,381	335 18	2,300
Nevada	1,485,505	163,718	1,445,449	3,094,672	72 83	1,495
Dakota..........	2,085.265	142,612	779,952	3,007,829	212 10	1,192
Montana.........	729,193	145,438	1,818,693	2,693,324	130 78	1,275
Idaho............	492,860	59,295	520,580	1,072,735	71 52	734
Washington......	3,978,341	280,551	2,103,343	6,371.235	265 97	1 689
Wyoming........	18,187	5,723	441,795	465,705	51 07	2,822
Colorado..... ...	3,385,748	272,604	2,871,102	6,529,454	163 79	1,010
Utah............	2,297,922	291,390	2,149,814	4.739,126	54 61	454
Arizona..........	161,340	20,105	143.996	325,441	33 70	253
New Mexico......	2,260,139	121,114	2,389,157	4.770.410	51 92	255
District Columbia	3,800,230	39,450	114,916	3,954,596	30 03	2,897

NUMBER AND PROPORTION OF PERSONS ENGAGED IN THE SEVERAL CLASSES OF OCCUPATIONS IN THE STATES AND TERRITORIES OF THE UNITED STATES, AS DEDUCED FROM THE CENSUS OF 1870.

States and Territories.	Number of persons in all occupations.	Number in agricultural occupations.		Number in professional and personal occupations.	
	Number.	*Number.*	*Per cent.*	*Number.*	*Per cent.*
United States	12,505,923	5,922,471	47.35	2,684,793	21.47
Alabama	365,258	291,628	79.84	42,125	11.54
Alaska	.....	.....	.....	.....	.....
Arizona	6,030	1,285	21.31	3,115	51.66
Arkansas	135,949	109,310	80.41	14,877	10.94
California	238,648	47,863	20.05	76,112	31.90
Colorado	17,583	6,462	36.75	3,625	20.62
Connecticut	193,421	43,653	22.57	38,704	20.01
Dakota	5,887	2,522	42.84	2,704	45 93
Delaware	40,313	15,973	39.62	11,389	28.25
District of Columbia	49,041	1,365	2.78	29,845	60.86
Florida	60,703	42,492	70	10,897	17.95
Georgia	444,678	336,145	75.59	64,083	14.41
Idaho	10,879	1.462	13.44	1 423	13.08
Illinois	742,015	376,441	50.73	151,931	20.48
Indiana	459,369	266,777	58.08	80,018	17.42
Indian Territory	.....	.....	.....	.....	.....
Iowa	344.276	210,263	61 07	58,484	17
Kansas	123 852	73,228	59.13	20,736	16.74
Kentucky	414,593	261,080	62.97	84,024	20.27
Louisiana	256,452	141 467	55.16	65,347	25.48
Maine	208,225	82,011	39.39	36,092	17.33
Maryland	258,543	80.449	31.12	79,226	30.64
Massachusetts	579,844	72,810	12.56	131,291	22.64
Michigan	404,164	187,211	46.32	104,728	25.91
Minnesota	132,657	75,157	56.65	28,330	21.36
Mississippi	318.850	259.199	81.29	40,522	12.71
Missouri	505,556	263,918	52.20	106,903	21.14
Montana	14,048	2,111	15.03	2,674	19.03
Nebraska	43 837	23,115	52.73	10,331	23.56
Nevada	26,911	2,070	6.69	7,431	27.61
New Hampshire	120,168	46,573	38.76	18,528	15 42
New Jersey	296,036	63,128	21.32	83,380	28.17
New Mexico	26,361	18,668	63.58	7,535	25.66
New York	1,491,018	374.323	25.10	405,339	27.19
North Carolina	351,299	269,238	76.64	51,290	14.60
Ohio	840,889	397,024	47.21	168,308	20.02
Oregon	30,651	13,248	43.22	6,090	19.88
Pennsylvania	1,020,544	260,051	25.48	283,000	27.73
Rhode Island	88,574	11,780	13.30	19,679	22.22
South Carolina	263,301	206,654	78 48	34,383	13.07
Tennessee	367,987	267,020	72.56	54,396	14.78
Texas	237,126	166,753	70.32	40,882	17.24
Utah	21,517	10,428	48.46	5,317	24.71
Vermont	108,763	57,983	53.31	21,032	19.34
Virginia	412,665	244,550	59.26	98,521	33.87
Washington	9,760	3,771	38 64	2,207	22.61
West Virginia	115,229	73,960	64.19	16,699	14.49
Wisconsin	292,808	159,687	54.53	58,070	19.83
Wyoming	6,645	165	2.48	3,170	47.71

NUMBER, ETC., OF PERSONS ENGAGED IN THE SEVERAL CLASSES OF OCCUPATIONS, ETC.—*Continued.*

States and Territories.	Number in trade and transportation.		Number in manufactures and mechanical and mining industries.		Total population.
	Number.	*Per cent.*	*Number.*	*Per cent.*	
United States	1,191,238	9.52	2,707,421	21.65	38,925,598
Alabama	14,435	3.95	17,070	4.67	996,992
Alaska	....	....	....	....	70,461
Arizona	591	9.80	1,039	17.23	41,710
Arkansas	5,491	4.04	6,271	4.61	484,471
California	33,165	13.90	81,598	34.15	582,031
Colorado	2,815	16.01	4 681	26.62	47,154
Connecticut	24,720	12.78	86,344	44.64	537,454
Dakota	204	3.47	457	7.76	40,501
Delaware	3,437	8.53	9,514	23.60	125,015
District of Columbia	6,126	12.48	11,705	23.88	131,700
Florida	3,023	4.98	4,2[illegible]1	7.07	188,248
Georgia	17,410	3.92	27,040	6.08	1,184,109
Idaho	721	6.63	7,273	66.85	20,583
Illinois	80,422	10.84	133,221	17.95	2,539,891
Indiana	36,517	7.94	76,057	16.56	1,680,637
Indian Territory	....	....	....	....	68,152
Iowa	28,210	8.18	47,319	13.74	1,194,320
Kansas	11,762	9.50	18,126	14.63	373,299
Kentucky	25,292	6.10	44,197	10.66	1,321,011
Louisiana	23,831	9.24	25,807	10.07	726,915
Maine	28,115	13.50	62,007	29.78	626,915
Maryland	35,542	13.75	63,326	24.49	780,894
Massachusetts	83,078	14.33	292,665	50.47	1,457,351
Michigan	29,588	7.32	82,637	20.45	1,187,234
Minnesota	10,582	7.98	18,588	14.01	446,056
Mississippi	9,148	2.87	9,981	3.13	827,922
Missouri	54,885	10.86	79,850	15.80	1,721,295
Montana	1,233	8.78	8,030	57.16	39,895
Nebraska	4,628	10.56	5,763	13.15	129,322
Nevada	3,621	13.46	13,789	51.24	58,711
New Hampshire	8,514	7.08	46,553	38.74	318,300
New Jersey	46,206	15.61	103,322	34.90	906,096
New Mexico	863	2.94	2,295	7.82	111,303
New York	234,581	15.73	476,775	31.98	4,387,464
North Carolina	10,179	2.90	20,592	5.86	1,071,361
Ohio	78,547	9.34	197,010	23.43	2,665,260
Oregon	2,619	8.54	8,694	28.36	101,883
Pennsylvania	121,253	11.88	356,240	34.91	3,522,050
Rhode Island	10,108	14.41	47,007	53.07	217,353
South Carolina	8,470	3.22	13,794	5.23	707,606
Tennessee	17,510	4.76	29,061	7.90	1,258,520
Texas	13,612	5.74	15,879	6.70	818,899
Utah	1,665	7.74	4,107	19.09	99,581
Vermont	7,132	6.56	22,616	20.79	330,551
Virginia	20,181	4.89	49,413	11.97	1,225,163
Washington	1,129	11.57	2,653	27.18	37,432
West Virginia	6,897	5.98	17,673	15.34	442,014
Wisconsin	21,534	7.35	53,517	18.28	1,064,985
Wyoming	1,646	24.77	1,664	25.04	11,518

VIEW OF OAK KNOLL IN THE NAPA VALLEY.

[A Pioneer Farm, 1856.]

PART SECOND.

THE FARMERS' GREAT AWAKENING.

CHAPTER VIII.

THE FARMERS IN COUNCIL.

"The day is coming, aye, it is near, when working men shall rule this nation."—*David Broderick.*

GATHERING OF THE CLUBS—MR. HYATT'S TELLING REPORT ON SHIPPING—PROPOSAL FOR A CONVENTION—EXPRESSIONS OF OPINION—A SUMMARY OF COMPLAINTS—ORGANIZATION OF THE FARMERS' UNION AT SACRAMENTO—FRAUDULENT WHEAT QUOTATIONS.

DURING the years 1871–2, the farmers of California began to feel the necessity of combining for their own protection and improvement. The feeling of discontent with their condition, and the conviction that their difficulties were not inseparable from their calling, was almost universal. The wheat growers had the largest interests at stake, and were mostly concerned in the question of reducing the cost of transportation, but the fruit growers were even more strongly resolved to strike for freedom from the exactions and combinations of middle-men, who, they insisted, were receiving the lion's share of the profits. The farmers seemed everywhere fully awake to the idea that an intelligent coöperation could best be effected by associations confined to those engaged in agriculture. A club was gathered in Sacramento on the 7th of December, 1871, and from this time onward the work of organization proceeded rapidly. Stockton drew to its club the intelligent farmers of the San Joaquin, and elected Dr. Holden as their President. At Oakland a "Farming, Horticultural and Industrial Club" was formed, for improvement in the theory and practice of agriculture, horticulture, and other industrial and domestic pursuits, which was presided over by the Professor of Agriculture, and held its meetings in the lecture room of the University. San José organized May 4, and opened by discussing the question of grain sacks. Napa had a large and influential club. Santa Cruz, Sonoma, Contra Costa and the neighboring counties, discussed a great variety of questions of local and general interest in their meetings, which were duly reported in the Rural Press. This exchange of views and experiences, not only between neighborhoods, but different sections of the State, was felt to be of great benefit, and it was truly surprising to see what a wide range of subjects were thus brought to the tests of experience.

Toward the end of the season, the clubs at Napa and Sacramento laid before the other associations a proposal for a convention during the State Fair in September, requesting each to appoint delegates, and by previous expressions of opinion, indicate what was to be considered. This request met with universal approval, and large delegations were appointed.

The subjects which most profoundly interested the farmers, are indicated by the following extracts from their proceedings, as published at the time.

The report of the committee at the Oakland Club, August 23, 1872, embodied the results of their investigations into the shipping business;

To demonstrate the urgent necessity of a league or association among farmers to prevent the Shylocks, who are preying upon them, from carrying off all the farmers' profits, and making them mere hewers of wood, and drawers of water, and delvers in the soil, to benefit a few heartless grain speculators, let us look at the manner in which the grain market has been manipulated the present season in California. We are told that the prices here are governed by the prices of grain in Liverpool. How is this?

On the 2d day of August, instant, the Liverpool market for California wheat was quoted at 11s. 8d., and the same day, in San Francisco, at $1 55 to $1 60 per hundred pounds. On the 12th of August, instant, the Liverpool quotations were 12s. 4d.; and on the 13th, the next day, in San Francisco, the speculators paid only $1 60 for "good shipping." Here, it will be seen, was an advance in the Liverpool market, from the 2d of August to the 13th, from 11s. 8d. to 12s. 4d., or over fifteen cents; and how did the San Francisco market respond? How much did the wheat buyers of San Francisco advance the prices? Not one cent.

Again, on the 21st of September of last year, the Liverpool market was quoted at 12s. 8d., only 4d. more than on the 13th of August of this year, and wheat was then (in September) selling in the San Francisco market at $2 70; while this August, with the Liverpool market at 12s. 4d. (only 4d. less), they pay but $1 60 per cental—a difference between last year and this of $1 10 against the California farmer, when the difference should be but 4d., or less than eight cents, making a clean shave of $1 02 on every cental, or over sixty cents on every bushel. It seems that while these speculators pay out but $5 more for freight, they pay $22 per ton less this year than the last for wheat.

But we are told by these wheat sharps, these bread buccaneers, that the present low price of wheat in the California market is necessarily caused by the high price of freights, the increased charges for shipping, and because they are obliged to pay £4, or $20 per ton to Liverpool. Is this true? Is this the legitimate cause of depressing the price of wheat? Let us prick this pretty bubble and see it collapse. Twenty dollars per ton is one cent per pound. Now, to offset for the high rates of freight now charged the farmer; to have made last year's profits compare with those of this year, the freight last year ought to have been forty cents a ton less than nothing. But what were the actual freights paid last autumn? We find it noted in the Daily Bulletin of November 15th, "grain to Liverpool direct, £2," and as high as £2 7s. 6d., or nearly $12 (according to a recent number of the Alta California), was paid during that year. So that, instead of the buyers being able to pay us $2 70 per cental for wheat in San Francisco, by reason of its being carried to Liverpool for nothing, they were paying ten dollars a ton or over, or half a cent per pound; add which to the present price of wheat, $1 60, and we have $2 10 per cental as the present value of wheat in this market; and this is what the farmer ought now to receive, and would receive, but for the disreputable "rings" formed to monopolize the carrying trade.

But do these bread buccaneers really pay £4 or $20 per ton freight? It is well understood that the chief mogul of the buccaneers chartered a large number of ships more than he was prospectively in need of for legitimate purposes, at £2 to £3, and then pretended to re-charter them to his fellow-clansmen of the "ring" at £4 per ton, or thereabouts. That's what makes this pretext of high freights, and not the real scarcity of ships. There are numbers of disengaged vessels in our harbor every week, and more arriving daily. Wheat is now being shipped from Philadelphia to Liverpool, at $6 per ton, and by steamer at that. Does this indicate a scarcity of shipping?

Here we find these remorseless speculators (if their re-charters are genuine), making the snug sum of $5 or more on every ton, or $5,000 on each ship of one thousand tons capacity, at the expense of the farmer, to say nothing of the advance the speculators get in buying wheat at $1 60 and selling it at over $3 per cental. No wonder, under these circumstance, that we should see such paragraphs as the following, which we clip from a recent San Francisco daily paper:

"It is a curious fact, and one which has been observed by not a few, that when wheat is most wanted in this market, up go the Liverpool quotations, and, encouraged by a healthier market, in come the supplies; but on their arrival down go the Liverpool quotations, and this market instantly responds. Those who manipulate the wires must be in a very doubtful state regarding the wheat prospects by the uncertain and frequent changes made in the quotations."

Your committee can here only allude to the petit larceny attempt to swindle the farmers by the wheat sack extortion.

And now, what is to be done to counteract these plots against the interests of the farmer, and to enable the farmer to obtain a living price for his grain—the honest earnings of his hard labor, earned by the sweat of his brow, and by days of ceaseless toil and by nights of watchful care? Your committee are expected to suggest a remedy. The one proposed by the resolution of the Napa County Club, and endorsed by various agricultural associations of the kind in Sacramento, San Jose, San Joaquin and other places, to form Protective Unions by counties and districts, and to concentrate in a strong State Institution, meets the approval of your committee, with some modifications perhaps; but we deem it now too late to perfect any organization that shall be effective the present season. But farmers have the power to make their efforts felt, and at once; and that is by holding on to their grain crop until a fair price shall be offered. Those in immediate want of money can get what advances they may need on their wheat, and sell it when it reaches a living price. Compel these ship-grabbers to pay heavy demurrage on their empty vessels for a few months, and it will bring them to terms.

Let those speculators who attempt to "corner" the farmer, beware that they do not find themselves "cornered," as in a late remarkable instance in Chicago, resulting so disastrously to the buccaneers.

We regret there should be any antagonism between the farmer and the produce dealer. It is not the fault of the farmers; they only seek what is right and just; they ask only a reasonable compensation for their labor and capital; they are willing to live and let live. They are willing to sell their products at rates that will allow a fair margin of profits for the honest dealer, but they are not satisfied to have all their profits and earnings carried off by the speculators. Free trade and farmers' rights are what we seek. We cannot consent to be made the victims of dishonest combinations and over-reaching avarice and monopolies. Between the farm laborer, clamoring for increased wages, though far better paid in California than in any other country in the world, and the greedy middle-men and intriguing produce gamblers and grasping railroad monopolists and the insatiable tax-gatherer, the farmer, who can come out even at the close of the year, may well congratulate himself as a fortunate man. It is only indefatigable industry, keen sagacity and untiring perseverance, that will enable him to do this. All other callings and industries have their co-operative associations for their protection and advancement. The farmer must have his or he cannot prosper, nor attain those rewards of labor and industry that he has a right to claim.

Your committee would conclude by recommending that five delegates be chosen by the Oakland Farming, Horticultural and Industrial Club, to meet representatives from like associations in other portions of the State, at Sacramento, on Monday evening, September 22d (during the State Fair), as suggested by the Sacramento Club, to consider the propriety of an effective organization throughout the State, for their mutual protection and advantage.

Respectfully submitted, by

T. HART HYATT, } Committee.
CHR. BAGGE, }

In the Napa Club, Mr. Nash spoke very earnestly to the same subject. He said:

The great trouble with farmers of all classes was, after having produced their crops, to get adequately paid for them. They needed organization, as they had everything to contend with. The cost of hired help, mechanics' bills, and profits were extortionate. They have to give what is asked, and take what is offered. The costs of shipping eats up everything. What one thing can we raise and make a profit? Had spent some time with Mr. Lewellyn in Alameda county. He had found there that the farmers and fruit growers had combined and hired a steamboat to ship their produce. They don't ship any more by railroad, which used to charge them $1 50 per chest for small fruits. They now ship per steamer at 62½ cents, at which the boat is making money, and weeds and dog fennel are growing up around the depot.

In the present state of things, we are making nothing and can make nothing. It cost $1 per chest to pick my berries, and I have seen plenty of strawberries sold this year at $2 and $3 per hundred pounds. Everything is eaten up by expenses, leaving the farmers nothing. Many of them cannot keep the sheriff outside their fences. We must find out some plan of co-operation, such as they have in some places at the East, and have co-operative stores and shops, for our own protection. We may yet do something by a thorough and general organization.

In the Contra Costa Club, the President, Mr. Jones, said:

In regard to co-operation, the most of the small farmers labored under the difficulty of being obliged to hypothecate their crops, and consequently were under the control of capitalists. We see that capitalists are now controlling tonnage, and almost everything that the farmer requires. He thought that if farmers were thoroughly organized, they might control these matters. It would be a good thing if farmers would unite and create a capital so as to be able to relieve the small farmers in their time of need, and by this means enable them to get their small farms in good condition, so that in a few years they would be entirely independent of capitalists.

Mr. Porter said he supposed the object of all farmers would be to produce as much as possible themselves, such articles as they were obliged to have, because the cost of transporting all comes out of the farmer. There is no doubt that farmers might produce a great deal more than they do. If a farmer puts all his land in wheat, it takes up all his time; if he would put in less wheat and raise some of the articles he is compelled to buy, he would save more money and be better prepared to devote a portion of his time to something else. If a judicious system of exchanges could be instituted, it would do away with many of the fees of middle-men—a great saving to farmers. In regard to the securing of tonnage, he did not know that it would prove a disadvantage to us; it might be an advantage. If the buyers engage the tonnage to ship their own purchases of wheat, we will be benefitted; if they charter ships to sub-charter, then we are not benefitted.

Mr. Fish thought the system of farming, as now practiced, was ruinous to the owners of the land. We have to pay so many commissions that it leaves nothing to the small farmer; he thought the system of freights was in the hands of a monopoly; thought we ought to have a system of co-operation in regard to disposing of our crops. Those whose experience gave them the right to speak with authority, declared concerning the wheat market, that in no other State in the Union are the great body of wheat growers so completely under the thumb of one man as in California; no other State in which there is not something like competition in the market, and generally more than one outlet for the disposal of the surplus product. It is simply strange that one man only in California of those possessing ample means, should have been found with brains enough to have made some provision for the purchase and shipment of our wheat crop.

A summary of the farmers' complaints and their causes appeared in the Rural Press of September 7th. "In addition to the impositions practiced upon the farmers by middle-men, who crowd themselves in between the producer and consumer, and unnecessarily, and by every art in their power, increase the cost of all agricultural products as much as possible, while passing through their hands, we may mention another great wrong, the effect of which, particularly in this State, falls heavily upon the agriculturists. We refer to the additional rate of interest which is charged upon all moneys loaned in the country, over and above the rate charged for money loaned in the large towns and cities. For many years the savings and other banks of the cities refused to loan money even upon real estate which was not located within the city; thus, with wonderful stupidity, refusing to assist in the development of the agricultural resources of the State, upon which all other industries, and even the banking or money-loaning business itself, depends for its continued and permanent prosperity. Time has shown them their mistake by cities being forced into unnatural growth and beyond the necessities of the country, and consequent depreciation of city property and want of city demand for money.

"Being forced to keep their money laying in their vaults idle or seek loans in the country, they adopt the latter; but make it a rule to require country borrowers to pay from an eighth to a quarter per cent. more per month than they ask on city loans; thus still adhering to the suicidal policy of crippling the industry which lies at the foundation of the prosperity of other industries and of the State.

"This discrimination of the banks and moneyed men against the agricultural industries, is as unjust to the farmer as it is unwise in those who practice it. It induces or compels a forced system of cultivation without proper fertilization of the land. It prevents necessary improvements, without which the country cannot possess the appearance or reality of thrift. It compels the farmer to sell his grain at whatever he can get for it, thus throwing him into the clutches of another class of sharpers. The grain buyers conspire together to form rings and corners to catch the producer in a tight place and rob him of his crop—or, at least, of his legitimate profits thereon. It is a common remark in this country, that the price of grain is kept down after each harvest until after the bulk of it has passed out of the hands of the producers, and then, by combinations of the buyers, forced up to an illegitimate price, thus forcing from the consumers—the common laborers, mechanics and manufacturers of the State—an improper proportion of their wages and profits for the staple articles of life, and at the same time discouraging the introduction and success of manufacturing industries, upon which, and the additional consumers they would bring, the producers must depend for their home market—the most profitable and reliable market in any country.

"It would seem as though we had named difficulties enough, with which farmers are beset, to arouse them to united action for the purpose of breaking the chains which bind them down, but there are still others, compared to which those enumerated are but trifles. Chief among these is the *freight monopoly*. The whole carrying trade of the State is now virtually in the hands of one company. Whether it shall cost the farmers of the State one sixteenth, one eighth, one fourth or one half the value of their crops to move them to market, is absolutely at the discretion of an organization which has absorbed all the railroads and all the steamboat routes of the State. This company has it in its power to-day to reduce the cost of putting the surplus products of the State on the wharves of our seaport towns and cities to the least possible figure, and thus spread prosperity and contentment all over the State, and secure the good-will of the entire producing classes; or it has the power temporarily to extort an unjust and unreasonable amount for the performance of this labor, and thus oppress the agriculturists, drive prosperity and thrift from their doors, produce suffering and discontent throughout the land, and provoke the ill-will and the combined opposition of the people who have this labor to give and the freights to carry, and who, while acting as individuals, have no influence or power, but who, when forced to combine, will have all the influence and all the power.

"There is no proposition clearer than that a liberal policy, adopted and carried out by the capitalists, the produce dealers and grain buyers and freighting companies of the State toward the industrial classes, will result in the mutual benefit of all, in the increased population and redoubled prosperity of the State. Equally clear is the other proposition that the opposite policy will secure the opposite effect and will form a combination of those industrial classes for their own protection.

"The organization of the farmers' clubs throughout the State is one of the first fruits of this latter policy. It is an evidence that the farmers feel their wrongs and know and mean to apply the remedy. They have the power to regulate alike the rate of interest on money, and the rate of freights on railroads. They have the power to dispense with all middle-men, and by co-operative systems, to dispose of their own produce directly to the consumers, free of all commissions and all unnecessary charges."

The Sacramento convention brought together the following delegates:

Sonoma County Club—R. A. Thompson, A. W. Middleton, William H. Rector, Henderson Holmes, G. W. Davis, John Adams.

Napa County Club—J. B. Saul, James M. Thompson, W. H. Nash, Wm. Gouverneur Morris, T. L. Griggs, W. A. Truebody, J. M. Mayfield, W. A. Fisher.

Vacaville and Pleasant Valley Fruit Growers' Association—T. O. Bingham, Wm. Cantelow.

Sacramento County Farmers' Club—I. N. Hoag, S. N. Baker, W. S. Manlove, James Rutter, William M. Haynie.

Oakland Farming, Horticultural and Industrial Club—Dr. E. S. Carr, T. Hart Hyatt, Christian Bagge, A. D. Pryall, and A. T. Dewey.

Santa Clara County Club—W. H. Ware, Jesse Hobson, C. T. Settle, ——Chipman, Cary Peebles.

Sutter County Club—John McIlmoil, M. Wilson, C. P. Berry.

San Joaquin County Club—Dr. E. S. Holden, J. N. W. Hitchcock, Thomas C. Ketcham, C. Grattan, H. C. Wright, W. G. Phelps, James Smythe, L. H. Brannock.

Santa Cruz County Club—Benjamin Cahoon, J. R. Locke.

El Dorado County Club—G. G. Blanchard, Robert Chalmers.

Sonoma Vinicultural Club—W. M. McPherson Hill, Major J. R. Snyder, Wm. Hood.

T. Hart Hyatt submitted the following:

In view of the stern, exasperating fact that the farmers of California, when spared the calamity of a loss of crops from drought, floods, mildew, or blight, are met by a more withering scourge in the form of railroad monopolies and pestilent grain rings and bread-sharks, whereby the farmer is robbed of the fruits of his hard toil and life-long earnings, and left without enough in many cases to reimburse him for his expenditures, while the merciless speculators are fattening on their unjust gains, building palaces and sporting princely establishments on the plunder thus taken from the hard working farmer; and in view of the fact that nothing can be effectually done by the farmer without co-operative and vigilant, energetic, united action; therefore, be it

Resolved, That the convention deem it expedient forthwith to establish and organize a Farmers' Protective Union League, to be composed of the members of all the local agricultural and horticultural clubs and associations in the State, who may desire to join the league; and to hold semi-annual meetings alternately at Oakland, Marysville, Stockton, Napa City, San Jose, Sacramento, and at such other points as may be deemed practicable. That said league be organized under the laws of the State, and be duly incorporated, so far as it may be necessary to enable it to transact business in a legal manner; to be a business, not a sporting institution; that it appoint an Executive Central Committee, who shall be empowered to transact business for the league during the intervals of its regular meetings. The said league to have power and authority to organize and establish a Produce Exchange, a Farm Stock Exchange, and a Farmers' Savings, Deposit and Loan Bank; and to do all other things that may be found necessary to advance the rights of the farmers of California.

All seemed earnest in their action, and united and determined on the main objects of the association. The tenor of the general remarks showed a desire to strengthen the influence of the convention by calm, deliberate action, attempting no dictation and making no demands in any direction without the power to enforce them.

President Fisher recommended that warehouses be built at convenient points for shipment, where farmers can safely put their grain and keep it. It was suggested that foreign capital, or any other capital demanding a low interest, can ask for no safer security. The money can always be had when the grain is put up, and as long as it is needed and at rates that we can stand. Our great crops, once in our storehouses, we can also have the power to co-operate and deal directly with foreign buyers. We can show what we have in our hands, and they will know what ships can profitably be sent this way at the right time. Messrs. Blanchard, Phelps, Rector, Morris, and others favored building sufficient warehouses to carry out, as far as practicable, the objects desired.

Dr. Carr urged that there was a still higher work for the State Farmers' Club whereby they may secure the worthy object of getting fair prices for our products. Let us arrange to work up our own produce into brain and muscle. Encourage manufacturing, and diversified farming, giving all the needs and comforts of life cheaply. If low prices shall discourage sending enormous quantities of wheat out of the country annually, it may be in the end a blessing rather than a calamity. Wheat crops as now produced, year after year, are taking the cream of our rich and generous yielding soil. As our lands grow poorer, immigration and all industry is discouraged. It is the noble work of our Farmers' Club to bring about a better order of things and make the utmost of the rich resources that are within our reach on this highly favored coast.

Mr. Morris endorsed Dr. Carr's remarks, and stated that his taking the United States census returns for the State developed to him the fact that in a quite recent year one export of wheat brought us less money than we sent away for boots and shoes manufactured abroad. The census returns also bring painfully before us our lack of suitable employment of boys and girls. Occupation is needed for them, that we may have the right men and women of to-morrow to develop and increase our naturally rich possessions.

Mr. Blanchard counseled making the best of things beyond our present control. When we cannot build competing railroads, let farmers and fruit-growers combine, see what, unitedly, is the best they can do without the railroads—immediately and prospectively—and then show railroad men how they stand in their own light by keeping up high prices, preventing industry from being profitable, keeping back settlement, and retaining undeveloped districts for their slim trains to pass through. Talk business, drive sharp bargains. Railroad men have not all the brains and business tact, and producers have frequent opportunities to make points in their own favor.

A Constitution and By-Laws were adopted, and the following officers elected, viz: Hon. John Bidwell, President; J. R. Snyder, of Sonoma, E. P. Holden, of San Joaquin, T. Hart Hyatt, of Alameda, W. S. Manlove, of Sacramento, D. C. Feeley, of Santa Cruz, and W. H. Ware, of Santa Clara, Vice Presidents; I. N. Hoag, Secretary, and A. T. Dewey, Treasurer.

The farmers were now organized, but there was not yet sufficient unanimity of sentiment, or experience in management, to secure that without which sentiments and resolutions would prove of little avail, viz. incorporation.

The statement that the quotations of California wheat in Liverpool, were below the real market rates prevailing there, and that false telegraphic quotations had been intentionally made for the purpose of further depressing prices in California, was confirmed on the arrival by mail of the "Mark Lane Express," the representative of the produce interests of England, both agricultural and commercial. The loss to the farmers for August amounted to $168,870, which went into the pockets of the operators. For the year it would not have been less than $1,560,000—2,340,000.* An attempt was made to excuse these discrepancies, by the statement that the higher quotations from the "Mark Lane Express" were for "club," and those telegraphed for "average white wheat;" but inasmuch as the amount of "club" raised or shipped is trifling, this explanation only served to stimulate further inquiry, when it was found that these misquotations had been continued through the fourteen months, with one single exception. On the 28th of November, 1871, the true average price of wheat in Liverpool had been telegraphed. All the rest were from 1 cent to 22 cents; averaging 10 cents lower than the real quotations. Our own dailies had innocently published these fraudulent reports, based in some cases also upon grain circulars issued in England in the interest of the buyers. The "Mark Lane Express" alone remained above suspicion. What could be done about it? The farmers might protect themselves by the establishment of a Wheat Bureau in Liverpool, or of an agency authorized by the State Board, whose business it should be to tabulate imports, exports, crop returns, information as to prices brought by different grades, etc., etc.

The Rural Press summed up the subject in its issue of November 16, in a manner which gave the people at large an understanding of all its relations:

The average rate of tonnage for the last four months for charters effected in this port has been £4 15s., and the difference between this, and that really paid for ships chartered previous to arrival, has been £1 15s. per ton, or 42 cents per cental. This has been the average profit of those who received the principal part of the tonnage bound to our port for the last six or eight months, on every cental of wheat exported this harvest year. From the 1st of July to the 3d of November, the exports have amounted to 3,355,318 centals, which at 42 cents each, gives a profit of $1,409,235 55, at least one million dollars of which must have found its way into the pockets of a single firm. If this came out of the pocket of one

*See "Rural Press" of October and November, 1872.

speculator and went into those of another, we would not mind. And there is every reason to fear that a proportionally large sum will be extracted from the pockets of the farmers for the balance of the season. If this should be the case, and should the amount of wheat available for export, equal that which would be intimated by the estimates of some of our prominent men, the loss to the farmers and the gain to the speculators will not be less than $5,888,000. At nineteen bushels an acre, the loss to the farmer would be seven dollars and ninety-eight cents, or nearly eight dollars per acre, and on a farm of one thousand acres, producing such an average crop, the loss would be almost $8,000. It is high time then that farmers should awake to the situation. If taxes of this amount were levied on them, or attempted to be levied, they would rise in open rebellion, and yet they tamely submit to this imposition, or make a few feeble and ineffectual protests, and there the matter ends. It will be seen from our table that the average of freights for the eleven years ending December, 1871, was £2 10s. 8d. only. If the farmers of the State were united on the matter, they could freight ships or build them, and the cost of carrying wheat to Liverpool would not exceed £2 10s. With wheat for export equaling fourteen million centals, they would then save in one season, the sum of $7,560,000, or 54 cents per cental, or $10,260 on every farm of one thousand acres.

During the balance of the harvest year, with the vessels which have already loaded cargoes for England, and those on the way now known to be engaged, we have one hundred and seventy-seven vessels. Now, calculating by the average cargoes which have already been loaded, there would, supposing fourteen million centals to be available for exportation, be required four hundred and ten vessels. So that we require arrivals of one hundred and sixty-four more besides those already on the way known to be chartered for wheat in order to carry away the largest possible margin of export. Those at present available will carry away 10,151,658 centals; and there being now on the way to this port altogether one hundred and eighty-seven ships, this ensures us a far more satisfactory prospect for the balance of the year. In this connection we may mention a circumstance that has come under our notice during the last fortnight which shows how completely are the farmers at the mercy of the grain speculators.

A merchant in Visalia, whose interests are intimately connected with those of the farmers of his section, desired to assist them in obtaining better prices for their wheat, and in order to do so, he contracted at reasonable rates for a ship with one of our largest shipping houses in this city. The house in question generally bears a good name, but unfortunately the merchant only made a verbal contract with it. He was soon after approached by an agent of Mr. Monopoly or a party in his interest, who endeavored to obtain the ship from him. But the merchant was firm. This agent then says to him, "I suppose you expect to load the ship." The reply was, "Yes, certainly I do, I have engaged it, and shall send it." Whereupon Monopoly's representative rejoined, "Let me tell you, (or mark my words,) you won't send that ship." Within forty-eight hours the merchant received a notification from the house that they could not possibly let him have the ship.

We can give the names of the parties to any of our readers who may desire to have them. We have been accused of bringing charges on freight rings and grain rings needlessly, but we think that a perusal of our article, and a knowledge of such means as here shown to be made use of to keep all the available tonnage mainly in the hands of one house, will convince our readers that our denunciation of the unworthy means made use of to rob the farmers of this State, have been both timely and needed.

CHAPTER IX.

HOW THE CLUBS BECAME GRANGES.

Meeting of the Board of Directors: President Bidwell's Remarks: Major Snyder advocates Building Co-operative Warehouses: Judge McCune on Fares and Freights—Sonoma Club—Mass Meeting at Stockton: Thirty Thousand Dollars Subscribed — Mr. Baxter appears on the Scene — Convention at San Francisco— How the Grangers Negotiated for Sacks and Did'nt Get them—Gen. Bidwell's Address---A Lady's Suggestions ---Mr. Hallett on the Future of the Wheat Market---Convention Recommends the Formation of Granges: Winding Up of its Affairs.

The history of the Farmers' Union is virtually that of the emancipation of California agriculture from its oppressive burdens. It has been seen that the local clubs were the centers of influence, and the germinal points of enlightened public opinion, while the board of directors were active in perfecting plans for immediate relief. President Bidwell called a meeting of the board, in January, "to devise means by which the cost of moving and marketing the crops of the approaching season might be reduced, thus enabling the farmer to realize a larger percentage of profit. The charges for sacks and freight to a market at home or abroad were so great that the farmer was scarcely remunerated for his labor of production; and this state of things did not so much arise from natural causes as from the exorbitant exactions of those by whom the material for sacking, the money to move produce, and the means of transportation were provided. It was the interest and the duty of the farmers, by combined action, by organization, by financial or political power and influence, to endeavor to protect themselves; to demand, exact and enforce justice and common honesty from those with whom they deal. There is but one way for the farmers to succeed in the accomplishment of these objects, and that is the organization of local clubs, and the steady support of the State Club in its efforts in their behalf. If the farmers in all portions of the State will come together and form local clubs, and put themselves in correspondence and business relations with the State Farmers' Union, in such a manner as to authorize the officers of this association to act for and bind them under necessary moral and financial obligations, in my opinion, the relief which they seek can be obtained, to a great degree at least, and industrial prosperity may become general throughout the State.

"But, while the farmer remains aloof from his neighbors—while he continues to act on the selfish individual policy—other classes, such as importers and manufacturers of agricultural tools and implements, importers and manufacturers of sacks, common carriers, grain dealers, commission merchants and money loaners, will unite for the advancement of their own interests and ends, and will take undue and unjust advantages of the farmer; will oppress, prey upon him, and eat out his substance, and continue to keep him poor and dependent. Farmers now, unorganized, are weak and in a great degree helpless, and they have but little courage to make an effort to free themselves or better their condition; but let one hundred thousand farmers of this State unite together, and act as one man, through an honest and reliable organization, demanding only common justice, but exacting this to the last degree, and with a firm and united front, and there is no power in the land that can prevent the attainment of their just demands. The farming interests of the country need some wholesome legislation to place them on an equal footing with other occupations, and to relieve them from the exactions of heartless monopolies; and if farmers will but unite to send the proper men to represent them in our legislative halls, both State and National; will see to it that our judicial and executive offices are filled with honest, efficient and reliable men, it will then be but an easy matter to secure such legislation and such constitution and execution of the laws as their interests and the best interests of the State demand. For the purpose of emphasizing the idea, I repeat," said Gen. Bidwell, "and I wish I could sound it in the ears of every farmer in the State, the only salvation of the agricultural interests, the only safety to the individual interests of the farmer, is in union of interest and union of action."

Major J. R. Snyder, of Sonoma, warmly advocated the careful selection of county supervisors, looking toward the improvement of the roads; and also the building of co-operative farmers' warehouses. The taxing of growing crops was declared to be unjust and oppressive; and the Board resolved to call upon the local clubs for a repeal of the law at the next session of the Legislature.

Before the Stockton Club, Judge J. H. McCune gave an able address, which was afterwards widely circulated, on the carrying trade, and the subject of fares and freights. The Sonoma Club struck directly for an immediate incorporation. They said:

"It is manifest that while the moral benefits of a mere association of farmers are apparent, and much good may be derived therefrom, yet in order to market our crops cheaply, control freights, make successful war on monopolies obnoxious to our interests, we need some more effective machinery than that afforded by a mere social organization. There must be a financial and commercial element in our organization to make our power felt."

To carry out these ideas they made the following specific recommendations, which are interesting to us, at the present time, only as showing the clearness with which remedial measures were already outlined in the minds of the farmers:

1st. We recommend the incorporation of this Club, as provided by section two hundred and eighty-six of the Civil Code of the State, as a corporation "for the encouragement of, or business of agriculture, horticulture and stock-raising;" that we maintain our social character, as it is at present, so that none but those interested in the farmers' progress may be members thereof, and by which we may choose our associates.

2d. In order that a pecuniary profit may accrue, we recommend the incorporation of a "County Farmers' Union," upon the basis of a capital stock of say not less than $100,000, the paid-up capital of which shall be $10,000, and increased as necessity demands. Part of this stock may be taken by the several local or district farmers' clubs, and the remainder by farmers whose operations are large, and whose wants the local clubs could not supply. This County Union could enter the market, buy sacks at reduced rates, secure by the large interest of its operations cheap freight, both by ship and car, build or lease warehouses, accumulate funds for loaning to farmers, secured by storage of crops, and be the farmers' consignee and middle-men. The farmers holding stock would thus control both the capital and the crop, and could easily prevent it from being an engine of oppression. It need not necessarily be organized to secure profit and declare dividends; these results would be obtained by cheap freights and increased prices for produce, and the profit would be found in "farming." Each stockholder should be a member of a Farmers' Club.

3d. We also recommend the incorporation of the State Farmers' Union, with a capital of $1,000,000.

The benefits to be derived from this organization may be outlined as follows: The several clubs at their meetings can report the prospects of the crops from time to time, to the Union, and the probable amount of the several products; the estimates of the county thus made and forwarded promptly to the officers of the State Union, will enable them to make estimates of the number of sacks required, and the tonnage necessary to convey the crops to foreign markets.

The officers of the State Union, by observation of the prospects in foreign countries, and the East, will be enabled early to form an estimate of the value of the several products of export. Thus the farmers, by their agents, will be able to fix the prices of their own products, and by the moneys and credits established by and represented in these exportations, they will be able to maintain the prices they may agree upon.

Thus organized, thus combined for the maintenance of our rights, we will be able to bid defiance to the monopolists who have been preying upon us in the past; and if we cannot entirely dispose of the "middle-men," who stand between the producer and consumer, we shall be able at least to induce a more liberal division with us, of the fruits of our toil, to compel them to live less sumptuously, to ride in less elegant carriages, drawn by slower horses.

Nor was this all talk, as the liberal subscriptions to the stock of the local and county clubs bore testimony. All farmers, whether members of the clubs or not, were invited to coöperate in obtaining sacks at reduced prices. At the above-mentioned meeting of the Sonoma Club, Mr. Isaac De Turk proposed the establishment of an experimental farm, and supported his views by strong and well considered reasons.

The Dixon Club drew up a petition to Congress for the repeal of the duty on grain sacks, which was duly communicated to the other clubs for their signatures. On the 1st of March, there was an immense gathering of farmers at Stockton, to incorporate the San Joaquin Farmers' Union, with a proposed capital stock of $300,000.

This indeed looked like a "revolt of the field." "Farmers should combine against monopolists," said Mr. Paulsell; "and to protect their own interests, the association proposed to de-

W. H. BAXTER,
W. S. of State Grange of California.

vise some plan of getting to foreign and domestic markets without having their products go through the hands of so many middle-men; to import grain sacks direct, instead of allowing California merchants to swallow up the farmers' earnings by enormous profits." The sum of nineteen thousand dollars was subscribed on the spot, and eleven thousand subsequently, making a total of thirty thousand dollars on that Saturday afternoon.

By the first of April, there was a chain of farmers' organizations completed on the Pacific Coast, from El Monte in Los Angeles County, to Walla Walla, in Washington Territory. It began to appear likely that greater privacy in carrying on the large business interests contemplated by them, would be indispensable. In the Spring of 1871, W. H. Baxter, residing on his farm near Napa City, had communicated with the Secretary of the National Grange, with respect to the wants of agriculturists in California, the social isolation in which so many of them lived, and the exactions which they suffered. Certain plans for their relief had been shaping themselves in his mind, which, through this correspondence, he found anticipated, or met to a reasonable extent by the statements of the purposes and practical effects of that Order. In August, 1871, he received a commission as Deputy of the National Grange for California.

Mr. Baxter at once began to spread information with regard to the objects and advantages promised in the new organization, but his hearers, for the most part, were already members of clubs, and had no suspicion that any open organization would necessarily fail before the combination of intellect and capital with which the farmers had to contend. Patient and persistent, Mr. Baxter watched his opportunity, and was content to bide his time, which came even sooner than he expected, at the Farmers' Union Convention, which met in San Francisco, on the 8th of April, 1873, and was fully represented by delegations from all the Clubs, and by those who are now the leading Patrons in the State.

The convention was opened by an address from President Bidwell, who said:

We are convened as farmers and representatives of the farming and industrial interests of California. For several years a growing want has been felt among the farmers of the State for co-operation through a State organization, and that feeling found expression in the formation of this California Farmers' Union in September last, during the State Fair at Sacramento. In that movement there was something very American in its character—a directness, an ability to improvise, to meet emergency. In a word, there was something to be done, and they met and did it.

One of the grievances of the past year complained of by farmers is the enormous price imposed for sacks in which to market or store their wheat. Instead of eleven to thirteen cents, which would have been a fair price, they have had to pay fifteen to nineteen cents, or an aggregate overcharge in the State of half a million of dollars. Instead of $12 50 per ton freight on wheat from San Francisco to Liverpool, which would have been a fair rate, ocean tonnage became monopolized and demoralized, and farmers were made to suffer to the tune of probably $2,500,000 more. That interior freights are too high, all agree, and the overcharge on wheat alone may be within the actual limits if placed at half a million more. In how many other ways farmers are and have been unjustly taxed I will not undertake to enumerate. The aggregate totals, at a moderate estimate, cannot be stated at a lower figure than three to five millions; and the universal complaint of the farmers is that they are burdened beyond their ability to bear. [How many frugal and industrious farmers during the past year—which was one of overflowing abundance, and coincided with high prices and large demand in Liverpool and elsewhere—were obliged to borrow money to pay their State and County taxes ?]

At a meeting of your Board of Directors, convened January 3d last, in this city, the question of grain sacks for the coming harvest was considered. There was still time to order from Dundee, and a committee of the Board made every possible effort to arrange with a reliable house for a promise to furnish sacks at the lowest definite rate, and on such terms as to time and responsibility as the committee could recommend and the farmers afford to accept, with the view of communicating the information to the several clubs for their acceptance. For some time we were hopeful of success. But I must say, as one of the committee, we utterly failed to accomplish our mission in that respect. The parties could not do as we wished. After repeated delays, the manufacturers or the holders would not agree to a stipulated price, which would make it an object for farmers to accept.

This subject is submitted to your consideration, with the suggestion that the manufacture of sacks in this State should, by every means in our power, be encouraged as the only adequate remedy for existing wants in that respect.

In order to bring about efficiency on the part of your Board of Directors, and enable them to meet your reasonable expectations, I beg leave to suggest that at least the President, Treasurer and Secretary, if not a quorum of the Board, should reside in San Francisco or Sacramento (San Francisco, everything considered, would be preferable, I think), and have some certain place of business. The officers named must necessarily be on the Executive Committee, and it is indispensable, in my judgment, that they be where they can meet as often as necessary to transact business. I take it for granted that you are in earnest and mean business, and if so, you must have a habitation as well as a name.

Believing this to be absolutely necessary, if you propose to continue this State organization in any form whatever, with a capacity for usefulness, I propose to resign my position that you may be free to adopt any plan or measure giving promise of efficiency.

At this point, it may not be improper to take a view of the situation in another direction. Agriculture in California has many advantages, but it has also its disadvantages.

First, you have a soil of wonderful and varied productiveness. No other land teems with fruits and useful products of such rare excellence, and in so great variety and abundance. Look at the cereal capacity of your State. Take for instance wheat—bread, the staff of life. If a premium were offered for the smallest yield of wheat in this State—on any land timely and properly managed—it would be difficult, in my opinion, to establish a smaller showing than ten bushels per acre, in any ordinary or average season, from land chosen by any sane man, up to this date. On the other hand, sixty to seventy bushels per acre are not uncommon; twenty bushels per acre by no means an extravagant average in some sections; and estimating the aggregate product in the United States at three hundred million of bushels, your total for 1872 gives the enormous proportion of one twelfth of all the wheat raised in all the States and Territories of this extended and productive country.

Next, you have a climate so serene, salubrious, equable, reliable, and invigorating, that its fame is becoming world-wide; thousands are being attracted hither from the Atlantic sea-board and other countries, from considerations of climate alone.

You have almost six months of summer sun and cloudless skies to ripen your cereal crops, and give a harvest season, of which the people on the Atlantic side of the continent can have no conception.

You have another advantage in the lay of the land, and the almost perfect condition of the soil. While in other States and Territories vast outlays from the very beginning have been necessary to clear lands of timber, or to drain them because too wet, or to irrigate because too dry, or to fertilize because too poor; here in this favored sunny realm the lands cultivated have, with few exceptions, come to you from the hand of nature, ready for immediate use, and all you have had to do was literally "to sow and reap and gather into barns."

Nor is this all. The general topography of the grain regions has enabled farmers to introduce with advantage the most approved agricultural implements and machinery.

You sow grain as well as reap by horse-power; you thresh by steam-power; and you are, many of you at least, looking impatiently to the time in the near future, when you shall be able by steam to stir and pulverize the soil with greater profit than is possible by animal power.

In addition to the advantages named, your State abounds in mineral, pastoral, and other resources. But I cannot further dwell on the pleasant side of the picture (though in itself inexhaustible), except to remark that great as has been nature's lavishness, in points of mineral wealth, that of the soil has run past them, and become, and is henceforth to be, the leading and paramount interest.

But it is not all sunshine, even in California. As the brightest skies become overcast with the darkest clouds, and the richest soil produces the rankest weeds, so even in this favored land you have your trials and troubles. You can produce, but you have no reliable adequate markets at home or abroad for your products. Even when there happens to be a demand, combinations intervene and cut you off.

I submit, then, that it is our interest to unite in order to encourage manufactures and build up useful industries in our own State, and thereby enlarge home market; and in order to bring about reasonable transportation and other expenses, and enable you to go into the markets of the world, and compete with all the world with your surplus products. As it is now, we are, in comparison with the Atlantic coast, at a disadvantage of more than fifteen thousand miles (practically more than half the circumference of the globe), in order to reach Europe. And from this there is no escape. Your cargoes must double Cape Horn, or do worse, by doubling the Cape of Good Hope, or still worse, by doubling all the capes of Southern Asia, and thence through the Red Sea and the Suez Canal. The other lines—overland by rail and the Isthmus—are by their charges practically closed, and therefore I do not take them into account.

By the nearest feasible route, then, the Pacific Coast is the remotest place on earth furnishing bread to European markets. Nevertheless, enterprise and superior natural advantages enabled you for long years to contend against distance, and overcome obstacles innumerable, till you won for California as wide a reputation for bread and other agricultural products, as for the precious metals. You have made her name like that of Egypt of old, almost a synonym for plenty.

There is a limit beyond which burdens cannot be borne, even by California farmers. As long as freights, sacks, and other expenses left even a small margin, you said nothing. You could pay fair rates for every needful outlay, and still have a margin, though small, on which to base hopes for the future. You could afford to await the growth of home industries and the influx of population to the State, knowing, as you did, that she possessed the elements, though undeveloped, of a glorious future.

It is true the elements which bear so heavily on your prosperity are not the growth of a day, but they are none the less dangerous, for they have become well-nigh formidable.

But when speculation and reckless adventure organize against you, and demoralize every legitimate business, enhance every risk and increase every expense—in other words, when freight rings, grain rings, sack rings, and all sorts of combinations, regulate their own charges, dictate the prices of your produce, and practically block up every avenue between you and your markets—can you remain insensible, silent, apathetic?

Do we not owe it to ourselves as well as to those who are to come after us, to devise reasonable safeguards for the agricultural interests of our State, and to say with the united voices of forty thousand farmers, and the forty thousand more whose best interests are inseparable from the farming interest, that they shall not, with our consent, be enslaved.

What avail all your boasted advantages? What, though your soil is unsurpassed and you amaze the world with its productiveness; what, though your valleys and plains have been made ready for use by nature's lavish kindness, and give to labor larger returns than any other known country; what, though your landscape charms, your climate invigorates, and your cloudless skies give you a harvest season from June to October; of what advantage, I say, are all these, if you are to groan under oppression, lose the fruits of your labor and the control of your destiny?

Of course, farmers whose interests are indissolubly linked with the general welfare should not and do not propose to make an invasion on vested rights or retard legitimate industries of any kind whatsoever. They simply ask for protection.

I can say for myself, and I speak the sentiments of the farmers generally, as I believe, in the following declarations:

That agriculture is and ever must be the fundamental industry of this and all other prosperous States, and more than any other industry creates and sustains commerce and manufactures, and furnishes the material to feed and clothe the world.

That transportation is indispensable to agricultural prosperity, and that it is our duty, as farmers, to promote the construction of roads, canals, vessels and all modes of conveyance calculated to facilitate the movement of agricultural products.

That the charges on lines of transportation should be regulated by law, and not left to unlimited monopoly; and if such regulations be found impracticable on existing lines, they should be made applicable to all future lines, until reciprocal relations shall be fully established between the producer and the common carrier.

We declare that farmers and all others should be equal before the law; that all laws should be enacted without bias, and executed without partiality; and to this end we declare that neither farmers or others ought to furnish legislative, executive, or judicial officers with free passes, or in any manner do anything calculated to improperly influence them in the discharge of their public trust; and that no officer, or candidate for office, ought to accept, nor shall any officer, with our consent, be hereafter elected who will accept of a free pass, or other gift.

We declare that all laws taxing growing crops, mortgages, or book accounts, or other mere memoranda calculated to enhance interest on money, which farmers and others in need have to borrow, are wrong in principle and oppressive in operation, and ought to be repealed.

We declare that it is the duty of Congress to so regulate commerce among all the States of this Union that agriculture shall not be oppressed by unnecessary burdens.

We declare that these vital questions are above all party issues.

On the second day, the Committee on Resolutions reported the following, which were adopted:

Resolved, That the rates charged for freights over the railroads in this State are ruinous to our agricultural interests.

2d—That in our opinion the corporations operating these roads, being the creations of our laws, are, and should be, under the control of our statutes, and that the maximum rates of freights should be so fixed by statute as to prevent extortion, and leave the producer a margin of profit on his productions, and that way freights be charged only in proportion to the distance the freight is sent with the charge for through freight.

3d—That if we find it impracticable under present management of such roads to obtain a fair reduction of such freights, we will agitate the subject and insist that the railroads built by the money of government shall be operated by the government in the interests of the people, rather than by private persons for personal aggrandizement.

4th—That as these matters are political, we will so far make this a political body as to cast our votes and use our influence for such men for our State Legislature as will carry our views into effect.

5th — That inasmuch as the farmers of this State find themselves a prey to moneyed rings, in the matter of grain sacks, we refer this matter to the Executive Committee of this body, with instructions to consider the propriety of utilizing State-prison labor, either at San Quentin or Folsom, in the production of a sufficient number of sacks each year, for our home consumption, to be sold to the farmers at their actual cost, thus saving the profit now made from us by dealers.

6th—That our Executive Committee also consider such other remedies for the wrongs we now sustain in that regard, as shall, to them, seem practical.

7th—That there being less tariff on the raw material for sacks, we can and ought to provide ourselves with the manufactured article without paying any margin to mere dealers in sacks.

8th—That our Executive Committee consider and propose a plan for the organization of co-operative banking, which shall put the farmers of the State in the possession of means sufficient to protect themselves from the rings formed by capitalists to appropriate to themselves the profits of our industry.

9th—That the Executive Committee be requested to propose some plan for the co-operation of farmers in each locality in the sale of their products and the purchase of necessaries, with a view to retain among the producers the profits now made by mere dealers.

10th—That our Executive Committee also consider and provide a plan for stowing grain and other farmers' products, with a view to enable farmers to retain their crops till they can get for them the highest market value.

The Committee on Communications presented a very able paper, by Mrs. J. Preston Moore, delegate from the Oakland

Farmers' Club, embodying suggestions, "how to move the crop:"

By means of an agency under the control of the California Farmers' Union, to be constituted in the following manner:

1st.—The officers of the California Farmer's Union to be a Board of Directors, to meet quarterly or oftener, and pass upon all matters pertaining to the agency, to have free access to the books at all times, etc., call meetings, etc.

2d.—The agency to consist of three departments. (1) Financial. A manager to arrange sales and all money matters at home and abroad; to pay all transportation and other expenses in shipping the crop, and to have the general oversight of all the other departments. (2) Transportation. A man to attend to the receiving and receipting for the wheat, and bringing to shipping ports, making terms with railroads and vessels for carrying. (3) Shipping. A man to attend to the loading and storing, arranging the cargoes to the best advantage for sale. These three to constitute an Advisory Board, with power to appoint clerks and agents, and subject to the Board of Directors.

3d.—An agency in London under the control of the Advisory Board, to make sales by means of telegrams and letters.

4th.—Actual cost of transportation from places of production to points of shipment and other expenses, to be charged against wheat of each farmer, and to be deducted with interest from his proportionate amount of wheat sales.

5th.—The Advisory Board to decide relative value of each farmer's wheat at time of its receipt, according to relative value in the English market at the time. (This refers to different qualities as the difference between coast and other wheat.) There to be but two discriminating clauses against any farmers' wheat, viz: relative cost of transportation to shipping point, and relative quality of wheat.

6th.—Money to be advanced by agency to the farmers on, before or after receipt of wheat, according to percentage that may be agreed upon by Board of Directors, say up to ninety per cent. of its value at time of reception, and balance to be paid him on the yearly settlement of the whole crop, say in June.

7th.—The yearly average of prices obtained for whole crop, to be determined say in June, or earlier if possible, and each farmer credited up at sale of same, and finally settled with and paid in full. This settlement would involve all the elements of expenses and profits in the business of the year. Such an agency would save in all shipments the five per cent. on amount of freight, and in many cases the seven per cent. paid by the ships to the parties chartering. For instance, a vessel of 1,500 tons at £4 per ton for freight, would pay five per cent., $1,500 commission, and paid here as soon as loaded. This arrangement would save here for selling one per cent., and in England two to three and one half per cent.

Of course the farmers must furnish the business credit of the agency. Each club must decide the relative responsibility of its members, and enter into written obligations to meet this. The club must as a whole meet their responsibility, and look to its members for their proportion in case of loss. This will necessitate the incorporation of the clubs as the first step.

The State Board of Directors will decide the relative responsibility of each club, based on the amount of property each represents. To make these credits available, the members of each club will be responsible to the club, and the club to the Board of Directors. The Board, which ought to consist of the prominent and most responsible members of all the clubs, would be responsible to the agency, and thus give it the necessary credit. There is no doubt about the wealth of the agricultural interest, but to make it available to transact their business as they wish, it must be thrown into such legal and business form as will make it a security at once certain and convertible.

To reap the advantages of a farmers' bank the farmers must own it. To do this, it will be necessary for each farmer to set aside in a good year (such as this promises to be), a certain sum for the formation of the bank, and for which he would receive stock in the bank, and thus participate in the profits to the amount of his stock; and, as banks never pay less than one per cent. a month to their shareholders, and often more, this would be a good investment for the farmer. This bank would be under a separate agency. Each club would be largely interested in the welfare of this bank, and as each club would be well acquainted with the standing of each of its members, it would be necessary, before any member could get money, to make application to the club, and obtain a written recommendation from it. Thus the club guarantees each of its members to the bank, and in case of loss the club will have to pay and collect of its members whatever they fail to recover of the delinquent. This, of course, is for money obtained as advances. This bank would do a regular banking business, charging the regular rates of interest, but giving the farmer the same rates as business men in the city, and the preference.

A very important subject in this connection is the warehousing, or storing the wheat, in order that the rush of the sales may he distributed over a longer time, and thus holding the power over the shipping, which cannot afford to wait, and giving the agency a better chance to obtain better charter parties.

The Committee on Communications also reported, presenting the following memorials and petitions:

To the Honorable Representatives elect, and Senators of the Pacific States:

We, your constituents, farmers and laborers and others, carrying the industries and development of the States of the sunset slope, would most respectfully crave your attention to our wants; and through you, ask of Congress relief of a grievous burden—an uncalled-for tax upon our industries.

The farming interests of the States of California and Oregon are carried forward with great difficulties, when compared with the same interest East.

We seek the same market for the disposal of our grain, though three thousand miles farther west, and six thousand by the only route open to us—the sea. We have also the enormous expense of sacking our grain—forty to eighty dollars per thousand bushels; twelve million sacks to move the crop of 1872, in the State of California alone, averaging not less than fifteen cents a piece to your humble petitioners, the farmers of the State, making nearly two million dollars tax on the farmer to enter the market with his products in competition with his eastern brother, and six thousand miles more water freight too; and now, in addition to all that burden, the government has placed a tariff upon the importation of sacks, thirty and forty per cent., and material for manufacture. This is the last pound to the camel's burden, and is the chief cry we have for redress; and we would ask at your hands, that the tariff on jute and all material for sack manufacture be removed, and all duty on sacks be taken off, as far as the ports of California and Oregon are concerned. This would relieve the over-burdened farmer of California of about one half million dollars tax; as it is claimed by experts that the State manufactory can now compete with the foreign trade at one cent profit per sack; by the removal of tax on raw material it still has the more advantage, and we, your petitioners, will also gain, and not lose anything, as we do not raise the sack materials in the State. And we believe our eastern brothers will not complain when they see how much we already endure; and not unmindful of the great benefits to a State of home manufactories, we must say that the present Jute Company does not command our strong sympathies, as they have run the mills almost exclusively for the speculators, instead of the demands of the trade, with the greatest good to the greatest number.

All of the above is most respectfully submitted, and for relief we would ever pray.

To the Honorable, the Senate and House of Representatives in Congress assembled.

The undersigned petitioners, citizens of the United States, of the State of California, respectfully represent—

That all taxes should be as equally borne by all the people of the United States as possible. That a tax that reaches one part of the country and leaves the rest untouched, or nearly so, is manifestly unjust.

And your petitioners would further represent that in their opinion the import duty collected by the United States, of thirty to forty per cent. on our grain bags, and the material of which they are manufactured, is a tax which has almost entirely a local bearing; that it is unjust to, and discriminating against, the agricultural interests of the Pacific Coast; that while the grain surplus of the Atlantic States is moved to the sea-board, and thence to Europe in bulk, we, under an inexorable custom, are compelled to put ours in sacks for which we get no adequate return; that the import duty on the sacks used in California the past year amounts to over one half million of dollars, which is equivalent to a "direct export tax" of that amount upon the wheat crop of California; that said tax is bur-

densome and unjust; and we pray your honorable body to repeal the import duty on all burlap bags and all material of which they are manufactured, that they may be admitted free of duty, and your petitioners will ever pray, etc.

The Committee on Granges and Patrons of Husbandry reported as follows:

1st. The organization presents a medium of establishing and maintaining a better state of social and confidential relation among the farmers.

2d. The necessity of transacting our business within ourselves, without publishing our intentions to the world.

3d. The unprecedented success of this organization, the Atlantic States is a good evidence that it will, in a measure, meet our wants as an agricultural community; therefore,

Resolved—That it is, in the opinion of this body, expedient to establish among the farmers of the State, Granges of the Patrons of Husbandry.

Mr. Hallett, of Butte, by leave, read an essay upon the dangers to the wheat crop of California, which was adopted:

The future of the market for California surplus wheat presents, I think, some new aspects.

Great Britain is the buyer of the surplus breadstuffs of all the world. She procures supplies from Russia, Austria, Germany, France, Italy, Chili, the Atlantic and Pacific ports of the United States, to which must now be added Australia. The average annual import of great Britain is about three million of tons. The nearest sources of supply are the ports of the continent of Europe; next come the Atlantic ports of the United States; then Australia and Chili, and last California. The transit between these ports and Great Britain is by the ocean, and the cost of transportation is, therefore, in a general way, proportioned to the length of voyage. The price of breadstuff at the ports of export will be equal to the English price, less the cost of transportation thither, and less a further margin proportioned to the time required for transit, which provides for the interest on the money paid for the wheat, and the contingencies of the fluctuation in the English market. Hence, it follows that wheat at a California port must be sold lower than wheat of the same quality at the ports of any other exporting country in Christendom. And in reference to this item of quality, it must be remembered that the high grades of Baltic, of Chilian, of Australian and Western American, rate as high as Californian. The question to be investigated is, therefore, whether there is a definite prospect and danger that the surplus from those other countries which are in competition with California are likely to so supply the market in the near future as to reduce the selling cost of wheat at a California port to, or below the cost of production.

The facts necessary to be learned in order to arrive at a judgment

on this question, are not so numerous but that they be ascertained by an inquiry, which this body may set on foot.

Some of the points to be specifically answered are, as I understand them, these:

First—As I understand the area adapted to the growing of wheat in Western Russia and Eastern Austria is nearly, if not quite, adequate to the production of the entire surplus demand by England; that a lack of facilities for transportation has, in the past, prevented such production, just as lack of the same facilities prevented it in California; that with the supply of such facilities an increase of production is to be looked for, not unlike the increase which California has shown in the last, and promises in the next season. Even though the increase should not be affected in Russia with the same suddenness that has been effected by California energy, yet it may be expected to be equaled in two, three, or four seasons. Also, I understand that the facilities for wheat transportation in Russia have already been supplied by the railways built by the Government during the past two years, and which are still in progress; but the reason the surplus did not increase has been that those two years were bad ones, just as they were in California in 1870 and 1871; that the Russian and European crops generally were injured by floods and excessive wet; but a recurrence of such seasons is no more to be expected than drought in California; in fact, continual crops must be expected to maintain their "average" yield; that this average will be applied in Russia to an enormously increased area, and that this area is capable, with the increase of transportation facilities, of indefinite extension. And in order to perceive the full significance of this development, it is only necessary to remember that Russia regularly supplies two thirds of the total English import, or two million of tons out of three million. An increase of only one half, therefore, in her surplus, would suffice to supply the wants of Great Britain, to the exclusion of every other exporting country.

But France and Germany offer a larger surplus than that of California—which has been suspended the past two years, first, by the war, and next by a bad crop year—which has a prior chance in the English market; that is, which pays a lower transportation to get there; next comes the Russian surplus; and next that of the Atlantic American sea-board, paying a freight of only $5 to $7 per ton. Last of all are the Pacific ports of Chili, Australia and California, paying freights, which are at the comparative rates of $12, $15 or $20 per ton—of which California pays the highest. The difference between freights to England from New York and from San Francisco, is never less than half a cent. per pound.

Now, to show that we are not dealing with a speculative and remote danger, but with an actual and near one, it must be borne in mind that the price of first-quality wheat in England, in average seasons, during a series of years past, has been under $2 50 per one hundred pounds; it has even run as low, if I remember right, as $2. It was sold at these prices at a profit, by the exporting countries, which are still the competitors of California, and which have since increased their facilities for transportation; that is, their facilities for laying down their surplus in England in larger quantities and at less cost than ever before. Yet, at the prices of average seasons in England, in past years, California wheat would have to secure lower freights than there is now any reason to count on, in order to pay the cost of its production, with a surplus offering from the Continent increased beyond the old figures, the average English price will rule lower than there, and as we have seen, California wheat must then be shut out as a living crop.

The only point remaining to be inquired into, in this chain of reasoning, is the question whether continental producers can afford to lay down their surplus in England at the rates which will exclude California. Experience has shown that they can. But the facts attending that production, so far as I have been able to learn them—the almost nominal rates of wages paid in the wheat districts of Russia and Austria, with the improved facilities for transportation to the wheat ports, satisfy me that the wheat from these districts will cut out, not only California, but will cut out the surplus of our great West, even allowing it the benefit of the cheapest possible rates of transport to the Atlantic sea-board. If these facts as here suggested are all true, it is of the first importance to California producers to know them. The production of such a surplus as we have moved the past season, with the English market quoted at nine to ten shillings, would be as great a calamity as a drought. What could be done with the wheat? Absolutely nothing. It would not pay to harvest; there are not the animals in the State to eat it; it could not be ground for flour to China. Nothing could be done with it. And so far from this being an imaginary state of affairs, it is the state of affairs which we are to expect—which is probable—during the marketing of our harvest for 1874. And all the facts of the situation can be easily learned in time for our farmers to govern themselves.

Probably most of the information is already in the archives of the State Department at Washington, in the reports of the American Consuls at Odessa, Riga and Dantzig, or, perhaps, as to the new Russian railways, in the documents forwarded from the Minister at St. Petersburg. Or, if it is not there, a circular from the Department addressed to those officers, asking the specific information, would produce it; and the Department at the solicitation of this body, presented through our Representatives, would not hesitate, I am confident, to issue such a circular. If action be taken now, the information can be received by this organization by the time the next harvest is fully secured, and before the work for the following year is laid out.

The facts of the situation can be laid before every producer in the State, and he will go to work with his eyes open. Later in the season, as the reports of the condition and prospects of the continental crops are received, their full signification will be understood, and producers will act understandingly in the disposal of their crops. I believe the prospect to be, that a surplus of half a million tons of wheat in California in 1874 will not repay the cash outlay of making it; and I therefore feel that this organization cannot do a more useful thing than lay before the class whom it represents, the facts which will either confirm that belief or show it to be unfounded.

Prof. E. S. Carr offered the following resolution:

Resolved, That a diminished demand for our cereals in foreign markets being a reasonable expectation, that the Farmers' Union authorize the preparation of a report by a suitable committee upon the relative profits of other agricultural products suitable to our climate with a view to the encouragement of manufactures, a better home market, a more diversified, and consequently a more independent system of industry.

Prof. Carr spoke to his resolution, calling attention to the necessity of diversifying agricultural products to prevent depletion of the soil and to create home consumption, invite immigration, and work up home products.

Mr. Baxter was invited to address the Convention on the subject of the Order of Patrons of Husbandry; and, as if to enforce the views he laid down of the advantages of a secret organization, the sack committee, whose instructions had been to ascertain and report the best terms upon which sacks could be obtained for the coming crop, reported that no sacks could that day be obtained at the rates offered on the first day of the session. The proceedings of the Convention becoming known, some combination had been effected by which a very material advance in the price of sacks had been reached, and the farmers were again at the mercy of the operators. All the sacks in the eastern markets were but an item in the large prospective demand. The Convention at once passed a resolution authorizing the Executive Committee to incorporate a part or the whole of itself as a Branch Association, coöperative with the Farmers' Union, county and local incorporations, and proceeded to elect the following officers: President, John Bidwell; Secretary, I. N. Hoag; Treasurer, A. T. Dewey; Executive Committee, C. J. Cressey, of Stanislaus, J. V. Webster, of Oakland, J. D. Fowler, of Hollister, Prof. E. S. Carr, of the State University, Prof. Lippett, of Sonoma. The Convention then adjourned.

The "Farmers' Union" never met again, except for a final settlement of its affairs. President Bidwell said on that occasion, that its one year of existence had marked an era in California agriculture; the lesson of combination and coöperation had been learned, with a benefit to the farmers of not less than three million of dollars. The continuance of this work was formally turned over to the Granges, and the Union ceased to exist.

CHAPTER X.

THE ORDER OF PATRONS OF HUSBANDRY.

How Established---Messrs. Kelley and Saunders---A Cloud no Bigger than a Man's Hand--Significance of Names, "Grange" and "Patron"--Eligibility: Organization and First Officers: First Four Dispensations---Growth on the Upper Mississippi: Eighty Granges a Day in Iowa---Third Annual Session---What the Patrons Propose to Do--- Official Declaration of Purposes---Constitution and By-Laws.

"Industry requires its captains as well as war." During the last twenty years, the observant and philosophical watchman upon the walls of privilege, might have observed in various quarters the gathering of the clans of discontented laboring men. The doctrine of equal rights under the law, the power to enforce this doctrine through the ballot, had been gained; there was needed an organization through which these could manifest themselves. Political or financial combinations had felt secure during all the historical struggle between wealth and power on the one side, and numbers on the other, because, wherever combinations of workmen were not interdicted by law, advantage was taken of the diversity of interests among them, to neutralize their influence.

In France the antagonism of certain industrial interests was stimulated to an unnatural degree; in America, the same thing was accomplished by ranging the great body of agriculturists in separate political camps. The need of a great conciliating, centralizing influence was felt, before the civil war. It soon afterward became an imperative necessity, for the industry of the South was utterly paralyzed, while that of the North was staggering under burdens too great to be borne. The associations hitherto organized for the improvement of the farm, were utterly inadequate to cope with the monster monopolies which had taken a firm grasp of Congress and upon capital.

It was very natural that the great awakening should begin where the magnitude of the dangers was most apparent, viz: at the seat of government.

In January, 1866, under an order from President Andrew Johnson, Mr. O. H. Kelley, of the Agricultural Bureau, commenced a tour of inspection of the Southern States, during which he conversed freely with the farmers and planters, and came to the conclusion that the industrial reconstruction of that section would require the mutual aid and coöperation of the whole country. The political Union which had cost so much; which had watered the whole breadth of the land with tears; which the agriculture of the country had got to pay for with so many years of toil, required for its security a social and industrial union and harmony of interests, only to be reached by a close bond of association.

Mr. William Saunders, of the Bureau of Agriculture, an intelligent and thoughtful Scotchman, whose extensive correspondence had made him familiar with the struggles of the farmers in all sections of the country, entered warmly into the views expressed by Mr. Kelley on his return. Mr. Kelley had proposed, through some organizations like that of the Freemasons, to link the farmers into a solidarity. The originators of the movement were Mr. Kelley, Mr. William Saunders, then and at present Superintendent of the garden and grounds of the Department of Agriculture; Mr. William M. Ireland, Chief Clerk of the Finance office of the Postoffice Department; Mr. John R. Thompson, of the Treasury Department; Rev. Dr. John Trimble, of the Treasury Department, and Rev. A. B. Grosh, of the Department of Agriculture. On the 5th of August, 1867, they compiled the first degree of the Order of Patrons of Husbandry.

Eight days after, Mr. Saunders left Washington for St. Louis, with the purpose of establishing the Order in the West, thus opening the way for the labors of the chief apostle, Mr. Kelley, during the following year.

The generic name of the Order explains itself, and covers in a general way the requirements for membership. The word "Grange" is pure old English, used by the older as well as recent writers and poets, in the sense of a farm-stead or rural residence. In its symbolical application it means the hall or place of assembly of Grangers or Patrons of Husbandry, whatever their degree.

The National Grange was organized at Washington, at the residence of Mr. Saunders, on the evening of December 4, 1867, by the election of the following officers: Master, William Saunders, of the District of Columbia; Lecturer, J. R. Thompson, of Vermont; Overseer, Anson Bartlett, of Ohio; Steward, William Muir, of Pennsylvania; Assistant Steward, A. S. Moss, of New York; Chaplain, Rev. A. B. Grosh, of Pennsylvania; Treasurer, William M. Ireland, of Pennsylvania; Secretary, O. H. Kelley, of Minnesota; Gate Keeper, Edward F. Farris, of Illinois.

The next step was to test the workings of the ritual in a subordinate Grange. One was therefore formed, consisting of about sixty members. The first dispensation for a subordinate Grange was granted to an application from Harrisburg, Pennsylvania; the second to one from Fredonia, New York; the third to a Grange at Columbus, Ohio, and the fourth to one in Chicago. Only ten Granges were organized during the first year; at the end of the second, they numbered thirty-one.

The great center of the growth of the order was in the States bordering the Mississippi. In Iowa, subordinate Granges were formed in the spring of 1873, at the rate of from sixty to eighty a day. With irresistible power the great wave has increased and swelled in volume, until it has reached both oceans. It lifted the bowed head of the South; it included both sexes; it became a powerful educator. The only element to which any objection could be made, viz, that of secrecy, could not compromise it, while the work to which it was solemnly pledged, was pure and honorable. It was not a political organization; but in the words of the New York Tribune, it "altered the political equilibrium of the most steadfast States." Its objects and plans are well expressed in an address by Worthy Master Saunders, at the third annual session of the National Grange, February 4, 1870:

To increase the products of the earth, by increasing the knowledge of the producer, is the basis of our structure; to learn and apply the relations of science, so far as relates to the various products of the vegetable kingdom, and to diffuse the truths and general principles of the science and art of agriculture, are ultimate objects of our organization. We fully avail ourselves of the valuable results of scientific investigations in establishing principles (which, although sometimes difficult of discovery, are generally of easy application when properly understood), and seek to disseminate knowledge upon every subject that bears upon the increase of the productions and wealth of the nation.

One of the first duties of every Grange is to form a good library. This should be well supplied with elementary works in the various branches of natural history; standard works on agriculture, horticulture, pomology, physiology, rural architecture, landscape-gardening, breeding and raising of live-stock, and those of similar import. It is suggested that treatises on principles and fundamental laws should have special preference. The practices, more varied in their details, will be found from time to time in the periodicals devoted to these subjects.

The social relaxation from every-day duties and toils, inculcated and encouraged in the Order, is keenly appreciated by its members. The barriers to social intercourse that are thrown around society by despotic fashion, are ruthlessly thrown down with us, and we meet on a common footing, with a common object in view, viz, of receiving and contributing the highest enjoyments of civilized society. To make country homes and country society attractive, refined, and enjoyable; to balance exhaustive labors by instructive amusements and accomplishments, is part of our mission and our aim.

The admission of women to full membership, and their assistance in the workings of the Order, is proving of incalculable value; it is, indeed, doubtful whether the objects of the institution, especially in regard to the refinements of education, and all that tends to brighten hearths and enliven homes, could have been accomplished without their presence and aid.

In establishing an organization of this kind, we must not allow our energies to relax by an apparent indifference, or even avowed hostility to our cause. This we must expect, as there is no popular movement exempt from opposition. There is always a class of doubters who predict failures; others misconstrue motives, and still others who freely give opinions without investigating the objects sought to be attained, or the methods by which they are to be accomplished.

The secret ceremony of initiation of members has been objected to by a few persons; but we are already well convinced that the efficient discipline necessary to secure permanent organization could not be attained by any other means, thus completely realizing the only object that suggested its adoption; and it meets the warm approval of all those who have experienced the transitory existence of rural clubs and societies, and who recognize in our simple, but efficient rules, elements of success, based upon a solid and lasting foundation.

The Patrons of Husbandry propose: 1. To secure for themselves, through the Granges, social and educational advantages not otherwise attainable, and thereby, while improving their condition as a class, ennoble farm life, and render it attractive and desirable.

2. To give a full practical effect to the fraternal tie which unites them, in helping and protecting each other in case of sickness, bereavement, pecuniary misfortune, want, and danger of every kind.

3. To make themselves better and more successful farmers and planters, by means of the knowledge gained, the habits of industry, and method established, and the quickening of thought induced by intercourse and discussion.

4. To secure economies in the purchase of implements, fertilizers, and family supplies, and in transportation, as well as increased profits in the sale of the products of their labor, at the same time lessening the cost to the consumer.

5. To entirely abolish the credit system, in their ordinary transactions, always buying and selling on a cash basis, both among themselves and in their dealings with the outside world.

6. To encourage co-operation in trade, in farming, and in other branches of industry, especially those most intimately connected with agriculture.

7. To promote the true unity of the Republic, by drawing the best men and women of all parts of the country together in an organization which knows no sectional bounds—no prejudices—and owes no party allegiance.

DECLARATION OF PURPOSES.

Declaration of purposes of the National Grange, adopted at St. Louis, February, 1874; also by the State Grange of California, October 10, 1874:

Profoundly impressed with the truth that the National Grange of the United States should definitely proclaim to the world its general objects, we hereby unanimously make this Declaration of Purposes of the Patrons of Husbandry:

1. United by the strong and faithful tie of agriculture, we mutually resolve to labor for the good of our Order, our country, and mankind.

2. We heartily indorse the motto: "In essentials, unity; in non-essentials, liberty; in all things, charity."

3. We shall endeavor to advance our cause by laboring to accomplish the following objects:

To develop a better and higher manhood and womanhood among ourselves. To enhance the comforts and attractions of our homes, and strengthen our attachments to our pursuits. To foster mutual understanding and co-operation. To maintain inviolate our laws, and to emulate each other in labor to hasten the good time coming. To reduce our expenses, both individual and corporate. To diversify our crops, and crop no more than we can cultivate. To condense the weight of our exports, selling less in the bushel and more on hoof and in fleece; less in lint, and more in warp and woof. To systematize our work, and calculate intelligently on probabilities. To discountenance the credit system, the mortgage system, the fashion system, and every other system tending to prodigality and bankruptcy. We propose meeting together, talking together, working together, buying together, selling together, and in general acting together for our mutual protection and advancement, as occasion may require. We shall avoid litigation as much as possible by arbitration in the Grange. We shall constantly strive to secure entire harmony, good-will, vital brotherhood among ourselves, and to make our Order perpetual. We shall earnestly endeavor to suppress personal, local, sectional, and national prejudices, all unhealthy rivalry, all selfish ambition. Faithful adherence to these principles will insure our mental, moral, social, and material advancement.

4. For our business interests, we desire to bring producers and consumers, farmers and manufacturers, into the most direct and friendly relations possible. Hence we must dispense with a surplus of middle-men; not that we are unfriendly to them, but we do

not need them. Their surplus and their exactions diminish our profits. We wage no aggressive warfare against any other interests whatever. On the contrary, all our acts and all our efforts, so far as business is concerned, are not only for the benefit of the producer and consumer, but also for all other interests that tend to bring these two parties into speedy and economical contact. Hence we hold that transportation companies of every kind are necessary to our success, that their interests are intimately connected with our interests, and harmonious action is mutually advantageous, keeping in view the first sentence in our declaration of principles of action, that "Individual happiness depends upon general prosperity." We shall, therefore, advocate for every State the increase in every practicable way, of all facilities for transporting cheaply to the seaboard, or between home producers and consumers, all the productions of our country. We adopt it as our fixed purpose to "open out the channels in nature's great arteries that the life-blood of commerce may flow freely." We are not enemies of railroads, navigation and irrigation canals, nor of any corporation that will advance our industrial interests, nor of any laboring classes. In our noble Order there is no communism, no agrarianism. We are opposed to such spirit and management of any corporation or enterprise as tends to oppress the people and rob them of their just profits. We are not enemies to capital, but we oppose the tyranny of monopolies. We long to see the antagonism between capital and labor removed by common consent, and by an enlightened statesmanship worthy of the nineteenth century. We are opposed to excessive salaries, high rates of interest, and exorbitant per cent. profits of producers. We desire only self-protection and the protection of every true interest of our land by legitimate transactions, legitimate trade, and legitimate profits. We shall advance the cause of education among ourselves and for our children, by all just means within our power. We especially advocate for our agricultural and industrial colleges that practical agriculture, domestic science, and all the arts which adorn the home, be taught in their courses of study.

5. We emphatically and sincerely assert the oft-repeated truth taught in our organic law, that the Grange, National, State, or Subordinate, is not a political or party organization. No Grange, if true to its obligations, can discuss political or religiqus questions, nor call political conventions, nor nominate candidates, nor even discuss their merits in its meetings. Yet the priciples we teach underlie all true politics, all true statemanship, and, if properly carried out, will tend to purify the whole political atmosphere of our country. For we seek the greatest good to the greatest number. We must always bear in mind that no one, by becoming a Patron of Husbandry, gives up that inalienable right and duty which belongs to every American citizen, to take a proper interest in the politics of his country. On the contrary, it is right for every member to do all in his power legitimately to influence for good any political party to which he belongs. It is his duty to do all he can in his own party to put down bribery, corruption, and trickery; to see that none but competent, faithful, and honest men, who will unflinchingly stand by our industrial interests, are nominated for all

positions of trust; and to have carried out the principle which should always characterize every Patron, that the office should seek the man, and not the man the office. We acknowledge the broad principle that difference of opinion is no crime, and hold that "progress toward truth is made by difference of opinion," while "the fault lies in bitterness of controversy." We desire a proper equality, equity, and fairness; protection for the weak, restraint upon the strong; in short, justly distributed burdens and justly distributed power. These are American ideas, the very essence of American independence, and to advocate the contrary is unworthy of the sons and daughters of an American republic. We cherish the belief that sectionalism is, and of right should be, dead and buried with the past. Our work is for the future. In our agricultural brotherhood and its purposes, we shall recognize no North, no South, no East, no West. It is reserved by every patron, as the right of a freeman, to affiliate with any party that will best carry out his principles.

6. Ours being peculiarly a farmers' institution, we cannot admit all to our ranks. Many are excluded by the nature of our organization, not because they are professional men, or artisans, or laborers, but because they have not a sufficient direct interest in tilling the soil, or may have some interest in conflict with our purposes. But we appeal to all good citizens for their cordial co-operation to assist in our efforts toward reform, that we may eventually remove from our midst the last vestige of tyranny and corruption. We hail the general desire for fraternal harmony, equitable compromises, and earnest co-operation, as an omen of our future success.

7. It shall be an abiding principle with us to relieve any of our oppressed and suffering brotherhood by any means at our command. Last, but not least, we proclaim it among our purposes to inculcate a proper appreciation of the abilities and sphere of woman, as is indicated by admitting her to membership and position in our Order. Imploring the continued assistance of our Divine Master to guide us in our work, we here pledge ourselves to faithful and harmonious labor for all future time, to return by our united efforts to the wisdom, justice, fraternity, and political purity of our forefathers.

CONSTITUTION OF THE NATIONAL GRANGE OF THE ORDER OF PATRONS OF HUSBANDRY.

PREAMBLE.

Human happiness is the acme of earthly ambition. Individual happiness depends upon general prosperity.

The prosperity of a nation is in proportion to the value of its productions.

The soil is the source from whence we derive all that constitutes wealth. without it we would have no agriculture, no manufactures, no commerce. Of all the material gifts of the Creator, the various productions of the vegetable world are of the first importance. The art of agriculture is the parent and precursor of all arts, and its products the foundation of all wealth.

The productions of the earth are subject to the influence of natural laws, invariable and indisputable; the amount produced will consequently be in proportion to the intelligence of the producer, and success will depend upon his knowledge of the action of these laws, and the proper application of their principles.

Hence, knowledge is the foundation of happiness.

The ultimate object of this organization is for mutual instruction and protection; to lighten labor by diffusing a knowledge of its aims and purposes; expand the mind by tracing the beautiful laws the Great Creator has established in the universe, and to enlarge our views of creative wisdom and power.

To those who read aright, history proves that in all ages society is fragmentary, and successful results of general welfare can be secured only by general effort. Unity of action cannot be acquired without discipline, and discipline cannot be enforced without significant organization; hence, we have a ceremony of initiation which binds us in mutual fraternity as with a band of iron; but although its influence is so powerful, its application is as gentle as that of the silken thread that binds a wreath of flowers.

The Patrons of Husbandry consist of the following organization:

Subordinate Granges.

First Degree: Maid, (woman,) Laborer, (man.)
Second Degree: Shepherdess, (woman,) Cultivator, (man.)
Third Degree: Gleaner, (woman,) Harvester, (man.)
Fourth Degree: Matron, (woman,) Husbandman, (man.)

State Grange.

SECTION 1. Fifth degree. Pomona, (Faith.) Composed of the Masters of Subordinate Granges and their wives, who are Matrons, provided that when the number of Subordinate Granges in any State becomes so great as to render it necessary, the State Grange may, in such manner as it may determine, reduce its representatives by providing for the election of a certain proportion of those entitled to membership in the State Grange from each county; and the members so chosen shall constitute the State Grange.

Sec. 2. There may be established District or County Granges in the fifth degree, not to exceed one in each county, composed of Masters and Past Masters of Subordinate Granges, and their wives, who are Matrons, and such fourth degree members (not to exceed three), as may be elected thereto by the Subordinate Granges, under such regulations as may be established by State Granges. Such District or County Granges shall have charge of the educational and business interests of the Order in their respective districts, and shall encourage, strengthen and aid the Subordinate Granges represented therein. Dispensations for such District or County Granges shall issue from the State Grange, and under such regulations as the State Grange may adopt.

National Grange.

Sixth Degree: Flora, (Charity.)

Composed of Masters of State Granges and their wives who have taken the degree of Pomona, and the officers and members of the Executive Committee of the National Grange.

Seventh Degree: Ceres, (Faith.)

Members of the National Grange who have served one year therein, may become members of this degree upon application and election. It has charge of the secret work of the Order, and shall be a court of impeachment of all officers of the National Grange.

Members of this degree are honorary members of the National Grange, and are eligible to offices therein, but not entitled to vote.

CONSTITUTION.

ARTICLE I.—Section 1. The officers of a Grange, either National, State, or Subordinate, consist of and rank as follows: Master, Overseer, Lecturer, Steward, Assistant Steward, Chaplain, Treasurer, Secretary, Gate-keeper, Ceres, Pomona, Flora, and Lady Assistant Steward. It is their duty to see that the laws of the Order are carried out.

Sec. 2. In the Subordinate Granges they shall be chosen annually at the regular meeting in December, and installed at the regular meeting in January, or as soon thereafter as practicable; in the State Granges, once in two years, and in the National Grange once in three years. All elections to be by ballot.

Vacancies by death or resignation to be filled at a special election at the next regular meeting thereof—officers so chosen to serve until the annual meeting.

Sec. 3. The Master of the National Grange may appoint members of the Order as deputies to organize Granges where no State Grange exists.

Sec. 4. There shall be an Executive Committee of the National Grange, consisting of five members, whose term of office shall be three years.

Sec. 5. The officers of the respective Granges shall be addressed as "worthy."

Article II.—Section 1. Subordinate Granges shall meet at least once each month, and may hold intermediate meetings.

Sec. 2. State Granges shall meet annually at such time and place as the Grange shall, from year to year, determine.

Sec. 3. The National Grange shall meet annually on the third Wednesday in November, at such place as the Grange may, from year to year, determine. Should the National Grange adjourn without selecting the place of meeting, the Executive Committee shall appoint the place and notify the Secretary of the National Grange and the Masters of the State Granges at least thirty days before the day appointed.

Article III.—The National Grange, at its annual session, may frame, amend, or repeal such laws as the good of the Order may require. All laws of State and Subordinate Granges must conform to this Constitution and the laws adopted by the National Grange.

Article IV.—The Ritual adopted by the National Grange shall be used in all Subordinate Granges, and any desired alteration in the same must be submitted to, and receive the sanction of the National Grange.

Article V.—Any person engaged in agricultural pursuits and having no interest in conflict with our purposes, of the age of sixteen years, duly proposed, elected, and complying with the rules and regulations of the Order, is entitled to membership and the benefit of the degrees taken. Every application must be accompanied by the fee of membership. If rejected the money will be refunded. Applications must be certified by members, and balloted for at a subsequent meeting. It shall require three negative votes to reject an applicant.

Article VI.—The minimum fee for membership in a Subordinate Grange shall be, for men, five dollars, and for women, two dollars, for the four degrees, except charter members, who shall pay—men, three dollars, and women, fifty cents.

Article VII.—Section 1. The minimum of regular monthly dues shall be ten cents from each member, and each Grange may otherwise regulate its own dues.

Sec. 2. The Secretary of each Subordinate Grange shall report quarterly to the Secretary of the State Grange the names of all persons initiated during the quarter, and pay to the Secretary of the State Grange one dollar for each man, and fifty cents for each woman initiated during the quarter. Also a quarterly due of six cents for each member, said report to be approved and forwarded at the first session of the Grange in each quarter.

Sec. 3. The Secretary of the State Grange shall pay to the Treasurer of the State Grange all moneys coming into his hands, at least once every ten days, taking his receipt therefor; and shall report quarterly to the Secretary of the National Grange the membership in the State.

Sec. 4. The Treasurer of each State Grange shall deposit to the credit of the National Grange of Patrons of Husbandry, with some Banking or Trust company, to be selected by the Executive Committee, in quarterly instalments, the annual due of five cents of each member in his State, and forward the receipts of the same to the Treasurer of the National Grange.

Sec. 5. All moneys deposited with said company shall be paid out only upon the drafts of the Treasurer approved by the Master and countersigned by the Secretary.

Sec. 6. No State Grange shall be entitled to representation in the National Grange whose dues are unpaid for more than one quarter.

Article VIII.—Section 1. All charters and dispensations issue directly from the National Grange.

Sec. 2. Nine men and four women having received the four Subordinate degrees, may receive a dispensation to organize a Subordinate Grange.

Sec. 3. Applications for dispensations or charters shall be made to the Secretary of the National Grange, and be signed by the persons applying for the same, and be accompanied by a fee of fifteen dollars.

Sec. 4. Charter members are those persons only whose names are upon the application, and whose fees were paid at the time of organization. Their number shall not be less than nine men and four women, nor more than twenty men and twenty women.

Sec. 5. Fifteen Subordinate Granges working in a State can apply for authority to organize a State Grange.

Sec. 6. Where State Granges are organized, dispensations for the organization of the Subordinate Granges heretofore issued shall be replaced by Charter from the National Grange without further fee; and thereafter all applications for Charters for Subordinate Granges shall pass through the office of the Master of the State Grange, and must be approved by him before they are issued by the National Grange. When so issued, the Charter shall pass through the office of the Secretary of the State Grange and receive the signature and official seal of that office.

Sec. 7. No Grange shall confer more than one degree on the same person at the same meeting.

Article IX.—The duties of the officers of the National, State and Subordinate Granges shall be prescribed by the laws of the same.

Article X.—Section 1. The Treasurers of the National, State and Subordinate Granges shall give bonds, to be approved by the officers of their respective Granges.

Sec. 2. In all Granges bills must be approved by the Master, and countersigned by the Secretary, before the Treasurer can pay the same.

Article XI.—Religious or political questions will not be tolerated as subjects of discussion in the work of the Order, and no political or religious tests for membership shall be applied.

Article XIII.—The Master of the National Grange and the members of the Executive Committee shall be empowered to suspend from office any officer of the National Grange who may prove inefficient or derelict in the discharge of his duty, subject to appeal to the next session thereafter of the National Grange.

Article XIV.—This Constitution can be altered or amended by a two thirds vote of the National Grange at any annual meeting, and when such alteration or amendment shall have been ratified by three fourths of the State Granges, and the same reported to the Secretary of the National Grange, it shall be of full force.

[Our readers will observe, by comparing it with the Constitution as it existed before the meeting at St. Louis, that the new Constitution, as herewith given, changes entirely the status of Past Masters and their wives, as members of the National Grange and of State Granges. Formerly, as honorary members of these bodies, they could attend at their own expense, take part in debate, serve on committees, be eligible to office, in short, be active members in every way, except to vote. In the National Grange, under the old law, if it was deemed expedient to appoint them on standing committees to report at the next session, it could be done, and their expenses paid out of the treasury. Under the new law all this is changed. In State Granges Past Masters and their wives can now attend if they wish to and "look on" as fifth degree members. In the National Grange, ditto, as sixth degree members. If their past experience and training are of any value, it goes for naught. That is all. In other words, the National and State Granges are now more exclusive in their privileges than formerly. The changes in the new Constitution were in force at the late session of the National Grange, and will be in force at all sessions of State Granges for the ensuing year.

Of the amendments proposed at St. Louis, all were ratified and became laws, except four, namely, those relating to—

1. The seven founders becoming life members.
2. Past Masters of National Granges, and their wives.
3. Increase of representation.
4. Increase of membership fees.

These four were lost.

It is important for our members, everywhere, to observe that as the Constitution now stands (Art. VIII., Sec. 7), different degrees can be conferred on different persons at the same meeting, but not on the same person. It is equally important to observe that, according to Art. V., to be eligible to become a member in future, they must be engaged in agriculture as a pursuit, and must have no interest conflicting with the purposes of our Order.]

BY-LAWS.

Article I.—The fourth day of December, the birthday of the Patrons of Husbandry, shall be celebrated as the anniversary of the Order.

Article II.—Not less than the representation of twenty States present at any meeting of the National Grange, shall constitute a quorum for the transaction of business.

Article III.—Questions of law and usage arising in Subordinate Granges, shall be decided by the Master, subject to an appeal to the Master of the State Grange. Questions of law and usage arising in the State Grange, or brought by appeal from the Subordinate Grange, shall be decided by the Master of the State Grange, subject to an appeal to the Master of the National Grange, whose decision thereon shall be final.

Article IV.—It shall be the duty of the Master to preside at meetings of the National Grange; to see that all officers and members of committees properly perform their respective duties; to see that the Constitution, By-Laws and resolutions of the National Grange, and the usages of the Order are observed and obeyed, and generally to perform all duties pertaining to such office.

Article V.—It shall be the duty of the Secretary to keep a record of all proceedings of the National Grange; to keep a just and true account of all moneys received and deposited by him in the fiscal agency; to countersign all drafts drawn by the Treasurer; to conduct the correspondence of the National Grange; and to perform such other duties appertaining to the office as may be required by the Master and Executive Committee.

It shall be his duty, at least once each week, to deposit with the fiscal agency holding the funds of the National Grange, all moneys that may have come into his hands, and forward a duplicate receipt therefor to the Treasurer, and to make a full report of all transactions to the National Grange at each annual session.

It shall be his further duty to procure a monthly report from the fiscal agency, with whom the funds of the National Grange are deposited, of all moneys received and paid out by them during each month, and send a copy of such report to the Executive Committee and the Master of the National Grange.

He shall give bond in such sum and with such security as may be approved by the Executive Committee.

Article VI.—Section 1. It shall be the duty of the Treasurer to issue all drafts upon the fiscal agency of the Order, said drafts having been previously approved by the Master, and countersigned by the Secretary of the National Grange.

Sec. 2. He shall report monthly to the Master of the National Grange, a statement of all moneys deposited to his credit in the fiscal agency, and of all drafts signed by him during the previous month.

Sec. 3. He shall report to the National Grange at each annual session, a statement of all moneys deposited in the fiscal agency, and of all drafts signed by him since his last annual report.

Sec. 4. It shall be his duty to collect all interest accruing on investments made by the Executive Committee, and to deposit the same in the fiscal agency.

Article VII.—It shall be the duty of the Lecturer to visit, for the good of the Order, such portions of the United States as the Master or the Executive Committee may direct, for which services he shall receive compensation.

Article VIII.—Section 1. It shall be the duty of the Executive Committee to exercise a general supervision of the affairs of the Order during the recess of the National Grange. They shall have authority to act on all matters of interest to the Order, when the National Grange is not in session; shall provide for the welfare of the Order in business matters; and shall report their acts in detail to the National Grange, on the first day of its annual meeting.

Sec. 2. It shall be the duty of the Executive Committee to furnish to the Masters of the several State Granges, at the commencement of each quarter, a statement of the receipts and disbursements of all moneys by the National Grange during the preceding quarter.

Sec. 3. The Executive Committee shall, at the close of each annual session of the National Grange, appoint two of their number, who, together with the Worthy Master of the National Grange, shall constitute a Court of Appeals, to which shall be referred all appeals that may be taken to the National Grange. The Worthy Master, as President of the Court, shall convene the Court whenever the business in his hands shall make it necessary, and when thus convened, the Court shall try all cases coming before it, or continue the same as the equities of each case may demand.

It shall prescribe its own mode of procedure; its decisions shall be final and must be reported to the next session of the National Grange.

Article IX.—Section 1. Such compensation for time and service shall be given the Master, Lecturer, Secretary, Treasurer, and Executive Committee, as the National Grange may, from time to time, determine.

Sec. 2. Whenever General Deputies are appointed by the Master of the National Grange, said Deputies shall receive such compensation for time and services as may be determined by the Master and the Executive Committee; provided, in no case shall pay from the National Grange be given General Deputies in any State after the formation of its State Grange.

Article X.—Section 1. The financial reports of Subordinate Granges shall be made on the first day of January, the first day of April, the first day of July, and the first day of October.

Sec. 2. State Granges shall date their financial existence three months after the first day of January, first day of April, first day of July, and the first day of October, immediately following their organization.

Sec. 3. The financial year of the National Grange shall close on the 30th day of September.

Article XI.—Each session of the National Grange shall fix the compensation of its members.

Article XII.—Special meetings of the National Grange shall be called by the Master upon the application of the Masters of twenty State Granges, one month's notice of such meeting being given to all members of the National Grange. No alterations or amendments to the By-Laws or Ritual shall be made at any special meeting.

Article XIII.—Upon the demand of five members, the ayes and noes may be called on any question, and when so called, shall be entered by the Secretary upon his minutes.

Article XIV.—Past-Masters are Masters who have been duly elected and installed, and who have served out the term for which they were elected.

Article XV.—Vacancies in office may be filled at any regular meeting of the Grange.

Article XVI.—Two or more Subordinate Granges may be consolidated in the manner following, to wit:—

Application for permission to consolidate shall be made to the Master of the State Grange and his consent obtained. One of the consolidating Granges shall then vote to surrender its Charter and to consolidate with the other; and the other must vote to receive all the members of the surrendering Grange.

A copy of each vote, duly authenticated, must be transmitted to the Secretary of the State Grange, and the surrendered charter must be returned to the National Grange, through the office of the Secretary of the State Grange, with the fact and date of its surrender and consolidation endorsed thereon, authenticated by the seal and signature of the Secretary of the State Grange; provided, that nothing herein contained shall be construed to authorize the surrender of the charter of a Grange in which nine men and four women shall desire to continue the organization thereof.

Article XVII.—Section 1. In case satisfactory evidence shall come to the Master of a State Grange, that a Grange has been organized contrary to the laws and usages of the Order, or is working in violation of the same, it shall be the duty of the Master to suspend such offending Grange, and at once forward to the Master of the National Grange notice of the same, together with the evidence in the case, who shall, if in his opinion the good of the Order requires such action, revoke the Charter of such offending Grange.

Sec. 2. Granges, whose Charters are thus revoked, may appeal to the National Grange at its next session for the final action of that body,

Article XVIII.—Members of the State and Subordinate Granges shall be amenable to their respective Granges under such regulations as may be prescribed by the State Granges for the trial of causes in their respective jurisdictions; provided that members of the Subordinate Granges shall be allowed the right of appeal to their State Granges, and members of the State Grange shall be allowed the right of appeal to the Court of Appeals.

ARTICLE XIX.—Each officer required by law to report to the National Grange at its annual sessions, shall furnish, in connection with his report, an itemized statement of the expenses of his office for the current year.

ARTICLE XX.—The Secretary of each State Grange shall send to the Secretary of the National Grange, two printed copies of the proceedings of his State Grange, as soon as practicable after each annual session, and also copies of the Constitution and By-Laws of his State Grange, and the Secretary of the National Grange shall preserve, in his office, one copy of each of these documents.

ARTICLE XXI.—All communications, circulars, and all other documents transmitted by the officers of the National Grange, or any department thereof, to the Subordinate Granges, shall pass through the office of the State Grange to which they belong.

ARTICLE XXII.—These By-Laws may be altered or amended at any annual meeting of the National Grange by a two thirds vote of the members present.

ELIGIBILITY.

Of all applicants, either for charter membership or otherwise, the questions should be asked:

1st—Are they "engaged in agricultural pursuits?"

2d—Have they "any interests in conflict with our purposes?"

If they are not engaged in agricultural pursuits they are not eligible. If they have any conflicting interest they are not eligible. Organizing officers and the members decide these points.

The amendment which embodies the above restriction was brought in at the St. Louis meeting in 1874; more explicitly defining the original requirement. Like all other amendments it required the ratification of twenty-seven State and Territorial Granges. It is now the law of admission, but not an *ex post facto* law; is not retroactive, and cannot affect any member already in the Grange.

RULINGS.

To the Rulings of our Worthy Master Adams, masters and members in all the States must render a cheerful obedience, until an appeal may be sustained by the National Grange.

A married woman derives her eligibility to become a member of a Grange from the eligibility of her husband, and if he is not eligible and worthy of being admitted to the Grange, the wife should not be admitted alone. It is not safe or good policy to admit married women to the Grange whose husbands are opposed to our Order, or who, being eligible, have no disposition to join it. Unless the by-laws of a Subordinate Grange fix a time which must elapse before a new application can be made for a rejected candidate, there is nothing in the National Constitution to prohibit the application being renewed at any subsequent meeting.

If the Master of a Grange has good reason to believe that some of the members have cast black balls by mistake, he should, before declaring the result of the ballot, make such statement and recommend another ballot. If, however, he declares the ballot, and the members themselves are satisfied a mistake has been made, it will be in order for some one to move for a reconsideration. And if a majority of the members vote to reconsider, the ballot may be taken over again and the result must be final. A ballot can only be reconsidered at the same meeting the vote is declared.

The Treasurer's report of the National Grange for 1874 has been made public. The total receipts were $132,151 28, of which $129,315 00 was for dispensations to 8,621 Granges; $1,261 68 for dues from Iowa, Illinois and Wisconsin. These are the only States from which dues are reported, and nothing was received from Iowa of dues for 1873. The expenses for the year seem to have been $79,343 75, leaving a balance in the treasury of $52,807 53. The largest item of expense was for printing--$29,314 40.

The salaries amounted to $5,416 67—of which Secretary Kelley received $3,500. The contingent expenses were $13,-840 81. There was paid to deputies $5,983 35; to Executive Committee, $1,039 00; traveling expenses, $1,188 00; mileage, $546 80. It seems the treasury was empty at the beginning of the year, and owed Secretary Kelly, $3,321 74.

The National Grange has seventy thousand dollars invested in registered sixes. The investment was made through the Farmers' Loan and Trust Company, in New York, which acts as financial agent for the Grange. This company is one of the strongest and safest in the country, having gone through all the panics and financial crises without suspension or question of its integrity or ability to meet every obligation. If, however, the company should fail, remember that the bonds are registered, and so have the entire security of the nation's good faith. Besides this bond investment, there is a working fund, varying, of course, but averaging about twenty thousand dollars. This fund is also on deposit with the financial agent in New York, and a monthly report is made by the agent to each member of the Executive Committee, setting forth the amount on deposit from day to day, with the receipts and disbursements.

The Secretary of the National Grange also sends weekly to each member of the Executive Committee a full statement of the amount of money received and disbursed through his office. No money is paid out by the financial agent without the order of the Worthy Master, countersigned by the Secretary, the orders being made at the request of the Executive Committee.

The Committee also directs all purchases, and audits all bills; so that not a dollar is expended without its knowledge. The Treasurer keeps an accurate account of all moneys, and countersigns orders before they are paid by the financial agent. Accounts are opened upon the books of the Secretary with the several State Granges, and each is duly credited with all moneys received from it, and charged with whatever is disbursed for its benefit. The balance, less its proportional share of the expenses of the National Grange, shows what we will call the deposit of that Grange with the National Grange. These balances or deposits are held as sacred trusts for the benefit of the State Granges, to be used, as during the past year, to the amount of more than twelve thousand dollars, in the relief of suffering, or in such other manner as may be determined on hereafter. More than twelve thousand dollars has been expended during the year for the relief of suffering from grasshoppers, from floods, and from other disasters; the several amounts having been paid back to the State Granges, out of their deposits, and so far as possible in proportion to those deposits.

The general disposition of the Order is toward a reduction of salaries, the abolition of the supply feature, and, disregarding all party ties, to act unitedly for the common good of all classes, and for the whole country.

CHAPTER XI.

WHAT HAS BEEN ACCOMPLISHED.

Growth—Causes of Numerical Strength—Granges of the First and Second Growth—Investments and Savings—General and Incidental Benefits—Worthy Master Adams' Address at Charleston: Summary of Proceedings: What was Done about the Texas Pacific Railroad, and Why it was Done.

In 1873 ten States were represented in the meeting of the National Grange. In 1874 the number had swelled to thirty-one, and the business of the Central Bureau, at Washington, required a heavy staff for its successful prosecution. No great enterprises are moved without a corresponding outlay of brain and money power; but it was marvelous to the uninitiated, to see what the "little drops of water and little grains of sand," falling so quietly from the coffers of the Subordinate Granges, were accomplishing when gathered together. The monopolists who had thought the farmers' movement unlikely to "prove much of a shower," began to lay in a stock of umbrellas. They also began to devise schemes for dividing and creating distrust within the body of the Order. But so thoroughly had the organization prepared itself for any stress of weather; so strong was it on its central principle that "the good of the whole could only be reached by the perfection of its parts," that its growth has scarcely been checked by even momentary disasters.

It was not until the fall of 1873, however, that, owing to the agitation prevailing throughout the United States in respect to monopolies, especially oppressive in the North-west, the power of the Grange began to be felt in the land. From the original centers of its strength, without any effort at propogandism, it had spread in all directions; in truth, it had a center in every true Patron, from which an unconscious influence proceeded, until at the opening of the year 1875, its membership was estimated at not less than one million four hundred and thirty thousand. There were other negative causes for this unprecedented growth, among which may be named class-spirit, a debauched currency, protective tariff, railroad combinations, combinations of manufactures, plow-makers and others. The Granges of the first period may be termed the fighting Granges; for they bore the brunt of the great conflict with monopolies, and led the way to concession and peace. They had unpleasant things to say, and they said them in unmistakable English. Some excesses of zeal were exhibited, and the Western Granges narrowly escaped the fate of becoming a third political party. It must be admitted by all that they possessed wise and temperate leaders. Dudley W. Adams, the present W. M. of the National Grange, and Colonel Cochrane, Master of the Wisconsin State Grange, declined nominations for the highest offices in their respective States.

The Order now contains, in round numbers, twenty-two thousand Subordinate Granges, distributed as follows: Missouri, Iowa, and Indiana, each two thousand; Illinois and Kentucky, each one thousand five hundred; Kansas, one thousand three hundred; Ohio and Tennessee, each one thousand one hundred; Texas, eight hundred; Georgia, seven hundred; Alabama and

Mississippi, six hundred and fifty; Minnesota, Michigan, Wisconsin, Arkansas, each five hundred and fifty to five hundred and seventy-five; Nebraska, six hundred; North Carolina, four hundred and sixty; Virginia and Pennsylvania, each four hundred; South Carolina, three hundred and twenty-five; New York, two hundred and seventy-three; California, two hundred and fifty; Louisiana, two hundred and ten; Oregon, one hundred and seventy-five; Washington Territory, (under jurisdiction of Oregon,) fifty-two. Vermont, West Virginia, Maryland, Florida, New Jersey, Colorado, Massachusetts, Wyoming Territory, Maine, Dakota, New Hampshire, Canada, Montana, Delaware, Idaho, Nevada, and Connecticut, make the grand total at the present time, not less than a million and a half. Complete statistics of each State, or of the whole membership, are not given to the public, for obvious reasons.

It will be seen that the South and the South-west are the strongest in proportion to their population. But at the present moment the Granges are multiplying in the Eastern States with great rapidity. North and South are linked by the Grange into an industrial and fraternal unity; and are already proving the benefits of coöperation in commercial exchanges.

The "Granges of the second growth," Missouri, Michigan and Wisconsin, have especially devoted themselves to the promotion of business enterprises; have been careful and economical, and have "held aloof from politics." In Missouri, however, so many Grangers found themselves in the legislature, that it was proposed to organize a Legislative Grange, while Wisconsin, under a Granger Governor, carried her legislative war upon the railroads to a successful termination.

The Patrons have invested their capital as follows: In Grange banks; in direct trade unions; in elevators and warehouses; in grist-mills; in pork-packing houses; in bag factories and brick yards; in blacksmith shops, machine and implement works; in broom factories; in cotton-gins, and cotton-yarn factories, in the South; in fruit-canning establishments; in transportation enterprises by rail, ship, and boat; in homestead associations, coöperative land companies, immigration associations and insurance companies. Not less than \$18,000,000 is thus invested. The estimate of savings through coöperation is \$100 per head for four hundred thousand active Grangers.

During the past year one hundred and fifty headers have been built and sold in Nebraska alone. The price has been $150 each, while the dealers were charging $325—a discount of 54 per cent., and a total saving in first cost of $26,250.

Over three hundred Werner harvesters have been built in the three States of Iowa, Nebraska and Minnesota, and sold at $140, a saving on each machine of $80, and a total saving to the buyers of $24,000. The orders for the Werner this year very far exceeded the capacity of the factories to supply, and next year it is thought that three thousand of them will be called for. They have everywhere given entire satisfaction when well made and in the hands of competent operators. In a recent trial in Minnesota between the Werner, the Marsh and the Massillon, the Werner was adjudged the best of the three. Fully fifteen hundred cultivators have been made and sold during the past year, the price being $18 to $20 50 for an implement in every way as good as those generally sold for $30 to $35. The coming season a spring-tooth sulky rake will be made and offered for about $25, such an one as now brings $35 to $45. These rakes will be made at Des Moines and Dubuque, and probably at other places also. A seeder will also be offered for about $40. It is called the gang-plow seeder, and is equal in value to those now sold for $65 to $75.

A Bessemer steel beam plow is now making at Des Moines, at the Given plow-works, which can be sold for $18. Mr. Given will fill Patrons' orders first at that price, while others must wait to be served afterwards, and at a higher price. These plows are first-class in every respect, far superior and much lighter than any ordinary iron beam plow.

A mower is now making in New York, of which our Order will have entire control. All the parts usually made of iron are of Bessemer steel; the movement is very simple, and the draft light. It is provided with self-oiling boxes, which require attention but two or three times a week, and generally it is first-class in all its parts. It will be sold in Iowa, freight paid, for not more than seventy-five dollars.

Arrangements will soon be completed to get sugars and syrups direct from members of our Order in Louisiana through the agency in New Orleans. Samples and prices are promised. Prices of syrups, of course, vary with the market; but last year the best pure cane syrups were sold in New Orleans for thirty-five cents per gallon.

The agency in New Orleans is now ready to receive flour, corn, bacon, and other western products, in exchange for sugars, syrups, etc., which the South has to spare.

In general, it may be said that the business operations of the Order have more than tripled during the past year. Business agencies are established in more than twenty-five States, including all the Western, Southern and Pacific States; and in the Eastern States such agencies are rapidly multiplying, and while increasing in numbers they are perfecting their plans of doing business. Col. Shankland is in constant correspondence with the several agents, and is making numerous journeys to attend their conventions. County and district agencies, auxiliary to the State agencies, are forming everywhere, and all are increasing in efficiency as they learn the routine of business, and as the members of the Order learn the facilities and savings of the agencies.

For example: In Iowa more than half the elevators are now in the hands of Patrons, and elevator companies, coöperative stores and mutual insurance companies are constantly increasing. Some of them, while saving largely for their customers, are also making large profits for themselves. Of course their success depends much on the experience, tact, zeal and honesty of the agent in charge; but in a general way it may be said that all are doing well and meeting the expectations of their founders. By way of illustration, a fire insurance company in Wisconsin, which is carrying four hundred and fifty thousand dollars of risks on the following plan—payment of one dollar and fifty cents for survey and policy, and one tenth of one per cent. on the risk—has not lost a dollar in a year.

A State and National organization of colored men, has been formed at the South, not political in its character, which claims to be an auxiliary to our Order and which desires to receive its supplies through our agencies. Indeed, already several carloads of goods have been furnished them in this way.

Under the special charge of Col. Aikin, of South Carolina, another member of the Executive Committee of the National Grange, the collating and publishing of information about the crops and markets is a matter fast assuming vast consequence. His reports are more complete in their statistics and more prompt in their issue than the corresponding reports of the Government Bureau of Agriculture. It is hoped to be able soon, by means of the accurate information which the Granges furnish at home, and the facilities of corresponding agencies abroad, to lay before our members, each month, a comprehensive digest of the condition of the markets and the prospects of the crops throughout the world, which will guide them both in their planting and their sales.

One of the best features of the organization of the Patrons of Husbandry is the settlement of differences, whether pecuniary or otherwise, between members, by arbitration. Instead of going to law, and feeing lawyers, officers and courts, and spending time and money to secure some legal or technical advantage of a neighbor, by the plan introduced in the Granges all these little questions of dispute are now settled in an equitable and generally in an amicable manner by reference to committees or arbitrators consisting of mutual friends. It is true that this plan deprives the lawyers, officers and courts of a great deal of business, and, consequently, of a great deal of money; but, while they are the losers in a pecuniary way, the farmers are the gainers, not only in a pecuniary sense, but in many other ways. Friendship between individuals is thus promoted and maintained; neighborhood difficulties are avoided, and the whole community of farmers are greatly the gainers; while outsiders are none the wiser. This is certainly a very commendable and valuable feature of the Order.

Upon such articles as tea, sugar, coffee, kerosene, etc., the average saving has been from five to fifteen per cent.; clothing from ten to twenty per cent.; machines and implements from thirty-five to forty per cent. This work is mostly done through the State agencies; that of Indiana exceeded two hundred and fifty thousand dollars last year. The New York Evening Post sums up the general benefits of the Grangers' organization, as follows:

> The railroads have been taught that there is a higher power, viz: public opinion, which they cannot wantonly defy. A body of regulating laws has been collected and tested (in Wisconsin), which will serve as a guide and foundation for all future and more final and just legislation.
>
> The agriculturists have partially awaked to the fact that the chief cause of their troubles is "protection;" that they are systematically and legally plundered for the sake of the Eastern manufacturer; that cheap transportation, by means of road-bed, rails and rolling stock, swollen in cost by a high tariff, is an impossible thing. The

high tariff makes the annual repairs on our railroads cost millions of dollars more than they should; and the farmers, in the form of dearer freights, must pay these needless millions forever. "Whoever would be free, himself must cast the vote."

The annual address of Worthy Master Adams, at the last session of the National Grange, held at Charleston, February, 1875, will be read with pleasure by every Patron, and received as the most authoritative expression of the sentiments which will govern the future of the Order in the United States:

Patrons of Husbandry: From the snow-clad hills, the flowery vales, the golden shore, and prairie lands we meet together by the historic palmetto. Not as nomads who gather at a shrine in obedience to a sentiment do we come, but as chosen representatives of the fraternity, whose object is the moral and material advancement of the greatest industrial interests of the great republic. Standing as we do to-day upon the narrow line which divides the past from the future, about to step forward into that time which is all unseen by human eye, it behooves us to well scrutinize the track behind us, that we gain thereby some clue to the path before. One year ago, we met beyond the Father of Waters, and congratulated ourselves on the growth and strength of our gigantic young Order. To-day, by the ever-sounding seas, we proudly proclaim that our members have increased one hundred-fold. Two more sister States (Maine and Montana), have joined our ranks, and the few remaining ones are joyfully on the way. The work has spread from ocean to ocean. The winds have wafted the sounds across, and now they come back like echoes from the other shore, asking us to extend to other people a helping hand. This uprising and organizing of a great and scattered interest has not a parallel in the history of the world. The magnitude and force of the movement has surprised its friends, and astonished and alarmed its foes. It has burst upon us with the suddenness of the erratic comet, yet promises to remain with the brilliancy and permanency of the sun. It found the agriculture of the nation unorganized, isolated, unrecognized, weak, plodding, and their voices virtually unheard in the councils of the land. To-day, they are organized, united, strong, thoughtful, and duly respected and recognized as one of the great powers that be. Though much has now been done in awakening thought and clearing the field, yet we have but just stepped upon the mount and caught a faint glimpse of the promised land. Right before us it lies awaiting our possession. But ere we fairly reach the goal and fully possess the land, we see a wide and dreary waste is to be crossed, which will tax to our utmost our prudence, our perseverance, and our valor.

The positions of honor and trust, the avenues to great wealth, the molding of the political, financial and educational institutions of the nation, have long been in the hands of members of other callings. This monopoly will not be given up without a struggle; and whoever enlists in the Patrons of Husbandry, in the expectation of an easy victory, reckons without his host. Our movement has been and will be met by a most determined and persistent warfare—every means which talent, wealth and place can command, will be used. So, while we believe in the goodness of God and the justice of our cause, we must maintain unbroken ranks and keep our powder dry. In many of the States, the work of organizing Granges has been nearly completed, and the noise and enthusiasm attending it, is succeeded by comparative silence. The Order is there passing through the ordeal which shall reveal its weakness or display its strength. Though enthusiasm and noise were very suitable and efficient means to kindle the flame, they are not the materials with which to maintain a steady and lasting heat.

To preserve the vantage ground we have gained, and ensure permanence and further advancement, we must be able to show to our members and the world, that material and moral gain does and will result from our organization. We must keep our ranks full, our faith strong, our work pure, and our actions wise. One year ago I called the attention of this body to the fact that the Subordinate Granges are the foundation and life of our Order, and urged the necessity of aiding them by devising profitable and agreeable plans of work and recreation, so that the present membership and interest would not only be maintained, but increased. Owing to a press of business, no action was taken in this matter, and the Subordinate Granges have been thrown on their own resources. I am happy to announce that most of them have been equal to the emergency, but many of the weaker have languished and failed simply for want of a little paternal aid and counsel in their infancy. We cannot afford to thus allow the weak (for whom especially we should provide), to fall by the wayside. It is our stern duty, and should be an unmixed pleasure to tend, direct and uphold them. If we fail in this, we fail in carrying out one of our cardinal principles. Let me then most earnestly request you to give this subject your attention as one of the most important which ever came before you. It would be impossible, even were it desirable, at this time to discern all the grave subjects which will demand your attention, but there are some which I cannot pass without a brief notice.

Prominent among these is the subject of transportation, in which every citizen has an interest, either as a producer or consumer. There is a deep-seated and well-founded conviction that the present modes of carrying commodities are uselessly expensive. The people and the government have liberally aided in the construction of railroads and canals in the expectation that increased facilities would result in the cheaper rates of transportation.

We relied implicitly on the idea that by building numerous routes we would attain the benefits of competition, and secure fair rates; but sad experience has fully proven that increase in number and strength of transportation companies only results in more gigantic and oppressive combinations. Though we have some powerful lines between the north-west and north-east, yet instead of their competing to reduce rates, they have, within a few days, formed a new combination, by which western bound freights have been advanced. To remedy this alarming and growing evil the people, in their individual capacity, are powerless, and only through their united action as sovereigns can they obtain redress. In some of the States something of this has been done, but it has been necessarily fragmentary and wholly inoperative on through freights. It is utterly impracticable for the several States to act in concert through the different legislatures. I see, then, no solution of this question, but for the people of the several States, through their representatives to the General Government, to stretch out their strong arm between the people and those corporations. I know I speak the sentiments of the people, when I say we would do no wrong to the capital nominally invested in railroads. We fully recognize their capacity for good, and all their just claims, but we demand justice and protection for the people.

But even if railroads do carry at fair rates, still the fact stares us in the face, that transportation of heavy commodities is at least an expensive luxury, and our true policy is to bring producer and consumer nearer together, and so lessen the transporting. We, of the South and West especially, should spare no pains to introduce and foster manufactures in our midst, that we be not obliged to transport our raw material out and the manufactured article in. We of the East, where manufactures are many and strong, should, with equal assiduity, promote the cultivation of the raw material, that the terrible strain on transportation be lessened.

I have long ago said that the history of the world or its present condition does not afford a single example of a country which has remained permanently prosperous by the production and exportation of the raw material, but their tendency is all the time toward a condition of dependence and poverty. This position has not been disputed, and I believe cannot be. How important, then, that we cultivate the most amicable relations between all the productive industries, as only by mutual development can we be mutually prosperous, and the whole body politic be maintained in vigorous health.

A thousand years ago learned and thoughtful chemists devoted the energies of a lifetime to a vain search for the wonderful philosopher's stone, whose magic touch should convert the baser metals into purest gold, and thus fill the whole world at once with wealth and luxury. To-day we have numerous citizens who are eagerly pursuing the same phantom. They are torturing their poor brains to devise some plan whose talismanic power will transmute bits of printed paper into countless millions of actual money of such a subtle nature that true as the needle to the pole, it shall go straight to the pockets of the poor, and like a subtle "Will-o'-the-wisp," forever evade the clutches of the rich.

It is an indisputable fact that our country is now seriously suffering from a derangement of finances. We need not to be at a loss to know the cause. It is a solemn reality that our country has passed through a most wasting civil war. It cost us in money, time lost, industry disturbed, material destroyed, production stopped, more than ten billions of dollars. That immense sum was in four years subtracted from the wealth of the country. It was consumed, and is forever gone. It made us comparatively poor. To bridge over the emergency of the hour, the government issued great volumes of irredeemable paper currency, which we used as money, and thus for a time disguised and hid our poverty. By using this currency our judgment of values became more and more confused as we drifted further from the world's standard. We totally failed to realize our changed circumstances and to inaugurate a corresponding system of economy and industry, and, consequently, with an inheritance of debt, extravagant habits and distorted judgment of values, we have been incessantly drifting to leeward. Out of this trouble there is no royal road. Only by a return to habits of industry and economy, guided by intelligence, can we regain our wealth and remove our load of debt. As an auxiliary to this, we want a staple and sound currency, that shall be a reliable measure of values, and recognized as such by all the civilized world. For we may gain this truth from others and our own history, that an irredeemable, fluctuating currency always favors speculators and sharpers, at the expense of those engaged in productive industry.

In an order like ours, which is still in the formative state, it has not seemed strange that many cases have presented themselves during the past year which were provided for by no written law. To meet these emergencies it has devolved upon me, as the chief executive officer of the Order, to make numerous rules for our temporary guidance. These have been placed in the hands of your committee for arrangement, and will be submitted for your consideration.

Some cases have arisen involving points of such doubtful expediency that I have hesitated about taking the responsibility of making rulings. To cover these additional legislation will be needed. An amendment to the Constitution has been adopted and ratified, providing for County Granges, under the direction of State Granges. I am fully convinced, from visiting several States, that the widest possible difference will exist in the organization and management of these Granges in the different States. Under proper and efficient rule they cannot fail to be of eminent value to the Order, but if loosely and carelessly constructed they will be a source of endless annoyance and confusion. As the Masters of all the State Granges are here together in council, it might be well for this body to prepare a complete system of management of Fifth Degree County Granges, and send it to the States. This would not, of course, go to the States as law, but recommended as a plan prepared by and embodying the combined judgment of the Masters of all the State Granges. I doubt not such a plan would be generally welcomed, and would tend to produce uniformity in the work in the several States.

The principal office of the National Grange, under the management of our Worthy Secretary, is each year assuming a more systematic and perfect shape. The amount of business done and the manner of doing it, will be fully shown in his report.

It is an agreeable fact to state that the revenues of the National Grange have been above the expenditures, thus leaving a balance in the treasury, as will appear by the report of the Worthy Treasurer.

This subject of our finances is one upon which the members of our Order are particularly and very properly quite sensitive, and we owe it, not only to them, but to ourselves, that the receipts and disbursement of all moneys be conducted in a manner which will commend itself to the judgment of business men.

In our work as a body, and in our association with each other as sisters and brothers, let our deportment be such as to cast a halo over the noble occupation we follow, unite in closer bonds our great fraternity, and intensify the patriotic affection we feel for our common country.

Following is a summary of the proceedings of the National Grange, at its last session as furnished by Bro. J. W. A. Wright:

1. The emphatic request for Congressional aid, with proper restrictions, to the Texas Pacific Railroad.

2. Action favoring the construction of a double steel track railway from the Mississippi river near St. Louis, to the Atlantic at some northern point.

3. Resolutions favoring the speedy completion of the Spartansburg and Asheville Railroad, thus connecting Chicago and other western cities with the Atlantic at Charleston, by a route of one hundred miles shorter than by any other.

4. Hearty approval of the resolutions of the Agricultural Association of Georgia, which recommend the construction of canals to connect the Ohio and Tennessee rivers with the Atlantic.

5. Recommendation of government aid to repair the levees on the Mississippi.

6. Advocating the opening, by national aid, of the mouth of the Mississippi.

7. Request to Congress for reduction of tax on tobacco.

8. Expressed opposition to an injurious extension of patent rights.

9. Recommendations with regard to the Centennial Exposition at Philadelphia.

10. Resolutions favoring the early completion of the Washington National Monument.

11. Adoption of the Constitution of the National Grange, as amended at the last session, and ratified by three fourths of the State Granges.

12. Other important amendments to the Constitution and By-Laws.

13. Careful preparation, for the use of the Order, of a Parliamentary Guide and a Digest of Decisions on Constitutional Questions.

14. Decisions to move the headquarters of the National Grange from Washington to some point in the West, which the members of the Executive Committee are to select.

15. Distribution of part of the funds of the National Grange, as a loan without interest to the different State Granges. This loan is in the proportion of two dollars and fifty cents to each Subordinate Grange in each State, but it is not intended to be divided among the Subordinate Granges.

16. Additional safeguards have been thrown around the expenditure of the funds of the National Grange for the ensuing year, looking chiefly to economy.

17. No one result of this session was more satisfactory than the proof that, in spite of all malicious assertions of hostile papers to the contrary, our worthy Secretary and Treasurer have handled all the funds entrusted to their keeping, with the most perfect integrity.

18. The election of members of the Executive Committee was an important matter. At the last session it was determined to increase the number from three to five. D. W. Aiken, of South Carolina, is re-elected for three years, and the two new members are D. T. Chase, of New Hampshire, and John T. Jones, of Arkansas. R. E. Shankland, of Iowa, continues for two years, and William Saunders, of Washington City, for one year.

19. The National Grange will meet in San Francisco next November, if, on investigation, it is found that the expense to its Treasury will not be too great.

20. An important change made by the ratification and final adoption of the new Constitution is, that Past Masters are no longer, as such, even honorary members of the National or State Granges.

The following is a report of the Committee and the resolutions adopted concerning the Texas Pacific Railroad:

Your committee, to whom was referred resolutions of the Texas State Grange, and of numerous other bodies in different sections of the United States, to extend its aid to the Texas Pacific Railroad, have had the same under consideration, and ask to make this report:

Your committee have viewed with great interest the expressions of approval and appeals to Congress to forward this great work, emanating from the State Granges and Boards of Trade, from the Pacific to the Atlantic, and are impressed with the great and obvious benefits which would result to this whole nation by the speedy completion of this road: and as it is an enterprise too vast to depend alone for its success upon private capital, equal justice to all sections of our common country requires aid of the National Government to forward this work, under the proper restrictions and safeguards, insuring the Government against loss, and the people against unjust impositions and discriminations.

Your committee therefore submit the following resolution:

That this National Grange earnestly invites the attention of Congress to the necessity of a speedy completion of the Texas Pacific Railroad, and asks of that body reasonable aid to the company, which has inaugurated this great national enterprise, under such cautionary restrictions and safeguards as the prudence and wisdom of Congress may devise to guarantee the Government against loss, and protect the agricultural interests of every section of the country against unjust discriminations in the price of transportation.

The reasons for the action of the National Grange are thus explained by Worthy Master Hamilton:

The friends of the Texas Pacific, when they came before the National Grange, never asked for anything which might prove injurious—they merely asked the endorsement of the agriculturists of our country to a bill then before Congress, which was intended and well calculated to develop the resources of millions of fertile acres of our territory, open up beautiful homes for thousands of our fellow citizens, check the monopoly already existing in the carrying trade across this continent, between Asia and the cities and sea-board on our Atlantic coast; add to the national population, the national industry and the national wealth; increase the taxable resources of the country, add to its revenues and lessen the public debt. They urged it was a public duty to utilize the enormous national capital that now lies idle in the vast southern region between Texas and the Pacific coast. They pointed to that vast national domain, capable of producing untold quantities of corn, wheat, wine, cotton, wool and stock; and which, from its want of accessibility and distance from market, could not be profitably brought under cultivation. This wealth, with the rich mines of gold, silver, lead, copper, and coal in Southern Colorado, New Mexico, Arizona, Southern Utah, Nevada, and Southern California, was shown to be unavailable to the nation by reason of distance from mercantile centers and cost of transportation.

Justice to the Southern States demanded that they should have the same rights and facilities to develop their material wealth and increase their productions as had been extended to the Middle and Northern States. Their products, cotton, tobacco, rice, and sugar, are of great value to the nation, and the Northern and Middle States have a direct interest in everything which has a tendency to stimulate the growth of agricultural products in the South.

Our military commanders, Generals Grant, Sherman, Sheridan, Hancock, Meiggs and Ingalls, have all testified that the extension of the railroad from our south-western frontier to the Pacific coast is a military necessity, and that it would substantially end our Indian troubles by the facilities it would give the military to control these wild and savage people.

The bill indorsed by the National Grange, and which it recommended to the speedy action of Congress, does not ask for one acre of the public domain, beyond what may be needed for roadway and stations, nor one dollar as a gift from the public treasury, nor any bonds, the principle or interest of which the government was expected to pay,—none of these were asked for—but simply that the government would guarantee an interest of six per cent. upon the bonds of the road, to the extent of $30,000 per mile, agreed that every guard and restriction necessary to prevent extortion, or unjust discrimination, or fraud of any kind, either towards the people or bond-holders, should be placed by Congress in the franchise.

The security offered against loss on this guarantee is vast and comprehensive. First, the road surrenders every acre of the valuable lands hitherto obtained. Second, it gives the whole of its earnings for transportation for the government. Third, it gives ten per cent. of the entire gross receipts of the road. Fourth, in default of payment the road itself becomes forfeit. Was better security ever exacted by capitalist?

The propriety and security of this great work was so apparent to the members of the National Grange, that the vote, in regard to it, was almost a unit. The Masters from Iowa, Illinois, Missouri, and other States, where Patrons have been contending so earnestly against railroad monopolies, were so well satisfied of the benefits and advantages to be derived from opening another great thoroughfare across our country from Atlantic to Pacific shore, and that

J. W. A. WRIGHT.

P. W. M., and Present Lecturer of State Grange of California.

all necessary guards and restrictions to prevent imposition and fraud would be thrown around it, gave it their hearty support; and not one of them had an idea their action was in the least degree a departure from the principles which should control the action of Grangers, or a violation of the objects and purposes of the Patrons of Husbandry, as fully set forth and given to the world in our Platform of Principles.

CHAPTER XII.

ANNALS OF THE STATE GRANGE OF CALIFORNIA.

Organization at Napa—Representation: Address of N. W. Garretson: Specific Objects Stated Resolutions: State Book of Plans: Election of Officers and Executive Committee: Agencies Provided for—First Annual Meeting—One Hundred and Four Granges in Three Months—Worthy Master Wright's Address—Report of Committee on Irrigation: Committee of Inquiry into Agricultural Department of University—Election of Officers for Two Ensuing Years—Presentation to Bro. Garretson—Installation—Prof. Carr's Lecture—Constitution and By-Laws.

The organization of the State Grange of California took place at Napa, on the 15th of July, 1873, scarcely three months after the adjournment of the Farmers' Union Convention. Meanwhile, a special deputy from the National Grange had been busy organizing the necessary number of Subordinate Granges, which were now convened; the First President of the State Agricultural Society, Hon. J. M. Hamilton, Worthy Master of Guenoc Grange, appeared among the good men and true, who had been active members of the Union, and upon whose shoulders the burden of responsibility was afterward cast.

The following Granges were represented by their proper officers:

W. H. Baxter and Mrs. Baxter, Napa Grange; W. A. Fisher, Past Master, Napa Grange; E. B. Stiles, W. San Joaquin Grange; J. D. Spencer and Mrs. Spencer, Stanislaus Grange; T. Hart Hyatt, Vacaville Grange; W. M. Thorp and Mrs. Thorp, Chico Grange; J. B. Jolley and Mrs. Jolley, Merced Grange; J. D. Reyburn and Mrs. Reyburn, Salida Grange; R. C. Haile, Suisun Valley Grange; G. W. Henning, San Jose Grange; J. D. Fowler, Hollister Grange; W. S. Manlove and Mrs. Manlove, Sacramento Grange; W. M. Jackson and Mrs. Jackson, Yolo Grange; Nelson Carr and Mrs. N. Carr, Bennett Valley Grange; G. W. Davis and Mrs. G. W. Davis, Santa Rosa Grange; T. H. Merry and Mrs. T. H. Merry, Healdsburg Grange; J. A. Clark, Elmira Grange; J. C. Merryfield and Mrs. Merryfield, Dixon Grange; J. M. Hamilton, Guenoc Grange; J. M. Mayfield, Yountville Grange; J. J. Hicok, Grand Island Grange; L. W. Walker, Petaluma Grange; N. L. Allen, Salinas Grange; J. W. A. Wright, Turlock Grange; G. B. Crane and Mrs. G. B. Crane, St. Helena Grange; I. G. Gardner and Mrs. I. G. Gardner, Greyson Grange; B. V. Weeks, Pescadero Grange; J. H. Hegeler and Mrs. J. H. Hegeler, Bodega Grange; A. T. Dewey and Mrs. A. T. Dewey, Temescal Grange.

N. W. Garretson, representing the Worthy Master of the National Grange, opened the session with an eloquent and instructive address. He said:

It seems but as yesterday, (so short is the time,) since your now fair and beautiful State was unreclaimed, unsought and unvalued but for its gold. Its civilization was confined to mining camps, and its bread and fruit supplied from distant fields. Very soon, however, it was demonstrated that the capabilities of these valleys for producing the cereals were great, and their adaptation to fruit culture unrivaled. The effect of this was, not only to change the dreams of emigrants to this land of perpetual summer and sunshine, but it marked a change also in their character. Women, the refining guardians of our race, now swelled the caravan that stretched across the plains and poured over the mountain ranges or that landed from the crowded steamers. Men and women with strong arms and brave hearts were now coming to make homes and plant upon the Pacific Coast a new civilization. Your experiences in reaching California then, though bitter at the time, are garnered with the traveled past, and serve you now—a store of wonders to repeat to those who now cross the continent, borne in palaces of luxuriant ease.

I am presuaded that in no State have the industries found so rapid a development as in California. At a single bound she takes rank as the first wheat-producing State in the Union, exporting last year to England alone not less than five hundred thousand tons. While the products of your gold fields have been great, and have largely swelled the treasuries of the world, the product of your wheat fields, under judicious tillage, will be far greater, affording a more abiding wealth, and promising a far more stable prosperity. The fertility of your soil is equalled only by the enterprise and intelligence of its tillers.

I utter these words as the sum of my observations since I have come among you. I think I see in the farmers of California a discerning intelligence not so general elsewhere. With this characteristic attribute, these men might have successfully prosecuted almost any business pursuit; but seeing the wondrous capabilities for profitable production offered by the diversity of soil and climate in this summer-land, their hearts responded to the invitations of nature, to the comfort and enjoyment of farm life, to that pursuit above all others, God-given and ennobling—Agriculture.

Little did they dream while their thoughts were given to this work, that many of those they fed were combining for the impoverishment of their benefactors. Yet it is true that these men, who stand between you and the market, and whose duty it is to transfer and distribute the products of your labor to and among the consumers of the same, for a reasonable toll, have combined to flank the law of "demand and supply," forming rings and corners at your expense, and are gambling recklessly and wickedly — your rights and your money being their stakes. They have gotten to themselves fortunes, and, to complete their work, these ill-gotten gains are employed as a corruption-fund, to turn aside the arm of justice, and buy the men to whom you have intrusted your dearest interests in the State and National Legislatures. Laws that have sheltered you from the rapacity of these capital combinations are quickly repealed, and other laws are enacted by which other rings are formed to prey as vampires upon your material and industrial interests.

Extravagant salaries, without precedent elsewhere, are fixed for your public functionaries, while the system of prodigality is inaugurated, which, if continued, must terminate in your bankruptcy; for, to meet this unwise expenditure of public funds, heavy assessments of taxes must be made, in the apportionment of which a discrimination, as unscrupulous as it is invidious, is made against the farmer in the interest of the money power.

This work of public corruption and labor-impoverishment, to which I have alluded, is by no means confined to California, but is wide-spread and threatening throughout our whole country. Its deadly leaven has been at work in the councils of our nation, and threatens to-day, more than any other agency, the overthrow of our free government. At the sight of developments within the few months past at Washington, good men grow sick and turn away.

As unpromising as this picture makes our future, we have grounds for hope, for the people are the source of power; and, thank God, they are waking up all over the land—in almost every hamlet and school-house. The farmers, yes, and the farmers' wives—God bless them—are in council. For a like purpose you are convened to-day, as American citizens, as representatives of the great producing interests of California, and as representatives from your respective Granges, to consider the state of the country, and to discuss the necessities of the hour. We are here to form the California State Grange of Patrons of Husbandry. You will remember that the eyes of the oppressed farmers, all over this State, are turned to you for relief, while your enemies will most diligently scrutinize your every act. Conscious, then, of the weight and importance of your duties here, you will, as the State Grange, define for the Order, in this State, a line of future action, which, in your judgment will, at the earliest possible day, most surely emancipate labor from the despotism of capital combinations; one that will bring about the needed reform in your State and inter-State commerce, and drive from places of honor and trust the corrupt horde who have fattened upon your substance.

With clean hands and pure hearts should we come to such a work. Therefore let each lay upon the common altar of this new Order whatever he may have of selfish ambition, or of mercenary motive, and, joining hands, let us covenant, upon the very threshold of our organization, that the meetings, the counsels and the labors of the Order in California, shall be dedicated to the cause of justice and humanity.

That we pledge each to the other that we will labor faithfully, patiently, earnestly and persistently, to purify the moral, social, business and political atmosphere of our State and Nation, bearing ever in mind that if we would triumph in the unequal conflict upon which we now enter, we must fear God, obey our laws and maintain our honor, not forgetting that a good Matron, as also a good Husbandman, is noted at all times and everywhere for his or her fidelity.

The specific objects were declared to be:

1. To establish coöperative systems of trade, thus bringing producers and consumers as near together as possible.

2. To establish banks from which farmers could obtain loans at reasonable interest.

3. To make arrangements for the purchase of farming implements, sacks and machinery, directly from manufacturers.

4. To obtain direct shipments on more favorable terms, and storage at lower rates; drawing upon their products advances at the lowest rates of interest.

5. To secure the establishment of Grange stores; and,

6. The gradual substitution of the cash for the credit system; and, finally,

7. The eventual introduction of shipment in bulk.

The Convention resolved: To labor for the reduction of railroad fares and freights, by using all legitimate means to obtain the necessary legislation; for the reduction of port charges; for the introduction of European laborers; for an increase of tonnage for "our own purposes;" for irrigation; for the elevation and increase of our mechanical industry, all of which work was distributed among proper committees.

As a record of Grange intelligence, and in order to secure a full expression of feeling upon the methods in which these objects were to be carried out, every member of Subordinate Granges was invited to present a concisely written plan, to be classified and kept as a State Book of Plans.

It was also resolved to offer two premiums for the best plan for a general system of coöperation.

The election of officers resulted as follows: J. W. A. Wright, Master; J. M. Hamilton, Overseer; Thos. H. Merry, Lecturer; N. L. Allen, Steward; W. M. Jackson, Assistant Steward; W.

A. Fisher, Treasurer; W. H. Baxter, Secretary; J. D. Fowler, Gate Keeper; T. H. Hyatt, Chaplain; Mrs. I. G. Gardner, Lady Assistant Steward; Mrs. G. W. Davis, Ceres; Mrs. W. H. Baxter, Pomona; Mrs. J. H. Hegeler, Flora.

Resolutions were passed authorizing the Executive Committee, consisting of Brothers Jolley, of Merced county; Merryfield, of Solano county; Allen, of Monterey county, Gardner, of Stanislaus county; Thorp, of Butte county, and Mayfield, of Napa county, to employ a central Business Agent in the city of San Francisco, under bonds and guaranties which should prevent the use of such agency for speculative purposes.

It was furthermore resolved, "to be expedient that the State Grange should have an agent or correspondent residing at Liverpool, authorized to charter ships in the proper season to convey grain crops to European or other markets; to make arrangements for advances of money on cargoes of grain, and on such other securities as the farmer may be able to command, at the lowest rates of interest; also to have laborers and emigrants sent out to California by ships coming hither for cargoes, etc."

The fullest exchanges of information between the Subordinate Granges and the State Agent, between the latter and State Agents of other State Granges, was recommended and provided for. The State Grange then adjourned.

FIRST ANNUAL MEETING.

At the first annual meeting of the California State Grange, held October 14, 1873, at San José, the following Granges were represented:

Alameda County.—Livermore Grange, Daniel Inman, Master; Temescal Grange, Oakland, Alfred T. Dewey, Master.

Butte County.—Chico Grange, W. M. Thorp, Master; Nord Grange, G. W. Colby, Master.

Colusa County.—Antelope Valley Grange, H. A. Logan, Master; Grand Island Grange, J. J. Hicok, Master; Plaza Grange, Olimpo, F. C. Graves, Master; Princeton Grange, Princeton, A. D. Logan, Master; Funk Slough Grange, E. C. Hunter, Master; Spring Valley Grange, D. H. Arnold, Master; Willows Grange, J. W. Zumwalt, Master.

Contra Costa County.—Danville Grange, Danville, Chas. Wood, Master.

El Dorado County.—Pilot Hill Grange, Pilot Hill, P. D. Brown, Master.

Humboldt County.—Kiwelatti Grange, Arcata, Lewis R. Wood, Master; Table Bluff Grange, Jackson Sawyer, Master; Ferndale

Grange, F. Z. Boynton, Master; Elk River Grange, Theodore Meyer, Master.

LAKE COUNTY.—Guenoc Grange, Guenoc, J. M. Hamilton, Master.

LOS ANGELES COUNTY.—Los Angeles Grange, T. A. Garey, Master.

MERCED COUNTY.—Badger Flat Grange, W. F. Clarke, Master; Merced Grange, H. B. Jolley, Master.

MONTEREY COUNTY.—Hollister Grange, J. D. Fowler, Master; Pajaro Grange, D. M. Clough, Master; Salinas Grange, N. L. Allen, Master.

NAPA COUNTY.—Napa Grange, W. H. Baxter, Master; St. Helena Grange, G. B. Crane, Master; Yountville Grange, J. M. Mayfield, Master.

SAN LUIS OBISPO COUNTY.—Cambria Grange, Rufus Rigdon, Master; Moro City Grange, A. J. Mothersead, Master; Old Creek Grange, Isaac Flood, Master; San Luis Obispo Grange, Wm. Jackson, Master.

SANTA BARBARA COUNTY.—Carpenteria Grange, O. N. Cadwell, Master; Santa Barbara Grange, O. L. Abbott, Master; Santa Maria Grange, Joel Miller, Master.

SAN JOAQUIN COUNTY.—Castoria Grange, Samuel Gower, Master; Linden Grange, John Wasley, Master; Lodi Grange, J. W. Kearny, Master; Liberty Grange, Justus Schomp, Master; Rustic Grange, J. A. Shepherd, Master; Stockton Grange, Andrew Wolfe, Master; West San Joaquin Grange, E. B. Stiles, Master; Woodbridge Grange, J. L. Hutson, Master.

STANISLAUS COUNTY.—Ceres Grange, W. B. Harp, Master; Grayson Grange, I. G. Gardner, Master; Salida Grange, Joseph Reyburn, Master; Stanislaus Grange, J. D. Spencer, Master; Turlock Grange, J. W. A. Wright, Master; Waterford Grange, R. R. Warder, Master.

SOLANO COUNTY.—Dixon Grange, J. C. Merryfield, Master; Suisun Valley Grange, R. C. Haile, Master; Vacaville Grange, E. R. Thurbur, Master.

SONOMA COUNTY.—Bennett Valley Grange, Nelson Carr, Master; Bodega Grange, J. H. Hegeler, Master; Cloverdale Grange, Chas. H. Cooley, Master; Healdsburg Grange, T. H. Merry, Master; Petaluma Grange, L. W. Walker, Master, D. G. Heald, Secretary; Santa Rosa Grange, Geo. W. Davis, Master; Sonoma Grange, Leonard Goss, Master; Windsor Grange, A. B. Nalley, Master.

SACRAMENTO COUNTY.—Sacramento Grange, W. S. Manlove, Master.

SANTA CLARA COUNTY.—San Jose Grange, G. W. Henning, Master; Santa Clara Grange, Cary Peebles, Master.

SAN MATEO COUNTY.—Pescadero Grange, B. V. Weeks, Master.

SUTTER COUNTY.—Sutter Grange, W. C. Smith, Master; Yuba City Grange, T. B. Hull, Master.

SANTA CRUZ COUNTY.—Santa Cruz Grange, Benj. Cahoon, Master.

VENTURA COUNTY.—Saticoy Grange, Milton Wasson, Master.

YOLO COUNTY.—Antelope Grange, W. G. Clark, Master; Buckeye Grange, Wm. Sims, Master; Capay Valley Grange, R. R. Darby, Master; Hungry Hollow Grange, G. L. Parker, Master; West

Grafton Grange, A. W. Morris, Master; Yolo Grange, W. M. Jackson, Master. Total, 104.

PAST MASTERS PRESENT.—Napa, W. A. Fisher; San Jose, Oliver Cottle.

MATRONS PRESENT.—Badger Flat Grange, Mrs. S. J. Clarke; Bennett Valley Grange, H. L. Carr; Bodega Grange, R. L. Hegeler; Chico Grange, S. J. Thorp; Cloverdale Grange, E. N. Cooley; Danville Grange, C. A. Wood; Elmira Grange, A. Clark; Grayson Grange, S. M. Gardner; Hollister Grange, S. F. Fowler; Healdsburg Grange, E. E. Merry; Linden Grange, C. E. Wasley; Lodi Grange, E. M. Kearny; Liberty Grange, H. J. Schomp; Merced Grange, L. W. Jolley; Napa Grange, S. C. Baxter; Nord Grange, C. A. Colby; Old Creek Grange, Elizabeth Flood; Petaluma Grange, Jane Walker; Sacramento Grange, F. L. Manlove; Salinas Grange, C. L. Allen; Santa Barbara Grange, L. E. Abbott; Santa Maria Grange, Charlotte Miller; Saticoy Grange, S. E. A. Higgins; Stanislaus Grange, M. A. Spencer; St. Helena Grange, Mrs. Frank Crane; Stockton Grange, A. Wolf; Yolo Grange, Kate Jackson; San Jose Grange, Mrs. O. Cottle.

COMMITTEES.—The following committees were appointed during the session:

Publication Committee.—J. D. Spencer, T. A. Garey, A. J. Mothersead.

Immigration Committee.—R. C. Haile, W. A. Fisher, Leonard Goss.

Signal Bureau Committee.—W. S. Manlove, T. A. Garey, J. W. A. Wright.

Irrigation Committee.—H. B. Jolley, E. B. Stiles, Wm. M. Jackson, J. W. A. Wright, T. A. Garey.

Auditing Committee.—O. L. Abbott, Nelson Carr, L. W. Walker.

Committee on Constitution and By-Laws.—J. D. Fowler, G. W. Henning, E. B. Higgins, W. H. Baxter, I. G. Gardner.

Committee on Resolutions.—W. S. Manlove, G. W. Colby, O. L. Abbott.

Trade and Banks.—W. A. Fisher, G. W. Davis, N. L. Allen, J. D. Spencer, G. B. Crane, A. T. Dewey, J. J. Hicok, Oliver Cottle, R. C. Haile.

Education and University.—J. W. A. Wright, W. H. Baxter, O. L. Abbott.

On the second day the State Grange being opened in due form, N. W. Garretson, Deputy of the National Grange, and Daniel Clark, Master of the Oregon State Grange, and fraternal delegate to this Grange, were introduced by Worthy Master Wright, as follows:

Fellow Patrons of the State of California: A hearty welcome to our first annual meeting. And heartily do we greet you, our brother, who first gave life to the body of our Order on this coast. To this household of our brotherhood, we welcome you cordially, after your additional labor of love for two months by which you have brought into existence another State Grange out of our lamentable chaos of farmers, which, strange to say, has existed from Adam's day to this. And cordially do we welcome you, my brother, who as the Worthy Master of the new State Grange, represent among us, our monopoly-ridden brothers of Oregon and Washington. We rejoice to have you both with us, that you may share our happiness and our work.

On the 15th of July, three months ago, the State Grange of California was organized with delegates from twenty-eight Subordinate Granges. To-day we meet for fraternal greeting and earnest work, as the representatives of one hundred and four Granges throughout the State of California, while our visiting brother represents sixty-five Granges for Oregon and Washington. Rapid as may seem the growth of our Order upon the Pacific Coast, especially when we remember that the past three months are among the busiest of the year, it has been slow in comparison with its progress throughout the United States. Although our National Grange was first organized December 4, 1867, when it convened in Washington City, January 7, 1873, for its sixth annual session, there were, as officially announced, but one thousand three hundred and fifty-nine Subordinate Granges in the United States, and three in Canada. By our latest official reports, there are now seven thousand three hundred in the United States, and eight in Canada. This shows an increase of some six thousand Granges in nine months time. Nearly half of these, or some two thousand eight hundred, have been added in the last three months; for when our State Grange adjourned in July, the number officially reported was four thousand five hundred and thirty-four. In the month of August alone, eight hundred and twenty-nine Granges were organized in the various States and Territories, and fifty-one in one day. In January last, but ten State Granges had been organized, although Subordinate Granges existed in twenty-two States. To-day there are twenty State Granges, and the Order is found in thirty-one States and three Territories. Nor is it confined to America alone. The farmers of Great Britain have written to our American Granges to know the principles of our organization. They tell us that they too are forming such associations, and wish to make their work conform with ours. Our Ritual is being translated into German, that the farmers of Germany may enjoy the benefits which our Order proposes to secure for its members. So broad then are our principles of unity, harmony and brotherhood, so well do they meet a common want of the human race for social, mental and moral advancement, for improvements in agriculture and in our business transactions, that our noble institution is not only national, but is fast becoming international and cosmopolitan in its character.

Should any still doubt the excellence of our Order to meet the farmers' wants, or dread its secrecy, or fear that it is political, or may in some way interfere with their personal independence, or if any of its other features appear objectionable, when superficially examined, is not this grand rallying of the tillers of the soil under the banner of the Patrons of Husbandry, a sufficient answer to all such doubts? Has its success ever been surpassed in the history of any secret organization? And this too among farmers, who, as a class, are extremely cautious and slow to move. Had we not found in it all the elements of success, we should long since have abandoned it. But the better it is understood, the more popular it becomes.

We find one of the most attractive features of our Order in this fact: its growth is not confined to any section of our country. While Iowa takes the lead as our banner State, with over 1,800 Granges, the following figures show a corresponding increase of Subordinate Granges in various Northern and Southern States, since the middle of July: Kansas, from 315 to 597; Indiana, from 238 to 435; Ohio, from 72 to 151; Missouri, from 416 to 879; Tennessee, from 50 to 175; Mississippi, from 149 to 378; Alabama, from 14 to 96. This, recollect, is the increase during the last three months. Yes, our brotherhood is equally valued in all parts of our land. It extends from the granite hills of New England to the mountain-girt valleys of the Pacific. Our brothers and sisters are rallying from the rice and cotton, and sugar lands, which are fanned by the balmy breezes of the Atlantic and the Gulf of Mexico, as well as from the grain and stock farms that are swept by the bracing winds of our Northern lakes. And we feel alike toward all the members of our brotherhood For in the handling of our productions, and in supplying our wants, we have suffered from like impositions and like oppression, and, on common ground, we now seek the same redress, the same independence, to be gained by lawful, peaceful means.

Let our thoughts dwell for a moment on some of our principles and purposes which are liable to be misunderstood and misrepresented. We do not make war against railroads and other internal improvements, but against the spirit of their management. We would rejoice to see in our valleys and mountains a network of railways, and a thorough system of mining, irrigating and navigable canals; they would support and give employment to millions of happy people, and would, when seconded by deep plowing and thorough cultivation, give absolute certainty to calculations on crops and investments; yes, would truly make an earthly paradise of our parched and suffering valleys. We wish to see them succeed. But we do not wish to see them so endowed and managed as to enable those controlling them, to grow rich by preying upon the necessities of our people. We want the water of our State, as well as the air, which the Creator has made the freest of all things on earth, to be kept as free as human laws can make it, consistent with the success of human enterprise, for impartial distribution to supply the wants of our producing classes.

We do not make war upon mere concentrated capital, called, under some of its forms, monopoly. Capital and labor must go hand in hand for the successful development of any country. But we oppose the tyranny of all such monpolies as become oppressive. If we cannot create a monopoly without making it oppressive, we say, "Don't create it." If we cannot correct any existing monopoly so that it will cease to be oppressive, we say, "Put it down, if it can be done."

We do not make war upon just freights and fair profits, but only upon those which are made exorbitant and burdensome by the men who handle our productions and supply our wants.

We do not wage war against fair rates of interest. But we do not think it is right for the moneyed men of our land to get from twelve to twenty-four per cent. upon their loans, and spend their days in tapestried homes and luxurious offices, while the hard-fisted sons of the soil cannot realize two per cent., nay, cannot realize any profits, as the reward of that earnest and unceasing labor, which furnishes bread for millions of our race.

We would like to see such a division of profits made, that while it would take nothing from the welfare and happiness of the capitalist, it would enable our producing and laboring classes to supply their homes with more of the comforts and enjoyments of life.

We make no war on labor, for the whole Grange movement is in friendship to our laboring, as well as our producing classes.

The truth is, we wage war on no other interests. We only demand our rights, without wishing to trample on any rights of our most exalted or humblest citizens. We are merely unwilling for our farming interests to remain the only ones unprotected, while we have all the bills to pay. It is the inequality, the want of equity, the preferences and privileges of the few over the many, to which we are opposed. A proper equality, equity and fairness, protection for the weak, restraint upon the strong, in short, justly-distributed burdens and justly-distributed power, are American ideas, the very essence of American independence, and to advocate the contrary is unworthy of the sons of an American republic.

Our Order, as has been repeated, is not a political organization. We do not even allow the discussion of political questions inside the Grange; but as farmers, who in the past have been an oppressed class, and have borne our oppression too silently, we are allowed to say this much: If our present system of trade and our present political organizations can be so modified and controlled as to secure what we justly require and demand, we shall be content: but if we find that any system of trade or any political party stands between us and our rights as farmers, we say, in imitation of our brothers in Illinois, "Let them all die." We wish always to bear in mind that we do not expect to accomplish our purposes, as producers, by our own unaided efforts, but we hope our demands will appear so just, when properly understood, that every reasonable and ungrasping capitalist, banker, trader, representative of the press, railroad man, grain-buyer, warehouse-keeper, ship-owner—yes, all who are engaged in the development of our industries—every professional and laboring man; nay, more, every uncorrupt and incorruptible politician and office-holder, will heartily aid us in our work. We need their co-operation; but we candidly confess that, as ours is peculiarly a farmers' institution, we want the aid of most of these classes outside the gate. If they really have the will to help us, they can do so quite as effectually—and perhaps more so—without being allowed to enter the sacred portals of the Grange.

We wish to remove from our hearts all jealousies, and hatred, and bitterness of feeling toward others, and to co-operate cordially with all associations, and men who will sincerely labor with us for the accomplishment of our purposes, to secure the good of our fellow beings. Especially are we in sympathy with that enterprising representative of the laboring classes of England, Mr. Joseph Arch. We heartily welcome him to America, and hope he will visit our Coast, that he may learn whether the capacities of our climate, soil, and other resources can meet his wants. We should rejoice to be able to furnish homes for tens of thousands of his people.

Indeed, Patrons, pardon me, if, in view of the silent work of reform which is steadily going on throughout our land, I seem to go too far in saying, we have lived to see a day of glory for the farmers of America. It is not here alone that this good work is going on, but throughout the length and breadth of our land, and it is extending to other lands. Yet let us encourage no spirit of boasting. In all due reverence would I remind you of the sacred words, "Glory to God in the highest, peace on earth, good will toward men." But there is a part that remains for us to do. In all its truth, let us practice the advice not to forget the precepts of our Order. Oh, let us remember, at all times, the fraternal tie and all the requirements of the sacred obligations which bind us together. Let it be our study to understand, and our pride to obey them. We should cultivate a spirit of obedience toward those we place in authority. If we think or know a Patron has so far forgotten his duty as to be guilty of a wrong, let us throw a veil of charity over all that has been done amiss. Let us not openly condemn, until he has been proved guilty by the proper authority. Let us remember, it is one of our first duties to protect all our members, however humble may be their position among us, from any misrepresentations, especially from the vile tongue of slander, which may be used against them. Let us ever strive to put the best, rather than the worst, construction upon the acts of every brother or sister of our Order. Let us be up and doing. Be firm, be prudent, be earnest, be true, and success will as surely follow our efforts as the mid-day's sun shall continue to shine.

To insure the highest degree of success we must impress upon our members the vast importance of preserving the secrecy not only of our unwritten work, but of all our business arrangements. Never forget, these are for Grange members only. Secrecy is the invaluable means of keeping our own counsel. Let us continue to work together in harmony, for the accomplishment of our purposes. Let us act, rather than talk. Remember everything depends on action —action—action! Who can tell the good that, with the blessing of Providence, may be accomplished for our race and nation, and for every race and nation by our united efforts, with the aid of all good citizens! Who can tell what the result may be when the nations of the earth shall assemble in 1876 to celebrate in one grand jubilee the hundredth anniversary of American liberty, equality, and independence—the children of Washington, Putnam and Jefferson, our farmer leaders, who nobly led American farmers a hundred years ago!

Brothers and sisters, again congratulating you on the solid work accomplished since we last met, let me express to you my heartfelt thanks for your undeserved kindness toward myself personally. I can only assure you that I have endeavored to labor faithfully to redeem my pledge, that I would perform the duties of this responsible position to the best of my ability during my short term of office. Pardon me for any errors I may have committed in serving you. Believe my assurance, that my heart and hand are fully with my brother farmers in this work, and ever shall be.

We declare to the world, that "Human happiness is the acme of earthly ambition," and that "Knowledge is the foundation of happiness." We should ask no greater happiness for our future lives than successful labor, wherever duty calls, with our fellow Patrons of Husbandry, for the good of all mankind. For my own part, I confess that never have I enjoyed the true happiness of life more fully than I have in the performance of the duties which have fallen to my lot. During the few remaining days of my term of office, let me feel assured of your kind forbearance and the constant assistance of your valuable counsels.

I have the pleasure of introducing to you Bro. Daniel Clark, Worthy Master of Oregon and Washington State Grange, who comes with Brother Garretson as fraternal delegate to our present session.

Bro. Clark thanked the brethren for the hearty welcome extended, and congratulated them on their remarkable success in this State. The movement is a grand one, and we hope to accomplish great things for the producers of this coast and nation. As fraternal delegate from Oregon and Washington Territory, he was here to cement yet more closely the relationship between the farmers of the different sections of our great Pacific Slope.

He will be able to take back a report that shall make glad the hearts of the people up North. The great wall of partition has been broken down, and henceforth we will all work as one people. He gave every assurance of hearty co-operation on the part of the Patrons of his jurisdiction in all matters pertaining to the interest of the Order.

Bro. Clark was followed by Deputy Garretson, who said:

It was not necessary for him to repeat assurances of his pleasure at meeting us again. He could not express his feeling—was not gifted with an eloquent tongue. He rejoiced in our success. Four months ago this movement in this State was in embryo—the first Subordinate Grange was just organized. Now, behold! Subordinate Granges extend along a line from north to south a distance of seventeen hundred miles, from San Bernardino in Southern California to Dayton in Washington Territory. They are planted for the redemption of humanity.

On going to Oregon he found twenty Sub-Granges ready to organize. They take hold with a will—they are baptized with the spirit of reform. He found, four hundred miles in the interior, a fertile belt of country well populated, with every natural facility for home making and fortune making, yet in a most deplorable condition. The Columbia river is their only outlet to the ocean. Its falls had been seized upon by a monopoly, the Oregon Steam Navigation Company, and these farmers there were bottled up and corked in. While the government has been building railroads and princely monopolies, it has neglected the husbandmen of the north. They look to this jurisdiction to help them secure an appropriation to open the Columbia river, and to relieve the Willamette river of the obstruction to navigation. He thanked the Grange again for their greeting, and begged that, while others were laboring in the field, he might be permitted to retire to a fence corner.

The Committee on Transportation and Legislation reported as follows:

Your committee, to whom was referred that portion of the "Declaration of Purposes of the State Grange" of California having reference to the subject of transportation and legislation, beg leave to report, first: It has been said that "cheap transportation of persons and property is a national necessity." Nowhere can the force of this axiom be more fully realized than here in our favored State. With a territory great in extent, affording within its limits the preductions of both torrid and temperate zones, with a climate varied as its productions, and with a population gathered from all parts of the globe, we can readily understand how facilities for bringing producer and consumer together will contribute to our comfort and convenience. Our wheat, our wool, our wines, our fruit, our minerals, all sources of wealth, health and luxury, must be transported either in a raw or manufactured state; to fetch and carry them, so that the greatest good will ensue to the greatest number, is a study well worthy of the political economist, and its solution will remove an oppressive burden which now hangs like a millstone around the neck of the producer of our State. Our present avenues for transportation of freight are either insufficient or do not perform their proper work. Our inland water courses are blockaded for months during the dry season by sand bars and shoals. The exorbitant rates in many cases charged for transportation on railroads make the cost of moving our crops to market almost prohibitory, and in years of plenty the producer can scarcely realize the cost of production. These things, with the unjust discrimination sometimes made, cause fluctuations, which at times unduly excite, at other times depress and destroy the agricultural and manufacturing interests of our State, and have a tendency even to depopulate it.

While we recognize in the railway an effectual instrument to aid in developing the agricultural resources of the State, and believe that the public interests of the country and its producers would be subserved by fostering the further development of the railway system, provided such a judicious management can be obtained as will secure equitable and just treatment in the way of fares and freight to all localities through which they pass, yet we are satisfied that the present system of building and managing railroads is injurious to the best interests of the producers:

1st. In companies having such special privileges granted them as enable them, after obtaining large subsidies and stock subscriptions from individuals, corporations and counties, to depreciate the value of stock to such an extent as to enable an interested ring to secure the entire control of the road and deprive those who aided in its construction, by furnishing funds, from having any voice in the management of it. Then giving this ring the power to build and equip the road at a fictitious cost, the profits of which go into their own pockets, and farther permitting them, in order to have large dividends, to compel the producer, consumer and traveler to pay excessive fare and freight on such road.

2d. In permitting the consolidation of what should be rival lines in our State, inasmuch as such action is contrary to public policy in building strong monopolies which defy competition, facilitates the charging of exorbitant rates and discriminates unjustly in favor of or against localities, and enables such monopolies to attain their objects, by introducing in our legislative and judicial halls, and by the use of our safeguards for their own selfish ends, to carry out a policy which builds up the carrier at the expense of the producer or consumer. Farmers should encourage the opening and establishing of new routes, under proper restrictions, and retain controlling interest in them. Canals from interior points to communicate with our navigable streams should be constructed; narrow-gauge railways, so much cheaper in construction and operation than the present broad-gauge, are well adapted to cheap transportation, and would help meet the exigencies required. All farmers, as well as Patrons of Husbandry, should unite in an effort to secure a reduction of freight and fare and charges on inland as well as ocean routes, and withhold their voice, their votes and subscription from all transporting corporations which will not agree that such uniform, equitable rates shall be fixed by the State authorities as will afford a fair remuneration to them, and, at the same time, will not be an oppressive burden to the producer and consumer.

Another and true way to correct and alleviate the present trouble and assist the producer of this State, would be to create a home consumption for our products by encouraging and drawing to us manufactories. These, by affording us consumers at home, would do away with all need of transportation of much that is now surplus. If a moiety of the subsidies, by farmers to railroads in this State, had been invested in manufactories, our population would have been so increased that the home market for produce would be double what it is now. If the demand for transportation was curtailed this much, the surplus we have to spare would find a ready market at compensating rates.

The subject of oceanic and internal transportation is of such a varied nature and of such vast importance, that your committee have approached it with reluctance. Especially as the whole subject is now in the hands of the special committee of the United States Senate, who, with a great deal of care and considerable expense, are now gathering facts and statistics to make a report which will, no doubt, be made public in time to enable us to derive as much or more real information and benefit therefrom, than from any report your committee, with the limited means at their command, could possibly make.

The agriculturists of this as well as other States, may justly complain of the unequal burdens imposed upon them for the support of State and Federal governments, while they receive no more, and in many cases not near so much, care and protection from the Government as other industries; yet the statistics show the producers (we include in this class, the farmer, the stockman, the fruit-grower and the mechanic), either directly or indirectly, pay nearly all the taxes that are required for the machinery of the Government. Our lands are taxed, our stock is taxed, our crops are taxed, our improvements are taxed, and in addition to this we pay most of the tax and tariff which is required by the Government from manufacturers. We pay in addition to the cost of transportation on all articles which are brought from abroad, whether of luxury or comfort, the revenue which the Government receives from their importation.

The capitalist who has money invested in bonds or other securities, or is engaged in manufactures, compels the party who uses or consumes the same to pay all the tax which is imposed on him, so that it matters not to him how excessive or onerous the tariff may be. All he has to do is to add the percentage necessary to cover this expense and collect it without diminishing his profits. The Government has fallen into the hands of the consumers rather than the producers of the country, and per consequence a system of unjust discrimination has been adopted and carried out, which makes the producers mere hewers of wood and drawers of water, to their more favored fellow citizens.

This state of affairs has been brought about mainly by the fact that the producers, as a class, have had their time so occupied with the attention necessary to the successful management of the particular industry in which they are engaged, that they could not or have not taken that active part in the administration and control of State and National affairs which they should. Demagogues have usurped power; chicanery and fraud have been successfully used to control the masses; party tactics and selfish intrigue have been permitted to usurp the place of brain and muscle.

The remedy for this is for the producers to arouse from their lethargy, to awake from their slumbers, and not only assist but carry out the measures necessary to reform these abuses. Let their power be seen, and felt, and heard in every part of our Government; in the administration of their local affairs, in our legislative forums, in our judicial halls. Let the mechanics and farmers see to it that none but good, honest and true men fill our State and county offices, none but the true representatives of our interests appear for us either in our State or National capital, men who are closely identified with the bone and sinew of the land, who have suffered from the same ills as ourselves, who have felt the crushing, grinding power of the monopolies which have weighed us down.

We respectfully submit as the most practical way to accomplish these objects and secure the reforms we need, that such legislation shall be had as will make in each county the District Attorney ex-officio chairman of the Board of Supervisors, with the power to veto all appropriations made by the Board for the payment of moneys which in his judgment are illegal or not actually necessary for public uses. The District Attorney to be liable on his official bond for any malfeasance in office while acting as Chairman of the Boards. This, we believe, would effectually check the extravagant and illegal appropriations so often made, and provide for the impartial action of bodies which combine the functions of the legislative, judicial and executive branches of government without, in many cases, being able to properly discharge the duties of either.

Again, believing as we do, that the subject of freights and fares of railroads should be controlled by the Legislature, their rights to do so having generally been admitted under those powers which give the States the right to compel common carriers to establish reasonable rates of freight or fare (the Supreme Court of Minnesota has so decided, and the statutes of New York and Massachusetts expressly declare it), we, therefore, propose that our Legislature at its next session, do establish a uniform standard of fares and freights on the railroads and steamboats of this State, which shall give a reasonable and just remuneration for the distance traveled and service performed. These rates to be conclusive and absolute, but subject to revision at specified times by the Legislature, and that a commission of three or five tax-paying citizens be appointed by the Legislature, whose duty shall be executive and supervisory, to whom shall be referred all matters of controversy growing out of any illegal charges, or arbitrary and oppressive acts on the part of railways or steamers, and who shall see that these carriers comply with the requirements of their charters, and perform all the services for which they were created. The commission would afford protection and redress to every individual having dealings with the companies, without obliging them to apply to the courts at great expense or delay.

In order to secure more uniform and equal taxation, we recommend that the duties enjoined upon our assessors be more definite and specific, and penalties be inflicted upon them when it can be shown that they have made unfair or unjust discrimination in fixing valuation or assessing land and property in the same locality, or when they consent to receive any special favors from large property holders or tax payers, even if it is but a railroad pass.

We recommend that our representatives, both at Sacramento and at Washington, be petitioned to interfere in our behalf, and redress our grievances by carrying out the measures proposed, or if the plans suggested are not practicable, or will not have the desired effect, let them devise some other way by which taxation shall be reduced and made uniform and equal; freight and fares be regulated so as to prevent unjust discrimination and oppressive rates; additional facilities for transportation be encouraged and built up, and the agricultural and mechanical industries of our country receive more fostering care from the heads of our government.

Adopted.

J. M. Hamilton,
T. H. Merry,
G. W. Henning.

The Committee on Irrigation reported as follows:

We find it impracticable at this time, even if we wished to do so, to report the draft for a bill for presentation to the Legislature of this State, providing for a general system of supplying water for irrigating, mining, and other purposes. The draft for such a bill, is, from the nature and novelty of the subject to be treated, a work difficult in itself, and requiring, in its proper execution, a more accurate judgment, greater skill and a more thorough knowledge of legislation than your committee feel that they possess. After mature deliberation, we have reached the conviction that a general bill, applicable to the whole State, can, and ought to be prepared, perfected, and enacted into a law, having for its objects the utilizing of all the inland waters of the State, and their uniform and equitable division and distribution, under the authority and control of the State, among the actual land owners of the State, regardless of whether such lands yield to the hand of industry precious metals only, or the less precious, but far more indispensable article of bread. And to accomplish these ends we recommend the appointment of a committee by this State Grange, to be composed of five members, with authority to prepare, or cause to be prepared, the draft for a bill to be presented to the next Legislature, and in that regard to expend such sums of money as they shall deem to be necessary; and we further recommend that the several Subordinate Granges of this State shall petition the next Legislature of California for the enactment of a general law, having for its design the carrying into effect the objects above mentioned.

Recognizing the natural division of our seasons into dry and rainy, and that the farmers of the State are wholly dependent for remunerative crops upon a sufficient supply of water—and recognizing and looking fully in the face the further fact, that nearly all of the inland waters of the State, available for the purposes of irrigation, are now under either the practical or asserted control of corporations, or confederated capital, in some form, we earnestly recommend the adoption of the following declaration of principles, as expressive of our purposes in that regard:

1st. We hold that the inland waters of this State, not claimed by the general government for navigation purposes, its lakes, rivers and streams, are, and of right ought to be, the property of the State, or of the people thereof, subject to their use and control, through their creature, the Legislature of the State, and that each inhabitant of the State is of right as much entitled to the use and benefit of his equitable proportion of the inland waters of the State, as he is to a sufficiency of the free air of heaven.

2d. That the asserted proposition, that a few, or any number of men, can, under the forms and privileges of a corporation, lay claim to, and hold, as private property, the first right, or exclusive privilege to use, for their own gain, to the impoverishment of the general public, any of the inland waters of this State, is false. That it is indefensible in law or equity, and an unblushing outrage on the people, and especially the farmers of this State.

3d. That it is not only the right, but the duty of the Legislature of this State, to at once take and retain the control of all the inland waters of this State, and by a general law, so far as it does not conflict with any of the rights of the general government, provide the mode and means for dividing and surveying the whole State into Irrigation Districts, and of distributing under fixed, equitable rules, the waters of each District among the land and mine owners thereof, whose land and mines are susceptible of being advantageously supplied with water. That the State should pay the cost of laying out and surveying the several districts; that the lands and mines of each district, susceptible of being advantageously supplied with water, should, by a tax levied thereon, pay for the construction of, and keeping in repair, the canals and other means of conveying the water, and for that purpose each district should be authorized to issue its bonds. And further, that in order to secure the inhabitants of this State in their right to the use of the inland waters therein, the Legislature should, at its next session, provide a way for condemning every and all actual asserted or pretended prior right, privilege or franchise to, or in the use of any of the inland waters of this State, whether held or claimed by individuals or corporations, and the same should be condemned to the public use of supplying the lands and mines of this State with water, and the price of the thing condemned should be paid out of the District fund.

All of which is respectfully submitted.

H. B. Jolley,
Wm. M. Jackson,
Edwin B. Stiles.

Brother Stiles offered the following resolutions:

Resolved—1st. That the Committee on Irrigation proceed, immediately after the adjournment of this State Grange, to provide or cause to be provided, for presentation to the Legislature of the State of California, at its coming session, a bill founded upon the general principles laid down in their report, this day offered to the State Grange, providing for a general system of Irrigation throughout the State.

2d. That the said Committee be, and are hereby instructed, to provide printed petitions asking the Legislature to pass a law for a General System of Irrigation throughout the State, and cause the same to be distributed throughout the State to the Subordinate Granges, and that each Subordinate Grange be requested to appoint a committee to circulate the same, and obtain the largest amount of signatures possible to the same, and that the same be returned to the Worthy Secretary of the State Grange, prior to the 25th day of November, 1873, and by him returned to the Committee on Irrigation.

3d. That it be made the special duty of each Master of Subordinate Granges to impress upon the members of his Grange the great importance of immediate action; to the end that any bill presented to the Legislature may have the full benefit of all the influence which this State Grange can exert, and an influence which even political demagogues dare not disregard.

On Friday, 17th, the election of officers for the ensuing two years was held, and resulted as follows:

Master—J. M. Hamilton, Guenoc, Lake County. *Overseer*—O. L. Abbott, Santa Barbara. *Lecturer*—J. W. A. Wright, Turlock, Stanislaus County. *Steward*—N. L. Allen, Salinas. *Asssistant Steward*—Wm. M. Jackson, Woodland. *Chaplain*—I. C. Gardner, Grayson. *Treasurer*—W. A. Fisher, Napa. *Secretary*—W. H. Baxter, Napa. *Gate Keeper*—R. R. Warder, Waterford, Stanislaus County. *Ceres*—Mrs. G. W. Davis, Santa Rosa. *Pomona*—Mrs. S. C. Baxter,

Napa. *Flora*—Mrs. R. S. Hegeler, Bodega. *Lady Assistant Steward*—Mrs. S. M. Gardner.

A recess was ordered, during which Worthy Master elect, on behalf of committee appointed for that purpose, presented to Bro. N. W. Garretson, Deputy Master of National Grange, a beautiful silver service, as a testimonial of appreciation and fraternal regard. Bro. Garretson responded briefly as follows:

Accepting then this precious offering as a testimonial, not only of your loyalty to the principles that I officially represent, but also of your kind appreciation of my feeble services in their establishment on this coast, I tender you in the name of the National Grange of our Order, and also in my own behalf, unaffected and unmeasured thanks. I shall preserve with care this gift, that is rendered thrice precious by the recollections of this day, and the noble patronhood of California. With this valued token of your regards I shall soon pass your great mountain chain, from the lofty summit of which I may for the last time look into the valleys of this coast; the abodes of those I have learned to love so well. The thought of parting with them saddens me, even now, for I shall leave my heart behind. I shall go from you to gather with the patron hosts of the great Mississippi Valley, to join in their harvest song and to sit down at their harvest feasts. Then, I will speak of you, and of your loving hearts, and words of cheer. And when old winter shall gather about him the northern winds, and sweep down in snowy tempests upon my prairie home, I will gather my little ones around the fireside and talk of this coast. I will tell them of the loving and generous dwellers here, and how pained I was to part with them. I will show them this beautiful cane, from the brothers of the State Grange of Oregon, and also these jewels, the gift of my sisters there. I will then point to this solid silver bar, the product of your own fair State and the valued and valuable testimonial of your regards, and before laying my little ones down to sleep, and while their infant lips are employed with their evening prayer they will think of you (and lisp my father's friends). And when months and years shall have come and gone, and I perchance shall be forgotten here, if in the stillness of the night, you should hear whispered at your pillow in accents of gratitude and love a friendly presence near—be not afraid, for it will be me. God bless you.

The silver service was all of modern style and of exquisitely wrought patterns, consisting of forty-three pieces, the whole laid in a large and substantial leather-bound case. In addition to this was a butter dish which attracted much attention for its elegance and novelty of construction.

After recess the Grange proceeded to elect an Executive Committee for the ensuing term, as follows:

J. M. Hamilton, W. M., chairman, Lake county; J. G. Gardner, Stanislaus county; J. C. Merryfield, Solano county; H. B. Jolley, Merced county; Thos. A. Garey, Los Angeles county; G. W. Colby, Butte county; A. B. Nally, Sonoma county.

The following resolutions, offered by W. H. Baxter, were adopted:

Resolved, That a committee of three be appointed on the subject of agricultural education. Said committee to inquire particularly into the Agricultural Department of the State University—what improvements, if any, should be made, and what legislation, if any, is required to secure to the farmers of the State the full benefits of the Agricultural College grant.

Resolved, That the true meaning and intent of the Congressional grant (see Act of eighteen hundred and sixty-two), was to establish primarily, "Agricultural" or "Mechanics Arts" Colleges, and that the funds derived therefrom should be first applied to these purposes, and that the State should render such aid as may be necessary. Such colleges should be mainly under the control of men engaged in these pursuits, and should be practical as well as theoretical.

J. W. A. Wright, W. H. Baxter, and O. L. Abbott, were appointed on this committee.

The Grange then proceeded to the installation of officers.

Previous to the ceremony of installation, a richly-mounted gold-headed cane was presented to Worthy Master Wright, by the Executive Committee, as a token of fraternal regard and appreciation of his services.

In retiring, Worthy Master J. W. A. Wright, spoke as follows:

Having been called to labor in another portion of the field, and while I am willing to serve you wherever I can, I confess to a feeling of no small relief, now that I surrender into most competent hands the very trying and laborious duties of Master of the State Grange of California.

And to you, my brother, who relieve me, I would say: We are not yet safe beyond the dangerous shores of our harbor. Keep a sharp look-out for hidden rocks and reefs. We are on a treacherous coast for so large a ship as ours. Storms may arise at any hour. But when they come, stand at the helm, and see that all our officers and crew shall do their duty. I am sure you will.

You will find that our ship is staunch and true. Be vigilant that none come on board who have no right to be in our counsels. Should any come who have no right to be here, let them understand that if you find they are the cause of any storms likely to prevent a safe voyage, you will make Jonahs of them all.

May success attend your efforts, our brother from Oregon, in the new field over which you have been called to preside. Assure our brothers of your jurisdiction, when you return to them, that the

Patrons of California will cordially co-operate with them in any measures that can secure our mutual interests. Your welfare is ours. Success and happiness attend you, our brother from Iowa, on your return to a joyous home. May your useful life long be spared, that you may continue to labor, as we are sure you have among us, with an eye single to the good of our Order.

To you, brothers and sisters of San Jose Grange, we return our thanks for the courtesies you have shown us during our session. With all my heart, I thank you for the handsome and valued testimonial of your regard.

To all of you, my brother officers and friends, at this parting hour, my feelings go out in earnest sympathy and fraternal love, strengthened by the memories of the past. Believe me, I shall ever be willing to labor with you in any part of our symbolic field for the successful accomplishment of our purposes. Let us remember, my brothers and sisters, "a good name is rather to be chosen than great riches, and loving favor rather than silver and gold."

Accept my thanks for all your fraternal kindness toward me. God bless and preserve you all, and grant continued prosperity to our cause.

Brother, I cheerfully transfer to you the gavel, as Master of the State Grange of California.

Worthy Master Hamilton made some feeling and appropriate remarks on taking his seat.

Dr. E. S. Carr, Professor of Agriculture of the California State University, (Worthy Lecturer of Temescal Grange), gave an interesting address, a portion only of which we are permitted to present to our readers:

In coming before the Patrons of Husbandry, I lay down the role of instructor, and sit as a learner in the common school of experience —as a fellow laborer with you for a common end, viz: the advancement of the industrial classes. I have been about the State a good deal in pursuance of my duties as Agricultural Professor in the People's University, finding more opportunities to learn than to teach, and I have learned much of the difficulties you have to contend with; perhaps I have seen more plainly than you could yourselves that the greatest was the lack of ready, trained intelligence in meeting those difficulties, or in other words, allowing the brains of others to use your hands for their own, rather than your benefit. Here as elsewhere, labor has been a blind giant, conscious of his strength, yet impotent to use it for his own advantage. And here as elsewhere, the giant's eyes are opened at last, to see how little mere strength is worth, without skill to direct and utilize it.

Dr. Carr then proceeded to show that "education" must go into the ballot, before the laboring man, even in America, could maintain his personal and industrial rights; because it is the key to order and organization. Intellectual faculty is capital; it is a blessed and most hopeful sign of the times that men are organizing everywhere, not only for relief and protection, but for improvement and social unity. The speaker drew a vivid picture of the disabilities of agricultural laborers in England, and showed how much they had already accomplished by peaceable co-operation. Chancellor Lowe struck the key-note of their position, when he said in the British Parliament: "Let us educate our new masters." D'Israeli, speaking of the first efforts of this patient, long-suffering class toward their own emancipation, said: "We have long been mortgaging industry to protect property, and the hour of foreclosure has come."

The great watchwords of the time are education and association. Both these desiderata are fully recognized in this organization, so unprecedented in its growth, so beneficent in its aims, so wide reaching in its influence. Of all combinations originating under strong necessities for resistance, it is the least revolutionary, the most patient and progressive. It is no part of our business to foster enmities and widen differences between capital and labor—but on the contrary to learn how these can be associated into a true equality. Capital in the hands of educated labor is not one tool, but many, the grandest piece of its complex machinery. The increasing subdivision and specialization of labor is a sufficient guaranty that the principles of co-operation will never work adversely to the interests of capital.

These views were amply and variously presented and illustrated in their educational, political and social aspects. While the Granges would never become political in a narrow and partisan sense, any more than churches are, the speaker said he believed they were destined to become an immense power in the purification of our politics by carrying into them a higher sense of responsibility, and the more direct and constant influence of our best womanhood.

Resolutions complimentary to Bro. Daniel Clark, W. M. of Oregon, and to Bro. N. W. Garretson, Deputy of the National Grange, Patrons of Husbandry, were unanimously adopted.

It was moved by J. W. A. Wright that the State Grange of California include in its memorial to Congress a petition for the requisite appropriations to improve the navigation of the Columbia and Willamette rivers, as such improvement is absolutely necessary to relieve the farmers, who depend upon them as commercial avenues, from the oppression of existing monopolists. Adopted.

The following resolutions were also offered by Bro. Wright:

Resolved, That the State Grange of California is in full sympathy with the mission to this country of Mr. Joseph Arch of England, and that we cordially invite him to visit our Pacific Coast with a view to bringing among us immigrants from the laboring classes of Europe, whom he represents.

Resolved, That the Committee on Immigration be instructed to communicate this invitation to Mr. Joseph Arch, and report his answer to the Executive Committee. Adopted.

State Agent, G. P. Kellogg, and Mr. Walcott, of E. E.

Morgan's Sons, were present, by invitation, during a recess in the evening, and enjoyed a social interview, after which the State Grange was formally adjourned.

CHAPTER XIII.

CONSTITUTION OF THE CALIFORNIA STATE GRANGE, PATRONS OF HUSBANDRY.

ARTICLE I.—This Grange shall be known and designated as the California State Grange of the Patrons of Husbandry.

ARTICLE II.—The membership of the State Grange shall consist of Masters of the Subordinate Granges and their wives, who are Matrons. Past Masters and their wives who are Matrons, are honorary members, and are eligible to hold office, but not entitled to vote.

ARTICLE III.—Section 1. The officers of State or Subordinate Granges shall consist of and rank as follows: Master, Overseer, Lecturer, Steward, Assistant Steward, Chaplain, Treasurer, Secretary, Gate Keeper, Ceres, Pomona, Flora, and Lady Assistant Steward. It is their duty to see that the laws of the Order are carried out.

Sec. 2. In the Subordinate Granges they shall be chosen annually; in the State Grange once in two years. All elections to be by ballot, and a majority shall elect. Vacancies by death or resignation to be filled at a special election at the next regular meeting thereof—officers so chosen to serve until the annual meeting.

Sec. 3. There shall be an Executive Committee of the State Grange, consisting of six members, whose term of office shall be two years, three of whom shall be elected each year.

Sec. 4. The officers of the respective Granges shall be addressed as "Worthy."

ARTICLE IV.—The State Grange shall hold its regular annual meetings on the first Tuesday in October, at such place as the Grange may from time to time determine. Special meetings may be called by the Executive Committee, by giving written notice to each Subordinate Grange, thirty days preceding, or by a vote of the Grange at a regular meeting.

ARTICLE V.—Section 1. One third of all Subordinate Granges entitled to representation, shall constitute a quorum for the transaction of business.

Sec. 2. The Ritual adopted by the National Grange, shall be used in all Subordinate Granges, and any desired alteration in the same must be submitted to, and receive the sanction of the National Grange.

ARTICLE VI.—Section 1. Any person interested in agricultural pursuits, of the age of sixteen years (female), and eighteen years (male), duly proposed, elected, and complying with the rules and regulations of the Order, may be admitted to membership and the benefit of the degrees taken. Every application must be accompanied by the fee of membership. If rejected, the money will be refunded. Applications must be certified by members, and balloted for at a subsequent meeting. It shall require three negative votes to reject an applicant.

Sec. 2. No member who is not actually engaged in agricultural pursuits, shall hold office in this Grange.

Sec. 3. No person shall hold at one time more than one office provided for by this Constitution.

ARTICLE VII.—The minimum fee for membership in a Subordinate Grange shall be, for men, five dollars, and for women, two dollars, for the four degrees, except charter members, who shall pay—men, three dollars, and women, fifty cents.

ARTICLE VIII.—Section 1. The minimum of regular monthly dues shall be ten cents from each member, and each Grange may otherwise regulate its own dues.

Sec. 2. The Secretary of each Subordinate Grange shall report quarterly to the Secretary of the State Grange, the names of all persons initiated or passed to higher degrees.

Sec. 3. The Treasurer of each Subordinate Grange shall report quarterly; and pay to the Treasurer of the State Grange the sum of one dollar for each man, and fifty cents for each woman initiated during that quarter; also, a quarterly due of six cents for each member.

Sec. 4. The Secretary of the State Grange shall report quarterly to the Secretary of the National Grange the membership in this State, and the degrees conferred during the quarter.

Sec. 5. The Treasurer of the State Grange shall deposit to the credit of the National Grange of Patrons of Husbandry with some Banking or Trust Company in New York, (to be selected by the Executive Committee,) in quarterly installments, the annual due of ten cents for each member in this State, and forward the receipts for the same to the Treasurer of the National Grange.

Sec. 6. All moneys deposited with said company shall be paid out only upon the drafts of the Treasurer signed by the Master, and countersigned by the Secretary.

Sec. 7. No State Grange shall be entitled to representation in the National Grange, whose dues are unpaid for more than one quarter.

Sec. 8. The fiscal year of this and Subordinate Granges shall commence on the first day of January, and end on the last day of December in each year.

Article IX.—Section 1. Reports from subordinate Granges relative to crops, implements, stock, or any other matters called for by the National Grange, must be certified to by the Master and Secretary, and under seal of the Grange giving the same.

Sec. 2. All printed matter on whatever subject, and all information issued by the National or State to Subordinate Granges, shall be made known to the members without unnecessary delay.

Sec. 3. If any brothers or sisters of the Order are sick, it shall be the duty of the Patrons to visit them, and see that they are well provided with all things needful.

Sec. 4. Any member found guilty of wanton cruelty to animals shall be expelled from the order.

Sec. 5. The officers of Subordinate Granges shall be on the alert in devising means by which the interests of the whole Order may be advanced; but no plan of work shall be adopted by State or Subordinate Granges without first submitting it to, and receiving the sanction of, the National Grange.

Article X.—Section 1. All charters and dispensations issue directly from the National Grange.

Sec. 2. Nine men and four women having received the four Subordinate Degrees, may receive a dispensation to organize a Subordinate Grange.

Sec. 3. Applications for dispensations shall be made to the Secretary of the National Grange, and be signed by the persons applying for the same, and be accompanied by a fee of fifteen dollars.

Sec. 4. Charter members are those persons *only* whose names are upon the application, and whose fees were paid at the time of organization. Their number shall not be less than nine men and four women, nor more than twenty men and ten women.

Sec. 5. Fifteen Subordinate Granges working in a State, can apply for authority to organize a State Grange.

Sec. 6. When State Granges are organized, dispensations will be replaced by charters, issued without further fee.

Sec. 7. All charters must pass through the State Granges for record, and receive the seal and official signatures of the same.

Sec. 8. No Grange shall confer more than one degree (either *First, Second, Third* or *Fourth*) at the same meeting.

Sec. 9. After a State Grange is organized, all applications for charters must pass through the same and be approved by the Master and Secretary.

Article XI.—The duties of the officers of the State and Subordinate Granges shall be prescribed by the laws of the same.

Article 12.—Section 1. The Treasurers of the State and Subordinate Granges shall give bonds to be approved by the officers of their respective Granges.

Sec. 2. In all Granges bills must be approved by the Master, and countersigned by the Secretary, before the Treasurer can pay the same.

Article XIII.—Religious or political questions will not be tolerated as subjects of discussion in the work of the Order, and no political or religious tests for membership shall be applied.

Article XIV.—Any brother or sister who is in good standing, clear of the books of the Grange, and who has attained to the Fourth Degree, is entitled to a withdrawal-card, upon the payment of the sum of one dollar. Persons bearing such cards may be admitted, without additional fees, to membership in another Subordinate Grange, but shall be subject to the same form of petition, examination and ballot, as those first applying for membership, except that a majority vote shall elect them.

Article XV.—Persons making application for membership in our Order shall apply to the Subordinate Grange nearest to them, unless good and sufficient reasons exist for doing otherwise. In such cases, the Grange to which application is made, shall judge the reasons, and may consult the Grange nearest the applicant.

Article XVI.—It shall be lawful for Subordinate Granges to form themselves into Councils for the purpose of facilitating the transaction of business, buying, selling and shipping, or such other purposes as may seem for the good of the Order. They shall be governed, and the membership regulated, by such laws as the Council may, from time to time, make, not in conflict with the Constitutions of the National and State Granges. They may elect a business agent to act in concert with the Executive Committee; and it shall be their duty to inform the Master of any irregularities practiced by Deputies within their jurisdiction.

Article XVII.—Section 1. The Executive Committee shall be empowered to try and suspend from office any officer of the State Grange who may prove inefficient or derelict in the discharge of his duty—subject to appeal to the ensuing session of the State Grange.

Sec. 2. A Master of a Subordinate Grange is amenable to a Court constituted by the Grange of which he is a member, and an appeal lays from such Court to the State Grange.

Article XVIII.—This Constitution may be amended at any regular meeting of the State Grange, provided that any proposed amendment shall have been presented to the Executive Committee, and by it reported to the Masters of Subordinate Granges, three months previous to the meeting of the State Grange.

BY-LAWS OF THE CALIFORNIA STATE GRANGE.

Article I.—Section 1. It shall be the duty of the Master to preside at all meetings of the Grange; to see that all officers and members of committees properly perform their respective duties; to see that the Constitution of the National Grange, the By-Laws of this State Grange, and the usages of the Order, are observed and obeyed; to sign all drafts upon the Treasury, and to perform all other duties usually pertaining to such office.

Sec. 2. It shall be the duty of Masters of Subordinate Granges to take charge of all books and papers containing the work of the Order, private instructions, etc., and they shall not allow the same out of their possession, except for use in the Grange.

Sec. 3. It shall be the duty of the Overseer to assist the Master in preserving order; to preside over the Grange in the absence of the Master, and in case of the vacancy of the office of Master, he shall fill the same until the next annual meeting.

Sec. 4. The duties of Lecturer shall be such as usually devolve upon that officer in a Subordinate Grange. He shall also visit Subordinate Granges throughout the State, when requested to do so by the Executive Committee.

Sec. 5. It shall be the duty of the Steward to have charge of the inner Gate, and perform such other duties as are required by the Ritual.

Sec. 6. The Assistant Steward shall assist the Steward in the performance of his duties.

Sec. 7. The Secretary shall keep an accurate record of all proceedings of the Grange, make out all necessary returns to the National Grange, keep the accounts of the Subordinate Granges with the State Grange, and pay over quarterly to the Treasurer all moneys coming into his hands and take his receipt for the same. He shall also keep a complete register of the names and numbers of all Subordinate Granges, and the names and addresses of Masters and Secretaries.

Sec. 8. It shall be the duty of the Treasurer to receive all moneys, giving his receipt for the same; to keep an accurate occount thereof, and pay all orders of the Grange signed by the Master and Secretary; to render a full account of his office at each annual meeting, and deliver to his successor in office all moneys, books and papers pertaining to his office; and he shall give bonds in a sufficient amount to secure the money that may be placed in his hands—said bonds to be approved by the Executive Committee.

Sec. 9. The Treasurer of each Subordinate Grange shall report quarterly, and shall pay to the Secretary of the State Grange the sum of one dollar for each man and fifty cents for each woman initiated during the quarter; also a quarterly due of six cents for each member. He shall send at the same time a duplicate of his report to the Secretary of the State Grange. The Treasurer of the State Grange shall send a receipt to Treasurers of Subordinate Granges, and a duplicate to the Secretary of the State Grange.

Sec. 10. The Treasurer of the State Grange shall keep his balance with the Grangers' Bank of California.

Sec. 11. The Treasurers and Secretaries of Subordinate Granges shall file copies of their quarterly reports certified by the Master.

Sec. 12. The Gate Keeper shall see that the Gates are properly guarded, and shall have charge of all property committed to his keeping.

Article II.—Section 1. All Committees, unless otherwise ordered, shall consist of three members, and shall be appointed—two by the Master and one by the Overseer. All Committees shall be composed of both brothers and sisters, unless otherwise specially provided.

Sec. 2. At the regular annual meeting a Committee on Finance shall be appointed, whose duty it shall be to audit all accounts previous to their being paid. To them shall be referred the reports of the Secretary and Treasurer for examination.

Sec. 3. The Executive Committee shall consist of the Master, who shall be Chairman, and six members elected by ballot, who shall hold office for two years, three being elected each year. But no two shall be elected from the same county. They shall have authority to act on all matters of interest to the Order, when the State Grange is not in session; shall provide for the welfare of the Order in business matters, and shall report their acts in detail to the State Grange on the first day of its annual meeting. They shall also make such report at special meetings of the State Grange as the good of the Order may demand.

Sec. 4. The Executive Committee shall hold its regular meetings quarterly on the first Tuesday of January, April, July and October.

Article III.—The Secretary shall see that the quarterly dues of the Subordinate Granges are promptly paid, and in case the dues remain delinquent two quarters, the delinquent Grange shall be reported to the Master of the State Grange. On receiving such notice it shall be the duty of the Master to warn the delinquent Grange, and if the dues are not forwarded in thirty days, the Master shall advise the Master of the National Grange of such delinquency, and recommend the revocal of the charter of the delinquent Grange; and any Grange whose charter has been thus revoked may petition the State Grange for re-instatement.

Article IV.—Subordinate Granges shall defray the expenses of their delegates to the State Grange.

Article V.—The Master of the State Grange shall appoint at least one deputy in each county, where a proper person can be found, who is a Master or Past Master, whose duty it shall be to organize new Granges, upon application being made to him by proper persons residing in his district; to install officers of Granges when the same have been elected; and to be vigilant that no disorder shall obtain in the Grange under his jurisdiction, and to promptly report any such disorder to the Master. They shall have exclusive jurisdiction in their respective districts, and their rulings on questions of law and points of order shall be respected, until overruled by the Master of the State Grange. They shall receive for organizing new Granges their necessary expenses. They shall be appointed for one year, subject to removal for cause by the Master. No other Granges shall hereafter be recognized except those organized by Deputies as herein specified, excepting only those organized by the Master of the State Grange, or one especially deputized by him.

Article VI.—Section 1. An appeal may be taken from the decision of the Master of a Subordinate Grange to the District Deputy, and from thence to the Master of the State Grange.

Sec. 2. On trials, an appeal from the judgment of a Subordinate Grange, lies to the State Grange, and must be presented to the Executive Committee at least ten days prior to the meeting of the State Grange.

Article VII.—Section 1. Any member of a Subordinate Grange, who may wish to change his pursuit, or enter into new business relations which may bring him in conflict with the interests of the Grange, must first obtain consent of his Grange.

Sec. 2. Persons holding a membership in any Subordinate Grange within this jurisdiction, who may so change their pursuit, or become so associated in business relation that their pecuniary interests are in conflict with the interests of the Order, or with the attainment of any of the objects of this Order, shall be deemed to have forfeited their membership in the Grange. And it shall be the duty of any Subordinate Grange in which such person may hold membership, upon written complaint and charge being made by ten members of the Order, to institute an investigation of such sharge; and if upon investigation it shall appear that it is founded upon facts, said Subordinate Grange shall without delay expel such unworthy person from its fellowship, giving thereof the notice required by law.

Sec. 3. It is further provided that if any member of our Order shall reflect disgrace upon the same by grossly immoral or improper conduct, or if his acts shall show that he is in sympathy with our enemies, and is disposed to obstruct or defeat the work of our Order, rather than aid in the attainment of its objects, such person shall be adjudged to have forfeited his membership, and upon proof being made of his guilt, he shall be expelled from the Grange.

Sec. 4. Upon the filing with the Master of any Subordinate Grange the complaint of ten members of our Order, specifically charging that any member of his Grange is guilty of a violation of any of the provisions of Sections 1 and 2 of this article, it shall be his duty to investigate, without delay, the ground upon which such charges are made, using reasonable diligence to bring the offender to trial thereon, and notifying said complainants and defendants of the time and place at which said investigation will be had.

Sec. 5. It is further provided that, should any Subordinate Grange with which a complaint is filed, as provided in Section 3 of this Article, refuse to entertain said complaint, or neglect to bring its accused member to a speedy trial thereon, it shall thereby forfeit its membership in this body, with all benefits accruing therefrom; and it shall be the duty of the Master of the State Grange to recommend to the Master of the National Grange, the revocation of the charter of said offending Grange.

Sec. 6. An accused party shall have one week's notice of the time at which a Committee of Investigation will be raised, and all such Committees shall be elected by ballot.

Sec. 7. Secretaries of Subordinate Granges shall report to the Secretary of this Grange the names of all persons expelled from their respective Granges, and he shall report the same quarterly to all Subordinate Granges in the State.

Article VIII. A ballot on application for membership in a Subordinate Grange, may be reconsidered at any time prior to initiation, immediately upon application of three members, or after one week's notice by one member.

Article IX.—These By-Laws may be amended at any regular meeting of this Grange by a vote of two thirds of the members present.

RULES OF ORDER.

1. When the presiding officer takes the chair, the officers and members shall take their respective stations, and at the sound of the gavel there shall be a general silence. The Grange shall then proceed to open in regular form.

2. No question shall be stated unless moved by two members, or be open for consideration unless stated by the Master. And when a question is before the Grange no motion shall be received, unless to close; to lay on the table; the previous question; to postpone; to refer, or to amend. They shall have precedence in the order in which they are arranged, the first three of which shall be decided without debate.

3. Any member may call for a division of a question when the sense of it will permit.

4. The yeas and nays shall be ordered by the Master, on the call of any member, duly seconded.

5. After any question (except of indefinite postponement) has been decided, any member who voted in the majority may, at the same or next meeting, move for a reconsideration thereof; but no discussion of the main question shall be allowed unless reconsidered.

6. No member shall speak more than once on the same subject, until all the members wishing to speak have had an opportunity to do so, or more than twice without permission from the chair. And no member, while speaking, shall name another by his or her proper name, but shall use the appropriate designation belonging to his or her standing in the Grange.

7. The Master or any other member may call a brother or sister to order while speaking; when the debate shall be suspended, and the brother or sister shall not speak until the point of order be determined, unless to appeal from the chair, when he or she may use the words following, and no others: "Master, I respectfully appeal from the decision of the chair to the Grange." Whereupon the Grange shall proceed to vote on the question: "Will the Grange sustain the decision of the chair?"

8. When a brother or sister intends to speak on a question, he or she shall rise in his or her place and respectfully address his or her remarks to the Worthy Master, confining him or herself to the question, and avoid personality. Should more than one member rise to speak at the same time, the Worthy Master shall determine who is entitled to the floor.

9. When a brother or sister has been called to order by the Worthy Master for the manifestation of temper or improper feeling, he or she shall not be allowed to speak again on the subject under discussion in the Grange, at that meeting, except to apologize.

10. On a call of five members, a majority of the Grange may demand that the previous question shall be put, which shall always be in this form: "Shall the main question now be put?" And until it is decided shall preclude all amendments to the main question and all further debate.

11. All motions or resolutions offered in the Grange shall be reduced to writing, if required.

12. When standing or special committees are appointed, the individual first named is considered the chairman, although each has a right to elect its own chairman. Committees are required to meet and attend to the matters assigned to them with regularity, and not by separate consultation, or in a loose and indefinite manner.

13. The Worthy Master, by virtue of his office, may attend all meetings of committees, take part in their deliberations (without voting, however), and urge them to action. (In the appointment of committees, the Worthy Master, who should ever preserve a courteous and conciliatory deportment to all, not overlooking the humblest member, has many opportunities for bringing humble merit into notice, and of testing and making available the capabilities of those around him. He should carefully avoid both petulancy and favoritism, and act with strict impartiality.)

14. In all cases, not herein provided, "Cushing's Manual" shall be our parliamentary law.

CHAPTER XIV.

BUSINESS OPERATIONS AND ORGANIZATIONS.

Agency Established in San Francisco—Mr. A. F. Walcott Appears for E. E. Morgan's Sons—Firm Endorsed by Prominent Houses—Agreements and Precautions—State Agent—Competition Produces Better Prices—Savings of the First Year—Grangers' Bank Meeting—Organization—Dairy Agency—Stanislaus Savings and Loan Society—Warehouse at Modesto—Davisville Grange Incorporates—Colusa County Bank—Waterford—Warehouses and Business Associations.

Shortly after the adjournment of the State Grange the Executive Committee met at the Russ House in San Francisco, to carry out one of the most difficult tasks ever undertaken by men unacquainted with each other, and with the modes of carrying out such extensive business transactions in the great commercial centers. They considered it their wisest course to form an alliance with some well established house, and for this purpose various firms were invited to a friendly conference.

Among these appeared the old and well known house of E. E. Morgan's Sons, shipping merchants between New York and Liverpool, represented in San Francisco by their local agent and managing partner, Mr. A. F. Walcott.

The advantages offered by this firm appeared to the Committee such as to warrant a careful examination into his standing and references. A special committee, consisting of Brothers Merryfield, Jolley, and Mayfield, after visiting the London and San Francisco Bank, the Fireman's Fund Insurance Company, and other responsible firms, reported the house of Morgan's Sons as sound and good, with credit at the London and San Francisco Bank for half a million of dollars. The arrangements entered into were that the Executive Committee should employ an agent of their own, who should have full access to the books of the shipping firm to examine therein any accounts with Patrons of Husbandry; to all telegraphic and other communications from Liverpool or other markets relative to prices, rates, or other matters bearing on the interests of the farmers, in consideration of which, the committee agreed to use their influence throughout the State to secure the shipping of Patrons' produce through the above mentioned firm. Great care and deliberation was required in the choice of the Grangers' agent, who must be a thorough business man, and above suspicion. They did not fix upon any one at that session, nor until a circular letter had been sent to each of the Subordinate Granges, asking them to name such parties as were competent and willing to serve. The election fell upon G. P. Kellogg, of Salinas, who qualified by filing bonds to the amount of two hundred thousand dollars, and entered at once upon his varied and difficult task.

He took rooms in the building occupied by Morgan's Sons, and immediately put the Granges in possession of all the information commanded by the firm. In order to relieve patrons of limited means, who were compelled to realize at once on their crop, the Executive Committee requested Mr. Walcott to add to his sole business of shipper, that of purchaser, which he promised to do to the extent of twenty or thirty thousand tons. So lively was the competition pushed by the old wheat ring, that in a very few weeks the prices went up even higher than the Liverpool quotations would warrant, and Mr. Walcott, having entered into this competition, extended his purchases from thirty to nearly a hundred thousand tons. The price steadily rose from $1 50 per cental to $2 37½. Meanwhile, the State Agent, watching closely to see that his employers were fairly dealt with, was making favorable terms with dealers in implements and importers, as will be seen in the official reports. Mr. I. G. Gardner, a member of the Executive Committee, acted as assistant to Mr. Kellogg, until the resignation of the latter in January, 1874, when the Committee placed Mr. Gardner in full charge, tendering their own security for the faithful performance of his duties.

The efficiency with which these obligations were met, is best shown by the footing-up of the operations of the first year, as follows:—

Amount saved on sacks, $450,000; amount saved on tonnage, at $5 per ton, $3,000,000; amount saved on agricultural implements, $160,000; amount saved on groceries and general merchandise, $200,000; amount saved on grain of 1873-74, at 15 cts. per cental—9,000,000 centals—$1,350,000. Total, $5,160,000.

The magnitude of these operations, and the growing confidence of the people in the agency, already warranted the establishment of a Grangers' Bank.

Early in April, 1874, the Executive Committee issued a call

THE GRANGERS' BANK; Offices of Fire Insurance Association and Executive Committee, Corner California and Leidesdorff Streets, San Francisco.

THE GRANGERS' BUSINESS ASSOCIATION,
Corner of Market and Fremont Streets, San Francisco.

for a convention, to consider ways and means to give greater unity and efficiency to their business operations. On the 21st, two hundred delegates, representing one hundred and thirty-one Granges, met in San Francisco, for a comparison of views. After a full discussion, it was

> "Resolved—That a general system of banks and warehouses, with a central bank in San Francisco, is an absolute necessity for the future success of the Order."

A committee of seven was appointed to prepare a plan of organization, which was substantially the same as that afterward adopted. $500,000 was subscribed to the capital stock, which was fixed at $5,000,000, in 50,000 shares of $100 each. It was resolved to incur no expense until after $100,000 should have actually been paid in by the stockholders.

The committee on warehousing reported a plan for the establishment of a general warehouse or depot for the sale of Granger's products, and for branch warehouses or storage companies, to be established under regulations of the Executive Committee.

The question of shipping in bulk also came up for consideration. It was—

> "Resolved, That this Convention endorse the proposition to change the system of handling and shipping grain in sacks, now in operation in this State, to a system of handling in bulk.
>
> "Resolved, That from this day, we, as farmers and producers of wheat and other produce in California, will work for the change of the system above referred to."

Mr. A. F. Walcott was introduced by the Executive Committee, and gave a full explanation of the shipping interest, the state of the foreign market, and replied to inquiries which Patrons desired to make, in respect to his agency. The confidence which Mr. Walcott had inspired in the large body of farmers with whom he had business relations, resulted in his election to the Presidency of the bank, when it went into operation, some three months later. The Secretary of the State Grange was also appointed Secretary of the bank corporation.

The Grangers' Bank of California is organized under the Statute of 1872, known as the Civil Code. Its capital stock is fixed at five million ($5,000,000) dollars, divided into fifty thousand (50,000) shares of the par value of one hundred ($100) dollars each. Its place of business is in the City and County of San Francisco, State of California. This bank has been organized for the purpose of enabling the Patrons of California to secure to themselves such advantages in obtaining money for use in the agricultural portions of the State upon as favorable terms as it can be obtained in the city for commercial purposes; believing that the landed security of the agriculturist is equal to, if not better than city property as a basis of credit, and at the same time giving people of every class an opportunity of safely and profitably investing their money.

A careful perusal of the By-Laws will show that they are so framed as to have all the safeguards, not inconsistent with law, that it is possible for them to have.

BY-LAWS OF THE GRANGERS' BANK OF CALIFORNIA.

ARTICLE 1. The name of this Corporation shall be "GRANGERS' BANK OF CALIFORNIA."

ART. 2. The principal place of business shall be in the City and County of San Francisco, and State of California.

ART. 3. The bank shall have a capital stock of five million of dollars, divided into fifty thousand shares, of the par value of one hundred dollars each.

ART. 4. None but Patrons of Husbandry, or corporations composed exclusively of Patrons of Husbandry, shall be permitted to subscribe to the capital stock of this bank, and such persons or incorporations shall not be permitted to subscribe in excess of five hundred shares.

ART. 5. Stockholders of this bank shall be such persons or corporations as may have executed, or shall hereafter execute a subscription to the capital stock in form such as the Board of Directors may prescribe, and shall pay to the cashier of the bank all called assessments, or any person to whom said stock has been duly assigned.

ART. 6. The powers of the corporation shall be vested in a Board of eleven (11) Directors, who shall be elected by the stockholders at the annual meeting, and shall hold their office for the term of one year, and until their successors are elected and qualified.

ART. 7. The Directors shall be stockholders of the corporation, and Patrons of Husbandry, resident of the State of California, and citizens of the United States, and shall hold at least five shares of the capital stock.

ART. 8. A majority of the whole number of Directors shall constitute a quorum for the transaction of business, and every decision of a majority of the persons duly assembled as a Board (if not in conflict with these By-Laws), shall be valid as a corporate act.

ART. 9. Regular meetings of the Board of Directors shall be held at the office of the corporation, at least once in every two months, and at such other times as the Board of Directors may direct, and special meetings of the Board of Directors shall be held at the same place, upon the call of the President; and it shall be the duty of the President, Vice President, or Cashier to call special meetings upon request of five Directors, or upon request of stockholders representing one quarter of the stock issued. No notice need be given of the regular meetings, in addition to that furnished by this Article; but of special meetings, the President or Cashier shall cause all Directors residing outside of San Francisco, to be notified by mail or telegraph, mailing the same seven days prior to such meeting, and all Directors residing and being in the city and county of San Francisco, and to any others to whom it is practicable to give such personal notice, to be personally notified.

Art. 10. Whenever a vacancy shall occur in the office of any Director, by death, resignation, or other cause, the Board of Directors shall appoint a successor for his unexpired term. Provided, that if more than one vacancy shall occur in the Board in any year, a meeting of the stockholders shall be called by the Board of Directors within thirty days, giving at least twenty days' notice of such meeting, by advertising the same in some newspaper published daily in the city of San Francisco, for the purpose of filling such vacancy or vacancies.

Art. 11. Whenever any Director shall cease to be a stockholder, his office becomes *ipso faeto*, vacant; such vacancy shall be filled as provided in Article 10.

Art. 12. The Board of Directors shall elect from their number a President and Vice President of the corporation, who shall hold their office for one year.

Art. 13. The President or Vice President, or either of them, may be removed from office at any time on the vote of seven Directors in favor of such removal.

Art. 14. The Board of Directors shall appoint a cashier, an attorney, and such other officers, agents, clerks or servants, as the business of the bank shall require, define their powers and prescribe their duties, subject to the By-Laws, and shall fix the salaries or compensation to be paid all officers, agents, clerks, or servants of the corporation.

Art. 15. The President, Vice President and Cashier shall have charge and custody of the funds, property, books, papers, and other matters of the corporation, under such rules, regulations and restrictions as the Board of Directors shall prescribe in the By-Laws, or by express resolution from time to time made or passed.

Art. 16. The President, Vice President, and Cashier, shall have power to buy and sell bills of exchange, to make loans under such regulations and restrictions as may be fixed by resolutions of the Board of Directors, to keep the Common Seal, and each shall have the power to affix the same to all papers, instruments, or documents, on behalf of the Corporation, requiring the Seal; they shall each have the power to collect all moneys due the Corporation; to make, execute, and deliver all receipts, releases, acquittances, or other papers, writings, documents, or instruments on behalf of the Corporation, proper or necessary in the ordinary course of business of the Bank; and generally to carry on the business of the Corporation, subject to the control of the Board of Directors, expressed through the By-Laws, or such express resolutions as may from time to time be passed; and they shall each report to the Board of Directors, when required, each and everything by them, or either of them, transacted.

Art. 17. The President and Vice President shall not both be absent from the State at the same time, and in case of the absence of either from the Bank, his duties and powers shall devolve upon and be performed by the other; and each to be eligible to such office shall be a stockholder to the amount of five shares.

Art. 18. It shall be the duty of the President, and in his absence the Vice President, to preside at all meetings of the Board of Directors, and at all meetings of the stockholders of the Corporation.

Art. 19. It shall be the duty of the Cashier to keep or cause to be kept such books as the business of the Bank may require, under the control and instructions of the Board of Directors. He shall attend personally to the business of the Bank at such hours as the Board of Directors may determine. He shall also be required to give bonds for the faithful performance of his duties, in an amount to be fixed by the Board of Directors.

Art. 20. The Board of Directors shall appoint from their number a Finance Committee of three, whose duties shall be defined by resolution of the Board of Directors.

Art. 21. The Board of Directors shall appoint an Auditing Committee of three from their number, whose duty it shall be to count the cash and examine the books, vouchers, documents, papers, and other assets of the Bank; to report upon the same to the stockholders at their annual meetings, and to the Board of Directors from time to time, as they may direct.

Art. 22. The annual meeting of the stockholders for the election of Directors shall be held at the office of the Bank, on the second Tuesday of October of each year, at one o'clock P. M.

Art. 23. The call for the annual meeting of stockholders, and for the annual election of Directors shall be signed by the President, Vice President, or Cashier, and published at least once a week for four consecutive weeks next preceding the day of meeting, in at least three newspapers of general circulation throughout the State. If from any cause no quorum shall be present, the meeting may adjourn from time to time without further notice.

Art. 24. At all meetings of the stockholders one vote shall be counted for each share of stock not exceeding fifty share, and one additional vote shall be counted for each twenty-five shares, or fractional part of twenty-five shares in excess of fifty, upon which all called assessments have been paid. Each stockholder may be represented at any meeting of the stockholders by a proxy, who must also be a stockholder; provided said proxy shall have filed his credentials with the Cashier at least ten days next preceeding each meeting; provided further that no person shall be allowed to hold proxies representing more than one hundred votes.

Art. 25. The Board of Directors shall have power to regulate, from time to time, the rate of interest to be charged upon loans and allowed upon deposits.

Art. 26. All transfers of stock shall be subject to all debts and equities in favor of the Corporation, against the person or corporations making such transfer, and existing or arising prior to the regular transfer thereof upon the books of the Corporation; and no transfer of shares shall be made upon the books of the Corporation, until all dues and demands thereon, due to the Corporation from the party or parties representing such shares, shall have been paid.

Art. 27. All transfers of stock shall be made on the books of the Corporation, and no transfer shall be binding on the Corporation until so entered, or until all assessments thereon have been paid. No stock that has been transferred on the books of the Corporation within thirty days next preceding any meeting of the stockholders, shall be entitled to representation at said meeting.

Art. 28. Certificates of stock shall be issued to the original stockholders of this Bank, to the number of shares by each subscribed in the original articles of association, as evidence to each of the number of shares by him owned in the capital stock, and the manner of transferring shares shall be by endorsement and delivery of the certificates thereof, such endorsement being by the signature of the proprietor, or his or her attorney, or legal representative. No stock shall be transferred without the surrender of the certificate, and upon such surrender the word "cancelled" shall be written across the face of the certificate by the Cashier, and the signature of the officers shall be erased, and such certificate so cancelled, shall be preserved by pasting the same to the stub from which it was torn in the Certificate Book. The transfer books shall be closed for two days prior to the annual meeting and the payment of dividends, and the dividends shall be paid to the stockholders in whose names the stock shall stand when the books are closed.

Art. 29. The officers of the Bank are strictly prohibited from loaning its funds on mining stocks.

Art. 30. The Board of Directors shall have power to dispose of the stock of the Bank at rates not less than the par value, and after the first of October, 1874, may fix such premiums on the stock as in their judgment may be deemed just.

Art. 31. All persons subscribing to the capital stock of the Bank, are required to sign their names to the By-Laws.

The bank went into operation on the first of August, 1874, at 415 California street, San Francisco. Beautiful and commodious rooms, with the necessary private rooms attached, accommodate both the bank, the Executive Committee, Secretary, and other officers of the State Grange. Amid the surging throng of capitalists, speculators, and schemers, which crowd the money-changers' highway, is set the financial headquarters of our most important industry. It was created for the Patrons, with especial reference to small stockholders; $2,517,000 of the capital stock has been taken up, $2,000,000 is on deposit in the bank. Its stock is owned by one thousand five hundred and forty-three Patrons of Husbandry, and the number of depositors is correspondingly large. It is managed by the following Board of Directors:

J. V. Webster (President), of Alameda county; Calvin J. Cressey (Vice President), of Stanislaus county; Thos. McConnell, of Sacramento county; John G. Hill, of Ventura county; J. C. Merryfield, of Solano county; John Lewelling, of Napa county; Gilbert W. Colby, of Butte county; J. P. Chrisman, of Contra Costa county; F. J. Woodward, of San Joaquin county; C. S. Abbott, of Monterey county; F. A. Cressey, Secretary.

Current accounts are opened and conducted in the usual way, and interest at the rate of one quarter of one per cent. per month, is allowed on the minimum monthly balance. Deposit receipts in sums of fifty dollars and upwards received, and receipts given for the amounts, payable on thirty days' notice of withdrawal. These deposits bear interest at rates varying with the current rate of discount. Deposits for fixed periods are received, and interest allowed at the following rates: three months, six per cent.; six months, seven per cent.; one year, eight per cent.

About this time, the Executive Committee deemed it advisable to establish a Dairy Agency in San Francisco, and proceeded to appoint Mr. J. Hegeler, of Sonoma County, who opened a depot for the disposition of this class of products. The bonds of this sub-agency were fixed at twenty thousand dollars.

The Farmers' Saving and Loan Society of Stanislaus County had organized in March, 1873, and incorporated with a capital of two hundred and fifty thousand dollars. The spirit with which the farmers were pushing these various interests was shown at the meeting in Modesto, when four of their number took fifty thousand dollars' worth of stock. One hundred thousand dollars was subscribed on the spot.

The Grange Warehouse in Modesto was provided for in the same business-like manner, with a capital stock of one hundred thousand dollars.

Davisville Grange decided to incorporate with a capital stock of fifty thousand dollars.

Colusa County called its Bank meeting February 25th, 1874, and incorporated with a capital of two hundred and fifty thousand dollars, all of which was subscribed. As a local institution, under judicious management, it is a perfect success, and has benefited its patrons by relieving them of the necessity of borrowing money on call of men who were most likely to call just when wheat was on the rise.

Grand Island Grange, which had but thirteen members, incorporated, bought out their only merchant, and established a coöperative store.

Waterford Grange incorporated May 23d, 1873. A few days later, articles of incorporation were filed at the office of the Secretary of State, for Grangers' warehouses at Antelope Station, and at Antioch. Up to the present time, coöperative companies have been formed for storing grain, and warehouses established as follows:

At Modesto, Stanislaus county; at Merced City, Merced county; at Yuba City, Sutter county; at Woodland, Yolo county; at Colusa, Colusa county; at Dixon, Solano county; at Antioch, Contra Costa county. In other places warehouses have been leased, and in others they are projected to be built. Before the close of another season, we shall probably see Granger warehouses at Vallejo, Collinsville, Monterey, and other points convenient and accessible to large ships, and also at sundry stations along the lines of railroad in the interior. Thus it will be seen that when the Grangers talk of "handling their own products," they do not mean merely hauling them to town in their own wagons and selling them to the first bidder. They mean a vast system that will secure to the producer a fair price for his crops, and to the consumer the crop at a fair price —mutual protection against the impositions and extortions of middle-men.

There is another class of incorporations, all of which have grown into existence within the past year. First among them in point of time, and we believe also in magnitude, is the Farmers' Coöperative Union of San José. The capital stock is one hundred thousand dollars, of which the entire amount is subscribed. This Association set out by purchasing the stock and good will of Pfister & Co. for thirty thousand dollars. They have since increased the stock to perhaps eighty thousand dollars, have spread out so as to occupy several large store-rooms, and are in a most flourishing condition. They include in their invoices hardware, agricultural implements, and a general line of groceries.

The Grangers' Union of Stockton started a little more than a year ago, with two hundred and fifty thousand dollars capital, but by careful management has achieved a greater success in proportion to the actual investment than any similar institution on the coast.

The Farmers' Bank of Dixon, (Solano county) went into operation less than a year ago with a capital of two hundred thousand dollars, and like the others, is to-day giving testimony to the fact that farmers can conduct even a banking business with safety and profit.

The Grangers of Southern California being comparatively isolated, felt the necessity of coöperative exertions even more than the great wheat-growing counties had done. A coöperative store at Los Angeles, established with a capital of twenty-five thousand dollars, has been satisfactory beyond their expectations. The stock was mostly groceries and agricultural implements. The stockholders realize the difference in the net results of buying at wholesale for cash, and at retail on time. But they reach out toward larger benefits.

Their objects are stated to be:

1. The establishment of one or more stores, warehouses, etc.; the buying and selling of goods, machinery and agricultural products; the borrowing and loaning of money; the buying, holding and selling of such real estate as may be necessary for its own use; and the conduct of a general mercantile business.

2. Principal place of business, Los Angeles.

3. Capital stock one hundred thousand dollars, divided into two thousand shares of fifty dollars each, five dollars per share to be paid on or before April 1st, 1874, and the balance in installments, as may be called for by the Board of Directors, not to exceed ten dollars per share per annum.

4. None but Grange members can hold stock, and no person can hold more than ten shares.

5. Each family containing one Grange member can obtain all the privileges of the company by holding one share of stock.

6. Goods are to be sold to stockholders and their families at as near cost as possible, and the usual prices are to be charged all outsiders.

7. All farm produce is to be bought or handled on commission by the company.

8. Money to be loaned stockholders for legitimate farming operations at the lowest rates of interest.

It is also the intention of the company to assist stockholders in every way it can consistently with its own safety. It will, as soon as practicable, borrow funds with which to assist those who are now in the clutches of merchants or others, if such persons endeavor to oppress our members because they seek to better their condition by this method of coöperation. The company is organized for the benefit of its stockholders, and any system of relief to them that can be devised and safely carried out will be inaugurated for the common good.

Encouraged by the success of the experiments mentioned above, the Visalia Grangers have just opened a similar institution with a capital of one hundred thousand dollars. At Grand Island, Colusa County, one has recently been inaugurated, as also one at Meridian, Sutter County; but neither of these has been in operation long enough to show a balance sheet. Santa Barbara just now announces an incorporation with a capital of fifty thousand dollars, and we doubt not will soon give a good account of herself. San Buenaventura is also on the way, and sundry other places are discussing the matter, with every probability of soon reaching the point of incorporation. Everywhere the local merchants have displayed more or less hostility toward these enterprises, until they become satisfied that, if the Grangers were only let alone, they would pursue the "even tenor of their way," without making war on any legitimate business; and gradually matters have adjusted themselves so as to work without friction.

In addition to what has already been mentioned, the Grangers of the Salinas Valley have constructed a narrow-gauge railroad from Salinas City to Monterey, that they might get their grain from the field to the ship at the nearest point, and at the least cost. The Salinas is a large, fertile valley, opening out to the coast with a first-class harbor, and there is no reason why its products should not be shipped direct to European markets, thus avoiding the expensive carrying and handling *via* San Francisco. The Grangers saw the opportunity, seized it, and have made a grand success of the project, without detriment to any other interest. Other projects of a similar character are under discussion, with promises of success, and we see no reason why the Grangers, if they have the means, should not become railroad builders as well as anybody else.

The Farmers' Mutual Fire Insurance Company is another achievement, the present standing of which, after an existence of less than a year, would be ground of congratulation to any incorporation. It was worked up to its present efficient condition by J. D. Blanchar, a gentleman of long experience in insurance, who had retired to the quietude of a farm on account of ill health. He was a member of Napa Grange, and entered into the movement with his whole soul, appreciating, as most farmers could not, the great advantages of coöperation. The company was instituted with a capital stock of one hundred thousand dollars, all of which has since been paid up, to insure farm property on the mutual plan, at its actual cost, thereby saving to the farmers the amount they were obliged to contribute in other companies to cover losses on city property. A "cash plan" was also introduced, so as to enable the company to take risks on town property, granger stores, warehouses, etc. At the last meeting of the Directors, a proposition was made to further increase the capital stock to three hundred thousand dollars. The risks amount to about one million and a half, with no losses, and the company is classed A 1, by the Commissioner.

CONSTITUTION OF THE CALIFORNIA MUTUAL FIRE INSURANCE ASSOCIATION.

We, the undersigned, citizens of California, and Directors of The California Mutual Fire Insurance Association, in pursuance of the insurance laws of California, do hereby associate together for the purpose of forming an incorporated association, to insure dwelling houses, barns, or other buildings, and personal property in the same, belonging to farmers, against loss or damage by fire.

Officers.—J. D. Blanchar, President; I. G. Gardner, Vice President; G. P Kellogg, Treasurer; W. H. Baxter, Secretary.

Directors.—A. Wolf, J. D. Blanchar, I. G. Gardner, G. P. Kellogg, W. H. Baxter.

Trustees.—J. M. Hamilton, J. C. Merryfield, G. W. Colby, H. B. Jolly, A. Wolf, I. C. Steele, A. B. Nally, O. L. Abbott.

And we declare this instrument to be the Agreement and By-Laws of the Association by which it shall be governed, subject only to the Constitution and laws of the State.

Name.—This Association shall be known as the California Farmers' Mutual Fire Insurance Association; and its principal place of business shall be in the City and County of San Francisco, State of California.

Annual Meeting.—The Annual Meeting shall be held on the first Tuesday of October of each year, at San Francisco, and may be adjourned from time to time until the business is completed. No other notice than these By-Laws need be given for the Annual Meetings. Special meetings may be called by the Secretary or President, or on the order of two Directors, and notice given by notification by mail.

Officers.—The officers of said Association shall consist of five (5) Directors, to be elected by ballot, at the annual meeting, by a majority vote of the stockholders present; and the Directors shall elect a President, Vice-President, Treasurer and Secretary. Ten shares or over will entitle a stockholder to one vote. Provided, in case there should be no election, the then incumbents of such offices shall hold over respectively until there is an election, and their successors have qualified, and any stockholder shall be eligible to hold office.

Duty of Officers.—Section 1. The Directors shall have power to appoint such officers and agents as they deem necessary, and to fix salaries and commissions of all officers and agents. They shall have power to make contracts, transfer property, and provide for a definite sum of money for insurance therein, or issue cash policies in lieu of being assessed. They shall audit all claims of the Association not otherwise provided for; determine the rates and time of insurance, amount of money to be deposited, and by virtue of their office shall become agents of the Association.

Sec. 2. The President shall sign all policies, inspect the books and accounts of the Association, and appoint officers *pro tem* to fill vacancies occasioned by death, removal or resignation of officers; preside at all meetings when present, and perform such other duties as may seem connected with his office, and required by the By-Laws. He shall attend to the commencement and prosecution of all suits or actions in which the Association, or any of its officers, as such, may or shall be interested, and in like manner defend against all such suits or actions.

Sec. 3. The Vice-President shall act at the exclusion of the President, whenever the President shall be absent, unable, or neglect from any cause whatever, to perform the duties required of him. When the President and Vice-President are absent from a meeting, the members may elect a President *pro tempore.*

Sec. 4. The Secretary or Deputy shall keep a record of the proceedings of all meetings, and keep all necessary books and accounts, file and preserve all papers, documents and instruments required to be kept in his office. He shall issue policies for the insurance of the property mentioned in the Charter, and he may cancel policies at any time for the non-fulfillment of the requirements of this Association, audit all claims on the part of the holder or holders thereof, and audit all claims presented against the Association for payment, and generally transact all business of the Association in the absence of the Board of Directors, not inconsistent with the By-Laws, and make all assessments against the persons insured, and draw all orders on the banks for money for losses and expenses of the Association, in accordance with the By-Laws; and he may appoint agents to receive applications for insurance, and shall make a report annually.

Sec. 5. It shall be the duty of the Treasurer to keep all moneys coming into his hands, subject to the order of the Secretary, for actual losses and expenses of the Association. He shall give bonds, with sufficient sureties, to an amount satisfactory to the Directors; and he shall make a report in writing at any time when required by the Board of Directors.

Any officer may be removed for neglect of duty, malfeasance, or misfeasance in office, by a majority vote of the Directors.

Fees and Assessments.—All persons insuring shall pay a fee of $5 00, which includes the issuance of the first policy for five years; and thereafter all policies issued or renewed shall be subject to, and pay $1 25 in U. S. Gold Coin.

And shall be ratably assessed, and are hereby bound to pay all their proportion of all losses and expenses happening to and accruing in or to said Association.

Withdrawal.—Any person may withdraw at any time, by paying her, his or their proportion of indebtedness to the Association, up to the time of their withdrawal and surrender of policy, when any balance due such person will be refunded.

Deposit Money.—Section 1. Each person insuring in this Association shall make a deposit of two per cent. on the amount for which his, her or their property is insured, for the purpose of meeting assessments for losses and expenses of the Association, and the money so received shall be deposited with the Grangers'. Bank of California, and a Certificate of Deposit issued to the depositor for the amount; the money so deposited to draw interest as may be agreed upon by the Directors with the Bank. And when the deposits in the said Bank shall amount to over fifty thousand dollars, the President, Vice-President, Secretary, Treasurer and Directors shall have power to withdraw from said Bank the excess of fifty thousand dollars, and deposit the amount so withdrawn with local banks in other parts of the State, or invest the same in real estate securities, school or county, or township or county bonds of this State, as they may deem prudent, and for the best interests of the insured.

Sec. 2. When a promissory note is given for the deposit-money, the insurance shall be good on said note, provided the policy shall not have been canceled; and in case a loss occurs previous to the payment of the said note, the Secretary shall retain out of the amount allowed for loss when adjusted, the amount of said note and interest.

Sec. 3. If, at the expiration of a policy, there is deposit-money on hand it will be refunded, by giving thirty days' notice, and also forwarding the certificate of deposit and the policy; and if it shall ever so happen that the deposit-money of any person insured should be insufficient to pay the proportion of losses and expenses of the Association for the time insured, the Secretary shall notify such person, and he, she or they, can withdraw, or deposit such an amount of money as the Board of Directors may deem sufficient to pay the proportion of losses and expenses for the unexpired term of the insurance.

INSURANCE.—Section 1. Property of those insuring may be removed at the pleasure of the owner, to any other locality where such property can be insured, if not more hazardous; the party must notify the Secretary of the removal, with a description of the new locality, and pay a fee of one dollar and twenty-five cents.

Sec. 2. Insurance in this Association shall be effected for five years, and all policies, and alterations in policies, shall expire in five years from date of first policy.

Sec. 3. Any person insured in this Association may have the policy canceled at any time, on making application to the Secretary, and returning the policy and certificate of deposit; and in ninety days the money deposited, less the amount of assessments and proportion of expenses, will be refunded; and the Secretary is authorized to cancel any policy whenever he deems advisable, after the Policy Note given becomes due, unless said note shall be renewed or paid within thirty days; and for non-conformance with the rules and regulations of the Association.

Sec. 4. The insurance shall cease upon the sale of the property insured, but the insurer shall be holden for all assessments, until the policies shall be legally withdrawn and canceled.

Sec. 5. If ashes are kept in a wooden box, cask or vessel of any kind of wood, in any buildings insured, that will endanger the same, or when out of doors, if not deposited twenty feet from buildings, the Association will not be responsible for any loss resulting therefrom. No stove pipe must come nearer than four inches of wood or other combustible material, unless protected by a funnel. Kerosene or fluid lamps must never be filled while burning. Smoking, or playing with matches, or carrying open or lighted lamps or candles in or about barn, or other places liable to take fire, are prohibited. Wooden fire-boards must be lined with zinc, sheet-iron, or tin, when a stovepive enters the chimney.

This Association will not be responsible for any loss occurring by or through the neglect of any portion of this section.

Sec. 6. Altering or improving any building does not affect the policy, provided these By-Laws are not violated, nor the risk increased by such alteration or improvement.

Sec. 7. Any person found guilty of fraud or false swearing, in any manner affecting the risk, will thereby forfeit his insurance.

Sec. 8. Upon the death of any person insured, the insurance will continue good to the heirs or legal representatives.

Sec. 9. Any person insured wishing to insure the same property in another association, must notify the Secretary and obtain consent.

Sec. 10. If the buildings insured shall at any time be used for the purpose of carrying on or exercising therein any trade, business or vocation denominated by insurance companies as hazardous, or extra hazardous, the insurance shall be null and void.

Sec. 11. Whenever any person having insurance in this company, shall mortgage the property insured, the policy shall thereby terminate and become void, unless upon written application to the Secretary he waive the said forfeiture, and give a written certificate of such waiver.

Sec. 12. This Association shall pay no more than five hundred dollars on any one animal.

Sec. 13. If any person shall allow any insured building to become vacated or unoccupied for a period to exceed thirty days, without the consent of the Secretary, the insurance on such building and its contents shall be null and void, until said building is again occupied.

Sec. 14. Every person applying for insurance shall make a true statement of the amount of incumbrance, if any, both real and personal.

Losses.—Section 1. In case of loss or damage by fire, the Secretary, or Director residing in the county in which the fire occurred, or both, or an agent, may proceed to investigate the cause and origin of such fire or damage, and ascertain by evidence the liability of the Association.

Sec. 2. When any person insured shall sustain a loss or damage by fire, he shall, within thirty days after such loss, deliver to the Secretary a particular statement in writing of such loss or damage, signed by him, and verified by his oath or affirmation, and also, if required, by proper vouchers, and stating also the whole cash value of the property lost or damaged; how the building was occupied, and by whom, at the time of the loss; how the fire originated as far as he knows or believes, and that the fire occurred by misfortune, and without fraud or evil practice; also declare whether any insurance existed thereon in any other company, and if so what amount; and if required, submit to a full examination.

Sec. 3. No person shall have claim for more than two thirds the value of buildings, or household furniture and wearing apparel, at the time destroyed, nor more than the amount of insurance; such loss to be determined by the Directors. But in case a disagreement shall arise between the insured and the Directors in regard to the settlement of loss by fire, the same shall be determined by three referees, not interested, mutually chosen by the insured and Directors, and their decision shall be final; and the reasonable expenses of such referees shall be equally borne by the Association and the loser.

Sec. 4. No claim for loss or damage shall be valid against the Association, unless presented within thirty days from the date of loss.

Sec. 5. In case of fire or loss or damage thereby, or by exposure to loss or damage thereby, it shall be the duty of the assured to use all possible diligence in saving and preserving the property; and if they fail to do so, this Association shall not be held answerable to make good the loss or damage sustained in consequence of such neglect; or from any loss occasioned by steam threshers.

Sec. 6. In case of any loss or damage to the property insured, it shall be optional with the Association to replace the articles lost or damaged with others of the same kind and equal quality, and to rebuild or repair the building or buildings, within a reasonable time, giving notice of their intention to do so within thirty days after the preliminary proofs shall have been received at the office of the Association.

Office.—Section 1. All policies issued shall be signed by the President and Secretary, and shall take effect at twelve o'clock, noon, on the date of the application.

Sec. 2. The fiscal year shall begin and close at twelve o'clock, noon, of the same day of the annual meeting.

Sec. 3. The books of the office of the Association shall be open for inspection during business hours.

Sec. 4. In case of a deficit or deficits arising from the non-collection of any assessments made for any purpose herein mentioned, provided for the assessing and collecting of sums to pay losses or damage by fire, or other purposes, another assessment can be made for such deficit or deficits.

HON. J. M. HAMILTON,
W. M. of State Grange of California.

CHAPTER XV.

THE SECOND ANNUAL MEETING.

LARGE ATTENDANCE—WORTHY MASTER HAMILTON'S ADDRESS—A GRANGE FUNERAL—FESTIVAL OF POMONA—IMPORTANT RESOLUTIONS—ABSTRACT OF REPORT OF STATE AGENT: OF THE EXECUTIVE COMMITTEE: OF THE TREASURER: OF THE LECTURER: OF THE MANAGER OF DAIRY PRODUCE DEPARTMENT: OF COMMITTEE ON THE AGRICULTURAL COLLEGE OF THE STATE UNIVERSITY: OF THE COMMITTEE ON IRRIGATION: OF THE COMMITTEE ON EDUCATION AND LABOR: OF THE COMMITTEE ON THE GOOD OF THE ORDER.

THE State Grange of California convened for its second annual session in Stockton on the 6th of October, 1874, and was opened by Worthy Master Hamilton, in the usual form; eighty Masters, seven Past Masters, and twenty-seven Matrons were present, and others were added from day to day, as the meeting progressed.

Not only was the time during three daily sessions crowded with work, but a daily meeting of the Fruit Growers was held, to dispose of questions affecting their interests alone. All Fourth Degree members were cordially invited to attend the session in that degree. The largest hall in Stockton, beautifully decorated with appropriate emblems of the plenteous harvest, was prepared for the occasion, to which the services of an excellent choir gave an additional charm.

From the instructive address of the Worthy Master, we gather the following report of progress and specific recommendations:

One year ago we numbered one hundred and four Granges, with a membership of three thousand one hundred and sixty-eight. To-day we report two hundred and thirty-one Granges, with a membership of eighteen thousand five hundred, to which may be added a membership of two hundred in the State of Nevada, at present under our jurisdiction.

Our Order has been progressing. It has made a steady and vigorous growth. Our power and strength have been appreciated. Our business arrangements have been so conducted that we have derived great good from them, but they have not been as effective as they should have been. This is from a variety of causes, among which may be placed that misunderstanding which seems to prevail in regard to the duties of Patrons to each other and to the Order. Our organic law provides for an association intended for co-operative purposes, each part of which is dependent upon some other to make it effective. These parts, taken singly, are but weak and imperfect; but when all are combined, they make a machine of wondrous power and utility. When we become Patrons, we agree to relinquish many individual rights we previously enjoyed, and bind ourselves to co-operate for certain purposes. These purposes are plainly prescribed, and, to a great extent, the mode of accomplishing them is pointed out. No Patron, no Grange, no Council—under the arrangement of our organic law—has any right to adopt any plan for business purposes, without first ascertaining whether such plan is in accord with the general good of the Order. No one can be allowed to carry out selfish views, and devise a system which, although advantageous to themselves, may be injurious to other members or other parts of the Order. Our strength lies in our united action, and in order to carry out our objects there must be no jarring, no clash, no discord; but all must work smoothly together, each must perform the duty assigned to it.

The general objects we have in view are so plain we need not err therein, but, hand in hand and shoulder to shoulder, we should keep step in our onward march, and be true to ourselves and to each other. In order to accomplish this, it is absolutely necessary that we must not only be united in our efforts, but we must adhere to plans formed by those we have placed in position for that purpose. If there are any who cannot do so, they are out of place. They may be with us, but they are not of us; their presence, their voices, their acts, are elements of weakness instead of strength, and we should avail ourselves of the ample means which have been provided by our laws to remove such from among us.

A due regard is not always observed to our obligation to keep secret the work of our Order; our business arrangements are often divulged without any intention of wrong doing. Patrons give some friend, or perhaps some member of their family, information as to some of the advantages we derive from our connection with the Order. This is wrong. Each one should always remember that they are pledged to strict secrecy in regard to all information of every kind they receive in the Grange.

No one has any right to divulge to an outsider what occurs within our gates—not a word spoken or an act taken of any kind. The business arrangements confided to us are not our own. They belong to others, and we have no right, either morally or legally, to use the property of others in such a way that the owners thereof may be injured by our act.

The Grangers' Bank is an institution growing out of our necessities. Without it we are destitute of an important auxiliary to carry out the plans and purposes we have in contemplation in regard to storing, shipping, and selling grain in the home and foreign markets, in the arrangements contemplated for the future, for procuring direct from manufacturers, on the most favorable terms, such articles as were needed by Patrons. With it, we have financial facilities afforded by which we can be assisted in the operation of our agencies, be aided in carrying our crops, and obtaining such money accommodations as from time to time are almost indispensable, without having to pay exorbitant rates of interest. Although a difference of opinion did exist among Patrons at the inception of the enterprise, as to the expediency of attempting to carry it through at the time, and the prospect of its final success, the bank is now an established fact. It has been in operation nearly three months, and the amount of business done through it, and the superior facilities it affords for the transaction of our business, are so apparent, that these differences have become almost entirely removed.

Patrons are now stockholders, I believe; fully double the number of shareholders in any other bank in California, and these are from every part of our State. By far the largest number of certificates are for a few shares of stock. Thus the responsibility for its proper management, and the benefit to be derived from it, are shared by so many members of our Order, that it is in reality, as well as name, the Grangers' Bank of California.

From the opportunity afforded me for observation, I am able to say that all the business transactions and all the financial arrangements are carried on in such a safe and conservative manner, that, as long as the present policy is pursued, I cannot see how any disaster can overtake it, or any injury arise from it. The interests of the stockholders are so well guarded, and their control and management of it so directly in their own hands, that nothing but gross neglect on the part of the friends of the Bank will ever allow any advantage to be taken of it, or a loss sustained by those investing money in it. Over 1,300 Patrons are now stockholders in the Bank, having 10,802 shares. This, I believe, is more than double the number of stockholders in any other bank in California, and they are from every part of the State. Thus the impossibility of its improper management.

The Grangers' Insurance Company meets a great want among the agriculturists of this State; and Patrons, instead of having to depend upon others to assist them in repairing losses, which from time to time are sustained from fire, have a friend of their own, bred and born in the Order, managed and controlled by themselves, of but a short existence, still fast assuming vast proportions; and from the rapidity with which Patrons are availing themselves of the security it affords them against losses, its popularity is becoming more and more manifest, and confidence in it is becoming stronger every day. Its policies embrace all the most improved features adopted by other fire associations; the care exercised in taking only what are termed by all underwriters first-class risks; the low rates of premium required—all recommend it strongly to the patronage of our Order, and all should unite in availing themselves of the benefits to be derived.

And now, Patrons, let me again remind you, we have our task before us, and all our ability will be taxed to devise plans to accomplish it; all our energies will be required to carry it into effect. If we are but true to ourselves and the cause we have espoused, by the light of the new era which has dawned, we will secure better and brighter days for the tillers of the soil than they have ever enjoyed. We will establish a test of true manhood, and make honor, honesty, and capacity the crucible in which to try men's fitness for place and power. When this is done, we will realize the benefits we have sought for, and then, but not until then, can we sit under our own vines and fig-trees without molestation, and enjoy the fruits of our labors.

The death of Sister Stephens, one of the charter members of the Stockton Grange, having occurred during this session, the State Grange adjourned for the purpose of attending her funeral, and with the solemn and impressive service of the Order, the remains of the deceased Sister were committed to the grave.

On the evening of the third day, the hall having been duly prepared, the Fifth Degree was conferred upon one hundred and four Masters and thirty-six Matrons; when the festival of Pomona was celebrated by two hundred of her votaries. The creed of the Patron requires that the social features of the Order be ever held as of the highest importance.

A great number of resolutions were presented and discussed during the session, which illustrated the benefits of the Grange in calling attention to defects in legislation, and the bearings of other pursuits and interests upon agriculture. Among the more important resolutions adopted were the following:

Whereas, The State Grange of California believes that conference and consultation with transportation companies is preferable to legislation, when it can accomplish the same. Therefore,

Resolved, That our Executive Committee be requested to confer with the Directors of the Central Pacific Railroad Company, and see if they cannot secure from them such reductions on freights and fares as may seem desirable and just; also, that they confer with other transportation companies of our coast for similar reductions.

Resolved, That in view of the great scarcity of domestic help in this State, it shall be the duty of the Executive Committee to take immediate steps to perfect such arrangements with the Order in the Atlantic States, as will enable us to import female help under the auspices of the Order.

Resolved, That the attention of the farmers of this State should be directed to the culture of cotton as one of the staples, thereby producing that diversity of products so necessary to develop our agricultural wealth.

Resolved, That as soon as the Secretary of the State Grange is notified of the ratification of the amendments to the Constitution of the National Grange by the proper authority, the Executive Committee of the State Grange are hereby authorized to establish regulations for the organization of County or District Granges.

Resolved, That the Executive Committee are hereby authorized to immediately mature a plan for the incorporation of the State Grange as a corporate body, for the purpose of carrying out the demands of our Order.

The various official reports furnished gratifying proof of the earnestness and economy with which the work of the Order had been prosecuted. They are necessarily presented here in a greatly abridged form. First in importance was the report of the State Agent, Bro. I. G. Gardner, as follows:

When the office was first opened, it had to contend with men brought up and trained in mercantile pursuits, who looked upon our movements with suspicion, well knowing that, should we preserve harmony amongst ourselves, great innovations would necessarily be made. I have spared neither time nor patience in the endeavor to place the office in a position that would compel the respect of its enemies, and protect, to the fullest extent, the interests of our Order.

The amount of money saved to purchasers, during the short period of my agency, has reached the sum of $15,000, while the expense of the same, including salary of agent, clerk-hire, etc., has been $411 66, over and above its earnings, which are derived from commission alone, at one half the rate charged by commission houses. During the greater portion of the time Bro. Kellogg was in the office, no commissions were charged. The business of the agency is increasing, and more confidence appears to exist in its operations as experience is acquired.

The direct savings upon actual purchases, through the agency, are insignificant, compared with the indirect influence such purchases have had on the general market throughout the State.

As the accompanying statement shows the amount of business in the matter of purchase done by the agency, the general effect of its influence has produced the following results. Last year, when there were short crops, and a large surplus of agricultural implements, the maximum discount that could be obtained on such implements, for cash, was five per cent.; and even this concession was made only to those whose experience taught them that a discount was due. In many cases, three per cent. was the greatest amount allowed.

This year, with an abundant harvest, causing a demand beyond the supply of agricultural implements, through the operations of this agency a discount of fifteen per cent., for cash, on the large purchases of implements by said agency, has been allowed. I estimate the reduction on groceries and general merchandise, by the efforts of this agency, to be five per cent. on $4,000,000—a clear saving to the Patrons of $200,000, over and above the present prices paid by those who do not and cannot belong to our organization.

On sacks, we have caused a reduction of one cent each, aside from the still greater reduction caused by the large importation thereof by E. E. Morgan's Sons, as per agreement with our Granges. The consumption of sacks this year has been 15,000,000, on which a clear saving has been made of one per cent., or $150,000 more.

Through the operations of E. E. Morgan's Sons, and the various other means made use of by the Executive Committee, we are enabled to give the following figures as the result of our operations for the first year:

Amount saved on sacks, $450,000; amount saved on tonnage, $5 per ton, $3,000,000; amount saved on agricultural implements, $160,000; amount saved on groceries and general merchandise, $200,000; amount saved on our own grain last year, 15c per cental, 9,000,000 centals, $1,350,000. Total, $5,160,000.

The Treasurer, W. A. Fisher, reported:

Receipts to June 30, 1874		$8,846 14
For dues and contingent fund contribution....	$7,598 14	
Commissions from agency	1,248 00	
		$8,846 14
Disbursed upon drafts to September 17, 1874..	$6,891 60	
Cash on hand in bank	1,954 64	
		$8,846 14

Report of Executive Committee:

The efforts put forth by them, were first directed toward carrying out your instructions with reference to legislative matters placed in their hands, viz: Irrigation, Public School Lands and the State University, the committees of which will make detailed reports.

The next, establishing an agency for the sale of Dairy Produce, the report of which will be presented under its proper head.

Then came the all absorbing and most vital of business matters for their consideration, that of providing sacks and tonnage for the coming season and this present crop. Their efforts in this direction have been made manifest by the circulars which have been sent to every Grange in the State, urging upon the members of the Order everywhere, to take such steps as the Committee believed to be necessary in order to carry out the principles of business for which we have combined; also in sending those who were informed upon the subjects, to visit and explain, so that all might understand in relation thereto, and understanding, all could work in harmony and unison toward solving the great and difficult problem of the "capability of the farmer to transact business for himself."

Then the momentous question of a financial institution forced itself upon them for consideration. The popular feeling and disposition seeming ripe, and the time propitious for its establishment, a convention was called, and the results are before you; although not under the control of the Executive Committee, or the State Grange, still inaugurated by them for the good of the members of the Order.

And, finally, they were called upon to consider the propriety of sanctioning another proposition, pregnant with good to the members of the Order and the farmers of the State; one that will save to them hundreds of thousands, aye, millions of dollars per annum, keeping in our own hands, instead of flowing into the coffers of those who have become millionaires from the hard earned dollars of the tillers of the soil, and whose affection for us is measured by the amount they can compel us to contribute to the stream flowing to their ocean of wealth. That proposition was the "California Farmers' Mutual Fire Insurance Association," like the bank, not under their control, but sanctioned and recommended by them for the good of the members of the Order, and farmers generally.

The actual cash expenses paid for railroad fare and hotel bills during the past year by the Executive Committee, is as follows:

Individual expenses: J. M. Hamilton, $278 65; I. G. Gardner, $155 50; J. C. Merryfield, $176 50. J. M. Mayfield (Old Committee), $43 25; G. W. Colby, $320; H, B. Jolley, $224 50; N. L, Allen (Old Committee), $84; W. M. Thorpe (Old Committee), $28; A. B. Nalley, $163 25; W. H. Baxter, Secretary, $135. Total $1,668 65. Printing bills, $34 50; printing, $337 51; Masters' attendance at N. G., $600; Masters' printing, $10 75; Lecturers, $171 50; Treasurer, $79 50; office of Secretary, $207 77; express charges on sundries, $53 60; State Grange agency, 2,318 85; salary of Secretary, 13 months, $1,300. Total $5,081 03. Total expenses as per account, $6,724 18.

The Lecturer, J. W. A. Wright, reported:

The first two weeks after our adjournment at San José, October 19th, 1873, were spent chiefly in work connected with the investigation and Memorial concerning the Agricultural and Mechanic Arts College of the State University, as will appear in the report of the University Committee. Eden Grange, Alameda County, was also organized October 25th, at Haywards, by request of the Worthy Deputy of Alameda County, Bro. Dewey; Oristimba, November 4th, and Cottonwood, November 10th. From December 9th to 31st, inclusive, my entire time was devoted to organizing Granges in Fresno, Tulare, and Kern counties. During this time I traveled seven hundred and fifty miles, and had the satisfaction of leaving fourteen good Granges in counties where our work had not been previously carried. The first twenty days of the new year were occupied almost exclusively in installations, chiefly by invitation, in Turlock, Rustic, Yuba City, Colusa, Meridian, Woodville, Napa, and St. Helena Granges. Two days of this time were also spent at Sacramento, in conference with the Worthy Master and Executive Committee, and members of the Senate and Assembly, to determine the best mode of proceeding with our Memorial on the University.

The following week was spent in making preparations to attend the meeting of the National Grange at St. Louis. As you are aware, Past Masters of State Granges are members of the National Grange, but no provision is made by that body to pay their expenses in attending its sessions, as they are only honorary members. Yet by the voluntary contributions of some of our fellow Patrons for the purpose, chiefly in Napa and St. Helena Granges, as they wished me to attend that meeting as your Past Master, and by the generous fees allowed by the Granges whose officers I installed, I was enabled to accompany our Worthy Master in that ever memorable session.

The next two months were spent in Alabama and Mississippi with my friends and family. I had thus an opportunity to confer with our southern brethren about the mutual interests of our Order, and it is most gratifying to be able to testify to the fact, that nowhere do you find more devotion to the principles of the Patrons of Husbandry than among our southern brothers and sisters, and their name is legion. They hail with joy the glad tidings from all parts of our land, that reform and harmony are fast becoming the watchwords of our people. None believe more strongly than they do the great truth, based upon the pure principles of the Grange, that "in our Union is our strength." They rejoice that the time has come, when in the work of the Grange, by the aid of its many outside friends, we find promise of an educator, a harmonizer, and a peacemaker, which, if used in good faith and with prudent action, can eventually be the salvation of our country. Let each of us at all times, fellow Patrons, so act as to lend whatever influence we may have to secure that great result so devoutly to be wished.

To sum up my efforts for the year, as it has resulted, allow me to report that since our last session, I have traveled over three thousand miles in our own State, some six thousand miles in attending the National Grange; have visited twenty-seven out of thirty-eight counties in California where Granges exist; have organized thirty-one Granges in addition to the nine organized while Master of the State Grange; have visited twenty-five Granges already organized, and there met members of more than one hundred neighboring Granges; have delivered seventy-eight addresses, of which some fifty were public; have rehearsed our unwritten work some eighty times in Granges, and hundreds of times in private; have written hundreds of letters, and devoted in all some two hundred days of my time to the interests of the Grange. These labors of the year have been a small tax upon the treasury of the State Grange, from which I have drawn less than one hundred and twenty dollars for my services; in addition to fees for organizing and installing, this has met my expenses and left me a small surplus. The duties of the office have been performed in the midst of many private disappointments, struggles and trials in the management of my own farm and business.

Report of John H. Hegeler, Manager of the Dairy Produce Department:

In representing to the Executive Committee of the California State Grange this report, I give the figures, suggestions, etc., so each may draw their own conclusions.

The house was opened informally for business on the first of January, 1874, during which month the sales amounted to $432 03; in February, to $2,423 48; in March, to $8,099 73; in April, to $9,742 16; in May, to $10,033 94; in June, to $10,209 88. In July, it dropped to $8,533 21; in August, $11,107 02; and in the last month, September, it ran up to $13,877 94, making a total for the first nine months of $74,460 36. The total number of shippers on the books is 301; the total commissions, $2,481 12; the total expense account amounts to $2,570 36, of which nearly $1,000 is for rents and $450 for store fixtures.

Charged to loss and gain, for bad debts and money otherwise lost in the course of business, $1,222 04, making a loss to the business, so far, of $1,311 28.

While I do not expect that the business will clear itself by the end of the year, yet I hope and believe, from the manner in which it increases, that it will be more than self-sustaining in another season. Everything seems to bid fair for the Grangers to do the great business in this line in the future. In fact this is now very generally admitted, even by those who, not many months ago, stigmatized us as not understanding the business, and that of necessity we would freeze out, as we had "neither credit nor capital."

To show how near freezing out we came, I will state that during the month of September there were received in San Francisco, from all sources, some eighty-three thousand pounds. Of this amount, there were received by us, nineteen thousand eight hundred and twelve pounds, or nearly one fourth of the whole amount; and when we come to know that there are forty-eight firms engaged in selling dairy produce at wholesale, we know that we are not going to die out yet awhile.

The matter of dried fruits deserves more than a passing notice. The fact that California-grown fruits are among the finest, at once gives us a prominent position among the fruit-growers of the world. But the mere matter of prominent position is not all we want—we must have a proper renumeration for our investment and our labor. As green fruits are so common and cheap in this State, we are compelled to look abroad for a market, and since the establishment of the various drying machines and apparatuses, this is now not so difficult as before. With this end in view, I have made permanent arrangements with the house of Miles, Carson & Co., in Philadelphia, who are probably the heaviest dealers in this commodity in the United States, to handle and sell for our house dried fruits, honey, and butter. I have every reason to believe the business will succeed.

In speaking of the business done, I speak usually of butter, as that is my principal business; yet there is much done in other commodities. Very nearly all the cheese of the Petaluma factory has found a market through the Grange agency, besides much dairy cheese; also eggs, poultry, potatoes, honey, and dried fruits. The matter of potatoes is an important interest, and requires more attention than it now receives. But when it comes to be considered more thoroughly, you will find it a very difficult thing to manage. For the special benefit of the potato-growers, I have employed the services of Wm. H. Alexander, who is also a Patron, and member of Tomales Grange, and who has had several years of experience in selling potatoes.

As to honey, it must find a market out of this State, to be profitable to the farmer.

Now, let us look at the practical results of our enterprise. There are now made in California, as near as can be approximated, about nine million nine hundred and twenty thousand six hundred and twenty-eight pounds of butter, besides cheese. Of this, about seven million nine hundred and thirty-six thousand pounds finds a market throughout the State. In looking over my account sales for the butter sold in 1872, which was an average year as to price, I find the average price per pound, for the first nine months, to be twenty-five and one-eighth cents, while this year, for the same dairy, during the same time, I find the price to have been thirty-three and one sixth cents per pound, a difference of eight and one twenty-fourth cents per pound, or a clear gain of six hundred and thirty-eight thousand two hundred and thirty-three dollars to the dairy interests of the State. This difference is, to a very great extent, traceable to the existence of the Grange store in San Francisco, for several reasons: one being that, to a very great extent, it prevents combinations against farmers to break the market. On the contrary, it has a tendency to create a sharp competition between the various dealers to get the highest possible price for their products.

One of the greatest wants of the dairy farmers is a bank that will supply them with means for prosecuting their business, and, at the same time, leave them free to sell their products as best they can. The manner in which this borrowing business is done in California is such that the commission merchants virtually own or control the entire products of the State by the advances they have made.

Banking and money loaning are no part of a legitimate commission business, and the man who goes to a merchant to borrow money on the article he is to sell, places himself at the mercy of that merchant. Moreover, every commission merchant is the agent of the farmer for whom he sells, and any business that is conducted in such a manner as to make a farmer's agent a speculator in his products must breed corruption.

Now, the proofs and illustrations. It has been the practice, since the building of the railroad across the continent, of our largest dairy produce commission houses, to send car-loads of butter East each season, about February, March, or April, as the openness of our winters enables us to make butter here much earlier than in the East. It always so happens that the butter market here "breaks up" just about the time our merchants get ready to ship East, and the price suddenly drops from forty or fifty cents per pound to twenty-five or thirty. And why not? The agent of the dairymen—the commission man—buys this butter, buys it of whom? Of the dairyman? No, he buys it of himself, to ship on a speculation of his own. This agent, then, fixes the price on the very article he buys. It is simply this: Hegeler, a commission merchant, sells to Hegeler, a speculator, ten tons of butter, and Hegeler, the merchant, fixes the price to Hegeler, the speculator. If any one thinks the dairymen profit by this kind of an arrangement, they see things in a different light from myself.

During the spring and summer much butter is packed, by both farmers and speculating commission merchants, who pack much of the butter consigned to them, and the process just explained of buying of themselves is here repeated. If the product is supposed to be short, every pound possible is bought, and prices are purposely held down till all is secured, which being done, the prices are at once put up. Yet, the dairyman is in no wise profited by this rise, as he has probably sold the products of his toil, while the profits of all this, the farmers' hard toiling, goes into the hands of middle-men speculators.

But you say it is not necessary always for the farmer to sell while prices are low—he, too, can hold on for the usual rise in price.

Very well, suppose I am a commission merchant, I buy all I can, say I buy two thirds of the yield, that is of the surplus, the remaining one third is held by the farmer; the fact becomes known to me. I am aware there is a surplus in the country. Then what do I do? I offer only my own butter for sale, while that which I hold in trust for the farmer, on consignment, I keep in the background, and do not offer for sale. I dispose of mine at a fair figure, and when I have sold all I have of my own, I then offer yours. But the butter market having been supplied, yours will form the surplus—the result must be as it was last year—a tumble in the prices. The one is sold at a good figure, while the other must suffer his to be slaughtered; as we are all human, and self-preservation being the first law of nature, it is hardly necessary to say that the party slaughtered is the farmer. It has been my study to look up the evils of this system of trade. They are necessarily evils of a system—perhaps there is no one who, under the same circumstances, would not take advantage of these business opportunities; and, therefore, we should not attack the persons engaged in it half so much as we should attack the system itself.

The remedy for all this is simple enough. It lies alone within ourselves—within the Grange, I mean. To this body, and to this body alone, will devolve this duty of transforming this great evil into a better and healthier mode of business. It lies simply in this: the farmer must become his own business man; he must be his own business manager; he must be his own salesman; he must, not only sow, but he must reap; and he must not cease to garner his products till he is done, and he is not done when he places his golden grain in his barn, but he shall have done when he has reaped the reward of his toil by a proper remuneration and exchange of his products for the necessaries of his life and household. No one can be so good an agent for the farmer as the farmer himself; or at least he should be the creature of the farmer, and not, as is now the case, the farmer the creature of the agent. My idea is, that the State Grange should own the business, and it is the duty of every Patron to patronize it to the fullest extent possible.

Second Annual Report of Brothers Jolley, Stiles and Wright, Committee on Irrigation:

While the past year has been one of unexampled prosperity in most parts of the State, it has also demonstrated the absolute necessity of the immediate adoption of some system of irrigation, which will enable hundreds of the small farmers of this State to retain their homes, which they cannot do, unless their farms afford them the means of support for their families.

The San Joaquin Valley, which seems destined to be the Garden of the Continent, and especially that part west of the San Joaquin River, has suffered to an alarming extent in the last year from drought, and we feel safe in calculating the loss at sufficient to construct a canal from Tulare Lake to Antioch.

In accordance with the instructions of this State Grange, and the Preamble and Resolutions adopted by this Grange at its last session, we prepared and printed five hundred copies of a petition to the Legislature for an act creating a general system of irrigation, setting forth the views in the aforesaid Resolutions, and caused the same to be distributed throughout the State to every Grange then organized. We also issued a circular letter to each Master, asking in the name of this State Grange his personal influence in furthering this enterprise, by obtaining signatures to these petitions. In such localities as have realized, by the saddest of experience, the great need of this measure, the petitions were very generally signed; and we were enabled to present the petition to the Legislature backed by the names of several thousand petitioners. We regret to say, that in some of those localities where the need of such a system is not as plainly felt, or where it would prove of less direct advantage than elsewhere, subordinate Granges refused to give their countenance and support to the measure, and disregarded the fact that this State Grange had authorized such effort, and considered it to be of vital importance to the agriculturists of this State. We believe it to be the grandest scheme, and entirely feasible withal, ever inaugurated in this State, and one which would, if successfully carried out, bring to us untold wealth, and fill our valleys with an immense population.

In conformity with the instructions of this Grange, your Committee prepared a "bill to provide for a general system of irrigation throughout the State," which system was to have been inaugurated and conducted by the State, authority vesting the rights to the water in the soil forever; and although imperfect, as human institutions always are, it would have been the initiative of one of the grandest enterprises yet projected for the benefit of the agriculturists of the State, and one than which no other is more needed at this day. As can be seen by reference to section 12, page 4, of this bill, it was required that the expenses on the part of the State, in carrying out the provisions of this act, should "in no case exceed the sum of thirty thousand dollars in any one year." So that the objection that it would have been a great expense to the State does not hold good.

The deep interest felt in the success of this measure induced a portion of your Committee to spend most of their time in Sacramento, during the time of preparing the bill and its pendency before those august bodies, the Senate and Assembly. Our efforts to discharge our trust as a Committee were ably seconded by West San Joaquin Grange, No. 3, which spared no expense in their power to secure the success of the measure, sending to the aid of your Committee its Worthy Overseer, to whom your Committee tender their sincere thanks for his earnest efforts.

Our bill was presented in the Assembly January 21st, 1874, by Brother Venable, of Los Angeles, and was known thereafter as "Venable's Bill." Your Committee would take this opportunity to publicly return their thanks to Brother Venable for his efforts in behalf of this great enterprise. After the usual delays attendant upon all Legislation, the bill was passed by the Assembly by a majority of thirty. The bill was then introduced in the Senate, and although there seemed to be little direct opposition to it, did not come up on its final passage until March 24th, 1874. The principle seemed generally accepted that something should be done, and the die seemed about to be cast in our favor; but on the eve of our triumph, a new party appeared in the field. The friends of that giant monopoly known as the San Joaquin & Kings River Canal Company, rushed to the State Capital in force, and in the few hours which intervened our defeat was accomplished, and on the next day the labor of the year was ignominiously defeated. How this was accomplished, we leave you to imagine. Their influence, whether exerted through *solid* argument or other wise, was more potent than the prayers of thousands of farmers.

Your Committee return thanks to the Executive Committee of this Grange for the aid extended by them, enabling one of our Committee to remain in the capital during the pendency of this question.

Your Committee would ask of this State Grange a renewed effort to accomplish this great enterprise, and recommend the discharge of the present Committee and the appointment of a new Committee, who shall be peculiarly alive to this great subject. In conclusion, your Committee would recommend to every Patron a careful perusal of the very able address, delivered by Hon. M. M. Estee, at the opening of the late State Fair, as being replete with facts and information of great importance to the farmers throughout the State.

Report of Committee on Good of the Order:

Whereas, It can be shown from statistics accessible to every one, that the insurance business of the State of California in 1873 amounted to $184,345,589, with a profit of $2,377,970, out of which the foreign companies do business in fire risks to the amount of $86,-094,960, with a net profit of $970,478; and that marine risks amount to a business of $56,823,425, with a profit of $973,980, of which business, $24,502,587 is done by foreign companies, with a net profit of $359,199, making a total net profit to the foreign companies doing business in this State, of $1,329,677; and,

Whereas, It is notorious that the whole, or a larger part of this immense sum is placed at the disposal of our opponents, the grain speculators, and other middle-men of San Francisco, and their agents in the interior of the State; and,

Whereas, The By-Laws of the California Farmers' Fire Insurance Association, an institution formed in our own Order, provides that all funds shall be deposited in the Grangers' Bank at San Francisco, thereby placing them where they will be used in our favor, instead of against us; and,

Whereas, This Company proposes to take fire risks on farm buildings at lower rates than have heretofore obtained, thus securing a material economy, in accordance with the principles of our Order; therefore, be it

Resolved, That it is the duty of every member of the Order to forward the interests of the Farmers' Mutual Fire Insurance Association, so far as can be done without conflicting with any private right or interest.

The efforts of the State Grange to put the Agricultural College upon a practical foundation, are presented in the report of the Standing Committee on Education and the University, J. W. A. Wright, W. H. Baxter and O. L. Abbott, as follows:

Having our duties mapped out for us, by the resolution passed at the first annual meeting, requiring us "to inquire particularly into the condition of the Agricultural Department of the State University, what improvements, if any, should be made, and what legislation, if any, is required to secure to the farmers of this State, the full benefits of the Agricultural College grant," etc., etc., your Committee went immediately to work, Brother Wright proceeding to Oakland to investigate, became acquainted with the President of the University and most of the Faculty, and collected as many facts as possible bearing upon the subject under consideration. Learning that the Mechanics' Deliberative Assembly of San Francisco, had, almost simultaneously with the State Grange, appointed a committee of three for a similar purpose, and to avoid any conflict of action between the representatives of the two great industrial classes of our State, whose interests are so clearly mutual in developing the agricultural and mechanical departments of our University, we determined, after several conferences, upon joint action by the two bodies. The result was a most cordial and happy unity of action between these industrial elements; and, after much deliberation and care, a joint memorial to the State Legislature was prepared, asking for such timely enactments and appropriations as would tend to properly develop and foster the industrial features of our great institution, in accordance with the evident intent of the organic Acts of Congress and the State Legislature. The Chairman of your Committee, in accordance with the wishes of the other members, spent the greater part of two weeks in such investigations and conferences; and in drafting, with the aid of Judge Sawyer, the Chairman of the Mechanics' Committee, the memorial aforesaid.

Early in January, he visited Sacramento, and laid the joint memorial before our Executive Committee, and they heartily endorsed it, as appears in the official copy. In conjunction with Worthy Master Hamilton, and other members of the Executive Committee, he presented and explained the memorial to our fellow Patrons in the Senate and Assembly, in whom we found able co-workers for this and all our petitions for reformatory legislative action.

At this memorable Grange Conference in our State Capital, a plan of proceedings was also agreed upon to present this memorial to the Legislature, and to prepare the necessary resolutions, and a bill to carry out the provisions asked for. This memorial is herewith presented as document "A."

Care should be taken, however, at all times, to distinguish between the investigation which resulted from our memorial, and another which was made at the same time, and which developed deplorable irregularities in applying funds for University buildings. These two investigations were entirely separate, but are too often confounded by those not fully posted as to the facts in the case.

Most of the after-work in the Legislature, which was brought about by our memorial, was left in the hands of our Worthy Bro.

Higbie, of Los Angeles, Chairman of the Assembly Committee on Education, who was ably seconded by numerous zealous members of our Order, and equally zealous representatives of the Mechanics' Association, whom the people had placed on guard in our legislative halls.

We must not, however, omit to mention, that while subsequent investigations in the Legislature were going on, and when Bros. Hamilton and Wright were absent at the National Grange in St. Louis, Bro. Baxter performed all the duties of the Committee. He went to Sacramento several times at the summons of the Investigating Committee. During some five or six weeks he devoted much of his time to answering questions of the Committee, and of some of the Regents with whom he was confronted.

It should be well understood by all of us, that none of the acts of this, or any other of our Grange Committees that visited Sacramento last winter, partook in the least of a partisan character; but appeals in behalf of our industrial interests were made impartially to our friends of every political party, and we found they met us without any regard to party distinctions. Hence our strength.

We should not fail to mention that our worthy brother, Professor Carr, gave us material aid in all this work, whenever he was called upon to do so.

The result of these many earnest efforts for the advancement of the great cause of industrial and practical, as well as of theoretical education on this Coast, was the hearty approval of the measures recommended in our joint memorial by the legislative Committees on Education, and the preparation of a bill enacting the necessary reforms, which was within an hour of the time of passing, when pledges came, understood to be authorized by the present Board of Regents, that if said bill was not passed, and the matter was dropped, Brother Carr, the able and experienced Professor of Agriculture in the State University, would not be interfered with, but would be permitted, in good faith, to carry out, under his most competent supervision, and by use of the liberal appropriations of the Legislature, the various ideas advanced in the joint memorial.

All these, and subsequent facts, however, are so fully and ably set forth in the unanswerable statements of Professor Carr, in his recent history of this entire struggle, that we deem it necessary merely to refer to his noble paper, which is filed herewith as document "B."

Unfortunately for the cause of industrial education, and unfortunately for the educational interests of a vast majority of the citizens of this State, the pledges given were believed to be reliable, and no further effort was made to pass the bill. Yet that bill would, unless killed by the Senate, have been a law within an hour after these pledges were made, and would at once and forever have removed the only obstacle that exists to making our valued University eventually one of the most complete embodiments of the true University idea in the world, an ornament to the cause of modern education, and a far greater honor to our State than we can ever hope to see it under the blighting hand of a selfish and moneyed aristocracy and monopoly, which, like all its kindred "rings" everywhere, has too long been at once the bane of our American institutions and the vampire which is slowly but surely withdrawing for itself the life-blood of our people.

The subsequent history of this movement, culminating in the summary, and, we believe, unjust removal of Professor Carr from the chair of Agriculture, is too well known to all of you to require repetition now. You are aware that the only answer of the Regents to the joint inquiry of the Committee of the State Grange and the Mechanics' Deliberative Assembly, as to the reason for Professor Carr's removal is, "unfitness and incompetency." They do not deign to tell us what they mean by "unfitness and incompetency." They do not condescend to give a single fact to prove this charge.

Hence, we can but believe the removal of our brother was unjust, and would here place on record our solemn protest against that act of the Board of Regents and the manner in which it was consummated.

Our investigations for the past year lead us to believe that the management of the financial affairs of the University, and especially of its agricultural and mechanical interests, has not been for the best interests of this noble institution, in whose complete and successful development the people of California, including, most certainly, its industrial classes, have a deep interest by our inalienable rights as American citizens in a representative government. In proof of this, we beg leave to call your attention to the following facts and figures:

We find that Congress "for the benefit of Agriculture and the Mechanic Arts," as indicated in the title of the Act of July 2, 1862, gave to the State of California one hundred and fifty thousand acres of land for the maintainance "of at least one college whose leading object should be, without excluding other scientific and classical studies, and including military tactics, to promote the liberal and practical eduation of the industrial classes in their several pursuits and professions in life."

That the administration of this grant, both in respect to the management of the fund and the educational provisions adopted, was confided to twenty-two Regents of the University of California—organized in March, 1868. The organic act of said University required that a College of Agriculture should first be established, that priority of development and of privileges should be accorded to it, and next to a College of Mechanic Arts, around these other colleges were required to be successively organized. We find that neither in the choice of Regents for said University, nearly all of whom are lawyers and capitalists of San Francisco, nor in the distribution of its instructional force or other educational facilities, have these plain requirements of the law been complied with.

Your Committee are satisfied that the facts presented in the memorial to the Legislature with respect to instruction in Agriculture and the Mechanic Arts, were well and correctly stated, the theoretical instruction in science related thereto being such only as is common in all colleges not industrial in their leading objects, with a solitary exception of a single professorship, viz.: that of Agriculture, since made vacant by the summary and as yet unexplained removal of Professor Carr. No practical instruction, either in Agriculture or the Mechanic Arts, has ever been given, nor has the manual labor system, required by law in connection with its construction, and made a prominent feature in other industrial colleges, been encouraged or practiced.

We find in the organic laws of the University provisions which virtually give absolute control of its property to the Regents, allowing them to sell, invest, reinvest, bestow, etc., to put their own construction upon the meaning of grants, gifts, and endowments, without requiring them to take any oath of office, with no guaranty for the rightful exercise of these powers and no redress, should they be abused. The terms of the organic act states that their office "shall be held and deemed exclusively a private trust." The presentation of the memorial of the State Grange and Mechanics to the Legislature, in compliance with the resolution at the San Jose meeting, resulted in a fuller exhibit of the financial affairs of the University than had previously appeared. A joint committee of the Senate and Assembly, appointed at their request, received from them as testimony an official report dated March 3, 1874, "which was carefully considered by them, unanimously adopted, and certified to as correct in all the particulars."

We find this report to contradict itself in important particulars, to be at variance with other facts well attested, and documentary evidence, especially in regard to the sale of lands donated by Congress, and the investment of the proceeds. The Regents tell us (in page 37 of their Statements) that they have either sold or contracted to sell the entire grant of 150,000 acres at $5 per acre in gold coin, net, 20 per cent. being paid down, and the remaining 80 per cent. bearing interest at 10 per cent., which should give a productive fund of $750,000, or an income of $75,000 per annum. With prudent management, this would be the value of the Congressional grant to-day, even at the low price (for California) of five dollars an acre. The law of Congress requires the proceeds from the grant to be invested in United States, State, or other safe stocks.

Paying no attention to this requirement, the Regents have invested it as follows: Of the $114,025 47 received of purchasers, $20,000 was invested in a vacant lot in the city of Oakland, for which the Agricultural department had no use whatever; $11,386 25 in paying interest on a debt injudiciously assumed by the Regents; $2,929 26 for some purpose not explained; amounting in all to $34,315 51, expended for the purchase of the Brayton estate, for which Regent Tompkins was agent. The remainder, $79,709 96, is deposited by the Treasurer of the University, Regent Ralston, in the Bank of California, of which Regent and Treasurer Ralston is President, and bears interest at six per cent per annum. while the Regents of the University, on a mortgage of $50,000, assumed in the purchase of tbe aforesaid Brayton estate, are paying nine per cent. per annum. The 80 per cent. credit upon $150,663 58 is in the form of notes bearing interest at the rate of 10 per cent. per annum. Applications on file with the Land Agent of the University, and certificates of deposit to the amount of $94,573 are now in his hands, and this money all or mostly in the Bank of California. No account for interest allowed appears in the exhibit of the Regents, though we learn that in connection with recent events interest has lately been paid. Four dollars credit per acre on 94,573 acres, amounting to $378,292, should have been drawing interest—otherwise the income from the Land Fund is diminished at the rate of $37,829 per annum.

A still more serious evil appears in the fact that the Regents have so framed their regulations that the purchaser is not obliged to pay interest on the credit portion of his purchase-money until his title is obtained. The time intervening between the application and rendering of patent may be extended for years while the land is occupied and cleared of timber. No bonds had been given guarding against such a contingency up to the first day of July last, while on page 36 of the Regents' Statements we find that 8,840 acres have been forfeited and returned to the Land Fund.

We have seen from the Regents' Statements that $79,709 96 of the Agricultural Land Fund was drawing six per cent. interest in the Bank of California, and $94,573 drawing no interest at all up to the 1st of July last, as appears from the books.

In the statements we are informed that "the remainder, $34,-315 51, was temporarily invested in the purchase of four full blocks, with extensive improvements, in the heart of the growing city of Oakland, being the property formerly owned by the College of California, and the Brayton estate. This property is subject to a mortgage of $50,000, bearing interest at the rate of nine per cent. per annum," (and they are loaning nearly twice the amount to the Bank of California at six per cent. at the same time!) "It has cost to date, including $11,386 25 paid as interest on the mortgage, the sum of $112,476 25, and is valued by the most competent experts at a minimum of $150,000." This statement is not correct. These four blocks cost the University far more than is here represented. Block No. 1, known as the College Block, cost the University $49,030 04. Other property was received with this block, and turned over to Mrs. Brayton in part payment for blocks Nos. 2 and 3. Blocks Nos. 2 and 3 cost $94,315 51, in this manner. The Regents assumed a $50,000 mortgage for Mrs. Brayton, "and transferred to the vendors the outside property, valued at about $30,000, adjoining the University site at Berkeley, which had been obtained from the College of California. The property (blocks Nos. 2 and 3) was thus obtained without any additional cash expenditure." On the $50,000 mortgage, $11,386 25 interest was paid by the Regents, and also, $2,-929 51 for some unexplained purpose, amounting to $94,315 51, the entire cost of blocks Nos. 2 and 3.

The fourth block, vacant, and of no use to the institution, was subsequently purchased of the Brayton estate for the sum of $20,-000. Block No. 1 cost $49,030 04; block Nos. 2 and 3 cost $80,-000; block Nos. 2 and 3 interest on mortgage $11,386 25; item for which no account is given, $2,929 26; block No. 4 cost $20,000. Total cost of four blocks "in the heart of the growing city of Oakland," as shown by the Regents, $163,345 55.

On the same statements, the following glaring misrepresentation appears with regard to these same blocks: "Since the removal of the University to Berkeley, this property is no longer essential. It is growing in value, however, year by year. Should it be deemed best to dispose of it, it will realize a sum, say $150,000 at least; sufficient to pay off the mortgage of $50,000, to repay the Land Fund the $34,315 51 borrowed, and leave a surplus of $65,684 49, yielding in the shape of profit a far larger interest upon the amount of the Land Fund invested than could possibly have been derived from any ordinary safe investment." This statement was designed to lead the Legislature of California to infer that the four blocks cost but $84,000, and that $65,000 had been gained by the speculation, when in fact these four blocks cost, years ago, $163,345 55, which was $13,345 55 more than the Regents claim them now to be worth, although in the heart of the growing city of Oakland.

If this were all that the Regents have so adroitly attempted to conceal, there would be less cause of complaint. The "outside property, valued at about $30,000, adjoining the University site at Berkeley, which had been obtained from the College of California," transferred to Mrs. Brayton, in part payment for blocks Nos. 2 and 3, was worth to the Agricultural Department of the University for experimental purposes, at least $200,000, which is probably not far from its present commerical value. This indicates that the Brayton job has cost the institution about $175,000, and robbed the experimental farm of nearly, if not quite, two hundred acres of ground essential in making up the necessary varieties of soil and location. The Regents estimate the remaining two hundred acres directly adjoining, although less valuable, and sheltered for horticulture, at one thousand dollars per acre, while the water rights parted with are practically inestimable.

Still further, your committee find that the Regents obtained from the College of California and other sources, nearly four hundred acres of land entirely by donation. The liabilities of the College of California assumed by the Regents, amounted to $49,030 04, a debt not equal to the amount realized on the College property, or Block No. 1, in the growing city of Oakland, at the recent sale. The Berkeley property was donated, and in some cases the terms of the deed are explicit, for an Agricultural College, and yet the choicest lands, those nearest the city of Oakland, lands rapidly advancing in value since the removal of the University, have been sold for a mere nominal sum, while of the two hundred acres remaining, only about five have been set apart for agriculture and horticulture. Not a spadeful of earth had been turned, or an agricultural experiment made, when the Committee appointed by the State Grange commenced its labors. Yet the Professor of Agriculture had been persistently and repeatedly calling attention to this, had submitted plans for work and for instruction by experts, plans for farm buildings, with estimates of cost, and such other information as was needed to secure intelligent action. In their reply to the Memorial of Grangers and Mechanics, of August 8th, 1874, the Regents, under date of September 1st, 1874, state that "within the past year the Berkeley property has been surveyed and mapped, and the right places marked out for agriculture, horticulture, botanical garden, and forestry." We find that as early as May, 1870, the Professor of Agriculture was asking to have these places marked out, and a definite working plan adopted, and that these requests were repeated year after year.

We find that the resolution of the Board authorizing Professor Carr to employ a gardener, passed September 18th, 1872, was made practically inoperative by failure to locate or mark out these "right places" for his operations, which has only been done "within the past year." The same is true of their statement that $500 was placed at the disposal of Professor Carr to secure the aid of competent lecturers on special subjects, no such money having been placed at his disposal, while his requests to have lectures from Dr. Strentzel and other competent parties named by him, with subjects and number of lectures specified, was disregarded.

On page sixty-eight of their Statements, the Regents say they have been "desirous of securing progress in the Department of Agriculture, and have asked for appropriations which would give it more efficiency. They have requested means for the improvement of the grounds." By turning back to page fifty-three of this extraordinary document, we find that they have expended $21,151 05 for such improvements, not one feature of which was agricultural or horticultural, a sum much larger than was required to carry out the wishes of the Professor of Agriculture, who was never consulted with regard to them. This sum was expended under the direction of Dr. Merritt, Chairman of the Committee on Buildings and Grounds, "exclusively as a private trust."

Your Committee cannot too strongly urge that the interest of the people of the State, and especially of the agricultural and other laboring classes, does not end with the administration of the Congressional grant, and the Agricultural and Mechanical Colleges. The Regents say that they have received from the State $412,694 79, exclusive of the $300,000 for building purposes; including this and the $80,000 appropriated last winter, we have the sum of $792,694 79. The income derived from other sources of endowment, subject to the disposition of the Regents as a "private trust," are the proceeds of seventy-two sections of "Seminary lands," of ten sections, given to the State for public buildings, the Act of endowment approved April 2, 1870, giving an income of $50,000 per annum, all of which add enormously to the resources of the institution, with prudent management. But neither in respect to the disposition of public lands, the employment of funds thence derived, or in the direction of the instructional force employed in the University, do we find the evidence we have diligently sought of the fitness or competency of the Board of Regents to manage an institution created for the benefit of the whole people. We find that, in consequence of their unfitness, incompetency, and bad management, the interest of the Agricultural College has been entirely subordinated, instead of being a leading one in the University, as the law requires; its future usefulness crippled by loss of lands of the greatest importance to practical education, and the prospect of an additional grant from Congress jeopardized, which would secure an additional income of $30,000 per annum.

In view of all these facts, we earnestly recommend to the Patrons of California and their friends to adopt such measures as will best remove, through the action of our next Legislature, the wrongs in the management of the State University, of which we think we most justly complain.

The memorial above referred to was also signed by Hon. E. D. Sawyer, C. C. Terrill, and M. J. Donovan, on the part of the Mechanics. It presented the case as follows:

Your petitioners, in behalf of the industrial classes of California, both agriculturists and mechanics, would respectfully call the attention of your honorable body to the condition and wants of the State University. We make this petition with all due deference to the Honorable Board of Regents and Faculty of our University, and with no desire to interfere improperly with any of their rights or duties. But we believe the interests of the people of the State, for whose benefit especially this noble institution was established, require that greater efficiency be given to the agricultural, mechanical, and other industrial instruction therein, without diminishing the usefulness of those departments already in successful operation.

Your petitioners find that the State University resulted from an Act of Congress entitled "An Act donating public lands to the several States and Territories which may provide Colleges for the benefit of agriculture and the mechanic arts." By this Act one hundred and fifty thousand acres (more or less) were donated to California. In accordance with this munificent provision of the United States Government, our Legislature passed an Act establishing a University, and prescribing that its most prominent features should be Colleges of Agriculture and Mechanic Arts. By reference to the last report from each of the thirty-eight States that shared in this national endowment to the Department of Agriculture at Washington, we find nearly every one of them carrying out both the letter and the spirit of the Act of Congress; "that they are attended by over three thousand students, most of whom are practically pursuing agricultural and mechanical studies," with well stocked farms, work-shops, and all necessary appliances of instruction.

In the same report, we read that "in California a farm of about two hundred acres has been provided for the Agricultural Department, but it has not been improved, nor are the students instructed in agriculture outside of the school-room. The Act of Congress requires that the "leading object" of the Industrial Universities shall be without excluding other scientific and classical studies, and including military tactics, to teach such branches of learning as are related to agriculture and the mechanic arts, in such manner as the Legislatures of the States may respectively prescribe, in order to promote the liberal and practical education of the industrial classes in their several pursuits. The organic Act creating the University requires that the College of Agriculture shall first be developed, "and next, that of the Mechanic Arts." We find that of the monthly appropriation (six thousand dollars) for the regular expenses only one twentieth is now devoted to the Agricultural Department, and that one Professor is discharging all the duties of instruction on the subjects related to it. No technical instruction in the mechanic arts has thus far been given.

The instructional force of the University (besides the President) is as follows:—One Professor of Latin and Greek, and two Assistants; one instructor in Hebrew; one Professor of Mathematics, and two Assistants; one Professor of Modern Languages, and two Assistants; one Professor of Chemistry, and two Assistants (advanced students;) one Professor of Physics and Mechanics; one Professor of Geology and Natural History; one Professor of Civil Engineering and Astronomy; one Professor of Rhetoric, History, and English Language; one instructor in Drawing; one Professor in Agriculture, Agricultural Chemistry, and Horticulture.

Your petitioners do, therefore, request, that in accordance with plans pursued at Cornell, the Massachusetts and Michigan Agricultural Colleges, the Universities of Missouri, Illinois, and many others (as may be seen from the report already referred to), that whatever State aid is granted for our University, and as rapidly as the income from the land sales is received, it may be "first of all applied to the extending of the Colleges of Agriculture and the Mechanic Arts, and all the departments of instruction which directly bear upon the studies pursued in them."

With this object in view, we earnestly recommend a sufficient appropriation to carry out the following objects:

First. The improvement of such portions of the University grounds as may be required to illustrate practically the subjects taught in the Department of Agriculture, and the adaptation of this State to various cultures. The erection of a plain, convenient, and commodious farm house, with suitable outhouses, to be occupied by the Professor of Agriculture, or some practical farmer to act under his direction. To this an orchard, vineyard, vegetable and flower garden, and a poultry yard should be attached; also, a propagating house, and, as soon as practicable, a conservatory. The culture of cereals, textiles, and other valuable vegetable productions; the rearing of stock, bees, and silk worms should be illustrated, on a small scale, epitomizing the entire range of agricultural industries.

Second. The appropriation of a sufficient amount to secure the necessary practical instruction in the mechanic arts; to provide blacksmiths', carpenters', cabinet and machine shops, and printing press, under the supervision of competent persons.

We by no means expect to accomplish all this at once, but we ask means to secure to the youth of our State, with proper economy and despatch, the advantages enjoyed by students of the best developed institutions which owe their existence to the same foundation. We desire that the grounds of our University, its museums, parks and gardens, may eventually become as instructive as those of the Garden of Plants at Paris; and that our College of Mechanic Arts may, without needless delay, rival the Technological School in Boston. We ask that in keeping with the educational standards of the age, the principles of object teaching and practical instruction be conducted in connection with the ideal and theoretical, and occupy in the chief school of the State, the position which their importance demands. We believe that nowhere will the dignity of labor be so strongly impressed upon the mind as in those higher institutions of learning, organized for the benefit of the most important class of laborers, where the acquisition of skill goes hand in hand with the acquisition of knowledge.

We find that the Board of Regents, as at present constituted, does not sufficiently represent the various portions and interests of the State. Though composed of gentlemen of the highest position and worth, they reside, mainly, in San Francisco and Oakland, and although they have been zealous in their efforts to secure the prosperity of the institution, we believe that the best interests of education would be promoted by an amendment of the Act so as to unify the University with the other departments of State education. We, therefore, respectfully ask such amendment of this Act, and of other Acts, as shall constitute a State Board of Education, having charge of the University, the Normal School, and other public schools, and to consist of fifteen Regents, viz: Seven ex-officio—the Governor, Lieutenant Governor, Speaker of the Assembly, State Superintendent of Public Instruction, President of the State Agricultural Society, Master of the State Grange, and President of the Mechanics' Institute of San Francisco; also two members from each Congressional District, to be appointed from their districts by the Governor, with the consent of the Senate, for their first terms, and afterward to be elected by the people as vacancies occur. We also recommend that any nine members shall constitute a quorum, as the Board of Education, or as the Board of Regents for the University, or as the Board of Trustees of the State Normal School. We ask that they may be so selected as to represent the various industrial interests, occupations, and professions of the citizens of the State.

The law (Article IV, section 1,450 of the new Code) clearly provides that the Secretary of the Board of Regents must be a practical farmer, and must reside and keep his office at the site of the University. These requirements having been hitherto disregarded, we recommend that the law be either rigidly enforced or essentially modified. It is generally understood that a portion of the lands donated by Congress for the purposes of industrial education in California, have been sold at five dollars per acre, one fifth of the amount having been paid down, and it is understood that the fund thus obtained has been used in paying professorships and scholarships in our University. But it is the misfortune of the people of California to know very little about these lands and their present condition, while they do know that in other States, in consequence of mismanagement, only a small part of the real value of school and University lands has been realized. In some instances timber lands valued at thirty and fifty dollars per acre have been taken up, the first payments made, the timber removed, and the lands forfeited. It is clearly the right of the people to have correct information on this subject.

We do therefore petition your honorable body that a University Committee be carefully selected from your number whose duty it shall be to examine fully, minutely, and impartially into the location and present condition of all lands donated to California for these purposes; to ascertain what has accrued from the sales thereof, and how the same has been expended; and that the necessary power be granted them to send for persons, books, and papers, to administer the necessary oaths, and take the testimony for the thorough investigation of the whole question, and that the results of such investigation be published without unnecessary delay, for the information of the people.

In view of the important fact that another bill was introduced into Congress, at the late session (by Mr. Morrill, the author of the original bill), which it is expected will be passed during the coming winter, giving to each of the industrial Universities in operation an additional grant of five hundred thousand acres, we also request that our Legislature memorialize Congress so to amend the law regarding the locations upon unsurveyed lands as to protect actual settlers in their improvements up to the time that the locator can make his selection by sections or subdivisions.

As a means of redress for seizures under the existing law, we also recommend that our Legislature forthwith pass an Act, providing that in all cases where contests have arisen, or may hereafter arise, before the Board of Regents of the University upon University lands, and the contestant shall feel aggrieved at the decision of said Board, he shall have the right of appeal to the District Court, by giving the usual notice of said appeal.

We respectfully recommend that all the University funds be kept in the State Treasury, subject only to order in proper form for University disbursements. As we are now informed that the funds hitherto appropriated are exhausted, and that additional appropriations will be required at the present session, to add other and needed improvements, in accordance with the original plan, your petitioners would respectfully ask that in addition to the sum required for monthly current expenses, the following be specifically appropriated: For farm, buildings, implements, stock, etc., twenty-five thousand dollars; for annual farm and garden expenses, payment of students and other labor, salary of farmer and gardener, expenses of lectures from experts in special cultures, agricultural, entomology, veterinary science, etc., collection and preparation of specimens for museum of agriculture, and incidental expenses, fifteen thousand dollars; for mechanical shops, printing press, steam engine, and their appurtenances, fifty thousand dollars; for annual expenses of mechanical shops, printing press, superintendence, students and skilled labor, collections of models and raw materials for museum of Mechanic Arts, lectures on technical subjects connected with mechanical pursuits by skilled persons, and incidental expenses, fifteen thousand dollars. It is expected that this will furnish the carpenters', cabinet work, and printing for the institution. It should be borne in mind that these departments are to be created, and that no part of the twenty thousand dollars already expended for chemical and physical apparatus, will supply their technical needs.

The completion of the central building, according to the original plan, is a prime necessity in accomplishing the great purpose of the University; for, in the absence of suitable rooms for the present Museum and Library, it has been considered necessary to occupy for this purpose, a part of the College of Agriculture, a building designed to supply the wants of this department, as is indicated by the appropriate and bountiful emblems that adorn its outer walls. In this exigency, the entire Agricultural Department is forced into the limited space of the north half of the basement of this splendid structure, thus placing in a subordinate position, which it was never intended to occupy, what should be the most prominent department of the State University.

We find that a building containing an Assembly Hall, Museum, etc,, can be erected of wood at a cost of one hundred and fifty thousand dollars; of brick, with granite facings, two hundred and fifty-six thousand dollars. The labor of students can be utilized in the construction of this and other needed edifices, and deserving young men can in this way be aided in paying a part at least of the expenses of their education. Suitable dwellings should at once be erected for the accommodation of the professors and club houses for the students upon the University grounds, for which a moderate rent might be charged. At present, both professors and students are compelled to live at Oakland, five miles distant, or to provide themselves accommodations in the yet sparsely-settled neighborhood of Berkeley, at an expense greater than their means will justify. The entire energies of the University body should be concentrated in and around its scholastic home.

In conclusion, we would repeat that it is not now our object to undervalue what has been so well done in the erection of buildings, of which the State may be justly proud; in the opening of the doors of the University to both sexes; in making its instruction in all departments free; in organizing the Military Department and Labor Corps; and in securing a Faculty of zealous and able men. But, believing that the first and highest employment of men is to feed, shelter, and clothe the world, we ask that the graduates of our industrial colleges may be "peers of scholars in mental culture, and peers of laborers in manual skill and physical development."

The relations of labor to study are admirably stated in the report of the Missouri University. "The pupil must study till he knows what should be done, why it should be done, and how. When this is done, the *intellectual* division of labor is finished. The pupil must labor till he can do work in the farm and shop with skill; then the *manual* division of an industrial education is finished. In agriculture, he should thus learn whatever is done on the farm, in the garden, orchard and nursery. If it is asked: 'Who shall direct the labors of the pupils?' we answer: 'The teacher of the principles put in practice, that useless and impracticable theories may not be introduced.'" Agriculture is far from being an exact science, and its conditions on this coast are peculiar. We ask that our University be made useful to the largest number of our citizens, by accurate annual reports of work done, experiments made, and results arrived at. Agriculture, in its various departments, should be so taught and practiced in our University as to send forth scientific farmers, whose labor and skill can utilize the soil and develop its greatest resources, while the mechanical department should graduate learned and skilled mechanics, who shall add dignity and worth to labor; and it is the earnest desire and purpose of agriculturists and mechanics of this State to make these great departments of industry the leading features of our State University, and for this purpose we expect your cordial co-operation, and such appropriations as are necessary. Nor do we think that any mechanical schools in San Francisco, valuable as they may become, can supply the place of the College of Mechanic Arts, as provided by the original plan of the State University. We also request the present Legislature to order that block letters be prepared and placed upon the east and west faces of the main building of the University, marking it for all time with the words, "Agricultural College of the University of California."

Document B. is omitted, as not properly belonging to the annals of the State Grange. It was a reply made by Professor Carr to these committees for a "full statement of the history of the Agricultural College, with a view to laying it before the people and the next Legislature."*

The following Report of the Committee on Education and Labor, was enthusiastically adopted:

When Congress, at the opening of its last session, appointed a Committee on Education and Labor, it seemed a recognition by the highest legislative body of the country, that these great interests are indissolubly connected. So we believe, and a thorough and practical education being the only means by which labor can be elevated, your committee desire to present a few suggestions with regard to improvements in our public schools, high schools, and university.

Our schools, both higher and lower, have naturally grown up on English models, and were then made to fit the needs of the aristocratic classes, rather than of working men and women. This is the reason why so much of our elementary instruction imparts a knowledge of words rather than of things.

Germany, France, and other European countries, are far ahead of England and America in both the quality and quantity of education furnished to the laboring classes, for they seek to impart skill, along

*On the occasion of Professor Carr's removal from the Agricultural Professorship of the University, (August, 1874,) Worthy Master Hamilton, who had been appointed a member of the Board of Regents, made this protest:

I protest against the summary removal of Professor Carr at this time:

1st—Because such removal will be in direct violation of pledges made by friends of the University to the House Committee on education of the last Legislature.

2d—I believe such an act is in opposition to the wishes of a large class of the friends of the University, viz., the agriculturists and mechanics of California, and will go far to confirm the belief that the vacating of the Chair of Professor of Agriculture at this time is more to gratify personal feeling than to subserve the public interest.

3d—Because such removal will have the effect of strengthening opposition to the present management, and give color to the charge now so openly preferred: That the President and Regents are striving to build up a purely literary institution at Berkeley at the expense of the agricultural and mechanical interests, and are thus diverting the University from the original purpose for which it was formed, by either ignoring entirely or making those objects secondary which the organic act declared should be primary ones.

4th—Because the summary dismissal of any Professor of the University for alleged incompetency, without first granting the accused the privilege of a hearing, and an opportunity to defend himself from the charges made against him, is demoralizing in its tendency, and is not in accordance with the principles of right and equity which should ever prevail in the management of the institution.

A great number of the Subordinate Granges sustained the action of their Worthy Master, and embodied their opposition to the present management of the University in the strongest terms.

with the merely mental training which is given them. They have consequently the best trained workmen in the world, both in agriculture and the arts, as all our best educators freely acknowledge.

To get more of this practical or technical education into our common schools, is a great desideratum, and for it two things are necessary. First, an enlightened public opinion, which will create a demand for improvement; and, second, better teachers and better books to meet the demand. The teachers should be able to "throw a light" upon all the subjects of common life, and the books should convey some definite knowledge adapted to the capacity of the pupil.

For instance, no study is better adapted to the comprehension of a child than elementary botany, which is made practical by what he daily sees done in agriculture and horticulture. Even young children should be encouraged to observe and collect the useful and wild plants of the neighborhood, to bring them to school, and to find out all about them. This finding out all about things is the alpha and omega of education. Putting the findings into practice is all there is of labor, except its drudgery.

These are simple principles which every Patron can recognize. Our watchword is "Progress." The three R's, "readin,' 'ritin' and 'rithmetic," are no longer sufficient for us; especially if these are fed out to us as dry husks, while all the juice is kept for the benefit of other pursuit. We, ourselves, want more knowledge of the natural sciences, and we want our children to have it secured to them at the period of their lives when such knowledge is gained most easily. We want suitable books to tell the children all about the plants, animals and birds with which they daily come in contact. If they do not exist, and there is no school, botany, or natural history for this coast, let them be made. In short, we want our children to grow up around us with a respect for our calling, even if they choose a different one, and so to fit them for it that they may carry it on by better methods to higher ends.

And, therefore, while we as Patrons mean to look very sharply at all proposed changes in our methods of instruction, and to "prove all things," as far as we are able, we also mean to change for the better whenever we can. We are aware that text-books, or the implements of instruction, are to be improved just as much as the implements of husbandry; and we believe that the new education will require them as fast as it is perfected.

Under our laws, wisely framed in this respect, all such changes must be gradual, thereby making them less oppressive. Though all matters relating especially to this subject are made the business of the State Board of Education, we nevertheless feel that it is within our province to present to that body, either through our own Executive Committee, or such other way as the Grange may direct, an expression of our sentiments; and therefore, suggest the adoption of the following resolutions:

Resolved, That it is the opinion of the State Grange of the Patrons of Husbandry that all our public institutions, from the primary school to the university, should be developed also in the direction of practical and technical education.

Resolved, That to this end elementary studies in botany and other branches of natural history, in their relations to agriculture and horticulture should be introduced into our district schools.

Resolved, That we desire the State Board of Education to encourage the preparation and gradual introduction of text-books which are adapted to the wants of this coast; and that, while protecting the people from unnecessary expense, it is their duty, other things being equal, to foster home industries in the selection of text-books, apparatus and furniture for our public schools.

Resolved, That our more advanced classes should be instructed in the rights and duties of American citizenship, viz: The "duty of earning a living," of obedience to the laws, respect for religion, the rights of property, the privileges and responsibilities of the ballot, what monopolies are, how industry of one kind creates another, etc.

The standing committees for the following year were announced by the Worthy Master as follows:

Resolutions—J. W. A. Wright, R. C. Haile, J. D. Spencer.

Constitution and By-Laws—A. T. Dewey, G. W. Henning, W. S. Manlove.

Finance—H. A. Oliver, J. Earl, and Sister Colby.

Good of the Order—J. D. Fowler, John Wasley, Ed. Hallett, Sisters Manlove and Carr.

Master's Message and other Reports—G. W. Colby, W. McPherson, J. M. Thompson.

Commercial Relations—James Shinn, R. G. Dean, H. M. Leonard.

Co-operation and Transportation—C. G. Bockens, Wm. Erkson, C. Cutter, Andrew Wolf, and Daniel Inman.

Education and Labor—Sister E. S. Carr, Brother Meyer (Humboldt,) and Sister Dean.

State University—O. L. Abbott, W. H. Baxter, J. W. A. Wright.

Immigration—O. L. Abbott, J. Earl, J. D. Spencer, J. B. Carrington, R. G. Dean, in addition to the old committee, which was continued.

Legislation—Thos. Fowler, W. K. Estelle, G. B. Crane.

Irrigation—H. B. Jolley, R. G. Dean, Ed. Evey, M. Lammers, J. A. Hutton.

Judiciary—J. D. Spencer, T. H. Merry, R. C. Haile, H. S. Case, D. Inman.

American Finance—J. W. A. Wright, E. S. Carr, W. McPherson Hill, O. L. Abbott, W. S. Manlove.

Grange Statistics—J. B. Carrington, Thos. A. Garey, J. D. Spencer.

Arrangements of Business—J. D. Fowler, Sister E. S. Carr, Ed. Hallett, Sister W. S. Manlove.

Centennial Committee—B. P. Kooser, J. W. A. Wright, H. B. Jolley, Andrew Wolf, O. L. Abbott.

Executive Committee—J. M. Hamilton, Chairman; J. C. Merryfield, G. W. Colby, A. B. Nalley, A. D. Logan, H. M. Leonard, J. M. Thompson.

The State Grange then adjourned to meet in San Francisco the second Tuesday in October, 1875.

CHAPTER XVI.

THE PATRONS' TRIALS AND TRIUMPHS.

THE WHEAT SHIPPING BUSINESS—THE WHEAT KING AND MR. WALCOTT—ADVANCE IN FREIGHTS IN 1872-3—EXAGGERATED ESTIMATES OF THE CROP OF 1874-5—MR. WALCOTT'S VARIOUS ENTERPRISES—THE SACK PURCHASE—FAILURE OF MORGAN'S SONS PROVES A BLESSING IN DISGUISE—CALLED MEETING OF THE GRANGE—PRACTICAL FELLOWSHIP—ALL'S WELL THAT ENDS WELL—DISCONTINUANCE OF DAIRY AND PRODUCE AGENCY—THE BUSINESS ASSOCIATION FORMED—OFFICERS AND ARTICLES OF INCORPORATION OF THE GRANGERS' BUSINESS ASSOCIATION.

THE reader who has patiently followed the history of the farmers' movement thus far, has not failed to notice the competition established in the years 1873 and 1874 between the agent of E. E. Morgan's Sons, Mr. Alfred Walcott, and the "Wheat King," Mr. Friedlander. The latter gentleman, of high standing in the business circles of San Francisco, had for many years controlled the grain shipping interests of the coast. He had numerous agents along the lines of railroads, and throughout the wheat-growing districts, and was ready to advance money to the farmers for the purchase of machinery, or to meet their pressing debts, to provide for harvesting expenses, purchase of sacks, pay of help, etc. The difficulties and ill-feeling which arose between the parties who had thus mortgaged their crop and the party who had the power to fix its value, was incident to the peculiar condition of wheat culture on this Coast, which had partaken largely of the speculative character which marks the transitional period of our industries.

So heavy were the operations of the single firm which combined the functions of money-lender, merchant and shipper, that any opposition which appeared was immediately absorbed, and the farmers were fully persuaded that firms purporting to act independently, with branch houses in Liverpool, were really the agents through whom the Wheat King received his orders for cargoes. The advances in the foreign markets being telegraphed to San Francisco three or four weeks before the great body of the farmers could avail themselves of it, the prices of wheat and rates of freight were practically beyond their control.

The appearance of a competitor whose paper was good for a

large amount with the London and San Francisco Bank, and whose policy had been announced as the upbuilding of a "slow, safe, permanent shipping business," was naturally welcomed by the Patrons. The crop of 1872–3 had been a large one; to move it Mr. Friedlander had chartered every available ship at from £3 10s. to £4 5s., and at once rushed the freight market up to £5 13s. In thus re-letting his low-priced vessels, a large profit was gained. It is a very difficult matter to form a correct estimate of the amount of the wheat crop, and the shipper has his risks as well as the farmer.

The Sacramento Record issued a circular of inquiry in 1873, containing a blank schedule to be filled up with the acreage and prospective yield of each of the principal crops, to which the leading farmers so generally responded, that this paper was able to lay before its readers what proved to be a correct estimate of the export of that year. A similar circular issued in May, 1874, warranted, on the testimony of the farmers, the extraordinary estimate of eight hundred and seventy-five thousand tons for shipment; four hundred and fifteen thousand tons more than the shipment of the previous year, including the Oregon wheat shipped from this port.

The crop of 1873–4 gave cargoes to two hundred and forty-seven ships, and was valued at $19,400,000.

The crop of 1874–5 would require four hundred and thirteen ships, and at the average prices of the previous year, was worth over $40,000,000. Mr. Walcott had made his own estimates, and had chartered some seventy vessels to arrive, at prices varying from £4 to £4 10s. By the time they did arrive, a surplus in the foreign market had lowered the price of wheat and of rates in San Francisco, and consequently the crop came forward slowly. Mr. Walcott had not only the Grangers' business on his hands, but in prospect commissions from farmers outside of the Order; nor was the wheat business the only one which had attracted his attention. One of the most important complications deserves to be mentioned here. We have seen how grievous a burden the farmers had felt the sack monoply to be upon the wheat industry, and in previous chapters have noticed their efforts to extricate themselves. In February, 1874, the agent employed by the Executive Committee, Mr. Gardner, called their attention to the fact that a corner was about to be made in sacks. A circular was immediately sent to all the

Subordinate Granges, advising them of the fact, and requesting them to signify whether they wished to import, and what number they were willing to take and pay for on delivery. There being no time to lose, Mr. Walcott took the responsibility, and at once ordered two million sacks from Dundee, which, becoming known to the wheat ring, they at once "unloaded," in many instances at less than cost prices. When the supply ordered by Mr. Walcott arrived, by steamship, thus further enhancing its cost, the sack market was at its lowest.

Meanwhile, the admiration of eastern Patrons was challenged by the sailing of the Grange fleet of California, loaded by the different Granges, some at Vallejo, some at Antioch, where it was demonstrated that vessels could be loaded without risk, and others at Oakland and San Francisco. The "doubting Thomases and unbelieving Philips" in the Eastern Granges were bidden by their masters to "get up and shake themselves," for while they had been "napping and grumbling, the Grange fleet of California, where the Order was little more than a year old, with a membership of sixteen thousand, had out-done Iowa, three and a half years old, with a membership of one hundred thousand." "Let us rejoice," they said, "that the farmers of California have courage and brains enough to enter the markets of Europe with their own produce, shipped on their own account. Who will now say that the millenium is not near at hand."

But the Grange fleet was destined to encounter financial storms and breakers, and the millenium of the monopolists, when "the lion and the lamb would lie down peaceably, with the lamb inside of the lion," was yet further off.

At the time of the failure, the firm of E. E. Morgan's Sons had loaded and dispatched seventeen cargoes of wheat for the Grangers, in 1874. Five of these were sent off in August, eight in September, and four in November. The Antioch, Colusa, Collinsville, Dixon, Hollister, Livermore, Merced, Modesto, Plainsburg, Stockton, Turlock and Yolo Granges, had engaged in this trade. These seventeen vessels carried over twenty thousand tons of wheat. With one exception, they were all chartered to arrive at £4 and upward. The firm had fifteen vessels then in port, under charter to load wheat, chiefly at 85s., though two got 87s. 6d., and one was taken on the spot at 60s. It appears that it was customary for the shippers to advance twenty dollars per ton on all grain as it was shipped, or received for shipment, the balance to be paid to the farmers when freight and commissions were deducted on the sale of the wheat in Liverpool, but some of the farmers had neglected to obtain these advances. Time must necessarily elapse before the cargoes could be heard from. What could be done? The Grange was not a corporate body; the Executive Committee were powerless to act in so grave an emergency. The London and San Francisco Bank withdrew its support from Mr. Walcott, and though the prominent firm of Daniel Meyer & Co. came at once to his relief, he was forced into bankruptcy.

The business of E. E. Morgan's Sons was complicated, and the Executive Committee who had access to his books and papers, found that time was required before definite statements could be made of losses and liabilities. Mr. Walcott had been doing a mixed business, within and outside of the Grange, and individual Patrons had been doing business with him on their own account, without consulting the State agent. The warfare which Mr. Walcott had waged with the wheat ring, had been an unequal one, for they could afford to lose a season's profit in breaking him down, trusting to an advance in the foreign demand. The confidence of the Grangers in Mr. Walcott's business talents was more than matched by that of the most experienced commercial houses in San Francisco, upon whom the weight of the failure fell even more heavily. Most unfortunately for himself, for his financial backers, and for a considerable number of Patrons who had trusted implicitly in his judgment and integrity, Mr. Walcott failed; but most fortunately for the success of the farmers' movement towards emancipation. Now, for the first time, the farmers had a true view of their helplessness, who knew how to grow a crop, but not how to dispose of it to their own advantage. The whole body of Patrons were now ready to incorporate, pay their own agents, and employ their own capital. The lesson was at once improved; and those who best understood how the disaster had happened, were the most patient and unshaken in their confidence in their officers, who labored day and night to lessen the severity of the loss.

Another blessing in disguise included in the failure, was that it demonstrated the moral status of the Order.

When, in August and September, it was seen that ships could be obtained at a much lower rate than that specified in Morgan's

Sons' charters; that sacks had fallen also, and that failure was inevitable, the Grangers were advised to repudiate a transaction not binding in law, and save themselves; but they did nothing of the kind. As a body, they stood by their agreements and by the firm, as will be seen in the resolutions of the Stockton meeting.

Mr. Walcott, who had previously resigned the Presidency of the Bank, turned over his books and unfinished business to the Executive Committee, who issued a circular proposing to take entire charge of the wheat and wool interests heretofore managed by him, and thus take advantage of the low prices of tonnage. A special meeting of the State Grange was also called to convene at San Francisco, on the 4th of November. At this meeting, attended by a large delegation from the Subordinate Granges, Mr. Walcott's books, accounts, etc., were presented for examination. He was present whenever desired, to give explanations, and the whole business interests of the Order were freely canvassed, resulting in renewed confidence in the prudence and fidelity of the Executive Committee. But no other feature of that meeting will so long be remembered by those who participated in it, as the noble spirit of fellowship which led those who had lost much in the failure of Morgan's Sons, to come to the relief of those who had lost their all.

Costly as the education in business had proved, it was felt to be worth all it had cost, and there was a determination to equalize the burden by substantial and immediate assistance to the greater sufferers.

The failure of Morgan's Sons undoubtedly hastened the foundation of the Grangers' Business Association, for the members were daily made to feel, in attempting to repair their losses, that faithfulness and ability counted for nothing, without authority to act as the legalized officers of a corporation. "Going to war without arms," was no longer to be thought of. It had been proposed to incorporate the State Grange, but that could not be done under the State laws. Whether to have one or several incorporations, was a serious question. The fruit growers, wool growers, and dairy interest, all required separate handling. It was finally resolved to include them all in one incorporation, in which those interests should be represented respectively, by men of their own choosing as directors.

Again, to define the scope of the organization was no easy

task. Having determined the necessity and feasibility of doing something, what, how, and how much, remained to be settled. While it was felt that anything that might become necessary to protect the commercial interests of Patrons was consistent with the scheme, it was clear that speculation was no part of a farmer's business. It was, therefore, determined to limit the functions of the incorporation to a factor's business, and the articles of agreement were framed accordingly. As Grangers, it is not intended to make war upon any legitimate business, nor to interrupt commerce in any of its established channels. But they do propose to protect themselves by all proper means, and to avoid all unnecessary expense in the transportation of their products, thereby securing better pay for their labor and the use of their capital. They do not object to reasonable commissions, but to extortion.

Another question that has very generally agitated the minds of Patrons, and that was thoroughly discussed by the convention, was the relative importance of local incorporations. It was deemed safe to leave it to Patrons to settle for themselves according to the circumstances of their respective localities. These local incorporations may become important auxiliaries to the Business Association, and the Association must, when once established, contribute largely to their success, by affording them facilities and connections for trade at the central market of the State, which, without it, they cannot have. While, therefore, the benefits are reciprocal, it seems more needful first to nurture the trunk, whence the branches may be sent out to cover with their beneficent shade every Grange and every Granger in the land.

Some idea of the amount of business that may be reasonably expected to be done by the Association during the present year, may be formed by considering the amount of transactions at San Francisco in agricultural and dairy products during the year 1874, of which the following is a reliable statement: dairy products—total value, $5,000,000; wheat—21,000,000 centals, at $1 70, total value, $35,700,000; wool—40,000,000 pounds, total value, $6,800,000; barley, oats, hay, etc.,—total value, $5,000,000; fruit crop—total value, $2,000,000; wine—total value, $4,000,000.

We omit all mention of poultry, eggs, beans, potatoes and other products, each of which amounts to a large business of itself. We have, however, mentioned enough to show an aggregate business of nearly $60,000,000 per annum. The proportion of this vast business which shall be diverted into this channel will depend upon the disposition of the members of the Order—inasmuch as the above statement is but an aggregation of the business done by the farmers of the State.

At 351 Market street, San Francisco, conveniently accessible to the wharves and depots, the Grangers' Business Association now stands ready to do its proper share of the farmers' commercial work. The Grange is now for the first time a completed organism, with producing, distributing and assimilating functions working harmoniously together for the material and social advancement of the tillers of the soil. By resolution of the Executive Committee, the Dairy and Business Agencies, which have accomplished so much for the benefit of the Patrons, are formally discontinued, and will hereafter constitute departments of the Business Association.

This Business Association, which promises to be of such substantial benefit to the farmer, is organized under the following

ARTICLES OF INCORPORATION.

KNOW ALL MEN BY THESE PRESENTS: That we, the undersigned, have this day associated ourselves together for the purpose of incorporating, under the laws of the State of California, a corporation to be known by the corporate name of "Grangers' Business Association, of California."

And we hereby certify that the purposes for which this corporation is formed, are: As factor and broker, and not otherwise, to deal in all kinds of agricultural produce, live stock, wool, agricultural implements, and general merchandise. Also, to ship grain and other merchandise to and from foreign and domestic ports, as factor and broker, and not otherwise. Also, to charter and load vessels to and from foreign and domestic ports, as factor and broker, and not otherwise.

That its principal place of business shall be in the city and county of San Francisco, State of California.

That the time of its existence shall be fifty years from and after the date of its incorporation.

That the number of its Directors or Trustees shall be eleven; and the names and residences of those who shall serve until the election of such officers and their qualification, are:

J. M. Hamilton, Lake County, California; J. C. Merryfield, Solano County, California; G. W. Colby, Butte County, California; A. B. Nalley, Sonoma County, California; J. M. Thompson, Napa County, California; A. D. Logan, Colusa County, California; H. M. Leonard, Santa Clara County, California; Wm. McP. Hill, Sonoma County, California; O. Hubbell, Marin County, California; G. P. Kellogg, Monterey County, California; D. Inman, Alameda County, California.

That the Capital Stock of this corporation shall be one million dollars ($1,000,000), in gold coin of the United States, divided into forty thousand shares of the par value of twenty-five dollars ($25) each.

In witness whereof, we have hereunto set our hands and seals, this 16th day of February, A. D. 1875.

G. W. COLBY,
W. MCPHERSON HILL,
J. C. MERRYFIELD,
A. B NALLEY,
A. D. LOGAN.

At a meeting held on February 18th, 1875, a complete organization was effected, with the following result:

BY-LAWS.

ARTICLE I. The name of this corporation shall be the GRANGERS' BUSINESS ASSOCIATION OF CALIFORNIA.

ARTICLE II. The said Corporation shall have a capital stock of one million dollars, gold coin of the United States, divided into forty thousand shares of twenty-five dollars each.

ARTICLE III. The principal place of business of said Corporation shall be at the City and County of San Francisco, State of California.

ARTICLE IV. None but Patrons of Husbandry shall be permitted to subscribe to the capital stock of this Corporation.

ARTICLE V. Stockholders of this Corporation shall be such persons or corporations, composed of Patrons, as may have executed or shall execute a subscription to the capital stock—in such form as the Board of Directors may prescribe—and shall pay to the said Corporation all duly levied and called assessments, or such persons or corporations as the stock may be duly assigned to in accordance with these By-Laws.

ARTICLE VI. The powers of the Corporation shall be vested in a Board of eleven Directors, who shall have been elected, and who shall hold office for the term of one year, or until their successors should have been elected and entered upon the discharge of their duties.

ARTICLE VII. The Directors shall be citizens of the United States, Patrons of Husbandry, and Stockholders in the Corporation, and hold, each, at least ten shares of the capital stock.

ARTICLE VIII. A majority of the whole number of Directors shall constitute a quorum for the transaction of business, and every decision of a majority of the persons duly assembled as a Board (if not in conflict with these By-Laws), shall be valid as an act of this Corporation.

ARTICLE IX. Regular meetings of the Board of Directors shall be held at the office of the Corporation, at least once in every three months, and at such other times as the Board of Directors may prescribe. Special meetings of the Board of Directors shall be held, at the same place, upon the call of the President or Vice-President. It shall be the duty of the President or Vice-President, in case from any cause the President cannot act, to call special meetings, either of the Board of Directors or of the stockholders, upon the written request of five directors, or upon the written request of stockholders representing one tenth of the stock issued. Due notice of such requested meeting of the stockholders shall be given by mail, and also by publication, as prescribed in Article XXIV of these By-Laws; and all business which could be transacted at a regular meeting of the stockholders may be done at such requested and specially called meeting. No notice of the regular meeting of the Board of Directors shall be requisite other than that prescribed herein; but of all special meetings the President or Vice President shall cause all Directors residing out of San Francisco to be notified by mail or telegraph; and all Directors residing and being in San Francisco, and any others to whom it is practicable to give such personal notice, shall be personally notified.

ARTICLE X. The Corporation shall have power, through its officers and employés to deal, as a factor, in all kinds of agricultural produce, live stock, wool, agricultural implements and general merchandise; and also, as a factor, to import and export all articles appropriate or fitting to agricultural pursuits.

ARTICLE XI. Whenever a vacancy shall occur in the Board of Directors by death, resignation or otherwise, the Board of Directors shall fill the same by appointing a successor for the unexpired term.

ARTICLE XII. Whenever any Director shall cease to be a stockholder, his office shall become *ipso facto*, vacant; and such vacancy shall be filled as provided in Article XI.

ARTICLE XIII. The Board of Directors shall elect from their number a President, and Vice President of the corporation, who shall hold their offices for one year, or until their successors are elected and entered upon the discharge of their official duties.

ARTICLE XIV. The President or Vice President, or either of them, may be removed from office at any time on the vote of seven Directors in favor of removal.

ARTICLE XV. The President and Vice President and Teasurer shall give bonds for the faithful discharge of their respective duties, in such sums as may be prescribed by the Board of Directors; and for their services shall receive such remuneration as may be fixed by said Board.

ARTICLE XVI. The Board of Directors shall have power to appoint a Secretary an Attorney, and such other officers, agents, clerks and servants, as the business of the Corporation may require, define their powers and prescribe their duties, subject to these By-Laws, and shall fix the salaries or other compensation to be paid to such officers, agents, clerks and servants of the Corporation.

ARTICLE XVII. The President and Vice President shall have charge and custody of the funds, property, books, papers and other matters of the Corporation, under such rules, regulations and restrictions as provided by these By-Laws, or the Board of Directors may prescribe by resolutions duly passed and entered upon the minutes of said Board.

ARTICLE XVIII. The President and Vice President shall not both be absent from the State at the same time, and in case of the absence of either, his duties and powers shall devolve upon and be performed by the other.

ARTICLE XIX. It shall be the duty of the President, and in his absence, the Vice President, to preside at all meetings of the Board of Directors, and at all meetings of the stockholders of the Corporation.

ARTICLE XX. It shall be the duty of the Secretary to record correctly all the proceedings of the stockholders at their meetings, and of the Board of Directors.

ARTICLE XXI. The Board of Directors shall, from their number, appoint an Auditing Committee of three, whose duty it shall be to count the cash, examine the books, vouchers, documents, papers, and other assets of the Corporation; to report upon the same to the stockholders at their annual meetings, and to the Board of Directors from time to time, as they may direct.

ARTICLE XXII. The Board of Directors shall, from their number, appoint a Finance Committee of three, whose duties shall be defined by resolution of the Board of Directors.

ARTICLE XXIII. The annual meeting of the stockholders for the election of Directors shall be held at the office of the Corporation, on the third Wednesday of February of each year, at ten o'clock A. M.

ARTICLE XXIV. The call for the annual meeting of stockholders, and for the annual election of Directors shall be signed by the President or Vice President, and be attested by the Secretary, and be published at least once a week, for four consecutive weeks next preceding the day of meeting, in at least three newspapers of general circulation throughout the State. If from any cause no quorum shall be present, the meeting may adjourn from time to time without further notice.

ARTICLE XXV.—All transfers of stock shall be subject to all debts and equities in favor of the Corporation against the person or Corporations making such transfer, and existing or arising prior to the regular transfer thereof upon the books of the Corporation; and no transfer of shares shall be made upon the books of the Corporation, until all dues and demands thereon, due to the Corporation, from the party or parties representing such shares, shall have been paid.

ARTICLE XXVI.—All transfers of stock shall be made on the books of the Corporation, and no transfer shall be binding on the Corporation until so entered, or until all assessments thereon have been paid. No stock that has been transferred on the books of the Corporation within thirty days next preceding any meeting of the stockholders, shall be entitled to representation at said meeting.

ARTICLE XXVII.—Certificates of stock shall be issued to the original stockholders of this Corporation, to the number of shares by each subscribed in the original articles of association, as evidence to each of the number of shares by him or her owned in the capital stock; and the manner of transferring shares shall be by endorsement and delivery of the certificate thereof, such endorsement being by the signature of the proprietor, or his or her attorney in fact, or legal representative. No stock shall be transferred without the surrender of the certificate, and upon such surrender the word "cancelled" shall be written across the face of the certificate by the Secretary, and the signatures of the officers shall be erased, and such certificate, so cancelled, shall be preserved by pasting the same to the stub from which it was torn, in the Certificate book. The transfer books shall be closed for two days prior to the annual meetings and the payment of dividends, and the dividends shall be paid to the persons in whose names they stand as stockholders at the time when the books are closed.

ARTICLE XXVIII.—All the net earnings and profits in said business of the Corporation, over and above actual expenses paid, or for which the Corporation is liable, shall, by dividends duly declared by the Board of Directors, be divided among the stockholders, *pro rata* their stock, and in no event shall indebtedness be incurred other than in the proper, legitimate business of the Corporation; provided, the amount of indebtedness that may be incurred, shall not exceed the amount of stock actually subscribed.

OFFICERS.—*President*, Daniel Inman; *Vice-President*, T. J. Brooke; *Treasurer*, John Llewellyn; *Attorney*, A. W. Thompson; *Secretary*, Wm. Vanderbilt; *Auditing Committee*, R. C. Haile, Thomas Flint, I. C. Steele. *Finance Committee*, Amos Adams, Thomas Upton, C. P. Kellogg.

Directors.—Daniel Inman, of Alameda County; Thomas Upton, of Merced County; T. J. Brooke, of San Joaquin County; I. C. Steele, of San Mateo County; Amos Adams, of Sacramento County; Wm. Vanderbilt of Marin County; John Llewellyn, of Napa County; Thomas Flint, of San Benito County; A. W. Thompson, of Sonoma County: R. C. Haile, of Solano County; G. P. Kellogg, of Monterey County.

PART THIRD.

GRANGE DIRECTORY.

CHAPTER XVII.

THE NATIONAL GRANGE.

OFFICERS:

Master—DUDLEY W. ADAMS, Waukon, Iowa.
Overseer—THOMAS TAYLOR, Columbia, South Carolina.
Lecturer—T. A. THOMPSON, Plainview, Wabash county, Minnesota.
Steward—A. J. VAUGHAN, Early Grove, Marshall county, Mississippi.
Assistant Steward—G. W. THOMPSON, New Brunswick, New Jersey.
Chaplain—Rev. A. B. GROSH, Washington, District of Columbia.
Treasurer—F. M. McDOWELL, Corning, New York.
Secretary—O. H. KELLEY, Washington, District of Columbia.
Gate Keeper—O. DINWIDDIE, Orchard Grove, Lake county, Indiana.
Ceres—MRS. D. W. ADAMS, Waukon, Iowa.
Pomona—MRS. O. H. KELLEY, Washington, District of Columbia.
Flora—MRS. J. C. ABBOTT, Clarkesville, Butler county, Iowa.
Lady Assistant Steward—MISS C. A. HALL, Washington, District of Columbia.

EXECUTIVE COMMITTEE:

WILLIAM SAUNDERS, Washington, District of Columbia.
D. WYATT AIKEN, Cokesbury, Abbeville county, South Carolina.
E. R. SHANKLAND, Dubuque, Iowa.

MEMBERS:

State.	Master.	Address.
Alabama	W. H. Chambers	Oswichee, Russell county.
Arkansas	John T. Jones	Helena, Phillips county.
California	J. M. Hamilton	Guenoc, Lake county.
Colorado	R. Q. Tenney	Fort Collins, Larimer county.
Delaware	(United with	Maryland.)
Dakota	E. B. Crew	Lodi, Clay county.
Florida	B. F. Wardlaw	Madison, Madison county.
Georgia	T. J. Smith	Oconee, C. R. R., Wash'ton co.
Illinois	Alonzo Golder	Rock Falls, Whitesides county.
Indiana	Henley James	Marion, Grant county.
Iowa	A. B. Smedley	Cresco, Howard county.
Idaho	(United with	Oregon.)
Kansas	M. E. Hudson	Mapleton, Bourbon county.
Kentucky	M. D. Davie	Beverly, Christian county.
Louisiana	H. W. L. Lewis	Osyka, Pike county.
Maine	Nelson Ham	Lewiston, Androscoggin county.
Maryland	Jos. T. Moore	Sandy Springs, Mont. county.
Massachusetts	Joseph P. Felton	Greenfield, Franklin county.
Michigan	S. F. Brown	Schoolcraft, Kalamazoo county.
Minnesota	S. E. Adams	Monticello, Wright county.
Mississippi	W. L. Hemingway	Carrollton, Carroll county.
Missouri	T. R. Allen	Allenton, St. Louis county.
Montana	Brigham Reed	Bozeman, Gallatin county.

State.	Master.	Address.
Nebraska	Wm. B. Porter	Plattsmouth, Cass county.
New Hampshire	Dudley T. Chase	Claremont, Sullivan county.
New Jersey	Edward Howland	Hammonton, Atlantic county.
New York	George D. Hinckley	Fredonia, Chatauqua county.
North Carolina	Columbus Mills	Concord, Cabarrus county.
Nevada	(United with	California.)
Ohio	S. H. Ellis	Springboro, Warren county.
Oregon	Daniel Clark	Salem, Marion county.
Pennsylvania	D. B. Mauger	Douglassville, Berks county
South Carolina	Thomas Taylor	Columbia, Richland county.
Tennessee	William Maxwell	Humboldt, Gibson county.
Texas	William W. Lang	Marlin, Falls county.
Vermont	E. P. Colton	Irasburg, Orleans county.
Virginia	J. W. White	Eureka Mills, Charlotte county.
West Virginia	B. M. Kitchen	Shanghai, Berkeley county.
Wisconsin	John Cochrane	Waupun, Fond du Lac county.
Washington	(United with	Oregon.)

CALIFORNIA STATE GRANGE.

OFFICERS.

Master—J. M. Hamilton, Guenoc, Lake county.
Overseer—O. L. Abbott, Santa Barbara, Santa Barbara county.
Lecturer—J. W. A. Wright, Borden, Fresno county.
Steward—N. L. Allen, Salinas, Monterey county.
Assistant Steward—Wm. M. Jackson, Woodland, Yolo county.
Chaplain—J. A. Hutton, Yolo, Yolo county.
Treasurer—J. B. Carrington, Denverton, Solano county.
Secretary—W. H. Baxter, 6 Leidesdorff street, San Francisco.
Gate Keeper—R. R. Warder, Waterford, Stanislaus county.
Ceres—Mrs. G. W. Davis, Santa Rosa, Sonoma county.
Pomona—Mrs. S. C. Baxter, Napa city, Napa county.
Flora—Mrs. R. S. Hegeler, Bodega, Sonoma county.
Lady Assistant Steward—Mrs. S. M. Gardner, Grayson, Stanislaus county.

EXECUTIVE COMMITTEE:

J. M. Hamilton, W. M., Chairman, Guenoc, Lake county.
I. G. Gardner, Grayson, Stanislaus county.
J. C. Merryfield, Dixon, Solano county.
H. M. Leonard, Santa Clara, Santa Clara county.
J. M. Thompson, Suscol, Napa county.
G. W. Colby, Nord, Butte county.
A. B. Nalley, Windsor, Sonoma county.

CALIFORNIA DISTRICT AND COUNTY COUNCILS:

Alameda County—Joel Russell, Haywood, M.; T. Hellar, S.

Los Angeles and San Bernardino District—T. A. Garey, Los Angeles, M.; J. F. Marquis, Anaheim, S.

Mendocino County—L. F. Long, Ukiah City, M.; J. A. Knox, Sanel, S.

Monterey and Santa Cruz District—J. R. Hebbron, M.; A. F. Richardson, S.

Napa District—J. D. Blanchar, M.; H. W. Haskell, S.

Sacramento, El Dorado and Placer District—Officers not reported.

San Luis Obispo County—A. J. Mothersead, M.; J. M. Mannon, S.

Santa Clara County—H. M. Leonard, M.; I. A. Wilcox, S. Regular meetings every three months, alternately at Santa Clara and San Jose.

Santa Barbara and San Luis Obispo District—Officers not reported.

Solano County—J. B. Carrington, M.; J. M. Jones, S.

Sonoma County—Wm. McPherson Hill, M.; S. T. Coulter, S.

STANISLAUS COUNTY—R. R. Warder, M.; Vital E. Bangs, S.
TULARE COUNTY—W. S. Babcock, M.; J. S. Urton, S.
VENTURA COUNTY COUNCIL—Daniel Rouillish, M,; James S. Harkey, S.
WEST SAN JOAQUIN DISTRICT, (Merced, San Joaquin and Stanislaus counties.) W. J. Miller, Oristimba, M.; Thomas A. Chapman, Oristimba, S.

LIST OF ORGANIZING DEPUTIES.

County.	Deputy.	Post-office.
Alameda	Thos. Heller	Eden.
Amador	H. Vanderpool	Plymouth.
Butte	Ed. Hallett	Chico.
Butte	Wm. M. Thorpe	Chico.
Butte	G. W. Colby	Nord.
Colusa	J. J. Hicok	Grand Island.
Colusa	D. H. Arnold	Spring Valley.
Contra Costa	R. G. Dean	Antioch.
El Dorado	A. J. Cristie.	Coloma.
Fresno	J. W. A. Wright	Borden.
Humboldt	H. W. Arbogast	Arcata.
Inyo	T. J. Furbee	Bishop's Creek
Lake	H. A. Oliver	Guenoc.
Los Angeles	Thos. A. Garey	Los Angeles.
Los Angeles	Ed. Evey	Anaheim.
Mendocino	R. M. Wilson	Cahto.
Merced	H. B. Jolley	Merced City.
Modoc	I. S. Mathews	Fort Jones.
Mono	T. J. Furbee	Bishop's Creek, Inyo.
Monterey	J. D. Fowler	Hollister.
Placer	A. D. Neher	Roseville.
Sacramento	W. S. Manlove	Sacramento.
San Benito	J. D. Fowler	Hollister.
San Francisco	I. G. Gardner	San Francisco.
San Francisco	J. H. Hegeler	San Francisco.
San Joaquin	A. Wolf	Stockton.
San Luis Obispo	A. J. Mothersead	Moro.
San Luis Obispo	Isaac Flood	Old Creek.
Santa Barbara	O. L. Abbott	Santa Barbara.
Santa Clara	G. W. Henning	San Jose.
Shasta	J. T. Dinsmore	Reading.
Siskiyou	I. S. Mathews	Fort Jones.
Solano	J. B. Carrington	Denverton.
Solano	R. C. Haile	Suisun.
Solano	J. C. Merryfield	Dixon.
Sonoma	Geo. W. Davis	Santa Rosa.
Sonoma	A. B. Nally	Windsor.
Sonoma	T. H. Merry	Healdsburg.
Stanislaus	J. D. Spencer	Modesto.
Stanislaus	J. D. Reyburn	Modesto.
Sutter	Geo. Ohleyer	Yuba City.
Tehama	A. J. Loomis	Farmington.
Tulare	M. S. Babcock	Kingston, Fresno.
Yolo	Wm. Sims	Buckeye.

GENERAL DEPUTIES.

Alameda	Ezra S. Carr	Oakland.
Fresno	J. W. A. Wright (W. L.)	Borden.
Lake	J. M. Hamilton (W. M.)	Guenoc.
San Francisco	W. H. Baxter (W. S.)	6 Liedesdorff Street.
San Francisco	John H. Hegeler	San Francisco.
Solano	John B. Carrington	Denverton.

NEVADA.

	A. J. Hatch	Reno.

CALIFORNIA SUBORDINATE GRANGES, ARRANGED BY COUNTIES

This list contains the names of Masters and Secretaries so far as reported, elected to serve during the year 1875. In Granges not reported we continue the names of last year's officers:

Name of Grange.	Master.	Secretary.	Post-office.
AMADOR COUNTY.			
Jackson Valley	Jesse D. Hamrick	Lansing J. Dooley	Ione City.
Plymouth	Harding Vanderpool	S. C. Wheeler	Plymouth.
South Sutter	Thos. Boyd	G. R. Richardson	South Sutter.
ALAMEDA COUNTY.			
Centerville	Jas. Shinn	M. B. Sturgis	Centerville.
Eden	Thos. Hellar	Wm. Pearce	Haywards.
Livermore	D. Inman	F. R. Fassett	Livermore.
Sunol	E. M. Carr	S. W. Millard	Sunol.
Temescal	J. V. Webster	John Collins	Oakland.
BUTTE COUNTY.			
Chico	E. Hallett	H. W. Barnes	Chico.
Evening Star	A. D. Nelson	A. M. Woodruff	Nelson.
Hamilton	H. L. Lasselle	Anson Brown	Biggs' Station.
Honcut	John C. Moore	D. F. Newbert	Moore's Station.
Nord	G. Van Woert	Peter Kern	Nord.
CALAVERAS COUNTY.			
Calaveras	M. F. Gregory	Mrs. Rodgers	Jenny Lind
COLUSA COUNTY.			
Antelope Valley	John Sites	P. Peterson	Antelope Valley
Center	D. Bebee	Mrs. Carrie Wellay	Colusa.
Colusa	J. O. Wilkins	R. Jones	Colusa.
Freshwater	P. S. Perdue	R. A. Wilsey	Colusa.
Funk Slough	L. D. McDow	E. C. Hunte.r	Colusa.
Grand Island	Wm. Ogden	J. H. Duffield	Grand Island.
Newville	B. N. Scribner	S. Osborne	Newville.
Plaza	M. Kendrick	J. W. Bower	Jacinto.
Princeton	R. R. Rush	P. H. Scott	Princeton.
Spring Valley	B. Lucas	T. Singleton	Spring Valley.
Union	J. F. Garr	W. W Dollings	Princeton.
Willows	J. W. Zumwalt	G. T. Hicklin	Princeton.
CONTRA COSTA COUNTY.			
Alhambra	J. Strentzell	W. A. Frazer	Martinez.
Antioch	M. A. Walton	J. D. Darby	Antioch.
Danville	C. Wood	J. R. Sydnor	Danville.
Point of Timber	H. C. McCabe	E. W. Carey	Point of Timber.
Walnut Creek	M. S. Gray	R. M. Jones	Walnut Creek.
EL DORADO COUNTY.			
Clarksville	R. T. Mills	I. Maltby	Clarksville.
El Dorado	C. G. Carpenter	J. M. B. Weatherwax	El Dorado.
Pilot Hill	John Bishop	A. J. Bayley	Pilot Hill.
Placerville	William Wiltse	H. G. Hulburd	Placerville.
Sutter Mill	J. G. O'Brien	H. Mahler	Coloma.
FRESNO COUNTY.			
Adams	T. P. Nelson	T. Wyatt	Big Dry Creek.
Borden	H. L. Patterson	J. Fontaine	Borden.
Fresno	D. C. Libby	F. Dusy	Fresno City.
Garretson	Jos. Burns	H. C. Higby	King's River.
Rising Star	W. W. Hagar	W. M. Poage	Panochi.
Sycamore	A. C. Bradford	J. A. Allen	Sycamore.

HUMBOLDT COUNTY.

Name of Grange.	Master.	Secretary.	Post-office.
Elk River	T. S. Stewaart	D. A. DeMerritt	Eureka.
Ferndale	F. Z. Boynton	E. C. Damon	Ferndale.
Kiwelattah	D. D. Averill	F. McPhee	Arcata.
Mattole	Jacob Miner	David Simmons	Petrolia.
Rohnerville	H. S. Case	S. Strong	Rohnerville
Table Bluff	J. Sawyer	E. Clark	Table Bluff.

INYO COUNTY.

Name of Grange.	Master.	Secretary.	Post-office.
Bishop's Creek	A. Dell	W. T. Wiswall	Bishop's Creek.
Independence	J. W. Symmes	D. Beurtis	Independence.
Lone Pine	J. J. McCall	A. H. Johnson	Lone Pine.

KERN COUNTY.

Name of Grange.	Master.	Secretary.	Post-office.
Bakersfield	J. R. Riley	P. D. Jewett	Bakersfield.
Cummings Valley	G. Thompson	T. Yates	Tehaichipa.
Linn's Valley	S. W. Woody	S. E. Reed	Glenville.
New River	W. Norton	L. G. Baker	Bakersfield.
Panama	H. D. Robb	J. F. Gordon	Bakersfield.
Rising Star	C. Valpey	J. W. Craycroft	Panoche.
Tehaichipa	J. Norboe	J. Prewett	Tehaichipa.
Weldon	J. B. Bartz	James Swan	Weldon.

LASSEN COUNTY.

Name of Grange.	Master.	Secretary.	Post-office.
Lakeside	Geo. H. Bingham	John Theodore	Janesville.

LAKE COUNTY.

Name of Grange.	Master.	Secretary.	Post-office.
Guenoc	T. Sopher	W. C. Greenfield	Guenoc.
Kelseyville	D. P. Shattuck	T. Ormiston	Kelseyville.
Lakeport	J. W. Boggs	N. Phelan	Lakeport.
Lower Lake	J. W. Howard	Lucy S. Wilson	Lower Lake.
Upper Lake	D. V. Thompson	D. Q. McCarty	Upper Lake.

LOS ANGELES COUNTY.

Name of Grange.	Master.	Secretary.	Post-office.
Alliance	J. D. Durfee	J. W. Mansfield,	El Monte,
Azusa	W. W. Maxey	J. C. Preston	El Monte
Compton	J. J. Morton	T. V. Kimble	Compton.
El Monte	J. T. Gordon	A.H. Hoyt	El Monte.
Enterprise	T. E. Alexander	Mrs. Alexander	Los Angeles.
Eureka	C. Burdick	P. C. Tonner	Spadra.
Fairview	E. Evey	J. M. Guinn	Anaheim.
Florence	Philip How	R. Ramsey	Los Angeles.
Fruitland	N. O. Stafford	L. H. Collins	Santa Anna.
Los Angeles	T. A. Garey	S. A. Waldron	Los Angeles.
Los Nietos,	F. B. Granlin	W. S. Reavis	Los Nietos.
New River	W. Newton	S. G. Baker	Los Nietos.
Orange	J. Beach	L. J. Lockhart	Orange.
Silver	H. L. Montgomery.	W. P. McDonald	Los Nietos.
Spadra	A. T. Currier	Jos. Wright	Spadra.
Vineland	A. B. Haywood	R. L. Freeman	Tustin City.
Westminster	M. B. Craig	W. F. Poor	Westminster.
Wellington	A. H. Hawley	J. N. Mann	Wellington.

MENDOCINO COUNTY

Name of Grange.	Master.	Secretary.	Post-office.
Cahto	H. Braden	H. Clark	Cahto.
Little Lake	A. P. Martin	W. A. Wright	Little Lake.
Manchester	B. F. McClure	W. F. McClure	Manchester.
Pomo	J. Mewhinney	G. B. Nichols	Pomo.
Potter Valley	L. A. Preston	Mrs. Slingerland	Potter Valley.
Round Valley	P. Handy	William Ford	Covelo.
Sanel	E. M. Carr	M. Gregory	Sanel.
Ukiah	Thos. A. Lucas	A. O. Carpenter	Ukiah.

MARIN COUNTY.

Name of Grange.	Master.	Secretary.	Post-office.
Nicasio	P. K. Austin	J. W. Noble	Nicasio.
Point Reyes	N. H. Stinson	A. H. Stinson	Point Reyes.
Tomales	Wm. Vanderbilt	R. H. Prince	Tomales.

MERCED COUNTY.

Name of Grange.	Master.	Secretary.	Post-office.
Badger Flat	A. P. Merrit	W. F. Clarke	Los Banos.
Cottonwood	J. L. Crittenden	J. M. Daley	Cottonwood.
Hopeton	John Buddle	T. Egleson	Hopeton.
Los Banos	A. P. Merrit	W. F. Smith	Los Banos.
Merced	W. E. Elliot	Jas. B. Ralston	Merced.
Plainsburg	P. Y. Welch	T. J. E. Wilcox	Plainsburg.
Snelling	Erastus Kelsey	Frank Larkin	Snelling.

MODOC COUNTY.

Name of Grange.	Master.	Secretary.	Post-office.
Modoc	A. V. Coffer	M. Waid	Willow Ranch.

MONTEREY COUNTY.

Name of Grange.	Master.	Secretary.	Post-office.
Hollister	R. Ruckledge	Mary E. Cowan	Hollister.
Morning Star	C. E. Williams	F. Blake	Castroville.
Pajaro	D. M. Clough	L. B. Johnson	Watsonville.
Salinas	J. R. Hebbron	Clara Westlake	Salinas.

NAPA COUNTY.

Name of Grange.	Master.	Secretary.	Post-office.
Berryessa	J. W Smittle	L. H. Buford	Monticello.
Calistoga	W. B. Pratt	C. H. Menefee	Calistoga.
Napa	J. B. Saul	A. A. R. Utting	Napa City.
Pope Valley	J. A. Van Arsdale	C. A. Booth	Pope Valley.
Rutherford	G. S. Burrege	H. W. Crabb	Yountville.
St. Helena	J. Llewellyn	Chas. A. Story	St. Helena.
Yountville	J. M. Mayfield	F. Griffin	Yountville.

NEVADA COUNTY.

Name of Grange.	Master.	Secretary.	Post-office.
Indian Springs	T. J. Robertson	L. Horton	Indian Springs.

PLACER COUNTY.

Name of Grange.	Master.	Secretary.	Post-office.
Lincoln	John Lewelling	A. Story	Lincoln.
New Castle	John C. Boggs	B. P. Tabor	New Castle.
Roseville	A. D. Usher	Robert Ward	Roseville
Sheridan	D. H. Long	S. J. Lewis	Sheridan.

PLUMAS COUNTY.

Name of Grange.	Master.	Secretary.	Post-office.
Plumas	A. J. Spoon	H. F. Lander	Sierra Valley.

SACRAMENTO COUNTY.

Name of Grange.	Master.	Secretary.	Post-office.
American River	J. A. Evans	W. W. Kilgore	Patterson.
Cosumnes	J. A. Elder	J. H. Atkins	Sheldon.
Elk Grove	Julius Everson	Delos Gage	Elk Grove.
Enterprise	G. J. Martin	W. A. Root	Brighton.
Florin	L. Fuscette	J. J. Bates	Florin.
Franklin	Amos Adams	P. R. Beckley	Franklin
Galt	J. C. Sawyer	J. L. Fifield	Galt.
Georgiana	F. M. Kittrell	G. A. Knott	Rio Vista.
Sacramento	W. S. Manlove	E. F. Aiken	Sacramento.
Sherman Island	J. M. Upham	W. M. Robbins	Emmaton.
Walnut Grove	S. Runyon	J. V. Prather	Walnut Grove.

SAN BENITO COUNTY.

Name of Grange.	Master.	Secretary.	Post-office.
Hollister	J. D. Fowler	S. F. Cowan	Hollister.
Mountain	G. Butterfield	J. W. Mathews	San Benito.

SAN BERNARDINO COUNTY.

Name of Grange.	Master.	Secretary.	Post-office.
Rincon	F. M. Slaughter	John Taylor	Rincon.
Riverside	W. B. Russell	G. W. Garcelon	Riverside.
San Bernardino	Geo. Lord	H. Goodell, Jr.	San Bernardino.

SAN DIEGO COUNTY.

Name of Grange.	Master.	Secretary.	Post-office.
Balena	C. O. Tucker	Mrs. C. O. Tucker	Balena,
Bear Valley	W. H. H. Dinwiddie	C. H. Moseley	Bear Valley.
San Bernardo	Z. Sikes	T. Duncan	San Bernardo.
San Luis Rey	M. E. Ormsby	L. J. Crombie	San Luis Rey.
San Jacinto	T. D. Henry	Mrs. M. Collins	San Jacinto.
National Ranch	F. A. Kimball	S. T. Blackmore	National Ranch.
Poway	J. F. Chapin	E. D. Frank	Poway.

SAN JOAQUIN COUNTY.

Name of Grange.	Master.	Secretary.	Post-office.
Atlanta	S. Myers	Mrs. J. W. Moore	Morano.
Castoria	F. J. Woodward	Eugene Kaye	Stockton.
Collegeville	P. P. Ward	S. R. Chalmers	Collegeville.
Elliot	Henry H. West	N. S. Misiner	Elliot.
Farmington	Wm. St. J. Rodgers	E. O. Long	Farmington.
Liberty	J. M. Wood	Victor Jahant	Acampo.
Linden	E. B. Cayswell	James Wasley	Linden.
Lockeford	G. C. Holman,	S. S. Stewart	Lockeford.
Lodi	John Parrott	Mrs. N. Crouch	Lodi.
Rustic	L. P. Whitman	H. C. Willis	Lathrop.
Stockton	T. L. Ketchim	E. N. Allen	Stockton.
Washington	J. W. Sollars	M. L. Cook	Washington.
West San Joaquin	C. E. Neeham	J. Quackenbush	Ellis.
Wildwood	E. D. Morrison	W. M. Muncey	Wildwood.
Woodbridge	Ezra Fiske	A. S. Thomas	Woodbridge

SAN LUIS OBISPO COUNTY.

Name of Grange.	Master.	Secretary.	Post-office.
Arroyo Grande	W. H. Nelson	B. J. Wood	Arroyo Grande.
Cambria	C. H. Ivins	H. Olmstead	Cambria.
Moro City	H. Y. Stanley	Jas. Allen	Moro City.
Old Creek	R. C. Swain	Chas. S. Clark	Old Creek.
Paso Robles	H. W. Rhyne	J. P. Mooky	Paso Robles.
San Luis Obispo	Wm. Jackson	E. L. Reed	San Luis Obispo.
Summit	J. V. N. Young	A. T. Foster	Paso Robles.

SAN MATEO COUNTY.

Name of Grange.	Master.	Secretary.	Post-office.
Crescent	H. M. Jewell	James Compton	Crescent.
La Honda	M. Woodhams	Mrs. Woodhams	La Honda.
Ocean View	I. G. Knowles	E. Robson	Ocean View.
Pescadero	B. V. Weeks	H. B. Sprague	Pescadero.
San Mateo	A. F. Green	C. E. Rowe	San Mateo.

SANTA BARBARA COUNTY.

Name of Grange.	Master.	Secretary.	Post-office.
Carpenteria	S. H. Olmstead	Henry Fish	Carpenteria.
Confidence	A. Copeland	J. T. Austin	Guadaloupe.
Santa Barbara	O. L. Abbott	V. F. Russell	Santa Barbara.
Santa Maria	S. G. Lockwood	S. J. Nicholson	Santa Maria.

SANTA CLARA COUNTY.

Name of Grange.	Master.	Secretary.	Post-office.
Gilroy	W. Z. Angeney	H. Coffin	Gilroy.
Mayfield	F. W. Weisshaar	J. Ponce	Mayfield.
San José	Wm. Erkson	Rufus Fish	San José.
Santa Clara	S. J. Jameson	I. A. Willcox	Santa Clara.
Saratoga	Willis Morrison	Mrs. J. Farwell	Saratoga.

SANTA CRUZ COUNTY.

Name of Grange.	Master.	Secretary.	Post-office.
Ben Lomond	John Burns	Jas. Burns	Santa Cruz.
Santa Cruz	G. C. Wardwell	T. Pilkington	Santa Cruz.
Watsonville	J. McCollin	Sarah Redman	Watsonville.

SHASTA COUNTY

Name of Grange.	Master.	Secretary.	Post-office.
Cottonwood	G. G. Kimball	John Barry	Cottonwood.
Millville	J. P. Webb	Geo. W. Welch	Millville.
Reading	J. F. Dinsmore	S. J. R. Gilbert	Reading.

SISKIYOU COUNTY.

Name of Grange.	Master.	Secretary.	Post-office.
Ætna	John McBride	T. S. Wilson	Ætna.
Fort Jones	J. S. Matthews	J. W. Tuttle	Fort Jones.
Mt. Bolivar	R. M. Hayden	J. A. Cole	Callahan's Ranch.

SOLANO COUNTY.

Name of Grange.	Master.	Secretary.	Post-office.
Binghampton	A. Bennett	E. A. Beardsley	Binghampton.
Denverton	J. B. Carrington	G. C. Arnold	Denverton.
Dixon	J. C. Merryfield	J. A. Ellis	Dixon.
Elmira	J. A. Clark	M. D. Cooper	Elmira.
Montezuma	T. Hooper	C. K. Marshall	Collinsville.
Rio Vista	A. B. Alsip	John H. Gardener	Rio Vista.
Rockville	W. A. Lattin	J. R. Morris	Cordelia.
Suisun Valley	J. M. Jones	Mrs. R. B. Canovan	Suisun Valley.
Vacaville	E. R. Thurbur	Oscar Dobbins	Vacaville.
Vallejo	S. S. Drake	Chas. B. Deming	Vallejo.

SONOMA COUNTY.

Name of Grange.	Master.	Secretary.	Post-office.
Bennett Valley	N. Carr	G. N. Whitaker	Santa Rosa.
Bloomfield	Wm. H. White	A. B. Glover	Bloomfield.
Bodega	E. S. Piune	E. H. Choney	Bodega
Cloverdale	Chas. H. Cooley	F. W. Davenport	Cloverdale.
Geyserville	C. P. Moore	H. Wiedersheim	Geyserville.
Healdsburg	B. B. Capell	W. M. Gladden	Healdsburg.
Petaluma	W. W. Chapman	Freeman Parker	Petaluma.
Santa Rosa	Geo. W. Davis	J. A. Obreen	Santa Rosa.
Sebastopol	J. M. Hudspeth	W. J. Hunt	Sebastopol.
Sonoma	Wm. McP. Hill	T. S. Cooper	Sonoma.
Two Rock	John R. Doss	J. C. Purvine	Two Rock.
Windsor	E. H. Barns	Edgar Lindsey	Windsor.

STANISLAUS COUNTY.

Name of Grange.	Master.	Secretary.	Post-office.
Bonita	J. W. Treadwell	A. B. Crook	Crow's Landing.
Ceres	H. W. Brouse	R. R. Whitmore	Ceres.
Grayson	Wm. Love	A. C. Lander	Grayson.
Oak Dale	A. S. Emery	C. B. Ingalls	Oak Dale.
Oristimba	W. J. Miller	E. H. Robison	Hill's Ferry
Salida	P. Vincent	A. H. Elmore	Modesto.
Stanislaus	V. E. Bangs	E. R. Turner	Modesto.
Turlock	C. S. Campbell	W. S. Robinson	Turlock.
Waterford	S. M. Gallup	J. Booth	Waterford.

SUTTER COUNTY.

Name of Grange.	Master.	Secretary.	Post-office.
North Butte	B. R. Spillman	J. D. Dow	North Butte.
South Sutter	Thos. Boyd	Geo. R. Richardson	South Sutter.
Sutter	W. C. Smith	J. M. Gladden	Meridian.
Yuba City	B. F. Walton	J. Hondy	Yuba City.

TEHAMA COUNTY.

Name of Grange.	Master.	Secretary.	Post-office.
Farmington	C. F. Foster	S. H. Loomis	Farmington.
New Salem	O. Harris	W. T. Hains	Paskento.
Red Bluff	R. H. Blossom	C. E. Fonda	Red Bluff.

TULARE COUNTY.

Name of Grange.	Master.	Secretary.	Post-office.
Christmas	W. M. Stuart	C. H. Robinson	Visalia.
Deep Creek	G. F. Jefferds	W. G. Pennebaker	Farmersville.
Franklin	W. L. Moreton	G. W. Camp	Grangeville.
Keystone	Erastus Axtell	N. B. Golden	Grangeville.
Lake	M. S. Babcock	Mrs. E. D. Simmons	Grangeville.
Mussel Slough	Wisley Underwood	Wm. Land	Grangeville.
Mount Whitney	G. W. Duncan	A. Thompson	Mount Whitney.
Tulare	D. E. Wilson	Victoria Wright	Tulare.
Tule River	E. H. Baker	Miss J. Gilmer	Portsville.
Visalia	T. Fowler	O. Blakely	Visalia.
Woodville	J. A. Slover	J. Stewart	Woodville.

TUOLUMNE COUNTY.

Name of Grange.	Master.	Secretary.	Post-office.
Sonora	G. C. Soulsby	R. F. Williams	Sonora.

VENTURA COUNTY.

Name of Grange.	Master.	Secretary.	Post-office.
Ojai	C. E. Soule	J. Hobart	Nordhoff.
Pleasant Valley	W. P. Ramsener	W. O. Wood	Pleasant Valley.
San Pedro,	W. H. Vinyard	D. D. DeNure	Hueneme.
Saticoy	Milton Wasson	Miss A. Baker	Saticoy.
Sesipe	S. A. Guiberson	T. Marple	San Buenaventura
Ventura	J. Willett	C. Preble	San Buenaventura

YOLO COUNTY.

Name of Grange.	Master.	Secretary.	Post-office.
Antelope	W. J. Clark	T. F. Hughes	Antelope.
Buckeye	Wm. Sims	L. Moody	Buckeye.
Cache Creek	S. A. Howard	R. B. Butler.	Cache Creek.
Capay Valley	J. N. Rhodes	Howland Bower	Capay Valley
Davisville	J. C. Campbell	W. Hand	Davisville.
Hungry Hollow	T. A. Gallup	Mrs. Partz	Oat Valley.
West Grafton	A. W. Morris	G. W. Parks	Yolo.
Yolo	J. A. Hutton	D. Schindler	Woodland.

YUBA COUNTY.

Name of Grange.	Master.	Secretary.	Post-office.
Marysville	C. G. Bockius	Jas. M. Cutts	Marysville.

NEVADA SUBORDINATE GRANGES.

ALFALFA, Reno, G. W. Huffaker, M.; T. B. Kloher, S.

EAGLE VALLEY, Eagle Valley, G. W. Chedig, M.; O. A. F. Gilbert, S.

CARSON VALLEY, Genoa, R. J. Livingstone, M.; J. S. Child, S.

WASHOE VALLEY, Franktown, Elias Owens, M.; G. D. Winters, S.

WELLINGTON, Wellington, Esmeralda county, A. H. Hawley, M.; J. N. Mann, S.

MERRITT, Mason Valley, Esmeralda county, Kimber Cleaver, M.; Clark Cleaver, S.

PARADISE, Paradise Valley, B. F. Riley, M.; W. Perkins, S.

WINNEMUCCA, Winnemucca, Wm. B. Haskell, M.; Hez. Barns, S.

ELKO, Elko, Jos. A. Tinker, M.; Jos. L. Keyser, S.

LANEVILLE, Laneville Valley, Edwin Odell, M.; Henry M. Freeman, S.

HALLECK, Camp Halleck Station, J. S. Fenn, M.; Maurice Geary, S.

STAR VALLEY, Humboldt Wells, D. E. Johnston, M.; Chas. J. Whitney, S.

CLOVER VALLEY, Humboldt Wells, F. Honeyman, M.; W. B. Raymond, S.

The Grange Record:

CONTAINING A LIST OF CHARTER MEMBERS OF EACH GRANGE IN CALIFORNIA AND NEVADA.

CALIFORNIA.

PILOT HILL GRANGE, No. 1.

Pilot Hill, El Dorado County.

Organized August 10, 1870, by A. A. Bayley, General Deputy.

P. D. Brown, Master,
A. J. Bayley, Secretary,
J. W. Davis,
A. A. Bayley,
John Bishop,
James H. Rose,
John Marshall,
C. S. Rogers,
Thos. Owens,
J. P. Bayley,
S. S. Blue,
A. Martin,
Wm. Norvall,
J. R. Clow,
Silas Hayes,
J. S. Martin,
T. T. Lovejoy,
Wm. H. Matherley,
George B. Mudd,
Mrs. C. H. Jones,
Mrs. S. C. Owens,
Mrs. P. D. Brown,
Mrs. G. B. Mudd,
Mrs. U. J. Bayley,
Miss Jane Jones,
Miss Mary Jones,
Miss A. R. Lovejoy,
Miss M. R. Brown,
Miss J. E. Bayley.

NAPA GRANGE, No. 2.

Napa, Napa County.

Organized March 8, 1873, by W. H. Baxter, General Deputy.

W. A. Fisher, Master,
J. Walter Ward, Secretary,
W. H. Nash,
Daniel Gridley,
L. W. Evey,
James M. Thompson,
T. H. Thompson,
Wm. Fleming,
Levi Hardman,
Paris Kilbourn,
J. M. Mansfield,
C. A. Menefee,
J. L. Marshall,
W. W. Smith,
Jas. B. Saul,
D. Squib,
A. A. R. Witting,
Wm. H. Winter,
G. W. Henning,
Mrs. W. H. Nash,
Mrs. C. Plass,
Mrs. Blanchar,
Mrs. J. M. Mansfield,
James Hill.

WEST SAN JOAQUIN GRANGE, No. 3.

Ellis, San Joaquin County.

Organized April 14, 1873, by W. H. Baxter, Deputy.

E. B. Stiles, Master,
H. W. Fassett, Secretary,
A. P. Stocking,
L. Gish,
J. Carroll,
C. D. Needham,
J. Field,
C. E. Needham,
M. Lammers,
P. T. Gomer,
Mrs. P. T. Gomer,
Alex. Girvan,
Wm. B. Hay,
Ellen Hay,
Mary E. King,
Olive L. Needham,
Julia E. Fox,
Savilla L. Hatfield,
Mrs. Lammers,
J. Chrisman,
W. Haynes,
Charles B. Geddes,
Amelia R. Geddes,
Kate Girvan.

STANISLAUS GRANGE, No. 4.

MODESTO, STANISLAUS COUNTY.

Organized April 15, 1873, by W. H. Baxter, Deputy.

J. D. Spencer, Master,
Wm. S. McHenry, Sec'y,
T. D. Harp,
W. B. Wood,
J. R. Briggs,
Garrison Turner,
D. T. Curtis,
Miss Mary J. Webster,
Mrs. Luella Curtis,
Lizzie J. Turner,
F. S. Bentley,
C. J. Cressey,
John Murphy,
J. D. Hart,
A. M. McHenry,
F. H. Ross,
Mrs. F. H. Ross,
Mrs. S. Royes,
Stephen Royes,
James McHenry,
B. Drake,
G. B. Douglass.

VACAVILLE GRANGE, No. 5.

VACAVILLE, SOLANO COUNTY.

Organized April 18, 1873, by W. H. Baxter, Deputy.

T. Hart Hyatt, Master,
T. Hart Hyatt, Jr., Sec'y,
W. J. Dobbins,
George Kay Miller,
Mrs. M. R. Miller,
W. C. Harris,
Mrs. W. C. Harris,
Wm. Cantelow,
Mrs. Wm. Cantelow,
Joseph Longmire,
Leonice Longmire,
Wm. Butcher,
W. B. Dairs,
Mrs. Emeline Dairs,
Miss Lula Hyatt,
Mrs. E. A. Dobbins,
M. R. Miller,
Ozias Bingham,
Josephine W. Bingham,
A. C. Hawkins,
E. R. Thurber,
Geo. N. Weldon,
Stephen Hill,
Mrs. L. Decker,
Mrs. M. R. Decker.

CHICO GRANGE, No. 6.

CHICO, BUTTE COUNTY.

Organized April 30, 1873, by W. H. Baxter, Secretary.

Wm. M. Thorp, Master,
Jonathan Martin, Sec'y,
Edward Hallett,
George W. Colby,
Allen Henry,
George Van Wert,
J. F. Jaggerd,
Jos. Eddy,
Mahlon Grey,
Willard Bassett.
J. M. Ball,
J. W. Scott,
M. Barnes,
J. B. Swain, Jr.,
H. Bay,
Mrs. E. Hallett,
Mrs. G. W. Colby,
Mrs. A. Henry,
Mrs. G. Van Wert,
Mrs. W. M. Thorp,
Mrs. I. Eddy,
Mrs. C. Bowman,
Mrs. C. E. Elliott.
R. M. Turner,
C. Bowman,
C. E. Elliott,
Wm. Van Wert,
H. York.

MERCED GRANGE, No. 7.

MERCED CITY, MERCED COUNTY.

Organized May 3, 1873, by W. H. Baxter, Deputy.

H. B. Jolley, Master,
H. M. Hamilton, Sec'y,
W. E. Elliott,
W. H. Atkinson,
Thomas Upton,
N. S. Rogers,
James A. Kieth,
M. D. Atwater,
W. S. Fowler,
E. R. Elliott,
F. V. Harmon,
F. G. Poor,
William W. Grey,
Clara M. Upton
Louisa W. Jolley,
Jennie Rogers,
Francis J. Kieth,
Laura A. Atwater,
Fannie A. Fowler,
Edward Clark,
Catherine Clark,
John A. Perry,
Orsina M. Grey.

SALIDA GRANGE, No. 8.

MURPHY'S PRECINCT, MODESTO, STANISLAUS COUNTY.

Organized May 6, 1873, by W. H. Baxter, Deputy.

J. D. Reyburn, Master,
L. Dickey, Secretary,
Henry Miller,
A. J. Carver,
Wm. H. Chance,
M. Byrum,
George Sherman,
Wm. R. Scanberg,
Wm. Wilkinson,
Wm. Shoemaker,
J. W. McDonald,
D. W. Dickey,
C. E. McDonald,
Mrs. C. E. Miller,
M. E. Reyburn,
Mrs. Chance,
Mrs. M. Byrum,
G. Usher,
S. E. Scanberg,
Anabel Wilkinson,
Mrs. Louise Shoemaker,
Miss Cora McDonald,
Melinda Shannon,
John W. McCarthy.

SUISUN VALLEY GRANGE, No. 9.

SUISUN, SOLANO COUNTY.

Organized May 9, 1873, by W. H. Baxter, Deputy.

R. C. Haile, Master,
A. T. Hatch, Secretary,
Hattie Haile,
L. S. Storg,
J. B. Lemon,
S. M. Best,
J. S. Wood,
J. M. Gassin,
Peter Long,
James L. Miles,
Geo. C. McMullen,
R. E. McMullen,
L. Abernathie,
J. H. Beauman,
G. H. Pangburn,
Adeline Pangburn,
Joseph Blake,
Mary Hatch,
Adeline Pangburn,
Jennie Lemon,
Isabella Best,
Ella J. Wood,
Mrs. A. Gossin,
Sarah A. Long,
Sampson Smith,
Thomas M. Swan,
J. G. Edwards,
John C. Kirby,
H. C. Henderson,
Ellen Cannon,
R. Keams.

SAN JOSE GRANGE, No. 10.

SAN JOSE, SANTA CLARA COUNTY.

Organized May 13, 1873, by W. H. Baxter, Deputy.

Oliver Cottle, Master,
S. H. Herring, Secretary,
B. F. Watkins,
J. M. Battee,
Hiram Pomeroy,
Marshall Pomeroy,
J. W. Haskell,
M. W. Drinkwater
A. J. Fowler,
James McLellan,
L. F. Chipman,
S. F. Ayer,
H. C. Paine,
E. M. Settle,
C. A. Ladd,
H. S. McClay,
L. J. Watkins,
S. J. Watkins,
Harriett Pomroy,
James Singleton,
Charles G. Thomas,
Joseph R. Holland,
Edmund Ladd,
Caleb Cadwell,
D. Campbell,
C. T. Settle,
P. A. Singleton,
Stella Cottle,
Harriet R. Cadwell.

HOLLISTER GRANGE, No. 11.

HOLLISTER, SAN BENITO COUNTY.

Organized May 14, 1873, by W. H. Baxter, Deputy.

J. D. Fowler, Master,
S. F. Cowan, Secretary,
C. D. Fowler,
Wm. H. Oliver,
W. P. Phillips,
A. Sally,
Elizabeth Sally,
K. D. Pearce,
Mrs. M. C. Pearce,
Patrick Cullen,
T. L. Williams,
H. W. Cothren,
J. A. Evans,
C. S. Phillips,
F. B. Nast,
Mark Pomeroy,
C. W. Pomeroy,
P. L. Nash,
Mrs. A. W. Nash,
L. H. Cook,
L. I. Cook,
Job Malsbury,
Jesse Ross,
R. Rucklidge,
E. Haslan,
F. M. Ware,
M. E. Cowan,
S. F. Fowler.

SACRAMENTO GRANGE, No. 12.

SACRAMENTO, SACRAMENTO COUNTY.

Organized May 17, 1873, by W. H. Baxter, Secretary.

W. S. Manlove, Master,
Wm. M. Haynie, Sec'y,
Mrs. F. L. Manlove,
R. S. Sackett,
Amos Adams,
James Holland,
Edward F. Aiken,
Robert Williamson,
William Kendall,
A. P. Smith,
Theo. K. Stewart,
Mrs. A. M. Haynie,
I. N. Hoag,
Mrs. I. N. Hoag.
Maria L. Rich,
George S. Rich,
A. S. Greenlaw,
Mrs. A. S. Greenlaw,
Mary L. Aiken,
A. E. Holland.

YOLO GRANGE, No. 13.

WOODLAND, YOLO COUNTY.

Organized May 19, 1873, by W. H. Baxter, Deputy.

Wm. M. Jackson, Master,
D. Schindler, Secretary,
Catherine Jackson,
E, R. Jackson,
Kate Jackson,
Mary O. Schindler,
W. S. Flournoy,
C. A. Flournoy,
R. B. Blowers,
Mary Blowers,
C. Barney,
Mrs. M. Barney,
J. J. Dexter,
Mrs. H. W. Dexter,
D. P. Diggs,
Mrs. J. E. Diggs,
Robert Roberts,
D. A. Roberts,
H. Deaner,
T. P. Pond,
Miss M. J. Naison,
W. W. Harrison,
H. Deaner.

POINT OF TIMBER GRANGE, No. 14.

POINT OF TIMBER, CONTRA COSTA COUNTY.

Organized May 20, 1873, by W. H. Baxter, Deputy.

R. G. Dean, Master,
J. E. W. Carey, Secretary,
Mrs. R. G. Dean,
I. H. Baldwin,
Mrs. Mary H. Baldwin,
James B. Henderson,
Thomas McCabe,
H. C. Gallagher,
A. Richardson,
C. H. Carey,
Delia Carey,
Minnie J. Carey
Mark A. Walton,
P. A. Henderson,
A. Plumley.

ELMIRA GRANGE, No. 15.

ELMIRA, VACA STATION, SOLANO COUNTY.

Organized May 27, 1873, by T. H. Hyatt, Deputy.

J. A. Clark, Master,
M. D. Cooper, Secretary,
Mrs. Annette Clark,
G. W. Frazer,
Mrs. A. E. Frazer,
D. C. Glen,
Mrs. Mary Glen,
James Wells,
Mrs. A. Wells,
Kenneth McPherson,
Mrs. J. B. McPherson,
S. T. Hoyt,
Mrs. Mary Hoyt,
M. L. Williams,
T. G. Frost,
S. Rippy,
Mrs. L. E. Rippy,
Mrs. L. E. Cooper,
C. C. Turner,
Jackson Turner,
R. W. Frost,
G. M. Gates,
Mrs. Sarah Gates,
W. H. Black,
J. B. Mefford,
F. M. Gates,
George Ranschart,
J. C. Suggs,
W. C. Swart,
Miss Mary Finley.

BENNETT VALLEY GRANGE, No. 16.

BENNETT VALLEY, SANTA ROSA, SONOMA COUNTY.

Organized May 27, 1873, by W. H. Baxter, Deputy.

Nelson Carr, Master,
J. H. Plank, Secretary,
Mrs. H. L. Carr,
Isaac De Turk,
B. Lacque,
Sarah A. Lacque,
Anna M. Lacque,
Aaron Lacque,
G. Lyman,
Mrs. C. Lyman,
Holeman Talbot,
Mrs. H. Talbot,
E. Peterson,
Susanna R. Plank,
John Burnham,
A. Burnham,
Joseph C. Burnham,
Mrs. A. Burnham,
G. W. Wilks,
Lovanda Wilks,
Walter Phillips,
Rettie Phillips,
George N. Whitaker,
Elmira E. Whitaker,
Daniel E. Miller.

SANTA ROSA GRANGE, No. 17.

SANTA ROSA, SONOMA COUNTY.

Organized May 28, 1873, by W. H. Baxter, Deputy.

G. W. Davis, Master,
J. A. O'Brien, Secretary,
Ellen R. Davis,
A. T. Coulter,
Rachel M. Coulter,
John Adams,
H. D. R. Adams,
H. P. Holmes,
Rebecca Holmes,
Willen W. Gauldin,
Richard Fulkerson,
Sallie Fulkerson,
Theodore Staley,
Crawford P. League,
O. J. Speenhoff,
R. A. Thompson,
S. C. Gauldin,

HEALDSBURG GRANGE, No. 18.

HEALDSBURG, SONOMA COUNTY.

Organized May 29, 1873, by W. H. Baxter, Deputy.

Thomas H. Merry, Master,
L. M. Holt, Secretary,
Mrs. T. H. Merry,
A. J. Spoon,
L. Alexander,
Ira Proctor,
Charles Alexander.
I. N. Stapp,
Alice Alexander,
William S. Moss,
A. Wagenseller,
Robert Finley,
D. Lamb,
R. Foster,
I. Le Leymance,
A. Bonton,
Elon Catlin,
Philip S. Peck,
H. C. Spencer,
Sarah A. Peck,
Rachel S. Spencer,
Nettie Tribbs,
Mary Dow,
Charles Alexander,
I. G. Dow,
H. Hammeken.

DIXON GRANGE, No. 19.

DIXON, SOLANO COUNTY.

Organized June 3, 1873, by W. H. Baxter, Deputy.

J. C. Merryfield, Master,
James A. Ellis, Secretary,
Susannah Merryfield,
J. S. Garnett,
Margaret Garnett,
Jos. Kline,
Jane Kline,
J. G. McMahon,
L. McMahon,
H. E. McCune,
B. S. McCune,
Jas. O. Johnson,
Thos. E. Kelley,
Mrs. E. Kelley,
A. McPherson,
S. McBride,
J. L. Read,
Henrietta E. Ellis,
J. M. Dudley,
Mrs. Dudley,
John Love,
Ellen Love,
Wm. Steel,
Abbie Steel,
F. E. Russell,
Mrs. F. Russell,
Florence Johnson,
Andrew Marshall,
Mrs. Marshall,
Mrs. McPherson,
Mrs. McBride,
B. R. Newell,
S. Radcliffe.

GUENOC GRANGE, No. 20.

GUENOC, LAKE COUNTY (removed to Middleton, Lake County).

Organized June 5, 1873, by W. H. Baxter, Deputy.

J. M. Hamilton, Master,
A. A. Ritchie, Secretary,
J. P. Brandt,
W. R. Matthews,
W. R. Coburn,
Mrs. C. Coburn,
A. H. Cheeney,
Mrs. A. H. Cheeney,
J. B. Greenfield,
Wm. C. Greenfield,
H. A. Oliver,
W. Matthews,
D. M. Copsey,
J. S. Capps,
W. G. Cannon,
Mrs. L. S. Cannon,
J. C. Murphy,
Mrs. J. A. Murphy,
John Good,
R. L. Hicks,
Jas. N. Hamilton,
S. A. Copsey,
Mrs. Copsey,
J. W. Brown,
Mrs. Brown.

YOUNTVILLE GRANGE, No. 21.

YOUNTVILLE, NAPA COUNTY.

Organized June 7, 1873, by W. H. Baxter, Deputy.

J. M. Mayfield, Master,
F. B. Hopper, Secretary,
Charles Hopper,
A. M. Crow,
Mrs. Crow.
J. Falkenstin,
L. Falkenstin,
H. H. Harris,
Mrs. L. Harris,
Mary E. Hopper,
William T. Bradley,
Mary C. Bradley,
J. W. Johnston,
A. M. Johnston,
Rosalie Mayfield.

GRAND ISLAND GRANGE, No. 22.

SYCAMORE (Grand Island), COLUSA COUNTY.

Organized June 10, 1873, by W. H. Baxter, Deputy.

J. J. Hickoc, Master,
J. C. Wilkins, Secretary,
William Ogden,
P. A. Earp,
W. S. Green,
J. O. Zumwalt,
Wm. Ash,
Howell Davis,
Mrs. S. Davis,
Mrs. Jane Horover,
Thomas Phillips,
Frank Boardman,
John Oman,
John Welch,
Isaac Howell,
Ed. Howell,
Jacob Myers,
C. Kopf,
R. S. Browning,
Moses Stinchfield,
Mrs. M. Stinchfield,
Mrs. M. V. Welsh,
Thomas Eddy,
Emma Ogden,
W. H. Pollard,
Oulda Pollard,
Wm. McClure,
James Hearen,
Gideon Giles,
M. E. Earp.

PETALUMA GRANGE, No. 23.

PETALUMA, SONOMA COUNTY.

Organized June 14, 1873, by W. H. Baxter, Deputy.

L. W. Walker, Master,
Daniel G. Heald, Secretary,
G. O. Green,
Alfred Symonds,
D. S. Sutton,
Hannah Sutton,
Nelson Wiswell,
Rosie C. Wiswell,
Wm. Comstock,
James W. Todd,
Louisa Skillman,
Theodore Skillman,
Elizabeth Heald,
John Neal,
H. Gibbs,
John Powell.

SALINAS GRANGE, No. 24.

SALINAS CITY, MONTEREY COUNTY.

Organized June 17, 1873, by W. H. Baxter, Deputy.

N. L. Allen, Master,
Samuel Cassidy, Secretary,
C. S. Abbott,
W. S. Stephens,
James R. Hebbron,
J. W. Trigh,
H. S. Bull,
Mrs. Kate Bull,
Ira Tucker,
Jeason Parson,
M. Hartnell,
H. Whisman,
I. G. Baxter,
J. C. Storm,
Mrs. C. L. Allen,
Miss Clara Abbott,
Ida C. Hebbron,
William Ford,
J. H. Campbell,
William Quentell,
C. Laird,
Mrs. H. Laird,
George Abbott,
Wm. F. Ramsey,
Annie Whisman.

CAMBRIA GRANGE, No. 25.

CAMBRIA, SAN LUIS OBISPO COUNTY.

Organized June 19, 1873, by W. H. Baxter, Deputy.

Rufus Rigdon, Master,
C. H. Ivins, Secretary,
L. Utley,
B. B. Tripp,
Alex Cook,
N. Steward,
J. D. Campbell,
E. A. Everett,
F. W. Utley,
J. Scott,
Mary Scott,
J. C. Mc Ferson,
G. Van Gorden,
Mrs. A. Van Gorden,
M: C. Morris,
M. B. Martin,
Mrs. M. E. Ivins,
Mrs. E. M. Utley,
Mrs. G. M. Blunt,
Mrs. A. Everett,
A. C. Buffington,
Wm. Cooper,
J. L. Leffingwell,
James M. Woods,
O. P. McFadden,
Mrs. V. J. McFadden,
Wm. Skinner,
G. W. Proctor,
Ira Van Gorden.

OLD CREEK GRANGE, No. 26.

OLD CREEK, SAN LUIS OBISPO COUNTY.

Organized June 20, 1873, by W. H. Baxter, Deputy.

Isaac Flood, Master,
Richard M. Preston, Sec'y,
Augus M. Hardie,
Nathaniel Nickolls,
Robert C. Swain,
Charles S. Clark,
Travis Phillips,
Samuel Kingery,
L. H. Draper,
Alexander Fraser,
John Greening,
James L. Kester,
Elizabeth Flood,
Mary V. Nuckolls,
Martha F. Phillips,
Jane S. Kingery,
Lula H. Preston,
Ruth A. Kester,
Mary J. Clark,
Sarah A. Nickolls,
Agnes Hardie,
Mary Jane Draper,
M. A. Greening.

MORO GRANGE, No. 27.

MORO, SAN LUIS OBISPO COUNTY.

Organized June 21, 1873, by W. H. Baxter, Secretary.

J. Mothersead, Master,
H. Y. Stanley, Secretary,
G. S. Alford,
Franklin Riley,
J. R. Cock,
T. J. Stephens,
G. F. Austin,
William Langlois,
D. H. Whitney,
G. C. Cock,
C. V. Shanver,
S. C. Stephens,
S. J. Cock,
F. W. Parker,
Mrs. H. G. Riley,
Mrs. C. A. Cock,
Miss Annie Cock,
Miss Lizzie Riley,
S. Langlois,
James Allen,
D. Taylor,
Mary Riley,
M. E. Austin,
A. O. Yates.

SAN LUIS OBISPO GRANGE, No. 28.

SAN LUIS OBISPO, SAN LUIS OBISPO COUNTY.

Organized June 23, 1873, by W. H. Baxter, Secretary.

William Jackson, Master,
G. W. Smith, Secretary,
G. W. Hampton,
D. M. Johnson,
Charles H. Johnson,
Samuel Cook,
E. Leff,
A. T. Brians,
E. L. Reed,
Joseph See,
J. W. Slack,
J. B. Hazen,
W. A. Dunbar,
Ira Johnson,
Sarah M. Johnson,
E. A. Johnson,
Nancy E. Barnett,
Mary M. Freeborn,
Mary C. Jackson,
Marie Leff,
May A. Johnson,
Elizabeth See,
J. L. Hazen,
H. I. Smith,
M. J. Reed,
Theresa Leff.

TURLOCK GRANGE, No. 29.

TURLOCK, STANISLAUS COUNTY.

Organized July 1st, 1873, by W. H. Baxter, Deputy.

J. W. A. Wright, Master,
J. A. Henderson, Secretary,
B. H. Dean,
M. J. Hall,
S. H. Crane,
John Warner,
A. S. Fulkerth,
E. Warner,
William Fulkerth,
Charles T. Campbell,
John Fox,
Edward McCabe,
Pleasant Henderson,
M. C. Monroe,
W. F. Huddleston,
James Kehoe,
Michael Kerrigan,
Mrs. J. Warner,
Mrs. A. S. Fulkerth,
Mrs. S. H. Crane,
Mrs. C. T. Campbell,
Mrs. M. J. Hall,
Mrs. W. Fulkerth,
Mrs. C. T. Campbell
Mrs. E. S. Russell,
Mrs. S. H. Jefferds,
Miss Ora Warner,
Miss Lilla Deane,
Richard Brown,
E. S. Russell,
S. H. Jefferds.

ST. HELENA GRANGE, No. 30.

St. Helena, Napa County.

Organized June 24th, 1873, by N. W. Garretson, Deputy.

G. B. Crane, Master,
J. L. Edwards, Secretary,
R. M. Chamberlin,
R. A. Haskin,
William Denning,
I. G. Norton,
A. Clock,
John York,
Guerdon Backus,
M. Vaun,
J. G. Sayward,
Charles Wheeler,
H. M. Allen,
D. O. Hunt,
David Edwards,
D. K. Rule,
F. K. Rule,
David Cole,
H. J. Allison,
H. A. Pellet,
Richard Garnett,
Mrs. R. M. Chamberlin,
Mrs. A. Clock,
Mrs. F. J. Crane,
Mrs. H. M. Allen,
Mrs. G. Backus,
Miss Carrie Backus,
Miss Louisa Allison,
Miss Kate V. Edwards,
Mrs. C. Wheeler,
Mrs. D. K. Rule.

GREYSON GRANGE, No. 31.

Greyson, Stanislaus County.

Organized June 6, 1873, by W. H. Baxter, Deputy.

I. G. Gardner, Master,
Geo. H. Copeland, Sec'y,
R. B. Smith,
N. D. Phelps,
J. W. Beuschoter,
R. Garner,
L. Funck,
J. H. Terry,
M. Frydendall,
L. L. Brown,
W. Love,
L. A. Richards,
A. Bronson,
Mrs. Julia Richards,
Miss Jennie Phelps,
Mrs. Sarah M. Gardner,
Mrs. E. T. Phelps.

PESCADERO GRANGE, No. 32.

Pescadero, San Mateo County.

Organized July 1, 1873, by N. W. Garretson, Deputy.

B. V. Weeks, Master,
H. B. Sprague, Secretary,
F. S. Morehead,
I. H. Osgood,
R. Knowles,
N. M. Brown,
J. S. Read,
L. Chandler,
S. Armes,
E. D. Moore,
R. W. Fogg,
Mrs. H. E. Reed,
Mrs. S. R. Corey,
Mrs. E. B. Moore,
Mrs. Olivia Morehead,
N. Corey,
J. B. Holinshead,
M. D. Hopkins,
J. Wilson,
J. Beeding.

WINDSOR GRANGE, No. 33.

Windsor, Sonoma County.

Organized July 8, 1873.

A. B. Nally, Master,
J. H. McClelland, Sec'y,
H. L. Runyon,
S. V. R. Klink,
Ben Clark,
H. I. Poole,
Edgar Lindsey,
I. W. Bailache,
E. H. Barnes.
R. A. Petray,
H. Marden,
E. Tants,
I. W. Calhoun,
M. T. Wallace,
Henry Bell,
Mrs. Martha Wallace,
Charles Clark,
Elinor L. Lindsey,
Mary M. Clark,
S. M. Calhoun,
Mrs. N. A. Kenneday,
Martha A. Clark,
Mrs. M. E. Pool,
George A. Morgan,
John M. Laughlin,
G. H. Kennedy,
William Brooks,
Mrs. Mary Barnes,
Mrs. S. B. Klink,
I. H. Loughlin.

BODEGA GRANGE, No. 34.

Bodega, Sonoma County.

Organized July 9, 1873, by W. H. Baxter, Deputy.

John H. Hegeler, Master,
W. Smith, Secretary,
A. S. Perrine,
E. H. Cheney,
Christian Warnekey,
D. J. Cunningham,
James Kee,
James Watson,
Henry Ross,
Mrs. J. H. Hegeler,
Mrs. A. S. Perrine,
Mrs. E. H. Cheney,
Mrs. Theresa Warnekey.

TEMESCAL GRANGE, No. 35.

OAKLAND TOWNSHIP, ALAMEDA COUNTY.

Organized July 10, 1873, by N. W. Garretson, Deputy.

A. T. Dewey, Master,
C. H. Dwinelle, Secretary,
Christian Bagge,
J. B. Woolsey,
John Kelsey,
J. V. Webster,
Charles Bagge,
Ezra S. Carr,
E. D. Harmon,
A. B. Dixon,
N. B. Byrne,
W. Applegarth,
H. G. Babcock,
John S. Collins,
Emily Bagge,
Mrs. A. T. Dewey,
Miss Elnora Bagge,
Mrs. Jeanne C. Carr,
Mrs. S. E. Dixon,
Mrs. Nellie G. Babcock,
P. H. Cordez,
W. B. Ewer.

LOS ANGELES GRANGE, No. 36.

LOS ANGELES, LOS ANGELES COUNTY.

Organized August 2, 1873, by W. H. Baxter, Deputy.

Thos. A. Garey, Master,
H. S. Parcels, Secretary,
J. Q. A. Stanley,
Milton Thomas,
T. D. Hancock,
J. M. Stewart,
R. M. Town,
J. H. Brewer,
C. E. White,
R. M. McCreary,
J. W. Potts,
A. N. Hamilton,
C. H. Hass,
Mrs. S. Hass,
Mrs. M. J. Stanley,
Mrs. E. C. Potts,
Mrs. E. E. Thomas,
Mrs. J. Hamilton,
Mrs. M. McCreary,
Mrs. M. M. Brewer.

COMPTON GRANGE, No. 37.

COMPTON, LOS ANGELES COUNTY.

Organized August 4, 1873, by W. H. Baxter, Deputy.

A. Higbie, Master,
J. A. Walker, Secretary,
J. E. McComas,
H. Burlingame,
H. H. Morton,
J. G. Hathorne,
Robert Orr,
G. D. Compton,
Emily Compton,
Timothy V. Kimball,
Sarah E. Burlingame,
Eda Kimball,
W. G. Goss,
Lilly T. Brower,
A. E. Putney,
Ada C. Steele,
C. W. Coltrin,
Amanda Walker,
Lizzie McComas,
J. J. Martin,
C. Martin,
Lewis A. Carey,
A. M. Peck,
F. W. Steele,
C. W, Turss,
Martha Coltrin,
C. B. Wright,
John Angelo,
Rebecca Angelo.

ENTERPRISE GRANGE, No. 38.

LA DOW, LOS ANGELES COUNTY.

Organized August 5, 1873, by W. H. Baxter, Deputy.

Y. C. Alexander, Master,
W. T. Henderson, Sec'y,
J. A. Nichols,
M. J. Golden,
A. M. Southworth,
R. K. McGue,
S. W. La Dow,
M. M. Green,
E. S. Butterworth,
C. M. Jenkins,
B. F. Shirley,
Mrs. William Dryden,
Mrs. S. I. Green,
Mrs. S. W. La Dow,
Mrs. Susan Brown,
Miss Fanny Dye,
Wm. Dryden,
J. H Snyder,
Milton Krytzler,
David Foster,
C. P. Switzer,
J. F. Lewis,
Henry Vogt,
John Erick,
J. B. Middleton,
Mrs. J. A. Nichols,
Mrs. M. A. Alexander,
Mrs. E. S. Buttersworth,
Miss M. E. Hall,
Miss Fanny Juden.

FAIRVIEW GRANGE, No. 39.

FAIRVIEW, LOS ANGELES COUNTY.

Organized August 6, 1873, by W. H. Baxter, Deputy.

Edward Evey, Master,
J. D. Taylor, Secretary,
J. J. Hill,
B. F. E. Kellogg,
Andrew Bittner,
D. W. C. Cowan,
John Gwin,
H. C. Kellogg,
Mrs. R. A. Evey,
Mrs. Mary O. Kellogg,
Miss Mary E. Kellogg,
Mrs. Marian Clark,
Miss Mary E. Austin,
Mrs. Gertrude Gwin,
Mrs. E. A. Gridley,
Byron Clark,
B. Snodgrass,
F. A. Gates,
G. A. Greely,
Rev. C. Gridley,
Wm. H. Hill,
Wm. M. Richter,
Thos. Boswell,
Wm. Neabeck,
Alex Henry,
Erastus Johnson,
Miss M. J. Boswell,
Miss Jeckie Snodgrass.

ORANGE GRANGE, No. 40.

RICHLAND, LOS ANGELES COUNTY.

Organized August 7, 1873, by W. H. Baxter, Deputy.

Thomas Brown, Master,
J. W. Anderson, Secretary,
Patterson Bowens,
C. M. Marshall,
S. N. Falkington,
J. H. Gregg,
Stephen McPherson,
Silas Yearnal,
Mrs. C. M. Hickox,
Mrs. A. Davenport,
Mrs. C. Marshall,
A. A. Falkington,
A. Hickox,
J. P. Shaffer,
E. W. Squires,
W. G. McPherson,
Joseph Beach,
Mrs. S. V. Gregg,
Mrs. Sarah M. Anderson.

SILVER GRANGE, No. 41,

LOS NIETOS (TOWN OF GALATIN), LOS ANGELES COUNTY.

Organized August 8, 1873, by W. H. Baxter, Deputy.

I. H. Burke, Master,
E. R. Wylie, Secretary,
R. H. Mayes,
Mrs. R. H. Mayes,
W. H. Pendleton, Sr.,
F. M. Matthew,
S. E. Matthew,
I. W. Doster,
S. S. Thompson,
Mrs. M. Thompson,
E. R. Wylie,
W. W. Standifer,
I. T. Carney,
J. W. Venable,
Jno. C. Ardis,
Wm. Wylie,
Hugh Forsman,
Elizabeth Forsman,
H. L. Montgomery,
M. B. Montgomery,
L. L. Bequette,
Mrs. M. A. Bequette,
A. Short,
Sarah A. Short,
D. W. Tuttle,
T. D. Cheney,
G. W. Pallett,
W. P. McDonald,
I. H. Burke,
Mary Burke,
M. B. Crawford,
A. C. Crawford,
S. G. Reynolds,
Dora Burnett.

NEW RIVER, No. 42.

NEW RIVER, LOS ANGLES COUNTY.

Organized August 9, 1873, by W. H. Baxter, Deputy.

R. B. Guthrie, Master,
D. S. Wardlaw, Secretary,
A. L. Sutton,
W. Newton,
I. S. Elliott,
T. J. Kerns,
D. M. Harlow,
C. J. Meek,
G. H. Sproul,
H. Schlesselman,
M. G. Settle,
S. G. Baker,
E. J. Elliott,
M. F. Harlow,
A. A. Sutton,
R. J. Meek,
I. W. Settle,
L. Wardlaw,
S. T. Corum,
D. B. Goodwin,
S. Holgate,
J. A. Montgomery,
S. T. Moore,
T. D. Sackett,
W. A. Sackett,
M. J. McGaugh,
Mrs. C. Newton,
Julia Holgate,
Susan A. Corwin,
S. A. Goodwin,
N. A. Guthrie.

EL MONTE GRANGE, No. 43.

LEXINGTON TOWNSHIP, EL MONTE, LOS ANGELES COUNTY.

Organized August 11, 1873, by W. H. Baxter, Deputy.

Geo. C. Gibbs, Master,
J. H. Grey, Secretary,
Josiah M. Grey,
Geo. H. Peck,
Mrs. G. H. Peck,
John T. Gordon,
A. J. Howard,
H. A. Messenger,
R. J. Floyd,
George H. Clark,
Sarah F. Clark,
M. F. Quin,
L. J. Hix,
Mrs. L. Hix,
L. S. Barnyard,
F. W. Gibson,
Wm. H. Winston,
W. S. Arnold,
Stephen Penfold,
Albert Gibbs,
L. Muth Rathmussen,
Peter Penfold,
E. A. Floyd,
Mrs. G. C. Gibbs,
Asa Ellis,
Mrs. A. Ellis,
E. Stallcup,
I. Avis,
Mrs. I. Avis.

LOS NIETOS GRANGE, No. 44.

OLD LOS NIETOS, LOS ANGELES COUNTY.

Organized August 12, 1873, by W. H. Baxter, Deputy.

E. B. Grandon, Master,
John F. Marquis, Sec'y,
J. E. Fulton,
W. S. Reavis,
J. W. Cate,
D. Y. Sorensen,
Jno. Condra,
M. B. Condit,
Thomas Harvey,
S. H. Butterfield,
James Stewart,
Mrs. J. F. Marquis,
Mrs. J. W. Cate,
Mrs. Villa Marquis,
Mrs. J. Mitts,
A. J. Hudson,
Daniel Standler,
E. Stockton,
J. Mitts,
Elan Martin,
Thomas Isbell,
W. H. Russell,
Mrs. M. B. Condit,
Mrs. S. E. Reavis,
Mrs. M. M. Fulton,
Mrs. E. Stockton,
Mrs. Louisa Isbell,
Mrs. Melissa Stockton,
R. S. Stroud,
I. W. Perkins.

SEBASTOPOL GRANGE, No. 45.

SEBASTOPOL, SONOMA COUNTY.

Organized August 15, 1873, by George W. Davis, Deputy.

J. M. Hudspeth, Master,
Joseph Purrington, Sec'y,
John Walker,
W. W. Petross,
James Grigson,
A. J. Peterson,
J. Marshal,
L. Ross,
John Gallagher,
A. Barnes,
William Bones,
Mrs. Elinor Walker,
Mrs. E. P. Berry,
Mrs. E. A. Hicks,
Mrs. Sidney Ross,
Mrs. Hattie Lappum,
H. E. Manifer,
B. B. Berry,
P. McChristian,
M. C. Hicks,
J. W. Sullivan,
Owen McChristian,
L. Harbine,
George A. Fruits,
H. Lappum,
Mrs. H. A. Petross,
Mrs. Eliza Grigson,
Mrs. Mary Sullivan,
Mrs. Eliza Harbine,
Mrs. Frances Purrington.

FRESHWATER GRANGE, No. 46.

FRESHWATER, COLUSA COUNTY.

Organized August 9, 1873, by J. J. Hicok, Deputy.

I. H. Durham, Master,
R. A. Wilsey, Secretary,
J. P. Rathbun,
J. C. White,
W. C. White,
W. A. Dunham,
Mrs. E. Graham,
Mrs. E. J. Dunham,
Mrs. R. A. Wilsey,
P. S. Pardue,
F. D. Graham,
M. J. Britton,
Mrs. M. Rathbourn,
L. H. Baker,
I. H. Dunham,
Mrs. B. C. Dunham,
James Catlin,
Mrs. Sarah Catlin,
William F. Lamburth,
Henry Marshall,
William Fulton,
William Bell,
Miss M. Marshall,
William Marshall.

WILLOWS GRANGE, No. 47.

MONROE, COLUSA COUNTY.

Organized August 11, 1873, by J. J. Hicok, Deputy.

J. W. Zumwalt, Master,
G. S. Hicklin, Secretary,
S. C. Longmire,
H. P. Grey,
Joseph Zumwalt,
W. G. Kung,
C. R. Summers,
I. H. Armfield,
P. H. Scott,
F. M. Luts,
F. McIntyre,
A. T. Stubblefield,
M. A. Zumwalt,
A. M. Stone,
Mrs. Amanda Armfield,
I. M. Clark,
C. K. West,
A. E. Duncan,
J. D. Mecum,
Benjamin Lee,
Charles Strong,
W. B. Small,
J. A. Towle,
Emily West,
Sarah I. Scott,
Adeline Longmire,
Mary Zumwalt,
Barbara E. Duncan.

COLUSA GRANGE, No. 48.

COLUSA, COLUSA COUNTY,

Organized August 15, 1873, by J. J. Hicok, Secretary.

I. F. Wilkins, Master,
E. B. Bainbridge, Sec'y,
Waller Colmes,
John P. Bainbridge,
Stephen Cooper,
Sarshel Cooper,
T. S. Coleman,
I. R. Wiert,
H. N. Yates,
J. S. Scoggins,
John K. Rowland,
Mrs. L. Kilgore,
Mrs. J. F. Wilkins,
Mrs. E. B. Bainbridge,
Peter Dolan,
I. R. Fryer,
I. M. Culp,
Logan Kilgore,
L. T. Stormer,
I. W. Walsh,
R. Jones,
John Cheney,
Mrs. J. P. Bainbridge,
Miss Mattie Stormer,
Mrs. J. G. Stormer,
I. F. Wilkins.

SATICOY GRANGE, No. 49.

SATICOY, VENTURA COUNTY.

Organized August 16, 1873, by W. H. Baxter, Deputy.

Milton Wasson, Master,
E. A. Duval, Secretary,
Joseph B. Kelsey,
E. B. Higgins,
Joseph Alderman,
Abner Haines,
Chas. O. Hara,
Mrs. M. A. Ellsworth.
Joseph L. Alderman,
Mrs. Maria A. Wasson,
Olney Whitesides,
Theo. A. Kelsey,
Jno. F. Cummins,
Mrs. E. A. Duval,
Daniel Ellsworth,
G. W. Crissman,
Wm. Evans,
Mahlon Thome,
Miss Mary E. Wasson,
Miss Helen D. Evans,
Mrs. M. E. Kelsey,
Mrs. E. C. Alderman,
J. K. Gries.

SANTA BARBARA GRANGE, No, 50.

SANTA BARBARA, SANTA BARBARA COUNTY.

Organized August 19, 1873, by W. H. Baxter, Deputy.

O. L. Abbott, Master,
Robert W. Smith, Sec'y,
J. C. Hamer,
J. A. Johnson,
W. E. Foster,
D. C. Mayfield,
M. H. Lane,
Joseph Pierson,
Elizabeth Pierson,
Sarah E. A. Higgins,
W. F. Russell,
Josephine Harton,
James M. Short,
M. Hickok,
T. H. B. Rosenberg,
Louisa Abbott,
Julia A. Foster,
Mary F. Hamer,
Jane Rosenberg,
C. Kenny,
Elvira Kenny,
Ada J. Eaton,
Virginia F. Russell,
Jesse Handford,
George Williams.

CARPENTERIA GRANGE, No. 51.

CARPENTERIA, SANTA BARBARA COUNTY.

Organized August 20, 1873, by W. H. Baxter, Deputy.

O. N. Cadwell, Master,
T. E. Thurmand, Sec'y,
James A. Blood,
Mrs. C. L. Blood,
Albert Doty,
Lucetta Doty,
Robert McAllister,
Dan Turner,
Frank Hartshorne,
G. E. Thurmand,
E. W. Thurmand,
J. L. Crane,
Jennette Crane,
John Pettigrew,
W. S. Callis,
W. J. Bradford,
James Ward,
Theo. Woods,
Clara Woods,
J. B. Wall,
E. H. Pierce,
M. A. Pierce,
John Walker,
Juliette Walker,
Emilia Walker,
H. D. Woods,
L. L. Woods,
T. A. Cravens,
Ben. Morris,
Jno. A. Walker,
M. E. Pettinger,
John Cross.

SANTA MARIA GRANGE, No. 52.

SANTA MARIA, (SUEZ,) SANTA BARBARA COUNTY.

Organized August 22, 1873, by W. H. Baxter, Secretary.

Joel Miller, Master,
M. D. Miller, Secretary,
J. Wheeler,
Mary D. Wheeler,
Sarah A. Wheeler,
Jeannette F. Wheeler
Speer McElhany,
Joel Miller,
John J. Prell,
Eliza Prell,
J. B. Linebaugh,
Susan M. Stowell,
Mary E. Stephens,
Henry Stowell,
Maurice Flynn,
R. D. Cook,
B. T. Wiley,
W. T. Morris,
J. M. McElhany,
Isaac Miller,
Annie Miller,
Maggie C. McElhany,
J. H. Harris,
Elizabeth Harris,
H. S. Sibley,
Charlotte Miller,
S. E. Linebaugh,
Milton D. Miller,
M. H. Stephens,
M. P. Nicholson,
L. L. Nicholson.

PLAZA GRANGE, No. 53.

MONROE (OLIMPO), COLUSA COUNTY.

Organized August 23, 1873, by J. J. Hicok, Deputy.

F. C. Graves, Master,
Wright F. Green, Sec'y,
M. Kendrick,
I. N. Mecum,
J. W. Williams,
M. R. Booth,
M. E. Pordyke,
A. J. Harris,
F. J. Kirkpatrick,
F. C. Graves,
Thomas E. Brown,
Norton Farnsworth,
Mrs. L. A. Fields,
Mrs. Nancy Carpenter,
Mrs. M. Kirkpatrick,
Mrs. E. Booth,
Miss Nellie Ashurst,
R. P. Gosén,
W. H. Carpenter,
Edmund Fields,
John Rice,
W. Norton,
R. Creed,
James A. Poague,
J. C. White,
R. D. Jones,
Mrs. Susan Harris,
Mrs. A. C. Kendrick,
Mrs. E. J. Brown,
Mrs. A. E. Williams,
Mrs. L. J. Graves.

CASTORIA GRANGE, No. 54.

CASTORIA (ELLIS), SAN JOAQUIN COUNTY.

Organized August 25, 1873, by Edwin B. Stiles, Deputy.

Sewall Gower, Master,
John H. Strahan, Secretary,
H. W. Cowell,
F. J. Woodward,
J. M. Barber,
I. H. Wolfe,
Joshua Cowell,
E. Benson,
F. A. Graves,
J. W. Seaver,
N. J. Sharp,
James Carter,
G. I. Chalmers,
Mrs. Chalmers,
S. A. Leavy,
Mrs. M. Martin,
Mrs. Loraine Cowell,
Mrs. Vinette Cowell,
Mrs. Medora Carter,
Mrs. M. A. Strahan
H. M. Ellis,
George W. Smith,
Mrs. Smith,
A. W. Brush,
Mrs. Brush,
Mrs. Gower,
Mrs. Leavy.

SONOMA GRANGE, No. 55.

SONOMA, SONOMA COUNTY.

Organized August 26, 1873, by G. W. Davis, Deputy.

Leonard Goss, Master,
Alfred V. Lammot, Sec'y,
William McPherson Hill,
A. S. Edwards,
A. F. Haraszthy,
David Burris,
William Burris,
Obed Chart,
W. A. Berry,
O. B. Shaw,
S. T. Craig,
O. W. Craig,
J. R. Snyder,
D. C. Young,
H. Appleton,
Maria E. Young,
Anna M. Harding,
Phebe Chart.

LINDEN GRANGE, No. 56.

LINDEN, SAN JOAQUIN COUNTY.

Organized August 28, 1873, by Edwin B. Stiles, Deputy.

John Wasley, Master,
James Wasley, Secretary,
David Lewis,
Mrs. M. A. Lewis,
John Patterson,
Mrs. E. Patterson,
J. W. Hill,
Mrs. Jane Hill,
A. S. Drais,
R. Latham,
Mrs. Jane Latham,
L. A. Morse,
Mrs. H. A. Morse,
E. B. Cogswell,
William F. Prather,
Thomas Wall,
N. E. Alling,
William Snow,
Mrs. J. Snow,
Mrs. C. Wasley,
S. H. Boardman,
Samuel Titus,
Mrs. Helen Titus,
P. Fitzgerald,
John Archers,
William H. Russell,
Mrs. J. Russell,
James Duncan,
George Klinger.

WATERFORD GRANGE, No. 57.

WATERFORD (HORR'S RANCH), STANISLAUS COUNTY.

Organized August 25, 1873, by J. W. A, Wright, Deputy.

R. R. Warder. Master,
W. C. Collins, Secretary,
Thomas Johnson,
S. M. Gallup,
James Kincaid,
R. H. Bentley,
L. C. Davis,
W. W. Baker,
W. C. Collins,
I. H. Finney,
W. P. Crow,
Wm. Fitzhue,
John Wooters,
J. W. Sheldon,
J. B. Booth,
Mrs. L. J. Pinkston,
Mrs. Jas. Kincaid,
Mrs. S. M. Gallup,
Mrs. W. C. Collins,
Miss L. A. Collins,
Mrs. L. C. Davis,
H. B. Davis,
L. H. Pinkston,
I. H. Barham,
W. J. Warder,
Wells Reynolds,
M. R. Harbert,
Mrs. I. H. Finney,
Mrs. J. Johnson,
Mrs. R. H. Bentley,
Mrs. J. H. Barham.

UNION GRANGE, No. 58.

UNION TOWNSHIP (PRINCETON), COLUSA COUNTY.

Organized August 13, 1873, by J. J. Hicok, Deputy.

W. Davis, Master,
J. L. McDaniel, Secretary,
M. Davis,
E. McDaniel,
John Garr,
Wm. Luman,
J. W. Bassett,
S. Thomas,
John Annond,
A. Beal,
J. L. McDaniel,
J. H. Black,
Stephen Miller,
James Bounds,
Samuel Peckwell,
S. N. Davis,
Mrs. S. A. McDaniel,
Mrs. Sarah Bassett,
Mrs. M. A. Luman,
Mrs. Ida Annond,
Mrs. E. McDaniel.

SPRING VALLEY GRANGE, No. 59.

SPRING VALLEY, COLUSA COUNTY.

Organized August 2, 1873, by J. J. Hicok, Deputy.

D. H. Arnold, Master,
J. B. Lucas, Secretary,
T. S. Asbreckel,
F. W. Lahn,
J. M. McElroy,
E. Haskins,
Wm. Kaorth,
L. T. Hayman,
W. C. Henny,
Henry Davidson,
A. R. Stone,
Mrs. H. J. Teel,
Mrs. E. W. Reed,
Mrs. Mary Hoskins,
Mrs. Amelia Julion,
Mrs. A. M. McElroy,
Joseph Wholform,
F. B. Reed,
Thomas Singleton,
Samuel Wattenberger,
H. I. Teel,
P. Grenell,
E. Weigel,
C. Richey,
F. Bushore,
Mrs. Sarah Haymond,
Mrs. Julian Lucas,
Mrs. B. Piechey,
Mrs. N. Arnold.

SUTTER GRANGE, No. 60.

MERIDIAN, SUTTER COUNTY.

Organized August 8, 1873, by J. J. Hicok, Deputy.

W. C. Smith, Master,
M. C. Hungerford, Sec.
Henry Burgett,
William Harris,
J. S. Davis,
J. G. Jones,
Joseph Johnson,
J. F. Fouts,
M. C. Hungerford,
Jacob Doty,
S. F. Davis,
Mrs. Minnie Doty,
Miss Joanna Fouts,
Mrs. A. O. Colclasure,
Mrs. S. E. Harris,
Mrs. E. Fouts,
F. A. Jones,
John Birk,
John H. Colclasure,
E. Jones,
William Johnson,
A. Moore,
H. C. Jones,
William Doty,
Mrs. Bell Jones,
Mrs. E. A. Smith,
Mrs. Maria Jones,
Mrs. E. Birks,
Nancy E. Moore.

SAN BERNARDINO GRANGE, No. 61.

SAN BERNARDINO, SAN BERNARDINO COUNTY.

Organized August 26, 1873, by Thomas A. Garey, Deputy.

E. G. Brown, Master,
John F. Gould, Secretary.
A. B. Anderson,
R. Shelton,
James T. Greves,
George D. Carlton,
Mrs. R. E. Gould,
R. Shelton,
William H. Gould,
John F. Gould,
Lewis F. Cram,
Mrs. Carrie W. Shelton,
Mrs. Ida Gould,
Mrs. M. E. Wills,
H. G. Clemments,
George Lord,
W T. Russell,
W. C. Wiseman,
A. Parker,
H. Saverkreup,
E. Sheldon,
Mrs. M. A. Parks,
Mrs. M. E. Coble.
Mrs. A. R. Wiseman,
Miss Ida M. Wills.

PRINCETON GRANGE, No. 62.

PRINCETON, COLUSA COUNTY.

Organized September 1, 1873, by J. J. Hicok, Deputy.

A. D. Logan, Master,
R. R. Rush, Secretary,
A. Coldern,
H. M. Moe,
F. M. Mayfield,
C. W. F. Jemison,
James Moe,
A. H. Patterson,
A. Oliver,
R. R. Rolston,
Mrs. Mary L. Coldern,
Miss Alice Cartmel,
Mrs. A. S. Helmstreet,
Mrs. F. M. Mayfield,
L. H. Helphenstein,
A. H. Helmstreet,
Charles High,
Michael O'Hore,
Philip O'Hore,
H. Jemison,
John Boggs,
F. Quint,
Mrs. M. B. Helphenstein,
Mrs. M. E Rush,
Mrs. C. High.

CLOVERDALE GRANGE, No. 63.

CLOVERDALE, SONOMA COUNTY.

Organized September 2, 1873, by T. H. Merry, Deputy.

Charles H. Cooley, Master,
D. M. Wambold, Secretary,
H. Keir,
Mrs. Keir,
J. G. Heald,
Mrs. R. Heald,
William H. Black,
William N. Waite,
Miss Mary Waite,
D. M. Wambold,
S. Larsson,
M. E. Black,
Robert E. Lewis,
J. M. Hartsock,
J. B. Cooley,
J. A. Carne,
J. F. Elam,
R. E. Lewis,
Mrs. E. N. Cooley,
S. Cook,
W. D. Sink,
Daniel Sink,
Mrs. P. Sink,
Mrs. Mary Waite,
W. M. Howell,
America Hall,
John Edwards,
A. Hartsock,
Samuel Larroson,
William Caldwell,
S. D. Howard,
D. W. Hall.

CERES GRANGE, No. 64.

WESTPORT (MODESTO), STANISLAUS COUNTY.

Organized August 31, 1873, by J. D. Spencer, Deputy.

W. B. Harp, Master,
M. B. Kittrell, Secretary,
L. C. St. Clair,
J. B. Sanders,
J. M. Berry,
E. Hatch,
S. W. Rush,
J. M. Henderson,
M. B. Kittrell,
L. L. Harwick,
Mrs. L. C. St. Clair,
Mrs. L. L. Harwick,
Mrs. M. B. Kittrell,
Mrs. J. M. Henderson,
Mrs. S. Ellenwood,
Mrs. P. Harp,
Miss M. Davis,
Miss M. Hatch.

YUBA CITY GRANGE, No. 65.

YUBA CITY, SUTTER COUNTY.

Organized September 9, 1873, by W. H. Baxter, Deputy.

F. B. Hull, Master.
S. R. Chandler, Sec'y
G. W. Carpenter,
Catherine Carpenter,
J. A. Wilkinson,
John C. Smith,
James Littlejohn,
R. Barnett,
Elizabeth Barnett,
W. W. Ashford,
Joseph Hardy,
Mrs. M. C. Hardy,
G. F. Starr,
Mrs. E. J. Starr,
O. M. Walton,
C. J. Bockius,
H. D. Littlejohn,
George Ohleyer,
Ellen Ohleyer,
Emily L. Wilkinson,
Mrs. S. E. Walton,
H. Pinney,
W. P. Harkey,
Clarinda E. Harkey,
B. F. Frisbie,
Mrs. M. J. Frisbie,
S. E. Wilson,
S. R. Chandler,
T. B. Hull,
James T. Smith,
Mrs. M. S. Smith.

EUREKA GRANGE, No. 66.

SAN JOSE TOWNSHIP (SPADRA), LOS ANGELES COUNTY.

Organized September 8, 1873, by Thos. A. Garey, Deputy.

P. C. Touner, Master,
Jos. Wright, Secretary,
Cyrus Burdick,
Mrs. A. M. Burdick,
A. Caldwell,
Joseph Fryer,
R. C. Fryer,
Littleton Fryer,
John Egan,
S. Hoofner,
Mrs. A. Humphreys,
W. F. Thompson,
R. S. Arnett,
Mrs. Bella Fryer,
Thomas Wright,
Miss Mollie Wright,
Miss Elsie Wright,
George Blake,
Mrs. N. Blake.
W. C. Martin,
Mrs. R. C. Martin,
W. T. Martin,
Mrs. M. Martin,
Samuel Arnett,
Miss Ella Arnett.

GEYSERVILLE GRANGE, No. 67.

GEYSERVILLE, SONOMA COUNTY.

Organized September 11, 1873, by Thos. H. Merry, Deputy.

Cal. M. Bosworth, Master,
R. R. Leigh, Secretary,
G. H. Jacobs,
N. H. Stiles,
J. R. Wisewiver,
Wm. S. Beeson,
Caroline W. Beeson,
Emmon Hamilton,
C. M. Bosworth,
Eli Cummings,
William Low,
Elizabeth Low,
Mrs. A. M. Jacobs,
A. G. Geigh,
Luella S. Walcott,
L. G. Ellis,
A. S. Bemick,
S. T. Caldwell,
G. H. Benjamin,
W. J. Powell,
Marcella Powell,
Cyrus P. Buckley,
Louisa Hamilton,
Mrs. C. M. Bosworth,
William Ellis,
Mrs. M. L. Morehouse,
C. P. Moore,
Electa Moore,
Henry Wiedersheim,
Kate Turner,
William Hixon.

SANTA CRUZ GRANGE, No. 68.

SANTA CRUZ, SANTA CRUZ COUNTY.

Organized September 13, 1873, by J. D. Fowler, Deputy.

B. Cahoon, Master,
J. W. Morgan, Secretary,
James L. Grover,
James Corcoran,
Henry Thurber,
Joseph Francis,
D. W. Madden,
D. C. Feeley,
M. J. Leonard,
Thomas Leonard,
Charlotte Cahoon,
E. B. Cahoon,
V. Humphrey,
Catherine Humphrey,
Henry Daubinbiss,
Martin Kinsley,
G. C. Wardwell,
H. Winkle,
John Doyle,
Benj. P. Kooser,
P. Leonard,
J. Archibald,
Mrs. J. Archibald.

LIBERTY GRANGE, No. 69.

ACAMPO TOWNSHIP, SAN JOAQUIN COUNTY.

Organized September 11, 1873, by J. W. A. Wright, Deputy,

Justus Schomp, Master,
J. J. Emlie, Secretary,
J. S. Crawford,
N. A. Knight,
Benj. Fugitt,
Peter Jahant,
T. M. Tracy,
H. W. Childs,
C. C. Fugitt,
W. R. Pearson,
J. Van Valkenburg,
S. R. Thorne,
Jno. Welsh,
Mrs. P. Jahant,
Mrs. J. M. Tracy,
Mrs. H. W. Child,
Mrs. J. Schomp,
Mrs. R. Thorne,
Mrs. A. J. Woods,
Miss Kate Childs,
J. N. Woods,
Victor Jahant,
James Nolan,
A. J. Woods,
Jno. Discoll,
Charles Neal,
Thos. Burns,
Mrs. N. A. Knight,
Mrs. J. Van Valkenburg,
Mrs. Victor Jahant.

STOCKTON GRANGE, No. 70.

STOCKTON, SAN JOAQUIN COUNTY.

Organized August 12, 1873, by J. W. A. Wright, Deputy.

Andrew Wolfe, Master,
Wm. G. Phelps, Sec.,
W. L. Overhizer,
T. E. Ketchum,
Andrew Showers,
J. Lander,
T. J. Brooke,
Freeman Mills,
I. Marsh,
Charles Sperry,
John Taylor,
W. D. Ashley,
S. V. Tredway,
Mrs. Chas. Sperry,
Mrs. George West,
Mrs. Wm. H. Fairchild,
Mrs. A. Burkett,
Mrs. W. L. Overhizer,
Mrs. T. J. Brooke,
Mrs. J. Marsh,
P. W. Dudley,
I. F. Harrison,
A. Burkett,
George West,
Wm. H. Fairchild,
H. E. Wright,
J. H. Cole,
Mrs. F. Mills,
Mrs. John Taylor,
Mrs. Andrew Wolfe.

SANTA CLARA GRANGE, No. 71.

SANTA CLARA, SANTA CLARA COUNTY.

Organized August 19, 1873, by George W. Henning, Deputy.

Carey Peebles, Master,
I. A. Wilcox, Secretary,
F. Garrigues,
J. J. Owen,
H. Goepper,
H. M. Leonard,
I. Knowles,
Mrs. A. Knowles,
B. F. Headen,
M. L. Grewell,
E. Vandine,
Frank Parks,
Rush McComus,
Miss M. Watkins,
Mrs. L. Smith,
B. F. Stinson,
I. N. Senter,
W. Oliver,
Mrs. J. A. Wilcox,
Benj. Craft,
A. Woodham,
L. J. Grewell,
Henry Sillick.

FRUITLAND GRANGE, No. 72.

TUSTIN CITY TOWNSHIP, LOS ANGELES COUNTY.

Organized September 15, 1873.

A. B. Hayward, Master,
Elton R. Nichols, Sec.,
D. H. Samis,
Columbus Tustin,
E. R. Nichols,
Wm. A. Abbott,
Thomas Cassad,
A. D. Stine,
I. T. Johnson,
N. O. Stafford,
A. T. Armstrong,
D. G. McClay,
Mrs. Julia Hayward,
Mrs. Mary Tustin,
Mrs. M. J. Armstrong,
Mrs. S. N. Stine,
Mrs. A. M. Robinson,
Robert McFadden,
Silas Ritchie,
Wm. H. Tedford,
J. J. Johnson,
S. W. Merritt,
A. T. Bates,
W. C. McClay,
I. T. Tedford,
Samuel Robinson,
Mrs. M. J. Nichols,
Mrs. Harriet C. Abbott,
Mrs. Sarah V. Cassad,
Mrs. M. A. Merrill,
Mrs. A. E. Tedford.

DAVISVILLE GRANGE, No. 73.

DAVISVILLE, YOLO COUNTY.

Organized September 23, 1873, by Wm. M. Jackson, Deputy,

Chas. E. Greene, Master,
John Krimmer, Secretary,
H. P. Martin,
Mrs. H. P. Martin,
Geo. W. Pierce.
Mrs. Geo. W. Pierce,
Rodney M. Bennett,
W. D. Wistine,
Mrs. Chas. E. Greene,
Dwight Cooley,
Andy McClary,
G. L. Luddington,
J. C. Campbell,
Mrs. W. D. Wistine.

ARROYO GRANDE GRANGE, No. 74.

ARROYO GRANDE, SAN LUIS OBISPO COUNTY.

Organized September 20, 1873, by A. J. Mothersead, Deputy.

David F. Newsom, Master,
D. F. Whittenberg, Sec'y,
W. H. Nelson,
James Morse,
Albert Fowler,
Frank Branch,
R. J. Branch,
R. F. Branch,
Jesse Castael,
James Brannan,
L. R. Branch,
Angelina Morse,
Susan Hess,
Eli Edwards,
Lizzie Nelson,
Sarah Fowler,
Susan Henry,
Angie Morse,
H. H. Johnston,
Henry Hess,
Daniel Henry,
Edward Shaw,
Annie Johnston.

ALLIANCE GRANGE, No. 75.

BOG DALE DISTRICT (EL MONTE), LOS ANGELES COUNTY.

Organized September 22, 1873, by Thos. A. Garey, Deputy.

S. S. Reeves, Master,
J. W. Marshall, Secretary,
James D. Durfee,
Charles Dougherty,
W. H. Guinn,
S. S. Reeves,
W. D. Cole,
George W. Durfee,
Mrs. Diantha Durfee,
Mrs. Henrietta Dukes,
Mrs. Lydia A. Reeves,
Miss Alice A. Reeves,
Miss Mary J. Reeves,
Mrs. A. J. Dougherty,
Alfred Gibson,
G. W. Mark,
A. S. Harris,
W. P. Cooper,
E. S. Harris,
J. A. Anderson,
A. V. Dunsmore,
Miss Fannie Mark,
Miss Jennie Mark,
Miss Martha Marshall,
Mrs. Mary A. Marshall.

LAKEPORT GRANGE, No. 76.

LAKEPORT, LAKE COUNTY.

Organized September 18, 1873, by J. M. Hamilton, Deputy.

I. C. W. Ingram, Master,
N. Phelan, Secretary,
J. J. Bruton,
J. S. McClintock,
N. Phelan,
William Gesner,
J. P. Denny,
B. D. Green,
I. F. Burger,
C. Sweigert,
John Jones,
A. Wittenburger,
Cyrus Cutler,
I. I. Hendricks,
W. A. Christy,
William Christy.
Robert McCullough,
P. M. Daley,
Mrs. Louisa Thompson,
Miss Mary Thompson,
Mrs. B. D. Green,
Mrs. J. F. Burger,
Mrs. J. McClintock,
Miss M. P. McClintock,
Mrs. L. C. Burriss,
Mrs. P. M. Daley,
Mrs. E. A. Hammock,
Mrs. J. W. Boggs,
J. W. Boggs,
J. C. Thompson.

LOWER LAKE GRANGE, No. 77.

LOWER LAKE, LAKE COUNTY.

Organized September 20, 1873, by J. M. Hamilton, Deputy.

Mack Matthews, Master,
G. H. Snow, Secretary,
W. H. Cunningham,
I. S. Fruits,
H. H. Wilson,
J. W. Howard,
Hanson Hazell,
James A. Harris,
Mack Matthews,
G. H. Snow,
I. D. Hendricks,
J. L. Jackson,
C. L. Wilson,
I. C. Crigler,
R. R. Nichols,
M. H. Hendricks,
E. Armstrong,
C. Stubbs,
M. M. Snow,
F. M. Herendon,
Rough Matthews,
A. E. Noel,
Edward Beckley,
O. J. Copsey,
Sarah M. Howard,
Nancy J. Cunningham,
S. T. Smith,
Jane Copsey,
L. S. Wilson,
Amanda Crigler,
A. R. Nichols,
E. A. DeWolf.

BADGER FLAT GRANGE, No. 78.

LOS BANOS, MERCED COUNTY.

Organized September 20, 1873, by J. W. A. Wright, Deputy.

W. F. Clark, Master,
Alfred Merritt, Secretary,
W. W. Parlin,
Sam'l Fowler,
Wm. Phillips,
James Torey,
Joseph Merritt,
Welcome Fowler,
William Stockton,
Jo. Friedman,
O. K. Jones,
J. W. Parker,
R. Alford,
Mrs. Sam'l Fowler,
Mrs. J. W. Parker,
Mrs. R. Alford,
George Taber,
Mrs. W. F. Clark,
Miss Jane Fowler,
Mrs. W. Phillips,
Mrs. W. W. Parlin,
N. H. Spencer,
John Fowler,
A. J. Fowler,
J. W. Maples,
Jesse Webb,
I. B. Yule,
Mrs. O. K. Jones,
Mrs. Jesse Webb,
Mrs. J. W. Maples.

LOS BANOS GRANGE, No. 79.

LOS BANOS, MERCED COUNTY.

Organized September 20, 1873, by J. W. A. Wright, Deputy.

Wm. M. Viney, Master,
H. C. Wainwright, Sec'y,
B. F. Davis,
G. H. Wiley,
William Jones,
Mrs. W. M. Viney,
Mrs. A. F. Munch,
Miss Mary Mitchell,
W. G. Jones,
Owen Hughes,
R. S. Vanderburg,
Henry Acker,
John Shaffer,
Mrs. S. J. Horner,
Mrs. John McGlashan,
Mrs. G. Shaffer,
Andrew McGlashan,
D. M. Wood,
G. F. Lawrence,
A. S. Munch,
Mrs. C. H. Wiley,
S. J. Horner,
Jno. McGlashan,
Jos. McCarthy,
Isaac Acner,
George Shaffer,
Jay Brown,
Mrs. B. F. Davis,
Mrs. J. Shaffer,
Mrs. A. McGlashan.

HOPETON GRANGE, No. 80.

HOPETON, MERCED COUNTY.

Organized September 23, 1873, by J. W. A. Wright, Deputy.

John Ruddle, Master,
Thomas Eagleson, Sec'y,
Fred Danner,
S. E. Smyer,
W. L. Coates,
Wm. Little,
A. S. Ellis,
B. Delashmutt,
Mrs. T. Eagleson,
T. J. Ramsey,
J. M. Strong,
John W. Collins,
A. C. McSwain,
Travis Marshall,
Mrs. T. J. Ramsey,
Mrs. A. C. McSwain,
Mrs. John Ruddle,
G. R. Scruggs,
Mrs. W. L. Silman,
Mrs. J. W. Collins,
Miss Laura Stockard,
Miss Alice Stockard,
W. W. Stockard,
W. L. Silman,
David P. Woodruff,
J. M. Scott,
J. H. Payne,
Cyrus Paine,
Mrs. J. M. Scott,
Mrs. V. Biggs.

BLOOMFIELD GRANGE, No. 81.

BLOOMFIELD, SONOMA COUNTY.

Organized September 25, 1873, by G. W. Davis, Deputy.

Wm. H. White, Master,
D. Bruner, Secretary,
William Lacost,
C. E. Colborn,
Isaac Kuffel,
A. B. Glover,
Mrs. A. B. Glover,
Wm. D. Canfield,
Wm. S. Edminster,
S. H. Church,
A. A. Boyington,
J. Boyington,
W. N. Wakefield,
Delia Edminster,
C. Parks,
W. W. Parks,
Wm. P. Hall,
Mrs. A. P. Hall,
Henry Hall,
D. H. Parks,
Ollie White,
Mrs. S. A Canfield,
Mrs. O. M. Colborn,
James Carvey,
Jesse B. Smith.

CACHE CREEK GRANGE, No. 82.

COTTONWOOD, YOLO COUNTY.

Organized September, 1873, by Wm. M. Jackson, Deputy.

D. B. Hurlburt, Master,
L. D. Stephen, Secretary,
H. Fredericks,
Mrs. M. Hurlburt,
H. Saling,
Mrs. C. F. Saling,
J. H. Norton,
Mrs. S. J. Norton,
J. Edger,
G. Shinn,
Mrs. A. Shinn,
C. Farlin,
N. Carbin,
B. W. Smith,
Miss M. Frederick,
G. N. Dameron,
R. G. Tadlock,
W. T. Cottle,
G. Woods,
D. Q. Adams,
L. D. Stephens,
E. R. Holton,
Mrs. S. J. Holton,
Mrs. E. Holton,
E. Sebald,
Mrs. E. Sebald,
Mrs. J. Margel,
W. N. Mardus.

RUSTIC GRANGE, No. 83.

LATHROP, SAN JOAQUIN COUNTY.

Organized September 29, 1873.

J. A. Shepherd, Master,
Henry Moore, Secretary,
George W. Haines,
W. R. Bailey,
Eugene Kay,
O. F. Atwood,
L. P. Whitman,
George W. Sperry,
Samuel W. Boice,
Thos. Gardner,
Joseph Heintz,
Mrs. J. K. Meyer,
Mrs. H. Moore,
Miss S. E. Shepherd,
Miss E. E. Shepherd,
J. K. Meyer,
Henry Moore,
Dennis Visher,
Mrs. S. W. Boice,
Mrs. J. Parks,
Mrs. D. Visher,
Miss Emma Sperry,
H. S. Howland,
Le Roscoe Howland,
Thos. Parks,
W. J. Reynolds,
Miss N. M. Haines,
Miss P. A. Sperry.

WOODBRIDGE GRANGE, No. 84.

WOODBRIDGE, SAN JOAQUIN COUNTY.

Organized September 30, 1873, by J. W. A. Wright, Deputy.

J. L. Hutson, Master,
A. McQueen, Secretary,
E. J. McIntosh,
E. Fisk,
C. L. Robinson,
G. H. Ashley,
G. W. Bressler,
A. McQueen,
H. G. Gillingham,
H. Beckman,
W. B. White,
T. J. Pope,
J. Hemphill,
Mrs. T. Henderson,
Mrs. J. L. Keagle,
Mrs. H. Beckman,
Mrs. E. Dayton,
Mrs. Perley,
Mrs. W. B. White,
Mrs. H. G. Gillingham,
Mrs. I. Emdy,
Dr. E. Dayton,
Thomas Henderson,
J. L. Keagle,
A. M. Hastner,
T. S. Moore,
A. R. Elliott,
I. Emdy,
H. C. Shattuck,
Mrs. G. H. Ashley,
Miss J. F. Bressler.

DANVILLE GRANGE, No. 85.

DANVILLE, CONTRA COSTA COUNTY.

Organized October 1, 1873, by R. G. Dean, Deputy.

Charles Wood, Master,
John B. Snyder, Sec'y,
John Stern,
Jonathan Hoag,
David N. Sherburn,
Robert B. Love,
Thomas Flournoy,
William Bell,
William W. Cox,
Isaac Russell,
Albert W. Stone,
Hugh Wiley,
Mrs. Mary Hoag,
Miss Livia Labaree,
Mrs. Francis Rice,
Mrs. Mary A. Jones,
John Camp,
James O. Boone,
Leonard Eddy,
Wade Hays,
Robert O. Baldwin,
Francis E. Mattison,
David A. Caldwell,
John W. Kerr,
Mrs. Sallie E. Boone,
Miss Lizzie Stern,
Mrs. Charles Wood,
Mrs. Amelia Love,
Miss Hattie Van Patten,
Mrs. Sarah Labaree.

ELK GROVE GRANGE, No. 86.

ELK GROVE, SACRAMENTO COUNTY.

Organized October 4, 1873, by W. T. Manlove, Deputy.

O. S. Freeman, Master,
Delos Gage, Secretary,
Julius Everson,
David Upton,
Sullivan Treat,
Mary Kerr,
George H. Kerr,
Martha Dixon,
Caroline M. Treat,
Asel B. Davis,
Joseph H. Kerr,
Thomas McConnell,
Louisa C. McConnell,
Alfred Dixon,
Wm. Parker,
Asa H. Simons
Ezra W. Simons,
Prudence Simons,
Alvira H. Everson,
Sobeiska Brown,
Agnes R. Gage,
Enoch Drew,
James Kent,
Milton Sherwood.

NORD GRANGE, No. 87.

NORD, BUTTE COUNTY.

Organized October 6, 1873, by W. M. Thorp, Deputy.

G. W. Colby, Master,
Lyman C. Cole, Secretary,
H. W. Steuben,
Charles Pettit,
William Vettel,
Alexander Ash,
J. R. Haughton,
John McIntyre,
Albert Carman,
Philander McCargar,
James McCargar,
Herman McCargar,
Mrs. G. W. Colby,
Mrs. Jane E. Ash,
Mrs. Adaline McCargar,
Mrs. Emeline Warren,
James F. Wright,
S. C. Bragg,
Lemuel Sweeny,
John B. Bragg,
Edward Warren,
Robert McCargar,
Lyman L. Cole,
Alexander Thrower,
John Thompson,
William Jasper,
Mrs. Charles Pettit,
Mrs. Eliza McCargar,
Mary Carlisle,
Mary Taylor,
Mrs. S. G. Bragg.

KIWELATTA GRANGE, No. 88.

ARCATA, HUMBOLDT COUNTY.

Organized September 30, 1873, by T. H. Merry, General Deputy.

Lewis K. Wood, Master,
D. D. Averill, Secretary,
Clarissa S. Wood,
David H. Tower,
J. J. Jule,
F. F. Lansdale,
H. L. Lansdale,
Naomi Handy,
Mary Handy,
John H. Pratt,
Calista Pratt,
James F. Denning,
S. Myers,
J. G. Dolson,
L. H. Jansen,
George Zehendner,
Daniel B. Judd,
Lucinda Averill,
J. Sowash,
Louisa Sowash,
David H. Tower,
Albert Hall,
Sophronia Hall,
James Sinclair,
Mary Sinclair,
James Burk,
Frank McFee,
G. B. Kneeland,
A. B. Kneeland,
D. N. Dilla,
H. W. Arbogast.

WEST GRAFTON GRANGE, No. 89.

WEST GRAFTON (YOLO), YOLO COUNTY.

Organized October 3, 1873, by W. M. Jackson, Deputy.

A. C. Morris, Master,
G. W. Parks, Secretary,
Jay Green,
F. Schleiman,
John McClintock,
L. L. Burr,
W. H. H. Dinwiddie,
J. G. Ely,
Mrs. Mary Leggett,
J. G. Bower, Jr.,
George Thacher,
J. F. Nason,
Mrs. Susan Bower,
Mrs. C. Wizard,
I. T. Hadley,
J. W. Brown,
I. G. Bowers,
Theo. Wizard,
Josiah Rinsella,
W. S. Manor,
A. W. Morris,
Mrs. Alice Mapes,
James M. Packman,
George W. Parks,
Mrs. Schleiman,
Mrs. Sarah Brown,
E. S. Grey.

CAPAY VALLEY GRANGE, No. 90.

CAPAY, YOLO COUNTY.

Organized October 4, 1873, by Wm. M. Jackson, Deputy.

R. R. Darby, Master,
P. M. Savage, Secretary,
J. P. Goodnow,
Jall Woods,
John M. Rhodes,
Tillie Walters,
Wm. H. Duncan,
P. M. Savage,
M. Lambert,
D. C. Rumsay,
R. R. Darby,
E. B. Walters,
Mrs. S. C. Darby,
Mrs. Helen Duncan,
Mrs. L. Savage.

LIVERMORE GRANGE, No. 91.

LIVERMORE, ALAMEDA COUNTY.

Organized October 8, 1873, by W. H. Baxter, Deputy.

Daniel Inman, Master,
F. R. Fassett, Secretary,
W. W. Wynn,
J. H. Taylor,
J. T. Taylor,
A. J. McDavid,
J. H. Mahinney,
Valentine Alviso,
J. T. Taylor,
Arthur St. Clair,
John Foscalina,
B. J. Salisbury,
Mrs. A. P. Francis,
Mrs. Mattie Rinaldo,
Mrs. Joanna Brackett,
Mrs. Mattie Bowles,
Joshua A. Neale,
E. S. Allen,
J. W. Clark,
E. P. Bragdon,
F. J. Clark,
E. P. Bragdon,
E. M. Carr,
J. H. Brackett,
Jesse Bowles,
Mrs. Adelia E. Taylor,
Mrs. Helen A. Fassett,
Mrs. M. Taylor,
Mrs. J. J. Inman,

LODI GRANGE, No. 92.

LODI, SAN JOAQUIN COUNTY.

Organized August 29, 1873, by J. W. A. Wright, Deputy.

J. W. Kearney, Master,
D. Dickerson, Secretary,
A. J. Ayres,
C. T. Elliott,
C. P. Allison,
Samuel Fredum,
Mrs. A. W. Gove,
Mrs. C. P. Allison,
J. M. Fowler,
A. W. Gove,
W. H. Post,
R. Woods,
D. Kettleman,
Mrs. J. M. Fowler,
Mrs. O. O. Norton,
Mrs. W. H. Post,
O. O. Norton,
John Parrot,
E. Lawrence,
Mrs. L. M. Morse,
Mrs. E. Lawrence,
John Gerard,
L. M. Morse,
J. Talmadge,
Stephen Purdy,
Frank Turner,
Mrs. J. W. Kearny,
Mrs. J. Gerard,
Mrs. J. Talmadge.

PAJARO GRANGE, No. 93.

WATSONVILLE, PAJARO TOWNSHIP, MONTEREY COUNTY.

Organized October 10, 1873, by J. D. Fowler, Deputy.

D. M. Clough, Master,
G. W. Roadhouse, Sec'y,
D. Crawford,
Mrs. D. Crawford,
D. M. Clough,
S. B. Marcus,
Alexander Keer,
J. E. Trofton,
J. J. Roadhouse,
John Olinger,
Peter Cox,
Mrs. Rebecca Cox,
Mrs. N. A. Uren,
N. A. Uren,
Mrs. C. E. Roadhouse.

AZUSA GRANGE, No. 94.

AZUSA TOWNSHIP (EL MONTE), LOS ANGELES COUNTY.

Organized October 3, 1873, by Thos. A. Garey, Deputy.

W. W. Maxey, Master,
J. C. Preston, Secretary,
Thos. Allen,
J. S. Thompson,
E. R. Thompson,
C. Thompson,
W. J. Dougherty,
I. C. Barnes,
G. W. Bohannan,
Mrs. Q. A. Allen,
Mrs. Lucy W. Maxey,
Mrs. Alvina Thompson,
Mrs. M. A. Justice,
Mrs. M. O. Dougherty,
Mrs. M. L. Preston,
Callie L. Dougherty,
Miss Ellen Barnes,
E. T. Justice,
D. L. Dougherty,
I. C. Preston,
I. T. Collins,
L. Barnes,
W. S. Neal,
Jas. Dougherty,
A. J. Justice,
J. H. Malone,
J. M. Casey,
D. G. Malone,
W. J. Deshield,
Mrs. E. Barnes,
Mrs. Indiana Justice.

FLORENCE GRANGE, No. 95.

FLORENCE (LOS ANGELES), LOS ANGELES COUNTY.

Organized October 6, 1873, by Thos. A. Garey, Deputy.

H. Gibson, Master,
Wm. Porter, Secretary,
H. C. Thomas,
R. B. Russell,
H. Gibson,
Josiah Russell,
John Willey,
E. J. Durell,
Thomas Gillette,
Charles Hazard,
H. P. Hiett,
Frank Farris,
Mrs. Janes,
D. Farris,
Mrs. Mary Farris,
Mrs. H. C. Thomas,
Mrs. R. M. Russell,
Mrs. Sue C. Spencer,
I. D. Farris,
William F. Farris,
I. F. Durell,
Louis L. Rice,
A. Nelson,
J. M. Spencer,
G. B. Farris,
Wm. Porter,
J. W. Wilkinson,
John Chapman,
Mrs. A. Gibson,
Mrs. N. J. Russell,
Miss L. J. Russell,
Mrs. P. D. H. Durell,
Miss Nannie Farris.

BUCKEYE GRANGE, No. 96.

BUCKEYE, YOLO COUNTY.

Organized October 6, 1873, by W. M. Jackson, Deputy

Wm. Sims, Master,
J. G. Allen, Secretary,
R. A. Daniels,
Daniel Robinson,
I. P. Grafton,
J. O. Maxwell,
Mrs. Anna Maxwell,
I. W. Norton,
Mrs. Eliza Norton,
F. G. Russell,
Miss Saphrona Ely,
T. C. Goodwin,
Mrs. Susan C. Goodwin,
W. O. Campbell,
Mrs. C. Campbell,
J. R. Briggs,
Mrs. Julia Briggs,
E. G. Bray,
Mrs. E. G. Bray,
J. G. Allin,
J. W. Ely,
Mrs. Cornelia Ely.

HUNGRY HOLLOW GRANGE, No. 97.

YOLO, YOLO COUNTY.

Organized October 7, 1873, by W. M. Jackson, Deputy.

G. L. Parker, Master,
G. L. Perkins, Secretary,
A. H. Nixson,
T. J. Parker,
T. J. Gallup,
J. M. Parker,
C. P. Du Bois,
Mrs. A. E. Dutton,
Mrs. E. M. Young,
G. L. Parker,
Mrs. M. C. Parker,
P. Fishback,
John A. Zimmerman,
C. O. Perkins,
C. H. Dresser,
Mrs. Alice W. Dresser,
J. B. Nixson,
J. E. Young,
N. E. Spaights,
I. M. Dutton,
J. B. Dungan,
Miss C. H. Dutton,
Mrs. Lizzy Parker,
R. J. Mattock,
Frederick Mast,
Mrs. J. O. Fishback,
Gottlieb Mast,
Gottlieb Rath,
Mrs. C. Parker,
Edwin Blodgett.

ANTELOPE GRANGE, No. 98.

ANTELOPE, YOLO COUNTY.

Organized October 8, 1873, by W. M. Jackson, Deputy.

W. J. Clark, Master,
C. L. M. Vaughn, Sec'y,
A. W. Dunigan,
Miss R. Dunigan,
L. Dunigan,
Henry Yarrick,
W. O. Dresser,
Wm. M. Campbell,
Mrs. S. S. Campbell,
A. B. Richmond,
S. W. Foster,
L. B. Lewis,
Mrs. S. A. Lewis,
D. L. Ashley,
L. C. Lane,
J. Y. De Rose,
Mrs. B. De Rose,
Wm. Dresser,
Mrs. H. S. Dresser,
J. D. Snelling,
Mrs. S. A. Vaughn,
H. Garrett,
Wm. B. Carter,
Miss M. C. Vaughn,
W. J. Clark,
Mrs. C. Clark,
Miss K. Burgoyne,
I. L. Rollins.

FUNK SLOUGH GRANGE, No. 99.

FUNK SLOUGH (COLUSA), COLUSA COUNTY.

Organized October 8, 1873, by J. J. Hicok, Deputy.

E. C. Hunter, Master,
Russell Delapp, Secretary,
I. F. Daley,
I. A. Sutton,
T. Harden,
G. Harden,
Oren Phelps,
O. V. Daley,
G. H. Abell,
T. H. Dodson,
C. A. Kupper,
Miss E. Benjamin,
Miss C. Benjamin,
Mrs. A. Alexander,
L. D. McDow,
T. B. McDow,
A. Alexander,
Mark Hubbard,
R. J. Barnes,
I. G. Wolfe,
J. D. Rice,
W. S. McClevy,
I. W. Daley,
G. W. Sutton,
Miss L. Daley,
Miss Anne Sutton,
Mrs. Dodson,
Mrs. L. J. McDow,
Mrs. S. E. McDow,
Mrs. T. Harden.

ANTELOPE VALLEY GRANGE, No. 100.

ANTELOPE VALLEY (COLUSA), COLUSA COUNTY.

Organized October 10, 1873, by J. J. Hicok, Deputy.

H. A. Logan, Master,
A. T. Welton, Secretary,
R. T. Clark,
Mrs. S. C. Clark,
P. Peterson,
Mrs. L. M. Peterson,
Mrs. M. B. Aycoke,
A. A. Seheaine,
Mrs. Jane Seheaine,
D. T. Seheaine,
Mrs. S. A. Logan,
I. A. Cleghorn,
Mrs. C. A. Cleghorn,
M. A. Cleghorn,
M. H. Sechaine,
Mrs. R. B. Sehaine,
John Rosenberg,
Wm. Rosenberg,
Arthur T. Welton,
H. H. Graham,
Mrs. R. J. Graham,
I. D. S. Taylor,
G. W. Cardwell,
Mrs. Rebecca Cardwell,
Elizabeth Seheaine.

TABLE BLUFF GRANGE, No. 101.

TABLE BLUFF, HUMBOLDT COUNTY.

Organized October 2, 1873, by T. H. Merry, General Deputy.

Jackson Sawyer, Master
B. H. C. Pollard, Sec'y,
Edwin P. Vance,
Samuel Foss,
Mary Foss,
A. S. Frost,
Charles C. Foss,
Patrick O'Rourke,
Catherine O'Rourke,
Louis Buyatte,
Minerva Buyatte,
Elan B. Long,
Elizabeth Long,
Jerry Quill,
Julia Quill,
I. P. Walsh,
Mary Walsh,
Hannah Pollard,
T. J. Knight,
H. P. Dothen,
T. Y. Clyde,
D. A. DeMeritt,
James Wolgamott,
O. McNulty,
Ellen McNulty,
John McNulty,
Hannah Sawyer,
E. Tiernay,
I. E. Still.
Patrick Quinn.

FERNDALE GRANGE, No. 102.

FERNDALE, HUMBOLDT COUNTY.

Organized October 3, 1873, by T. H. Merry, General Deputy.

F. Z. Boynton, Master,
Charles Barber, Sec'y,
Ann Boynton,
Addie Winfield,
William Stover,
James Smith,
Jane Smith,
Jacob Criss,
Martha J. Criss.
J. C. Dungan,
Mary E. Spencer,
William Williams,
R. S. Tyrrell,
John Smith,
Malvina Stover,
L. C. Church,
William Taylor,
J. R. Kinsley,
Orrin Chapman,
Sarah Chapman,
R. J. Bugbee,
G. G. Dudley,
Margaret Dudley,
Andrew Denman.
Rebecca Denman,
William H. Spencer,
George W. Griffith,
James S. Freeman,
Rebecca Freeman.
Joseph Davenport.

ROHNERVILLE GRANGE, No. 103.

RHONERVILLE, HUMBOLDT COUNTY.

Organized October 6, 1873, by T. H. Merry, General Deputy.

B. T. Jamison, Master,
Samuel Strong, Secretary,
A. D. Sevier,
Martha J. Jamison,
Sarah Sevier,
Maria G. Strong,
Sarah E. Strong,
Mrs. Caroline Beckwith,
H. S. Case,
Mrs. E. C. Case,
Homer Drake,
W. R. Worthington,
Elizabeth W. Worthington,
John W. Cooper,
C. S. Chamberlain,
Job Tower,
Wm. M. Henry,
A. H. Bradford,
L. C. Beckwith,
Matthew Perrott,
S. A. Perrott,
C. Hanson,
Rolla Bryant,
Lizzie Bryant.

ELK RIVER GRANGE, No. 104.

BUCKSPORT, HUMBOLDT COUNTY.

Organized October 7, 1873, by T. H. Merry, General Deputy.

Theodore Meyer, Master,
D. A. De Merritt, Sec'y,
F. L. Meyer,
Ella M. Williams,
S. B. Lane,
Alex. Forbes,
F. S. Shaw,
Sophronia C. Shaw,
Mrs. D. E. De Merritt,
Waterman Fields,
Ruth Ann Haw,
S. N. Stewart,
Joseph Scott Stewart,
S. O. Showers,
G. H. Shaw,
Margaret Shaw,
William Orton,
Jacob W. Gardner,
Sophia B. Gardner.

SNELLING GRANGE, No. 105.

SNELLING, MERCED COUNTY.

Organized October 23, 1873, by H. B. Jolley, District Deputy.

Daniel Yeizer, Master,
W. L. Hamlin, Secretary,
A. B. Anderson,
G. L. Baker,
W. G. Hardwick,
Mrs. W. L. Hamlin,
L. J. Burns,
S. R. Spears,
Mrs. Martha Spears,
Mrs. Mary E. Yeizer,
Erastus Kelsey,
Mrs. Malinda Kelsey,

EDEN GRANGE, No. 106.

HAYWARDS, ALAMEDA COUNTY.

Organized October 25, 1873, by J. W. A. Wright, P. M. & L. Cal. State Grange.

Thomas Hellar Master,
Wm. Owen, Secretary,
H. W. Rice,
Edwin Kimball,
H. Momsen,
George E. Baxter,
J. C. Ward,
Thos. A. Cunningham,
J. Shilling,
C. F. A. Bagge,
Tim Houschildt,
I. H. Wisener,
Charles Prouse,
Mrs. Mary Kimball,
Mrs. H. W. Rice,
Miss Emma Templeton,
Mrs. E. Hellar,
Mrs. R. L. Knox,
Miss S. M. McCrea,
Mrs. J. C. Momsen,
Wm. F. Hellar,
J. H. Prouse,
Joel Russell,
H. F. Nebas,
John Bagge,
Wm. Knox,
John Donkell,
Mrs. J. Russell,
Mrs. Ida C. Wielbye,
Mrs. Maria Bagge.

ROCKVILLE GRANGE, No. 107.

ROCKVILLE, SOLANO COUNTY.

Organized October 29, 1873, by W. H. Baxter, Deputy.

W. A. Lattin, Master,
J. R. Morris, Secretary,
R. H. McMillen,
A. Gambel,
A. S. Gambel,
J. M. Baldwin,
B. O. Foster,
P. A. Russell,
Rush Lattin,
E. Barbour,
J. McMullen,
Mrs. E. Barbour,
Mrs. C. J. Pitman,
Mrs. C. M. Baldwin,
H. D. Tisdale,
Mrs. Georgia Fliggle,
Mrs. McMorris,
Mrs. Amy Lattin,
Mrs. Kate Gambel,
Mrs. C. P. Foster,
J. E. Fliggle,
Mrs. A. M. Cox,
P. G. Cox.

KELSEYVILLE GRANGE, No. 108.

KELSEYVILLE, LAKE COUNTY.

Organized October 29, 1873, by J. M. Hamilton, W. M. Cal. State Grange.

D. P. Shattuck, Master,
J. Ormenston, Secretary,
G. W. Piner,
Barton Kelsey,
Seth Rickabaugh,
Z. C. Beardsley,
R. R. Robinson,
C. C. Barker,
Anderson Benson,
Thomas Ormenston,
John Shirley,
I. H. Renfrow,
James Tryon,
D. E. Mills,
Mrs. L. P. Ormenston,
Mrs. S. F. Piner,
Mrs. F. M. Stonebreaker,
Miss N. E. Stonebreaker,
Miss Blanche Ormenston,
Miss E. A. Beardsly.

UPPER LAKE GRANGE, No. 109.

UPPER LAKE, LAKE COUNTY.

Organized October 30, 1873, by J. M. Hamilton, W. M. Cal. State Grange.

D. V. Thompson, Master,
D. Q. McCurty, Secretary,
George A. Lyon,
George Thornington,
A. J. Doty,
Emry Townsend,
Henry Parmer,
J. B. Robinson,
M. Shepard,
Samuel Coombs,
M. Deniston,
W. W. Meredith,
Mrs. E. Ford,
Mrs. Lucy Meredith,
Nancy S. Parmer,
Miss E. Sleeper,
George Ford,
I. W. Doty,
M. Sleeper,
J. B. Howard,
L. T. Matcalf,
Jerome Sleeper,
R. C. Tallman,
Mrs. Sarah Doty,
Mrs. E. Townsend,
Mrs. Mary Coombs,
Mrs. I. J. Doty,
Mrs. M. C. Thompson,
Miss Betty Thompson.

ORISTIMBA GRANGE, No. 110.

HILL'S FERRY, STANISLAUS COUNTY.

Organized November 4, 1873, by J. W. A. Wright, Deputy.

W. J. Miller, Master,
Thos. A Chapman, Sec'y,
T. R. Hutchinson,
Tyler Bithin,
E. P. Bennett,
B. B. McGuire,
Mrs. S. M. McGuire,
Mrs. C. F. Hutchinson,
P. M. Peterson,
William Wilkinson,
L. S. Bennett,
D. W. Eachus,
W. S. Underwood,
Mrs. M. Newell,
Mrs. M. Ellen Underwood,
Mrs. S. J. Bithin,
W. L. Pryor,
Peter Hansen,
C. C. Eastin,
Mrs. J. W. Miller,
Miss J. E. Newell,
Arthur A. Bithin,
M. G. Bennett,
S. V. Porter,
S. J. Foxe,
W. Underwood,
B. D. Noxon,
Mrs. Mary E. Underwood,
Mrs. Susan Wilkinson,
Mrs. Emma C. Eastin.

ATLANTA GRANGE, No. 111.

ATLANTA, SAN JOAQUIN COUNTY.

Organized October 30, 1873, by E. B. Stiles, Deputy.

W. J. Campbell, Master,
Wm. Dempsey, Secretary,
A. W. Hunsacker,
Samuel Myers,
Levi Niciwinger,
Mrs. N. P. Hunsacker,
Mrs. T. M. Gardner,
Miss Emma T. Gardner,
Mrs. J. W. Moore,
Mrs. Lou Vischer,
Mrs. Margaret Miller,
Mrs. Jennie M. Lombard,
Mrs. Samuel Myers,
Putnam Vischer,
Isaac Kock,
David Lombard,
T. W. Gilbert,
T. M. Gardner,
I. W. Moore,
Ernst Wagner,
Joseph Frost,
Milton Miller,
D. L. Campbell,
H. H. Clendennin,
Mrs. Caroline W. Gilbert.

BONITA GRANGE, No. 112.

CROW'S LANDING, STANISLAUS COUNTY.

Organized November 1, 1873, by J. D. Spencer, Deputy.

J. W. Treadwell, Master,
A. B. Crook, Secretary,
James M. Bond,
B. R. Pierce,
W. E. Garrett,
W. C. Cattron,
A. G. Lucas,
Edward Loomis,
W. H. Battenfield,
Benjamin Fowler,
Mrs. S. A. Pierce,
Mrs. F. A. Loomis,
Mrs. M. P. Garrett,
Mrs. Amanda Hutton,
Mrs. S. T. Bond,
Wm. Fisher,
I. A. Clark,
M. V. Morin,
D. Hayes,
A. R. Kirkwood,
George Medrie,
F. M. Smith,
A. C. Hutton,
Mrs. L. A. Crook,
Miss R. J. Daniels,
Mrs. E. Treadwell,
Mrs. M. Hayes,
Mrs. Margaret Clark.

VALLEJO GRANGE, No. 113.

VALLEJO, SOLANO COUNTY.

Organized November 8, 1873, by W. H. Baxter, Deputy.

G. C. Pierson, Master,
Charles B. Deming, Sec'y,
Ira Austin,
George H. Greenwood,
William Carter,
A. P. Ryerson,
Mrs. Celia Hunter,
Mrs. Hattie Pearson,
Mrs. Lavina Wilson,
Mrs. Elizabeth Greenwood,
John F. Deming,
Chas. B. Deming,
Mrs. Annie G. Deming,
John Wilson,
James Hunter,
Gustavus C. Pierson,
B. B. Brown,
John Fletcher,
M. M. Carter,
S. S. Drake,
Mrs. Anna Carter,
Joseph Wilson,
Mrs. Hattie G. Deming.
Mrs. Thirza Drake,

UKIAH GRANGE, No. 114.

UKIAH CITY, MENDOCINO COUNTY.

Organized November 4, 1873, by T. H. Merry, Deputy.

W. D. White, Master,
N. O. Carpenter, Sec'y,
Elisha Weller,
John M. Morris,
Mary Morris,
J. B. Short,
Thos. R. Lucas,
Martha Lucas,
I. M. Faught,
Philip Howell,
Mark York,
Elizabeth Bartlett,
Helen Carpenter,
Samuel Orr,
G. W. Jackson,
J. C. Cook,
Frances Ouseley,
Nathan Bartlett,
Lavinia G. White,
L. M. Ruddick,
Charles Bartlett,
Mary E. Bartlett,
J. R. Henry,
S. C. Henry,
R. Clark,
A. O. Carpenter,
J. B. McClum,
M. W. Howard,
John Crawford,
Elizabeth Howell,
Clara S. Warmseller.

POTTER VALLEY GRANGE, No. 115.

POTTER VALLEY, MENDOCINO COUNTY.

Organized November 6, 1873, by Thos. H. Merry, Deputy.

John Mewhinney, Master,
Thos. McCowen, Sec'y,
Samuel Mewhinney,
Donah M. Mewhinney,
J. G. Bush,
Thaddeus Dashiels,
Samuel McCulloch,
J. R. Ross,
Life Farmer,
Catherine Farmer,
J. E. Carner,
H. Slingerland,
A. H. Slingerland,
J. B. Endicott,
Charles Raider,
J. M. Elliott,
Lavinia Grover,
Eli Jones,
Mary A. Smith,
George Burkhardt,
B. Pemberton,
R. Carner,
S. H. McCreary,
John Leonard,
Jos. Thornton,
Rebecca McCulloch,
Catherine Endicott,
C. J. H. Nichols,
G. B. Nichols,
Sarah Spencer.

COTTONWOOD GRANGE, No. 116.

HILL'S FERRY, COTTONWOOD TOWNSHIP, MERCED COUNTY.

Organized November 10, 1873, by J. W. A. Wright, P. M., L. Cal. S. G.

I. L. Crittenden, Master,
J. J. Doyle, Secretary,
W. F. Draper,
I. M. Daley,
Jerry Stergeon,
C. S. Johnson,
R. M. C. Hale,
E. L. Stergeon,
G. E. Mills,
I. T. Sparks,
Henry Whitworth,
G. Estes,
Wm. Eachus,
Mrs. A. Stergeon,
Mrs. M. E. Coyle,
Miss K. Sanford,
Mrs. C. Draper,
Mrs. A. M. Crittenden,
Miss Belle Tinnin,
Miss H. Campbell,
M. O. Babcock,
A. C. Tinnin,
Wm. Ruff,
Oscar Babcock,
R. Coyle,
L. Sweitzer,
Bates De Hart,
Mrs. I. A. Mills,
Mrs. S. E. Tinnin,
Mrs. M. E. Sparks.

WILDWOOD GRANGE, No. 117.

DENT (ATLANTA), SAN JOAQUIN COUNTY.

Organized November 12, 1873, by Edwin B. Stiles, Deputy.

Joseph Leighton, Master, E. J. F. Merouse, F. M. Furman,
A. B. Munson, Secretary, Mrs. Joanna Purvos, J. M. Purbos,
John Ward, Mrs. Mary Brown, Frank Stanley,
J. W. Gann, Georgie Ella Leighton, Wm. H. Snow,
A. H. D. McIntosh, Mrs. Hizziah Brown, Wm. M. Muncey,
Geo. E. Blanchard, Mrs. Maggie Pride, Mrs. Sarah Stanley,
Geo. N. Cole, I. S. Muncey, Mrs. Emma Marvin,
Wm. A. Bedford, Wm. Allen, Albima Allen,
G. W. Brown, Samuel Hall, Mrs. A. S. Munson,
J. H. Brown, I. B. Paynon, Miss Laura Dossey.

SARATOGA GRANGE, No. 118.

SARATOGA, SANTA CLARA COUNTY.

Organized November 10, 1873, by G. W. Henning, Deputy.

Francis Dresser, Master, S. P. Hutchinson, Wm. Pfeffer,
Jennie Farwell, Secretary, Willis Morrison, Wm. M. Reid,
Abyah McCall, Mrs. M. E. Hutchinson, E. M. Dresser,
Hobart N. Cutler, Mrs. S. M. Morrison, J. Cox,
I. C. Hutchinson, Mrs. J. Nickle, Mrs. A. M. McCall,
D. R. Scott, Mrs. E. S. Reid, Mrs. H. N. Cutler,
Jas. W. Loyst, Wm. Cox, Mrs. C. D. Dresser,
Andrew J. Loyst, F. B. Nickle,

WALNUT CREEK GRANGE, No. 119.

WALNUT CREEK, CONTRA COSTA COUNTY.

Organized November 15, 1873, by R. G. Dean, Deputy.

Nathaniel Jones, Master, Mrs. C. S. Hollinbeck, Wm. S. Huston,
Wm. R. Daley, Secretary, Mrs. Mary A. Livingston, Walter Renwick,
John Larkey, Mrs. E. C. Jones, Mrs. E. C. Larkey,
D. F. McClellan, Mrs. Martha Renwick, Mrs. Lemantha Hammitt,
A. W. Hammett, Mrs. Esther M. Fales, Mrs. Mary S. Hickman,
Edward Worden, H. M. Hollinbeck, Mrs. M. L. Huston,
F. Langenkamp, S. B. Hickman, Miss Eliza J. Jones,
James T. Walker, John H. Livingston, Mrs. Mary C. Walker,
Orrin Fales,

CENTREVILLE GRANGE, No. 120.

CENTREVILLE, ALAMEDA COUNTY.

Organized November 18, 1873, by Wm. H. Baxter, Deputy.

James Shinn, Master, M. J. Overacker, E. Miehaus,
John L. Beard, Secretary, A. R. Hall, Rufus Denmark,
B. D. F. Clough, E. T. Randall, J. R. Clough,
Wm. Tyson, M. L. Babb, E. Tyson,
F. Perez, Comfort Healy, Mary G. Healy,
F. B. Granger, Samuel P. Marston, S. P. Osgood,
A. S. Clark, John Proctor, Mary Denmark,
Wm. Healy, L. E. Osgood, Mrs. H. Overacker,
John Lowrie, N. L. Babb, Mrs. C. S. Overacker,
Howard Overacker.

CONFIDENCE GRANGE, No. 121.

GAUDALUPE, SANTA BARBARA COUNTY.

Organized October 27, 1873, by O. L. Abbott, Deputy.

A. Copeland, Master,
J. F. Austin, Secretary,
H. C. Venable,
J. S. Miller,
Orrin Miller,
W. T. Scott,
T. W. Roberts,
B. O. Walker,
James A. Norris,
W. F. Johnston,
W. J. Cock,
E. J. Preston,
Azariah Kennedy,
John Biggs,
Elias Sansome,
W. J. Hudson,
Charles Silvarer,
Mrs. Mary M. Johnston,
Mrs. Sarah L. Walker,
Mrs. Hannah M. Cock,
Mrs. Nancy A. Preston,
Mrs. S. Copeland,
Mrs. M. A. Venable,
Mrs. S. E. Miller,
Mrs. L. G. Miller,
Mrs. Ellen D. Austin,
Mrs. Ellen Norris,
N. W. Best,
John W. Emrich,
W. A. Templeton.

GEORGIANA GRANGE, No. 122.

GEORGIANA (WALNUT GROVE), SACRAMENTO COUNTY.

Organized November 19, 1873, by W. S. Manlove, Deputy.

F. M. Kittrell, Master,
George A. Knott, Sec'y,
H. F. Smith,
C. P. Hensey,
J. P. Norman,
Peter Hanson,
I. N. Holt,
F. M. Pool,
J. H. Slayton,
Mrs. Mary A. Hensey,
Sarah A. Pool,
Sarah Raney,
Louisa Holt.

DENVERTON GRANGE, No. 123.

DENVERTON, SOLANO COUNTY.

Organized November 21, 1873, by James A. Clark, Deputy.

Jno. B. Carrington, Master,
G. C. Arnold, Secretary,
Mrs. H. P. Carrington,
John B. Roper,
Samuel Stewart,
Mrs. J. E. Stewart,
Wm. Bacon,
G. Y. Stewart,
John Bird,
Jas. Jones,
Mrs. S. F. Jones,
John Tomlie,
I. H. Bullard,
S. H. De Puy,
Mrs. H. E. De Puy,
James Blyth,
O. D. Ormsby,
T. C. Stewart,
Mrs. Grace Stewart,
Miss Mary E. Cook,
G. N. Daniels,
Nathan Barnes,
Mrs. E. H. Barnes,
C. E. Garfield,
Mrs. U. Garfield,
Wm. Spencer,
Mrs. Rebecca Spencer,
G. B. Eustace,
G. C. Arnold,
Mrs. S. J. Arnold,
R. H. Barkeway.

WATSONVILLE GRANGE, No. 124.

WATSONVILLE, SANTA CRUZ COUNTY.

Organized November 22, 1873, by J. D. Fowler, Deputy.

Joseph McCollum, Master,
A. F. Richardson, Sec'y,
E. A. Knowles,
R. T. Gallagher,
T. Martin,
A. Hanson,
J. C. Drew,
J. Struve,
Mrs. Adelia Ripley,
Mrs. Louisa Martin,
A. Cox,
Mrs. R. W. Cox,
Miss L. C. McNealy,
B Gallagher,
V. Westcott,
M. Gagner,
A. McNealey,
J. C. White,
L. A. Lee,
J. M. Ripley,
A. F. Richardson,
Mrs. E. McCollum,
Miss Lottie Knowles,
Mrs. H. M. Westcott,
Miss Mary Wiley.

CALISTOGA GRANGE, No. 125.

CALISTOGA, NAPA COUNTY.

Organized November 25, 1873, by J. M. Hamilton, W. M. Cal. S. G.

I. N. Bennett, Master,
L. Hopkins, Sec'y,
Andrew Safely,
James M. Wright,
J. C. Wright,
T. T. Walker,
John Martz,
Sebastian Martz,
Martin Martz,
Mrs. Lovina Cyrus,
Mrs. M. J. Martz,
John Hoover,
W. B. Pratt,
Peter Teal,
John Cyrus,
Isaac Bradley,
John C. Willoughby,
L. H. Hopkins,
Mrs. Catherine Bennett,
Miss Alice Bennett.

RED BLUFF GRANGE, No. 126.

RED BLUFF, TEHAMA COUNTY.

Organized November 26, 1873, by W. M. Thorp, Deputy.

R. H. Blossom, Master,
John Curtis, Secretary,
J. C. Tyler,
Mrs. J. C. Tyler,
Mrs. R. H. Blossom,
I. S. Cone,
Mrs. I. S. Cone,
L. B. Healy,
Mrs. L. B. Healy,
George B. Tabor,
H. A. Rawson,
Andrew Jelly,
N. Merrill,
Mrs. N. Merrill,
George Peels,
H. C. Copeland,
Mrs. H. C. Copeland,
Wm. B. Parker,
George Champlin,
Mrs. Geo. Champlin,
Samuel Jennison.

WESTMINSTER GRANGE, No. 127.

WESTMINSTER, LOS ANGELES COUNTY,

Organized November 19, 1873, by Thos. A. Garey, Deputy.

M. B. Craig, Master,
Henry Stephens, Secretary
L. P. Webber,
Robert Strong,
I. D. Bowley,
N. Frank Poor,
John Anderson,
John Mack,
G. M. Crittenden,
Lot M. Jaquette,
Robert Eccles,
George Danskin,
Mrs. George Danskin,
Amelia V. Lawton,
Mrs. V. C. Anderson,
Martha M. Edwards,
Converse Howe,
James Taylor,
Jesse Davis,
J. A. Davis,
D. W. Lawton,
Joseph Bingham,
Thos. Edwards,
James McFadden,
Sarah L. Patterson,
Ella A. Jaquette,
Mrs. Olive W. Stephens,
Julia G. Bowley,
Mrs. F. S. Bowley,
Mrs. W. C. McPherson.

RIVERSIDE GRANGE, No. 128.

RIVERSIDE, SAN BERNARDINO COUNTY.

Organized November 25, 1873, by Thos. A. Garey, Deputy

E. G. Brown, Master,
W. W. Kimball, Secretary,
P. S. Russell,
W. B. Russell,
J. P. Herbert,
A. J. Twogood,
J. W. North,
E. R. Pierce,
J. G. North,
C. E. Packard,
Mrs. M. A. Russell,
Mrs. Eliza M. Sheldon,
Mrs. M. T. Shugart,
Mrs. Arabella S. Lord,
Miss Josie Craig,
G. D. Carleton,
G. W. Garcelon,
G. H. Cleft,
T. L. Abel,
J. T. Tobias,
K. D. Shugart,
N. D. Millard,
Wm. Craig,
Miss Lettie C. Brown,
Mrs. Ann L. North,
Mrs. A. A. Pierce,
Mrs. Mary F. Garcelon.

ENTERPRISE GRANGE, No. 129.

Brighton, Sacramento County.

Organized December 12, 1873, by W. S. Manlove, Deputy.

Jasper M. Bell, Master,
Maurice Toomey, Sec'y,
Stephen M. Haynie,
A. A. Nordyke,
George Wilson,
J. Campbell,
H. A. Parker,
A. M. Gunter,
J. J. Martin,
Nelson Shaver,
Ada M. Shaver,
Mary C. Nordyke,
Euphernia Bell,
Marie W. Parker,
J. R. Gilleland,
R. S. Jamison,
M. Toomey,
J. D. Bennett,
R. J. Brown,
T. L. Williams,
John D. Morrison,
Al. Root,
Mary M. Gunter,
Margaret A. Haynie,
Sarah Martin,
Mary M. Brown.

FLORIN GRANGE, No. 130.

San Joaquin Township (Florin), Sacramento County.

Organized December 17, 1873, by W. S. Manlove.

Caleb Arnold, Master,
Wm. Scholefield, Sec'y,
William H. Starr,
Catharine A. Starr,
D. H. Buell,
Susan A. Buell,
Isaac Lea,
Mary J. Caottle,
J. J. Bates,
Charles Jackson,
Charles Lea,
G. H. Jones,
E. J. Taylor,
Celia A. Taylor,
David Rees,
Elizabeth Rees,
Daniel Buell,
Phebe Arnold,
C. A. Phillips,
Warren A. Smith.

LOCKFORD GRANGE, No. 131.

Lockford, San Joaquin County.

Organized December 29, 1873, by E. B. Stiles, Deputy.

G. C. Holman, Master,
Sol. G. Stewart, Secretary,
Jerome Rider,
B. P. Baird,
W. Moffatt,
B. Thomas,
J. F. McDowell,
C. R. Montgomery,
Mary A. Trethaway,
E. P. Meyerle,
Phoebe Stewart,
Thos. Clement,
John Trethaway,
Mrs. A. A. Meyerle,
John Carpenter,
Thomas Kenny,
Mrs. G. C. Holman,
F. C. Meyerle,
G. B. Ralph,
Elizabeth Ralph,
John McDowell,
A. J. Williams,
George Trethaway,
Mrs. Montgomery,
Mrs. Meyerle,
Mrs. T. Clements,
Mrs. Williams,
Jonathan Andrews,
Mrs. Carpenter.

GARRETSON GRANGE, No. 132.

Centreville (King's River,) Fresno County.

Organized December 10, 1873, by J. W. A. Wright, Deputy.

W. J. Hutchinson, Master,
W. W. Phillips, Secretary,
Joseph Burns,
W. L. Graves,
Andrew Jackson,
George Hobler,
Joseph Elliott,
A. H. Strathan,
L. W. Jones,
John Fuller,
John Carey,
Philip Weebe,
Mrs. J. Burns,
Mrs. J. Stephens,
Mrs. A. H. Strathan,
Mrs. L. V. Graves,
Mrs. A. Miles,
Miss A. A. Hutchinson.
Mrs. C. E. Phillips,
Jerome Stephens,
W. D. Mayhew,
Wm. Hutchings,
Joseph Imrie,
Robert Lacy,
Charles Hunter,
Allen Helm,
Mrs. J. Elliott,
Mrs. G. Hobler,
Mrs. A. Jackson.

FRESNO GRANGE, No. 133.

FRESNO, FRESNO COUNTY.

Organized December 10, 1873, by J. W. A. Wright.

H. W. Fassett, Master,
F. Dusy, Secretary,
Wm. Helm,
J. M. Amsa,
R. K. Estell,
G. W. Gretter,
G. A. Slocum,
Otto Brandt,
S. C. Smith,
W. M. Potter,
C. Walters,
S. Hamilton,
J. H. Bartlett,
Mrs. F. Dusy,
Mrs. M. J. Potter,
Mrs. M. Conklin,
Mrs. B. P. Gretter,
Miss E. L. Smith,
Mrs. M. Ross,
Mrs. F. Helm,
G. Dahl,
D. C. Libby,
W. M. Coolidge,
C. J. Hobler,
G. Helm,
F. E. Tadlock,
I. W. Tadlock,
Mrs. C. Walters,
Mrs. S. E. Freeman,
Mrs. D. C. Libby.

LAKE GRANGE, No. 134.

VISALIA, LAKE TOWNSHIP, TULARE COUNTY.

Organized December 11, 1873, by J. W. A. Wright.

M. S. Babcock, Master,
E. J. Bendick, Sec'y,
E. D. Simmons,
H. P. Grey,
J. F. Phillips,
H. W. Byron,
R. J. Wilson,
D. Rhoades,
J. Martin,
Henry Rhoades,
N. T. Gardner,
Andrew Foster,
G. Foster,
J. Robinson,
Mrs. J. Martin,
Mrs. N. J. Gardner,
Mrs. E. D. Simons,
Mrs. R. J. Grey,
Mrs. H. W. Byron,
Mrs. C. W. York,
R. P. Grey,
C. W. York,
W. R. Sullinger,
John Shores,
James Lebbey,
Jno. Heinlan,
Mrs. W. R. Sullinger,
Mrs. J. Shores,
Mrs. J. Sibley,
Mrs. H. Rhoades.

FRANKLIN GRANGE, No. 135.

VISALIA, LAKE TOWNSHIP, TULARE COUNTY.

Organized December 12, 1873, by J. W. A. Wright, Deputy.

F. Wyruck, Master,
A. B. Crowell, Sec'y,
M. W. Bloyd,
J. F. Betts,
Peter Kanawyer,
J. J. Kanawyer,
J. B. Fretwell,
John Chambers,
T. Jenkinson,
H. V. Harkins,
H. Johnson,
Aaron Jones,
James Jones,
I. J. Cole,
Mrs. Sarah Betts,
Mrs. M. B. Chambers,
Mrs. A. K. Kanawyer,
Steven Hicks,
Samuel Doyle,
A. B. Crowell,
Mrs. N. J. Wyruck,
Mrs. A. Bloyd,
Mrs. M. B. Chambers,
Mrs. N. J. Cole,
P. A. Kanawyer,
G. A. Hackett,
Chas. Hackett,
Mrs. M. J. Fretwell,
Mrs. P. A. Kanawyer,
Mrs. M. A. Kanawyer.

DEEP CREEK GRANGE, No. 136.

FARMERSVILLE, FARMERSVILLE TOWNSHIP, TULARE COUNTY.

Organized December 13, 1873, by J. W. A. Wright.

W. G. Pennebacker, M.,
F. J. Jefferds, Sec'y,
J. C. Goad,
G. F. Pennebacker,
D. Wood,
Wm. Davenport,
J. League,
B. Ballard,
F. G. Jeffards,
G. B. Catron,
Wm. Ballard,
A. H. Ballard,
A. Hinds,
Mrs. Carrie Wood,
Mrs. N. Jeffards,
Mrs. A. A. Davenport,
Mrs. LauraVanValkenburg,
Mrs. T. A. Allen,
Miss Katie Gilmer,
Mrs. S. J. Pennebacker,
W. J. Ellis,
L. Teague,
B. Miles,
Geo. Neilson,
A. W. Matthewson,
F. L. Castael,
A. Parker,
J. D. Vaugh,
Mrs. C. Miles,
Mrs. G. B. Catron,
Mrs. L. Matthewson,

TULE RIVER GRANGE, No. 137.

PORTERVILLE, TULARE COUNTY.

Organized December 16, 1873, by J. W. A. Wright.

G. A. Williamson, Master,
N. T. Blair, Secretary,
L. M. Bond,
J. B. Rumford,
L. P. Ford,
C. W. McKelvey,
C. S. Brown,
J. B. Hockett,
J. F. Griffin,
J. Hurton,
W. S. Henrahan,
D. M. Vance,
J. M. Owen,
Mrs. M. McKelvey,
Mrs. E. J. Sorrels,
Mrs. J. A. Loyd,
Mrs. Sarah Hadley,
Mrs. S. N. W. Rumford,
Miss Carrie Helton,
Miss L. A. Ford,
Anson Hadley,
Andrew S. Mapes,
S. C. Sorrels,
L. W. Lloyd,
J. W. Wilcoxon,
H. C. Kelley,
T. W. Hyndman,
Miss Caroline Leeds,
Mrs. M. J. Ford,
Miss Carrie Wilcoxon.

PANAMA GRANGE, No. 138.

PANAMA (BAKERSFIELD), KERN COUNTY.

Organized December 20, 1873, by J. W. A. Wright, Deputy.

H. D. Robb, Master,
J. F. Gordon, Secretary,
F. P. May,
J. W. Haworth,
O. B. Ormsby,
A. Noble,
J. Carlock,
Geo. Carlock,
J. M. Lundy,
C. B. Caldwell,
S. Baker,
I. S. Ellis,
O. Troy,
Mrs. P. E. Lundy,
Mrs. J. A. Ormsby,
Miss Phebe Stockton,
Mrs. M. B. Noble,
Mrs. A. Lundy,
Mrs. M. L. Caldwell,
Mrs. C. N. Carlock,
O. J. Lundy,
J. D. Stockton,
James Inglis,
Wm. N. Booth,
A. Charlton,
H. C. Loomis,
V. Barker,
Mrs. L. M. Stockton.
Mrs. A. H. May,
Mrs. E. E. Haworth.

BAKERSFIELD GRANGE, No. 139.

BAKERSFIELD, KERN COUNTY.

Organized December 22, 1873, by J. W. A. Wright, Deputy.

S. Jewett, Master,
Jerome Troy, Secretary,
L. S. Rogers,
J. S. Riley,
L. L. Reeder,
Walter James,
Robert Trewin,
J. S. Anderson,
P. A. Stine,
E. Tibbett,
P. Tibbett,
S. I. Jones,
D. W. Herndon,
Mrs. S. Rose,
Mrs. R. Tibbett,
Mrs. P. Tibbett,
Mrs. C. L. Rogers,
Mrs. A. Stine,
Mrs. L. James,
Mrs. E. Baker,
A. C. Marid,
C. H. Mayo,
M. W. Gates,
Allen Rose,
D. W. Walser,
A. A. Cochran,
P. D. Jewett,
Mrs. R. Reeder,
Mrs. J. D. Jewett,
Mrs. E. C. Jewett.

NEW RIVER GRANGE, No. 140.

NEW RIVER (BAKERSFIELD), KERN COUNTY.

Organized December 23, 1873, by J. W. A. Wright, Deputy.

John G. Dawes, Master,
James Dixon, Secretary,
P. C. May,
Wm. Canfield,
B. K. Said,
Wm. H. Gage,
I. R. Watson,
F. A. Tracy,
W. S. Brown,
R. J. Waldon,
Jas. J. Phillips,
E. S. Henley,
S. B. Henley,
Mrs. J. Said,
Mrs. M. J. Gage,
Miss Ella Said,
Miss Belle Gage,
Miss Kate Said,
Mrs. N. M. Watson,
G. W. Bevis,
Jesse Cole,
A. F. Gage,
Robert Plunkett,
R. Swift,
W. W. Drury,
Dave Chester,
Mrs. E. J. Brown,
Mrs. W. Canfield,
Mrs. J. Chester.

CHRISTMAS GRANGE, No. 141.

VISALIA, TULARE COUNTY.

Organized December 25, 1873, by J. W. A. Wright, Deputy.

A. B. Corey, Master,
W. H. Stuart, Secretary,
A. C. Jeffards,
Josephus Perrin,
J. L. Prather,
N. Archibald,
C. W. Flewellin,
G. W. Cotton,
B. F. McComb,
E. Y. Bock,
Thos. Gamlin,
Mrs. J. M. McQuiddy.
Mrs. L. Jeffards,
Mrs. M. E. Prather,
Mrs. M. A. Morton,
Mrs. Z. Lambert,
Mrs. F. A. Hatch,
Mrs. E. E. Bock,
Mrs. T. L. Gamlin,
Mrs. S. A. Cotton,
J. T. McQuiddy,
William Farmer,
N. T. Woodcock,
Wm. L. Morton,
J. Lambert,
J. R. Doty,
C. M. Hatch,
C. C. Lambert,
G. Slight,
Mrs. P. H. Doty.

VISALIA GRANGE, No. 142.

VISALIA, TULARE COUNTY.

Organized December 26, 1873, by J. W. A. Wright, Deputy.

Wiley Watson, Master,
H. C. Higby, Secretary,
J. P. Jones,
W. M. Meadows,
John Pogue,
B. G. Parker,
James Beck,
J. E. Lowry,
John Toombs,
G. W. Stephens,
W. H. Peck,
I. N. Peck,
W. R. Owens,
W. J. White,
Miss Mary Toombs,
Mrs. W. Watson,
Mrs. Mattie Harter,
Mrs. M. C. Parker,
Mrs. S. E. Peck,
Mrs. Belle Boyer,
Mrs. Traverse,
Wm. Smith,
John Cutler,
I. D. Keener,
Thos. Snider,
R. Bennett,
T. McGee,
Miss. S. R. Meadows,
Miss Mary N. Pogue,
Miss Alice Toombs.

ADAMS GRANGE, No. 143.

DRY CREEK, FRESNO COUNTY.

Organized December 27, 1873, by J. W. A. Wright, Deputy.

T. P Nelson, Master,
Thos. Wyatt, Secretary,
Thos. J. Hall,
Thos. Jeans,
J. P. Potter,
Logan F. Potter,
G. B. Jack,
W. W. Shipp,
E. H. Patterson,
R. B. Freeman,
David Ross,
P. O. McMahon,
W. B. Wyatt,
Mrs. Jane Hogle,
Mrs. M. Hieskell,
Mrs. M. H. Nelson,
Mrs. Mary Hall,
Mrs. M. B. Ross.
Miss Laura Jeans,
Mrs. S. F. Doak,
Mrs. Belle Jeans,
I. A. Jack,
David Barton,
T. S. Wyatt,
B. C. Wier,
J. M. Hieskell,
James Jeans,
A. M. Darwin,
Mrs. M. J. Shipp,
Mrs. M. Jack,
Mrs. C. C. Wier,

BORDEN GRANGE, No. 144.

BORDEN, FRESNO COUNTY.

Organized December 31, 1873, by J. W. A. Wright, Deputy.

J. W. A. Wright, Master,
J. H. Pickens, Secretary,
I. A. Pickens,
R. L. Dixon,
H. S. Patterson,
Joseph Borden, Jr.,
J. S. Pemberton,
J. G. Crowder,
W. S. Patterson,
Mrs. C. Dennett,
Mrs. J. A. Pemberton,
Mrs. J. Burcham,
Mrs. M. Patterson,
Mrs. F. Borden,
Miss Maggie Borden,
Mrs. M. E. Crowder,
L. A. Sledge,
W. B. Bennett,
John B. Fontaine,
H. St. J. Dixon,
I. Burcham.

ANTIOCH GRANGE, No. 145.

ANTIOCH, CONTRA COSTA COUNTY.

Organized December 27, 1873, by W. H. Baxter, Deputy,

J. P. Walton, Master,
James D. Darby, Sec'y,
Josiah Wells,
Mrs. Addie Wells,
W. J. Smith,
Delia T. Smith,
Wm. Ellsworth,
Wm. Gelchrist,
Thos. Shannon,
Wm. Davison,
Seth Davison,
C. L. Donaldson,
D. S. Hawkins,
Henry W. Baker,
J. W. Darby,
Sarah A. Sellers,
Wm. Sellers,
H. B. Jewett,
Phebe Jewett,
James Dukes,
T. O. Carter,
F. J. Quant,
Amanda M. Wells,
Abbott Sellers,
Jance C. Smith,
D. R. Benedict,
Phebe B. Benedict,
G. W. Kimball,
Wm. Wiggin Smith,
I. P. Walton,
A. G. Darby,

MARYSVILLE GRANGE, No. 146.

MARYSVILLE, YUBA COUNTY.

Organized January 9, 1874, by J. W. A. Wright, Deputy.

G. P. Bockius, Master,
James M. Cutts, Secretary,
L. P. Walker,
N. Sewell,
G. F. Kelser,
John Seaward,
A. Eaton,
H. S. Taylor,
W. H. Drum,
S. Grant,
Fred Grass,
Peter Grass,
Andrew Grass,
George R. Sanders,
Mrs. M. C. Brockins,
Mrs. M. Smith,
Mrs. A. W. Sewell,
Mrs. C. D. Kelser,
Mrs. M. E. Walker,
Miss Mary E. Eaton,
Miss Mollie Sewell,
Wm. D. Smith,
James Barry,
D. D. Fox,
George Shaw,
I. R. Bates,
E. A. Shepperd,
Christopher Westenhaver,
Mrs. H. S. Eaton,
Mrs. C. Taylor,
Mrs. J. Cutts.

FRANKLIN GRANGE, No. 147.

FRANKLIN (GEORGETOWN), SACRAMENTO COUNTY.

Organized January 10, 1874, by W. S. Manlove, Deputy.

Amos Adams, Master,
P. R. Beckley, Secretary,
Isaac F. Freeman.
George Morse,
J. M. Stephenson,
Thos. Anderson,
Martha Miller,
Amanda Moore,
Wm. Johnston,
J. W. Moore,
Troy Dye,
Fidelia Dye,
Sarah C. Beckley,
Eben Owen.

PLEASANT VALLEY GRANGE, No. 148.

PLEASANT VALLEY (SAN BUENAVENTURA) VENTURA COUNTY.

Organized January 10, 1874, by Milton Wasson, Deputy.

Dan. Rondebush, Master,
R. Browning, Secretary,
Charles Brooks,
Elmer Drake,
J. S. Harker,
J. B. Robins,
J. Sisson,
W. H. Walker,
John Mahan,
A. S. Clark,
N. O. Wood,
Miss Ollie Walbridge,
Miss Myra Walbridge,
Mrs. Sarah Walker,
Miss Libbie Sisson,
Mrs. Rachel Rondebush,
Joseph Davenport,
W. P. Ramsauer,
H. Evans,
I. B. George,
B. Z. Barnette,
E. P. Foster,
Wm. Hughes,
John Saviers,
Wm. Walbridge,
Mrs. L. A. Clark,
Miss Annie Wood,
Mrs. Ruth Brooks,
Mrs. N. R. George,
Mrs. H. Evans.

CLARKSVILLE GRANGE, No. 149.

CLARKSVILLE, EL DORADO COUNTY.

Organized January 13, 1874, by W. S. Manlove, Deputy,

Robert T. Mills, Master,
J. Malby, Secretary,
Charles Chapman,
Nettie Chapman,
John F. York,
W. D. Rantz,
Amelia T. Rantz,
J. E. Butler,
Elizabeth Mills,
Peter R. Willot,
C. F. Maltby,
Emma Woodward,
William Woodward,
A. Morrison,
Samuel Kyburz,
Rebecca S. Kyburz,
Albert B. Kyburz,
George C. Fitch,
Egbert L. Wilson,
Joseph Jouger,
Charles Porter,
S. Euer,
Clara S. Euer,
I. W. Wilson,
Carry E. Atwood.

MANCHESTER GRANGE, No. 150.

MANCHESTER (PUNTA ARENA), MENDOCINO COUNTY.

Organized January 14, 1873, by Thos. H. Merry,Deputy.

Joseph Wooden, Master,
B. F. McClure, Secretary,
C. B. Pease,
Mrs. C. B. Pease,
William Munro,
Adin Antrim,
Mary Antrim,
Mrs. M. J. Caughey,
Wm. Antrim,
W. R. Lane,
Mrs. C. W. Lane,
David Clanton,
W. F. McClure,
Joseph Shepard,
Mrs. J. Shepard,
Wm. Shoemaker,
John D. Taughey,
Hiram Gilmore,
Mrs. C. R. Gilmore,
D. F. Cain,
Mrs. D. P. Cain,
Clark Fairbanks,
G. W. Davis,
Mrs. A. A. Wooden,
A. B. Kendall,
Mrs. M. H. Kendall,
H. Veumngerholz,
S. S. Hoyt,
S. C. Hunter,
Mrs. S. M. Hoyt.

LITTLE LAKE GRANGE, No. 151.

LITTLE LAKE, MENDOCINO COUNTY.

Organized January 20, 1874, by T. H. Merry, Deputy.

G. B. Mast, Master,
Wm. A. Wright, Sec'y,
P. Muir,
R. V. Doggett,
I. S. Gardner,
I. H. Fettin,
M. C. Fettin,
W. V. Powell,
Mary A. Powell,
Daniel Lambert,
Miranda H. Lambert,
A. Simonson,
M. A. Simonson,
Z. Simonson,
A. P. Martin,
Hester Ann Sawyer,
Parmelia Mast,
E. J. Muir,
T. Hardwick,
S. E. Gardner,
F. L. Duncan,
Catherine Duncan,
Elijah Frost,
James Frost,
Jesse C. Thompson,
Peggy Sawyer,
S. Harten,
M. K. Sawyer,
Wm. A. Blosser,
John Robertson,

TWO ROCK GRANGE, No. 152.

TWO ROCK, SONOMA COUNTY.

Organized December 16, 1873, by J. H. Hegeler, Deputy.

John R. Doss, Master,
John H. Freeman, Sec'y,
W. D. Freeman,
J. Furgeson,
Wm. H. Thompson,
Howard Andrews,
John Pervine,
John R. Doss,
A. A. Brown,
Frank Freeman,
M. Laufenberg,
Hamilton Gaston,
Mrs. John Doss,
Mrs. H. E. Tower,
Mrs. Carrie Ent,
Mrs. Annie Hastead,
Mrs. G. Giberson,
Wm. H. Smith,
W. Church,
F. A. Tower,
Charles Giberson,
Wilbert Smith,
John H, Freeman,
Frank Hill,
N. A. Clark,
M. Johnson,
J. Malsead,
Mrs. Mary Freeman,
Mrs. M. M. Freeman,
Mrs. Emma M. Smith,
Mrs. Mary A. Brown,
Miss Hattie Ent,

TOMALES GRANGE, No. 153.

TOMALES, MARIN COUNTY.

Organized December, 17, 1873, by John H. Hegeler, Deputy.

Wm. Vanderbilt, Master,
R. H. Prince, Secretary,
S. C. Percival,
A. Doyle,
O. Hubbell,
Stanford Duncan,
Ed. Ladner,
John Buchanan,
A. S. Marshall,
Wm. Vanderbilt,
H. Guldager,
Henry Elpich,
Mrs. Phebe J. Huntley,
Miss Amelia Walters,
Mrs. F. W. Bemis,
Mrs. S. Duncan,
Mrs. D. B. Burbank,
Thos. J. Johnson,
F. A. Plank,
F. W. Bemis,
Conrad Stump,
Joseph Huntley,
D. B. Burbank,
Thos. M. Johnston,
Isaac Parker,
John Guglinelli,
Mrs. J. Parker,
Mrs. F. A. Plank,
Mrs. O. Hubbell,
Mrs. J. Huntley.

POINT REYES GRANGE, No. 154.

POINT REYES (OLEMA), MARIN COUNTY.

Organized December 20, 1873, by John H. Hegeler, Deputy.

N. H. Stenson, Master,
John A. Upton, Secretary,
T. B. Crandell,
Wm. P. Ruggles,
Wm. Evans,
S. E. Perham,
Henry Clausen,
James Whaley,
Thomas Whaley,
D. Hochreuter,
Mrs. John A. Upion,
Mrs. F. B. Crandall,
Mrs. Wm. P. Ruggles,
Mrs. Wm. Evans,
Mrs. S. C. Perham,
Mrs. James Whaley,
David Amos,
Chas. H. Johnson,
A. Huff,
Joseph Fay
A. N. Cleland,
A. H. Stenson,
A. K. Keyser,
N. Shafter,
R. E. Johnson,
R. A. Upton,
Mrs. Peck,
Mrs. A. Huff,
Mrs. A. N. Cleland,
Mrs. Henry Clausen.

NICASIO GRANGE, No. 155.

NICASIO, MARIN COUNTY.

Organized December 22, 1873, by John H. Hegeler, Deputy.

H. F. Taft, Master,
J. W. Noble, Secretary,
Frank Nasen,
George Boreham,
John Shaub,
Frank Rogers,
B. F. Partee,
Wm. F. Farley,
P. K. Austin,
R. B. Noble,
Thos. B. Roy,
Thos. Campbell,
Mrs. H. Fluis,
Mrs. C. W. Bull,
Mrs. C. J. Magee,
Mrs. J. W. Noble,
Mrs. B. F. Partee,
Richard Magee,
C. L. Estey,
Thos. H. Estey,
M. McNamara,
Wm. Reeding,
C. J. Magee,
Wm. Dixon,
Henry Fluis,
Mrs. Frank Nasen,
Mrs. H. F. Taft,
Mrs. Wm. Reeding,
Mrs. McNamara,
Mrs. John Shaub.

MAYFIELD GRANGE, No. 156.

MAYFIELD, SANTA CLARA COUNTY.

Organized January 31, 1874, by George W. Henning, Deputy.

F. W. Wieshaer, Master,
James M. Pitman, Sec'y,
A. J. Pitman,
Nathan Dawson,
Thos. Williams,
Sarah H. Grâs,
R. L. Boulware,
Wm. Paul,
Permelia Boulware,
G. D. Gleason,
P. Dowd,
J. D. Dixon,
Jno. Bradbury,
James A. Boulware,
Josephine E. Bowles,
W. W. Brown,
John Green.

OCEAN VIEW GRANGE, No. 157.

COLMA (SCHOOL-HOUSE STATION), SAN MATEO COUNTY.

Organized February 20, 1874, by W. H. Baxter, Deputy.

J. G. Knowles, Master,
Edward Robson, Sec'y.
A. J. Vanwinkle,
H. A. Knight,
Edward Charlton,
J. V. White,
Mrs. Vanwinkle,
Mrs. Kuine,
John Charlton,
F. E. Pierce,
B. Houbrick,
Robt. Ashburner,
Mrs. Ashburner,
Mrs. Knight,
Wm. Hall,
D. Hutchinson,
H. Jones,
J. Smith,
E. Robson,
J. Wright,
Mrs. J. Smith,
Mrs. Knowles,
W. H. Kuine,
Mrs. M. J. Charlton,
Ai. Willard,
C. W. Taber,
Mrs. L. Taber,
H. Schwerin,
H. Moran.

MONTEZUMA GRANGE, No. 158.

COLLINSVILLE, SOLANO COUNTY.

Organized January 23, 1874, by Robert C. Haile, Deputy.

Thos. F. Hooper, Master,
C. Knox Marshall, Sec'y,
C. H. Rice,
Wm. Jubb,
F. Unger,
C. M. Ish,
E. J. Upham,
M. Nelson,
H. R. Barker,
E. P. Sanborn,
Mrs. Delia Rice,
Mrs. S. E. Jubb,
Mrs. S. C. Shedd,
F. J. Taylor,
Wm. Quick,
D. Cushman,
Wm. Donell,
W. D. Hanson,
Jas. Galbraith,
Mrs. Augusta M. Hooper,
Mrs. S. A. Daniels,
Miss Addie Daniels,
Mrs. Mary Taylor,
Mrs. Mira Barker.

RIO VISTA GRANGE, No 159.

RIO VISTA, SOLANO COUNTY.

Organized January 24, 1874, by Robert C. Haile, Deputy.

A. B. Alsip, Master,
J. H. Gardner, Secretary,
R. Thrush,
Wm. Ewing,
E. Wilson,
Wm. Glenn,
J. W. Connolly,
I. T. Broady,
Chas. Peterson,
Alex. Curry,
A. W. Ellitt,
Miss Alice Williams,
Mrs. L. L. Alsip,
Miss E. M. Thrush,
Mrs. L. M. Thrush,
Mrs. J. W. Connolly,
J. W. Cameron,
John McCrary,
Wm. Williams,
Thos. Menzies,
John Johnson,
Daniel Stewart,
Charles Howard,
J. H. Hamilton,
I. M. Johnson,
Mrs. C. Cameron,
Miss S. A. Bicknell,
Miss J. J. Glenn,
Miss Margaret Menzies.

OAKDALE GRANGE, No. 160.

OAKDALE, STANISLAUS COUNTY.

Organized February 21, 1874, by J. D. Spencer, Deputy.

A. S. Emery, Master,
C. B. Ingalls, Secretary,
Theron Parker,
James Booth,
R. Rutherford,
F. G. Whitby,
G. F. La Clerk,
Wm. Lett,
C. R. Callender,
Mrs. Wm. Martin,
Mrs. Mary Crow,
Mrs. Mary Murphy,
Wm. Rutherford,
S. B. Callender,
D. Monroe,
Wm. Clavey,
W. H. Recker,
S. La Clerk,
J. C. Henderson,
T. G. Murphy,
Mrs. S. B. Ingalls,
Mrs. A. S. Emery,
Mrs. R. Lovell.

ROSEVILLE GRANGE, No. 161.

ROSEVILLE, PLACER COUNTY.

Organized March 6, 1874, by W. S. Manlove, Deputy.

A. D. Neher, Master,
J. N. Neher, Secretary,
George R. Grant,
Mary H. Grant,
I. G. Gould,
Catherine S. Gould,
D. W. Lewis,
G. W. Cavitt,
Rebecca Cavitt,
John McClurg,
I. F. Cross,
Sarah J. Cross,
L. L. Crocker,
Julia A. Crocker,
S. De Kay,
Mary L. Neher,
S. P. Neher,
Nicholas Mertes,
W. H. Murray,
H. F. Davis,
D. L. Allen,
H. Porter,
Amelia Porter,
Margaret Mertes,
George K. Kirby,
Daniel Stephenson,
Elizabeth Stephenson.

SAN PEDRO GRANGE, No. 162.

HUENEME (SAN BUENAVENTURA), VENTURA COUNTY.

Organized February 28, 1874, by Milton Wasson, Deputy.

I. Y. Saviers, Master,
D. D. De Nare, Sec'y,
S. D. Pinkard,
Thos. Alexander,
William Alexander,
Jacob Maulhardt,
John Borchard,
John G. Hill,
I. F. Woolley,
Walter H. Cook,
Newton Bagley,
Mrs. S. D. Pinkard,
Miss Minnie Alexander,
Miss Nettie J. Hill,
Mrs. Mary Borchard,
Mrs. Cassandra Woolley,
John H. Conrad,
I. E. Borchard,
Godfrid Maulhardt,
G. G. Glowner,
W. M. Neece,
Thos. H. Williams,
Louis Pfeiler,
Joseph S. Cook,
Mrs. Flora De Nure,
Mrs. N. W. Conrad,
Mrs. Mary E. Glowner,
Mrs. Sophia Maulhardt,
Mrs. Martha K. Saviers.

SUNOL GRANGE, No. 163.

SUÑOL, ALAMEDA COUNTY.

Organized March 7, 1874, by W. H. Baxter, Deputy.

Elijah M. Carr, Master,
S. W. Millard, Sec'y,
B. F. Cooper,
D. W. Baker,
Charles Duerr,
L. Austraumer,
G. J. Vanderwort,
W. S. Alexander,
Maria Carr,
T. N. Suñol,
Elizabeth A. Canavan,
James Bennett,
Jos. F. Black,
Mary E. Cooper,
Eliza A. Vanderwort,
Abbie M. Blake,
Dena Baker,
James Trimingham,
C. P. Blake,
Peter Canavan,
S. W. Millard,
Chas. Hadsell,
Michael Rogan,
P. McLachlan,
George Gregory,
John Arnett,
Leon E. Jones,
Naomi J. Baker,
Sarah Carr,
Augusta Trimingham,
Anna M. Hadsell.

SESPI GRANGE, No. 164.

SATICOY TOWNSHIP (SAN BUENAVENTURA), VENTURA COUNTY.

Organized March 13, 1874, by Milton Wasson, Deputy.

S. A. Guiberson, Master,
Thomas Marpels, Sec'y,
T. A. Sprague,
James Heaney,
Mrs T. Caswel,
C. H. Dickel,
Mrs. M. E. Guiberson,
Mrs. Lizzie Canaway,
Mrs. E. M. Dickel,
C. W. Edwards,
I. A. Canaway,
T. J. Casner,
Wm. Horton,
Mrs. E. C. Sprague,
Mrs. M. J. Edwards.

OJAI GRANGE, No. 165.

VENTURA (SAN BUENAVENTURA), VENTURA COUNTY.

Organized March 19, 1874, by Milton Wasson, Deputy.

C. E. Soule, Master,
Jos. Hobart, Secretary,
L. D. Roberts,
F. M. White,
G. T. Grow,
George L. Watters,
H. J. Dennison,
Joseph Hobart,
Theodore Todd,
S. C. Gray,
John Pinkerton,
Mrs. Georgie Jones,
Mrs. Adeline T. Grow,
Mrs. Sarah E. McLean,
Mrs. H. E. McKee,
Mrs. Margaret Dennison,
William Pine,
John Reeth,
John Larmer,
N. N. McLean,
W. S. McKee,
J. N. Jones,
J. M. Charles,
Rober Ayres,
Mrs. M. A. Roberts,
Mrs. Adeline Soule,
Mrs. M. E. Watters,
Mrs. M. E. Jones,
Mrs. Lucinda Grey.

RUTHERFORD GRANGE, No. 166.

RUTHERFORD (YOUNTVILLE), NAPA COUNTY.

Organized March 14, 1874, by W. H. Baxter, Deputy.

C. S. Burrage, Master,
H. W. Crabb, Secretary,
T. B. Edington,
C. W. Smith,
W. H. Sanders,
Adda Crabb,
T. Chopen,
John Bateman,
R. H. Garner,
Elizabeth Ritchie,
Amanda Garner,
Milla Crabb,
Cordelia Long,
Elizabeth Crabb,
Candace Ross,
Malvina Edington,
Mary A. Smith,
Reuben Long,
Wm. T. Ross,
M. G. Ritchie,
Frederick Willoughby,
Sarah A. Saunders,
Mattie Willoughby,
C. Bateman.

FARMINGTON GRANGE, No. 167.

FARMINGTON (TEHAMA), TEHAMA COUNTY.

Organized March 19, 1874, by G. W. Colby, Deputy.

Addison J. Loomis, Mast.,
S. H. Loomis, Secretary,
Arthur J. Chittenden,
James M. Rodgers,
James Specks,
S. P. Garvoutt,
Wm. Jewett,
C. F. Foster,
Vina E. Jewett,
Mary L. Best,
Catherine Specks,
M. C. Loomis,
R. Johnson,
C. C. Chittenden,
William McDane,
C. P. Rice,
Z. Best,
S. S. Stinchaum,
O. A. Loomis,
N. Garvoutt,
Mary Rice,
J. Mullen,
Martha J. Mullen,
Chas. C. White,
J. Boland.

GILROY GRANGE, No. 168.

GILROY, SANTA CLARA COUNTY.

Organized March 26, 1874, by G. W. Henning, Deputy.

W. Z. Augney, Master,
H. Coffin, Secratary,
E. Seaverly,
Mrs. E. Seaverly,
Hugh L. Jones,
Mrs. H. L. Jones,
Miss Corrinne Jones,
Frank M. Dunning,
H. Coffin,
D. B. Lillard,
W. Frank Oldham,
Ledyard Fine,
Miss —. Fine,
J. F. Freeman,
Mrs. J. F. Freeman,
J. Begg,
O. P. Reeve.

PLAINSBURG GRANGE, No. 169.

PLAINSBURG, MERCED COUNTY.

Organized April 3, 1874, by H. B. Jolley, Deputy.

P. Y. Welch, Master,
T. J. E. Wilcox, Sec'y,
H. N. Fish,
R. Earl,
R. M. Burchell,
Wm. Wynn,
Mrs. Wynn,
Ed Russell,
J. C. C. Russell,
Mrs. Russell,
H. Dewey,
Mrs. Dewey,
Mrs. Fish,
MissJeannette Spangleburg
S. Peak,
Mrs. C. Applegarth,
H. E. McCure,
N. S. Drew,
J. A. Barker,
Alex. Taylor,
A. Hassell,
E. Mason,
Mrs. Mason,
S. C. Johnson,
W. Johnson,
P. Y. Welch,
Eli Furman,
F. Furman,
Miss C. Anderson,
Mrs. Stonewood,
Miss Lula Peck.

BEN LOMOND GRANGE, No. 170.

BEN LOMOND (SANTA CRUZ), SANTA CRUZ COUNTY.

Organized April 4, 1874, by Geo. W. Henning, Deputy.

H. H. Buckles, Master,
Charles Craghill, Sec'y,
Robert Canham,
D. D. Tompkins,
B. P. Wright,
Alex. Leacht,
John Gray,
Mrs. E. F. Gray,
James Jones,
Fritz Quistorff,
Lewis Bregenza,
Mrs. C. Buckles,
Levi P. Sprague,
Charles Craghill,
Mrs. Chas. Craghill,
Mrs. Susan M. Craghill,
John Burns, Sr.,
John Burns, Jr.,
James Burns,
Miss Maggie Burns,
Minerva Canham,
Alvira Tompkins.

CENTRE GRANGE, No. 171.

CENTRAL DISTRICT (COLUSA), COLUSA COUNTY.

Organized November 20, 1873, by J. J. Hicok, Deputy.

J. B. Kimbull, Master,
W. G. Saunders, Secretary,
James Dowson,
E. Stewart,
D. Bebe,
J. K. Duncan,
Elias B. Duncan,
Henry Husted,
P. H. Williams,
Louis Ganthier,
H. C. Simmons,
Mrs. Anna Husted,
Miss Lucy A. Gilman,
Mrs. Carrie Webley,
Miss Sarah Becker,
H. B. Gay,
C. W. Marsh,
J. M. Grove,
W. G. Saunders,
John Duncan,
I. C. Smith,
Frank Becker,
Mrs. J. C. Smith,
Mrs. W. G. Saunders,
Miss R. Murphy,
Miss Lucy Duncan,
Mrs. Mary Zumwalt.

AMERICAN RIVER GRANGE, No. 172.

BRIGHTON (PATTERSON), SACRAMENTO COUNTY.

Organized March 23, 1874, by William S. Manlove, Deputy.

E. G. Morton, Sr., Master,
Cyrus Wilson, Secretary,
William Deterding,
James W. Kilgore,
George M. Kilgore,
J. A. Evans,
David W. Taylor,
A. W. Bryan,
T. G. Saulsburg,
Carl Halversen,
W. W. Brison,
Thomas Cox,
N. Kane,
Christina Deterding,
Elizabeth M. Criswel,
Metta Bryan,
Carrie Brison,
Amanda Kane,
M. L. Smith,
D. L. Williamson,
Edmund G. Morton, Jr.,
Claus Jorgenson,
George Hanlon,
George Saulsburg,
Claus Jorgenson,
John Studerous,
Emeline E. Kilgore,
Adaline D. Morton,
Addie Morton,
Nellie Williamson,
Laura J. M. Saulsburg.

MOUNTAIN GRANGE, No. 173.

SAN BENITO, SAN BENITO COUNTY.

Organized April 9, 1874, by J. D. Fowler, Deputy.

S. Kennedy, Master,
J. W. Matthews, Secretary,
C. P. Bryant,
D. M. Sellick,
J. Mantes,
F. R. Meyer,
Mrs. C. C. Butterfield,
Miss Mary Jane Kennedy,
Mrs. R. K. Blosser,
W. H. Blosser,
John D. Justice,
W. McCool,
J. F. Taylor,
B. Smith,
G. M. Butterfield,
Mrs. E. J. Pruett,
Miss S. M. Bryant,
Mrs. C. S. Bittey,
Ella Justice.

BINGHAMPTON GRANGE, No. 174.

BINGHAMPTON, SOLANO COUNTY.

Organized April 11, 1874, by Richard C. Haile.

Albert Bennett, Master,
Edgar A. Beardsley, Sec'y,
J. A. C. Thompson,
E. A. Beardsley,
C. S. Cushing,
G. C. McCray,
C. E. Irwin,
Wm. Johnson,
H. C. Gay
I. M. Bell,
S. M. Callton,
Mrs. E. L. McCray,
Mrs. M. E. Rychard,
Mrs. F. E. Gay,
Mrs. Helen Bell,
Mrs. Susan A. Mack,
J. B. Jameson,
Sherman Brown,
E. R. Miles,
H. H. McKinstry,
C. E. Plummer,
J. F. Brown,
George C. Mack,
J. Tuck,
F. B. Dodge,
Miss Ida Jameson,
Mrs. R. V. L. Bennett,
Mrs. Lucy Plummer,
Mrs. Etta Tuck,
Mrs. Ellen Cushing.

SAN MATEO GRANGE, No. 175.

SAN MATEO, SAN MATEO COUNTY.

Organized April 11, 1874, by B. N. Weeks, Deputy.

A. F. Green, Master,
W. H. Laurence, Secretary,
David S. McClellan,
W. Y. Price,
Levi Flagg,
W. M. Newhall,
Mrs. J. E. Butler,
Mrs. Orin Brown,
James Byrnes,
J. E. Butler,
John Spaulding,
Orin Brown,
Mrs. W. Y. Price,
Mary P. McClellan.

COSUMNES GRANGE, No. 176.

LEE (SHELDON), SACRAMENTO COUNTY.

Organized April 13, 1874, by W. S. Manlove, Deputy.

James A. Elder, Master,
J. H. Atkins, Secretary,
W. H. Lindsey, Jr.,
Owen Ingersoll,
Gilles Doty,
T. D. French,
Caroline L. French,
W. D. Hass,
C. W. Pierce,
Alice Elder,
Emma J. Richardson,
John W. Witt,
Mary Jane Witt,
Seth Macy,
Mary J. Hass.

RISING STAR GRANGE, No. 177.

PANOCHE, FRESNO COUNTY.

Organized April 18, 1874, by J. D. Fowler, Deputy.

Calvin Valpey, Master,
J. W. Craycroft, Secretary,
Mrs. L. S. Valpey,
A. D. Smith,
Mrs. Fannie Smith,
Wesley Shaw,
E. S. Keith,
Mrs. A. M. Keith,
Rhodes Gardner,
Mrs. E. Gardner,
Mrs. M. A. Craycroft,
Frank Enos,
Daniel Van Chief,
George Hinckley,
I. W. Ramsey,
Mrs. E. Ramsey,
W. H. Thornburg,
Mrs. O. S. Thornburg,
A. W. Hager,
F. Bennett.

EL DORADO GRANGE, No. 178.

El Dorado, El Dorado County.

Organized April 27, 1874, by W. S. Manlove, Deputy.

C. G. Carpenter, Master,
J. M. B. Wetherwax, Sec'y,
Philip Kramp,
W. H. Kramp,
Katherine Kramp,
Jacob Knizeley,
Fanny C. Knizeley,
C. D. Brooke,
Mary E. Brooks,
M. S. Robinson,
J. M. B. Wetherwax,
D. E. Norton,
Betsey A. Norton.
Sarah H. Carpenter,
C. G. Carpenter,
F. C. Carpenter,
John Bryan,
C. T. Foster,
Charlotte Foster,
Thomas Burns,
Cleora C. Burns,
N. Gilmore.

SUTTER MILL GRANGE, No. 179.

Coloma, El Dorado County.

Organized April 29, 1874, by W. S. Manlove, Deputy.

A. J. Christie, Master,
Henry Mahler, Secretary,
J. G. O'Brien,
Henrietta A. O'Brien,
Ornst Martensen,
Louisa Martensen.
W. D. Othietz,
E. Delory,
A. J. Peterson,
W. Stearns,
Wm. H. Hooper,
Aggie Mahler,
W. H. Valentine,
Mary Stearns,
Edith Vandershefter,
Anna A. Delory,
G. Bassé,
E. M. Smith,
Eliza J. Dobson,
Rebecca A. Poteel,
S. J. Poteel,
Andrew White,
H. B. Newell,
A. P. Christie,
Rosa McCay,
Robert Chalmers,
G. H. Bowser,
Abe Chalmers,
R. C. McKay,
Mary E. Delory,
Francis Vercamp.

GALT GRANGE, No. 180

Galt, Sacramento County.

Organized May 2, 1874.

J. C. Sawyer. Master,
J. L. Fifield, Secretary,
John McFarland,
B. F. Gates,
A. B. Bryant,
L. C. Young,
James H. Ferris,
E. Ray,
Angie Fifield,
E. M. Slater,
Rachel A. Wiser,
J. H. Sawyer,
Hiram Wiser,
B. F. Slater,
W. H. Young,
Hiram Chase,
Delia Wiser,
Fannie M. Bryant,
Augusta R. Sawyer.

NEWVILLE GRANGE, No. 181.

Newville, Colusa County.

Organized April 25, 1874, by J. J. Hicok, Deputy.

B. N. Scribner, Master.
Sullivan Osborne, Sec'y,
George O. Cobb,
Mrs. T. J. Cobb,
John R. Cobb,
James Tarleton,
Mrs. Rachel Tarleton,
B. F. Foreman,
Mrs. Arty Foreman,
Charles Neale,
Mrs. Joanna Osborne,
Alonzo Luce,
Mrs. Elizabeth Luce,
John A. Price,
Mrs. Ardell Price,
Mark Bailey,
Mrs. L. W. Bailey.

CALAVERAS GRANGE, No. 182.

JENNY LIND, CALAVERAS COUNTY.

Organized May 1, 1874, by John H. Hegeler, Deputy.

M. F. Gregory, Master,
A. Miles, Secretary,
Mrs. A. M. Gregory,
John W. Kirk,
Mrs. E. Kirk,
Chas. L. Williams,
Mrs. G. A. Williams,
Z. Taylor Vance,
John Baldwin,
Mrs. P. J. Hightower,
Louisa V. Baldwin,
Charles Morrill,
Miss Louisa Hightower,
Wm. H. Harper,
Mrs. N. E. Harper,
John S. Kirk,
W. Carson,
Christian Myers,
Robert Thompson,
Charles Topper,
Mrs. Rose Topper,
Clinton Gall,
Mrs. A. Gall.

ELLIOTT GRANGE, No. 183.

ELLIOTT, SAN JOAQUIN COUNTY.

Organized March 18, 1874, by E. B. Stiles, Deputy.

H. H. West, Master,
A. S. Misener, Secretary,
J. B. Greene,
D. W. Mooney,
Alex. Thompson,
M. E. Scott,
F. Ritter,
I. Wiltsie,
A. G. Dillon,
Mrs. Armena Greene,
Miss Mary Greene,
Mrs. Martha A. West,
Mrs. Caroline E. Misener,
Mrs. J. H. Dillon,
B. M. Greene,
M. Peter,
W. L. Campbell,
E. C. Greene,
M. Bovard,
L. W. Pounds,
J. F. Duntlin,
Mrs. Jennie A. Ritter,
Miss Martha Scott,
Miss Sarahette Thompson,
Mrs. Catherine Peter.

COLLEGEVILLE GRANGE, No. 184.

COLLEGEVILLE, SAN JOAQUIN COUNTY.

Organized March 19, 1874, by E. B. Stiles, Deputy.

Alex. Mayberry, Master,
J. C. McIntosh, Secretary,
T. Minahan,
S. K. Camp,
W. S. Camp,
W. T. Anglin,
W. N. Moss,
George F. Shackford,
Daniel Thomas,
James M. White.
J. F. Mullen,
Mrs. Josie M. Merwin,
Mrs. Sarah Haun,
Mrs. M. L. McIntosh,
Mrs. P. Camp,
Mrs. E. Mayberry,
George A. Beach,
H. W. Moss,
D. M. Walrad,
P. P. Ward.
B. McCabe,
D. C. McIntosh,
D. Pollock,
R. H. Walrad,
Franklin Faris,
Mrs. S. A. Connor,
Mrs. J. McKamy,
Miss Minerva McKamy,
Mrs. Pollock,
Mrs. Belinda Thomas.

FARMINGTON GRANGE, No. 185.

FARMINGTON, SAN JOAQUIN COUNTY.

Organized March 20, 1874, by E. B. Stiles, Deputy.

I. M. Groves, Master,
E. O. Long, Secretary,
C. H. Patterson,
J. E. Groves,
T. J. Drais,
M. J. Drais,
S. H. Anthony,
G. W. Andrews,
C. L. Rodgers,
J. R. Owens,
Jos. Manchester,
Mrs. E. M. Groves,
Mrs. E. Patterson,
Mrs. H. Long,
Mrs. C. Henry,
Mrs. S. N. Manchester,
J. R. Henry,
N. S. Harrold,
J. W. Smith,
J. G. Schrœder,
H. J. Bonham,
S. Shackford,
W. H. Derick,
J. J. Cross,
W. St. Rodgers,
Miss M. Kingsby,
Mrs. C. E. Schrœder,
Mrs. C. Drais,
Mrs. M. H. Andrews,
Mrs. E. Harrold.

VINELAND GRANGE, No. 186.

TUSTIN CITY, LOS ANGELES COUNTY.

Organized April 30, 1874, by Thos. A. Garey, Deputy.

A. B. Hayward, Master,
R. L. Freeman, Secretary,
Wm. Nettleton,
W. K. Robinson,
N. L. Harris,
C. A. Moore,
B. Wright,
J. Buck,
Mrs. C. A. Harris,
Mrs. S. J. Moore,
Mrs. M. Cates,
Mrs. S. A. Ritchie,
Mrs. B. J. Martin,
Miss Jennie E. Hayward,
C. Tustin,
M. Osborn,
W. W. Martin,
L. S. Robinson,
G. W. Freeman,
L. H. Stine,
T. B. Hulse,
T. Jacobs,
E. V. Stine,
Mrs. S. A. Stine,
Mrs. M. Tustin,
Miss H. C. Freeman,
Miss A. Keim.

LINCOLN GRANGE, No. 187.

LINCOLN, PLACER COUNTY.

Organized May 15, 1874, by W. S. Manlove, Deputy.

M. Waldron, Master,
J. S. Mariner, Secretary,
W. H. Tierner,
J. R. Nickerson,
Melvina Nickerson,
Anna Fuller,
James M. Tindall,
Tennessee B. Tindall,
Jas. A. Nickerson,
Octavia Nickerson,
Hans Anderson,
Alex. Cox,
A. J. Soule,
Sarah Carter,
Jacob Wilty,
Owen Clark,
Richard Fuller,
A. J. Boyden,
Peter Saling,
Lucinda S. Saling,
Chriss Crook,
Ellen M. Crook
H. Newton,
Martha A. Newton.

MORNING STAR GRANGE, No. 188.

CASTROVILLE, MONTEREY COUNTY.

Organized May 15, 1874, by J. D. Fowler, Deputy.

C. E. Williams, Master,
F. Blackie, Secretary,
Mrs. V. A. Williams,
W. A. Evans,
Mrs. H. Evans,
J. Withort,
J. Manteuffel,
R. Veuver,
J. Ball,
Fred. Brown,
Miss Tillie Brown,
Mrs. F. Armstrong,
H. C. Bryan,
Mrs. H. C. Bryan,
J. H. Ashley,
H. B. Scott,
Mrs. M. G. Scott,
C. R. Drumon,
A. Raine,
Mrs. M. Raine,
J. P. Armstrong,
T. McDonald.

VENTURA GRANGE, No. 189.

VENTURA (SAN BUENAVENTURA), VENTURA COUNTY.

Organized May 7, 1874, by Milton Wasson, Deputy.

J. Willett, Master,
Charles S. Preble, Sec'y,
Francis Barrow,
Charles S. Preble
Owen Merry,
Irwin Barnard,
Geo. D. Barrow.
J. M. Egbert,
Mrs. M. L. Barrow,
L. D. Chilson,
Mrs. M. E. Chilson,
Miss L. J. Merry,
Mrs. Mary Willett,
Miss Emily Barrow,
Henry Shaw,
J. Willett,
J. F. Hubbard,
Robert Calles,
J. C. Barrow,
Mrs. Phebe W. Barrow,
Mrs. Orpha Woods,
Mrs. Clara Bagley,
Miss Hattie J. Barrow,
Mrs. M. Hubbard.

COTTONWOOD GRANGE, No. 190.

COTTONWOOD, SHASTA COUNTY.

Organized May 25, 1874, by G. W. Colby, Deputy.

G. G. Kimball, Master,
John Barry, Secretary,
J. W. Span,
Wm. Ludwig,
Richard Owens,
Joseph Glass,
F. P. Glass,
J. Patterson,
M. W. Smith,
S. B. Sheldon,
C. A. Howard,
Mrs. M. E. Patterson,
Annie Nickols,
Elizabeth Span,
C. F. Glass,
Hattie Abel,
P. R. Richardson,
B. H. Pickett,
Wm. Lean,
C. P. Dunham,
E. Nickols,
James N. Patterson,
W. J. Eagleston,
H. Bosanki,
Thomas Grey,
Calvin Owens,
Wm. Wilcox,
Ann L. Smith,
Mrs. E. Lean,
N. M. Glass,
Grace Ann Patterson.

WALNUT GROVE GRANGE, No. 191.

WALNUT GROVE (COURTLAND), SACRAMENTO COUNTY.

Organized May 21, 1874, by W. S. Manlove, Deputy.

Sol. Runyon, Master,
J. V. Prather, Secretary,
S. A. Scearce,
F. M. Limbaugh,
E. W. Odell,
John W. Sharp,
Joseph Wise,
Adeline Runyon,
Cynthia L. Green,
Nancy J. Wise,
Levi Painter,
L. Wenser,
Dwight Holster,
P. B. Green,
A. J. Peck,
John Crofton,
Lizzie Dye,
Ephraim Dann,
Sperry Dye.

SHERMAN ISLAND GRANGE, No. 192.

EMMATON (SHERMAN ISLAND), SACRAMENTO COUNTY.

Organized May 22, 1874, by W. S. Manlove, Deputy.

J. M. Upham, Master,
W. M. Robins, Secretary,
W. H. Billings,
John E. Baker,
H. W. Baker, Jr.,
John McCall,
Thomas Cathers,
J. D. Sarles,
L. M. Upham,
W. G. Lemmond,
John Ferall,
Martha J. Bigelow,
D. S. Perry,
M. W. Blaboce,
O. A. Lindsey,
James Cathers,
A. J. Bigelow,
M. M. Robins,
P. K. Bigelow,
J. Palmer,
Emma O. Upham,
Emily P. Robins,
Catherine A. Baker.

SPADRA GRANGE, No. 193.

SPADRA, LOS ANGELES COUNTY.

Organized May 23, 1874, by Thos. A. Garey, Deputy.

A. T. Currier, Master,
Jno. Wright, Secretary,
T. D. Holladay,
A. H. Taft,
T. A. Caldwell,
D. R. Lilly,
J. H. Egan,
Richard Eads,
Joseph Malott,
William Jeffries,
Mrs. Rachel Eads,
Mrs. Lizzie Caldwell,
Miss Francis Fryer,
Mrs. Julia Holladay,
Miss Mary Shrewsbury,
A. M. Humphreys,
A. P. Monroe,
Henry Fryer,
W. S. Cook,
W. L. Marshall,
Wilson Beach,
Jere. Fryer,
Miss E. Lilly,
Mrs. M. A. Lilly,
Miss Louisa Fryer,
Mrs. Minnie Caldwell,
Mrs. A. J. Monroe.

EVENING STAR GRANGE, No. 194.

HAMILTON (NELSON STATION), BUTTE COUNTY.

Organized May 23, 1874, by Wm. M. Thorp, Deputy.

E. W. S. Woods, Master,
C. F. Butler, Secretary,
Jessie L. Warfield,
Wm. Downing,
Rufus Downing,
Edwin Pearson,
T. C. Pearson,
George Saunders,
A. M. Woodruff,
G. C. Nelson,
John Williams,
Virginia M. Warfield,
Lydia Woods,
May Downing,
Mrs. Howard,
Milton Mowry,
Chas. Howard,
Thos. Barnes,
Stephen Jones,
A. J. Conklin,
W. H. Moran,
I. W. Downing,
C. F. Butler,
Martha P. Warfield,
Emma Pierson,
Sallie Saunders,
Missouri Woodruff,
Ellen Bowles,
Mary Bradford.

REDDING GRANGE, No. 195.

REDDING, SHASTA COUNTY.

Organized May 27, 1874, by Wm. M. Thorp, Deputy.

Jos. F. Dinsmore, Master,
Sam. J. R. Gilbert, Sec'y,
H. C. Woodman,
W. H. Wilson,
Wm. Hawse,
E. A. Reid,
D. C. Johnson,
R. M. Johnson,
Daniel Robinson,
James McMullen,
J. J. Bell,
H. C. Ferrel,
Mrs. N. B. McLaughlin,
Mrs. Josephine Wilson,
Mrs. Sarah George,
A. Wood,
I. W. Dinsmore,
D. R. McLaughlin,
Geo. McFarland,
H. H. Loomis,
Jno. G. Wilson,
John George,
E. Anderson,
Rebecca Hawse,
Mrs. E. J. Woods,
Mrs. Anna Woodman,
Mrs. Anna Johnson,
Mrs. E. Anderson,
Miss Julie Johnson.

NEW SALEM GRANGE, No. 196.

PASKENTA, TEHAMA COUNTY.

Organized May 28, 1874, by W. M. Thorp, Deputy.

Oliver Harris, Master,
J. R. Whitlock, Sec'y,
James Wilder,
Stephen F. Harris,
John Fassen,
W. T. Harris,
M. Burt,
Cortland Harris,
Catharine A. Whitlock,
Julia A. Botkin,
Grace Haag,
Lucy Burt,
Margaret Harris,
W. F. Grey,
W. W. Botkin,
Elias Haag,
John Thompson,
I. W. Harris,
Caroline Wilder,
Mary Harris,
Susan M. Harris,
Emeline Blakely,
Mary Ann Harris.

POPE VALLEY GRANGE, No. 197.

POPE VALLEY, NAPA COUNTY.

Organized May 30, 1874, by J. M. Hamilton, W. M.

J. A. Van Arsdale, Master,
C. A. Booth, Secretary,
R. S. Hardin,
T. A. Varm,
John A. Hanna,
Henry Cole,
A. J. Dollarhide,
G. P. Wallace,
T. H. Ink,
R. J. Davenport,
George Swartz,
Mrs. J. A. Van Arsdale,
Mrs. G. P. Ink,
Mrs. G. P. Wallace,
Mrs. Jessie Barnet,
Miss Emma Booth,
Miss Ella Wallace,
John E. Williams,
Patrick Marrion,
Ed. Kean,
John Rose,
J. R. Booth,
C. A. Booth,
I. Booth,
Jesse Barnet,
J. J. Walters,
B. F. Wallace,
Mrs. John Hanna,
Mrs. R. J. Davenport,
Mrs. A. J. Dollarhide,
Miss Jennie Varm.

TULARE GRANGE, No. 198.

TULARE, TULARE COUNTY.

Organized May 28, 1874, by H. B. Jolley, Deputy.

D. E. Wilson, Master,
Victoria Wright, Sec'y,
I. N. Wright,
W. W. Wright,
Cynthia Wright,
Lizzie Wilson,
John Roach,
Agnes Roach,
Inza Roach,
I. A. Goodwin,
D. E. Wilson,
Mrs. F. Cartmill,
Sophia Cartmill,
William Small,
Vickie Wright,
Eli Williams,
Isabella Williams,
W. W. Wright, Jr.,
J. H. Hart.

WOODVILLE GRANGE, No. 199

WOODVILLE, TULARE COUNTY.

Organized May 29, 1874, by H. B. Jolley, Deputy.

I. A. Stover, Master,
J. Stewart, Secretary,
I. Chrisman,
J. Houston,
T. B. Fuguey,
T. J. Ruy,
W. Spense,
C. S. Lynch,
J. H. Grimsley,
R. J. King,
Mrs. F. E. Bensey,
Mrs. Mary Roach,
Mrs. Rachel Hensley,
Mrs. M. A. Lewis,
Mrs. E. J. Hensley,
W. Monroe,
C. C. Beebe,
R. McKee,
J. McFine,
I. P. Hensley,
Thomas Lewis,
Frederick Hensley,
Miss Jane Roach
Mrs. Virginia Ramy,
Mrs. J. M. Slover,
Mrs. Rebecca Beebe,
Mrs. M. A. Grimsley.

SHERIDAN GRANGE, No. 200.

SHERIDAN, PLACER COUNTY.

Organized May 29, 1874, by W. S. Manlove, Deputy.

D. H. Long, Master,
S. J. Lewis, Secretary,
J. W. Clark,
Charles Greetman,
John Storrs,
Miron Luce,
Lola C. Wheeler,
Emmett Botkin,
Louisa Greetman,
N. H. Kaschner,
Emily A. Beatty,
David H. Long,
J. T. Brock,
S. J. Lewis,
Thos. S. Barker,
W. H. Beatty,
Mary Kaschner,
H. S. Kempton,
S. R. Wilson,
Mary Stout.

MATTOLE GRANGE, No. 201.

PETROLIA, HUMBOLDT COUNTY.

Organized May 26, 1874, by Thos. H. Merry, Deputy.

Stephen Goff, Master,
D. J. Johnson, Secretary,
Mrs. Mary D. Goff,
M. J. Conklin,
Margaret Conklin,
Thos. Clark,
Jacob Miner,
Mrs. C. A. Miner,
J. W. Jamison,
John A. Coon,
David L. Marshall,
N. Crouch,
Sarah E. Marshall,
Jotham Bull,
James H. Goff,
A. McNett,
Mrs. Rosa Johnson,
Morgan Rudolph,
Mrs. R. A. Rudolph,
J. Wright,
Lucy A. Wright,
S. W. Gillett,
Mrs. H. A. Gillett,
Yost Benton,
Mrs. A. H. Benton,
David Simmons,
Mrs. M. A. Simmons,
Charles S. Cook,
Wm. Roberts,
Walker Hunter.

CAHTO GRANGE, No. 202.

Cahto, Mendocino County.

Organized June 1, 1874, by Thos. H. Merry, Deputy.

R. M. Wilson, Master,
J. P. Simpson, Secretary,
J. H. Braden,
Mrs. Frances Braden,
S. G. Williams,
Martha A. Williams,
Mrs. A. J. Grubb,
William Henry,
Elizabeth Henry,
Benj. S. Burns,
Eliza Burns,
S. M. Wilson,
Maggie Farly,
M. Vasser,
B. M. Wayman,
J. G. Burns,
W. B. Burns,
R. White,
Johnathan Thomas,
John M. Wilson,
G. N. Guibb,
I. I. Thomas,
Dorsinda Harelson,
O. R. Burnett,
I. F. Lammeth,
J. D. Wyman,
S. P. Beattie,
Mrs. E. A. Wilson,
Mrs. Mary F. Thomas,
G. W. Thomas.

PASO ROBLES GRANGE, No. 203.

Paso Robles, San Luis Obispo County.

Organized June 3, 1874, by A. J. Mothersead, Deputy.

H. W. Rhyne, Master,
J. P. Moody, Secretary,
I. M. Cummins,
D. W. Gilbert,
Mary Middaughs,
J. M. Cunningham,
D. E. Cummins,
T. E. A. Rhyne,
Esner Matthew,
D. F. Stockdale,
Gilbert Middaughs,
Minna Cummins,
H. S. F. Rhyne,
Nancy Gilbert,
A. Frick,
Nancy Tuley,
P. Kipple,
J. P. Moody,
B. Matthew,
Anna Cunningham,
Martha Moody.
G. W. Parrish,
Wm. Holden,
Rebecca Stockdale,
Rosetta Rhyne.

SANEL GRANGE, No. 204.

Sanel, Mendocino County.

Organized June 5, 1874, by Thos. H. Merry, Deputy.

Alex. Marshall, Master,
Jos. A. Knox, Secretary,
Mrs. A. Marshall,
Mrs. M. A. Edsoll,
E. H. Duncan,
Mrs. E. M. Duncan,
R. M. Parsons,
J. W. Daw,
Mrs. J. W. Daw,
Sarah Bickle,
E. Dooley,
Mary Daw,
Lucy E. Dooley,
Samuel Duncan,
Isaac Bickle,
Wm. E. Parsons,
T. S. Parsons.
O. R. Myers,
H. Willard,
T. J. Gallamore,
O. Howell,
Mrs. H. Stanley,
Mrs. J. W. Daw,
Miss M. J. Edsoll,
Mrs. L. F. Howell,
John McGlashen.

SYCAMORE GRANGE, No. 205.

Sycamore, Fresno County.

Organized June 6, 1874, by J. W. A. Wright, Deputy.

A. C. Bradford, Master.
Wm. A. Allen, Sec'y,
Alex. Kennedy,
Joel Bass,
John House,
James Allen,
J. R. McComb,
W. H. Parker,
Wm. A. Allen,
John West,
Mrs. R. Bass,
Mrs. N. Parker,
Mrs. Mary Kennedy,
Mrs. L. W. Bradford,
John Lamotte.

BENEYESSA GRANGE, No. 206.

MONTICELLO, NAPA COUNTY.

Organized June 12, 1874, by W. H. Baxter, Deputy.

J. W. Smittle, Master,
O. Schetter, Secretary,
C. Goslin,
M. C. Ish,
I. T. Ish,
R. D. Kincaid,
Cornelius Swietzer,
L. H. Swietzer,
J. C. Cunningham,
A. J. Wester,
Chas. Combs,
Isaac Swietzer,
Emma V. Schwitzer,
May Stafford,
Mollie Stafford,
Asa M. Jackson,
D. W. Carriger,
A. Stafford,
Peter Laflish,
J. Carrol Owen,
Chas. Seawell,
Nellie Gillespie,
Sallie Gillespie,
Angeline M. Gillespie,
Fannie Ish,
Lucy J. Jackson,
Elvira Combs.

SOUTH SUTTER GRANGE, No. 207.

PLEASANT GROVE, SUTTER COUNTY.

Organized June 13, 1874, by A. D. Neher, Deputy.

Thomas Boyd, Master,
Alex. Donaldson, Sec'y,
James Jones,
Geo. T. Boyd,
John W. Jones,
Terry Ballow,
Cyrus Briggs,
R. H. McClellan,
M. T. McClellan,
J. R. McClellan,
S. F. McClellan,
F. Saukey,
W. A. Goode,
Mrs. Susan Boyd,
Candace Richardson,
Alex. Donaldson,
Homer Saukey,
C. E. Hull,
Rebecca Jones,
John Morrison,
W. W. Monroe,
Geo. Richardson,
Charles Richardson.
M. T. Laros,
A. T. Jackson,
Wm. E. Roberts,
Daniel Carray,
Susan C. Boyd,
Mary J. Richardson.

SONORA GRANGE, No. 208.

SONORA, TUOLUMNE COUNTY.

Organized June 13, 1874, by J. D. Spencer, Deputy.

S. S. Turner, Master,
Robt. F. Williams, Sec'y,
E. M. Hampton,
Mrs. M. E. Hampton,
J. F. Ralph,
Mrs. E. A. Ralph,
John Pereira,
J. Leguarel,
George Soulsbys,
Mrs. E. Soulsbys,
R. Gilkey,
Mrs. E. J. Gilkey,
James B. Latimer,
M. E. Hyde,
E. N. Twist,
S. Allen,
W. H. Dickenson,
Mrs. E. Dickenson,
R. M. Chenoweth,
Mrs. Mary Williams,
M. W. Brooks,
Mrs. E. Brooks,
Mrs. J. Marks,
Mrs. S. A. E. Marks,
E. F. Hammers,
Mrs. E. A. Hammers,
I. Fergusson,
J. Blackburn,
Mrs. M. Blackburn.

LINN VALLEY GRANGE, No. 209

GLENVILLE, KERN COUNTY.

Organized June 18, 1874, by J. W. A. Wright, Deputy.

A. B. Du Brutz, Master,
S. E. Reed, Secretary,
J. F. Lewis,
L. W. Woody,
I. Pascoe,
J. Vanderen,
Joseph Morrison,
D. Laver,
T. E. Wilks,
David Scott,
J. M. Glenn,
E. Vaughn,
M. P. Blake,
Miss M. Early,
Mrs. M. A. Vaughn,
Mrs. Sarah Glenn,
Mrs. P. A. Morrison,
Mrs. Mary C. Wright,
Mrs. E. J. Towery,
Mrs. N. A. Pascoe,
James Prewett, Sr.,
N. S. Dauner,
Ed. Mahurin,
John Wicker,
J. R. Towery,
Henry Pascoe,
James Caruthers,
Miss C. Harvey,
Mrs. Mary Allen,
Mrs. E. Pascoe,

INDEPENDENCE GRANGE, No. 210.

INDEPENDENCE, INYO COUNTY.

Organized June 20, 1874, by J. W. A Wright, Deputy.

Josiah Earl, Master,
J. B. White, Secretary,
John Shephard,
J. W. Symmes,
D. D. Gunnison,
M. Garretson,
A. Wayland,
J. Vogt,
John Martin,
Owen Murphy,
J. Malone,
John Baxter,
S. A. Dinsmore,
Mrs. M. Shepherd,
Mrs. S. A. White,
Mrs. L. Wayland,
Mrs. H. Vogt,
Mrs. A. S. Earl,
Mrs. K. Gunnison,
Mrs. S. C. Martin,
B. Aiguerre,
C. A Walters,
F. Schamble,
E. Chagnette,
Louis McClure,
Chas. Kennedy,
W. M. Boyd,
Mrs. A. Chagnette,
Mrs. L. Walters,
Mrs. R. Schamble.

BISHOP CREEK GRANGE, No. 211.

BISHOP CREEK, INYO COUNTY.

Organized June 22, 1874, by J. W. A. Wright, Deputy.

T. J. Furbees, Master,
W. T. Wiswall, Secretary,
J. L. Garrettson,
B. H. Roberts,
John Clark,
Joseph Inman,
Andrew Dell,
E. D. Powers,
J. W. Wiswall,
O. D. Watson,
C. Munson,
W. G. Watson,
Wm. McLarren,
Mrs. A. Cromwell,
Mrs. C. Moats,
Mrs. E. McCrosky,
Mrs. M. A. Clark,
Mrs. A. Bowers,
Mrs. R. A. McLarren,
Mrs. M. Inman,
Jacob Powers,
O. Cromwell,
G. M. Clark,
George Collins,
H. Wamafield,
Wm. Bulbit,
Wm. Powers,
W. G. McCrosky,
Mrs. U. G. Monson,
Mrs. E. Roberts,
Mrs. S. A. Chamberlain.

LONE PINE GRANGE, No. 212.

LONE PINE, INYO COUNTY.

Organized June 23, 1874, by J. W. A. Wright, Deputy.

C. L. Jackson, Master,
R. A. Loomis, Secretary,
J. J. McCall,
Joseph Seely,
A. H. Johnson,
R. P. Ritgers,
G. W. Betty,
J. G. Dodge,
C. W. Johnson,
R. Vandyke,
John Dodge,
Mrs. M. Dodge,
Mrs. M. McCall,
Mrs. D. Johnson,
Mrs. A. B. Ritgers,
J. A. Ritgers,
Julius Roeper,
F. Albis,
Mrs. C. Vincentalli.

WELDON GRANGE, No. 213.

WELDON, KERN COUNTY.

Organized June 25, 1874, by J. W. A Wright, Deputy

R. T. Melvin, Master,
J. T. H. Grey, Sec'y,
W. J. Grant,
John F. Pyle,
G. F. Melvin,
Mrs. S. E. Gray,
I. L. Mack,
John Waterworth,
Thos. J. Elliott,
C. S. Collins,
Mrs. E. G. Stambler,
Mrs. A. L. Collins,
C. L. Brown,
A. A. Bermudez,
H. D. Strambler,
Joseph E. Miller,
H. T. Miller,
P. K. Brown,
Mrs. E. Bermudez,
Miss M. E. Elliott,
Mrs. M. J. Grant,
Mrs. F. J. Melvin.
Mrs. S. J. Miller,
Mrs. A. T. Riley,
J. B. Batz,
I. T. H. Gray.

TEHAICHIPA GRANGE, No. 214.

TEHAICHIPA, KERN COUNTY.

Organized June 29, 1874, by J. W. A. Wright, Deputy.

John Norboe, Master,
Jas. Prewett, Jr., Sec'y.
E. McVicker,
W. B. S. Brink,
W. S. Eastwood,
H. F. Wiggins,
Thos. H. Goodwin,
W. C. Wiggins,
Robert Taylor,
W. A. Taylor,
George Recq,
L. Gibson,
J. B. Malin,
Mrs. H. Williams,
Mrs. H. Whitlock,
Mrs. M. J. Green,
Mrs. L. Wiggins,
Mrs. J. Taylor,
Miss L. E. Butts,
Mrs. M. McVicker,
J. E. Williams,
Paul M. Norboe,
A. H. Butts,
L. D. Green,
T. M. Wiggins,
A. J. Degman,
A. Murphy,
Miss Martha Wiggins,
Mrs. E. Wiggins,
Mrs. E. A. Butts.

CUMMING'S VALLEY GRANGE, No. 215.

CUMMING'S VALLEY (TEHAICHIPA), KERN COUNTY.

Organized June 29, 1874, by J. W. A. Wright, Deputy.

Geo. M. Thompson, Mast'r,
T. M. Yates, Sec'y,
J. M. Brite,
P. P. Martin,
M. S. Freeman,
O. B. Wilson,
J. D. Chappell,
Jesse Davenport,
H. L. Todd,
Moses Hart,
I. N. Ellis,
Clint. Cudderback,
J. L. Hosack,
Mrs. E. Brite,
Mrs. R. Davenport,
Mrs. M. E. Cudderback,
Mrs. M. E. Martin,
Mrs. S. Cummings,
Mrs. S. Chappell,
Mrs. M. J. Freeman,
John Freeman,
N. J. McKaig,
George Cummings,
Lewis Smith,
Daniel Davenport,
J. B. Chamberlain,
Joseph Wagerer,
Mrs. M. McKaig,
Mrs. S. A. Ellis,
Mrs. J. Todd,

POMO GRANGE, No. 216.

POMO, MENDOCINO COUNTY.

Organized July 4, 1874, by T. H. Merry, Deputy.

John Mewhinney, Master,
G. B. Nichols, Secretary,
Daniel Mewhinney,
T. W. Dashiels,
Jennie Deselms,
B. Pemberton,
G. W. Pickle,
Isaac W. Grover,
Lavinia Grover,
B. B. Brown,
Life Farmer,
Wm. D. Jones,
Samuel Mewhinney,
J. Wattenburger,
John P. Bevans,
H. T. Cox,
H. Cox,
Martha Hughes,
David Wolvener,
Mrs. C. Farmer,
W. L. Jones,
L. P. Grover,
Mrs. Jane Miller,
Lewis Hall,
R. E. Madden,
Emma Madden,
L. J. Hall,
Martha Sellers,
Mrs. C. H. I. Nichols,
Stoddard Neil.

ROUND VALLEY GRANGE, No. 217.

ROUND VALLEY (COVELO), MENDOCINO COUNTY.

Organized July 7, 1874, by T. H. Merry, Deputy.

Philo Handy, Master,
J. A. Crawford, Secretary,
Nelson Brush,
Mrs. A. M. Brush,
Patrick K. Faulds,
S. Honbrook,
M. E. Honbrook,
I. A. Crawford,
A. E. McCombs,
Sarah H. McCombs,
I. A. Foster,
Joel Eveland,
J. Green Short,
Chas. H. Bourne,
F. M. Hughes,
C. H. Eberle,
L. C. Long,
E. R. Potter,
W. F. Moore,
Martha R. Moore,
W. P. Melendy,
Mary M. Melendy,
A. J. Shrum,
Wm. Pullen,
D. C. Dorman,
P. K. O'Farrell,
Mrs. Esther O'Farrell,
S. Foster.

MOUNT BOLIVAR GRANGE, No. 218.

CALLAHANS, SISKIYOU COUNTY.

Organized July 31, 1874, by J. W. A. Wright, Deputy.

R. M. Hayden, Master,
J. A. Cole, Secretary,
Wm. F. Chapman,
J. F. Forbes,
J. Comstock,
A. W. Wolford,
C. B. Sweet,
Mrs. S. A. Denny,
Mrs. J. E. Eddy,
Mrs. A. A. Guild,
Mrs. Clara Chapman,
Miss M. G. Eddy,
C. Schuler,
F. Knauft,
G. A. Eddy,
Jno. M. Messner,
Stephen Farrington,
Miss M. A. Sweet,
Mrs. Mary Blevius,
Mrs. M. A. Knauft,
Mrs. M. Farrington,

ÆTNA GRANGE, No. 219.

ÆTNA, SISKIYOU COUNTY.

Organized August 1, 1874, by J. W. A. Wright, Deputy.

J. W. McBride, Master,
J. M. Conaughy, Sec'y,
Jno. T. Moxley,
H. C. Cory,
L. S. Wilson,
E. F. Smith,
O. V. Green,
G. Wagoner,
Charles Hovenden,
Lewis Hughes,
Charles F. McConaughy,
Cord Sackman,
Geo. E. Davidson,
Mrs. S. E. Hovenden,
Mrs. S. M. Moxley,
J. M. Wolford,
Mrs. M. J. Shelley,
Mrs. A. A. Green,
Mrs. M. M. Wilson,
Mrs. M. E. Walker,
W. D. Shelley,
J. H. Walker,
J. McWalker,
Thos. Quigley,
P. A. Hartstrand,
Mrs. E. E. Smith,
Mrs. C. Hughes,
Mrs. M. Quigley,
S. M. Conaughy.

FORT JONES GRANGE, No. 220.

FORT JONES, SISKIYOU COUNTY.

Organized August 1, 1874, by J. W. A. Wright, Deputy.

J. S. Matthews, Master,
J. W. Tuttle, Secretary,
B. A. Godfrey,
J. A. Davidson,
J. R. Kinyon,
A. W. Evans,
D. B. Kingery,
J. Hamilton,
I. C. Wood,
A. S. Rantz,
M. Malayan,
Thos. Weddess,
George Bleything,
Mrs. H. R. Godfrey,
Miss Alice Davidson,
Mrs. C. M. Kingery,
Mrs. A. E. Matthews,
Mrs. F. E. Evans,
Miss A. B. Godfrey,
Mrs. L. A. Kinyon,
L. J. Williams,
Jeremiah Davidson,
Thos. Patten,
S. J. Luttrell,
Isaac Evans,
S. D. Varnum,
Merrill Evans,
Mrs. M. A. Davidson,
Mrs. Ellen Tuttle,
Mrs. M. Evans.

MILLVILLE GRANGE, No. 221.

MILLVILLE, SHASTA COUNTY.

Organized August 5, 1874, by J. W. A. Wright, Deputy.

E. Wagoner, Master,
Geo. W. Welch, Secretary,
J. L. Nichols,
J. W. Winsell,
A. Chatham,
T. D. Gault,
L. T. Benton,
Jno. P. Webb,
G. Fender,
J. Dunham,
C. Reineke,
T. J. Martin,
J. J. Kern,
Mrs. N. Hufford,
Mrs. S. A. Grant,
Mrs. S. A. Martin,
Mrs. J. Gault,
Mrs. E. R. Winsell,
Mrs. M. A. Keeney,
Mrs. M. F. Nichols,
John Ellis,
S. Hufford,
Wm. Tulloch,
W. Grant,
G. F. Schuler,
N. Harrington,
P. B. Langlois,
Mrs. H. Ellis,
Mrs. L. A. Dunham,
Mrs. H. D. Fender.

LA HONDA GRANGE, No. 222.

LA HONDA, SAN MATEO COUNTY,

Organized July 17, 1874, by B. V. Weeks, Deputy.

M. Woodhams, Master,
W. A. Saunders, Secretary,
Charles C. Rodgers,
Charles B. Sears,
Henry Wilber,
Henry Steinbarg,
Richard T. Ray,
Joseph W. Haskins,
Delia C. Johns,
Ella W. Weeks,
Wm. H. Monroe,
Isaac M. Baker,
Augustus A. Haskins,
Wm. H. Monroe,
Martha Ray,
Ettie E. Sears,
Emma L. Johns.

CRESCENT GRANGE, No. 223.

SPANISH TOWN (HALF MOON BAY), SAN MATEO COUNTY.

Organized August 8, 1874, by B. V. Weeks, Deputy.

H. M. Jewell, Master,
James Compton, Sec'y,
Robert Campbell,
John B. Lock,
Alonzo De Haro,
J. B. Gilchrist,
Mrs. M. Jewell,
Mrs. S. M. Hammond,
Mrs. Mary Johnston,
J. P. Johnston,
John Johnston,
W. A. Hammond,
John Holmes,
Mrs. J. Compton.

HAMILTON GRANGE, No. 224.

BIGGS STATION, BUTTE COUNTY.

Organized August 10, 1874, by J. W. A. Wright, Deputy.

H. L. Lassell, Master,
M. A. Randall, Secretary,
Daniel Streeter,
Darius Hurlburt,
Thomas Boulware,
W. M. Harrison,
V. S. Runnels,
W. W. Stone,
Virgil Randall,
H. C. Wilbur,
Anson Brown,
D. W. Card,
Silas Card,
Wm. Cross,
August McKillican,
Mrs. F. B. Card,
Miss H. L. Card,
Mrs. C. Harrison,
Mrs. M. E. Stone,
Mrs. E. M. Runnels,
Mrs. M. Lassell,
John Robinson,
C. A. Robinson,
C. M. Harrison,
John Clusky,
I. H. Rutledge,
Mrs. N. M. Randall,
Mrs. R. W. Randall,
Mrs. J. H. Rutledge,
Mrs. D. Hurlburt.

NORTH BUTTE GRANGE, No. 225.

NORTH BUTTE (YUBA CITY), SUTTER COUNTY.

Organized August 11, 1874, by J. W. A. Wright, Deputy.

B. R. Spilman, Master,
J. D. Dow, Secretary,
Otis Clark,
Wm. McMurtry,
Thos. S. Kersey,
W. T. Lamb,
Wm. Powell, Jr,
Aaron Pugh,
J. H. Myers,
Robt. Boyd,
Thos. S. Clyma,
A. H. Lamma,
Henry S. Graves,
Mrs. M. Spilman,
Mrs. M. Lindsey,
Mrs. E. Boyd,
Mrs. R. A. Clyma,
Mrs. N. T. Myers,
Mrs. J. Kersey,
Mrs. L. A. Clark,
J. N. Lindsey,
J. Stafford,
C. Williams,
Wm. T. Spilman,
Frank M. Clyma,
J. S. Boyd,
Jno. D. Spilman,
Mrs. S. C. McMurtry,
Mrs. E. Spilman,
Mrs. F. Lamma.

SUMMIT GRANGE, No. 226.

SUMMIT SCHOOL-HOUSE (PASO ROBLES), SAN LUIS OBISPO COUNTY.

Organized July 25, 1874, by A. J. Mothersead, Deputy.

J. N. Young, Master,
A. J. Foster, Secretary,
Anderson Smith,
S. P. Litton,
John Wilkinson,
Andrew Harris,
Peter Gillis,
David Pate,
Mrs. Almira Young,
Mrs. M. E. Smith,
Mrs. Lottie M. Foster.
Mrs. Minerva Litton,
Miss Lucy Young,
F. G. Young,
G. W. Richardson,
L. D. Brians,
A. T. Foster,
James M. Jackson,
Wm. Jackson,
Mrs. Sarah Harris,
Mrs. L. Wilkinson,
Mrs. Sarah Mesenheimer,
Mrs. R. A. Klink,
Miss Hattie Mesenheimer.

RINCON GRANGE, No. 227.

RINCON, SAN BERNARDINO COUNTY.

Organized August 15, 1874, by Thos. A. Garey, Deputy.

F. M. Slaughter, Master,
John Taylor, Secretary,
T. B. Walkinshaw,
J. C. Harris,
George Lord,
F. M. Wood,
J. M. Halloway,
S. B. Matthews,
Miss Flora Wood,
R. W. Rivas,
Bartlett Vines,
Mrs. M. M. Hatheway,
Mrs. S. J. Rivas,
Mrs. S. M. Harris,
Mrs. M. E. Wood,
Mrs. Margaret Taylor.

WASHINGTON GRANGE, No. 228.

ELIOTT (COMANCHE), SAN JOAQUIN COUNTY.

Organized August 28, 1874, by Andrew Wolf, Deputy.

W. B. Stamper, Master,
M. L. Cook, Secretary,
D. R. McIntire.
S. W. Sollars,
M. L. Cook,
Wm. McIntire,
C. H. Sittle,
S. O. Sollars,
A. A. Vansant,
Ozias Peter,
I. C. Blyther,
Mrs. Elizabeth Peter,
Mrs. Martha Sollars,
Miss L. L. Little,
Mrs. A. E. Blyther,
Mrs. L. L. Harris,
Mrs. R. Sollars,
Mrs. E. Leeman,
L. C. Leeman,
R. Lucas,
J. C. Deboldt,
John Hill,
John Harris,
Mrs. R. Lucas.

SAN JACINTO GRANGE, No. 229.

SAN JACINTO, SAN DIEGO COUNTY.

Organized August 29, 1874, by Thos. A. Garey, Deputy.

T. D. Henry, Master,
Mrs. Martha Collins, Sec'y,
G. A. Collins,
I. M. Benson,
John Wakefield,
Joseph Carroll,
John Flanegan,
Allen Bane,
Sydney Van Suven,
Mrs. J. E. Benson,
Mrs. Sarah Kennedy,
H. A. Hammer,
F. M. Fowler,
Mrs. Mary Kennedy,
Mrs. Martha Collins,
Mrs. Rosaline Fowler,
Miss Mary Worthington
Miss Jennie Marine,
Mrs. Mary Worthington,
Mrs. J. A. Hammer.

MT. WHITNEY GRANGE, No. 230.

MT. WHITNEY, TULARE COUNTY.

Organized September 12, 1874, by M. S. Babcock, Deputy.

G. W. Duncan, Master,
A. F. Thompson, Sec'y,
Charles Lawless,
O. P. H. Duncan,
R. Doran,
T. J. Snyder,
O. W. Catlin,
O. G. Foot,
J. W. Moore,
Mrs. M. E. Lawless,
Miss B. Murray,
Mrs. M. Duncan,
Miss M. Catlin,
Mrs. A. Catlin,
B. M. Hotchkiss,
L. H. Moore,
A. Fletcher,
Geo. Vincent,
James Brown,
L. W. Gregg,
Henry Witt,
Wm. Sturgeon,
Mrs. A. Foot,
Mrs. C. J. Doran,
Mrs. A. M. Hotchkiss,
Mrs. M. Moore,
Mrs. L. A. Duncan.

ALHAMBRA GRANGE, No. 231.

MARTINEZ, CONTRA COSTA COUNTY.

Organized September 12, 1874, by R. G. Dean, Deputy.

John Strentzel, Master,
Wm. A. Frazer, Sec'y,
Henry Roap,
Elam Barber,
Lawrence M. Smith,
Beverly R. Holliday,
James C. McHarry,
James McHarry,
Mrs. Ann McHarry,
James Stewart,
Alexander Boss,
Johnson Young,
Mrs. Ann Young,
Mrs. Elitha Boss,
Mrs. Lena Roap,
Miss L. W. Strentzel,
Mrs. J. A. Holliday,
Miss Mary A. J. Holliday,
William Dick,
Mrs. Sarah A. Dick,
James Kelley,
Mrs. Margaret Kelley,
M. R. Barber,
Orpha Barber.

PLYMOUTH GRANGE, No. 232.

PLYMOUTH, AMADOR COUNTY.

Organized October 2, 1874, by Wm. S. Manlove, Deputy.

H. Vanderpool, Master,
S. C. Wheeler, Secretary,
Jas. F. Gregg,
S. B. Rhoads,
James Wheeler,
R. M. Ford,
C. Hammack,
H. H. Bell,
H. H. Horton,
Jonathan Sallie,
Wm. K. McKenzie,
A. T. Cleaves,
Wm. J. Matthews,
E. S. Potter,
C. C. Forbes,
G. W. Humphreys,
Juliatha Wheeler,
Sarah Vanderpool,
Maria Ford,
Sarah E. Bell,
Sarah L. Horton,
Anna Hammack,
Sarah J. Sallie,
Melinda E. Williams,
Mary A. McKenzie.

HONCUT GRANGE, No. 233.

MOORE'S STATION, BUTTE COUNTY.

Organized October 3, 1874, by Wm. M. Thorp, Deputy.

John C. Moore, Master,
D. F. Newbert, Secretary,
W. Lealey,
A. J. Opdike,
L. C. Goodell,
R. W. Goodell,
M. Savage,
J. Robinson,
G. W. Underwood,
W. L. Moore,
John Keith,
John S. Devoe,
Mrs. B. A. Moore,
John L. Devoe,
D. P. Newbert,
S. P. Dunville,
A. L. Burdick,
Mrs. Eliza Underwood,
Mrs. Mary Lealy,
Mrs. Mary Robinson,
Hiram Folsom,
Mrs. Harriett Folsom,
Thomas Smuck.

JACKSON VALLEY GRANGE, No. 234.

IONE CITY, AMADOR COUNTY.

Organized November 18, 1874, by Harding Vanderpool, Deputy.

Jesse D. Hamrick, Master,
Lansing J. Dooley. Sec'y,
Wm. H. Prouty,
Charles S. Black,
James W. Parkinson,
James W. Violette,
James P. Martin,
Francis A. McMurray,
Henry Dillion,
Robert K. James,
William C. Thompson,
James Ritchie,
Christopher C. Prouty,
Mrs. Nancy H. Prouty,
Mrs. Elizabeth Hamrick,
Mrs. Lavinia J. Dillion,
Mrs. Sarah L. Black,
Mrs. Mary H. Prouty,
Mrs. C. C. McMurray,
Mrs. Anna M. James,
Mrs. Australia R. Prouty,
Christian Linegar.

NATIONAL RANCH GRANGE, No. 235.

NATIONAL CITY, SAN DIEGO COUNTY.

Organized November 24, 1874, by J. W. A. Wright, Deputy.

Frank A. Kimball, Master,
E. T. Blackmer, Sec'y,
G. L. Kimball,
M. B. Hammond,
D. W. Bryant,
J. M. Asher,
T. Walker,
W. C. Kimball,
R. D. Perry,
N. P. Rouland,
Mrs. S. C. Kimball,
Mrs. A. Hammer,
Miss S. J. Perry,
Mrs. J. A. Walker,
Mrs. L. B. Roberts,
Mrs. L. B. Kimball,
Mrs. F. M. Kimball,
L. Roberts,
R. S. Pardee,
L. L. Roberts,
John T. Farley,
Mrs. Mary Farley,
Mrs. S. A. Bryant,
Miss Susie Farley.

POWAY GRANGE, No. 236.

POWAY, SAN DIEGO COUNTY.

Organized November 25, 1874, by J. W. A. Wright, Deputy.

J. F. Chapin, Master,
E. D. French, Sec'y,
C. C. Watson,
J. H. Hicks,
Wm. Burroughs,
Fred. Reetzke,
A. L. Feeler,
S. G. Hand,
A. Mitchell,
A. J. Babb,
C. Paine,
Wm. McKerren,
A. H. Le Claise,
Geo. R. Hoffman,
Fisher Allen,
Charles Thompson,
Miss E. Hand,
Mrs. M. E. Walden,
Mrs. L. Kerren,
Mrs. C. S. French,
Mrs. M. S. Babb,
Mrs. T. M. Paine,
Miss Adeline Feeler,
Miss Katie Kerren,
Mrs. M. E. Abell,
Mrs. C. Watson,
Wallace W. Walden,
I. L. Cole,
T. J. Cambron,
S. P. Abell.

BALLENA GRANGE, No. 237.

BALLENA, SAN DIEGO COUNTY.

Organized November 27, 1874, by J. W. A. Wright, Deputy.

W. C. Billingsby, Master,
J. J. Sanderson, Sec'y,
C. O. Tucker,
C. W. Stone,
A. W. Luckett,
W. W. Littlepage,
M. V. Castner,
M. D. Putnam,
S. Stone,
Joseph Swycaffer,
M. Cassner,
Mrs. S. J. Stone,
Mrs. Maria Warnock,
Mrs. L. J. Putnam,
Mrs. M. J. Cassner,
Miss M. Stone,
Mrs. M. E. Billingsby,
Samuel Warnock,
George Bradley,
Robert Bradley,
Mrs. Martha Swycaffer,
Mrs. H. M. Tucker,
Miss Pauline Swycaffer.

BEAR VALLEY GRANGE, No. 238.

BEAR VALLEY, SAN DIEGO COUNTY.

Organized November 28, 1874, by J. W. A. Wright, Deputy.

W.H.H.Dinwiddie, Master,
C. H. Moseley, Secretary,
J. C. Hedden,
A. M. Striplin,
James A. Cook,
D. E. Bowman,
J. H. Antes,
Samuel Striplin,
E. L. Jones,
I. T. Adams,
J. Q. Adams,
Albert Striplin,
J. S. Shelby,
S. Van Piper,
Mrs. J. M. McMullen,
Mrs. C. W. Jones,
Mrs. P. J. Striplin,
Mrs. L. J. Hedden,
Mrs. H. M. Dinwiddie,
George Hedden,
Joseph Fleshman,
N. Jones,
Jas. M. Lovett,
M. Price,
Ambrose Welch,
Mrs. Nancy Hedden,
Mrs. A. Lovett,
Mrs. A. Price,
Mrs. Maria Antes,
Miss Ida Antes.

SAN BERNARDO GRANGE, No. 239.

SAN BERNARDO, SAN DIEGO COUNTY.

Organized November 28, 1874, by J. W. A. Wright, Deputy.

Z. Sikes, Master,
T. Duncan, Secretary,
Walter Sherman,
L. J. Foster,
F. E. Feeler,
W. F. Foster,
Wm. Ober,
B. E. Barker,
A. Montgomery,
Chas. McDougall,
Charles Ebb,
Henry Beneke,
J. Watson,
Mrs. M. E. Sikes,
Mrs. M. T. Jones,
Miss E. R. Sikes,
Mrs. Ida A. Duncan,
W. J. Whitney,
J. P. Jones,
J. Noble,
H. Case,
Thos. Dunn,
Mrs. K. Sikes,
Miss Angeline Feeler.

SAN LUIS REY GRANGE, No. 240.

San Luis Rey, San Diego County.

Organized November 30, 1874, by J. W. A. Wright, Deputy.

M. E. Ormsby, Master,
L. J. Crombie, Secretary,
Jas. M. Griffin,
John Griffin,
A. C. Kitching,
J. M. Kolb,
A. Freeman,
A. J. Van Mater,
Robert Ridge,
S. E. Wright,
Mrs. L. E. Crombie,
Mrs. M. J. Welty,
Mrs. L. M. Combs,
Mrs. P. Freeman,
Mrs. S. Griffin,
Mrs. P. E. Kitching,
Mrs. L. J. Kolb,
W. Griffin,
A. R. Davis,
S. M. Harbolt,
R. J. Welty,
Henry Combs,
Mrs. N. O. Ridge,
Mrs. M. E. Ormsby.

PLACERVILLE GRANGE, No. 241.

Placerville, El Dorado County.

Organized February 1, 1875, by A. J. Christie, Deputy.

William Wiltse, Master,
H. G. Hulburd, Secretary,
Wm. Lewis,
I. S. Bamber,
R. Miles,
Sarah Miles,
George W. Ray,
Ethelinda Ray,
A. S. Cook,
Mary J. Cook,
Frank Goyan,
Susie Goyan,
John P. Allen,
Christie Ann Allen,
Griffith L. Jones,
Joseph Lyon,
Isaac Tribbin,
Jacob Lyon,
Elizabeth Lyon,
Rachael G. Simons,
Eli Herrell,
John Kemp,
Thomas Ralph,
Biron H. Hurlburd,
C. H. Burnham,
Mary J. Groves.

NEW CASTLE GRANGE, No. 242.

New Castle, Placer County.

Organized January 9, 1875, by A. D. Neher, Deputy.

John C. Boggs, Master,
B. P. Tabor, Secretary,
Mrs. L. C. Boggs,
Miss I. A. Boggs,
I. H. Mitchell,
Mrs. G. A. Mitchell,
Wm. H. Brainerd,
Timothy Plant,
Mrs. Catherine Plant,
John H. Nixon,
D. E. Plantz,
Mrs. M. M. Plantz,
Geo. Perkins,
Mrs. H. R. Perkins,
W. J. Prosser,
Mrs. N. J. Prosser,
Charles Brown,
Wm. Puffer,
Mrs. Clara Puffer,
Wm. J. Lawrence,
Owen King,
Isaac Tabor,
B. P. Tabor.
J. A. Griffith,
G. W. Shrelkel,
Wm. Smith,
I. H. Campbell.

KEYSTONE GRANGE, No. 243.

Grangeville, Tulare County.

Organized February 27, 1875, by M. S. Babcock, Deputy.

Erastus Axtell, Master,
N. B. Golden, Secretary,
E. Manning,
J. M. Fuller,
J. W. Griffes,
R. Bascom,
R. S. Dodge,
A. Hogle,
Mrs. L. Bascom,
Mrs. C. A. Dodge,
Mrs. A. Manning,
J. Coffey,
Mrs. H. Axtell,
Mrs. M. E. Coffey,
Mrs. M. A. Hogle,
Mrs. N. Snyder,
Jno. Rodgers,
Mrs. E. Rodgers,
R. Dodge,
Mrs C. Stewart,
A. Brown,
A. Childs,
D. V. Fuller,
E. Kelly.

MUSSEL SLOUGH GRANGE, No. 244.

GRANGEVILLE, TULARE COUNTY.

Organized February 26, 1875, by M. S. Babcock, Deputy.

Wes. Underwood, Master,
Wm. Land, Secretary,
T. Standard,
J. P. Duncan,
J. Battenfeld,
Wm. Battenfeld,
S. R. Wilson,
T. H. McNamee,
J. Bigham,
George H. Battenfeld,
Mrs. A. Battenfeld,
F. F. Wilson,
Perry Mills,
Mrs. S. Mills,
Jno. Mills,
W. H. Whitesides,
E. Greffee,
Mrs. S. A. Duncan,
Mrs. M. J. Standard,
Mrs. T. McNamee,
Mrs. M. E. Underwood,
Miss M. Lavery,
G. W. Battenfeld,
Mrs. M. E. Battenfeld,
M. Dowdy,
A. F. Barnhill,
Mrs. S. A. Lane,
J. T. Yount,
Mrs. M. Yount.

MODOC GRANGE, No. 245.

WILLOW RANCH, MODOC COUNTY.

Organized April 9, 1875, by D. S. K. Buick, Deputy.

A. V. Coffer, Master,
M. Waid, Secretary,
L. E. Henderson,
S. A. Hamersley.
F. Vincent,
J. L. Sanborn,
W. A. Henderson,
J. T. Crawford,
A. Siets,
D. O. Bissell,
James Harver,
Mrs. E. D. Henderson,
Mrs. S. E. Hamersley,
Mrs. L. Hamersley,
Mrs. M. Siet,
M. C. Siet,
Mrs. M. J. Coffer,
Mrs. M. A. Glidden,
J. J. Kirk,
J. A. Glidden,
E. J. Keeney,
R. Robinett,
E. V. Coffer,
W. H. Siet,
Henry Williams,
O. P. Russell,
D. Wills,
L. Crawford,
M. Wills,
Mrs. L. W. Henderson,
Miss Mary Hazelton,
Mrs. M. Robinett,
Mrs. M. E. Cloud.

PLUMAS GRANGE, No. 246.

SIERRA VALLEY (RENO, NEVADA,) PLUMAS COUNTY.

Organized April 24, 1875, by A. J. Hatch, Deputy.

A. J. Spoon, Master,
H. F. Lander, Sec'y,
Mrs. Josephine Spoon,
Jacob Stiner,
O. McElroy.
Wm. A. Sperry.
Joseph Hathaway,
Henry Lander,
Joel Langdon,
James E. Goble,
B. F. Bobo,
Wm. Arms,
Mrs. M. P. Arms,
Alexander Kirby,
Mrs. A. Kirby,
Alice Stiner,
Mrs. M. E. Hinds,
Richard Martin,
Miller Beach,
D. C. Berry,
W. C. Bingham,
Henry Stiner,
Jesse H. Stiner,
A. B. Huntley,
S. B. Hinds,
Thos. Black,
Mrs. W. C. Bingham,
Mrs. W. E. Sperry,
Mrs. J. Langdon,
Mrs. J. Hathaway,
Allen Trimble.

INDIAN SPRINGS GRANGE, No. 247.

INDIAN SPRINGS, NEVADA COUNTY.

Organized April 29, 1875.

T. J. Robinson,
L. Horton,
P. L. Stull,
J. O. Marsh,
C. D. Gassaway,
John Perry,
H. L. Hatch,
M. P. Hatch,
Stephen F. Ball,
Mrs. Ball,
W. Emery,
Mrs. C. Robinson,
Mrs. E. M. Horton,
Mrs. Margaret Gassaway,
Benj. Sanford,
H. Hoffman,
Mrs. E. W. Hatch,
Mrs. J. Hatch,
Mary Stull,
Jennie Stull.

LAKESIDE GRANGE, No. 248.

JANESVILLE, LASSEN COUNTY.

Organized May 25, 1875, by A. J. Hatch, Deputy.

Geo H. Bingham, Master,
John Theodore, Sec'y,
D. D. Byers,
W. S. Hamilton,
L. Hicks,
B. H. Laritt,
B. D. Bass,
Geo. W. Fry,
W. M. McClelland,
J. P. Sharp,
H. H. McMurphy,
E. T. Slackford,
Mrs. D. A. McMurphy,
S. A. McClelland,
Miss F. E. McMurphy,
Miss J. M. McClelland,
Mrs. M. L. Fry,
Mrs. P. Parks,
S. Huffman,
Geo. H. Bangham,
W. M. Cain,
Wm. Lieth,
Charles Barham,
John Parks,
E. C. Parks,
John Thayer,
Mrs. Margaret Cain,
Mrs. Mary F. Bangham,
Mrs. P. A. Hamilton,
Miss J. Bass,
Miss Hattie Parks.

NEVADA GRANGES.

ALFALFA GRANGE, No. 1.

RENO, WASHOE COUNTY.

Organized June 5, 1874, by J. M. Hamilton, W. M.

A. J. Hatch, Master,
P. H. Kinney, Secretary,
H. M. Frost,
W. J. Marsh,
Chris. Higgins,
W. D. Masten,
B. S. James,
George DeRemet,
J. C. Smith,
Mrs. F. M. Smith,
O. C. Ross,
J. W. Lyle,
Mrs. H. F. Hatch,
Mrs. C. A. Norcross,
R. H. Kinney,
Wm. Steele,
Jos. Mayberry,
A. J. Hatch,
A. M. Lamb,
J. H. Stone,
T. W. Norcross,
Mrs. Jane Lake,
M. C. Lake,
Robt. Steele,
Wm. Wright,
G. W. Huffaker.

EAGLE VALLEY GRANGE, No. 2.

CARSON, ORMSBY COUNTY.

Organized June 9, 1874, by J. M. Hamilton, W. M.

G. W. Chedig, Master,
O. A. F. Gilbert, Sec'y,
A. D. Tredway,
I. A. Lovejoy,
I. T. Griffiths,
S. A. Nevers,
J. S. Neal,
Mrs. Eliza Nevers,
Mrs. E. J. Dow,
Mrs. L. M. Lovejoy,
M. Y. Stewart,
J. M. Gatewood,
M. C. Gardner,
Clark Simons,
G. W. Chedig,
Mrs. H. M. Gardner,
Mrs. M. Dow,
Mrs. V. B. Chedig.

CARSON VALLEY GRANGE, No. 3.

GENEVA, DOUGLASS COUNTY.

Organized June 10, 1874, by J. M. Hamilton, W. M.

R. Y. Singleton, Master,
J. S. Childs, Secretary,
A. P. Brockliss,
S. Singleton,
J. S. Bostor,
Peter W. Van Sickle,
Hugh Park,
W. H. Hill,
A. P. Squiers,
Mrs. Margaret Cook,
Mrs. Amelia Harvey,
Mrs. Rebecca Park,
Richard Cossor,
R. J. Livingston,
W. F. Bull,
Robert Falk,
John Gardner,
Mrs. Rebecca Singleton,
Mrs. Ann Carey,
Mrs. Isabella Livingston,
Mrs. Mary McCue.

WASHOE VALLEY GRANGE, No. 4.

Organized June 13, 1874, by J. M. Hamilton, W. M.

Elias Owens, Master,
George D. Winters, Sec'y,
Wm. Thompson,
Hugh Montgomery,
E. B. Towl,
C. F. Wooten,
S. M. Place,
James Twaddle,
Joseph Frey,
Ross Lewers,
Miss Mary A. Smith,
Mrs. Anna Crowder,
Miss Sarah Hughes,
Miss Ida Simons,
J. M. Hope,
H. B. McCune,
Lemuel Cook,
E. Twaddle,
B. F. Small,
G. W. Small,
H. L. Perkins,
A. Sauer,
C. Perkins,
Miss Ella Simons,
Mrs. V. O. Towl.

WELLINGTON GRANGE, No. 5.

WELLINGTON, ESMERALDA COUNTY.

Organized, September 19, 1874, by A. J. Hatch, Deputy.

A. H. Hawley, Master.
J. N. Mann, Secretary,
S. A. Sawyer,
T. B. Rickey,
D. C. Simpson,
J. N. Mann,
S. Kent,
W. L. Hall,
J. P. Davis,
Frank Rivers,
Mrs. F. Rivers,
Mrs. S. M. Burbank,
S. M. Burbank,
S. M. Burbank,
John McVicker,
Cyrus Smith,
W. R. Hutson,
Amos Burbank,
Mrs. J. Davis,
Mrs. S. A. Hawley,
Mrs. E. A. Simpson,
Miss Susie Hawley,
Miss V. Lynds,
Mrs. T. B. Rickey.

MERRITT GRANGE, No. 6.

MASON VALLEY, ESMERALDA COUNTY.

Organized September 20, 1874, by A. J. Hatch, Deputy.

Kimber Cleaver, Master,
Clark Cleaver, Secretary,
George Sayles,
W. B. Saunders,
C. Hernleven,
Thos. Shedden,
Chas. Osborne,
John Wheeler,
James Merritt,
Mrs. R. A. Cleaver,
Mrs. L. Saunders,
Mrs. M. Hernleven,
David Cooper,
J. B. Kasner,
G. B. Waldo,
W. H. Spragg,
Dennis Wiggins,
John Lancaster,
E. Green,
H. Stickenbaugh,
Mrs. F. Wheeler,
Mrs. Alice Spragg,
Mrs. L. Stickenbaugh.

PARADISE GRANGE, No. 7.

PARADISE VALLEY, HUMBOLDT COUNTY.

Organized August 29, 1874, by A. J. Hatch, Deputy.

B. F. Riley, Master,
C. A. Nichols, Secretary,
S. R. P. Pierce,
Thos. Shirley,
B. Fisher.
Chas. Kemler,
A. S. Trousdale,
Thos. Mullinax,
John Ross,
John Byrnes,
M. Kree,
R. H. Swartz,
Isabella Lemance,
Mrs. E. J. Riley,
Mary Shirley,
Susan A. Nichols,
Mary Fisher,
Catherine Kemler,
Chesley Lamance.

WINNEMUCCA GRANGE, No. 8.

WINNEMUCCA, HUMBOLDT COUNTY.

Organized March 6, 1875, by A. J. Hatch, Deputy.

Wm. B. Haskell, Master,
Hez. Barns, Secretary,
James Buckner,
H. Dalrymple,
E. P. Tiernay,
Wm. W. Cross,
Wm. Wear,
Charles Kesler,
John Basco,
J. F. Abel,
Robert Henderson,
J. F. Henderson,
Julia E. Tierney,
Delphine Dalrymple,
Eliza Buckner,
A. Kleinhaus,
Jos. Thomas,
A. J. Shepard,
E. Pocket,
Wm. Shaw,
Wm. H. Lowell,
L. L. Rickard,
Eliza J. Shaw,
Mary J. Henderson,
Minna Kesler,
May F. Ford,
Sarah O. Barns,
Lizzie Pocket,
Phebe Dalrymple.

ELKO GRANGE, No. 9.

Elko, Elko County.

Organized March 22, 1875, by A. J. Hatch, Deputy.

Joseph A. Tinker, Master,
Joseph L. Keyser, Sec'y,
A. L. Sherman,
J. P. Hough,
John Hunter,
E. Burner,
G. W. Letton,
G. B. Kittridge,
H. Tuttle,
E. L. Wetmore,
George Sietz,
H. A. Young,
Mrs. H. Tuttle,
Mrs. John Hunter,
E. S. Yeates,
J. F. Burner,
J. Hufford,
H. Green,
J. W. Parke,
Thos. Hunter,
Robert B. Hunter.
Joseph Cox,
Mrs. J. A. Tinker,
Mrs. G. W. Letton,
Miss Maggie Yeates,
Mrs. E. L. Wetmore,
Mrs. Janet Adams.

LAMOILLE GRANGE, No. 10.

Lamoille Valley, Elko County.

Organized March 23, 1875, by A. J. Hatch, Deputy.

Edwin Odell, Master,
Henry M. Freeman, Sec'y,
A. Wines,
J. H. Jewett,
Amelia T. Jewett,
William McComb,
Catharine McComb.
Jacob Laddie,
E. H. Byers,
Marshall E. Stottler,
A. B. Marvel,
Mary J. Trueman,
Mary Wines,
Wm. M. Biggs
Anna Biggs,
J. K. Smith,
A. F. Bacon,
Mrs. B. E. Byers,
Henry Thompson,
Patrick McDermott.

HALLECK GRANGE, No. 11.

Camp Halleck Station, Elko County.

Organized March 24, 1875, by A. J. Hatch, Deptuy.

I. S. Fenn, Master,
Maurice Geary, Sec'y,
J. J. Campbell,
Mrs. J. T. Campbell,
Hamilton McCain,
Luella Geary,
Roland Day,
Mrs. Harriet Day,
John D. Ables,
Mrs. A. E. Fenn,
Mrs. M. A. Ables,
Miss Emma Ables,
F. M. Harges,
F. J. Greenberg,
Mrs. A. Greenberg,
H. J. Keith,
Nathan Phillips.

STAR VALLEY GRANGE, No. 12

Star Valley (Humboldt Wells), Elko County.

Organized June 2, 1875, by Joseph A. Tinker, Deputy.

D. E. Johnston, Master,
Chas. J. Whitney, Sec'y,
W. W. Griswold,
T. F. Breunan,
James Mullen,
John Crossen,
Malcolm Hall,
George Ackiey,
Charles J. Whiting,
John Deering,
Mrs. William Weathers,
Mrs. Debbie Hall,
Mrs. W. W. Griswold,
Mrs. M. Crossen,
W. Weathers.

CLOVER VALLEY GRANGE, No. 13.

Clover Valley (Humboldt Wells), Elko County.

Organized June 6, 1875, by Joseph A. Tinker, Deputy.

F. Honeyman, Master,
W. B. Raymond Sec'y,
J. Wiseman,
Daniel Gilanders,
J. A. Steel,
M. Duval,
C. Stoner,
W. A. Wilcox,
C. H. Brassey,
F. M. Smith,
W. T. Weeks,
John Crocker,
J. E. Chase,
H. S. Tuttle,
Charles Lampman,
Mrs. S. Honeyman,
Mrs. May Honeyman,
Mrs. S. Duval,
Mrs. A. Smith,
Mrs. S. Brassey,
Mrs. F. Wiseman,
Mrs. E. Chase,
Mrs. J. E. Chase.

DANIEL CLARK,
W. M. of State Grange of Oregon.

OREGON STATE GRANGE.

OFFICERS:

Master—Daniel Clark, Marion county.
Overseer—William Cyrus, Linn county.
Lecturer—E. L. Smith, Olympia, Washington Territory.
Steward—W. M. Shelton, Walla Walla, Washington Territory.
Assistant Steward—W. M. Powers, Linn county.
Chaplain—M. Peterson, Jackson county.
Treasurer—S. P. Lee, Clackamas county.
Secretary—J. Henry Smith, Linn county.
Gate Keeper—A. A. Matthews, Douglas county.
Ceres—Mrs. Jane Cyrus, Linn county.
Pomona—Mrs. M. Powers, Linn county.
Flora—L. C. Reid, Yamhill county.
Lady Assistant Steward—Mrs. L. S. Folsom, Lane county.

EXECUTIVE COMMITTEE:

S. W. Brown, Clarke county, Washington Territory.
H. N. Hill, Lane county.
C. E. Moore, Benton county.
Orley Hull, Walla Walla.
E. Forbes, Clackamas county.
M. Fisk, Salem.

ORGANIZING DEPUTIES FOR 1875.

OREGON.

County.	Deputy.	Post-office.
Baker	Wm. Brown	Baker City.
Benton	Chas. E. Moore	Corvallis.
Benton	Jacob Modie	Corvallis.
Clatsop	R. W. Morrison	
Clackamas	E. Forbes	Oregon City.
Clackamas	A. R. Shipley	Oswego.
Columbia	J. M. McIntire	McIntire's Landing, Sauvie's Island.
Coos	J. Henry Schroeder	Ott.
Douglass	R. M. Gurney	Ten Mile.
Grant	D. B. Rhinehart	Cañon City.
Jackson	D. S. R. Buick	Ashland.
Lane	H. N. Hill	Junction.
Lane	Geo. R. Hamersley	Camp Creek.
Linn	Wm. Cyrus	Scio.
Linn	R. A. Irvine	Lebanon.
Marion	S. D. Hale	Peoria.
Marion	B. A. Witzel	Turner.
Multnomah	Jacob Johnson	East Portland.
Multnomah	W. J. Campbell	East Portland.
Polk	James Tatom	Dixie.
Tillamook	H. F. Holden	
Umatilla	John S. White	Weston.
Wasco	R. Mayes	The Dalles.
Wasco	J. H. Douthitt	Upper Ocheco.
Washington	T. D. Humphrey	Hillsboro.
Washington	Henry Buxton	Forest Grove.
Yamhill	Alex. Reid	McMinnville.
Yamhill	A. B. Henry	La Fayette.

WASHINGTON TERRITORY.

County	Deputy.	Post-office.
Clarke	H. M. Knapp	Mill Plain, or Vancouver.
Chehalis	M. Z. Goodell	Elma.
King	Julius Horton	Seattle.
Pierce	John S. Bozarth	Pekin.
Pacific	S. S. Markham.	Chehalis Point.
Thurston	E. L. Smith	Olympia.
Thurston	Wm. Packwood	Tenino.
Walla Walla	Wm. M. Shelton	Walla Walla.
Walla Walla	O. Hull	Walla Walla.

IDAHO TERRITORY.

Ada	M. Russell	Weiser.
Ada	L. F. Cartee	Boise City.
Nez Perce	S. S. Howard	Paradise Valley.
Nez Perce	W. C. Pierson	Mt. Idaho.

OREGON SUBORDINATE GRANGES.

ARRANGED BY COUNTIES.

BAKER COUNTY.

Name and Number.	Master.	Secretary.	P. O. of Secretary.
Baker City, 152	C. M. Fo-ter	S. H. Small	Baker City.
Eldorado, 153	Wm. Morfit	J. T. Locey	El Dorado.
Malheur, 170	E. W. Imbler	W. E. Thompson	El Dorado.
Wingville, 150	William Brown	C. W. James	Baker City.

BENTON COUNTY.

Alsea, 77	Mulkey Vernon	Silas Howell	Alsea Valley.
Kings Valley, 66	R. J. Grant	B. Cady	Kings Valley.
Laurel, 69	H. B. Nichols	A. C. Nichols	Monroe.
Locke, 15	Charles E. Moor	O. V. Motley	Corvallis.
Orleans, 50	J. McCune	William Winning	Corvallis.
Philomath, 13	E. Hartless	George Henkle	Corvallis.
Toledo, 168	Wm. Brazelton	Wm. Stitt	Newport.
Union (4), 154	W. L. Price	H. N. Bowman	Summit.
Willamette, 52	S. W. B. Smith	George M. Porter	Corvallis.

CLACKAMAS COUNTY.

Beaver Creek, 115	M. O. Gard	C. F. Beatie	Oregon City.
Canby, 135	S. A. Marks	Wm. Knight	Canby.
Cascade, 120	J. C. Branham	Henry McGugin	Sandy.
Damascus, 41	James P. Chitwood	Norman Darling	Damascus.
Eagle Creek, 2	F. W. Foster	E. Forbes	Damascus.
Harding, 122	W. L. Holcomb	T. E. Lacey	Norton.
Highland, 70	A. Nicholas	W. J. Allison	Oregon City.
Highland Grove, 136	Randolph Stricklin	Chas. T. Hickman	Highland.
Marshfield, 1	T. J. Matlock	J. M. Mills	Clackamas.
Molalla, 40	John H. Smith	J. A. Wright	Molalla.
Mountain View, 142	James W. Offield	A. Carmichael	Canby.
Mount Zion, 121	John Tate	W. H. Livermore	Zion.
Needy, 81	John Ring	A. A. Arington	Needy.
Oswego, 175	C. W. Bryant	A. R. Shipley	Oswego.
Spring Water, 108	Henry Rowley	A. A. Southworth	Norton.
Upper Molalla, 83	Franklin W. Vaughn	Samuel Engle	Needy.

CLATSOP COUNTY.

Clatsop, 156	John A. Packard	Josiah West	Skipanon.
Young's River, 172	A. H. Sale	John Davis	Astoria.

COLUMBIA COUNTY.

Name and Number.	Master.	Secretary.	P. O. of Secretary.
Columbia City, 177	Geo. W. Maxwell	S. L. Lovell	Columbia City.
Klalskanine, 182	E. W. Congers	Mrs. A. J. Congers	Klalskanine.
North Union, 176	E. S. Bryant	Z. S. Bryant	Marshland.
Scappoose, 144	W. W. Mars	M. Pomeroy	Gosa's Landing.

COOS COUNTY.

Name and Number.	Master.	Secretary.	P. O. of Secretary.
Coos River, 45	Charles Higgins	Samuel Beavens	Coos River.
Coguille City, 167	Wm. Morris	James Aikens	Isthmus.
Halls Prairie, 164	J. Henry Schroeder	E. S. Spurgeon	Coquille City.
Laurel, 180	S. L. Leneve	R. H. Rosa	Randolph.
Maple, 171	Charles Wilkins	Henry Schroeder	Hermansville.
North Coquille, 173	J. H. Roach	J. S. Cocke	Dora.

DOUGLAS COUNTY.

Name and Number.	Master.	Secretary.	P. O. of Secretary.
Canyonville, 109	N. Cornutt	Geo. W. Riddle	Canyonville.
Elkton, 149	James M. Stark	D. W. Stearns	Elkton.
Mount Scott, 151	J. L. Thornton	R. A. Roper	Roseburg.
Myrtle, 59	W. J. Hayes	F. M. Gabbert	Myrtle Creek.
Umpqua, 28	Plinn Cooper	Nat Webb	Roseburg.
Union (2), 51	William Thornton	James Byron	Ten Mile.
Wilbur, 114	James N. Dodge	G W. Grubb	Wilbur.
Yoncalla, 78	Abraham Lamb	John H. McClure	Yoncalla.

GRANT COUNTY.

Name and Number.	Master.	Secretary.	P. O. of Secretary.
Canyon City, 161	D. B. Rhinehart	E. S. Penfield	Canyon City.
Daniel Clark, 162	J. G. Cozort	George Shearer	Prairie City.
Mount Vernon, 163	Robert E. Damon	Henry H. Davis	Canyon City.

JACKSON COUNTY.

Name and Number.	Master.	Secretary.	P. O. of Secretary.
Applegate, 138	Lyman Chappell	Wm. Ray	Jacksonville.
Ashland, 87	A. D. Helman	J. D. Fountain	Ashland.
Central Point, 124	Martin Peterson	George R. Hamrick	Jacksonville.
Eagle Point, 123	H. J. Terrill	Levi Yenkim	Brownsburg.
Harmony Point, 137	Thomas Wright	Lizzy B. Kincaid	Jacksonville.
Jacksonville, 88	F. M. Plymale	Isaac W. Berry	Jacksonville.
Oakland, 86	J. F. Rice	William Thiel	Oakland.
Phœnix, 104	J. S. Herron	J. M. Hoxie	Phœnix.
Sam's Valley, 113	J. S. March	B. F. Wade	Sam's Valley.
Washington, 181	Wm. W. Fidler	Frank A. Knox	Applegate.

JOSEPHINE COUNTY.

Name and Number.	Master.	Secretary.	P. O. of Secretary.
Kirbyville, 178	J. B. Siffers	D. Fiester	Kirbyville.
Josephine, 179	Joseph Pollock	T. F. Coxton	Leland.

LAKE COUNTY.

Name and Number.	Master.	Secretary.	P. O. of Secretary.
Hot Springs	J. J. Charlton	R. H. Danlack	Fort Bidwell.

LANE COUNTY.

Name and Number.	Master.	Secretary.	P. O. of Secretary.
Cayota, 55	S. S. Stephens	C. D. W. Huffman	Spencer Creek.
Charity, 76	M. Wilkins	F. M. Wilkins	Willamette Forks.
Creswell, 64	Roscoe Knox	G. S. Gilfry	Cresswell.
Eugene City, 56	Jesse Cox	J. F. Smith	Eugene City.
Fall Creek, 146	M. L. Wilmot	Wm. Eaton	Rattlesnake.
Fir Butte, 118	W. P. Chesher	Joseph H. Green	Eugene City.
Franklin, 155	W. G. Miller	S. Lewis	Franklin.
Goshen, 101	W. R. Dillard	A. K. Patterson	Goshen.
Grand Prairie, 26	Allen Bond	J. C. Jennings	Junction City.
Junction City, 43	F. W. Folsom	J. E. Houston	Junction City.
McKenzie, 107	Joseph McLane	W. A. Walcott	Camp Creek.
Mohawk, 147	Henry Parsons	Asahel Spencer	Eugene City.

LANE COUNTY—*Continued.*

Name and Number.	Master.	Secretary.	P. O. of Secretary.
Pleasant Grove, 139	A. J. Zumwalt	L. G. Belknap	Eugene City.
Pleasant Hill, 65	W. H. H. McClure	R. M. Mulholland	Pleasant Hill.
Spencer Butte, 126	James F. Amis	Joseph Bailey	Spencer Creek.
Springfield, 12	John Kelley	John Stewart	Eugene City.
Union (1), 17	Hynson Smyth	J. H. Furgeson	Junction City.

LINN COUNTY.

Name and Number.	Master.	Secretary.	P. O. of Secretary.
Banner, 165	J. A. Riggs	Robert Glass	Crawfordsville.
Beaver, 44	W. C. Foren	C. L. Morris	Lebanon and Scio.
Brownsville, 19	A. W. Stanard	G. C. Blakely	Brownsville.
Center, 97	W. J. Philpott	Z. B. Moss	Sweet Home.
Charity (2), 103	F. M. Kiser	P. H. Wigle	Harrisburg.
Corinthian, 8	W. F. Alexander	E. Haner	Albany.
Cottage Grove, 75	A. H. Spare	J. H. Shortridge	Cottage Grove.
Grand Prairie, 10	Isaac Hayes	Daniel Ray	Albany.
Happy Home, 46	J. R. South	G. B. McKinney	Scio and Lebanon.
Harmony, 23	S. A. Dawson	H. Powell	Albany.
Harrisburg, 11	Wm. McCulloch	J. P. Alford	Harrisburg.
Hope, 24	L. F. Smith	C. P. Davis	Albany.
Jordan Valley, 42	John Bryant	A. T. McCally	Scio.
Knox Butte, 22	M. H. Wilds	Milton Houston	Albany.
Lebanon, 21	S. A. Nickerson	Frank Pike	Lebanon.
Oak Plain, 6	J. H. Bramwell	T. J. Black	Halsey.
Peoria, 116	S. D. Haley	T. L. Porter	Peoria.
Santiam, 37	W. Cyrus	N. Crabtree	Scio.
Sandridge, 57	M. Scott	G. W. Cooper	Albany.
Scio, 36	Thos. McMunkers	J. F. Miller	Scio.
Shedd, 9	W. M. Powers	H. B. Sprenger	Shedd.
Siuselaw, 54	D. B. Cartwright	F. M. Nighswander	Cartwright.
Soap Creek, 14	Jacob Modie	R. D. Murray	Albany.
Sodaville, 85	W. B. Gibson	C. C. Burgo	Lebanon.
Syracuse, 53	S. T. Jones	H. Johnson	Millers Station.
Tangent, 7	James W. Jordan	E. P. McClure	Tangent.

MARION COUNTY.

Name and Number.	Master.	Secretary.	P. O. of Secretary.
Abiqua, 133	Willis Donegon	W. F. Eastham	Monitor.
Butte Creek, 82	Enoch Skirvin	J. R. White	Butte Creek.
Butteville, 74	John W. Grimm	J. D. Crawford	Butteville.
Chehulpan, 68	Jesse Parish	W. W. Steiner	Jefferson.
Fairview (2), 141	H. E. Ankeny	T. C. Jorey	Salem.
Gervais, 140	W. H. Ringo	M. A. Wade	Gervais.
Howell Prairie, 80	Wm. Sappingfield	J. G. Moore	Silverton.
Hubbards, 132	R. A. Ross	Jas. A. Cochran	Hubbard.
Mount Vernon, 134	J. H. Haddley	N. Scott	Silverton.
Rock Point, 48	J. Downing	G. W. Hunt	Sublimity.
Round Prairie, 106	Wm. Hubbard	D. H. La Follett	Brooks.
Salem, 17	M. Fisk	John Minto	Salem.
Turner, 18	B. A. Witzel	W. M. Hilleary	Turner.
Woodburn, 79	G. W. Dimmick	Wm. Darst	Woodburn.

MULTNOMAH COUNTY.

Name and Number.	Master.	Secretary.	P. O. of Secretary.
Acme, 166	W. Munger	T. H. Prince	Portland.
Evening Star, 27	W. J. Campbell	H. T. Campbell	E. Portland.
Fairview, 131	D. F. Buxton	James Brand	E. Portland.
Multnomah, 71	John Moore	J. S. Newell	E. Portland.
Powell Valley, 84	T. K. Williams	S. B. Whithington	Powell Valley.
Sauvies Island, 143	J. M. McIntire	Marissa Bouser	Sauvie's Island.
Western Star, 145	William Forrest	K. F. Kuetemeyer	Willamette Stongh.
Willamette, 119	William Bybee	S. E. Paddock	Portland.

POLK COUNTY.

Name and Number.	Master.	Secretary.	P. O. of Secretary.
Buena Vista, 4	J. B. Stump	M. Scrafford	Buena Vista.
Dallas, 61	Robert Clow	J. B. Riggs	Dallas.
Garretson, 60	A. G. Shurtleff	H. Alexander	Bethel.
Mill Creek, 91	B. B. Branson	W. H. Kuykendall	Grand Round.
Monmouth, 5	Langdon Bentley	Ira F. M. Butler	Monmouth.
Mono, 25	Isaac Staats	H. C. McTimonds	Lewisville.
Oak Point, 3	F. A. Patterson	J. G. Sears	Dixie.
Perrydale, 30	J. Stouffer	P. C. Sears	Perrydale.
Spring Valley, 62	W. A. Henry	Thomas Pierce	Eola.

TILLAMOOK COUNTY.

Fidelity, 174	H. F. Holden	W. T. Newcomb	Tillamook.

UMATILLA COUNTY.

Alta, 96	L. P. Davidson	E. Gilliam	Pilot Rock.
Butter Creek,	S. G. Lightfoot	J. S. Vinson	Butter Creek.
Lone Star, 160	W. D. Gilliam	W. A. Booth	Mitchell.
Meadowville, 94	A. L. Gordon	T. Benson	Umatilla City.
Midway, 95	J. H. Chase	H. C. Meyers	Heppner.
Milton, 29	Wm. M. Steen	Thomas K. McCoy	Walla Walla City.
Pendleton, 93	Wm. H. Barnhart	J. H. Sharon	Pendleton.
Weston, 34	Robert Jamieson	Hugh McArthur	Weston.
Wild Horse, 35	T. J. Kirk	D. A. Richards	Weston.

UNION COUNTY.

Cove, 128	N. B. Rees	Otho Eckersley	Cove.
La Grande, 127	Abner W. Waters	Daniel Chaplain	La Grande.
Powder River, 169	T. O. Bryant	H. D. Cassidy	Uniontown.
Summerville, 130	W. B. Hamilton	W. H. Parreut	Summerville.
Union (3), 129	Wm. Hutchinson	John Creighton	Union.

WASCO COUNTY.

Barlows Gate, 157	John End	Albert Savage	Tygh Valley.
Dalles, 39	Robert Mays	E. P. Roberts	The Dalles.
Ocheco, 159	J. H. Douthitt	Mrs. E. A. Freeland	Upper Ocheco.
Prineville, 158	E. Barnes	S. R. Slayton	Prineville.
Wasco, 38	J. J. Griffin	G. H. Barnett	The Dalles.

WASHINGTON COUNTY.

Beaverton, 100	Thos. Tucker	R. B. Wilmot	Beaverton.
Butte, 148	J. A. Richardson	S. D. Powell	Tualatin.
Columbia, 89	James Imbrie	Francis Kennedy	Glencoe.
Cornelius, 63	H. C. Raymond	G. A. Guild	Cornelius.
Farmington, 110	J. S. Grey	Alfred Davis	Scholls Ferry.
Forest Grove, 67	Henry Buxton	H. T. Buxton	Forest Grove.
Greenville, 49	Daniel Baker	W. R. Barrett	Greenville.
Hillsboro, 73	T. D. Humphreys	J. H. Sewell	Hillsboro.
Wapatoo, 90	S. W. Sappington	Isaac Chrisman	Gaston.
Tualatin, 111	John Krase	James Barstow	Tualatin.
Washington, 99	Isaac Ball	W. W. Gibbs	Tualatin.
West Union, 72	David Lennox	George Blish	West Union.

YAMHILL COUNTY.

Amity, 102	J. J. Henderson	J. R. Sawyer	Amity.
Chehalem, 92	S. Brutscher	J. J. Haynes	Newberg.
Excelsior, 16	B. F. Lewis	I. E. Coovert	Dayton.
La Fayette, 32	A. B. Henry	C. F. Royal	La Fayette.
McMinnville, 31	Alex. Reed	D. O. Durham	McMinnville.
North Yamhill, 33	R. R. Laughlin	J. W. Stewart	North Yamhill.
Sheridan, 98	Wm. Savage	Thos. E. Fristoe	Sheridan.
Unity, 112	S. S. Whitcomb	R. Pettyjohn	La Fayette.
West Chehalem, 125	T. B. Nel-on	George Noble	West Chehalem.
Willamette (2), 105	William Crosier	Peter Barendregt	Wheatland.

WASHINGTON TERRITORY SUBORDINATE GRANGES.

ARRANGED BY COUNTIES.

CHEHALIS COUNTY.

Name and Number.	Master.	Secretary.	P. O. of Secretary.
Central, 63	Joseph Castro	Justin Chenowith	Chehalis Station.
Chehalis, 26	W. Z. Goodell	W. A. Anderson	Elma.
Montesano, 18	J. E. Metcalf	S. S. Markham	Montesano.
Oakville, 27	George E. Smith.	Mrs. D M. Newton	Oakville.
Sharon, 51	D. J. Gladdis	J. A. Ridings	Sharon.

CLARK COUNTY.

Name and Number.	Master.	Secretary.	P. O. of Secretary.
Brush Prairie, 25	Isaac Diedtreich	Jesse Holbrook	Brush Prairie.
Central (2), 31	Geo. W. Proebstel	Wm. S. Douthitt	Vancouver.
Fern Prairie, 30	Chas. Zeek	Jasper M. Blair	Vancouver.
La Centre, 48	Thomas J. Carroll	D. A. McNalf	Lewis River.
Maple Grove, 45	D. L. Russell	John H. Fletcher	Battle Ground.
Mill Plain, 24	G. W. Evans	Hamilton Graham	Vancouver.
Oriental, 57	J. S. Hathaway	J. B. Hathaway	Vancouver.
Union Ridge, 46	David R. Fales	Minnie Hathaway	Union Ridge.
Vaucover, 54	S. W. Brown	J. C. Hileman	Vaucouver.
Washugul, 32	James A. Kerns	Charles T. Stiles	Vaucouver.

COWLITZ COUNTY.

Name and Number.	Master.	Secretary.	P. O. of Secretary.
Freeport, 58	George P. Gray	Jasper D. Stone	Pekin.
Rising Sun, 58	Nathan Davis	C. Calahan	Pekin.

KING COUNTY.

Name and Number.	Master.	Secretary.	P. O. of Secretary.
Alpha, 55	———	T. S. Sloane	Squak.
Duwamish, 11	John T. Jordon	Wm. M. Myers	Seattle.
Maple, 60	Henry Oliver	Joseph Alexander	Centerville.
Skagit, 61	W. H. Sartwell	Daniel Gage	Skagit.
Snogualamie, 39	James Taylor	Cyrus Dorst	Fall City.
White River, 9	Charles W. Lawton	T. McClellan	White River.

KLICKITAT COUNTY.

Name and Number.	Master.	Secretary.	P. O. of Secretary.
Klickitat, 49	R. W. Helm	H. T. Lewis	Klickitat City.
Nanum, 53	B. W. Frisbee	A. B. Ford	Ellensburg.

LEWIS COUNTY.

Name and Number.	Master.	Secretary.	P. O. of Secretary.
Boisford, 34	J. H. Miller	Jay Stillman	Boisfort.
Claquato, 19	F. M. Pearson	Brad W. Davis	Claquato.
Cowlitz, 35	H. Howe	G. D. Laughlin	Cowlitz.
Grand Mound, 20	J. S. French	John F. Brewer	Centreville.
Skookum Chuck, 33	John Tullis	B. S. McElroy	Skookum Chuck.

MASON COUNTY.

Name and Number.	Master.	Secretary.	P. O. of Secretary.
Home, 56	T. W. McDonald	F. H. Cook	Olympia.

PIERCE COUNTY.

Name and Number.	Master.	Secretary.	P. O. of Secretary.
Puyallup, 41	W. C. Kincaid.	Mary F. Meeker	Puyallup.

STEILACOOM COUNTY.

Name and Number.	Master.	Secretary.	P. O. of Secretary.
Muck, 40	William Lyle	M. F. Hawk	Steilacoom.

STEPHENS COUNTY.

Name and Number.	Master.	Secretary.	P. O. of Secretary.
Pine Grove, 17	F. A. Dashiel	L. Blain	Pine Grove.

THURSTON COUNTY.

Name and Number.	Master.	Secretary.	P. O. of Secretary.
Olympia, 10	L. G. Abbott	Albert A. Manning	Olympia.
Unity, 21	M. N. Ensbergen	Oliver Shead	Skookum Chuk.
Yelm, 28	E. Longmire	Wm. Martin.	Yelm.

WALLA WALLA COUNTY.

Name and Number.	Master.	Secretary.	P. O. of Secretary.
Battle Creek, 8	Wm. E. Ayres	Thos. Throssel	Dayton &Waitsburg.
Blue Mountain, 3	William M. Shelton	John F. Brewer	Walla Walla City.
Central, 22	G. T. Welch	Epps Hardy	Waitsburg.
Dayton, 2	J. B. Shrum	O. C. White	Dayton.
Dixie, 5	W. S. Gilliam	W. J. P. McKern	Walla Walla City.
Harmony, 6	W. W. Sherry	J. A. Starner	Dayton.
Pataha, 13	J. L. Rounds	T. McBrierly	Dayton.
Spring Valley, 23	C. C. Cram	D. R. Harris	Waitsburg.
Union, 12	George Geer	P. M. Smith	Pataha Prairie
Waitsburg, 1	J. W. Highland	Mrs. N. J. A. Simons	Waitsburg.
Walla Walla, 4	Frank Shelton	James Simonton	Walla Walla City.
Wallula, 29	G. D. Goodwin	Wm. Martin	Wallula.

WAKKIACUM COUNTY.

Skamakawa, 64	James W. Smith	Fred. E. Strong	Skamakawa.

WHATCOM COUNTY.

Fidalgo, 38	H. C. Barkhouser	C. N. White	Fidalgo.
Nooksachk, 37	Wm. Hampton	James H. Reed	Nooksachk.
Swinomish, 50	R. E. Whitney	E. A. Sisson	La Conner.
Whatcom, 36	A. C. Marston	M. D. Smith	Whatcom.

WHITMAN COUNTY.

Cour d'Alene, 16	W. A. Nickols	Wm. King	Colfax.
Excelsior, 14	Philip O. Cox	Marion Davis	Colfax.
Palause, 44	H. S. Burlingame	E. M. Downing	Colfax.
Pioneer, 15	Lewis Ringer	W. J. Hamilton	Colfax.

WHITBY'S ISLAND.

Oak Harbor, 63	Thos. P. Hastie	John W. Gillespie	Cove Land.
Whitby's Island, 42	B. F. Loveland	E. B. Ebey	Cowperville.

YACKIMA COUNTY.

Yackima, 52	G. S. Taylor	W. W. Dickenson	Selah & Stannum.

IDAHO TERRITORY SUBORDINATE GRANGES.

Arranged by Counties.

ADA COUNTY.

Boise, 3	L. F. Cartee	George D. Ellis	Boise City.
Dixie, 8	T. B. Gess	B. F. Young	Middleton.
Dry Creek	Henry L. Owings	I. W. Herald	Boise City.
Eureka, 9			
Emmettsville, 12	J. A. Bennett	W. F. Cavanah	Emmettsville.
Horse Shoe Bend, 10.			
Lower Boise, 7			
Middleton, 6			
Payette, 11	Sampson Reed	I. E. Fouts	Falk's Store.
Salubria, 14	John G. Curtis	Alexander Allison	Salubria.
Shelton, 4	Joseph Wilson	David Heron	Boise City.
Star, 5	D. W. Touch	C. I. Simpson	Boise City.
Weiser, 13	Nelsoe Haven	A. F. Helt	Weiser.

NEZ PERCE COUNTY.

Charity, 15	W. C. Pearson	J. H. Robinson	Mount Idaho.
Nez Perce, 1	W. C. Brittain	D. J. Hayfield	Pine Creek.
Paradise, 2	John A. Emery	Wm. Howard	Paradise.
Stepto, 43	J. H. Cousins	F. Hanna	Paradise.

PART FOURTH.

Aids and Obstacles to Agriculture on the Pacific Coast.

CHAPTER XVIII.

LAND MONOPOLY.

"The source of public security and social permanence is the attachment of the freeholder to his home. The State should seek to promote an intensive rather than an extensive agriculture.—*Prof. Thompson.*

Mr. J. Stuart Mill's Axiom—The Public Domain, and its Distribution—Lands in California—Prosperity shown by the Proportion of Farms to Population—Disposition of State Lands—Effects of Consolidation of Landed Interest in England—Spanish and Mexican Domination—Mexican Grants, and a Discreditable Chapter of History—Bounty of the Federal Government—How the State Lands have been Manipulated—Discrepancy between Federal and State Laws—Eastern College and Indian Scrip—Swamp and Tide Lands—Agricultural College Grant—Railroad Grants—California Peerage, and Status of our Landlords—Discrimination in Taxation--Remedies.

Not one, but many questions of vital importance to the public welfare, are involved in an intelligent opinion of the true relations of man and land. The interest which the whole people and successive generations have in its division and distribution, appears to justify peculiar legislation, inasmuch as it belongs to no other kind of property. Mr. J. Stuart Mill laid it down as a political axiom, that the "land, the gift of nature to all, cannot be considered property in the same absolute sense as that in which no one has any interest but ourselves."

A recent American writer, Prof. Robert Ellis Thompson, in a chapter on the national economy of land, says, that "the duty of the State extends to the improvement of the land and the laborer upon it. It may justly be said that this is true of the duty of the State toward any form of industry; but from the peculiar relation of agriculture to the very existence of the nation, the State stands in a relation of far greater responsibility here. Many of those who most incline to exclude the State from all activity in the sphere of industrial interests, are quite ready to admit that where motives of public policy call for interference, the land-owner may fairly be treated as the trustee or steward of the national property; not in any absolute sense the owner." It will not be questioned that laws which prevent or retard cultivation, are prejudicial to the welfare of the State; the Englishman who turns men off from his land to create a wilderness for his game is as much an enemy to civilization as the savage who struggles to preserve his wilderness intact. As the ancient doggerel hath it:

"It is a sin for man or woman
To steal a goose from off the common;
But who shall plead that man's excuse,
Who steals the common from the goose."

Coleridge long ago pointed out the evil influence of the commercial or trading spirit upon the rural economy of England, as leading men to regard the production and cheapening of commodities as the one great end of all activity, and taking away from the landlord a sense of duty to the land and its cultivators. The end of labor is not in the things produced, but in the elevation of the producer.

Mr. William R. Hooper, in an interesting article upon our public lands, in Harper's Magazine of January, 1871, gives us a brief history of the public domain, and the uses to which it has been applied:

In the very infancy of our existence as a nation, before the adoption of the Constitution, the ownership and control of the public lands was the chief obstacle to union. The question was creditably and magnanimously adjusted, however, by the owning States giving their outlying lands to the general government. New York took the lead, in 1781; Virginia followed in 1784, with a cession of the great Northwestern territory; Massachusetts relinquished her claims in 1785; and Connecticut, Georgia, the Carolinas, and other States, gave up their rights within a year or two afterward.

By the treaty of peace with Europe in 1783, our western boundary was fixed at the middle of the Mississippi, and the outlaying lands then belonging to the States, in severalty, and subsequently ceded to the general government as above stated, amounted to 226,-

000,000 acres. By the treaty with France in 1803, the treaty with Spain in 1818, the treaties with Mexico in 1848 and 1853, and the treaty with Russia in 1867, we increased our public domain over seven fold, adding over 1,609,000,000 acres to the national territory. We thus became possessed of a total of 1,834,990,400 acres of land—a domain sufficiently extensive to make twenty-five countries each of the size of England, Ireland, Scotland, and Wales combined, and capable of supporting a population of 720,000,000 of people of the average density of Great Britain, or more than half the population now living on the globe.

In the early days of the Republic, our public lands were chiefly valued as an anticipated source of public wealth; but under the pressure of progress, this idea has given way, and the lands are now chiefly used as a stimulus to immigration, in aid of public improvements, and to supply a homestead to every one who will live on them. About 440,000,000 of acres, in all, have been disposed of by sale, pre-emption and homestead rights, and grants to schools, canals, railroads, etc.. Some 70,000,000 acres more have been surveyed and are now in the market. And there are over 1,300,000,000 acres of wild lands yet unsurveyed.

During the first eleven years of our constitutional existence, land was only taken up at the rate of 100,000 acres a year. In 1806, the sales realized $705,245. During the war of 1812, the sales largely fell off; but with the return of peace, they gradually recuperated, until in 1819 they netted about $3,000,000. The sales for 1835, realized $14,000,000; and for 1836, they netted $21,000,000—the largest year's sales ever made. In 1842, the sales run down to nearly $1,000,000. From 1850 to 1855, they averaged about $10,000,000 a year. In 1862—the rebellion being in progress—they amounted to only $125,048. Since the war, they have increased to an average of about $300,000 a year.

The very wise and beneficent policy of setting apart a specific portion of the public lands for the establishment and support of common schools, is practiced by no other government but ours. The policy originated at a very early period of our history. In the first "Ordinance for ascertaining the mode of disposing of lands in the Western territory," Congress directed that every sixteenth section of every township, should be reserved for schools; and subsequently gave every thirty-sixth section to the same purpose. Over 78,000,000 acres have been set apart under these and similar acts, besides about 7,000,000 acres for agricultural colleges.

The chief glory of our public land system, however, is the homestead policy, under the operation of which more of the people own the homes they occupy, than in any other nation in the world. The number of homestead entries in the last year alone, made twice the number of freeholders in the United States that England possesses, with her ten centuries of civilized existence.

The policy of the National or State governments, in donating lands for public improvements, or for educational purposes, however meritorious in intention, may well be questioned, for it has been the most fruitful source of public corruption and land monopoly, and has probably done more to retard the development of California, than any other single cause. The benefits have accrued mainly to speculators, while the evil effects extend throughout the whole social organism.

Had the proceeds of the sale of lands granted by the United States for educational purposes, been kept in the treasury, and the interest thereon annually paid to the proper officers of States or institutions, according to the provisions of Morrill's Congressional Bill for the further endowment of Agricultural Colleges, (1872,) millions would have been saved to the educational interest, and many of these evils obviated.

The relations of all our industries, and our very existence as a republican government, are bound up in the freedom of land. Not an acre of our public domain should ever have been parted with, except for homestead purposes, for actual settlement and use, and for national parks, or conservatories of native animals and plants.

The public domain is distributed throughout the States of the interior, and especially those west of the Mississippi. Texas owns her own land; California contained 100,000,000 acres in 1870; the rest is to be found mainly in the territories, as follows :

Territories.	Total Acres.	Acres Unappropriated.
Washington,	44,796,160.00	40,976,976.60
New Mexico,	77,568,640.00	70,677,735.83
Utah,	54,065,043.20	48,659,916.27
Dakota,	96,596,128.50	90,567,020.47
Colorado,	66,880,000.00	62,382,773.26
Montana	92,016,640.00	86,768,100.09
Arizona,	72,906,240.00	68,855,730.00
Idaho,	55,228,160.00	52,103,783.04
Wyoming,	62,645,068.00	59,163,834.49
Indian,	44,154,240.00	44,154,240.00

The amount not disposed of on the 30th of June, 1870, was 1,387,732,209 acres. From this must be deducted, for water surface, at least 80,000,000 acres; Alaska, 369,000,000 acres; grants to railroad and other corporations, 200,000,000 acres.

Senator Stewart puts the amount of the public domain which is fit for homestead purposes, at 332,000,000 of acres. Of the 447,000,000 of acres disposed of by the government, he says not 100,000,000 has passed directly into the hands of cultivators.

Our public domain, therefore, can by no means be considered limitless; the normal rate of increase of our population, (35 per cent.,) will give us a population, in 1920, of 171,771,610; from which the reader may infer that the land question is already one of the greatest concerns of American statesmanship.

The report of the United States General Land Office, for the year 1871, gives the following information in regard to the lands in California on the 1st of June of that year. The area of the State is set down at 120,847,840 acres, of which but 33,900,633 have been surveyed up to 1871; leaving unsurveyed 87,047,207. Of the 33,900,633 acres surveyed, less than eight millions have been confirmed to private claimants. The condition of the remainder is as follows:

	ACRES.
Sold	3,591,816
School	5,569,990
Swamp Lands	969,702
University	46,080
Indian Scrip	38,425
Agricultural Colleges	52,213
Railroad Grants	694,684
Internal Improvements	500,000
Homestead Act of 1862	709,386
Scrip Locations	935,335
Government Sections	6,400
Military Reservations	511,052
Floating Scrip	80
Total	11,026,163
Total to private claimants	7,784,303
Surveyed lands still in possession of the Government	15,900,167
Total surveyed	33,900,633

We will now look a little more closely at the relations between "God's Country," and "Landlords." The best land the sun shines upon; "Time's latest offspring and the last," should have given the American people a better chance and a fairer future than they had even yet known. The State fails in one of its highest obligations, unless it takes means to secure that the manner in which the land is held, the mode and degree of its division shall be the most favorable for drawing the greatest benefit from its productive resources. A comparison, which can easily be made from the census report between the number of farms and the value of personal property thereon, and the number of land owners, tells the story. For instance: Wisconsin, in 1870, had 102,904 farms, only thirty-two of which contains more than 1,000 acres. In California five hundred and sixteen men owned 8,685,439 acres, nearly double the area of Massachusetts, and about one fifth of the arable land of the State.

In Fresno County there are forty-eight land-holders, that own from five to seventy-nine thousand acres each. In Santa Barbara forty-four men own over a million acres. Sixteen men in California own over eighty-four square miles.

At the present moment it is estimated that 40,000,000 acres in the State deserve to be considered tillable. 22,000,000 acres have been disposed of, including 8,000,000 acres covered by Mexican grants; 7,500,000 acres given for educational purposes; 4,000,000 sold; 600,000 given as homestead claims, and 800,000 granted to the State as swamp land. The railroad lands cover 30,000,000 of acres, but patents have been given for only a small portion of this amount.

We all know what the concentration of land ownership into the hands of a few persons has done for England. At the time of the Norman conquest, the population was supposed to have been a million and a half, and there is in existence a written roll of over 45,000 land-owners. In 1861, with a population of 20,000,000, the number of land-owners is 30,000. Millions of acres are kept out of cultivation in parks and forests; and within the last twenty-five years two and a half millions of the population of Great Britain have emigrated; while every twentieth man of those that remain is a pauper.

Two regions of the United States were ready for land monopoly to take refuge in, when driven from its European strongholds, viz., New Mexico and California. The foundation was laid in grants of large areas of the best agricultural and grazing lands therein, made by the Spanish and Mexican authorities to individuals. The indefinite character of Mexican grants, their boundaries being generally defined by some river or irregular mountain range, never surveyed or ascertained until they became the property of the United States, has led to endless litigation in both Federal and State courts. In 1835 the secularization of the Missions took place, their property being distributed among the few rancheros which had grown up under their shelter, or otherwise passing into the public treasury. The era of Spanish domination lasted fifty-three years; that of Mexican rule and pastoral life twenty-four. During the latter period men were too scarce to give any value to land. To every citizen a town lot was given; and every man who wanted an extensive cattle range, got it without trouble from the Mexican government. Nominally, the grants were limited to eleven leagues (a Mexican league contains 4,438 acres,) but practically they were made to cover pretty much everything a man wanted, especially after they passed from the original claimants into American hands. "If the history of the Mexican grants is ever written, it will be a history of greed, perjury, spoliation and high handed robbery, for which it will be difficult to find a parallel. Indefiniteness of boundaries has given such an opportunity for these spoliations, that while they have proved a curse to California, their original owners have reaped no commensurate benefit; at a very early day they passed into other hands."*

Not all the great landlords of California have obtained their possessions by fraudulent means; a good many of the Anglo Saxon settlers were grafted upon the Spanish families by marriage. Five Carillos of Santa Barbara, and three of Santa Rosa, thus endowed adventurous Americaños with their worldly goods of lands and cattle.

The able and exhaustive pamphlet we have referred to will lead the curious reader through many of the devious windings of our land affairs. Between bogus claims, possessory rights, and the splendid opportunity thus given for the foundation of lawyers' fortunes, the government lands of California have cost more to the settler than any equal amount in the United States. The Mexican land policy is not responsible for the unnumbered wrongs which it has done to the future welfare of the State, any more than lawyers are responsible for sin; it has furnished the pretext under which the land-grabber could thrive, to the exclusion of the actual settler.

GRANTS TO THE STATE.

Under Section VI. of Act of Congress, passed March 3, 1853,† California received from the federal government, the sixteenth

* "Our Land Policy," by Henry George.

† Surveyor-General's Report for 1873.

and thirty-sixth sections in each township, or indemnity therefor in cases where the State cannot perfect her title on account of Spanish grants, or prior sales by the United States. This grant comprises one-eighteenth of the land in the State, or an aggregate of about six millions of acres. About one third, or two millions of acres of this land is located within the mineral belt.

Under Section IV. of Act of September 28, 1850, the State is granted all the swamp and overflowed lands within her border.

Under Section VIII. of Act of September 4, 1841, the State is granted five hundred thousand acres for the purposes of internal improvement.

Under Section XII. of Act of March 3, 1853, the State is granted seventy-two sections, or 46,080 acres, for the use of a seminary of learning.

Under Section XIII. of the same Act, ten sections for the purpose of the erection of public buildings.

Under the Act of July 2, 1862, one hundred and fifty thousand acres for the benefit of agriculture and the mechanic arts.

By virtue of her sovereignty the State is owner of all the salt, marsh and tide-lands within her borders.

Had the State of California, on the receipt of these magnificent gifts, protected the settler instead of the speculator, our newspapers would not be asking to-day, "What shall we do with the immigrants?" But she appears to have offered, through her land laws, a premium to speculation, which is unexampled in the history of States. The floating titles of her Mexican grants, the floating character of swamp lands, and the large floating grant of "lieu," or indemnity lands, which may be located on any unappropriated government land, have made the Golden State the paradise of lawyers. Capital was not needed where a combination between lawyers, legislators, and speculators would enrich all three at the expense of the settler and the great future of the State.

The machinery was so well oiled that though a Governor could say in his message, "Our land system seems to be mainly framed to facilitate the acquisition of large bodies of land by capitalists or corporations, either as donations or at nominal prices," no effectual remedy has ever been applied. One illustration of the system must suffice: "To purchase land of the State, an application must be filed in the State Land Office, describing the land by range, township, and section, and stating under what grant the title is asked. This application must be accompanied by a fee of five dollars. The Surveyor-General then issues a certificate to the applicant, and sends the application to the United States Land Office, for certification that the land is free, before he approves the application, and demands payment. If there be in the United States Land Office no record of pre-emption, homestead, or other occupation, the United States Register marks the land off on his map, but he does not certify to the State Surveyor-General until he gets his fee. The payment of this fee, and return of the certificate, depend upon the applicant, whose interest it is not to get it until he wishes to pay for his land. Thus, by the payment of five dollars, a whole section of United States land can be shut up from the settler. There are 1,244,696 acres monopolized in this way, (which the immigrant can buy for from ten to twenty dollars per acre,) then the speculator goes to the United States Land Office, pays the Register's fee, gets his approved certificate, and pays the State $1 25 per acre!" The difference between what settlers have to pay and what they ought to pay, would have defrayed the expenses of their transportation twice over.

The general laws of the United States provide, that until land is offered at public sale, there is no way of getting it, save by actual occupation of not over 160 acres to each individual. Until the land is surveyed, and the plats filed, there can be no title, and no record can be made of pre-emption.

But by the State law of March 8th, 1868, which repealed all previous laws, all restrictions of amount, or use, except as to the sixteenth and thirty-sixth township sections first granted, were swept away. Even with respect to these, the applicant was not required to swear that he wanted the land for settlement, or wanted it for himself. Again, the actual settlers, upon the sixteenth and thirty-sixth sections above referred to, under this law, could only be protected in their occupancy for six months after its passage, after which date the protection extended only sixty days. Many a settler, in hitherto undisputed possession, knew nothing of these enactments until they received notice that another party had a clear title to their farms. As if this were not enough, a special bill was passed legalizing all applications for State lands, even where the affidavits by which they were supported did not conform to the requirements of the law, either in form or substance.*

Again, the best parts of the agricultural lands of the State were sold before there was any demand for them for agricultural purposes. Eastern agricultural-scrip locations covered whole townships, up to the year 1867, and gave unlimited opportunity for the further monopolization of large tracts.

The law is now amended, so as to limit the purchaser to three sections in any township. The speculator, formerly, had only to go east, buy up the scrip with greenbacks, when greenbacks were low, locate his scrip under the most favorable conditions to himself, and become a landlord. One speculator has thus obtained 350,000 acres, which has been mostly rented to cultivators who furnished themselves, and pay him one fourth of the crop. Patents have been issued in a similar way for Indian scrip. A great deal of this college and Indian scrip has been so obtained that the lands have not cost their present owners more than fifty cents an acre, which they have been able to hold, not only keeping out settlers, but often robbing those who had already come of their improved farms. Few had money enough to defend themselves in the Courts, where defense would have been possible; but the settler upon unsurveyed lands had no defense.

What is a land patent? A patent issued by the government of the United States, is legal and conclusive evidence of title to the land described therein. No equitable interest, however strong, to land described in such a patent, can provide at law against the patent.

When two patents have been issued for the same land, the general rule is, that the elder patent shall prevail. When it is evident that a junior patent has been issued pursuant to legal authority, and the elder patent has not, the former will prevail. If a patent shall have been issued by mistake, and the person holding the same refuses to deliver it up for correction or cancellation, the President may direct another one to issue to the same, or to another person, reciting therein the errors in the first. As a general rule the government will not issue misrepresentation of facts, or such a mistake as affects the substantial rights of parties, it may be set aside, or a trust declared, and a conveyance decreed by a court of equity, to be made to the party entitled.

Another fine opportunity for founding a permament landed aristocracy was given by the State in her management of swamp and overflowed lands. The speculator, having seen that the State proved a better nursing mother to his interests than the United States, was interested in getting the largest possible quantity of land under her jurisdiction. The Surveyor-General says: "The conflicting claims of the State and the United States for the past ten years, have rendered uncertain the title to a large amount of land sold by the State as swamp and overflowed. Surveys for a large amount of land which the State had previously sold, have been received—the re-survey having been made by the second party apparently on the hypothesis that the original sale was illegal. There are also many conflicts caused by two or more surveys having been made for the same tract. In such cases an appeal to the courts is necessary. A large area of land has also been surveyed and returned to this office as swamp and overflowed which is not shown to be such either by State segregations or United States maps." Lands are so held to-day, which cannot be cultivated without irrigation.*

Under the possessory law of California, which allows both individuals and corporations to make some temporary enclosure or abode good for a possessory right, pre-emption settlers have been kept and driven away. Tracts of from two to twenty thousand acres of government land are thus held by State laws.

Even the tide-lands have not been safe from the operations of the grabber. The Surveyor-General says: "In some cases long, narrow strips were surveyed by the owners of the adjacent high lands, to protect themselves; but often these surveys were made in the interest of parties who did not own any land in the vicinity, evidently with the view of obtaining control of the water front."

More than seven hundred and fifty thousand acres of Eastern Agricultural College Scrip has been located in California. Realizing too little from the munificent scheme of the national

* The reader who desires to know more of this subject is referred to the "Reports of the Joint Committees on Swamp and Overflowed Lands and Land Monopoly," presented at the Twentieth Session of the Legislature of California.

government, to keep such colleges above board, in many cases not over fifty cents an acre, the grant has been a questionable blessing; it may be considered as a tax put upon the settlers of the new States to support the colleges of the older and richer ones. The Agricultural College Scrip of California was located under special privileges, and has been sold for five dollars an acre. Who were the holders of this scrip, or to whom some of the best timbered lands in Humboldt and other counties have been sold for five dollars an acre, the public have never been informed, the property of the University being administered as a private trust. The University has a special officer in charge of these lands, given solely "for the benefit of agriculture and the mechanic arts."

The grants made to railroads of California have been as follows: To the Western and Central Pacific of ten alternate sections, on each side, per mile, (12,800 acres;) to the Southern Pacific, ditto, with ten miles on each side, from which to make up deficiencies; to the Stockton and Copperopolis of five alternate sections on each side, and twenty miles on each side, in which to make up deficiencies; to the Texas Pacific, and to the connecting branch of the Southern Pacific, ten alternate sections, with ten miles for deficiencies, made in the year 1871. The greater part of this land is unsurveyed, and the settler upon the government sections must take his chances whether he gets upon it or not. Settlers who have purchased of the railroad are few; the best farming lands having been sold to "Land Companies," who, it is asserted, stand in peculiar relations to the railroad. The railroads are in no haste to sell, foreseeing the inevitable rise in the value of their immense property.

The effect of all these monopolies is to keep lands out of the hands of the army of industrialists who would flock to God's country by hundreds of thousands, could this pressure be removed.

The following list, or "Blue Book," of our Land Peerage, is taken from Hittell's Resources of California, and other reliable sources. The reader is referred to the reports of the Board of Equalization for further details:

Those who own from 100,000 to 500,000 acres (some of which is in scattered tracts):

Wm. S. Chapman	350,000
Miller & Lux, from 228,000 to	450,000

Gen. Houghton, Ex-State Surveyor, estimated from 200,000 to	300,000
Gen. Beale, Ex-United States Surveyor-General 200,000 to	300,000
Charles McLaughlin	141,000
Isaac Friedlander	125,900
Bixby, Flint & Co	150,000
S. R. Throckmorton (Mendocino)	146,000
Thos. Fowler, Fresno, Tulare & Kern	200,000
G. W. Roberts (swamp)	120,000
Philadelphia Petroleum Company	160,000
Los Angeles Land Company	101,000
Dibblee & Hollister	97,000
Irvine, Flint & Co	77,000
A. P. Moore	63,000
Estate of Arques (Monterey county)	71,000
Pioche & Bayerque	69,000
Jesse D. Carr	47,000
John Forster	88,000
Miguel Pedroreno	47,000
E. De Celis	56,000
Alfred Robinson (Trustee)	42,000
Beale & Baker	53,000
W. C. Ralston	44,000
C. Paige	60,000
James Lick	51,000
Lloyd Tevis	43,000
J. H. Redington	45,000
J. W. Moore	48,000
E. Applegarth	49,000
J. W. Pedrie	47,000
E. St. John & Co	42,000
J. W. Mitchell	42,000
A. Weill	48,000
H. & W. Pierce	53,000
J. W. Moore	48,000
L. T. Barton	47,000
E. Conway	42,000
Hollister & Cooper	41,000
P. W. Murphy	54,000
F. Steele	44,000

Number of estates over 44,000 acres, forty-four; between 30,000 and 40,000, twenty-three; between 20,000 and 30,000, fifty-five; between 10,000 and 20,000, one hundred and forty-eight; and between 5,000 and 10,000, two hundred and thirty-eight. The entire number of estates over 5,000 each in extent, is four hundred and fifty-three. Let us see how these large land-holders are assessed. An unjust discrimination appears to have been made in the assessments of taxes in the State between farming and grazing lands, even where these were lying side by side. Great bodies of unimproved lands have been put down at mere nominal rates, while the farmer who plows, sows and reaps his two or three hundred acres sees assessments raised upon his labors at the rate of three or four hundred per cent. Enormous quantities of lands owned by the monopolists are assessed at one half or even one fourth the value at which they are being sold. W. C. Ralston's lands were assessed at $2 00 per acre in 1871; Miller & Lux's at from $1 00 to $1 50 per acre; Isaac Friedlander's land was assessed in 1871 at $2 00 per acre, while he sold the same year to Chapman & Montgomery 28,850 acres for $115,445; $4 00 per acre.

Experience has proved that the laws of competition and enlightened self-interest have not been a sufficient check upon the tendency towards railroad monopoly through concentration; and we shall find that our laws of inheritance and the natural fluctuations of property will not abate the evils, and prove a sufficient check upon land monopoly. A general feeling prevails that land investments are the safest as well as the most profitable, when obtained as so many of ours have been with a trifling outlay of capital. The tendency to concentration is the natural one as the value of land increases; and it is especially dangerous where the processes of machine culture can be carried on as advantageously as in California. "We are not only putting large bodies of our lands into the hands of a few persons, but we are doing our best to keep them there. Our whole past policy is of a piece—tending with irresistible force to make us a nation of landlords and tenants, of great capitalists and poverty-stricken employes." The remedy is to be found in changing the mode of taxation, and in a revision and honest administration of our laws in the interest of the whole people.

CHAPTER XIX.

WATER MONOPOLY AND IRRIGATION.

Canal and Water Companies, how Authorized—Legislation Favorable to Monopolies—Los Angeles Convention—Voice of the People—Gov. Downey's Address—Memorial of Colorado to Congress—Congress Appoints Irrigation Commissioners for California—Mr. Brereton's Views of Agriculture in the San Joaquin Valley—Conclusions Arrived at by the Commissioners.

Under "An Act to authorize the incorporation of companies for the construction of canals, for the transportation of passengers and freights, or for the purpose of irrigation or water power, or the conveyance of water for mining and manufacturing purposes, or for all such purposes," approved May 14, 1862, and another Act, bearing date April 2, 1870, nearly all the waters of California, now required for irrigation, are controlled by corporations or private individuals.

An Act of Congress, approved July 26, 1866, provides: "That whenever, by priority of possession, rights to the use of the water for mining, agricultural, manufacturing, or other purposes, have vested and accrued, and the same are recognized and acknowledged by the local customs, laws and decisions of the Courts, the possessors and owners of such vested rights shall be maintained and protected in the same, and the right of way for the construction of ditches and canals for the purposes aforesaid, is hereby acknowledged and confirmed."

Under these laws, a large amount of capital has already been invested. It is easy to see how a monopoly may spring up under their protection, and grow to such great proportions as seriously to retard the agricultural development of the State.

The reader will remember that one of the most important questions which has come before the State Grange, is that of water monopoly and irrigation, and that the efforts of the Patrons to secure desired action of the Legislature of 1873, proved unavailing. In the autumn of that year, a convention had been held at Los Angeles, for the same object, and had adopted the following preamble and resolutions:

Whereas, In our rivers and mountain lakes, there is a large amount of water not utilized, which if properly developed would irrigate a large area, and thus greatly enhance the taxable values of our agricultural lands; and,

Whereas, Our mountains are pierced with numerous and convenient cañons, which it is believed may be dammed, and used for reservoirs, and the river streams which sink, may be saved by submerged dams, or stone-lined ditches made into river beds, and flowing thence into reservoirs, and from thence distributed over a large territory; and,

Whereas, The agricultural riparian and common law and water rights have been, are, and continue to be, violently antagonistic and provocative of constant litigation, personal and neighborhood quarrels, all of which must be exaggerated and aggravated with an increased population; and,

Whereas, The public are prevented from using a large proportion of their own water, by pretended claims of individuals, which is against public interest, the spirit of our institutions, and not to be tolerated; and,

Whereas, The *individual* policy has never been, nor can ever be equal to properly managing this great question, which is of State, if not of national interest;

Therefore, It is resolved, by the delegates appointed at the mass convention held at Gallatin, October 9th, 1873, to meet at Los Angeles, 25th October, 1873, to consider means for developing and distributing the waters of Los Angeles county, for agricultural purposes, with the view of furnishing a basis for legislation during the coming winter, as follows:

Article I.—Sec. 1. That it is the positive duty of the State of California, to possess and control all the waters in the State, which may be used for irrigating, (except springs rising on private lands,) without delay.

Sec. 2. And, where ownership of water is exercised to the public detriment, except in the case of springs rising on private land, to provide for denouncing and paying an equitable value for the same.

Sec. 3. To prohibit the acquirement of private rights to water which may be used for irrigating, except to springs rising on private property, and except as may be permitted under a general water law.

Sec. 4. To declare all waters which may be used for irrigating, including waters from springs after they shall have passed the land owned by the party on which springs may have risen, to belong to the State, and to be for the use of the public.

Article II.—Sec. 1. That it is the duty of the State to employ able engineers to make a thorough examination of our rivers, cañons, etc., and report as to the feasibility of increasing the water supply, and of storing the same in reservoirs, etc., for future use.

Article III.—Section 1. It is the duty of the State to create a new department of the government, to have cognizance of all matters pertaining to water development and irrigation. Said department to consist of—

1. A State Superintendent, who shall be assisted by an advisory board of —— engineers and —— civilians.
2. One Superintendent for each county where irrigating is practiced.
3. Three Commissioners for each water district.
4. The details necessary to complete the above, are most respectfully left with the Legislature.

Sec. 2. Lands irrigable by one stream and its tributaries, to constitute not more than two districts, and if possible not more than one.

Sec. 3. Water to be sold in all cases; but irrigators privileged to buy in proportion to acres to be cultivated in that water year.

Sec. 4. Irrigating head to be defined in inches.

Sec. 5. Present water laws to be revised.

Sec. 6. Properly existing water rights, in any contemplated change, should be respected.

Sec. 7. That a system of taxation should be devised, by which lands to be brought under irrigation can pay the major part of the expense incident thereto, and that the additional taxation raised from such lands should be reimbursed to the extent of the cost of development.

Resolved, That the advancement of the State of California in civilization and material prosperity, will greatly depend upon a proper system of water laws.

Resolved, That a copy of the above be furnished his Excellency, the Governor, and the honorable members of the Assembly, and the honorable Senators, with the request that they will urge legislation as above desired.

On motion, it was further resolved:

1 That his Excellency, the Governor, is especially called to urge upon the coming Legislature the propriety of appointing a special commission, with power to visit all parts of the State, to examine into the above questions, and to report at the earliest practicable moment, in the coming session of the Legislature.

2. That Generals Volney E. Howard and John R. McConnel, and Geo. H. Smith, Esq., be requested to draw a suitable water bill for Los Angeles county, in conjunction with the above named committee, and with our Legislative delegation, and that it be done in time for the coming Legislature.

An address was then given by ex-Governor Downey, which was extensively read and circulated, and is so replete with valuable suggestions as to require no apology for its introduction here. He said:

I approach this subject, of so much importance to Los Angeles county and the people of the whole State, with a degree of fear that individual interests will clash with any system that may be proposed for the general good. First of all, the paucity of rainfall renders irrigation a necessity for the greater part of our lands. Secondly, as a fertilizer it perpetually renovates our fields, as the waters carry in solution nearly all the elements required for the organic composition of vegetable life. Thirdly, it enables the farmer to select his time of planting and harvesting; and, fourthly, it enables him to destroy the numerous pests that infest his soil, in the shape of squirrels, gophers, rats, etc. I do not propose to deprive any man of the use of water that he now has, nor do I think that any Legislature would attempt to legislate away any rights vested or acquired; but for the good of the whole State, I suggest that the Commonwealth assert its jurisdiction over every stream in the State, and enact such equitable laws as will extend their usefulness to their utmost capacity. The riparian rights, or proprietary rights, maintained in England and recognized in many of our States as the law governing rivers and streams, do not apply to California. The laws of Spain and Mexico retained these in their sovereign capacity, and the State of California falls heir to this precious inheritance for the benefit of its citizens. It will be seen by an examination of the eight hundred and odd grants made to citizens of this State by those governments that this right is expressly reserved to the nation as public *servitudis*. If, then, our Legislature assumes its proper jurisdiction it will be no stretch of power to prescribe the mode and manner of the distribution of this important element, and settle at once a subject that has given so much annoyance.

The law of proprietary rights existing in England was once the law of France and the other continental communities, but Louis the Fourteenth had the wisdom to see that it was embarassing the welfare of the nation, and that wise monarch caused the nation to assume exclusive control of the arteries of the nation's wealth, and his example has been followed by others. The Republic of Chili has done likewise, and to this fact the beautiful system of irrigation of Chili and Lombardy is indebted.

There is, without doubt, sufficient water passing annually through this valley, under proper management, to irrigate all the land between the mountains and the sea. Individual communities and settlers have neither the means nor sagacity to utilize it, and therefore the State should step in and say how it shall be done; whether the State can do it through its proper officers, or how companies, under proper restrictions as to charges, shall do it. There should be no water allowed to run down to the sea in winter unutilized. It should be carried in a thousand conduits through the valley, and, rain or no rain, we should irrigate our lands in winter, thus destroying the vermin that honeycomb our subsoil, and that destroy and break capillary attraction. If we thus throw into our land an additional number of inches of water and break the surface as soon as a team can walk over it after irrigation, we will, with any ordinary rainfall, secure an abundant small grain crop, and keep our lands forever renovated. Our streams must be sheet piled to the bed-rock at points where they emerge from the foot-hills, so as to bring their full flow to the surface, and then main ditches ramified from the dam in wood, cement pipe, or sheet iron or earthen pipes. The loss from evaporation and absorption is so great that our slovenly open ditch system will not serve our purpose.

It is unnecessary to review the practice of Egypt, Babylon and Syria to show what irrigation did for those countries, nor to allude to the perpetual renovation of the valley of the Nile from natural and artificial irrigation. We have only to refer to the productiveness of comparative sand hills here in this country, that have produced the same crops for seventy years in succession without the aid of manure and owe this to the ever-restoring qualities of irrigation; we refer to England, Ireland and Scotland, that have a humid atmosphere and an average rainfall of twenty-seven inches per annum and that have called in the aid of irrigation as a restorative to their lands and made their meadows yield ten tons of hay per acre when but one ton could be produced before. It must be borne in mind that our ditches should always keep full, that we should keep our dams always in repair, that tree planting and vine planting cannot be successfully carried out unless your ditch is ready to run behind you, and that it is no time to be called on to go to work on your ditches when you should be plowing, planting and seeding, and that if you neglect this you will all want water at the same time and cannot possibly procure it. All who have the good fortune to have artesian wells should have reservoirs; if not they are but little use, and are only a willful waste of a gift of Providence, to be swallowed in the next squirrel hole, or a nuisance to impede transit or devitalize some flat that would otherwise be productive.

The Legislature should take bold ground on this subject and compel well-owners to put on taps or build reservoirs to be called upon at the proper time to perform their part in adding to the general wealth of the State. It is a rational conclusion to come to that if every man who bores a well and suffers the flow to be carried off by our trade winds, perhaps to the valley of the Mississippi, we are the losers, and the fountain of supply will be exhausted. This suggestion may look like interfering with the private rights of citizens, but the maxim that partial evil is universal good comes in, and that every civilized man must surrender a portion of his natural liberty for the good of society is also a maxim well understood and happily appreciated in this Republic.

There are but few localities in this country that water cannot be had in from eight to thirty feet from the surface. Surely, then, any man can contrive means to water ten acres in trees with a simple lift pump, windmill or horse-power, and those who can afford it could have an Ericsson engine which is the cheapest and simplest means in which the agency of heat is brought to bear as a power. It can be started in the morning with a basket of chips or corn cobs, the door closed on it and when the fuel goes out the engine stops its work, and there is neither danger or trouble attending it. We should all have tanks and reservoirs, for when we want to use our water we must have it in a greater body than a pump or even an artesian well can supply it. Wherever there is a natural depression on our lands or a ravine, we should throw an embankment across it and construct our ponds. They will be our greatest wealth, food for ducks and geese.

You can raise your own fish, and these ponds will be found better than any manure pile, with the grand advantage that its own gravity will distribute it on our fields without the aid of cart or shovel, only requiring intelligent direction to guide it in its mission of good. Every owner of an artesian well has the power at hand to drive hydraulic rams; they are the cheapest motive power in existence and nearer perpetual motion than any contrivance yet invented. They are always in repair and can be used to raise the flow of your artesian wells to elevated tanks and reservoirs, which will enable the farmer to utilize his high or elevated slopes and supply the economy of his chambers, kitchen and barn yard.

Some of the ideas advanced may seem bold and novel, but when I first advanced the idea in my annual message, 1861, to the Legislature that stock-raisers had a co-equal obligation to prevent trespass as the cultivator to defend it, it was looked upon as equally novel and bold; the result, however, shows that land never assumed value nor stock a price in this country until it was adopted, although some of my best friends denounced it as wild and visionary.

I have given this subject of irrigation much thought: I have had much experience in the distribution of water; I have had friendly litigation as riparian proprietor, with my good friend ex-Governor Pico. Fourteen years ago he had a few straggling Sonoriños cultivating perhaps in all 1,000 acres, and I could not obtain water below him to irrigate sixty acres; he declared there was not water enough for himself. There are now 12,000 acres in cultivation on what was then my farm, and with proper management we can irrigate to the sea with the same supply that then existed. The same example will apply to the Los Angeles and Santa Ana rivers. That it requires bold and comprehensive legislation will be apparent to all thinking men; that American citizens will submit to any equitable law, passed by the Legislature for the preservation and just distribution of the waters of our rivers and streams, their history in the past will warrant.

That the time has arrived for legislative action to be taken is patent to all, and that it should be general and properly guarded is manifest from the general voice of the whole people.

About the time of the Los Angeles Convention, a similar meeting was held in Denver, Colorado, the results of which were embodied in an eminently practical memorial which was presented at the following session of Congress. This memorial prays for the enactment of a law embracing the following general provisions:

1. To grant to the several States and Territories named in the preamble to this memorial, one half of all the arid lands, not mineral, within their borders; said lands, or the proceeds thereof, to be devoted to the construction of irrigating canals and reservoirs for the reclamation of said arid and waste lands.

2. That the construction and maintenance of irrigating canals and reservoirs shall be under the exclusive control and direction of the Territory or State, as sole owner thereof, under such laws, rules and regulations as the Legislature thereof shall from time to time provide.

3. That the Territorial and State Legislatures shall have power to make all needful rules and regulations, and take all needful steps for the proper construction and maintenance of such canals, and that such power shall include the power to provide by law for the issuing of the bonds of the Territory or State for the construction of such canals.

4. That the proceeds of said lands herein granted shall be kept as an exclusive fund by the Territory or State; first, for the payment of the principal and interest of all bonds so issued as aforesaid; second, that any balance remaining after the payment of the bonds issued as aforesaid shall be used in the maintenance of said canals, as the Legislature of said Territory or State shall from time to time by law direct.

5. That any lands within said Territory or State which shall be filed under the provisions of the pre-emption and homestead laws of the United States after the passage of this Act, shall be subject to the operation of this Act, if the said lands shall be brought under irrigation by the construction of said canals.

6. That the lands donated to the several States and Territories herein named, and the remainder of the public domain therein belonging to the General Government, shall be disposed of under revised and more strict pre-emption and homestead laws than are now in force, and that no title shall issue until the claimant shall be a *bona fide*, actual settler upon the land claimed.

While the attention of the people at large was thus directed, an Act of Congress had been passed, March 3, 1873, authorizing a commission to examine and report a system of irrigation for the San Joaquin, Tulare and Sacramento valleys. By the terms of the act, the President was to select for this duty, army engineers or officers of the Coast Survey then stationed on the Pacific, allowing such officers to associate with themselves in the work, the chief of the Geological Survey, and one other civilian distinguished for his knowledge of the subject.

The board thus authorized, consisted of Col. B. S. Alexander, Major George H. Mendell, of the Army Corps, and Prof. George Davidson, of the Coast Survey, who were expected to carry out the provisions of the Act of Congress on the meagre appropriation of five thousand dollars.

The United States Commissioners invited the co-operation of Mr. R. M. Brereton, who declined their proposal, but whose views upon agriculture in the San Joaquin valley are worthy of a careful reading in connection with the Commissioners' report. He says:

Having carefully observed the climate of this valley during the past three years, and the results obtained from irrigation and deep plowing, I have found that neither irrigation nor deep plowing will secure the wheat that ripens between the middle of May and the middle of June from being shriveled by the north winds. These north winds blast even the young leaves of the willow, ash, sycamore, and orchard trees; and no amount of moisture in the soil, or vigorous growth of the plant, seems to prevent the grain, when in the dough or ripening period, from becoming shriveled by these desiccating winds.

I find that the Sonora wheat, which ripened nearly a month sooner than the Chili and Australian, and before the north winds prevailed, yielded a fine, plump, white grain, while the others, which matured later and during the period of the north winds, yielded a shriveled and dark-colored grain, although the plant was of a more vigorous growth, yielding more straw, and having larger and longer heads than the Sonora.

I am satisfied that to make wheat-cultivation a success on the west side of this valley, it must be made to ripen early before the north winds set in, or else it must be made a late or fall crop, to be harvested in October. To secure the first the land must be watered the end of September and beginning of October, in order to start the seed. This will enable the plant to make from three to five inches growth before the winter rains and cold weather set in, when it will harden and stool out. During December and January, in adobe or clayey soil, wheat grows very slowly, on account of the cold weather, and under the present system of cultivation the main growth of the plant is during the months of March, April, and May. By giving the plant two months' growth before the cold weather sets in, the roots will have had time to get down deep below the action of any degree of frost known in the valley, and being two months ahead of the growth of the plant raised by the winter rains, will necessarily mature much earlier.

With regard to the second choice, there are no north winds after the beginning of July, and corn, cotton, and tobacco are never found blasted. The days are shorter in August, September, and October, and the nights are cooler than in April, May, and June; evaporation is much less and dew is deposited; consequently, grain, under the influence of irrigation, grows better, and will mature sooner than grain sown under present auspices.

The great drawback to wheat cultivation on the west side of this valley, in addition to the loss from shriveling, is the cost of transportation. The river is only navigable for a few days during the winter freshets, and during May and June, when the snows are melting. If the grain were harvested in May, it could be shipped during the period of high water; and if it were harvested in October and beginning of November, it could be shipped during the winter freshets, or on the first rise of the water in May.

If my ideas are correct, the farmers of this valley can, with irrigation at their command, make agriculture a perfect success, and seedtime and harvest will follow the year throughout, without failure. It would be better, I think, to build at once the main canals right through to tide-water, for the sake of transportation and cheap communication with San Francisco. Irrigation from such canals will follow by a gradual process, as population flows in, and the fact of these main canals meandering for two hundred miles through this immense valley, and offering facilities of transportation to the farmer at rates of two dollars a ton, where it now costs eight to ten dollars, will tend to encourage a more rapid settlement of the lands, notwithstanding the serious drawback which now exists in the fact of the large bulk of the best lands being in the hands of a few land speculators.

The average yield of wheat from irrigation, where the grain has not been affected by north winds, has been over thirty bushels an acre, and where the north winds have affected it, sixteen bushels. In European countries I find from recent records that the average of wheat in bushels per acre in different countries is as follows: England and Scotland, 28 bushels; Ireland, 23; France, 14; Belgium, 21; Russia, 17; Silesia, 10; Austria, 15.

I am sure that the farmers in this valley do not pay sufficient attention to deep plowing and working the land to secure a good tilth.

Where land has been much cultivated and tramped by stock, the soil lying immediately below the two or three inches of cultivated surface has a hard layer or pan, caused by the pressure of the jole of the plow, and by the treading of stock. It is difficult for grain-roots to penetrate this hard layer, and therefore they have only this depth of soil to depend upon for moisture and nourishment. In loose, rich soil I have seen wheat-roots over three feet long. Below this hard layer the soil is more open, and contains moisture held there by capillary action. Farmers can see for themselves the practical workings of this capillary action in the soils by observing a flower-pot filled with dry soil, and placed in a saucer containing water. This action is precisely that of an oil-lamp fed by the wick. If the ground is not plowed deep, the rain falling on the surface will not penetrate this hard layer, but will either run off the surface or become evaporated. By plowing deep and surrounding the fields with levees, so as to cause the rain to be absorbed into the soil, far greater farming results can be obtained than at present, even without irrigation.

Each inch in depth of water on an acre is upward of one hundred tons in weight. A good crop of wheat, say twenty-eight to thirty bushels, with its straw, just before it is in the blossom, will weigh about ten tons, and contains about three fourths of one tenth of an inch of water, or about seventy-five per cent.

It is found in England that wheat, barley, and clover exhale during five months' growth more than two hundred times their dry weight of water. To grow half a ton of wheat grain to the acre, with its straw, which will weigh about a ton, or one and one half tons of grain and straw together, requires three hundred tons, or a depth of three inches to the acre in England. The evaporation in this valley is probably double that of England, and therefore six hundred tons, or six inches depth of water would be necessary.

Land that is hard, smooth, and free of vegetation, reflects the solar heat, whereas land that is broken up and porous absorbs it during the day, and radiates it during the night, and consequently causes a greater deposit of dew from the vapor in the atmosphere, caused by evaporation during the day. This thorough cultivation and the system of deep plowing, if carried out throughout this valley, must, I think, reduce the present summer temperature, as the solar heat, instead of being reflected and heating the air would be absorbed and radiated by the loosened surface, and the temperature being lowered, the winds would be reduced, and the evaporation would be lessened, and therefore both grain and grass crops would thrive better during the hot season.

Liebig, in his letters on agriculture, says: "With the chemical properties of soils there is associated a physical quality not less remarkable in its nature and influence, viz: the power which they possess of attracting moisture from the air, and condensing it in their pores." "When in a hot summer the surface of the ground is dried, and there is no apparent moisture by capillary attraction from their lower strata, the powerful attraction of the soil for the vapors of water in the air provides the means for supporting vegetation." "The vapor of water which is thus condensed by the soil is derived from two sources: During the night the temperature of the air falls, the tension of its watery vapor becomes less, and then without the temperature of the air falling to the dew-point, there follows through the attraction of the soil, absorption of moisture (with ammonia and carbonic acid) accompanied by evolution of heat, which moderates the cooling of the ground from radiation.

"A second source from which the dry soil derives its moisture by absorption is presented by the deeper-lying moist strata. From these a constant distillation of water is taking place toward the surface, accompanied by a corresponding evolution of heat in the upper strata on its absorption.

"In the above facts we recognize one of the most remarkable natural laws. The outermost crust of the earth is destined for the development of organic life, and its broken particles are endowed, by the wisest arrangement, with the power of collecting all the elements of food which are essential for the purpose."

The hot, dry winds in this valley and in the Colorado desert, and the excessive heat of these plains are simply local, and created by the hard, unbroken surface of the plains, reflecting instead of absorbing the solar heat.

That which absorbs heat best, reflects heat worst, and that which radiates most, also absorbs most heat, and hence rough, loose, and porous soils, such as cultivated soils, freely radiate by night the heat which they absorb by day, in consequence of which they become cooled down, and condense the vapor of the air into dew.

This immense valley, being to the east of the ocean, becomes first heated by the solar rays, and as the heated air ascends, the cooler air from the west rushes in through the Pacheco and other passes to supply its place, causing a prevailing wind, and this wind becomes hotter and hotter from the reflected heat as it passes along the hard and uncultivated surface of the valley.

I do not believe that the Colorado desert is the cause of the hot winds in the San Joaquin valley, because heated air must ascend, and being lighter than cold, denser air must pass over and not displace it. Hot winds are therefore due to local causes; and it is not the hot air of the Colorado desert that creates the hot winds of this valley. By deep plowing and carefully pulverizing the soil of these immense plains, the farmers and land-owners have it in their power to alter the climate of the valley, and to abate the force of the prevailing winds. By keeping the soil open and porous, they enable it to absorb the solar heat, instead of reflecting it; and also enable it to absorb carbonic acid, etc., which are food for plants, and thus render the air less unhealthy. The air being cooler, evaporation will be lessened, and more rain and dew will fall.

I believe that the farmers would obtain better results if they would plow up or cultivate the land as soon as the grain crop is removed. An eminent agricultural chemist, has calculated that a well-made fallow insures a supply of nitrogen equal to two cwt. of Peruvian guano per acre—worth $4 per cwt.

I am sure that canals built for transportation in the first instance, between Tulare lake and tide-water, will pay a fair interest on the capital invested therein. In time this would be supplemented by the receipts from sales of water for irrigation. With canals available for navigation and irrigation, and with a system of agriculture more in accordance with the present climate, I believe the San Joaquin valley can be made the most productive and reliable portion of the agricultural lands of the State.

The report of the United States Commissioners covers ninety octavo pages, and is accompanied by a map which embraces the San Joaquin, Tulare and Sacramento valleys, showing the Sierra Nevada mountains on the east side of the valley, and the Coast Range on the west side to the summits; the "great valley of California," with all its lakes, rivers and creeks, with their catchment-areas, the overflowed and swamp lands (one million two hundred and twenty-five thousand acres), the division into counties, and the township lines of the United

States surveys, the railroads and principal towns. On this map, which alone is worth the cost of the commission, the railroads are laid down; the canals that have been projected and actually surveyed, and the hypothetical system of irrigating canals. Other valuable charts are added to the report, illustrating the irrigation systems in other countries.

The conclusions arrived at by the Commissioners, are as follows:

1. That there are large bodies of fertile land in the great valley of California—extensive plains, in fact—that require irrigation to make them productive, and that the natural features of these plains are favorable to artificial irrigation.

2. That there is an abundance of water for the irrigation of all land on the eastern side of the valley by canals from the rivers.

3. While there is a scarcity of water on the western side of the valley, at the necessary elevation, particularly on the western side of the San Joaquin and Tulare valleys, yet there is sufficient water attainable there, and at a sufficient elevation, to irrigate large areas of land on that side.

4. That irrigation is much needed, particularly in the San Joaquin and Tulare valleys. The productions of these valleys could be increased many fold by a comprehensive system of irrigation. The value of the irrigable land, and of the revenue derived from it, both by the State and by the people, will be increased in the same ratio.

5. The cost of a comprehensive system of irrigation for these valleys will be great, but as the different portions are not equally in want of irrigation, the complete system may be the work of time.

6. Irrigation is but little understood in this country, either by our engineers, who must design, plan, lay out and execute the works for that purpose, or by the farmers, who are to use the water when it is brought alongside their farms.

7. That the experience of other countries appears to prove that no extensive system of irrigation can ever be devised or executed by the farmers themselves, in consequence of the impossibility of forming proper combinations or associations for that purpose. That, while small enterprises may be undertaken by the farmers in particular cases, it would not be in accordance with the experience of the world to expect of them

the means or inclination to that co-operation which would be necessary to construct irrigating-works involving large expenditures. That enterprises of this character, if built at all, must be built by the State or by private capital.

8. That it is the duty of the government, both State and national, to encourage irrigation; and the first step in that direction ought to be to make a complete instrumental reconnoissance of the country to be irrigated, embracing the sources from whence the irrigating-canals ought to commence, gauging the flow of the rivers and streams, and defining the boundaries of the natural districts of irrigation into which the country is divided.

9. Then, when it is proposed to irrigate any particular district, an accurate topographical survey of that district should be made, so that the canal and other necessary works for its irrigation may be designed on an intelligent and comprehensive system, and in harmony with the neighboring canals, and these works executed in the most economical manner. In this way, every farmer will be informed, before he will be called upon to contribute to the works of irrigation, whether or not his land is irrigable; and, if it is, of the quantity of water he will obtain; the exact place or places where it will be delivered to him, and of its probable cost.

10. While these surveys are being made, we think it would be a step in the right direction if the government of the United States, as well as of the State of California, would inaugurate measures for obtaining from foreign countries all possible information relating to the more modern systems of irrigation in these countries, and for disseminating this information throughout this country.

11. After the necessary reconnoissance shall have been made, and a knowledge of the most improved systems of irrigation in other countries has been obtained, the general system of irrigation can be properly planned, and the outline of the principal works determined, the laws under which a proper system of irrigation for the great valley can then be decided upon intelligently, the country divided into those natural districts which its topographical features require, and all, or nearly all, the land-owners will then know what benefits they are to derive from irrigation. Light will be thrown on a subject which is now in comparative darkness; unnecessary clashing of private

interests can be avoided or harmonized. The rights of water which have given so much trouble in other countries, where the laws regulating these rights have grown up with their system of irrigation, and, as history teaches us, have often been made for the benefit of private parties or particular districts of country, can be established beforehand, if not for all time, at least, on the principle of "the greatest good for the greatest number."

12. That, while the irrigation of these plains would probably be effected in the cheapest and most thorough manner by a comprehensive system of canals, such as we have sketched, we by no means recommend that all irrigation should await the development of such a system. We are taught, by the experience of other countries, to expect such development to be the work of many years. In the mean time, ten or twenty or fifty farmers having lands so situated as to be irrigable from a neighboring stream, may desire to construct the works necessary for that purpose, to be operated for their benefit, or they may desire to enter into an agreement with other parties, who shall build the required works. In either case, if the proposed works do not conflict with the general system of irrigation, we believe that such an enterprise should be permitted and encouraged by the State.

13. As a matter of public policy, it is desirable that the land and water should be joined together, never to be cut asunder; that the farmers should enjoy in perpetuity the use of the water necessary for the irrigation of their respective lands; that when the land is sold, the right to water shall also be sold with it, and that neither should be sold separately.

14. That the parties chiefly benefited by irrigation are the farmers or land-owners. That there is every reason to believe that the value of land in the driest districts will be appreciated many fold; that it results from this that the lands should, as far as possible, pay for the construction of the necessary works.

15. That the State and counties will be directly benefited by the appreciation of land, and by the increase of wealth in their revenues from taxation. That, consequently, it may be good policy for them to aid such enterprises.

16. That there is this difficulty in the way of the proposition that the lands shall pay for the canals, namely, that in many places the lands at present are not worth more than $5

per acre, if so much, and that the irrigation-works may cost $10 per acre.

17. That whatever aid is given by the State or county, should be extended in a cautious way. That in many parts of the country where irrigation will ultimately best repay expenditure, there are now no people; that the population must be imported, the houses, barns, and equipments of the farms, must be created before returns can follow the investment. That for these reasons, we must look for a comparatively slow development of the country.

18. That while we believe, as we have already stated, that the best policy is for farmers to build and own the canals, we also believe that where the farmers are unable to build, and where the State is unable or unwilling to build, it may be, and it probably will be, the best policy to invite the aid of private enterprise. We refer to numerous instances in Spain and Italy, where this system is now in successful operation, in support of our opinion.

19. That private companies undertaking such enterprises, should be subjected to certain conditions, some of which are as follows:

That after a stated period, the franchise shall lapse in favor of the State, or of the irrigators; or that, after a certain period, the State shall have the right to purchase, on certain previously-defined conditions. That the price of water shall be fixed by agreement, each party in interest being represented by arbiters. That the State shall have the right to charter an association of irrigators to administer the works, the company merely selling the water, and having nothing to do with it after it leaves the channels, the association making all arrangements for its distribution, and for the collection of the water-rates. This latter provision has several advantages: It relieves the company from the odious duty of discriminating in times of scarcity, and from the endless disputes which attend the distribution of water, and puts the responsibility where it belongs—on the irrigators. It favors each irrigator; for he becomes a member of a company, which is strong enough to stand up for its rights in any contest with the capitalists.

For a successful system of this kind, we refer to the "Association for irrigation in the Vercelles, Italy," given elsewhere in this report. That we see no reason why the rights of farmers and the rights of capitalists may not be adjusted by some such plan, on the basis of justice and of mutual interest. We observe that the conditions just referred to place a company of capitalists in the light of temporary owners, and that they contemplate a period when the works shall be owned by the State, or by the farmers.

20. That there is no reason to suppose that, for a long time, capital will look upon this kind of investment with favor. The financial history of most irrigating enterprises in other countries, is not favorable, so far as the interests of the shareholders are concerned. It may be a question for the State to consider whether it is a good policy to offer any special inducements in aid of such enterprises.

21. That the relation of the United States to the irrigation of California, is for the most part indirect, but that, in the southern end of the valley, between Visalia and Bakersfield, and south of this town, it is believed that the United States own many thousand acres of lands which are capable of irrigation; that most of this land cannot be cultivated under existing circumstances; that it has no value, except for pasturage, during part of the year; that, if irrigated, its value would be increased many fold; that under these circumstances, it may be a question whether the United States ought not, in some way, to encourage the irrigation of these lands.

22. That when any canals are built, the State should establish a system of inspection, by which a proper construction shall be assured; that the quantity of water to be taken from a river at its mean stage, for the irrigation of a definite quantity of land, should be fixed by a reasonable rule, so that those who come later shall not find all the water taken up, and so that proper drainage shall be secured.

23. That such supervision will probably be distasteful to the parties concerned; that, nevertheless, we believe it is essential to future prosperity, and that its neglect now will bring a fruitful crop of contentions in the future, will delay the development of the country, and that by making irrigation unhealthful, it may make it odious.

24. That the water-rights of the streams now taken up for mining purposes in the mountains, do not conflict with the irrigation of the plains, the water being returned to the natural channels above the points where it will be taken out for irrigation, at least for many years to come.

CHAPTER XX.

THE IRRIGATION PROBLEM.

"Irrigation commenced in necessity, and has been pursued ever since for profit. It is not an experiment resting upon the future to prove its advantage or uselessness, but a success, tested by the most careful inquiry, made by the most civilized nations of the world."—*Hon. M. M. Estee.*

Cost of Irrigation—Loss by Absorption—Amount of Water Required per Acre—Amount Used in Foreign Countries—Primary, Secondary, and Tertiary Ditches—Bases of Estimates—Ownership of Water—Mr. Estee's Views concerning Legislation—Italian Authorities Quoted—Dr. Ryer's Hints toward a Solution of the Problem—Irrigation and Public Health.

From the annual address given before the State Agricultural Society in September, 1874, we have, with the author's consent, taken not only the heading of the following chapter, but much of its contents. Indeed, so little can be added to the report of the commissioners so liberally quoted, and to Mr. Estee's presentation of the subject, that we deem it for the interest of those most deeply concerned in the solution of this great problem, to content ourselves with the effort to extend their benefits. The Commissioners have thus counted the cost of irrigation:

Before making an estimate of the cost of canals, it is necessary to inquire how much water is required to irrigate an acre of land. It will readily be understood that the quantity will depend upon a number of considerations, such as the character of the soil, whether sandy or clayey; upon the character of the substratum, whether pervious or impervious; and upon the depth of inclination of an impervious stratum. It will also depend upon the character of the cultivation. Rice and sugar fields, vegetable-gardens, orchards, and meadows require more water than cereals.

The present staples of this country are cereals. There is some cotton and tobacco cultivation, which will probably be extended; and, with abundance of water, we shall doubtless have a good deal of alfalfa or lucerne grass. Every farmer will have a little orchard, and will raise the vegetables required for home consumption.

The evaporation is high in the interior valleys of the State, quite equal to that in Madrid, where it is about thirteen inches in July.

The amount of water lost by absorption in the bed and banks of the canal, is an unknown and variable quantity. In the absence of extra data upon these points, we may for the present adopt the rule laid down by engineers for other countries of similar climate, and estimate the loss of water from these causes at fifteen per cent.

The rivers of California generally run full for about seven months. The rains of the winter increase their discharge, and the melting of the snows keeps it up, so that we may say that the streams from the Sierra Nevadas are well supplied with water from December to

August. The streams from the coast range have no snow reservoirs of much extent, and are generally dry in summer.

Let us assume that the streams on the east side of the valley are well supplied with water for two hundred days in the year, and, to make up for the overestimate on this point, let us neglect their flow for the remainder of the year.

How much land ought a cubic foot of water, supplied every second for two hundred days, to irrigate?

We will make a further supposition that the water is used for fourteen hours out of the twenty-four. Irrigation at night is practiced in other countries, and we may be assured that in seasons of scarcity it will be here, if it shall prove necessary to save the crops. One day's supply will put twelve inches of water over an acre, or two inches of water over six acres, and in two hundred days a supply of a cubic foot per second, will cover two hundred acres with twelve inches of water.

Wheat planted in October or November on summer-fallowed land, well watered when the rivers are high, will probably make a good crop without further watering, except what it gets from the winter rains, even when they prove scanty.

Wheat planted in January or February will probably need one or two irrigations, or three inches each to make a crop. Wheat or barley planted later, and with irrigating facilities, (there seems to be no reason why, in these hot valleys, the sowing-time may not be extended to April,) will probably ripen with twelve inches of water judiciously applied. We know that good crops of wheat are raised without irrigating, when there is a rain-fall of twelve inches, or even less, which comes at the required times.

On the tule or reclaimed lands, barley sowed after wheat harvest has been gathered comes to maturity.

The water required for cotton will probably not exceed that necessary for wheat. Rice cultivation is so unhealthful that its introduction into California will hardly be looked upon with favor.

Alfalfa, if cut five times for hay, will require twelve inches of water or more, depending on the nature of the soil; this in addition to the usual rain-fall.

There is another point to be considered. The whole of the land commanded by the canal will not be irrigated; some of it will be waste or unsuitable for cultivation; some will be fallow, and if we add the areas taken up by the roads, fences, buildings, farm-yards, etc., we ought, according to experience elsewhere, to deduct one fourth, at least, from the irrigable lands. This deduction, we assume, will make up for any kind of cultivation, such as gardens, orchards, etc., requiring larger supplies of water.

Our opinion is, therefore, that a reasonable allowance for the land commanded by the canals is one cubic foot a second for each two hundred acres.

In seasons when there is a great surplus of water, there can be no objection to a more liberal use of it, but it seems to us indispensable that the State should lay down a general rule. There ought to be an established allotment, which may vary in different districts. The cultivators who came first ought not to be allowed to appropriate more water than they require, because, if they do, those who come after will not be able to procure a fair supply.

There are probably exceptional places where the lower average of rain-fall and porosity of the soil may combine to require a larger allotment of water than we have assigned. Such places are about Tulare Lake, on the west side of the great valley. There is no cultivation in these portions, and before the occasion may arise to irrigate them, further information will probably be available to enable the proper conclusion to be reached.

As the population of the irrigated districts increases there will be an increased demand for water, and it will probably result that the allowance which is sufficient in this generation, may prove entirely inadequate fifty years in the future.

When the State makes the survey elsewhere recommended in this report, we will learn both how much water and how much land there is, and will be enabled to proportion the supply to be granted.

It may then be a question, in seasons of scarcity, whether a smaller supply of water will be given to the whole land, or a larger supply to a portion of it.

There is so much variety on this point, in the circumstances of climate, soil and cultivation, and so much difference in the statements of different authorities, that we cannot derive from the experience of other countries, any definite conclusions applicable to our own; but as a matter of interest it will not be amiss to mention the duty of water in other irrigating districts.

In North India a cubic foot of water per second irrigates five acres per day.

Taking the interval of irrigation at forty days, we have the duty of two hundred acres for one foot a second for cereals.

In Granada a canal for the Genil irrigates, of wheat, barley and vines, two hundred and forty acres per cubic foot.

In Valencia, where it is very hot, wheat is watered four or five times, giving about two hundred acres per foot.

In Elche, where water is very scarce, a cubic foot goes as far as to irrigate one thousand acres. Wheat here, in some years, scarcely requires artificial watering.

Rice-fields, in different parts of the world, vary from thirty to sixty, and even eighty acres, to the cubic foot.

In the heavy monsoons of India, ninety acres per foot are irrigated. In some of the *huertas* or gardens in Valencia, only from thirteen to twenty acres per foot are irrigated. Here, however, there are at least two crops a year, and a part is devoted to rice.

The grants for six recent canals in Spain run from seventy acres per foot to two hundred and sixty acres per foot. Assuming, then, that a cubic foot per second will water two hundred acres of land, we proceed to give some considerations in regard to the probable cost of construction of the canals and their primary ditches.

The secondary and tertiary ditches will, it is supposed, be made by the cultivators. They can be made by the farmer in seasons of leisure, and in the general case their cost will hardly be felt. The case will be somewhat different with the cultivator who farms on a large scale, and who is obliged to hire laborers.

It is plain, on the slightest consideration, that the cost of a canal will be so dependent on local and special circumstances that it is impossible to deduce a perfectly satisfactory conclusion from a given or hypothetical case.

The dam, the character of the soil, the quantity of land to be irrigated, the manner in which it is disposed, the relative remoteness, and the resources and population along the line are all elements which vary from case to case, and either of which may effect the cost by a very considerable per centage.

Still it seems essential to know within some limits the probable cost.

If a canal is to cost $100 per acre irrigated, the subject may be dismissed without any further consideration. It is plain that we cannot afford to pay that price. If, on the other hand, canals may be built for five or twice five dollars per acre, it is equally plain that now or before many years we shall be able to afford them, and shall have a fair prospect of return from such investment.

The value of the estimate which we proceed to give, will be understood from what proceeds.

Let us take the most favorable case that can happen, namely, when the excavation equals the embankment. We assume a canal to carry 315 cubic feet of water per second, having the dimensions given in the figure. Deducting from this 15 per cent. for loss, the water available for irrigation is 268 cubic feet, which will irrigate 53,600 acres. If we suppose the irrigable land to lie on one side of the canal, in a strip five miles wide, and that the ground permits straight parallel primary ditches spaced one mile apart, it follows that for each mile of canal there must be five miles of primary ditches, and that the quantity of irrigable land for each mile of canal will be 3,200 acres. Deducting one fourth for land not actually watered, we shall have 2,400 acres of irrigable land for each mile of canal.

Let us take a primary ditch of capacity to carry 50 feet of water per second. Allowing for loss, this size will be rather more than sufficient to cover the 2,400 acres with three inches of water in seven days and seven nights. The canal can fill at the same time six of the primary ditches, so that in seven days 14,400 acres can be covered with three inches of water, only six of the primary being full at the time. And in twenty-six days three inches of water may be put over the whole amount of the land, namely, 53,600 acres.

If the water is used only for fourteen hours each day, the time necessary to go over all the land with three inches of water will be forty-five days.

Under our hypothesis, in order to irrigate 2,400 acres, we must build one mile of main canal and five miles of primary ditches. Placing the excavation at 30 cents per cubic yard, we find the cost per acre to be about $5.

The section of the main canal will diminish towards its lower end, but to be on the safe side, so far as cost is concerned, we keep it of uniform size. The price of excavation may be somewhat in excess of its actual cost in some places; but inasmuch as in it are included all incidental and contingent expenses, we believe it is not far from correct. We have omitted from this calculation all estimates for inequality of the ground, by reason of which the amount of excavation may be considerably increased; all expense due to the fact that generally one or several miles of canal have to be made at its head before the water is high enough relatively to the adjoining land to irrigate it, and we do not include the cost of a dam, which generally will be indispensable. Neither do we include the cost of head-works or of the bridges and sluices which will be required, or of the measures that may be necessary to pass the drainage of the country into, over, or under the canal. We do not estimate for these points, for the reason that no estimate can be made, the circumstances in no two cases being the same.

Speaking generally, we are of the opinion that the omitted points will cost as much as the excavation, and hence, that the rate per acre just given should be double.

This brings us to the conclusion that it will cost about $10 per acre to irrigate these valleys.

It is, however, to be remarked, that large portions of the eastern side of the San Joaquin Valley are underlaid two or three feet from the surface by a hard stratum, which it will be necessary to blast, or, if not blasted, the canals must be very shallow. This fact leads us to believe that the cost per acre in these sections will be increased twenty-five to thirty-three per cent. above the estimate already given.

The irrigation of the foot-hills will of course cost more. Here the problem will be more similar to that presented in other countries. So far as we are able to judge from descriptions given by writers, we are inclined to believe that the physical conditions in these valleys are unexceptionably favorable for irrigation. This fact accounts in a great measure for the smallness of our estimates, as compared with the actual cost of canals in Spain, for instance, where the price of labor is so much cheaper than it is in California.

A further reason for this difference lies in the character of the constructions. The dams, head-works, and sluices of foreign works are made of masonry, and in the most thorough manner. In California all these constructions will for many years be of wood. It is cheaper, with the present rates of interest, to build of wood, and to rebuild when the works decay, than to construct once for all of masonry.

The cheapest canal that we find in Spain is that from the Esla, which cost fifteen dollars per acre. The other modern canals in Spain have cost more than twice as much. There are no longer in these old countries any lands which admit of easy irrigation, and on all these lines there is a great deal of heavy work in excavating, tunneling, aqueducts, and in revetment-walls, which the valley works in California will not require.

Having thus been furnished with approximate data for an estimate of the cost, the main element in the problem, we are prepared to consider the question of the ownership of the water.

In most countries where irrigation has proved successful, the ownership of the water remains in the sovereignty, and the sovereignty either grants the right to its use in canal companies, or making the canals, and rents water to those desiring to irrigate. Our American law of riparian ownership, and the recognized doctrine that each navigable stream is a highway, open alike to the use of the whole people, and especially the ease by which private parties acquire title to great water-courses, will necessarily cut a large figure in the disposition of this important question. If the State owned and controlled the fee to all our water-courses, so that no private enterprise or individual could acquire a legal right to any of the waters, any more than they could to a public highway, then terms could be imposed (the fee remaining in the State,) so that large inducements could be offered to private capital to invest in irrigating canals, while a reasonable and just protection against monopoly was assured to the people.

There is still another view, which presents itself for consideration. The right to the use of a reasonable amount of water is incident to the ownership of the land adjacent to it, and neither the State, nor any individual or corporation in the State, ought to be permitted to divert and take from its natural channel, or from the valley through which it runs, the water of any of the streams of the State, if it be needed there; but the amount only that is needed should be retained for riparian owners. To say that the waters of the San Joaquin may be transferred from that great valley, and used for the purpose of irrigating lands located either all upon the one side of the river or remote from it, when it is required there, will be to admit that the people of one portion of the State may do an act which will deprive the people of another section of the means of subsistence.

Yet the riparian ownership should be limited to the amount of water that is actually needed. The man who owns the right to an article like water, in a climate like ours, without taking any steps towards a useful appropriation of it, is as great a monopolist as he who owns and uses it as a means of oppression.

In a country like this, where a large portion of the year is rainless, a monopoly of the water is as dangerous to the prosperity of the country as a monopoly of the air we breathe; and yet, when we reflect that it requires the expenditure of a sum of money greater far than any estimate which has hitherto been made, to dig canals through our valleys large enough to answer the purposes of irrigation on a grand scale, we can realize how difficult it is to avoid a monopoly of this character; for every exclusive right necessarily amounts to a monopoly.

What can be done, and ought to be done, is to regulate its use and its price by legislation; not to prohibit or limit its use. There is a labor side to this question that can be only protected by legislation. Labor is weak and unprotected. Capital is strong and united, and can protect itself. The people, at this time, would undoubtedly object to the State, or the counties of the State, taking an interest in this enterprise. The subject is new to us; the profit not understood, or at least uncertain; the work vast and expensive; the interest local, as it could afford but a small advantage to the mining counties; therefore, private capital must be chiefly looked to for this purpose.

Already, some of the most wealthy, shrewd and enterprising business men of the Coast have given this subject a start in the right direction. They have, with the usual forethought and care of large moneyed interests, examined every side of it here presented for consideration, and have thus early mapped off a system of irrigation for at least one of the great valleys of the State (the San Joaquin), of the most comprehensive character. This has been contemplated simply as an investment. Money is rarely public spirited or patriotic. It moves in the channels of good investments and large interests. It is a mistake of its possessor if it gets out of these channels. You may therefore rest assured that these capitalists knew the value of this enterprise before they embarked in it.

As before stated, in Northern Italy, as in India, the government possesses the right of property in all running waters. In Lombardy, grants of the water in perpetuity have been made; but, says Captain Baird Smith, who is a standard authority on irrigation, "The grant of such material as water, the value of which must necessarily go on augmenting with the progress of agriculture, is an injustice toward the government and people. * * * * Hence I am distinctly of the opinion that for the government of India to follow the example of Lombardy in parting forever with its right of property in the waters of the country, on the receipt of sums which cannot possibly represent the real value of the article, would be unwise, not only as regards its own interests, but also those of the irrigating community. For there is no point better established by experience in Northern Italy, and particularly in Lombardy, than that the selfishness of the grantees of water in perpetuity has been one of the most serious obstacles to the development of irrigation."

"Acting on the principle that they had the right to do what they liked with their own, they were in the habit of arbitrarily suspending the supplies of water to some, of increasing as they saw fit the prices to be paid by others, and in a word pushing to its utmost limits the right of absolute property purchased by them from the State."

"But an agriculture," continues our authority, "founded under such an arbitrary system, cannot advance."

M. Giovanetti, a distinguished Italian lawyer and statesman, traces with a master hand the history of property in water in Italy; and after showing that the State claimed no property as such, in the bed of the river or islands, he says: "Nor does the State claim the water as a patrimony for the community, but simply to place beyond the reach of private appropriation all that was naturally designed for the common good."

As respects California irrigation, this in time will be another of the problems of doubtful solution. Here under our laws the ownership of the water of the unnavigable streams of the State can be acquired by the first appropriator. No legislation at this time could change this rule, or afford an ample remedy, for much of the water is already in private hands.

The only power, then, left in the State, and one which sooner or later it must exercise, is to regulate the use and the price of water for irrigation, not with the view of making the property in water less valuable, but to avoid oppression and discrimination, and thus make it, like all public enterprises, of value to the whole people.

It has recently been held, by the highest judicial tribunal in Italy, "that canals of irrigation are not to be regarded as works designed solely for the benefit of their original constructors, but that the general good of the community has to be considered, as well as the benefit of the individuals running them."

No sensible man will countenance the lawless idea that what a man owns is not his to enjoy, be it much or little, but is the part of wisdom to profit by the experience of the past, and so far as possible protect by law those who cannot protect themselves, and thus guard with a jealous eye the best interests of the producers of the State.

In this State and in this climate, if we should give to any one set of individuals the fee of the waters of the State for irrigation, whether such persons live upon the banks of rivers or remote from them, and the State have no right to regulate their use, although it would be of small value and little importance now, in a few years it would be of immense value and of the greatest importance to the farming community. It would give to the men who controlled the water or owned the canals the power, should they choose to exercise it, of controlling every farmer who depended on irrigation for his crops, or upon a water ditch for his stock. It would soon have a relation to public affairs that no power but revolution could conquer or control. It would imperil the great future already marked out for us, and set us back on the scale of advancement a quarter of a century.

The magnitude of the questions involved in the water supply of the San Joaquin Valley, and the probability that it will be one of the most prominent before future Legislatures, warrants a careful and critical examination of all sides of this subject. The Granges desire equity to all, and the good of all, and will be guided by these principles through the mazes of conflicting interests which harass the limitation of powers already in the hands of strong and skillful combinations. Dr. M. W. Ryer, (in the Rural Press of May 1st, 1875,) has, it appears to us, come most nearly to a solution of the irrigation problem. He says:

The question how to frame a law of association so that the ownership of the water and the land may go together, should be considered by every politician in the State, and no candidate for legislative office should be considered competent until he presents to his constituents the draft of a law covering land and water ownership.

We have found that, by association, lands may be reclaimed from overflow. Why, by the application of similar laws, may not lands be irrigated?

To the question, Why has not reclamation been more successful? the answer is, California engineers have tried to exclude water from lands by building levees of turf and spongy soil, upon land which floats on a bed of mud and water. The most insane engineer in existence will still retain sense enough to tell you that the first rule of leveeing, is to ditch through the turf, and then get solid earth from the bottom of the river by dredging machines, or earth containing no vegetation, from the nearest practical place, and to base the levee upon the hard pan or solid earth beneath; for levees, as buildings, require unyielding foundations.

The law of 1868 sets forth that the owners of a majority of the land in any district, may associate, and then elect trustees. These trustees may appoint engineers to make plans and estimate the cost of the work necessary to reclamation. Upon these plans and estimates, the Board of Supervisors, if they approve them, direct three commissioners to jointly view the land, and assess upon each and every acre to be reclaimed or benefited thereby, a tax proportionate to the whole expense, and to the benefits which will result from such work; said tax to be collected and paid into the county treasury, and shall be paid out for works of reclamation, upon the order of the Board of Trustees, when approved by the Board of Supervisors. This tax is enforced by the District Attorney of the county, in a manner similar to the enforcement of the collection of State and county taxes. With a few amendments, the reclamation laws are sufficient to reclaim the lands, and keep the control and ownership of the levees within the hands of the owners of the land.

Two incomplete and inefficient acts were passed upon irrigation at the last session of the Legislature. These acts may be so altered and amended as to render irrigation by association entirely practicable. The legislation needed should cover the following points:

1. The Surveyor-General of the State should lay off the land of the State with reference to irrigation, and set forth the proper water supply to each district, and the place and manner of taking it.

2. The owners of a majority of land susceptible of irrigation, should be enabled to form a district.

3. Trustees should be elected by the owners of the majority of the land in the district.

4. Trustees shall apply to the Surveyor-General of the State to designate the water supply proper to the district, and the land outside of the district necessary for canals or other work. As soon as the land and water is thus designated, the trustees shall immediately take possession of the same and hold them as property of the district.

The trustees shall employ an engineer to make plans, surveys, and estimates of the works, necessary to irrigation.

5. The Attorney-General of the State shall immediately seize, condemn and appropriate such water and land, as the Surveyor-General shall designate as necessary to the district, when the owners of such water-sources or land shall establish in Court the amount they have actually expended in works connected with such water supply or land, and the actual value at the time of seizure, without reference to any future or prospective values. Then the trustees of the district, approved by the Board of Supervisors, may order the amount paid out of funds belonging to the district. But no prospective damages to the owners of water or land shall be allowed by the Courts, or paid by order of the trustees. The

appropriation of the water and land should be immediate and irrevocable; the litigation for damages may take place afterward.

6. To furnish the money necessary to works of irrigation, there should be commissioners appointed by the Board of Supervisors, or, when in two or more countries, by the joint action of the Supervisors of the counties; these commissioners to assess upon each and every acre a tax proportionate to the whole expense as estimated by the engineers employed by the trustees, and to the benefits, either directly or indirectly, which will result from such works.

7. These assessments to be collected by the District Attorney of the county in which the land lies, or by some State officer appointed for the purpose, and the amount collected to be immediately paid into the county treasury and there subject to the order of the trustees when appointed by the Supervisors. But no order to be paid except for work actually done or in compliance with the judgment and orders of a court. Warrants drawn by the trustees to draw interest at ten per cent. per annum until paid.

8. Assessment to the full amount necessary should be made by the commissioners upon the estimates formed by the engineers employed by the trustees of the district; but the trustees shall call in only installments of this tax large enough to cover the works which must be completed within six months from date of call. All assessments to be a lien upon the land and work its forfeiture unless paid.

9. All contracts to be let to the lowest bidder for cash, and all contracts to be let in small sections, after due advertisement. Thus giving the poor man an opportunity of paying his assessment by his own labor.

10. The district thus formed shall own the water forever, and no land not included in the district, and which has not paid for the works of irrigation at the time the works are constructed, shall have the use of this water, except on such terms as the officers of the district may dictate; for the land-owner who will not assist in the enterprise should have none of its privileges.

If the State should actually own and build canals for irrigation, canal rings, as in New York, may be formed. And if it is proper to construct them in one place, why not in fifty places? The owners of gravel and placer claims will not understand why the land speculator should have State bonds to assist him, when other great interests of the State require assistance. The tule land-owner will equally demand assistance, and thus, when the State begins to issue bonds, who can tell the stopping place?

Few farmers on these plains count their acres by less than hundreds, and speculators count by thousands. If they form districts and prove to the world that they intend to irrigate, their lands will rapidly advance in value, and thus before they have to pay their first assessment they can sell one half their land for enough to pay for irrigating the other half. Now, as one acre irrigated is worth ten not irrigated, it seems a fair proposition that they should, if necessary, sell a portion to improve the other. State aid, except to assist in the formation of districts and the condemning to their use the waters of the rivers, should not be extended to the owners of the land.

The entangling alliance of State with land sharps will be fruitful of no public good. As almost all have more land than they can properly work after irrigation, let them sell a part to enhance the value of the remainder.

Let it be understood by all who read this article that it is written for the purpose of urging men of legislative capacity to frame an effective law upon a most difficult subject, as the above is but a crude and unfinished sketch.

How to wrest from the water-grabbers the waters of the State will puzzle many able men, and the legislator who can frame an act to do so should be well appreciated by his fellow-men. It may save much trouble in the Legislature, and enable our law makers to approach the subject with more intelligence if some of the legal minds of the State would publish in the journals of the day the outline or draft of a law applicable to the case, for no hasty legislation can properly encompass the great questions involved.

Another relation of irrigation to the public welfare must not be overlooked in our attention to its vast material benefits.

At a meeting of the California State Medical Society, Dr. Carr introduced the following resolution, which was adopted:

Whereas, The matter of irrigation is one of vital importance to the agricultural interests of California; and,

Whereas, The same is more or less connected with the health of the whole community; therefore,

Resolved, That each member of this society be earnestly requested to gather all the statistics and information in their several localities in regard to the effect of mining and irrigating ditches or canals upon the public health, and report the same to the Chairman of the Committee on Hygiene, at their earliest convenience.

CHAPTER XXI.

TRANSPORTATION.

"Transportation is King."

Results of Railroad Investigation by Congress—Committee, how Formed—Exhaustive Researches—Magnitude of Interests Involved—Inadequacy of Means of Transportation—Defects and Abuses—Discriminations and Extortions—Stock Watering—Capitalization of Earnings—Construction Rings—Unjust Discriminations—General Extravagance and Corruption of Railway Management—Combinations and Consolidations—Nominal Capital and Fictitious Stock—Excess of Capital over Actual Stock—Illustrations—How Evils may be Remedied—Summary of Conclusions and Recommendations—Congress may Regulate Inter-State Transportation.

The greatest drawback to the development of agriculture in California is the distance of our markets, and the lack of stimulus given by the rapid development of manufactures. The triple arms of industry mutually support each other with strength proportionate to their nearness. We have a personal interest in the consumer who is also our neighbor. In the farmers' war upon monopolies, it has not always been remembered that before the era of railroads it was estimated that the cost of carriage of a bushel of corn one hundred and sixty miles was equal to its value. Railroad carriage extended the distance point at which the value was consumed by transportation to fifteen hundred miles. Still another element in this question has been overlooked by the farmers. Protective duties are in a large measure responsible for the present high cost of railway construction and maintenance. Mr. Edward Atkinson, of Boston, in an address delivered four years ago, showed that the direct effect of the duty of fourteen dollars a ton of two thousand pounds on railroad iron in 1869, was to tax the industry and transportation interests ten million dollars; of which amount one fourth went into the national treasury, and three-fourths into the hands of the iron masters. This sum would build four hundred and fifty miles of railroad on the western prairies, where the consumption of iron is about ninety tons, and the actual cost does not exceed twenty-four thousand dollars.

Believing that no greater service can be rendered to the Agricultural classes of the Pacific Coast than to place before them in a condensed form the conclusions which have been reached by National and State Committees upon the vast and complicated question of Railroad Transportation, I have, in the following pages, summarized the more important documents which treat upon this subject.

The railroad legislation in own State is so recent, and the means of obtaining full information concerning it so accessible, that I have chosen to give all the space allotted to this objective point of the great farmers' movement to Eastern authorities instead of our own.

The report of the Select Congressional Committee on Transportation, appointed during the session of 1872–3, consisting of Roscoe Conkling, T. M. Norwood, N. G. Davis and John W. Johnston, fills nearly fifteen hundred octavo pages. They were authorized to sit at such places as they might designate during the recess; had every facility at their command; and being empowered to call for persons and papers, were able to obtain and to collate an almost infinite number of details never before brought within the public reach. They say:

Perhaps the most extraordinary feature of our governmental policy touching the vast internal trade of the nation is the apparent indifference and neglect with which it has been treated. While detailed information has been obtained by the Government, under customs and revenue laws, in relation to commerce with foreign countries, no means have been provided for collecting accurate statistics concerning the vastly more important interests of internal commerce. No officer of the Government has ever been charged with the duty of collecting information on this subject, and the legislator who desires to inform himself concerning the nature, extent, value, or necessities of our immense internal trade, or of its relations to foreign commerce, must patiently grope his way through the statistics furnished by boards of trade, chambers of commerce, and transportation companies. Even the census reports, which purport to contain an inventory of the property and business pursuits of the people, and which in some matters descend to the minutest details, are silent with regard to the billions of dollars represented by railways and other instruments of internal transportation, and to the much greater values of commodities annually moved by them.

We have no means of measuring accurately the magnitude of this trade, but its colossal proportions may be inferred from two or three known facts. The value of commodities moved by the railroads in 1872 is estimated at over $10,000,000,000, and their gross receipts reached the emormous sum of $473,241,055. The commerce of the cities of the Ohio river alone has been carefully estimated at over $1,600,000,000 per annum. The value of our internal commerce is many times greater than our trade with all foreign nations, and the amount annually paid for transportation is more than double the entire revenues of the Government.

Concisely stated, the defects and abuses alleged against the existing systems of transportation are: insufficient facilities, unfair discriminations, and extortionate charges. With reference to the matter of facilities, it is believed that the improvements of natural waterways and the construction of additional channels of water communication have been wholly inadequate to the growing demands of trade; and by reason of this neglect on the part of the Government, the commerce of the country has been compelled to accept the more expensive methods afforded by railroads; and that railway companies, having thus secured a substantial monopoly of the business of transportation, have failed to recognize their responsibilities to the public, or to meet the just demands of the rapidly increasing commerce between the interior and the seaboard.

Discriminating and extortionate charges, however, constitute the chief grounds of complaint. The principal causes which are supposed to produce such charges, and which have aggravated and intensified the public discontent, may be summarized as follows:

1. "Stock-watering," a well known process by which the capital stock of a company is largely increased for purely speculative purposes, without any corresponding expenditure on the part of its recipients.

2. Capitalization of surplus earnings. By this process, the net profits, over and above the amount paid on interest and dividends, are supposed to be expended in permanent improvements, and charged up to capital account, for which additional stock is issued, and increased charges rendered necessary to meet the increased dividends required. It is insisted that this is a double form of taxation; first, in the exorbitant charges from which such surplus profits are derived; and, second, in the conversion of such surplus into capital-stock, thereby compelling the business of the country to pay increased charges on all future transactions, in order to provide dividends on capital thus unjustly obtained. It is argued with great force, that as all the legitimate claims of railroad companies are met by the public, when it has paid a fair and reasonable return for the capital invested and services rendered, any surplus earnings expended in improvements should inure to its benefit, instead of being made the basis of future exactions. In brief, the people believe that by this process they are first robbed, and then compelled to pay interest on their own money.

3. The introduction of intermediate agencies, such as car-companies, fast freight lines, etc.

4. "Construction rings" and other means by which the managers are supposed to make large profits in the building of railways, which are charged up to the cost of the road.

5. Unfair adjustments of through and local rates, and unjust discriminations against certain localities, whereby one community is compelled to pay unreasonable charges in order that another more favored may pay less than the services are worth.

6. General extravagance and corruption in railway management, whereby favorites are enriched and the public impoverished.

7. Combinations and consolidations of railway companies, by which free competition is destroyed, and the producing and commercial interests of the country handed over to the control of monopolies, who are thereby enabled to enforce upon the public the exorbitant rates rendered necessary by the causes above named.

8. The system of operating fast and slow trains on the same road, whereby the cost of freight movement is believed to be largely increased. This is perhaps the misfortune rather than the fault of railway companies. It is doubtless a necessity growing out of the conditions under which our railway system has been developed.

Of the defects and abuses above enumerated, perhaps none have contributed so much to the general discontent and indignation as the increase of railway capital by "stock-watering," and capitalization of surplus earnings. It is fully conceded that a fair and even liberal remuneration should be paid for capital actually invested, but that the industry of the country should be taxed for all time to meet dividends on paper-capital, is indignantly denied.

To what extent the nominal railway capital of the country is represented by fictitious stock is not easy to determine. The manner in which railway accounts are usually kept, renders it very difficult for the managers themselves to state what proportion of the entire cost of a given road was paid by the stockholders, and what part from the surplus earnings. Replacements and improvements are constantly being made, and paid for out of current receipts. It is quite impossible for the committee to obtain accurate information on this point, without going into a detailed investigation of the accounts of the several companies extending over a long series of years, and involving in many cases the cross-examination of reluctant witnesses, which would have consumed the entire time of the committee, to the exclusion of all other matters. Enough is known of the extent and vicious effects of stock manipulations to justify the adoption of prompt and efficient means for their prevention in the future.

Assuming the estimates of three most important railways to be approximately correct, we have an excess of capital over actual cost, on these three lines, as follows:

Name of Line.	Present Capital in Stock and Bonds.	Probable Actual Cost.	Excess of Capital over Actual Cost.
Erie Line, New York to Dunkirk, 459 miles	$108,807,000	$40,000,000	$68,807,000
New York Central Line to Chicago, 980 miles	190,188,137	75,000,000	115,188,137
Pennsylvania Line, from Philadelphia to Chicago, 890 miles	78,290,374	67,000,000	11,290,374
Totals	$377,285,511	$182,000,000	$195,285,511

Making a total of over $195,000,000, on which to pay a dividend of ten per cent. per annum, the commerce between the west and the east must annually contribute over $19,000,000. In the presence of such facts as these, and with no assurance that the evils of stock inflation are to be restrained in the future, it is not surprising that the murmurs of discontent have swollen into a storm of popular indignation, which will only be appeased by a thorough and radical reform, or by opening up new channels of commerce which shall relieve the public from absolute dependence upon those, which by reason of stock speculations, are rendered incapable of performing the service required at reasonable rates.

The following general summary of the conclusions and recommendations of the committee are respectfully submitted:

1. One of the most important problems demanding solution at the hands of the American statesman, is, by what means shall cheap and ample facilities be provided for the interchange of commodities between the different sections of our widely extended country.

2. In the selection of means for the accomplishment of this object, Congress may, in its discretion, and under its responsibility to the people, prescribe the rules and regulations by which the instruments, vehicles, and agencies employed in transporting persons and commodities from one State into and through another, shall be governed, whether such transportation be by land or by water.

3. The power "to regulate commerce" includes the power to aid and facilitate it by the employment of such means as may be appropriate and plainly adapted to that end; and hence Congress may, in its discretion improve or create channels of commerce on land, or by water.

They therefore recommend for present action the following:

1. That all railway companies, freight lines, and other persons or organizations of common carriers, engaged in transporting passengers or freights from one State into or through another, be required, under proper penalties, to make publication at every point of shipment from one State to another, of their rates and fares, embracing all the particulars regarding distance, classifications, rates, special tariffs, drawbacks, etc., and that they be prohibited from increasing such rates above the limit named in the publication without reasonable notice to the public to be prescribed by law.

2. That combinations and consolidations with parallel or competing lines are evils of such magnitude as to demand prompt, vigorous measures for their prevention.

3. That all railway companies, freight lines, and other organizations of common carriers, employed in transporting grain from one State into or through another, should be required, under proper regulations and penalties to be provided by law, to receipt for quantity, and to deliver the same at its destination.

4. That all railway companies and freight organizations, receiving freights in one State to be delivered in another, and whose lines touch at any river or lake port, be prohibited from charging more to or from such port than for any greater distance on the same line.

5. Stock-inflations, generally known as "stock-waterings," are wholly indefensible, but the remedy for this evil seems to fall peculiarly within the province of the States who have created the corporations from which such practices proceed. The evil is believed to be of such magnitnde as to require prompt and efficient State action for its prevention, and to justify any measures that may be proper and within the range of national authority.

6. It is believed by the committee that great good would result from the passage of State laws prohibiting officers of railway companies from owning or holding, directly or indirectly, any interest in any "non-co-operative freight-line" or car company, operated upon the railroad with which they are connected in such official capacity.

7. For the purpose of procuring and laying before Congress and the country such complete and reliable information concerning the business of transportation and the wants of commerce as will enable Congress to legislate intelligently on this subject, it is recommended that a bureau of commerce, in one of the Executive Departments of the Government, be charged with the duty of collecting and reporting to Congress information concerning our internal trade and commerce and be clothed with the authority of law, under regulations to be prescribed by the head of such department, to require each and every railway and other transportation company engaged in inter-State transportation, to make a report, under oath of the proper officer of such company, at least once a year, which report shall embrace among other facts, the following, viz.: 1. The rates and fares charged on all points of shipment on its line in one State, to all points of destination in another State, including classifications and distances, and all drawbacks, deductions and discriminations. 2. A full and detailed statement of receipts and expenditures, in-

cluding the compensation paid to officers, agents, and employees of the company. 3. The amount of stock and bonds issued, the price at which they were sold, and the disposition made of the funds from said sale. 4. The amount and value of commodities transported during the year, as nearly as the same can be ascertained.

8. Though the existence of the Federal power to regulate commerce to the extent maintained in this report, is believed to be essential to the maintenance of perfect equality among the States as to commercial rights; to the prevention of unjust and invidious distinctions which local jealousies or interests might be disposed to introduce, to the proper restraints of consolidated corporate power, and to the correction of many of its existing evils, your committee are unanimously of the opinion that the problem of cheap transportation is to be solved through competition, as hereinafter stated, rather than by direct congressional regulation of existing lines.

9. Competition, which is to secure and maintain cheap transportation, must embrace two essential conditions: First—It must be controlled by a power with which combination will be impossible. Second—It must operate through cheaper and more ample channels of commerce than are now provided.

10. Railway competition, when regulated by its own laws, will not effect the object; because it exists only to a very limited extent in certain localities, it is always unreliable and inefficient, and it invariably ends in combination. Hence, additional railway lines, under the control of private corporations, will afford no substantial relief, because self-interest will inevitably lead them into combination with existing lines.

11. The only means of securing and maintaining reliable and effective competition between railways is through national or State ownership, or control of one or more lines, which, being unable to enter into combinations, will serve as regulators of other lines.

12. One or more double-track freight railways, honestly and thoroughly constructed, owned and controlled by the Government, and operated at a low rate of speed, would doubtless be able to carry at a much less cost than can be under the present system of operating fast and slow trains on the same road, and, being incapable of entering into combinations, would, no doubt, serve as a very valuable regulator of all existing railroads within the range of their influences.

13. The uniform testimony deduced from practical results in this country, and throughout the commercial world, is, that water routes, when properly located, not only afford the cheapest and best known means of transport for all heavy, bulky, and cheap commodities, but that they are also the natural competitors, and most effective regulators of railway transportation.

CHAPTER XXII.

RAILROAD LEGISLATION AND INVESTIGATION IN WISCONSIN.

RAILROAD LEGISLATION IN WISCONSIN—ABSTRACT OF THE POTTER LAW—ABSTRACT OF REPORT OF COMMISSIONERS—NATURE OF THE CONTROVERSY BETWEEN THE PEOPLE AND THE RAILROADS—SELF-INTEREST OF CORPORATIONS NOT A SUFFICIENT GUARANTY AGAINST EXTORTIONS—COMPETITION TENDS TO CONSOLIDATION—EVILS OF RAILWAY CONSTRUCTION AND MANAGEMENT—CAUSES OF UNDUE COST—CONSTRUCTION ON CREDIT—CORRUPT LETTING OF CONTRACTS—MISAPPROPRIATION OF LAND GRANTS—ILLINOIS LAW—SUPERVISORY DUTY OF STATES HOLDING LAND GRANTS—ILLINOIS DECISION.

ANOTHER source from which we have drawn largely, is the "First Annual Report of the Railroad Commissioners of the State of Wisconsin," lately published.

The people of that State had been eager for railroads. To build the first road, they had mortgaged their farms to the amount of over $4,000,000, and had granted other charters in excess of the real demand, and through unbounded confidence had failed to secure their own interests by proper guaranties. They had been taught by signal experiences the power of railroad corporations over legislatures. So far from being inimical to railroads, the contrary was true. They had "suffered long and were kind," until unjust discrimination in the matter of freights roused their indignation, and hastened the favorable hearing of their complaints. The strength of the Grange made them masters of the situation; a Granger Governor, perfectly familiar with the history of the roads and with legislation, was in the executive chair. This turning of the tables resulted in the passage of what is known as the "Potter Law," by the Legislature of 1873–4. This law classified the roads, determined a tariff for fares and freights according to such classification, and affixed severe penalties to its violation. The Supreme Court of the United States had held that the right of a company owning a road, to fix its rate or charges, was an "attribute of ownership." The railroad companies, therefore, declared the Potter law unconstitutional, and courteously informed the Governor, through their respective presidents, of their determination to resist it. The Governor as courteously, in a "proclamation," announced his intention to enforce it. By successive steps, the case finally reached the Supreme Court. The opinion of Chief Justice Ryan was rendered on the 15th of

September, 1874; an injunction was granted "including all the railroads of the State," and the Wisconsin Railroad war closed in the declaration, through the President of the Chicago, Milwaukee and St. Paul Railroad Company, that, "as law-abiding citizens, the railroads would at once conform to the decision of the Court, and endeavor to obey it, in good faith, until it should be reversed by a decision of the Supreme Court of the United States, or until the law was repealed by the Legislature."

These two reports are an education in railroading, and we commend their careful reading to every Patron who desires to secure the great ends of these exhaustive investigations. The fact that the conclusions arrived at by these two independent committees are so nearly identical, seems to give them such additional weight as to justify the large space given them in this work:

To a considerable extent, the interests of the railroad corporations and the public are in harmony; thus it is clearly for the real interest of the corporations to build good and safe roads, and upon lines that will accommodate the largest number of people and the greatest amount of traffic; and yet, practically, they not unfrequently disregard both these elements:

First, because the wisdom and foresight that should eminently characterize the management of railways are often wanting; and,

Secondly, because the managers are not unfrequently in their places for the sole purpose of promoting their own personal ends. But again, there are cases in which the interest of railway corporations and the public are opposed. For example, it is the interest of the companies to prevent the building of competing roads; to hamper and embarrass rival lines already established; to force such traffic as they are able to command over as much of their own lines respectively as possible, though it be at the expense of time and other advantage on the part of the shipper.

For all these reasons, and others that might be named, the insufficiency of self-interest on the part of companies, as a protection to the public, has been long recognized.

Again, competition is an unequal reliance, though it is so invariably applicable as a restraint in all sorts of trades, professions, and ordinary commercial enterprises, that it is not surprising how long it has misled the public and legislative bodies. It always serves as a protection where it is full and permanently maintained, as well in matters of transportation as in the case of the trades and most individual enterprises. But therein lies the difficulty. Competition implies freedom of the operator, both as to material and forces. In case of the ordinary avocations, this freedom is practically quite complete; the materials and the labor to be used can be had in the open market, and fair purchase is protected by the active interest of those who have them to sell.

With regard to competition between railroad companies, this natural law is not certainly operative. There is neither freedom of means nor of forces. A road once built cannot be placed in any market the company pleases and compete for freight, as the manufacturer can compete for his raw material, or the merchant vessel for a cargo. It can only offer its facilities and bide its time. Should no rival spring up to contest the field, it can command the produce of the section of country tributary to it, on its own terms, so that it leaves barely margin of profit enough to the producer and dealer to induce production and delivery. And if, by-and-by, a rival line should be established, and the traffic should be less than equal to the carrying capacity of both, the two are almost sure, after fruitless efforts to drive each other from the field, to form a combination, agreeing either to demand equal rates, agreed upon, or to "pool" their earnings.

This point having been reached, the public have no ground of hope, except in the possibility of a falling out of the companies, and a renewal of the competition which gave origin to the compact. For the companies themselves, there seems, in most cases, to be no safety but in a still closer union, under an act of consolidation from which there is no breaking away.

The controversy, then, is irrepressible, if the reliance is upon economical laws alone; being a conflict between the necessities of society on the one hand, and the natural selfishness of strong monopolies on the other.

We will now consider other difficulties and evils of railway construction and management. To make the matter worse, the roads are often so constructed, and railway transportation so managed, as to almost compel heavy exactions on the part of the railway companies, and lead to dissatisfaction and condemnation on the part of the public. An overshadowing evil attendant upon railway construction and operation is the fact that all railway enterprise is the result of individual interest and purpose, subject to no harmonizing general control. To avoid inconvenience and losses, consequent upon discordant management, the companies themselves are impelled to consolidation by a constant law of self-interest, which the public have regarded with hostility and distrust. The result must and should be an appreciation of the fact that the true interest of the public, as well as of the corporations, lies in the direction of better organized and less discordant expenditure of energy and capital, and in the adoption of more comprehensive principles of legislation to that end. The facts ought to be realized not only that discriminations by exorbitant charges upon one locality at the expense of another, is an evil to be discouraged, but also that legislation discouraging investment by encouraging ruinous competition is equally to be deplored.

Prominent among these evils is the primary one of unwarrantable cost. A road having been built as economically as possible, no one can reasonably make complaint of charges that yield only a moderate per cent. of profit on the investment. Indeed, the public are willing that they who put their money into railways should have a very liberal profit, since it is attended with more risk than is the investment of money in many other ways. But if a road has cost thousands of dollars per mile more than it ought, owing to want of skill and judgment on the part of the company, or if there is reason to believe that the assumed cost is not the real cost—the difference having gone into the hands of the officers, or their friends acting in the capacity of contractors or "promoters,"—then it is natural that there should be an unwillingness to allow even a moderate per cent. on the declared cost.

Unfortunately, these mere hints of dishonest management find warrant in actual facts in all countries.

If we inquire into the causes of undue cost of railways, they will be found with but little difficulty. Prominent among them are the following:

1. Slight pecuniary interest of the managers.
2. Construction on credit.

It is not essential that every dollar necessary to build a road should be in bank before the work of construction begins; if it were, few roads in a region of country like ours, where there is but little spare capital, would be built. A reasonable amount of credit is legitimate, indeed often absolutely essential; but since the use of it adds greatly to the cost of building, it should in all cases be employed as sparingly as possible.

3. Injudicious location of lines.

This particular cause of undue cost will be best appreciated by skillful engineers, who cannot have failed to note how very often lines of railway are made to cost much more than was necessary by careless surveys. But one need not be more than an ordinary engineer, or even a professional engineer at all, to detect expensive blunders of this sort on every hand—blunders which not only occasion a large increase in the cost of construction, but also a permanent extra expense of working.

4. Corrupt letting of contracts.

Probably the system of construction by "rings" formed inside to operate outside, for the private gain of individual officers and their friends, is, of all causes of excessive cost, the most prolific. Of course there are many railway officers too honorable to resort to measures for private advantage which involve the robbery of stockholders and creditors; but such practices are nevertheless so common as to make it somewhat doubtful whether they do not constitute the rule rather than the exception. Sometimes they are carried on by directors and officers openly, but oftener, of course, under cover. We would not be understood as branding every construction company, composed in whole or in part of officers and members of the company contracted with, as guilty of fraudulent dealings with stockholders. A construction company possesses some advantages for conducting the work of construction which a chartered railroad company does not possess—especially if many of the directors of the railway company are non-resident—and the undersigned have knowledge of some such who are believed to conduct the business of building in that way solely, because of these advantages, and wholly in the interest of the stockholders who compose the railway company. They are forced to believe, however, that the number of those who thus manage is comparatively small.

It is impossible to estimate with any degree of accuracy the amount of the burden upon the industry of this country by fraudulent building contracts, but it is safely assumed to be enormous.

5. Fraudulent purchase of lines.

Kindred to the corrupt letting of contracts is the wrong of purchasing lines already owned, at prices far above their real value, the excess being divided secretly between the "ring" managers of the two companies. Transactions of this sort are usually managed with such adroitness that detection is difficult, if not impossible; but the cases are neither few nor far to seek in which the evidence is convincing that the terms conceded by purchasers must be accounted for either on the ground of dishonesty or lack of judgment.

6. Misappropriation of land grants.

The American government is the only one that has adopted the policy of making donations of the public lands of the country to aid in the construction of internal improvements, looking at the industrial progress of the nation.

In view of the newness of the country, the deficiency of cash capital for the construction of expensive works, and the extent and variety of its material resources, which must otherwise long remain undeveloped, this policy may have appeared at the time to be a wise one; indeed, it has promoted the industrial prosperity of the nation.

In the case of the trans-continental railways, the Union and the Central, already in use, and the Northern and Southern, now in construction—there was still another motive that influenced the government to bestow the immense grants they have received. The rebellion had taught us the danger of disintegration. The Atlantic and Pacific States were so removed that there was danger of an early political falling apart; there was need, therefore, that these great divisions of our common country be brought into closer relations. This was the argument.

Unhappily, experience has shown that there is another side to this question of government aid in the construction of railways—that land grants, how much soever needed for the encouragement of improvements in the interest of industry and commerce, have by no means been an unmixed good—that, in view of the corruptions engendered, and the public demoralization they have produced, it is quite doubtful whether they have not been a curse rather than a benefit.

In the act of conferring lands upon the Illinois Central Railroad Company, the State of Illinois made an honorable exception to the general rule, requiring, as a condition of receiving a grant, that the company should annually pay into the public treasury seven per cent. of its gross earnings, a sum now amounting, we believe, to something over three quarters of a million of dollars. So far as we know, this act of a provident Legislature stands conspicuous as being the only instance in which the interests of the public, in grants made to the States to aid in the construction of railways, have been carefully protected.

The lands granted to Iowa and Minnesota, as well as to Missouri, Kansas, and Nebraska, have been given to the roads in those States, without other condition than the construction of the roads within a given date.

The result has been that the company managers have, in many cases, so planned the disposal of them as to promote their own personal, rather than public ends. In some instances, where it was possible to raise the funds for construction without making the lands the basis of securities, the roads have been built at a heavy sacrifice in the way of discounts, to be subsequently paid by the industry of the country, and the lands have been wholly or almost entirely appropriated to the private use of the builders.

So far as we have learned, the lands granted to Iowa have only in a small degree lessened to the public the cost of the roads in aid of whose construction they were given.

The people of Minnesota have hardly been more fortunate. Their land grants for the construction of railroads amounted to 9,965,500 acres. We do not find, either, that the State attempted to protect the rights of the people in reference to these lands, or that railroad companies upon whom they were conferred have so used them as to reduce the cost of the roads.

By the report of the Commissioner of the General Land Office for 1873, the total quantity of land received from grants to aid railroads in Wisconsin, was 3,412,358 21-100 acres. The value placed by the United States upon the alternate even sections being $2 50 per acre, that is the minimum given at which these lands can be estimated, but it is believed that the actual value of these lands should not be placed at less than double that sum, or a total of $17,061,791 05, and it will probably very much exceed this amount.

These grants of land were placed at the disposal of the State, with a view to the reduction of the absolute cost of railroads to the people, and thus encourage their construction. Such being the case, it would seem that an essential condition on which the lands were donated would require the exercise of a supervisory care over the manner of their application, on the part of the State, in order to be certain that they were not diverted from the objects intended, and the interests of the people neglected. By a singular oversight, no such provision seems ever to have been adopted. The grants were handed over to the several companies on the simple condition that their respective roads should be constructed.

In the case of the grant of 600,000 acres received by the Chicago and Northwestern Railway Company, to aid in the construction of that part of its road extending from Fond du Lac to the Michigan State line, taking the appraisal of that company itself for the first two hundred and forty sections ($12 per acre), and estimating the value of the balance at only $5 per acre, we have a valuation sufficient to yield almost $35,000 per mile for the whole distance to which the grant applies. When we consider that this company applied for and received still further aid from municipal corporations on the line of the road, it would seem as though, at least, the ordinary precaution of seeing that this munificent grant had not been needlessly mismanaged would have been taken by the State, especially as section thirty of the act making the grant contains the admonitory provision, "that the said lands hereby granted to said State, shall be subject to the the disposal of the legislature thereof, for the purposes aforesaid, and no other."

This subject is of special interest at this time in view of the judicial dicision lately rendered in Illinois, in which it is laid down as a rule "that directors of railroad companies were not absolute in their powers; that they were but trustees to manage the estate of stockholders, and could no more abuse their trust, or waste and squander the property of the stockholder than could any trustee or executor, or other person charged with a fiduciary duty."

The lands are received by the State as a trust, and are confided to the company to carry it into operation. The State, therefore, is responsible to the people for the faithful application of the trust.

The State provides, that while the lands are under its care, no part of the same shall be depredated upon, and that they shall be preserved intact for the purposes for which they were donated. It would seem still more necessary that the duty so assumed should be supplemented by a careful supervision of the same after the disposal of the grant, and until the final application of the proceeds therefrom is made, adequate security should be required for such faithful application. Indeed, in the spirit of the decision above referred to, if there should appear a reasonable apprehension that the lands donated had been diverted, wasted, or squandered, it may well be considered if it be not the further duty of the State to require such equitable adjustment thereof as a judicial investigation should determine.

CHAPTER XXIII.

MANAGEMENT OF RAILROADS IN OPERATION.

Management of Railroads in Operation—Railroads as Merchants—Rings—American Genius Displayed in Stock Watering—Unskillful Management—Excessive Charges—Railroad side of the Question—Benefits Conferred—Public Character of Railways Established—Necessity of Control and Consequent Right of Supervision—Interests of Capital Require Control—Insecurity of Railroad Investments—How Control may be Exercised—Faulty Legislation—Summary of Conclusions—Ohio Commissioners on Railroad Rates.

Two things have tended to confuse the ideas of farmers on the railroad question, viz., a lack of knowledge of the modes in which such vast business enterprises are conducted, and the crude and often conflicting treatment of the subject by the press. Politicians have found the agitation of this subject profitable for their own purposes, and, between the intemperate denunciations of "Grangers run wild," and the still more unfair treatment of the farmers' movement against monopolies, by a few Eastern journals, hundreds of readers have been trying to find the medial line of truth. To all such we especially commend the summing up of the Wisconsin Commissioners' report:

It were well did the evil of mismanagement confine itself to the period of construction. On the contrary, however, it is well understood by all those who are familiar with the management of railroads that there are many ways in which officers can, if so inclined, accumulate fortunes without using capital of their own, and wholly at the cost of the stockholders. Among them is the use of company funds for the handling of grain and produce; paying therefor a price enough higher than unaided buyers can afford to pay, to give them the command of the market, and shipping the same over their own lines free of charge, or at nominal charges. Another is, to arrange with buyers privately to carry their shipments at a price next to nothing—dividing the profits.

Practices like these are believed to be common, and help to account for the rapidity with which railway officials sometimes grow rich on moderate salaries. They also suggest the reason why railroads are sometimes made to facilitate the commercial growth and prosperity of one town or village to the great disadvantage, perhaps total ruin, of another. If private speculations on the part of railway managers are not discovered in all such cases, it is more than likely, because pains have been taken to conceal them.

The same sort of evils appear in another guise, and on a larger scale, where a private inside "ring" is formed for the purchase of lands, mines, docks, and harbors, and the sale of them for a large advance to the company the "ring" officially represents. The stockholders are duly advised of the great importance of the property to the future of the road, while congratulating them on the very favorable terms on which it was purchased, and there the matter ends.

But the giant evil under the head of dishonest management is undue inflation of stock. A fraudulent contract, the building and buying in of roads to be foisted upon the company managed, as well as the building up and killing out of cities and villages, usually require time, skill in manœuvering, and careful concealment of the operator's hand. Not so with stock watering. Here the cardinal qualities are, daring and deafness to the protestation of justice. The law is silent, and up to a certain limit the public must have transportation, no matter what the cost. This practice is probably confined to no one country, but it is doubtful, perhaps, whether any other railway managers in the world have a genius for it equal to the American. For illustration of the magnificant scale on which it is sometimes conducted, we have but to look at a single through line from Chicago to New York—the line formed by the Lake Shore and Michigan Southern, the New York Central and Hudson River Railways, whose total *waterings* within the past few years are alleged to exceed in amount $80,000,000. The interest on this sum at eight per cent. is $6,400,000. And since the tariffs on these several roads gauged to yield that per cent. on nominal capital, it is manifest that this one through line of railways is annually laying this enormous tax of over $6,000 000 upon the earnings of those who support it, in order that the holders of the stock may reap an annual dividend of some sixteen per cent. on the real cost.

If this be the tribute paid by the west on one line of railway, with a mileage less than one-seventieth of that of the United States, what must be the burden imposed by this cause upon the industry of the whole country?

Not a little of the poverty of which some railway companies complain, and not a little of the ill-feeling here and there manifested towards them, is due to the want of skill and good judgment in conducting their practical affairs. In too many instances they appear to act on the theory that the railway company is alike superior to the will of the State, and independent of popular favor; and naturally enough, in such cases, this view of the matter enters into the understanding of all subordinate officers and employes.

The subject of unjust discriminations has been already alluded to. Such discriminations are not always made, however, in the interest of managers, or the friends of managers. Sometimes they have origin in the false impression that they are essential to the business prosperity of the company. A prominent shipper is supposed to be able and fully disposed to advance the interest of the company in some manner, and is thought, on this account, to be entitled to special favors.

Another evil of practical railway management, and a crying one in this country, is inefficiency. No one who has traveled extensively upon European railways, can have failed to note that a certain slackness is too common with us in every department of the service.

The system of book-keeping is rarely such that the general agent, the chief-engineer, the superintendent, or the general manager can report, under three months time, the exact amount and kind of business done, the cost to the company of operating any one division of its road, or the average cost per passenger or ton of freight per mile, or the cost per train-mile. Scarcely anything is done with that scrupulous precision, efficiency, and thoroughness so much more common in Europe, and so very essential to economy, comfort, and security elsewhere.

Unjust charges for transportation are commonly denounced, because just here is the point of universal and painful contrast between the public and the corporations. And yet, in most cases, they are only the immediate result of the more primary evils already noticed. They are the symptoms in many cases, rather than the disease. Considered as an evil in themselves, they are hard to deal with, for the reason that, beyond the rather uncertain limit, it is quite impossible for any one not possessed of the data for a nice mathematical calculation to say whether this tariff or that is excessive.

If, in the absence of such data, the attempt is made to determine the question by a comparison of the tariffs of different roads, such method is likely to be found unsatisfactory, owing to the great number of modifying circumstances that require to be taken into the account. But leaving out of view causes and particulars, it is unquestionable that the public in almost every State have had to pay more for transportation than should have been necessary; certainly more than was compatible with the welfare of the industrial classes.

THE RAILROAD SIDE OF THE QUESTION.

Having thus dwelt at considerable length on the evils of railway management, it is essential to a just consideration of the measures to be employed for their correction, that we should recur for a moment to the very important part railroads have played in promoting the industrial, social and political progress of the world.

To present in detail the beneficial results of railways is of course impossible. They are at once innumerable and immeasurable. Nor is it possible to make a summary that will convey an adequate general conception of the benefits they have conferred.

Having mileage enough for a continuous track six times around the entire globe; moving annually a tonnage of some twenty thousand million dollars in value, the passengers scarcely less in number than the population of the whole earth; stimulating the productive forces of industry everywhere; rendering easy many otherwise impossible exchanges of products between different countries; leading to commercial treaties which else had not been effected for generations to come; promoting social as well as business relations between widely separated communities; binding together as a homogeneous people, the inhabitants of remote and unlike divisions of a common country; encouraging friendly intercourse between the people of many lands; and so helping to establish a brotherhood of the nations, the railway is everywhere justly regarded as being foremost among civilizing agencies.

For these reasons it is believed that there is but little danger that the $6,000,000,000 of capital said to be invested in railways will be sacrificed, or that the people of any country will knowingly cripple this immensely important interest.

The problem to be solved simply stated, is this: how to devise a system of control in the interest of the public, that will, at the same time, be entirely just to the railway corporations?

From the survey of the history of railroading in the United States, and in foreign countries, the Wisconsin Railroad Commissioners report the following general conclusions as unavoidable.

1. That the public character of railways is fully established.

One form of argument in high quarters against the exercise of public supervision, is embraced in the proposition that corporations have transportation to sell, and the purchase of the article, or privilege so offered, like that of all other commodities in market, is at the option of the purchaser. But the conditions of sale in this case come under none of the ordinary conditions of human traffic. The original right to construct and operate a railway is an emanation of sovereignty, grounded on public considerations, and having explicit reference to public, as well as private use and profit. The question of power is already substantially and fortunately settled as to our own State. The subsidiary question of the necessity and propriety of judiciously exercising that power when possessed, is equally settled in the opinion of the civilized world. We know of no government in Europe which has not already exercised this power, not with reference to the special ends of arbitrary government, but with the purpose of defending the people from the encroachments of consolidated wealth, manifest in the form of corporate monopoly.

2. That the consequent right, and the necessity of control, are nowhere in doubt.

It appears that the right of the State to exercise supervision over railway corporations, has been recognized wherever the subject has received material consideration—that it has been asserted by chambers and parliaments in all the countries of Europe, as well as by the legislatures of this country, and that it has been sustained and confirmed by the higher courts. Such conclusions are unavoidable, having their foundations in the common law, and in the very nature and relations of society.

3. That control is demanded by the public interests.

This proposition is now so well established, that there can be none to dispute it. The people have rights which inhere in the very nature of the case, and are inalienable. No legislature conferred them, and none can take them away. Governments may define these rights, and throw around them the safeguards of law, and this much they are bound to do. They are also bound to do it wisely and justly.

The facts which demand the intervention of public authority are enforced and multiplied by all experience and investigation. Not merely in the theory of law, but as a practical fact, railways have become public highways, and all classes of our people are as dependent upon their wholesome management, as upon the wholesome management of any other public property. The assumption on the part of the advocates of non-intervention, that the public has a choice between other methods of transportation and transportation by rail, is without actual truth. If the choice exists, that choice cannot be exercised, except upon such conditions as to render the privilege nugatory. As to large masses of freight, and a considerable portion of passenger travel, rapid transit by rail is the only available alternative presented. And were the fact otherwise, it is impossible to presume, under any known axiom of good government, that interests so vast and manifold as to involve the fundamental conditions of public progress and prosperity, should be surrendered to the undisputed determination of a personal discretion, based solely upon considerations of private or corporate profit.

4. That control is demanded in the interest of capital.

Most assuredly, the relations of our people to capital are not to be ignored. We are not under any circumstances to overlook the grave fact that the material interests of our State are vitally dependent upon the safety and ample remuneration of future investment in railway construction. A consultation of the comparative statistics of this report will show that the industries of the State are far more dependent upon future investment than past expenditure in this direction; and we know of no consideration of material interest or public morals which can counsel indifference to the honorable claim of capital to ample consideration for all legitimate expenditure.

Protection of capital from mismanagement.

It will not be assumed, however, that the interests of capital itself can be best promoted by the mismanagement of railways, or by the imposition of extortionate rates, or unjust discriminations. And judicious legislation should prohibit nothing more. The world over, capital prefers moderate returns on reliable security, rather than excessive returns upon unreliable security. The price of railway stock and bonds in any market depends less upon the rate of interest promised than upon the character of the enterprises upon which they are based. Most of all, they depend upon the legitimate management of the property in which the purchase-money is invested.

The history of all railway management furnishes an instructive lesson upon this topic. It is an almost unbroken history of broken faith and depreciated credit. Stocks originally sold under sanguine assurances of large returns, have become worthless paper. Bonds doubly assured on their face, and by every apparent source of security, in many cases, possess but a speculative and uncertain value.

The insecurity of railway investments at the present time, is such, that popular confidence in railway stocks has practically departed. No farmer, no merchant, no retired capitalist seeks to invest his surplus funds or labor in any railway company in which he does not himself possess control. And this want of confidence and refusal to contribute to public enterprisse of this class, are in no manner measured by the real merits of the enterprise itself. On the contrary, they are the fruit of the common judgment, that railway capital is the sport of speculative management.

Nor does this want of confidence extend to stock subscriptions alone. The bonded debts of railway companies are also rapidly becoming the object of suspicion. And this on precisely the same ground that originally deteriorated the market value of capital stock. The stock is no longer regarded as the representative of legitimate capital. Sold at a discount, inflated, unlimited by law, and often misappropriated, its actual amount and value ultimately become subject to the discretion of the managing board. The bonded debt, subject to the same conditions and influence, is liable to the same possible dilution and depreciation.

Let us look at the public consequences of insecurity for capital.

The tendency to financial demoralization, wholly prejudicial to regular investment, is of startling import in all its history and possible consequences. One of the immediate results is the fact that the public is held responsible for the payment of interest on a vast capital, nominal and not actual, and rendered nominal, at least in great part, by means which no intelligent judgment can sanction or approve.

5. That the necessity for control is a growing one.

That the demand for a judicious control is a growing one, is apparent from the rapid development of our country, and the consequent need of increased facilities, duly guaranteed and protected. It is especially apparent in the case of the northwestern States, whose resources are so incalculable, and whose growth in population has been so unprecedented during the recent years. Here are millions of an industrious, energetic, and progressible people, gathered from all parts of the new and old world, for the very purpose of availing themselves of the extraordinary opportunities afforded by our fertile soils, our forests of timber, and our rich and varied mineral resources. They came as to the garden spot of the whole world, and they will make it a garden in fact, if their industry is properly encouraged.

Transportation, easy, prompt, and cheap, is a condition of the growth of this new empire, which the economist cannot fail to recognize, and, with legislatures, cannot ignore. Somehow it must be insured, or a nation's growth is retarded.

The remaining questions are those of kind and degree.

What should be the form and nature of the control to be exercised, and to what extent is it proper to carry it? are in fact the questions which at this moment agitate the public mind in so many countries. They are doubtless in the way of settlement, but they are not settled. Indeed, as we have seen, scarcely any two States or countries fully agree as to either of them. One is trying full ownership by government, the State working the roads. Another prefers government ownership, the roads being leased to private corporations. Another, mixed ownership, the State owning and operating, or leasing, a part of the roads, and allowing companies to operate the rest. Another charters companies, assists them with money, and puts them under ministerial restraint, not only forbidding but preventing competition. Another creates companies, and leaves them to carry on the business of transportation pretty much as they like, but concentrates the best thought and the largest powers of the government deemed judicious, upon the matter of consolidations, with a view to prevent them. And yet others practice upon the theory of total non-interference.

SUMMARY OF CONCLUSIONS.

Having thus completed as full and careful a survey as possible of the whole field of inquiry, the commissioners present the following summary of the more important conclusions they have formed.

The only form of railway control likely to prove successful under present conditions, is the legislative, supplemented by direct supervision; the legislature laying down general rules of action, but leaving the application and enforcement of those rules to a commission. A judicious application of this method requires:

1. A determination, by the commissioners, of the actual cash value of each railroad; such value not to be greater than the actual cost thereof, and the valuation subject to legislative revision.

2. An annual determination of the gross and net earnings of each company, from the reports of companies, by actual inspection of books and affairs, and by all other practicable methods.

3. A division of roads into two classes; the first class including all roads paying a reasonable compensation on valuation, and the second class including all other roads.

4. A maximum of rates of fare and freights for roads ascertained to belong to the first class; such maximum being subject to legislative revision.

5. No restriction of earnings upon roads of the second class, except by way of remedying unjust discriminations.

6. A prohibition of unjust discriminations and unreasonable or excessive rates on all roads; any person complaining of discrimination or extortionate charges having the right to appeal to the board

of commissioners, under such rules as to evidence of facts as the commissioners may determine; the board determining the fact of discrimination on evidence and notice to both sides, and its conclusions to be *prima facie* evidence as to fact of discrimination, or of unreasonable charges.

7. Additional police regulations, especially as to running connections, and the passage of freight from one road to another.

8. Limited power of the commissioners to require repair of roads, improvement of roads or rolling stock, and increased accommodations for passenger travel.

9. Full and complete publicity of rates of fare and freight.

10. Publicity of all important contracts and agreements between railway companies, and of their business transactions generally.

11. Greater uniformity and completeness of accounts, as well as greater fullness and frequency of reports.

12. Adequate penalties for the falsification or concealment of earnings and expenditures, or other facts.

13. Efficient means for the prompt enforcement of all provisions of the law, at the expense of the State.

The annual report of the Ohio Commissioner of Railroads discusses at length the question of legislative enactments fixing railroad rates. We give the following extract:

For thirty years the British parliament and American legislatures have been making futile attempts to regulate this matter of rates by statutory enactments. The system of "equal mileage rates," so persistently urged by certain advocates of reform, and so often a subject of legislation, is evidently impracticable, and in contravention of the recognized rules of trade and the established principles upon which the business of the country is conducted. The advocates of equal mileage rates, however, object to the application of this business custom to rates upon railways, because, as is said, "they are built for the public use," and every citizen or customer is entitled equally to the benefits to be derived from them, regardless of his means or condition; and that an application of this rule would give the large shipper, or man who traveled most, advantages that he who shipped less or traveled little could not obtain. While we concede that the benefits and blessings of public improvements should be the equal inheritance of all, and dispensed to each upon the same conditions, a discrimination in rates upon account of quantity, distance, or like contingency does not impair the proposition; nor can it be considered an unnatural or unjust rule which extends them to all upon the same terms. A railway company makes more money, with less annoyance and cost, in doing the business of the large shipper, than that of the small one, though the rates per ton are less to the former.

There is, however, a kind of discrimination not only unjust, but which should be discontinued and prohibited. When the business of shippers is similar in kind and quantity, and can be done by the company at about the same cost, but through personal interest, friendship, or for any other reason of this nature, a discrimination is made in favor of one which is not extended to others, the act is reprehensible, and violates the spirit and intent of the privileges granted by the State. The same is true of localities; no privileges or concessions should be made in rates or facilities for transportation to one locality which are not granted to all similarly situated upon the same terms.

The impropriety and impracticability of fixing unyielding and inflexible rates for transportation by general laws, applicable to all roads, or by special acts applying to particular roads, or classes of roads, seems too apparent to need comment. The almost unlimited differences in the condition of our roads, affected by location, grades, curves, equipment, regularity of business, management, changes in earnings caused by construction of branches by developing new industries, opening new mines, or making new connections, and the innumerable and diverse matters which come in to affect or change their status for better or worse, but develop the folly of attempts to regulate rate of transportation by inflexible law. Such acts, or those intended to govern rates upon the basis of gross earnings or net income, can be of but temporary value. They demand such frequent changes, in order to be efficient or just, as to be of little service, and fail to accomplish the purpose desired. Laws which may be applicable and well adjusted to-day, may be quite the reverse a few months hence. General laws fixing rates which may rest lightly and not perceptibly affect the operation of roads well located, with light grades, and well managed, would be quite oppressive and burdensome to those less fortunate. A schedule which would make the lowest practicable rates under which some of our roads could do business and maintain an existence, would be far above rates now charged upon other lines more fortunately situated.

Laws fixing maximum rates, and intended solely to prevent extortion or excess in charges, may be consistently enforced ; but the adjustment of rates below this must necessarily be governed by the results of experience and the dictates of enlightened judgment.

The Massachusetts Railroad Commissioners recently, in effect, complimented and indorsed the Granger movement in their admission that it has established three important principles, viz: The accountability of railroads to the public, as well as to their stockholders ; the necessity and advantage of dealing equitably with all men ; and the existence of a broad distinction between a railroad corporation and a manufacturing company.

CHAPTER XXIV.

RAILROADS IN CALIFORNIA.

California Railroads: Routes, Length and Gauge—Senator Cole on the Public Interest in Railroads—Mr. Stanford's Report on the Financial Condition of the Central Pacific—The Railways of the World—Funded Debt and net Earnings of the Railroads of the United States.

No State has a greater interest in the harmonious adjustment of the question of transportation than California. Within her borders there is neither present nor prospective competition. The establishment of a true and cordial reciprocity between the railroads and the people, is not only a great essential of prosperity, but is entirely practicable and probable. The principles established in the searching investigations which we have summarized, are applicable here as elsewhere; but the practical working out of the problem is simplified here, by the fact that there are but two parties whose interests require to be harmonized. In a speech made in San Francisco, on the 23d of September, 1872, Senator Cole thus spoke of railroads in general, and of what had been contributed to those in California:

The inspection of a railroad map of the United States shows the country netted all over with railroads. Particularly is this the case in the northern Atlantic States. A more careful inquiry discloses the fact that 63,000 miles of road are now completed and in actual use. If they were stretched across the continent they would make twenty-five entire railroads from ocean to ocean, and give us a Pacific Railway every fifty miles from the British Possessions quite to the frontier of Mexico. Or, if running north and south, they would span the country fifty times or every fifty miles from the Atlantic to the Pacific. There is a mile of railroad to every one hundred voters, and if these roads, as is alleged, have cost $40,000 a mile, there is an investment in such property equal to $400 to every man, or $60 to every man, woman and child in the land. These roads have all been constructed and many of them rebuilt several times within the past forty years. I can myself remember the beginning of railroads in the United States, but the end no man can see. For the last ten years they have increased much more rapidly, in proportion, than the population, and this will probably continue for many years to come, and until all parts of the country are abundantly accommodated with the iron rail. Nothing can limit their construction but the supply of material and capital, and these are without limit. Ties can be grown, should necessity require it, and the mountains of iron, already discovered, are absolutely inexhaustible.

The question as to where railways shall be permanently established, is merely a question of time. Where they are not wanted they will not be built, or if built will not long be maintained; and where they are wanted, their construction is certain, notwithstanding arguments to the contrary, which may be drawn from slight delays and unimportant variations. Railroads, as a general rule, conform to the requirements of business; and it has rarely happened that the persons having their construction in charge have had the temerity to disregard such demands.

The Central and Western Pacific Railroad Companies, now one and the same concern, have received from the United States Government, in interest-bearing bonds, the sum of $27,855,680, and they are moreover authorized to issue their own first-mortgage bonds, to take precedence of the Government bonds, as a security upon the road, to an equal extent; so that they have actually received aid from the United States Government, in the form of bonds and securities, to the enormous amount of $55,711,360; besides which the Government has paid interest for them amounting to $6,164,720 49. How much the Central Company has up to date realized out of 15,000,000 acres, more or less, of lands donated to them by the General Government, the books of the real estate department of that huge concern alone will show; but counting the sales and assets together, and the amount in value cannot be less than $10,000,000. Numerous towns and cities have been laid out by the company along their lines, and these must all be counted under this head making the sum in all probability far in excess of $10,000,000 a year—her share of this annual gift from the Commonwealth of California to the thrifty firm known as the Central Pacific Railroad Company. Besides the million and a half thus guaranteed by the State, other millions have been donated directly by the people of the different cities and counties. I find that about forty special laws have been passed by our Legislature, authorizing gifts of money and bonds to railroad companies, to say nothing about other acts granting lands and privileges of one sort and another, and the five per cent. law, so-called, of the session of 1869. The amounts authorized to be given by the several counties and cities under these forty odd acts, at different times, range from $50,000 up to a million dollars each; and a partial list of them may be interesting for reference at the present time:

Yuba county	$ 200,000	Stanislaus county	$ 25,000
Sutter county	50,000	Alameda county	220,000
Solano county	200,000	San Francisco county	1,000,000
Yolo county	50,000	Sacramento county	300,000
San Mateo county	100,000	Calaveras county	50,000
San Francisco county	600,000	Tuolumne county	50,000
Santa Clara county	200,000	El Dorado county	100,000
Placer county	100,000	Calaveras county	50,000
Santa Clara county	200,000	Napa county	70,000
San Mateo county	100,000	Stanislaus county	25.000
San Francisco county	300,000	Yuba county	65,000
Los Angeles city	50,000	Yolo county	100,000
Los Angeles county	100,000	Los Angeles county	150,000
San Joaquin county	250,000	Los Angeles city	75,000
Placerville city	100,000	Plumas county	230,000
San Joaquin county	100,000	Sutter county	50,000
El Dorado county	200,000	San Joaquin county	200,000
Placer county	250,000	Stockton city	300,000
Santa Clara county	150,000	San Francisco	1,000,000

Total, $6,360,000. It is not exactly known how much assistance has been actually rendered in pursuance of these statutes, but it amounts to a good number of millions.

In addition to all these enumerated gifts and guarantees of money and lands and bonds from the Federal Government, the State and several cities and counties have granted bonds and franchises of inestimable value; as at Vallejo, at Sacramento, at Marysville, at San Jose, at Stockton and other places, besides the enormous donations of submerged and other lands in and adjoining Oakland and San Francisco, comprising a thousand or two acres in the former city, and in the latter, including the right of way to her southern border, literally hundreds of acres more prospectively, and in the immediate future worth millions upon millions of dollars. Such a record of munificent donations to railroads can be found in no other State in the Union, nor, indeed, anything at all comparable to it. California, in this particular, stands entirely alone, peerless in her generosity.

The force of the people is now so well organized for self-protection, through the Grange and other movements, that it rests with them to correct abuses; and it is to be hoped, availing themselves of experience elsewhere, they may do it in a manner which will require no after revision and correction. Thus far the spirit of conciliation and compromise has marked the intercourse of the Grange and Railroad authorities in this State.

Reports of California Railroad Companies (except the Central Pacific) Filed in the Office of the Secretary of State, for the Year ending December 31, 1874.

TERMINAL RAILWAY COMPANY.

Capital Stock	$4,000,000 00
Subscribed and paid in	27,500 00
Expended for purchase of Land and Construction	30,399 92
Amount of Indebtedness	2,899 92
Receipts and Dividends	

NORTHERN RAILROAD COMPANY.

Capital Stock	8,400,000 00
Subscribed	210,500 00
Paid in	21,050 00
Expended for Land and Construction	41,511 85
Indebtedness	41,586 90
Receipts, Freights, and Dividends	

SACRAMENTO VALLEY RAILROAD COMPANY.

Capital Stock	1,000,000 00
Subscribed	492,380 00
Received	180,964 31
Freight transported	50,906 32
Current Expenses	127,968 00
Dividends	

STOCKTON AND COPPEROPOLIS RAILWAY COMPANY.

Capital Stock	1,500,000 00
Subscribed	48,000 00
Paid in	4,800 00
Expended for Building	607,492 20
Indebtedness	1,238,783 34
Amount due the Company	491,000 00
Receipts	26,061 73
Freight transported	8,757 tons
Current Expenses, etc.	83,540 64
Dividends	

STOCKTON AND VISALIA RAILROAD COMPANY.

Capital Stock	$5,550,000 00
Subscribed	186,500 00
Paid in	71,802 00
Paid for Lands, Construction, etc	877,183 08
Indebtedness	891,000 00
Receipts	63,292 76
Freight transported	21,267 tons
Current Expenses, etc.	63,627 58

The following is an extract from the Annual Report of the Central Pacific Railroad Company, for 1873, bearing date July 14, 1874:

Mr. Stanford, the President of the Company, reports as follows: Capital stock (authorized), $100,000,000; capital stock subscribed, $62,608,800; capital stock paid in, $54,275,500; subscribed and held in trust for the Company, $8,333,300.

The indebtedness of the company is as follows: Funded debt, less sinking fund, $53,248,268 30; United States subsidy bonds, $27,-885,680 00; total, $81,133,948 30. The assets are as follows: 1,219 miles main line of railroad and telegraph, sidings, wharves, depots, steam ferries, etc., $131,419,110 53; equipments, real estate for use of road, telegraph intruments and material on hand, $9,960,-029 33; Sacramento river steamers, (cost,) $853,569 41; balance of accounts outstanding after deducting obligations, $1,666,787 34; farming lands, estimated value, $29,306,000 00. Undivided half 60 acres land in Mission Bay, in San Francisco; 500 acres water front at Oakland; about 140 acres and water front at Sacramento—estimated value, independent of improvements, $7,750,000 00; cash, $1,584,661 71. Total, $182,540,158 32.

The anticipations in the annual report for 1872, in relation to increase of business, have been realized, and we may expect as much greater increase for the year 1874. The increase of population of the State by immigration during the year 1873, was 34,000; this year it promises to be much greater. The harvest is abundant, and unusual prosperity prevails throughout the State.

At the last session of the Legislature, the question of change in the law in regard to freights and fares, was largely discussed, and, as a conclusion, no legislation was had. But an important principle was recognized, viz: that as a question of sound political economy, railroad companies should be assured of stability in the laws regulating their tariffs.

To this end, and because the good faith of the State in this respect had been questioned, four special bills were passed conferring rights upon associations to build as many separate lines of railroads, with varying tariff rates—in some cases increasing the rates above those of the General Incorporation law, and in many others decreasing them. The main and only object of the companies in accepting these special Acts, so far as they accept less rates than those provided in the general law, was to secure themselves against future legislation in reducing their rates. It was openly stated, and it was clearly true, that unless they could have a guaranty that the income of the lines to be constructed should not be interfered with by legislative control of tariffs, the roads could not obtain credit, and could not be built. No other benefits over these to be had by the General Corporation law, were gained by these special Acts, and there was nothing else to justify their passage by the Legislature, or their approval by the Governor. And it is clear that if railroads are to be built by other organizations than the Government, they must be left as free to make profits, under the law as it exists at the time of their organization, as others making investments in any species of property. It is just, and has its foundation in the soundest political economy. The fact that the State exercises its right of eminent domain to secure the right of way for the construction of railroads, is in itself an evidence of their great public utility, and it is only this that justifies it in the exercise of its right of eminent domain to procure the right of way. This exercise of eminent domain is made for the benefit of the public, and not for that of the corporation, which must pay the full value of all it takes for right of way, and which from that time holds it and controls it as private property. Can it be wise to discourage investments that are so unqualifiedly stamped by the State as beneficial to the public? Whether there is a reserve power to the State to regulate the tariffs of railroads, other than the limitation of the general Corporation Law, is a mooted question. Whatever the power, it is applicable to every corporation formed under it, whatever its business or objects. But, however this may be, the exercise of it, if its exists, must ultimately be regulated by justice, and by sound and correct principles. In the passage of the special bills, before alluded to, this principle was evidently recognized. The people seem to have acquiesced in the action of the Legislature, and we may confidently look for a full recognition of the principle hereafter. The question is now being largely discussed throughout the United States, and if the principle is correct, we may rest with confidence that the good faith and intelligence of the people will recognize it, and upon this good faith and intelligence must the railroads of the present and future rely. Decisions by the Courts, upholding a law that is repugnant to the will of the people, will avail nothing; but the majority will protect individuals in the right. The railroad companies are made up of individuals, and a wrong to one of these is a wrong to the whole people. And the question at last resolves itself into this, that either individuals must be protected in their investments in railroads, and allowed to make such profits as their enterprise commands, or the State must own and construct railroads, or railroading must cease. There is no such thing as separating control and ownership. Control is ownership. If the exigencies of the State shall require it, to assume partial or complete control of any species of property, good faith will compel it to provide compensation accordingly, as it does when it exercises the right of eminent domain, and takes private property for public use. The financial and business prospects of the company were never brighter. The end of each year in its history seems to more than realize the promises of the beginning.

From the report of General Superintendent Towne, it appears that the gross earnings were: Coin, $7,643,469 58; currency, $5,220,-483 40. The operating expenses amounted to $4,929,684 09 in gold, and $39,587 43 in currency. The percentage of expenses to earnings was 40.47. The earnings over operating expenses for the year amounted to $8,245,302 54, an increase of more than $1,000,000 over the profits of the preceding year's operations. The total number of passengers transported was 3,280,171, being an increase over 1872 of 276,197. The revenue from this department was, in coin, $2,235,942 81; in currency, $2,182,474 61. Total tonnage for 1873 was 2,057,204,628 pounds; total for 1872, 1,881,646,021 pounds, showing an increase of 175,558,607 pounds, or 9.33 per cent. The earnings from this department were as follows: Coin, $4,989,996 21; currency, $2,472,898 71, showing an increase in coin earnings of $251,143 13, and an increase in currency earnings of $244,307 21.

The number of miles of road operated was 1,218.93. The total land grants owned by the company amount to 11,722,400 acres. The total sales of land by the company from its organization to June 30, 1874, amounted to 358,818.73 acres, which were disposed of for $1,459,768 38, being an average of a little more than $4 12½ per acre. The Land Agent says that the number of sales is increasing from year to year, and the prices steadily increase in proportion. He is the authority for the statement that within the last three months 12,000 farmers and mechanics seeking homes have come to California.

CALIFORNIA RAILROADS.

There are 1,261 miles of wide gauge railroad completed and in operation in this State (all of which is four feet eight and one half inch gauge) to wit:

CENTRAL PACIFIC RAILROAD.	Miles.
Oakland to State line	276
Oakland to Brooklyn	6
Oakland to Alameda	2
Alameda to Haywards	15
Niles to San Jose	18
Lathrop to Goshen	146
Roseville to Redding	151
Total	614

SOUTHERN PACIFIC RAILROAD.	
San Francisco to Tres Pinos	101
Carnadero to Soledad	60
Goshen to Sumner	74
Los Angeles to San Fernando	29
Los Angeles towards San Bernardino	29
Total	293

LOS ANGELES AND SAN PEDRO RAILROAD.	
Los Angeles to Wilmington	22
Branch to Anaheim via Los Nietos	21
Total	43

CALIFORNIA PACIFIC RAILROAD.	
Vallejo to Sacramento	60
Davisville to Knight's Landing	18
Napa Junction to Calistoga	35
Total	113

VACA RAILROAD.

Vaca Station to Vacaville........ 6

SACRAMENTO VALLEY RAILROAD.

Sacramento to Folsom........ 23

PLACERVILLE AND SACRAMENTO VALLEY RAILROAD.

Folsom to Shingle Springs........ 26

CALIFORNIA NORTHERN RAILROAD.

Marysville to Oroville........ 27

STOCKTON AND VISALLA RAILROAD.

Stockton to Oakdale........ 33

STOCKTON AND COPPEROPOLIS RAILROAD.

Peters to Milton........ 12

SAN FRANCISCO AND NORTH PACIFIC RAILROAD.

Donahue to Cloverdale........ 56

MOUNT DIABLO RAILROADS.

Nortonville to New York........ 7
Somersville to Pittsburg........ 5

Total........ 12

RAILROAD.

San Rafael to San Quentin........ 3

VISALIA RAILROAD.

Visalia to Goshen........ 7

In addition to the wide-gauge roads, there are narrow gauge railroads, to wit:

San Francisco and North Pacific Coast Railroad, Saucelito toward Russian river, 30 miles, completed.

Salinas and Monterey Railroad, 18½ miles, was completed during the past season.

The Colfax and Nevada Narrow-gauge Road, 23 miles in length, is under contract, and to be completed next season.

The Watsonville and Santa Cruz Narrow-gauge Railroad, 22 miles in length, is now being constructed, and will be complete next season.

RECAPITULATION.	Miles.
Broad-gauge........	1,261
Narrow-gauge........	48½
Narrow-gauge under construction........	45
Total........	1,354½

STATEMENT SHOWING FUNDED DEBT AND NET EARNINGS OF THE RAILROADS OF THE UNITED STATES.

Railroad Network in	Bonds and Debt.	Net Earnings Required to Pay 7 per Cent.	Actual Net Earnings.	Amount Left for Dividends.
Western States..........	$883,794,823	$62,265,637	$72,464,212	$10,198,575
Middle States..........	477,199,070	33,403,934	69,280,585	35,876,651
New England States....	122,224,449	8,555,711	15,061,777	6,506,066
Southern States........	280,846,999	19,659,289	18,145,349	1,513,940
Pacific States..........	102,839,109	7,198,247	8,858,639	1,660,392
Totals..........	$1,836,904,450	$128,583,311	$183,810,562	$53,226,251

THE RAILWAYS OF THE WORLD.

COUNTRIES.	Date, Jan 1st.	Mileage.	Sq. Miles to 1 M. of Railway.	Cost per Mile.	Total Cost.
United States—					
New England	1874	5,314	12.9	$47,840	$263,697,778
Middle States	1874	14,019	9.9	67,736	1,126,702,107
Western States	1874	33,772	30.7	52,125	1,730,728,234
Southern States	1874	15,353	51.4	36,994	509,324,106
Pacific States	1874	2,193	209.0	95,590	154,090,809
Total United States	1873	70,651	...	$53,556	$3,784,542,934
Canada	1870	2,928	148.0	70,160	205,428,480
Mexico	1873	300	3,435.0	54,920	16,476,000
Honduras	1873	62	638.0	95,000	5,890,000
Costa Rica	....	82	318.0	90,000	7,380,000
NORTH AMERICA	....	74,023	......	$54,303	$4,019,717,414
Great Britain and Ireland	1874	16,082	8.0	$182,912	$2,941,601,540
France	1872	10,706	19.0	158,714	1,716,333,196
Belgium	1872	1,892	6.0	106,987	202,419,404
Switzerland	1871	820	18.0	87,134	71,448,220
Spain	1870	3,801	54.0	107,156	407,229,956
Portugal	1869	453	81.0	101,317	45,896,601
Italy	1871	3.895	27.0	89,712	349,428,240
Austria and Hungary	1872	7,529	30.0	73,915	556,506,035
Germany	1873	13,066	15.0	88,493	1,156,249,538
Netherlands	1872	1,045	13.0	97,202	101,575,045
Denmark	1872	530	28.0	57,114	30,270,420
Sweden and Norway	1873	1,049	292.0	66,438	69,693,462
Russia	1872	7,279	280.0	166,477	1,214,782,669
Turkey	1873	488	3,720.0	46,829	22,852,552
Roumania	1871	507	90.0	46,729	23,691,603
Greece	....	100	199.0	50,000	5,000,000
EUROPE	....	69,260	......	128,718	$8,915,048.501
British India	1870	4,182	230.0	100,500	450,271,000
ASIA	....	4,182	230.0	$100,500	$420,271,000
Egypt	1870	737	907.0	$96,504	$71,123,448
Cape of Good Hope	1873	134	5,000.0	92,103	12,341,802
AFRICA	....	871	......	95,826	$83,465,250
AUSTRALIA	1870	1,058	2,404.0	$99,622	$105,400,076
Brazil	1872	410	7,573.0	$201,157	$82,474,370
Paraguay	1873	44	2,334.0	89,790	3,950,760
Uraguay	1873	57	1,290.0	86,000	4,902,000
Argentine Confederacy	1872	875	955.0	53,918	47,178,250
Colombia	1873	65	6,600.0	166,667	10,833,355
Peru	1873	375	1,340.0	56,410	21,153,750
Chili	1872	452	298.0	61,309	27,711,668
SOUTH AMERICA	....	2,278	......	87,008	$198,204,153
Grand Totals	...	151,632	......	$90,627	$13,742,106,394

CHAPTER XXV.

AGRICULTURAL EDUCATION IN THE PUBLIC SCHOOLS.

"The ten commandments and a handicraft make a good and wholesome equipment to commence life with. A man must learn to stand upright upon his own feet, to respect himself, to be independent of charity or accident. It is only on this basis that any superstructure of intellectual cultivation worth having can possibly be built."—*Froude.*

First urged by Massachusetts Agricultural Society—Manual of Agriculture Prepared—Action taken by other States—Obstacles to Success—Professor Turner on Text-book Monopolies—Superintendent Northrup's Views on the Educational Value of Labor.

It must be conceded by all, that one of the greatest obstacles to the farmer's progress has been a defective and unsuitable education, and that the specific training required to lift his calling to a level with the highest of human occupations, is not to be obtained without an appeal to the ballot-box. Since the year 1860, the importance of industrial education in general, and of agricultural instruction in our common schools, has been urged upon the public by teachers eminent for broad and enlightened views, and by equally eminent farmers, trained in all the learning of our higher institutions. The Massachusetts State Board of Agriculture gave, fifteen years ago, the following reasons for asking the State Legislature for the passage of an act authorizing the introduction of a Manual of Agriculture into all the schools of the commonwealth:

The foundation for the intelligent pursuit of every business is laid in our common school system. So far as it goes, it answers every purpose, and if any complaint could be made, it would be, perhaps, that it aimed at too much—that some things are taught that might better be omitted. One fact, however, is certain, that nothing is taught in our public schools which have any special bearing upon the future education of that large class whose lives are devoted to the cultivation of the soil, and stranger still, this class is the only one that cannot get the special instruction necessary for it anywhere else. There are private schools, academies, and colleges for the education of youth for other callings in life, but not for the farmer, who requires, more that any other class, a special training for his profession. The fact that the greater proportion of all labor is farm labor, seems to have been overlooked in the studies prescribed in the common schools. The simple teachings which appeal to the daily senses and to natural objects, have been too much neglected. Without desiring to go into a minute criticism upon the instruction which is afforded, we claim a place for agriculture in the system of public education; and assert the right to have introduced a few elementary studies which might profitably occupy a portion of the time of every child, whatever his future occupation might be, but which are of inestimable benefit to those who are to become farmers. These studies cannot be commenced too early, for they are the germs of all future development, the vitality of which is never lost, but they must be planted early, if it is hoped to reach a full harvest.

If a person, who had the ability to perform whatever he undertook, should offer to the people of this commonwealth a secret, by which in twenty years the productive value of the lands throughout the whole State would be doubled without any more outlay than is now required, what would that secret be worth? The diffusion of general agricultural education would accomplish this object; nay, go far beyond it, in less time than has been named, and at an expense so trifling as to be hardly worth mentioning, in view of the benefits which would flow from it. There is no other way to effect this so easily, so cheaply, and so advantageously to the moral as well as material wealth of the State, as by commencing this education at an early period in the future farmer's life in our public schools.

Constant complaint is made that the pursuit of a farmer is unpopular with the young. That it is all hard work and no corresponding reward. That a farmer does not rank as high in the estimation of the community as other classes of professions. There is much truth in all this, and there are good reasons for it. Let us compare the education of a farmer with that of other professions. The boy who is to become a farmer leaves school at sixteen or seventeen, and commences work upon the farm—mere work, without one idea ever given to him as to the nature of the soil out of which he is to obtain his livelihood; without a thought as to the various processes connected with the beautiful laws of vegetation; without the slightest idea of races or breeds of cattle, and with not one general principle to guide him, and to make intelligent the labor he is performing. Now, this cannot be said of any other profession or industrial pursuit, although this one, more than any other demands all the previous preparation which it is possible to give, by instilling into the mind, when young and perceptive, those general principles and teachings which lie at the foundation of all success, and of all that future knowledge which practice and observation would, with a proper previous training, be sure to give. Thus it is that labor to the boy who is to become the future farmer is irksome at the best, but in most cases it is worse than this—it is deadening to the mental faculties, at the time when they are most capable of being quickened and improved.

Compare this with other pursuits, from the youth who is intended for one of the learned professions, and whose preparation continues for years after the age at which the boy is condemned to the farm, to the lad who goes to the counting-room or the factory, where the work is comparatively light, and where the mind is amused and intellect excited. Is it any wonder that farming is unpopular under these circumstances; or, is it surprising that farmers with such an education for their pursuit, should not hold their proper place in public estimation? How completely would this be changed were boys educated for this pursuit, and brought up to the standard of skill and intelligence that is necessary, in order to enter successfully upon any other industrial career? It is education which gives dignity to the man, be his profession what it may; and there is no calling which would rank higher than that of the farmer, if those who enter upon it were sufficiently educated to make it successful and profitable.

This committee proposed as the first step in furnishing agricultural education:

1. The engrafting upon our common school education the study of the elementary principles of geology, of agricultural chemistry, of physiology, and of botany.

They propose that these shall be taught by manuals, in the usual form of question and answer, and that they shall be confined to the plainest leading principles applicable to the cultivation of the soil, and prepared in such a manner that it will not depend altogether upon the knowledge of the instructor to make them of use to the learner.

It is only necessary to appeal to the individual experience of every one for a just estimate of the importance of this simple and inexpensive measure. Our children would, from this slight addition to their studies, learn something which would every day be more and more deeply implanted in their minds by their daily walks in the school-room. They could not see a tree send forth its leaves, its flowers, its fruits; or the fresh sod turned over by the plow; or the rain fall from the heavens; or the sun shine upon the earth, without attaching to these now unheeded operations a meaning and a significance, and without inspiring in their minds a spirit of investigation and inquiry, which would be preparing them for the practical pursuits of after-life.

The vital principle in the plan proposed is to start the education of the future farmer at the earliest possible period; and to do this, the commencement must be in our public schools, while the other parts of the boy's education are going on. But it must not stop here. It has already been remarked that special schools, academies and colleges, exist for the instruction of youths intended for every other career in life except that of a farmer. They leave the public schools, where they have been well prepared, to enter upon the special education for the professions for which they are designed, while the boy who is to become a farmer is left to shift for himself. He is dropped upon the farm, as it were, wholly unfitted, wholly unprepared to reap any advantage from what he has already been taught. His education stops short, just at the moment when a very moderate degree of special instruction would fit him to enter life with every prospect of success. To supply this absolute want the committee proposed the establishment of—

2. An agricultural school, with a farm attached to it, in each county, to be devoted exclusively to agricultural instruction, uniting science with correct practice.

These county schools need not be expensive undertakings. They should be commenced upon the plan of educating youths in the best methods of farm management, connecting with it such knowledge of the science and theory of agriculture, as can be obtained by devoting a portion of the time to study, under competent instructors. At these schools system, economy, the right adaptation of means to ends, the knowledge of what can be cultivated with profit, by learning to calculate the cost of production,—in short the doing of everything, with the reason for doing it, to be shown by a satisfactory result,—these are the main points to be observed in establishing them.

Many other States have taken similar action. The prominent farmers of Illinois urged the preparation and introduction of works on the elements of natural history into the public schools. The State Teachers' Association of Wisconsin, in the winter of 1874–5, recommended a revision of the school course, with the same object in view. The combined influence of the great publishing houses, whose interests were against change, and of the body of teachers, who are generally conservative, have thus far prevented the effectual prosecution of this much needed reform. Hear what Prof. Turner, of Illinois, says of the influence of text-book monopolies on the public schools :

We take the child out of God's natural industrial university and send him to school, where, at best, only a fraction of his entire manhood can be properly developed; and after all we do not fit pupils for actual life, even in those elemental studies, after forty weeks' school per annum, as well as they used to be fitted in ten weeks half a century ago, yet we never had better teachers or brighter children than now.

One prime cause of this result is, that the bookmakers and publishers have, in fact, assumed about as absolute control of our public schools as the politicians have of our postoffices. Rich publishing houses have offered as high as seventy thousand dollars for the introduction of a single book into a State. And yet not one of these books teach us the things which it is our chief interest to know, and our protracted school drill on the elements leaves no room for anything else. I wish to make room for some of the subjects that underlie the industrial arts. For botany, and entomology, and zoology, for instance. The State of Illinois spends, say, twelve millions of dollars on her common schools, and looses every year from ten millions to twenty millions of dollars from noxious insects, and Dr. LeBarron, our State Entomologist, tells us that about one hundred species do all this mischief. Now, I would have these insects, every mother's son of them, with pins in their backs, put up in a show-case in every public school in the State, and I would have every child know them by sight, as well as he knows his father's cows and horses; instead of having one or two lone men to look after their habits and remedies, I would turn millions of eyes directly and intelligently upon them, and thus prepare for their amelioration and cure. I would have this whether or no the child knew there was such a word as Entomology in the English language.

The hard-working American people want to know something about our continent, our life-work, our bodies, and bones, and souls, our duties and destinies in the great republic in which we live. Compared with this, all other knowledge is of little importance to us.

I look to the agricultural and industrial classes to lift us out of this monkeydom of precedent, into the true freedom of American citizenship. The common school must be their chief instrument. All that is needful is that every man should quietly set about improving his own school, in his own district, as fast and as fully as he can.

Few men have done better service to the cause of industrial education than Hon. B. G. Northrup, the State Superintendent of Schools in Connecticut. He says:

Every child's education is deficient who has not learned to work in some useful form of industry. Labor aids in disciplining the intellect and energizing the character. Especially does farm work task and test the mind, by leading a boy to plan and contrive, to adapt means to ends, in a great variety of ways, and under constantly varying circumstances. With all our improved gymnastics, none is better than manual labor, when it is cheerfully and intelligently performed, and especially farm work. The ambition for easier lives and more genteel employments, and the silly but common notion, that labor is menial, that the tools of the trades and the farm are badges of servility, have greatly lessened apprenticeships. These pernicious notions ought to be refuted in our schools, and our youth should there be taught the dignity and necessity of labor, and its vital relations to all human excellence and progress, the evils of indolence, the absurdity of the prevalent passion for city life, and the wide-spread aversion to manual labor. A practical knowledge of some industrial pursuit is an important element in intellectual culture. Every man should have one vocation, and as many avocations as possible. Let us imitate the Hebrews, among whom labor is always honorable; and no matter what a man's rank, he must be trained to work.

And I would add, let us imitate the Germans, whose training schools for girls include every subject required to be understood by the mistress of a family, employing either a very limited, or the most ample income. It is my opinion that the best influences which can be brought to bear upon the minds of boys and girls, will be found in early recognizing them as a part of the productive wealth of the home. The withdrawal of our scholars from the performance of daily duties and services, is an education in shirking and shiftlessness, just at the period when the opposite habits should be formed.

It is not to be supposed that farmers' sons will all desire to become farmers, nor is it desirable that they should. The broad term "technical education," comprises all the leading industries. It means the acquisition of skill, as well as theoretical knowledge, in whatever pursuit the student may choose.

The provisions made by the national and State governments for this training in all our leading industries, will be considered in the following chapter.

CHAPTER XXVI.

HIGHER AGRICULTURAL EDUCATION.

"The nation most quickly promoting the intellectual development of its industrial population must advance as surely as the country neglecting it must inevitably retrograde."—*Liebig.*

"The time is not far distant when science and manipulative skill must be joined together.' —*Humboldt.*

How Provided for by Foreign Governments: France: Germany: Russia—Beginnings in the United States—The Congressional Grant—Evasions and Perversions—An Example of Good Faith—The Record of California.

In the educational system of the future, attention will be specially directed to the technical element, since this alone can train each portion of the community to the full enjoyment of its resources, and bring to it an intelligent appreciation of its duties. It is the only training which will enable a man "to do cleverly what he undertakes, suiting his actions to his purpose, and his living to his means."

It would be a most interesting and profitable task to review the immense progress which has already been made in Europe, in the special science and art schools; but we must confine ourselves to the subject of agricultural education, and look for our modes in those countries where the art of agriculture is the most highly developed and completely systematized.

We find, according to a report from the French Minister of Agriculture, made last year to our Bureau at Washington, that the French system of agricultural education embraces three classes of schools: First, a central university or agronomic institute; next, three intermediate or high schools, called regional schools, from their special adaptation to the needs of the northern, western, and southern portions of the empire. I quote, as models for our imitation in California:

The school of Grignon, in the department of Seine-et-Oise, not far from Paris, which devotes special attention to *grande culture*, to grasses, cereals, and industrial crops, to stock-breeding and to the agricultural and viticultural interests of northern France generally. An agricultural station is attached to the institution. The school of Grand Jouan, in the department of Loire-Inférieure, studies especially the best methods of bringing virgin lands under cultivation, mixed pastoral husbandry, tenant farming, natural meadows, live-stock breeding, industrial and fruit crops, and the agricultural industries of the western departments in general. The school of Montpellier, in the department Hérault, represents the agricultural peculiarities of the Mediterranean region, embracing live-stock breeding, the replanting of forests, irrigation, silk culture and manufacture, and the agricultural, pomological, and viticultural interests of the region of the olive, the mulberry and the orange. It has a sericultural and a viticultural station attached.

These and all other agricultural schools are under the direction of the minister of agriculture and commerce, to whom applications for admission are addressed. By special indulgence foreign students may be admitted. Each applicant must present a record of his birth, a certificate of moral character from his mayor, a medical certificate, showing that he has been vaccinated or has had the varioloid, and a satisfactorily indorsed obligation to pay the tuition charges at the beginning of each term. Pupils are divided into internal and external pupils, and free hearers. The latter are admitted by the director of the school, who notifies the minister of the fact. Applicants are examined in arithmetic, algebra, plain geometry, (four books,) surveying, draughting, leveling, physics, hydrostatics, hydraulics, chemistry, geography, etc. A bachelor of science is exempt from this examination.

The courses of theoretic study embrace agriculture, horticulture, viticulture, silviculture, sericulture, natural history in all its branches, zoology, and zootechny, physics, mechanics, chemistry, meteorology, mineralogy, geology, topographical engineering, agricultural construction, rural economy and legislation, rights of administration, agricultural book-keeping, etc. Practical instruction embraces laboratory practice, analysis of soils, fertilizers, agricultural products, etc., water gauging, canal construction, irrigation, agricultural machinery, manipulation of fruits and vines, live-stock management, cereal, grass, and industrial crops, fabrication of alcohol, wine, and oil, farm management, etc. Pupils passing a satisfactory examination on the completion of these courses receive a certificate or diploma. These graduates may, upon the completion of an additional course, receive the degree of agricultural engineer. Of these latter graduates a few may obtain two years "stages" in private or public agricultural establishments. These "*stagiaires*" may be sent to study the agricultural resources of foreign countries, and to investigate special subjects, presenting a memoir of their investigations to the administration. Internal or boarding pupils pay a charge for tuition and board of 750 francs per annum; external pupils and free hearers are charged 200 francs per annum for tuition. The school at Montpellier does not receive boarding pupils.

The third grade embraces the primary or farm schools, of which there are forty-three in operation in various localities. These are established by decree of the minister of agriculture designating the name, location, number, and age of pupils or "apprentices," the length and character of the course of study, the *personnel* and salaries of the board of instruction, etc. In the pastoral regions schools are allowed to receive one apprentice for every four or five hectares (10 to 13 acres) in the cultivable domain attached; in the regions where grain-culture is pursued thirty pupils are allowed for each 100 hectares, (247 acres.) Each school must accommodate at least twenty-five. Great care is exercised to make the number of pupils proportionate to the work to be performed. The age of admission varies from fifteen to thirty years. The government pays the director 270 francs per annum for the board of each apprentice. Apprentices perform the labor of cultivation, and receive regular wages. They also pursue a prescribed course of study, and are at regular intervals examined thereon. The director, who is either owner or tenant holder of the domain, receives for his remuneration a salary of 2,400 francs per annum besides the profits of cultivation.

The course of study, which generally lasts but two years, is of the most practical character, though some schools enlarge their theoretical and literary instruction. The board of instruction consists of the director, who is also professor of agriculture, horticulture, zootechny, etc., a superintendent of accounts, whose office is to supply the lack of primary instruction and to teach proper methods of keeping farm accounts, etc.; a gardener and nursery-keeper, whose duty is to teach practical horticulture; an overseer of laborers, and a veterinary surgeon. Each school has a farm varying from 100 to 1,100 acres, generally well stocked with farm-animals, and furnished with the most approved farm-implements. Every facility is offered for thorough practical instruction in agriculture, horticulture, viticulture, stock-raising and management, business management, etc. Each school aims to suit its instruction and cultivation to the regions in which it is located. A complete record of the operations of these schools would afford facilities for a most satisfactory general study of French agriculture.

Besides the foregoing schools, several institutions for instruction in special branches have been established. Among these are the three veterinary schools at Alfort, Lyons, and Toulouse. These are under the supervision of the departmental prefects. The course of study embraces four years, and comprehends physics, meteorology, chemistry, botany, geology, zoology, anatomy, physiology, hygiene, zootechny, special and general pathology, medical and surgical therapeutics, pharmacy, sanitary police, medical jurisprudence, etc. The board of instruction consists of a director and five professors, with a number of tutors necessary to give proper instruction to all the pupils.

There is also a school of shepherds located at the Bergerie of Rambouillet, the national sheep farm of France. It is intended to train young men in the management of flocks. It is open to pupils from all parts of France. Their course of instruction lasts two years, and no charge of tuition is made. The chief shepherd exercises them in the management of all operations of sheep husbandry, lambing, weaning, castration, pairing, gestation, parturition, shearing, fold-ing, feeding, slaughtering, preparation for market, etc. They are taught the best treatment of sick animals. They also cultivate the land. If their primary instruction is defective, it is supplied by special teaching. Their instruction is tested and completed by the sub-director. After two years of pupilage, if they pass a satisfactory examination, they receive a certificate with a premium of 300 francs. If they do not pass this examination, they receive only 200 francs.

In Prussia the government requires that every child shall be educated; assuming that it is the right and duty of the State to protect itself from ignorance, the most fruitful source of crime, as well as crime itself. She enjoys the enviable reputation of being first among nations in this respect. All Germany, Austria, and of late Russia, are imitating her example, and act on the principle that the farmer and mechanic must have as thorough an education as the lawyer, doctor, or clergyman. To insure this, they have established special schools, with every appliance of land, buildings and apparatus; taking students from the higher classes of the public schools or otherwise, and training them for their pursuits as superintendents, overseers, or laborers. A description of one which has served for a model to the rest of Europe will suffice for all:

The Royal Land and Forest Academy of Wurtemberg is situated at Hohenheim, a few miles from Stutgard. You will find there a large farm, adjoining a government forest of five thousand acres (these practical Germans know the importance of taking care of and cultivating trees); about twenty acres, divided into one hundred plats, are used for experimental purposes, where all questions based upon soils and their preparation, methods of culture of new plants, are tested; a botanical garden, covering several acres, exhibiting all the varieties of plants which can be grown in that climate; there is a beet sugar factory, a brewery, a distillery, a starch factory, a vinegar factory, a malting and fruit-growing establishment, a silk worm establishment, and machine shops, where agricultural implements are made and mended, this department being expected to furnish the rest of Germany with the best models.

All the studies are pursued in connection with actual practice in the field and forest, and embrace the general principles of agriculture, composition and quality of soils, special plant culture, meadow culture, grape, hop, and tobacco culture, fruit culture, vegetable culture, breeding of domestic animals in general, horses, cattle, sheep, and smaller animals, silkworm culture, bee culture, dairying, and practical farm business. Parallel with this practical instruction, there is carried along through the course of study arithmetic and algebra, bookkeeping, a knowledge of the laws and principles of taxation, physics, general and agricultural chemistry, geology, vegetable physiology and zoology, veterinary science, and study of forest trees and their uses. There you will find in the highest departments, sons of the gentry, fitting themselves for the general management of estates; ambitious young men from the middle classes, fitting themselves for stewards ; and lower down the sons of peasants, between the ages of fourteen and eighteen, who wish to become familiar with the routine of farm work, and who spend three or four hours in study, and the rest in actual labor. Any one can have instructions in the special subjects taught. Besides, there is a course of three weeks of public school vacation in which common school teachers are posted up in the general principles of agriculture —an example worthy of imitation.

Nor is this all that those governments are doing for this branch of industry. Scattered around in various neighborhoods, are what are called experimental stations, where twelve to twenty acres are divided into small sections for experiments in fertilizers, rotation of crops, with a chemical laboratory and professor attached, and accommodations for animals, that questions of breeding, feeding and fattening may be settled. These are nurseries for professors in the secondary schools, which are supported by government. Equally thorough and comprehensive are the " building schools" in Prussia. At Holzminden, one of these has five hundred pupils; and at Neinberg, in Hanoverian Prussia, is one of the same grade for machinists and millwrights, masons, carpenters and joiners, cabinet-makers and locksmiths. France, before the war, had taken the lead in technical education. There was hardly a town which had not its school of design ; and even in Great Britain from ninety thousand to one hundred thousand pupils are annually receiving this kind of instruction.

But it is from Russia, who has been making such immense advances in developing all her resources, that we might draw the most striking example for imitation. In 1856 she founded the Imperial Agricultural Institute at Gorigoritz, embracing primary, intermediate, and superior departments. Then rapidly followed the creation of numerous establishments for the production of silk, with departments for instruction in the art; schools of horticulture, farm schools, model farms, special schools for the culture of flax, all distributed with a liberality almost profuse, over the vast territory of the empire, according to the nature of the soil and climate, and the habit and needs of the people. Then followed in quick succession the great agricultural museum at St. Petersburg, with numerous smaller ones in various parts of the country ; schools in Bessarabia, in Caucasia, and, last of all, the great Academy of Agriculture and Forestry near Moscow, to which the government makes an annual appropriation of $100,000. In Caucasia the tuition is not only made free, but small incomes are secured to meet the expenses of students. At Tiflis they have a school for teaching the applications of science to horticulture, arboriculture, bee, vine and silk culture, where they give board, lodging, clothing, and books to a limited number of pupils, with $40 for the first year, $64 for the second, $72 for the third, and $80 for the fourth and last year ; and all this does not adequately illustrate the spirit and energy with which the government is pushing forward the noble work of educating the agricultural classes.

We will now trace the progress of Agricultural Education in our own country.

Hon. G. M. Pinney, who has given an admirable summary of the movement, its importance, its aim and scope, in his noble pamphlet on the New Education, says:

> The political considerations which dictate a course of thorough education for our agriculturists, are quite as important as any which are connected with the subject as a pursuit. Our farmers should understand our government as well as our soil. They should be as capable of comprehending human as natural laws, and should know how the evils of state are to be remedied, as well as the evils of their crops. It is this sort of an education that our government is seeking to introduce through the various colleges which have been established by its munificence.
>
> These classes, which perform so important an office in all the industrial enterprises of our State and country, cannot discharge a higher or holier duty for humanity in this age, than to see that the object of Congress in the "New Education" is accomplished. They alone, can do it. The reform is in their hands. If it fails to realize all that is promised for it—all the most sanguine expectations of its founders, the blame will be theirs. It is emphatically a trust confided to their intelligence and energy.

One of the first, if not the very first definite movement toward the endowment of agricultural colleges, was a presentation of a memorial from the Pacific Coast to the Congress of 1853, by Warren & Son, in the Senate, and there approved and unanimously referred to the Committee on Education. It ably set forth the agricultural capacity of California, its growing importance as an agricultural State, and the unexampled facilities afforded for every department of agricultural education. It attracted respectful attention from eminent friends of agriculture in the Eastern States. Our greatest men had already urged the consecration of our public lands to the education of the people. Europe had moved in the establishment of agricultural and mechanical schools; Congress had given those liberal endowments to "higher seminaries of learning" in the younger States, on which the noble universities of Michigan, Wisconsin, Iowa and others, are founded. But nothing was done to elevate our industries through education until July, 1862, when Congress, under the sound of hostile cannon, legislated into being, the great comprehensive system of industrial and scientific education, a system which was to give dignity to labor, and "knit into its very core" practical with theoretical knowledge of all the sciences and arts bearing upon agriculture and mechanic arts. The measure had met with violent opposition from "optimists, pessimists, sham economists, hold-backs and do-nothings." Buchanan had killed it once with a veto, but at last our statesmen carried it through, and Morrill's bill, with Abraham Lincoln's signature, became one of the significant facts of our national history.

Colleges crowded forward to avail themselves of the grant. Denominational schools of all stripes and colors insisted upon dividing and sharing in its benefits. Twenty different institutions presented their claims to it in the New York Legislature alone. There was great danger that the benefits of the grant would be lost between the army of speculators in public lands and the army of obstructionists to the educational ideas it embodied, a danger not yet averted. Reckless waste and gross violation of public trust, had in many States attended the administration of the seminary lands. It was feared that this would prove true of the Agricultural College grant also. In every Western State a handful of men stood between these two fires, under every conceivable form of secret opposition and open hostility, to hold this precious legacy inviolate; and that they have so far succeeded is due to the fact that they appealed directly to the common sense of the people.

The first section of the Act of Congress (approved July 22, 1862) "donating public lands to the several States and Territories which may provide colleges for the benefit of agriculture and the mechanic arts," provides that a quantity of land equal to 30,000 acres for each Senator and Representative of the State in Congress be given for the purpose named. Section two prescribes how the land shall be apportioned, located and sold. Section three, that all expenses should be paid by the States to which the lands belong. Section four provides:

> That all moneys derived from the sale of the lands aforesaid by the States to which the lands are apportioned, and from the sales of land scrip hereinbefore provided for, shall be invested in stocks of the United States, or of the States, or some other safe stocks, yielding not less than five per centum upon the par value of said stocks; and that the money so invested shall constitute a perpetual fund, the capital of which shall remain forever undiminished (except so far as may be provided in Section five of this Act), and the interest of which shall be inviolably appropriated, by each State which may take and claim the benefit of this Act, to the endowment, support and maintenance of at least one College, where the leading object

shall be, without excluding other scientific and classical studies, and including military tactics, to teach such branches of learning as are related to agriculture and the mechanic arts, in such manner as the Legislatures of the States may respectively prescribe, in order to promote the liberal and practical education of the industrial classes in the several pursuits and professions in life.

There can be no doubt that Congress meant to endow schools that would bear the same relation to those pursuits that schools of law and medicine do to those professions. As far as this is done, the results are all that could reasonably be expected. Where they are managed in the interests of other pursuits, as in our own case, they are not eminent successes. The question as to who is to blame can easily be settled by inquiring who has the responsibility; for in a matter like this, ignorance is not a valid plea. Farmers and mechanics must take the management of institutions, designed for their benefit, into their own hands, if they would have them succeed. No other classes are or can be so deeply interested in their success.

The average time since the opening of the thirty-nine Agricultural Colleges, enjoying the national benefaction, is less than five years. Twenty-four of them had, two years ago, an attendance of 2,604 students, with 321 instructors—an average of 109 and 12.3, respectively; while the 217 old institutions (from 30 to 100 years old) which reported their collegiate and past graduate students, in the same year, had 20,866, and 3,018 instructors, an average of 95 and 13.8, respectively. They have called out State and individual donations to a very large amount. Thirteen of them have thus received $2,923,550. Eighteen, not including the richest, Cornell, possess property and funds to the amount of $8,272,382. Neither is it true that nineteen twentieths of their graduates never take to agriculture for a living.

Massachusetts is not an agricultural State, but she says of the fifty-seven graduates of her Agricultural College: "A large portion of them have engaged in agricultural and horticultural pursuits." Michigan says of her sixty-seven graduates: "A large portion of them have devoted themselves to agricultural pursuits." Maine, Massachusetts, Michigan, Iowa, are making educated farmers by the hundreds in Agricultural Colleges, separated from the overpowering influence of literary and purely scientific education. The difference in results is in the omission of the practical, for the quality and quantity of theoretical instruction is nearly the same in both cases. And more than all, the difference is in the spirit of the administrative or directing power of the institutions.

The Agricultural College of Alabama has two hundred acres of land, good college buildings and apparatus, one hundred and three students, thirty-nine of whom are pursuing agricultural and mechanical studies.

Arkansas Industrial University has a farm of one hundred and sixty acres, and one hundred and eighty-three students, of whom fifty are in the agricultural and mechanical course.

Illinois Industrial University had in 1873 an experimental farm of two hundred and thirteen, and a model farm of four hundred and ten acres, with three hundred and eighty-one students—males, three hundred and twenty-eight; females, fifty-three. In agricultural course, sixty-eight; architectural, four; chemical, fourteen; civil engineering, forty-five; commercial, four; electric, eighty-four; horticultural, eleven; literature and science, forty-four; mechanical engineering, thirty-three; military, fifteen; mining engineering, three; unassigned, forty-five.

The Agricultural College of Indiana has a farm of one hundred and eighty-four acres.

Iowa Agricultural College has a farm of seven hundred and ten acres, devoted to nearly all kinds of fruits, shrubs, grains, and stock, and has two hundred and sixty-five students. The graduating class for 1872 contained twenty-six, of whom seventeen were in the agricultural course.

Kansas Agricultural College has two hundred and sixty acres, devoted to nearly all kinds of fruits, grains, stock, etc., suited to that latitude, with two hundred students under practical instruction.

Kentucky Agricultural College has two hundred and twenty-five acres of land, with fine stock, fruit, etc., and two hundred and seventeen students. Nineteen twentieths of all the labor on the farm is done by the students, for which they receive pay. Live stock on the farm is valued at five thousand dollars; crop valuation, five thousand dollars.

Maryland Agricultural College has a fine farm, animals, fruits, grains, etc., and one hundred and forty-seven students.

Massachusetts Agricultural College has three hundred and eighty-four acres, upon which was raised, in 1873, four hundred and eighty bushels shelled corn, five hundred bushels potatoes, forty-eight tons sugar beets, one hundred bushels rye, fifty bushels barley, three hundred bushels of oats, two tons of millet, three hundred tons of apples, and two hundred and eight tons hay, produced by one hundred and seventy-one students, laboring six hours each week on the farm, during intervals of study, under practical instruction.

The Institute of Technology, at Boston, has three hundred and fifty-six students.

The Agricultural College of Michigan has a good farm, well cultivated, and devoted to the various grains, fruits, plants, etc. Special attention given to the improved varieties of stock, cattle, sheep, and hogs. Number of students, one hundred and thirty-one, who perform four fifths of the farm labor.

Minnesota College of Agriculture and Mechanical Arts has a good farm under cultivation. Number of students, three hundred and fifty-four; of this number, one hundred and seventeen were pursuing agricultural or mechanical studies.

The College of Agricultural and Mechanical Arts, Mississippi, has one hundred and ten acres of land; forty-two students receive practical instructions from the Professor of Agriculture.

Missouri Agricultural and Mechanical College has six hundred acres, well cultivated; the best varieties of blooded stock; has raised large quantities of corn, oats, potatoes, hay, grapes, etc. Number of students, three hundred and twenty-two, who are instructed in practical agriculture, and have performed three fourths of the labor on the farm.

The College of Agriculture, University of Nebraska, has a farm of four hundred and eighty acres. Number of students, one hundred and thirty, with twenty-five in agricultural department.

Dartmouth College has four hundred and eight students. The Commissioner of Agriculture says: "The number of students in this college has nearly doubled during the present year," (1873.) Whether this increase is attributable, in any degree, to the establishment of the College of Agriculture and Mechanic Arts with the College proper, he does not say.

The Scientific School and School of Agriculture, New Brunswick, New Jersey, has fifty students.

Cornell University Agricultural College, New York, has a

farm of two hundred acres, well cultivated, raising, already, all kinds of fruits, grains, etc., common to the climate. Number of students, five hundred and twenty-five; two hundred and seven in the agricultural department.

In Oregon, the Agricultural College has one hundred and sixty-five students, with twenty-two in the Department of Agriculture and Mechanics.

The Agricultural College of Pennsylvania has a very fine college farm of three hundred acres, and three experimental farms, each containing one hundred acres. The course of study has been scientific, experimental, and practical. Number of students, one hundred and fifty.

The University of Wisconsin has five hundred and seventeen students; ninety-three in the agricultural, and one hundred and thirty-nine in the female college.

From the foregoing, it would appear that the agricultural colleges of the various States have been a success, when consideration is taken of the time they have been organized, and the prejudice existing in many of our higher institutions of learning, not only against labor, agricultural or mechanical, but also against the establishment of agricultural colleges, as such, in which the farmer and mechanic might receive a thoroughly scientific and practical education for his calling. In our opinion, the indisputable facts herein contained, from such a source, should settle this question of success beyond controversy. As an example of good faith in the management, and sound common sense in the application of the grant to its purposes, we quote from the Hand-Book of the Kansas State Agricultural College:

1. We understand, the "industrial classes" to embrace all those whose vocations or pursuits ordinarily require a greater exercise of manual or mechanical, than of purely mental labor. It is impossible to draw a sharply defined line between the industrial and professional classes, for every occupation demands both mental and manual effort. But for the purpose of marking the general boundaries, which in our opinion, should divide agricultural from other colleges, we accept the recognized distinction between the mechanic or industrial, and the liberal arts as given by Webster; the industrial arts are those in which the hands and body are more concerned than the mind, the liberal arts are those in which the mind and imagination are chiefly concerned.

2. While not necessarily ignoring other and minor objects, the leading and controlling object of these institutions should be to teach such branches of learning as are related to agriculture and

the mechanic arts. Prominence should be given to those branches in the degree in which they are actually used by the farmer or mechanic.

3. As against the opinion that the aim of these colleges should be to make thoroughly educated men, we affirm that their greater aim should be to make men thoroughly educated farmers, and for three reasons: First—A student may receive the highest scholastic education afforded by universities, and yet know nothing of practical farming. Second—Although we hold that the mental faculties are as well disciplined by the mastery of those sciences which relate most directly to agriculture as by the study of any other branches of learning, and therefore that mental development can as truly be gained in agricultural as in other colleges; yet we affirm, that their greater aim should be to teach the farmer how best to apply the truths of science in the management of his farm, and how most to profit thereby. Third—The primary aim of literary colleges is and has been for centuries, to discipline the mind, other purposes being secondary. The doors of these noble institutions are open alike to the children of the industrial and professional classes. It is therefore neither necessary, economical or wise for the State to maintain an agricultural college which shall seek to do the same thing for the same purpose.

For the purpose of defining the policy of the Board of Regents of the Kansas State Agricultural College, and as a guide to the faculty in preparing a curriculum, it was—

Resolved, That the object of the institution is to impart a liberal and practical education to those who desire to qualify themselves for the actual practice of agriculture, the mechanic trades, or industrial arts. Prominence shall be given to agriculture and these arts in the proportion that they are severally followed in the State of Kansas. Prominence shall be given to the several branches of learning which relate to agriculture and the mechanic arts, according to the directness and value of their relation.

The difference between the line pursued in Kansas and that of the other Agricultural Colleges seems to be: They take as an objective point the graduation of agricultural experts, who shall act as missionaries to working farmers; the Kansas College makes its objective point the graduation of a capable farmer, able to make his living by farming. Their theory is that of the Normal School, training teachers who shall instruct scholars; the Kansas theory is that of training the scholar. Along the mechanical branch they seek to graduate master-builders or superintendents of machine shops; the Kansas College, to graduate intelligent and skillful carpenters, masons, and blacksmiths. The former strike for the industries considered the highest, and believe that in reaching them they include all below; the latter strikes for those most commonly followed in this State, and by successfully mastering them, expects to climb up to the rarest, because, with them, where five agricultural scientists can make a living, five thousand capable farmers can more than make a living; and where five master mechanics, or architects, can obtain employment, five times as many can command wages. The Regents and President of this remarkable college further declare, that whenever their masters, the Legislature of the State, wish the enterprise conducted upon other and antagonistic principles, "our resignations are most heartily at their service, because, whatever else may need to be tried, there is no use in repeating the experiment of flying a literary kite with an agricultural tail, so often made in various quarters; which, though a pleasant regential and professional amusement, and quite attractive to an immediate locality, has not a cent of money in it for the industrial student whose estate pays for the kite."

Whether the professional and regential amusement above referred to, of flying a literary kite with an agricultural tail, has been pursued in carrying out the provisions of the agricultural grant in California, we leave the reader to judge from the testimony of the memorial of the joint committee of Grangers and Mechanics (see pages 186–193); from the report of the joint legislative committee, and the almost unanimous expression of the friends of industrial education.

It is not a pleasant duty to point out the causes of failure, but as Mr. Gladstone said, all questions of reform are summed up in the one word, repeal; so in this case, it is necessary to show what legislation is needed to make this noble trust productive and available to the classes for whose benefit it was designed,

The share of California in the national gift was 150,000 acres of land. On her admission into the Union, California received seventy-two sections of land, which was her portion of the fund for higher seminaries of learning, and had appropriated them to the endowment and support of a University.

By Act of the Legislature, March 31, 1866, an Agricultural, Mining and Mechanical Art College, with a Board of Directors, was established. It never went into operation. The Act was repealed by the Act organizing the University, which became a law March 23, 1868.

The question of location was an important one. The committee to whom this was referred finally decided against Napa, San José, and other desirable points, in favor of Alameda county, in the neighborhood of Oakland. The final choice of a site was afterward determined by the action of the College of California.

The question arose here, as it had elsewhere: "Shall we have an independent agricultural and mechanical college, or make such colleges, with that of mining, parts of a comprehensive plan?" There appears to have been no one in California at that time to sound a warning note against the dangers of subversion, which had already appeared in older States; and though there were many enthusiastic friends of "University education," ready to bear a hand in the building of the young University, there were none to emphasize the practical features of education in agriculture and the mechanic arts.

Before and after the formal organization of the University, overtures were made to the College of California, already in successful operation in Oakland, with an able faculty and fully organized classes, to effect its disorganization and the transfer of its classes, buildings, lands, liabilities, and assets, to the new institution, in which a "College of Letters" might be co-existent, though it could not take precedence. Its property was estimated to be worth $80,000.

Its founder, Henry Durant, was the pioneer of the higher literary education on this coast. When the transfer was legally effected, on the condition of the uninterrupted continuance of its classes, there was no recognition of the eminent services of Mr. Durant to education, in the formation of the new Board; nor was the intent of the donors carried out according to their understanding of what was practicable or "in good faith" toward themselves or the people of the State. Among these trustees were some of the best educated men in the community, with a large experience and knowledge of the peculiar industrial conditions of the coast, such as Sherman Day, Henry Durant, and others. Into whose hands was the execution of this great, though "private trust," committed? A careful reading of the organic Act will show that nearly all the responsibility was thrown upon the Governor. Besides the six *ex-officio* members, there were eight appointed members "to be nominated by the Governor, by and with the consent of the Senate," and the remaining eight members were to be "chosen from the body of the State," by the official and appointed members, to hold their office for the term of sixteen years, according to classification. All vacancies were to be filled by appointments of the Governor, who did not make any appointments until after the adjournment of the Legislature, thus dispensing with confirmations. He then chose Samuel Merritt, John T. Doyle, Richard P. Hammond, John W. Dwinelle, Horatio Stebbins, Lawrence Archer, William Watt, and Samuel B. McKee.

The first meeting was held on the 19th of June, 1868, when these appointed Regents proceeded to elect Isaac Friedlander, Edward Tompkins, J. Mora Moss, S. F. Butterworth, A. J. Moulder, A. J. Bowie, Frederick F. Low, and John B. Felton. Not a single representative of the agricultural or mechanical classes appear among these names.

The first business which engaged the attention of the now complete Board was the disposition of the lands. This was put into the hands of a committee, of which Mr. Friedlander was chairman. Not long afterward Regent Friedlander resigned, and Louis Sachs, of San Francisco, was appointed in his place. On the second of March, 1869, the Board received a proposition "from a responsible party to purchase the entire tract of one hundred and fifty thousand acres for $3 50 per acre in gold."

This party was no other than the ex-Regent and chairman of the Land Committee, Mr. Friedlander, whose proposition was declined. An Act had just been passed through Congress conferring exceptional privileges upon the State of California in the matter of locating its lands.

The Board had full power under the organic Act to "locate and sell such lands for such price and on such terms as they shall prescribe."

These specialties of land location are not generally known, as no report has ever been published giving a list of the parties to whom the land certificates have been issued. It is manifestly desirable that the public should be fully informed of every point connected with the administration of the grant.

The organization of an agricultural college, therefore, became incidental to a more comprehensive plan, instead of a leading object in the very foundation. Still, the organic Act creating the University was sufficiently plain in its provisions, had they been carried out in good faith.

It provides that the College of Agriculture shall be first established; but in selecting the professors and instructors for the said College of Agriculture, the Regents shall, so far as is in their power, select persons possessing such requirements in their several vocations as will enable them to discharge the duties of professors in the several colleges of mechanic arts, of mines and of civil engineering. As soon as practicable a system of moderate manual labor shall be established in connection with the Agricultural College, and upon its agricultural and ornamental grounds, having for its object practical education in agriculture, landscape gardening, the health of the students, and to afford them an opportunity by their earnings of defraying a portion of the expenses of their education. These advantages shall be open, in the first instance, to students in the College of Agriculture, who shall be entitled to a preference in that behalf.

It further provides that the College of Mechanic Arts shall next be established, etc., and that the said Board of Regents shall always bear in mind that the College of Agriculture and the College of Mechanic Arts, are an especial object of their care and superintendence, and that they shall be considered and treated as entitled, primarily, to the use of the funds donated for their establishment and maintenance by the said Act of Congress.

It also provides that the College of Mines and the College of Civil Engineering shall be next established, etc.

It specifically provides "that the College of Letters shall be co-existent with the aforesaid College of Arts. But the provisions regarding the order in which the said colleges shall be organized, shall not be construed as directing or permitting the organization of any of the specified colleges to be unnecessarily delayed, but only as indicating the order in which the colleges shall be organized, beginning with the College of Agriculture and adding in succession to the body of instructors in that and the other colleges such other instructors as may be necessary to organize the other colleges successively in the order above indicated."

It provides "that a practical agriculturist by profession, competent to superintend the working of the agricultural farm, and of sufficient scientific acquirements to discharge the duties of Secretary of the Board of Regents, as prescribed in this Act, shall be chosen by said Board as their Secretary. The Board of Regents may also appoint a Treasurer of the University, and prescribe the form and sureties of his bond as such, which shall be executed, approved by them, and filed with the Secretary before any such Treasurer shall go into office. The Secretary and Treasurer shall be subject to summary removal by the Board of Regents."

Section 16 requires the Secretary to reside at and keep his office at the University, for important reasons hereinafter enumerated.

I feel justified in saying that the condition of the Agricultural College is not due to a defective plan of organization, as far as its educational features are concerned. Its defects lie in the extraordinary powers conferred upon the Governor and Board of Regents—powers which leave the property of the University in their hands, to be "managed, invested, re-invested, sold, transferred, and in all respects managed, and the proceeds thereof used, bestowed, invested and re-invested by the said Board of Regents," (see Section 12 of the organic Act), while (see Section 11 ditto,) "no member of the Board of Regents or of the University (perhaps this refers to the Treasurer) shall be deemed a public officer by virtue of such membership, or required to take any oath of office, but his employment as such shall be held and deemed to be exclusively a private trust."

We have thus far presented the anomaly of an institution created by a public fund, endowed from the public treasury, supported by public taxation, four of whose administrators hold their positions only as State officers, which is to all intents and purposes a private institution, beyond the reach of penalties, of the press, or of public censure for malfeasance in office.

The amended Codes provide that "the Regents may invest any of the permanent funds of the University which are now or may hereafter be in their custody in productive unincumbered real estate in this State," (see section 1415 of Political Code of California,) and that if the terms of any grant, gift, devise, or bequest are impracticable in the conditions imposed, such grant, gift, devise, or bequest shall not thereby fail, but such conditions may be rejected, and the "intent of the donor carried out as near as may be," etc. These large privileges have been exercised as freely as they were conferred. The grant of Congress to "provide colleges for the benefit of agriculture and mechanic arts," they tell us, was "really granted for the encouragement of all branches of modern scientific instruction, and was so construed in the application of it to the University of California."

Seven members of the Board constitute a quorum. Of these the Advisory Committee (five) will always be a majority, and the President is now entitled to a vote. It is easy to see, therefore, how a large body of twenty-three members may be controlled and managed by skillful combinations.

The Board of Regents, as at present constituted, is an anomaly in the history of democratic institutions. It is virtually a self-perpetuating close corporation, managing a property already worth more than a million dollars, commanding an important and constantly increasing political influence. Already the skillful dispensing of patronage has made itself felt at Berkeley. What it may become in the future requires no illustration.

It should be remembered that the State is not only the trustee of the national benefaction, but that the people have freely given of their substance, over eight hundred thousand dollars, for buildings and the maintenance of the University.

Another hindrance to the prosperity of the Agricultural College of the University is the want of land upon which to carry out farming operations on a scale commensurate with the magnitude of this interest in California. Since the sale of nearly two hundred acres of the University domain, (see page 191,) it will be impossible to exhibit the varied capacities of this State for agriculture and horticulture on the present site, or to carry out a manual labor system which will judiciously employ and train the students for their work. In nearly every other Agricultural College in the country manual labor is made obligatory, and it should be in every College, upon this foundation.

No way could be devised to give a stronger or more lasting direction to the taste of young men and women for these pursuits, than their association as students in the labors of the horticultural school and the farm. Four years of practical and theoretical training of the right kind, of such a body of students as California is even now ready to furnish, would, in my judgment, prove an incalculable benefit. It is the proper function of the public school to train the young for a respectable position in the industrial state. The Agricultural and Mechanical College should complete this training; its diploma should have a money value, as a certificate of educated power. This cannot be done without means and appliances for the acquirement of skill. "This acquisition of skill requires physical labor, just as the acquisition of science requires mental labor. Hence, physical labor should be compulsory, in the same sense and for the same purpose that mental labor is compulsory, and in no other. As long as a student feels that he is gaining either knowledge or skill that will be valuable to him as a farmer, he will work in the field, or nursery, or shop, as cheerfully as he plays, and more cheerfully than many study."

What is the education of most of our students worth on graduation day? Many a commencement occasion has brought to me only a painful sense of the utter helplessness of the young men and women graduates to make a living. I have received scores of letters from students, one, two, and three years after leaving college, asking for advice, for positions, for help in making their way in the world; for their training had only fitted them for the professions, and these are overcrowded and full. Now, suppose this training had been industrial—equal in every respect to the other, but differently directed. As a skilled mechanic, as a foreman or manager of a farm, or farmer on his own hook, he can at once command sixty dollars a month; he has not to wait from two to five years to wedge his way into a paying practice. The wages of a young man from sixteen to twenty years of age are worth, including his board, at least thirty dollars a month, or the interest on $3,600, at the rate of ten per cent. If he comes out of college a skillful mechanic or farmer, he has doubled his capital; if he has only got ready to begin the study of a profession, he has in a strictly business point of view, sunk it in a venture which may or may not reimburse him after many years. If he has made the great and almost universal mistake of studying without a definite purpose or aim, without a definite occupation to which his efforts have been constantly directed, this is almost certain to be true. As President Anderson, of the Kansas College, says: "It is time for men to look the educational question squarely in the face, and to substitute common sense for traditional and groundless sentimentality."

We are now beginning to understand that a sound mind is not to be expected in an unsound or half-developed body, and even the purely literary colleges are encouraging competitive muscularity in a way that would have caused John Harvard and Elihu Yale to shake in their shoes. What is there more interesting in a boat race than in a plowing match? Is the power ignoble which is applied to the spade or the plane, and otherwise when it holds the ball club, or boxing glove? Is it so much greater an accomplishment to say horse in half a dozen languages, than to know how to breed and care for one, until the beast has become more than half human in his beauty and intelligence? Is all the verbiage with which our schools are loaded down until physicians are crying out against the murder of the innocents, so much better than "paying knowledge to future farmers, paying skill to future mechanics, self support and God-birthed liberty to women?"

Another thing for the farmers to consider seriously in respect to the necessities of agricultural education is, that we need one institution at least free from the temptations to college extravagence, where plain living and high thinking can be illustrated in all the appointments. Extravagant buildings, which in some States have cost more than the principal of the congressional grant, no matter how they are obtained, are undesirable for our purposes and work.

President Anderson, of Kansas, once a resident of the Golden State, thus pictures his ideal of the Agricultural College of the future:

Some day, and somewhere, there will be an agricultural college looking so much like the grounds and buildings of a prosperous farmer, who did his own repairing and manufacturing, that we of the present happening by, would mistake it for a little hamlet of thriving artisans, built in the heart of rich and well-tilled fields. Nothing in its appearance would suggest our notion of the typical college. Its barns, sheds, yards and arrangements would embody the idea of the greatest utility at the least cost. Its implements, stock, and fields would show them to be used for real profit. Its orchards and gardens would not only reveal the success of the owner, but, also, his full determination to enjoy the fruit with the labor. We would be quite certain that it was only such a farm—the best specimen of the highest type—were it not for the presence of cheap, stone buildings, one or two stories, scattered among the trees; all of them more resembling mechanics' shops than anything else; some exactly, others, not exactly; and yet no two alike. One would be used for teaching practical agriculture, but would as little prompt our idea of a recitation room as the whole cluster would that of an imposing college edifice. While there would be seats for hearers, and a place for a speaker, yet the latter would most suggest a circus ring for the exhibition of short-horns, when short-horns were discussed; of horses, pigs, or sheep; of surgical operations; of plows, harrows, or reapers. The walls would be lined with photographs of famous herds, working models of farm machinery, the grain and stock of cereals. Part of its surrounding ground would be belted with every variety of growing grasses; and another would be for the draft-test of implements, or the trial of student skill. In fact, it would look, and be so like an actual workshop of real farming as not, even in the remotest way, to squint toward the article generally yclept "scientific agriculture." The interior of another shop, a few rods distant, and equally inexpensive, with its grafting-tables, potting benches, packing-room, working green-house, and, outside hot-beds and thrifty nursery grounds, would look so much like "gardening for profit" as to throw us completely off the trail of botany, as a pure science. Another would be a force shop, where light, heat, water, sound and electricity were made to reveal their laws, habits and effects, and to do their industrial work. The constant use of its appliances by busy students, in sacrilegious defiance of the rule, "Don't touch the apparatus," italicized with professional emphasis, would instantly satisfy us that there was nothing "collegiate" there, and that it was only a workshop where men had to become skillful workmen! There would be a mathematical shop, so much like a counting and drawing room, no one could be surprised when it led into an inventor's and pattern-maker's room, and its winding up in a machine-shop. There would be an English shop, remarkably like a printing-office; and the "Printer's Hand-Book" of that day might strike us an admirable drill in the art of using the English language, as well as in that of sticking type—almost as good **as** a grammar! There would be a woman's workshop, where the pale Hortense, at heart a good deal more sensible, earnest, and womanly than society supposes, would strive for the bloom and "faculty" of Mary. The blessed Mrs. Grundy would be dead! And there would be a mason's, carpenter's, and smith's shops. Not a shop of them would cost $5,000; and some, not half of it; because they would be shops, warm, light, cheerful, but *workshops*—not requiring costly foundations and tall, heavy walls, not finished as are parlors, nor wasting space in broad corridors. And they would not have been fore-ordained by men of a previous generation, who, to save the lives of the best of them, could not possibly have foretold just what buildings such a college would need. As, in the process of its growth, a want had been felt, its shop was supplied; and each generation had footed its own bills. No! it would not look like our great colleges; but very remarkably like a nest of real educational workshops, where flesh and blood students acquired marketable skill for industrial labor. In it, drill in the art would have greater prominence than the stringing of facts on the threads of a system; and the requirements of the art would serve as a skimmer to lift the cream of science as needed. Knowledge would be shoved paying end first, and not everlastingly philosophic end first. For the world has gotten back to the history of its own experience, where art was the Columbus, discovering science. In it, educational common sense would have supplanted uncommon educational nonsense. And leaving it, the newly fledged graduate, as does the newly fledged "jour.," would at once earn a living. Such an Agricultural College would be in keeping with its object, with the requirements and genius of labor, with itself! And, too, it would be in keeping with a rich, broad State, carpeted by emerald grasses, belted by golden grain, clumped with orchards, moving with herds, clustering with villages, threaded by railroads, flecked with countless smoke-offerings from the altars of industry to the god of labor.

Some day; somewhere; somehow!

CHAPTER XXVII.

THE INDUSTRIAL EDUCATION OF WOMEN.

"It is strange that a mother, educated as most mothers of the present day are, and who as wife and housekeeper has keenly felt her own ignorance of subjects that should have been taught, and her want of skill that might have been acquired, can be content to give her daughter the same unreal preparation for real life. And it is exceedingly strange that a father, long familiar with the distress suddenly wrought by financial changes, should religiously exclude from his daughter's education all knowledge of business, and every possibility of earning a woman's living, except at the needle, wash-tub, or piano."—J. A. Anderson.

Woman as an Industrialist—The Field of Domestic Life—Her Vocations as a Paid Laborer—Housekeeping as a Fine Art—Training Schools for Women in America and in Europe.

The wise man in the Book of Proverbs put a high estimate on the good housewife. He insisted that, although many daughters had done virtuously, she excelled all. Yet, as he does not mention her by name; as we have Deborah spoken of for her wisdom, or Ruth for her comeliness, or many others made prominent by their influence upon the men of the period, we take her as the representative of a class, and know from the condition of the household arts in Palestine, that a good housekeeper was almost as great a desideratum in their days as in our own. So, also, the Greeks praised the women of the hearth, though we do not know their names; while we know how Aspasia beguiled Socrates with the graces of her conversation, and that Sappho took her seat by divine right rather than by a nomination among the poets. We know that neither in Greece nor in Palestine, at a period when poets and prophets abounded, was there a home in which any of us would have willingly lived for a single week; nor was there for ages afterwards such a recognition of human rights, of the dignity of womanhood, or the sacredness of the home, as could create a progressive home-building civilization. We have seen in the earlier chapters of this work how the ancient civilizations were built upon slavery, which bore equally upon the sexes. In following the historical development of industry, we shall find that woman has at all times borne her full share of the burdens of the industrialist, in addition to those which are hers by virtue of her organic constitution.

In considering the question of her education, therefore, we should cover the whole field of her industrial and special functions, and provide whatever is needed to give her the highest possible efficiency in both. That we have been doing this in our higher schools, no reflective person will claim; and as for our public schools, our mistaken policy in them is not only injurious but alarming in its effects upon the female pupils.

"If viewed from the standpoint of actual instead of ideal life, the course of study followed in the average female seminary will logically appear as a standing wonder. It has been so long in use that the principle of it may be judged by the results actually produced. Apart from an effort to discipline the mind, which can as well be done by the acquisition of useful as of useless knowledge, its chief purpose seems to be that of furnishing intelligent playthings for men possessing exhaustless wealth." Ninety-nine out of a hundred women are called upon to do some domestic work every day of their lives, and yet not a ninety-ninth part of the girl's time is spent in preparation for it. She has a training fitted for the professional actress, preacher, astronomer, and usually leaves school without the possibility or the inclination of putting these acquirements to practical use. The uses of knowledge are not kept sufficiently before the minds of scholars of either sex, an evil which is especially hurtful to young women. Suppose, for instance, the goal to be reached by every girl in getting an education is how to prepare for doing a wife's and mother's work well and faithfully, and that every school should say, as the Kansas trustees declare with regard to their Agricultural College: "Prominence shall here be given to such branches of learning as relate to home culture and the household arts; according to the directness and value of such relation," would we not, in all human probability, work a speedy change in the results?

Again, every student in the Cornell University, whatever his aim, and to whatever college he belongs, is required to hear one full course of lectures on agriculture, on the ground of the importance of its relations to national and individual welfare. Now, suppose every school thus recognized the value of the domestic arts, and every young woman was obliged to pursue the studies bearing upon these, up to a certain point, would not this be justified by the universality of the application and use of such studies? We are aware that a mountain of prejudice must be overcome before these improvements upon our present system can be effected. A beginning has already been made. There are now five or six institutions of great merit, which have for their object the training of women as industrialists, in which everything relating to the home and family are made prominent subjects of study. These institutions, like the one in Needham, Mass., recently endowed by Mr. and Mrs. Henry Durant, by the gift of a million of dollars, are for special training of housekeepers, telegraph operators, engravers, pattern-makers, accountants, etc. They are intended to cover very different ground from the colleges and seminaries; to brighten the pale faces hurrying from attic to workshop in our large cities, with better wages for better work. But there are others still, which occupy middle ground, where those who make the loaf and those who eat it, are benefited alike. One of them, in the city of Gotha, Germany, enjoys the highest reputation on the continent of Europe, and draws pupils from Greece, Russia, Italy, and England.

Among other things its accomplished principal, Dr. Kohler, gives a series of what are called lecture conversations upon the science of domestic economy. We daily witness events where men, supposed to be worth millions of dollars, are stricken with bankruptcy as with the palsy, and reduced to poverty; and the evil results of such a calamity are often needlessly increased by an utter ignorance on the part of wives and daughters of the purchasing value of money and its uses as applied to household affairs. An American educator says:

We were present in the Kohler School, at Gotha, at several of these interesting lectures, in which the professor discussed with his pupils every phase of domestic economy. For the purpose of affording to American teachers the opportunity of fathoming its scope, and simply as an illustration of method, and not for the absolute value of the suggestions, we shall quote one of the lectures in detail:

"Young ladies," says the professor, "suppose that you had to keep house, either as a wife or as a daughter, and that the family consisted of two grown members and three children, and that the income was twelve hundred dollars a year, how would you spend it to the greatest advantage and comfort? If you had to reside in a rented dwelling, what kind of a house could you afford to lease? What proportion of this twelve hundred dollars, in justice to all other necessities and requirements, should be expended for rent? What number of rooms are essential? Would a garden be an advantage; and, if so, how large? What are the prices of house rent in the city of Gotha?"

This field of inquiry seemed to be entirely new, and few pupils were prepared to answer. The professor then said: "Make inquiries; let us know how many rooms a family so circumstanced could afford, so as not to entrench too largely upon other necessary expenditures."

The next inquiry of importance is the question of nourishment. The professor said: "Ladies, for to-day's dinner,"—many of the pupils being boarders,—"as you know, we had rice soup, beef, and vegetables, for the first course; sausage and potatoes for the second; and pudding for dessert; can you tell me what was the cost of that dinner per person?" They could not. "What is the price of beef? What is the price of potatoes?" They did not know. "For to-day I will excuse you; but when we take up this subject again, you must be better informed. Inquire of your mothers or friends, for it is of importance to you to know the values of the necessities of life."

Coming back to the initial point, the annual income, the conversational lecture involved a thorough sifting of the details. Its chief value lay in its minute examination, so that every pupil could make either an additional inquiry or relevant suggestion. After a thorough canvass of the house-rent question, the conclusion was reached that a family, with the income specified, could afford one hundred and fifty dollars per annum for house-rent in that city. In other words, after surveying the whole field, the conclusion was reached that one hundred and fifty dollars house-rent would be a proper proportion of the whole expenditure, and that any considerable increase in that direction would tend to diminish the comfort of the family in matters equally essential.

The discussions of the questions of proper nourishment and its relations to price, health, and comfort, were continued through a number of sessions. Not merely were the prices brought forward, but the questions: What kinds of food contain the most nourishment? How to secure a reasonable variety consistently with economy? and how various dishes can be prepared and waste prevented? were treated in the same suggestive and familiar manner. In fact, these conversations were so genial, and withal so dignified, so pleasant, and, for girls, so interesting, that the pupils looked forward to them with anticipations of both pleasure and profit. Questions were submitted by pupils, and the zest with which the discussion was followed up, showed that not merely was the topic in itself congenial, but that they appreciated its important relations to their future welfare. After a final and exhaustive review, it was determined that, with the existing prices of food in the city of Gotha, a family, with the income stated, could afford to spend three hundred dollars a year for food.

The next great question was the one of clothing. How shall we be clothed? The consideration of what are the chief requisites for clothing? brought out a number of answers. The first one—Germany being a cold country—was, quite naturally, that it should afford the requisite warmth and protection in winter. This was followed by the suggestions that it should be suited to the season; that it should be handsome in appearance; unchangeable in color, of firm and durable texture. The wearing apparel of the grown members of the household was first considered, and the cost of silk, woolen, linen, cotton, broadcloth, and cassimere was discussed. The relations of colors to each other, and their correspondence with the complexion of the wearer, were also discussed; and in this field the ladies were able to contribute many interesting observations.

It was finally concluded, after a number of conversations, carried on twice a week, that $300 a year would clothe the family in a neat and respectable manner. Incidentally the question of making over garments was brought up, and strange as it may seem to us, that part of the question which treated of the limits to which re-making or turning can be carried with advantage was brought prominently forward; for in that country careful women often go to the extreme of repairing and making over garments when they no longer pay for the labor expended on them.

One feature upon which the professor dwelt most emphatically was the ever-recurring incidental or extraordinary expenses of the family; and this is a matter of importance to both sexes and to all classes. The breaking of a pitcher does not happen every day, but in the aggregate there is an ever-recurring wear and tear of furniture and household goods, which, as these articles must be replaced at irregular periods, constitute what is called incidental or extraordinary expenses, though they are as truly ordinary expenses as any other. The keeping in repair of furniture and other household necessaries requires an average expenditure of $100 per annum, and $50 more may well be kept in reserve to meet the demand for literary and religious expenditures, and to provide for sickness, family presents, amusements, etc. In a growing family, $50 must be set apart for educational purposes; and the father may be considered an economic man if $50 suffices for his incidental expenses, particularly if—as in the case with most Germans—he is addicted to the use of wine and tobacco. $50 are also needed for fuel, the economic use of which, and the various kinds to be used, forms an interesting and profitable topic. Finally, the expenditures foot up as follows:

For house-rent	$150 00
For clothing	300 00
For food	300 00
For special expenditures	100 00
For extraordinary expenditures	50 00
For education	50 00
For fuel	50 00
For incidentals	50 00
Total	$1,050 00

This leaves about $150 as a savings-fund, and is as little as ought to be saved in times of prosperity; for as children grow larger, and it may be desirable to send a son to the University, and as the family may increase and times may change, no man ought to spend regularly a larger portion of his income than is here set forth.

But many men in Germany have not an income of $1,200. The great majority must live on $800, and even less. Let us, then, consider the question how a similar family can live on $800, remain out of debt, and be comfortable and respectable. The first question is, "Where can we retrench?" We must at once cut down the rent to $80 per annum. We must retrench in the article of food, but the reduction here must not be too great, because a certain amount and quality are absolutely necessary to keep the family in good working condition. It will cost us $250 at least. Then we must dress plainly; we must use simple, strong woollen goods. This will enable us to reduce this expenditure to $180. Thus all the household expenses are revised, and while enforcing previous lessons, these new discussions give to them a pleasant variety. These careful and well digested reviews of the various phases of domestic economy are exceedingly attractive to the pupils, in part, doubtless, because they can ventilate the theories—which nearly every young woman cherishes in her heart of domestic life.

In this manner a young woman becomes so thoroughly acquainted with the demands and details of domestic economy that she has well defined ideas, based upon reality and reflection. Far from encouraging the husband or father—the purchasing power of whose income she knows—in extravagance, or in the waste of money in some particular direction, to the diminution of other necessary comforts, she will be prepared to resist temptation herself, and to give sufficient reasons why the income should not be misdirected.

Instead of looking upon marriage as a New Jerusalem, where troubles cannot intrude, she is prepared to bear her share of the great responsibilities and to assume a portion of its ever-increasing cares. Thus the woman becomes self-poised, firm in character, ready to adapt herself to the varying changes of fortune, and to meet with courage the vicissitudes of life. Her children will also be taught that frugality and economy, with the careful use of clothing and household goods, furnish the only true way to prosperity.

Is not the average woman, when thus thoroughly equipped with a large store of practical information, better fitted to be a successful wife and mother, than if her time had been taken up exclusively with the study of geography, mathematics, grammar, and history? will she not be better prepared to avoid the danger of bankruptcy of her husband, and the terrible and harrowing course of "keeping up appearances," in which every comfort is sacrificed to the supposed requirements of social position?

We all know that the happiness of married life is worn out by the ever-recurring annoyances of little things. "Empty pots are filled with contention," is a proverb, in substance, of many nations, and the divorce courts are often called in as a last resort—and a most terrible one they are—when the struggle between impecuniosity on the one hand, and desires for extravagant expenditures on the other, have turned the love of early days into gall and wormwood.

In view of these facts, so common that they must have come under the observation of all, it is to be hoped that these features of special female education will receive full and fair discussion, so that these new studies, with such modifications as experience shall suggest, may be introduced into our high schools and academies for advanced female pupils.

We are the more certain that these methods are deserving of recognition and adoption, because the schools of the city of Gotha enjoy a high reputation upon the continent. The seminary for the education of male teachers and the common schools, under the zealous care of school director, Dr. Mobius, and the Kindergarten seminary, under Dr. Kohler, have earned so great a reputation that pupils from Greece, Russia, Hungary, and England, in increasing numbers, are being matriculated. This reputation for thorough and useful training is, moreover, based upon an unselfish devotion and a love for the cause, as rare as it is delightful.*

With the foundation thus indicated, it is easy to see how a young woman may be prepared to make the most of her resources; and not less, but all the more fully, should she be trained who has thousands, instead of hundreds, at her command, and whose duty it manifestly is to employ and adequately repay the labor of others less favored. Equally with the poorest does she need to be taught how to order her home without waste, discord, or confusion; to use upon it the fine artistic taste developed by the highest culture, and to apply scientific principles to the relief of necessary labor from what is mere drudgery.

In several of the institutions deriving their support from the grant of Congress, these principles are so far recognized as to require that their benefits shall be equal to both sexes, though not necessarily alike. A school of domestic science is one of the departments of the Illinois Industrial University, and in Nebraska the remunerative labor system encourages the young women to carry on the housework under competent supervision, in a way that does not retard their intellectual progress. "It is just as feasible to give practice in cooking with pleasure and profit to the pupil, as it is to give laboratory practice in chemistry, and no more expensive."

Many of the specialties which should be adequately provided for in an agricultural college are especially adapted to fit woman for her position as an industrialist, such as bee-keeping, silk culture, the culture and preservation of small fruits, floriculture, and the related industry of extracts and perfumes, dairy management, poultry management, etc., etc. Through the efforts of women in the Grange it is to be hoped an influence may be brought to bear upon our educational system; introducing such changes as are needed to fit the daughters of California for wife or motherhood; which, by making each of them the mistress of some industrial art, will, perchance, enable them to keep a roof

* Report of Bureau of Education for 1874.

over their heads in widowhood, and which will honorably secure the single woman from the temptations of dependence. What is true of employments related to agriculture is equally true of the adaptation of many in the mechanical range, which, under a wise re-distribution of labor, would naturally be assigned to women. A paying knowledge of drawing, painting, engraving, of photography and stenography, and of telegraphy, will be given to "our girls" in the College of Mechanic Arts whenever the true design of the Congressional endowment is realized.

CHAPTER XXVIII.

PAPER MONEY AND A PROTECTIVE TARIFF.

"I do hereby invite all farmers east and west, all Grangers north and south, and all other true men, to unite with me in raising a cry that shall pierce the dulled ears of our rulers—an honest cry for an honest dollar."—*Professor A. L. Perry, before Nebraska Agricultural Society.*

False Lights—General Principles—What Currency is—Legislation Required—Professor Perry's Views—Dialogue between Bonamy Price and the New York Capitalists—Origin of Tariffs—Effects of Protection upon Agricultural Industry—Tariffs Take but never Give.

A true, clear and comprehensive definition of the terms in daily use, in which the various relations of money are considered, is the first step toward an understanding of the many problems connected with our system of finance.

We have brought together, in this chapter, several of the most recent and pertinent discussions upon our currency, and nearly related subjects. Many of our writers upon political economy are more like astrologers, than astronomers or teachers of true science; they are seeking for a philosopher's stone, which will transmute not only the baser metals, but rags into gold. We have endeavored to make such selections from eminent authorities as shall least confuse the mind of the reader.

Mr. Charles Sears lays down the following propositions concerning money:

Material wealth is a symbol of social power. Equitable distribution of wealth through equivalent exchange is evidence of social health. Equivalent exchange is the natural law of exchange and is essential to the permanence of society. Money is a representative sign of wealth—a symbol of common title by which ownership of property is transferred. It is evidence of property; the equivalent of exchange. Therefore, the true basis of monetary issue is property;

not one commodity only, as gold, nor credit, nor population, but all commodities—the entire taxable property of the commonwealth. Money having this basis would be representative money, the money of the people, the sovereign money. The volume of money required for producing, utilizing and exchanging property is necessarily determined by the same law which governs production and exchange, viz., demand for use. Enough money for equivalent exchange is the law of volume. Therefore, arbitrary limitation of the volume of money is a violation of the natural law of exchange, and is void of right, as would be a like limitation of production and exchange. Arbitrary limitation of the volume of money has been the principal measure of class power to secure the monopoly of money; a necessary result of such limitation has been forced credits. Credit is the immediate parent of bankruptcy, and periods of bankruptcy have been the harvest times of the money monopolists. Therefore, arbitrary limitation of money issue should cease.

The right of monetary issue is a sovereign right, to be held and maintained by the people for the common benefit. The delegation of this right to corporations is the surrender of the central attribute of sovereignty; is void of constitutional sanction; is conferring upon a subordinate irresponsible power and plenary dominion over industry and commerce. Therefore, the people should resume their right over the issue and circulation of money.

Value is determined by agreement between parties to exchange, and the final standard of value is use. Gold is not the standard of value, but like other commodities, its value depends upon its power of exchange.

The legal dollar is a certain measure or counter of value. Its weight, twenty-five and eight tenths grains of gold, nine tenths fine, is the standard weight and quality of the monetary unit.

The volume of gold and the purchasing power of the dollar vary widely, as do those of other commodities. The use of gold in payment of interest upon national debt, and in adjusting balances of trade between nations, confer upon it the character of universal or international money. These uses, use in the arts and private hoarding, absorb nearly the entire volume, leaving little available for domestic exchange, and are reasons conclusive against making gold the sole basis of national or domestic money.

Promissory notes are evidences of debts. Such notes are not money, and the attempt to circulate them as money is an attempt to evade the force of the natural law, which has necessarily resulted in failure. Such notes were spurious tokens, and their proffered use as money should be prohibited.

A currency is inflated when the volume issued exceeds that of its basis. The so-called "specie basis currency" notes, promissory of specie payment, have been issued "nominally in the ratio of four dollars currency to one dollar coin, supposed to be in bank; but, in fact, six dollars of currency to one dollar of coin." The paper currency of the past, therefore, has been inflated to the extent of five hundred per cent.

A currency is redeemable when all of it can be redeemed in the substance signified or thing promised; therefore, with only one dollar of coin to redeem six dollars of promissory notes, the specie basis currency was always an irredeemable currency, and has so proved upon the general demand for liquidation whatever may have been the disproportion of coin to currency, five sixths of it in later years having been pure fiction, analogous to certificate for large sums against which there is no deposit. This currency was never the equivalent of exchange. It represented corporate monopoly, and its issue was a fraud, which has wrought destruction to the values of labor, property and commerce; therefore, the authority to issue such inflated, irredeemable, fraudulent currency should be abrogated.

Certificates of actual specie deposits are the only honest, redeemable specie basis currency. The exchange of property for representative money is equivalent exchange; is giving specie property for a title to any property of equal value; is redemption of such money in the substance represented; is accomplishing the primary object of money. The redemption of such money by government for taxes and dues, is equitable public redemption. The optional interchange of representative money, and public bonds bearing equitable interest will be the regulator of currency volume, and prevent artificial expansion and contraction. It will leave the currency free to expand and contract in accordance with the industrial demand. If at any time the volume be insufficient, bonds will be surrendered for money; while any temporary excess of money will be retired in favor of bonds, so that only the volume required for active use will be kept in circulation, and the speculative centers will not be gorged with idle money.

Evils specially incident to our finances, industries and commerce, are due to the want of a rational theory of monetary issue, a simple system of financial administration. The erroneous assumption that gold is the standard of value, and the consequent futile attempts to maintain a four-fold paper currency at par with gold, and the creation of an overwhelming national monopoly by surrendering to corporate power the public right of issuing currency, have made the empirical interference of government with the natural laws of production and exchange, a constant necessity, ending in perpetual failure.

Acts of Congress are required as follows: An act instituting a complete domestic monetary system, providing in such act for the issue of public currency representative of property and redeemable on demand in public bonds, and for the issue of public bonds, payable on demand and in public currency; such currency to be legal tender, non-interest bearing money, and receivable at par for all public dues, and such bonds to bear interest not to exceed three and sixty-five hundredths per cent. per annum, and the bonds and currency to liquidate other forms of the public debt. An act repealing all grants of authority to corporations, associations, or individuals to issue money. An act to prohibit the issue of notes promissory of specie payment, to circulate as money, other than certificates of specie deposit.

Professor Arthur L. Perry, of Williams College, a well known teacher, and authority on Political Economy, says:

The greatest foe the farmers of this country have had for the past dozen years has been the paper money. There is nothing mysterious about a silver dollar. There is nothing magical about it. It is just so much silver metal stamped, but the stamp adds only a slight fraction to its value. It took honest labor to get this silver out of the earth, refine, alloy, and coin it, and therefore it is just the thing to help exchange other things that have cost honest labor. This dollar is just like a bushel of wheat; it has cost something; it is adapted to a human want, and therefore it is good for something. Labor for labor is the law of exchange, and therefore the dollar that has cost labor is the only honest dollar. It is the only dollar about which there is no trick. It is the only dollar that defrauds nobody. It is a real equivalent. It is indeed only a tool to help exchange other things, but it is an honest tool. We take it only to part with it again, but when we take it we get an equivalent for what we give, and when we part with it we give an equivalent for what we get. Money is indeed a medium to exchange other things with, but it is of vast consequence that the medium be a good medium, a real medium, an intelligible medium, a medium that gives no advantage in the exchange to either party.

Moreover, this silver dollar is the same thing year in and year out. The first silver dollar was coined in this country in 1794, just eighty years ago, and there was put into it 371¼ grains of pure silver, and that quantity of pure silver has been put into every dollar coined since; so that, so far as the word dollar has depended on the silver coin of that name, (and the same principles of course apply to the gold dollar,) the word has had a steady significance. Men knew what they were talking about when they were bargaining in dollars. The thing dollar was a perfectly definite thing, and consequently the denomination dollar was a steady denomination. In values you reckon in dollars just as in grains you reckon in bushels. Gold and silver money give you steady denomination dollars to reckon in, to bargain by, to make calculations with. As things, dollars are a medium to exchange other things with; as denominations, dollars are a measure of all other values whatsoever; and it is impossible to have steady denominations unless you have steady coin dollars behind them.

I now hold in my hand a so-called paper dollar. It is not a dollar at all. It is only a promise to pay a dollar. Read it and you will see that it is so: "The United States will pay to bearer one dollar." It carries the truth upon its very face. It is only a promise. Unfortunately, also, it is a promise that has not been kept. It is an unfulfilled promise. Worse than that, it is a promise that the promiser refuses to fulfill. It is a broken promise. It is a dishonest promise. It is failed paper. Because it is an unfulfilled promise, it is of course worth less than that which it promises to pay. It is depreciated. It always has been depreciated, and it is depreciated now. It has been at times very much depreciated. Now, we have seen that the dollar as a thing is a medium helping exchange all other things, and also that the dollar as a denomination is a measure measuring all other values. But a measure of other things should itself be uniform. A bushel measure should be the same thing year in and year out—to buy and sell by. A yard-stick should be thirty-six inches long, no more and no less, made of solid material that just holds its own, and not of india rubber, expansible and contractible, of one length to-day and another to-morrow, and nobody knows what length the next time.

This very dollar bill has fluctuated in value as compared with a gold dollar all the way from thirty-five cents up to ninety-three cents and a fraction; and yet, we have been calling it a dollar all the while; we have been estimating our property in these dancing dollars; we have been buying when the dollar was at one value, and selling when it has been at another; a bushel measure holding three pecks at one time, four pecks at another time, and five pecks at another, is much more sensible than such a variable dollar, inasmuch as the bushel only measures grain, while the dollar, in the way of estimate, bargain, or sale, attempts to measure all values whatsoever. During the year 1873 there was a variation of thirteen per cent. in the value of this paper dollar as compared with gold—from one hundred and six and one half to one hundred and nineteen and one half, and now almost back again. These constant fluctuations in paper money—and they are inherent in it unless the paper is instantly convertible into gold—make it abominable as a measure of value for everybody, and particularly for farmers. An inconvertible paper money always depreciated and always variable is worse for farmers than for almost anybody else; first, on the ground of its depreciation, and second, on the ground of its variability. As the value of money goes down, of course general prices tend to rise; but, unfortunately, they do not rise equally, nor in equal times; and some prices do not rise at all. For example, manufactured goods are quickest to experience a rise of price owing to a depreciation of the currency, because as a rule manufacturers are intelligent men, and know the tendency of depreciated money to depreciate more, and thus hasten to insure themselves by putting a higher price on their goods. Wages rise much more slowly than goods, and never proportionably, because laborers do not well understand the situation, and never act quickly enough to insure themselves; and so they are always great sufferers from a depreciated money. Real estate rises slowly and irregularly, though at times tumultuously, under such money, and never on the average so high as manufactured goods rise; while agricultural products, some parts of which are exported to foreign countries, scarcely rise in price at all. The reason for this is, that the foreign gold price of that part which is exported largely determines the home price of the whole crop. There is only one wholesale price of wheat of the same grade in New York city, whether it is for export or whether it is for home consumption. The gold price in Liverpool determines the currency price in New York just so long as any wheat is exported; and the price in New York determines the price in Chicago and Omaha. If the premium on gold, in consequence of the use of a depreciated currency, were as high as the average rise of prices arising from that depreciation, it would not be so unjust; but it never is; gold is generally the cheapest thing a-going, so soon as an inferior currency has demonetized it and thrown it out of demand; and the whole consequence to farmers of the use of such a poor money is, that they have to pay a great deal more for all that they need to buy, and only get a little more or nothing at all for all that they have to sell. Wheat was no higher in currency in 1873 than it was in gold in 1860; hams were not; lard was not; and salt pork was not. These are all exportable agricultural products whose current price is determined by the gold money of the world's great market. These things are what farmers sell. But harnesses, boots and shoes, hats and caps, blankets, all manner of clothing, were much higher in 1873 than they were in 1860. These manufactures are what farmers have to buy. The mischief of paper money is, that it affects different classes differently, and the largest class the most injuriously of all. It raises some prices much, other prices little, and still other prices not at all. Some prices are raised quickly and pretty regularly, and other prices are raised slowly and irregularly; so that the shrewd ones always take advantage of the ignorant ones, and the dishonest ones of the honest ones. The whole trick of the thing is a trick of distribution. Some men may get rich out of it, but this is always at the expense of other men. All classes of the people are ultimately great losers in wealth and reputation from the destruction of the staple measure of value—from disturbing the meaning of the word dollar. A huge crop of defaulters, and of failures, and of bursted speculations, and of ruined reputations, are always the harvest of that sowing. But farmers always have been and always will be the greatest losers from rag-money; partly for the reason that I have just given, namely, that what they have to buy is enhanced in price by it, while what they have to sell is not enhanced in price by it; and partly, also, because it takes the farmer almost a year to realize on his crops, and he cannot meanwhile insure himself against the inevitable changes in the currency. The dollar in which he calculates the expenses of his crop is almost sure not to be the dollar in which he realizes the results of his crops. He cannot calculate. He cannot insure himself. He is helpless. The manufacturer who turns off his product weekly or monthly can vary his prices weekly or monthly, and save himself at least in part; but the farmer, poor man, can do no such thing. He is at the mercy of currency-tinkers, because all our paper money is only a promise to pay, and an unfulfilled promise at that; because it is depreciated far below the solid money of the world's market; because it is variable in value from day to day and from year to year, unsettling the measure of all other values; because such money always stimulates speculation and hampers productive industry; because it corrupts public morals, undermines honesty, and makes defaulters, by destroying the staple standard of value; because it unjustly distributes the rewards of industry, and cheats by wholesale the whole farming interests, and because such money has always been followed by these results wheresoever the experiment of using it has been tried.

Professor Bonamy Price fills the chair of Political Economy, in Oxford, England. In the year 1869, he issued what is regarded in Europe as the standard work on the "Problems of Currency."

During the autumn of 1874. he visited the United States, and was eagerly questioned by the bankers and capitalists of the East, with reference to his views on American Finance. The following, concerning the same, is taken from the "New York Tribune:"

Q. Professor Price, what do you think of the currency of the United States?

A. Simply that it is a shocking bad currency. But mind, if a currency is thoroughly convertible I don't think it is of great importance that there should be a large stock of gold. Provided the currency is issued by an issuer who is perfectly safe, thoroughly responsible for the debt, the public won't ask gold in exchange for his notes. They would rather have the notes. In Scotland at this moment a one-pound note is distinctly preferred to a sovereign. It is carried about much more easily; it has got a number upon it and it does its works perfectly. It is of the same value as a sovereign, and that implies that it is convertible. If that is only so a country may go on with very little gold and almost all paper, when the latter is of equal value with the former.

Q. Suppose the three great nations, England, France, and Germany, should all adopt the principle of using little coin, where is the gold they now use going to? What is to become of it?

A. The effect would be that gold would undoubtedly become cheaper. It would all flow back into the stores and shops and be locked up. It would be a large mass of property for which there was no use. The owners of this gold would have to do precisely as owners of notes would do—sell cheaper. In the case of currency it is not that metal should be worth one shilling of twenty shillings, but that its value should not be changeable; but a fifteen-shilling sovereign, or a ten-shilling sovereign, is just as good as a twenty. The only trouble is, that for the same business you carry twice the weight.

Q. As a matter of fact these three nations—England, France, and Germany—by adopting the course this county has, can sink the value of gold one-half?

A. On the other hand, you must remember that if it had not been for California and Australia, it is quite certain the price of gold must have gone up, and why? Because the world has opened so desperately fast. There are so many more people and so many more wants. In all those old countries they cannot deal with paper. The Russian will not take American greenbacks, nor in the very heart of Russia will they take English notes. You must pay in gold. But to come back to America. One very favorable circumstance in America is that the very ignorance of the people makes them more receptive of first principles than people in England. The English bankers are doing so well that they detest of all things any inquiries as to the nature of their business. Now here you are in trouble about your currency, and there is a receptivity of first principles which is to me very attractive.

Q. Suppose you were to propose legislation on the subject of the currency, what step would you advise?

A. I would take measures steadily to make the currency fulfill its only end—the exchanging of goods—and that embraces every idea and object connected with the currency.

Q. You consider it a fundamental principle that paper should be convertible into specie on demand?

A. As I have said before, inconvertible currency is so vicious, so radically bad, that I feel no interest in makeshifts. There is only one step to be taken—amputation.

Q. That is to say, contraction?

A. That is not contraction, but the extinction of inconvertible paper. Anything short of the extinction of the currency is so radically and fundamentally bad that I have no interest in comparing the relative goodness or badness of any expedients.

Q. How would you extinguish it?

A. You recollect the Bank of England was forbidden to pay. That was from mere alarm, from fright and the popular ignorance of banking.

Q. It is precisely the same here. Our National Treasury is forbidden to pay?

A. Ah! but the motive is different. The inconvertible currency of your country is a tax. By means of this species of paper the Government has got hold of the property of the nation, and it has kept it. The property has gone and the public in the place of it has got a species of paper. It is the Government's business to restore the property, clearly. In England at the close of the last century in the agitation of war, and banking being very unfamiliar then, the Government got desperately frightened. The Bank of England was going to be stopped and ruined. In a state of war and panic everybody likes to lock up his property in a commodity that is a reality. Then people rushed for gold.

Q. Was not the case very much the same here?

A. No. The motive here was simply as it was in France, Italy, and Austria. The Government wanted to get hold of the property of the country without paying for it, and the inconvertible currency is a tax. Government got the powder, shot, guns, soldier's clothes for nothing but a species of paper. That, in my idea, is a tax.

Q. Do you think Secretary McCulloch was pursuing the right policy?

A. Decidedly he was, and the only right thing to do now is to follow his example. In the case of the Bank of England three years were given, I believe, for resumption. The act providing for a return to cash payments was passed 1819. At the end of three years the bank paper was to become convertible paper. To illustrate an important principle let me mention here that during a very considerable time, while the bank restriction was going on, the inconvertible paper did not fall to a discount. In the latter years it did fall to a discount, so that a guinea became worth twenty-seven shillings in paper. That is a very instructive fact if we ask ourselves the question "how is that? Why were the bank note and the guinea of equal value for several years, and of unequal value in later years?" The reason is this, that in the earlier years of restriction—which was the injunction placed by the Government on the Bank, as being a great national institution, not to pay its notes in gold—the Bank did not issue more notes than the nation wanted for use. Consequently there was no excess; and I mean by "use," notes actually wanted to pass from hand to hand for the purpose of buying and selling. Precisely as in a purely gold currency, if there are more dollars issued than the public can use, they are sure to be locked up in some storehouse or other. The public won't keep them and won't have them. Just the same if you have fifty hats. You can't use more than two or three of them, and the rest must be locked up. It is the same with sovereigns and notes. If I give you one thousand metallic sovereigns, you cannot use them. By you, I am speaking of the public generally. You must send them into the cellar.

Q. Is it true that this California gold has had the effect to raise prices?

A. I do not believe it, although it is generally assumed by most economists. My answer to the claim is simply this—not proven. I don't see a single sign of the value of gold having declined in consequence of the Australian and California discoveries.

Q, Who should issue the currency, the Government or banks?

A. Who the issuer is, is of no consequence as to the action of currency. If it is inconvertible and a legal tender, then the depreciation is great. The only object of currency is to exchange goods, precisely as the only object of the Batavia steamboat was to bring me and fellow-passengers from England, and the goods on board also. They are both tools—one to carry us across the water, the other to enable one man to get his goods into another man's hands, and that, I say, is the only object of currency.

Q. You consider, as an essential part of that object, that there should be some consistency in the value of the currency?

A. The constancy of the value comes in in this way: There is a transaction between A. and B. A. has got ten bales of cotton to sell, and B. has nothing to give you for it but pieces of metal. A. knows what his cotton costs him, and between them both they know the value of those pieces of metal in the world, because they know what they can get for them in the shops—so many pounds of tea in one shop, so many hats from the hatter, so many boats from the boat builder. A. says, "Give me your metal and I will give you my cotton for it." That is the action of currency. It is a tool; and why is it wanted? Here is the secret of all currency: I am a grower of sugar in Louisiana, and you are a grower of cotton. I want to buy your cotton. I say to you, "Take my sugar and get rid of your cotton." You say, "I have no use for your sugar. Have you not got some yellow metal? Give me that metal and I will give you my cotton. Then I can go with that metal and buy what I want." This is the function of currency. Money was devised entirely for that and nothing else. The hatter might starve before he would find a butcher or a baker that wanted a hat. If it was not for currency he might starve before he got his bread. The fact is, a nation could not exist without currency. The vice of inconvertible currency is, that it has other ends and objects.

Q. How as to debts, mortgages, etc.?

A. The nature of these things is not altered by debts and mortgages. Every operation of credit is only this: that I have not got a dollar to-day and will give it to-morrow. Whether the debt is for a million or ten millions, or a national debt, even, or a basket of peaches, it is all the same in principle; but it does not alter the fact that the metallic dollar has got to be given as a pledge. The doctrine is the same.

Q. The steadiness in the value of the gold secures justice?

A. Certainly; because you have an article of real value; but in the case of inconvertible currency, when you bring me a legal-tender note and tell me it is as good as a dollar, that the Government is bound to pay it, I say directly, "If you had brought me a metallic dollar I could take it to a jeweler and sell it. I could not lose. At the worst, I could melt it and sell it as metal, and therefore I am paid." But if I find you bringing me a piece of paper which the United States Government says shall be paid, and does not say when, I say that it is not payment, and if I take it I must charge you something for the risk I run. The first quality of a currency is that it must have a permanent value. We cannot say positively that gold never changes in value, but the change is so little that the difference practically is nothing, If gold should jump up as it did in Elizabeth's time, through the lowering of the standard, it would be as bad as paper, because it would miss the one quality that people rely upon—permanency of value. The American currency is not to be trusted. It has destroyed its one great function—that of being a guarantee to the taker of it that he will get things of equal value. Nothing is more abominable than going to a dealer and being compelled to ask the relative prices of gold and currency. It is the same as asking of a ship, "Is she half rotten, or wholly rotten?"

Q. People out West know that all this is so, but they say, if they go back to the old standard they have got to pay ten per cent. more than they owe?

A. That may be. That is the punishment for getting into bad ways. My answer is: Is a nation to be permanently injured because it has done the wrong thing? Because some individuals must suffer, therefore must all suffer on their account? No. It is one of the consequences of sin. I admit the statement to be true that there must be suffering. In England they gave three years and diminished the suffering as much as possible; but to say that because we have sinned we must go on sinning, on account of contingent suffering, is absurd. If it is a good political argument, I have nothing tc say.

Q. What do you consider the evils of an inconvertible currency of fixed amount, as ours was up to within a year?

A. The answer is, the quantity of notes may be the same, unchanged, but the quantity that a nation wants for use may vary enormously, and therefore the fluctuation of value may go on. That is one of the curses of it. There is less currency wanted in England now than there was three years ago. Our currency simply goes out of commission. There is no disturbance in the value of it. But in the case of an inconvertible currency, suppose you only want three fourths, owing to circumstances such as now exist. It is very clear the quantity of notes remaining unchanged won't prevent depreciation in value, because every man in America wants only three notes this year where four were wanted last year. That is the state of things now. The evil is not mitigated. The demand for use is not itself stable, and never can be in any people, unless it be in an Indian village, where the quantity of currency does not change much. A nation changes greatly in its demand for currency. Travel is a great consumer of currency. It is the trade of all trades which demands ready money.

Q. Do you think the course of the Bank of France the last year, in taking in its notes, has inflicted any injury upon the trade of their country?

A. It cannot upon trade; it can upon individuals. It can only attack people who have got debts to receive or pay. The trade itself will be benefited. The nation, then, is not injured, but the individual.

Q. It must fall most heavily upon the producing classes, who are almost always in debt?

A. Very well; give them more time. Postpone the change. That is a question for statesmen to settle. An economist cannot settle it. It depends upon the exigencies of a nation. My argument is to the principle. In some cases you may restore the gold value in six months, in others you may wait six years. In either case I go back to what I said before—that the nation must not suffer forever to save individuals from suffering temporarily.

Q. You regard money as the universal barter, a medium to help the exchange of commodity for commodity?

A. The science of all trade is the exchange of two commodities of equal value. The cotton has a value which is the cost of producing cotton. The gold has a value of its own, which is the cost of getting it out of the mine. The exchange of cotton for gold is the exchange of articles of equal value. That makes a thoroughly sound currency. The only reason you are obliged to pass through gold is, as I said before, because trade would be stopped but for its intervention. The sellers of goods would not, in most cases, want the articles buyers had to offer them.

Q. The only way for that immediate barter is through gold, or paper for which gold can be had?

A. Yes; but it does not follow that because gold can be had for that paper that the man who has got the paper will go and get the gold. The only thing is that he feels he can get the gold with it if he wants to.

Q. Why should not the Government be the issuer of convertible notes and derive the profit from them?

A. The answer is this: You cannot get the President of the United States into the Bankruptcy Court. You can put the Directors of the Bank of England into it. You cannot rely upon convertibility with a party of politicians. You can't lock them up in a prison if they don't pay up, but you can the Bank of England, and break it up if it does not give you your gold. In economical principle one is as good as the other, but in political principle the difference is enormous. The public would not believe in any paper issued by the Government direct. The principle, as I said before, is sound. The profit belongs to the nation, but a government or a parliament are bad issuers of notes pledged to be paid on demand.

Q. The best thing the Government could do under the circumstances, under a convertible currency, would be to allow a free issue of bank notes, but to tax the issuer?

A. I don't say free issue, but I believe the intermediate agency of some private corporation is the true method.

Q. To require, as now, the security of United States bonds would be a good provision under a convertible currency?

A. Yes. I have always advocated the principle that the deposit of such things as national bonds is a legitimate and proper security to be required of the issuer of notes. If you have private issuers of public money the nation has the right to say to such private issuers, "You must guarantee to us not only that we can put you into the courts, but something more—that you shall have the means." Another illustration. In 1825, the English nation incurred great disasters from banks breaking which had the right of issuing notes, and in not a few instances those notes were only paid at half a crown to the pound. It is against all principle that such a thing should be possible in public money. Therefore, that led to the suppression of the one pound note, which was a mistake, and it led ultimately to that clause of the Bank Charter act which will in time extinguish the whole private circulation of England, and leave only notes of the Bank of England.

Q. The present condition on which national bank notes are issued, viz., the deposit of United States bonds with the Treasurer, would then be a safe rule for the issue of convertible notes, or free banking, as we call it?

A. Provided the notes are effectually realizable in gold on demand, there can be no possible objection, and there may be great advantage in any quantity of notes being on sale to the public, provided they are rendered perfectly safe by the deposit of adequate security.

Q. But this rule would not be a safe one with inconvertible currency?

A. If this rule is applied to inconvertible currency it does nothing to avert the disastrous vice of the currency losing its one indispensable feature of not fluctuating in value.

Q. There is no system of redemption of one kind of inconvertible paper with another that will mitigate the evils of incontrovertible currency?

A. I call that all hocus pocus.

Q. You consider the premium on gold, as quoted here on the street, as a tolerably accurate measure of the depreciation?

A. I presume so. I am not aware of any circumstances showing it is not.

Q. Is the common dread of contraction among our people well founded?

A. Not at all. There is great confusion in the meaning of the word money. Very little of the business of these great modern nations is transacted by money proper—currency. It is a mere trifle—mere change. The money is not the thing lent by banks or by lenders. Do you suppose if I wanted to borrow £20,000 of my banker, in London, for a mercantile operation, I should touch one sovereign or bank note? Do you suppose the trade between England and the United States is done by currency? Do you suppose the grain of the western men is paid for in currency? It is a fatal fallacy to identify currency—the means of exchanging property—with the property itself which is exchanged. Trade is an exchange of property. The money is very necessary as a measure, but it is not the trade.

Q. You don't think there is anything to be said in favor of the usury laws in this or any other country?

A. Laws limiting interest are not only bad, but absurd. They are always evaded. They are mischievous and nonsensical. Your banks here are limited to seven per cent. When the loan of money is really worth more than seven per cent., then people don't go to the banks, but somewhere else. You can't get anything for less than it is worth.

Professor Perry, from whom we have already quoted, says:

Next to the irredeemable paper money, the greatest obstacle to the prosperity of the farmers of the United States at the present moment is the so-called protective tariff. This is not so bad as it was two or three years ago. It has been twice reduced and simplified, in the fear that the honest indignation of the people would otherwise overthrow it altogether. But it is still bad enough; it is still too bad. It is an old trick of the devil, to take a good word and cover up with it an evil thing. Precisely this is done whenever the word "Protective" is applied to any tariff. The word protective is a good word when used in its legitimate sense. As signifying the security of person and property under a good government, it is an admirable word, and describes an indispensable thing; but as applied to a tariff, the word is full of deceit, inasmuch as a tariff from its very nature cannot "protect" anybody or anything. It can redistribute property by raising the prices of some things and depressing the prices of other things, but it cannot possibly raise the average prices of things in general. The trick of a potective tariff is just the same as the trick of paper money, the juggler's trick of putting existing things in strange places. A tariff creates nothing, produces nothing, adds nothing to existing wealth, but it distributes a great deal; and we must now examine this matter, especially in its bearing on the farmers.

There is a town in Spain, situated in the narrowest part of the Strait of Gibraltar, on the southernmost point of the kingdom, which is named Tarifa, in honor of Tarif Ibn Malik, a Berber chief who first landed here from Africa to reconnoiter the country, before the conquest of Spain by the Mohammedan Moors, in the eighth century of our Lord. These Moors occupied parts of Spain until the year of the discovery of America, 1492; and it was in the joy of her heart at the fortunate conquest of Grenada, their last stronghold, that Queen Isabella pledged her jewels to the enterprise of Columbus. The Moors built a castle at Tarifa which commanded the strait, and during their domination in Spain, compelled all vessels passing through the strait to stop and pay "duties" to them, at such rates as they dictated; and from this custom thus originating at Tarifa, the word *tariff*, derived from the name of that town, passed into the English and other European languages. The name tariff accordingly has not a very respectable origin; for those "duties" were nothing in the world but blackmail; they were the equivalent for no service rendered; they conferred no benefits on anybody except the robber-like receivers of the money; they were commanded and paid under compulsion; and they took just so much out without return from the profits of the voyages of the ships which passed inward and outward through the strait.

This origin of the name throws considerable light on the nature of the thing. The modern tariff is a more complicated piece of machinery than the ancient Moorish one, but that ancient one gave the pitch to the tune that has been sung by all tariffs ever since. In one respect that tariff was more respectable than almost any other ever laid—it was perfectly simple and above board. There was no hypocrisy about it. The Moors wanted money; they were in a position to extort it, and they took it without compunction, apology, or pretenses of any kind. They did not pretend that they were "protecting" their victims while compelling them to pay tribute. It was indeed downright robbery, but it was done on the square. It was an open, straightforward, daylight performance; and in this point of view contrasts strongly, as we shall see shortly, with some modern tariffs which pretend to benefit the people, while they really impoverish them. They are enacted in the name of patriotism and righteousness, but when one looks narrowly into them, he sees that they have remained true at bottom to the spirit of their origin. The thing tariff corresponds pretty well to the name tariff.

Tariffs take, but never give. At first sight a tariff seems to be nothing but a series of taxes on certain foreign goods. One may read a Tariff Act from beginning to end, or begin in the middle and read both ways, and he will find nothing but demands repeated over and over again. "Thou shalt pay!" is the only word that a tariff utters or can utter. I will quote from the tariff now in force in this country, from a copy just received from the Secretary of the Treasury, as codified and re-enacted in June last, premising that the demands quoted are taken at random under the different schedules, and premising also that there are by actual count just seven hundred and fifty-six different rates of duty specified to be assessed upon different things and classes of things. For example: Spool-thread, six cents per dozen, and thirty-five per centum; slates and slate-pencils, thirty-five per centum; aniline dyes, fifty cents per pound, and thirty-five per centum; woolen shawls, fifty cents per pound, and thirty-five per centum; bunting, twenty cents per square yard, and thirty-five per centum; ready-made clothing, fifty cents per pound, and forty per centum; webbing for shoes, fifty cents per pound, and fifty per centum; hand-saws, one dollar per dozen, and thirty per centum; hair-pins (iron), fifty-six per centum; druggets and bockings, twenty-five cents per square yard, and thirty-five per centum.

These, and all the rest, are demands. A tariff gives nothing. It takes. At its best estate, when most simple and honest, when there are no "protective" features in it, and no combination of specific and *ad valorem* duties on the same article, which is a device of "protection," as in some of the samples above given, a tariff is a body of taxes, which the people have to pay. It is needful to note this distinctly at the outset; because there are some people who seem to think a tariff has a sort of creative power; that it is a positive, productive agent; that it can do good; that it has something to confer. Not so. From the very nature of it, it pours nothing in, but only takes something out. Its sign is minus and not plus. It comes to take something *from* the people, and not to give anything *to* the people.

The United States has been accustomed, from the beginning of the government under the present constitution, to raise the principal part of its revenue from tariff-taxes on imported goods. These taxes, of course, raise the price of the goods on which they are laid considerably more to the consumers than the amount of the tax itself, because the tax having to be advanced by the importer and the jobber, becomes larger from the profits on the money advanced; and frequently, also, the tax is made a cover or excuse, under which the consumer is charged a sum additional to the original tax and the profits on it. In the ultimate price of the taxed goods the consumer pays for the goods, pays the tax and all profits on the tax, and frequently also something additional under cover of the tax. There are decided objections, as we shall see, to raising a revenue in this way, even when the sole purpose in laying the duties is to get revenue, and when the duties are so adjusted as that the government really gets the most that the people have to pay in consequence of the duties. It is very plain, that whatever tariff-taxes are levied solely for the sake of the revenue to be derived from them, they ought to be laid in accordance with these fundamental principles:—first, on goods like tea and coffee, for example, which are wholly imported from abroad, and not also grown or made at home, otherwise the tax on the portion imported will also incidentally raise the price of the portion produced at home, and the people will have to pay more in consequence of the tax than the government gets in revenue, because the government only gets the tax on the part imported. Second, if such taxes are to be productive, they must be levied at comparatively low rates, so as not to interfere essentially with the bringing in of the goods, or encourage smuggling at all, for in either of those cases the revenue from the importations would fall off. Third, the taxes should be simple, so that everybody can calculate their amount, and know how much of the price paid is owing to the tax; and it is just as much for the interest of the revenue as for that of the people that these taxes should be simple and honest, so that both importers and consumers, calculating them beforehand and knowing just how much the government is to take, will not be deterred from importing and buying by indefinite taxes; and, fourth, it is agreeable to reason and has been found true in experience that it is not needful to levy even low rates on all articles imported, in order to realize as large revenue, but only on certain classes of them, so as to burden at as few points as possible the on-going of international and profitable exchanges. Laid strictly on these four principles, which are very important: (one) on goods wholly imported, (two) at low rates, (three) at simple rates easily calculable, (four) on few classes of goods used by almost everybody, tariff-taxes, though objectionable because falling unequally on rich and poor, are yet endurable, and are infinitely preferable to the tariff-taxes laid at present in this country.

The English, after having violated for a long time every one of these four fundamental principles, now at length levy their tariff-taxes in strict accordance with them. I quote from the Monthly Report of the Bureau of Statistics of the United States for December, 1872, the following facts:—All tariff duties in Great Britain are levied under nine heads, as follows:—One, tobacco; two, sugars; three, tea, coffee, chickory, and cocoa; four, spirits; five, wines; six, dried fruits; seven, malt products; eight, table ware; nine, playing cards. The taxes on these are all specific, that is, by the pound, gallon, dozen, and so on, so that anybody can calculate them; they are laid on things exclusively imported, or, whenever they are not, as in the case of spirits and malts, a corresponding excise tax is put on the domestic product, so that the government gets all that the people are compelled to pay as the result of the tariff-taxes; and while the duties in some cases may be said to be high, they are not so high in any case as to discourage the importation of the things on which they are laid. There is no tariff-tax on any portion of the food of the people, except sugars; no tariff-tax on any article of clothing; and no tariff-tax on any raw materials or implements of production. This tariff of Great Britain, which can almost be written on the palm of one's hand, yielded, in the fiscal year 1872, $101,630,000 of revenue, which was $3 20 for each man, woman, and child in the United Kingdom. If there are to be tariffs at all, this is the only form of a tariff that even approaches towards justice and equality. Taxes on stimulants and sugar, which yield almost the whole of British customs' revenue, are as unexceptionable as any taxes on commodities can be, because everybody uses them in some form, and because it is optional with everybody how much of them they shall use. But we shall see that there is a more excellent way of taxation than this.

The only just taxation is the taxation of incomes, because the net annual income is the exact gains of one's exchanges for the year; and as one can only pay his taxes out of the gains of his exchanges, the taxes ought to be proportioned to those gains. In a country organized as this is, in which there are municipal, state and national taxes, the local authorities ought to ascertain (and they would surely be able to ascertain) the net income of every person within their limits; and, taxing this income a certain fraction for local purposes, then report it to the state for another fraction of state taxation; and then the state, reporting incomes to the nation, would be the medium, through its local officers, of collecting the third fraction for national purposes. Under this plan one set of local officers could gather all three kinds of taxes at one time in the cheapest possible way; custom houses and national internal revenue offices, with all their political abuses and pecuniary corruptions, could be abolished; it would make no difference where the property was located, whether in one's own state or elsewhere, or whence the income was drawn, whether from commodities or services or credits,—a man's domicil would mark the place of his taxation, and he would be taxed throughout exactly in proportion to his income. The more you think about this scheme the better you will like it, and the fewer objections and more excellence you will see in it; but I have no expectation of seeing it adopted in my time, because habits and prejudices are against it, political parties could make nothing out of it, and personal aggrandizements would have no chance in connection with it. The towns, counties, and states will probably continue to raise their taxes on real estate and corporations; and the nation will long continue to raise its revenue by excise and by tariff.

But protective tariffs, so-called, will doubtless pass off from our statute-books, as they have already passed out of the laws of Great Britain, Belgium, and largely also of France, because they are monstrously unjust; because by raising the price of the corresponding domestic article as well as of the foregin article taxed, they make the people pay in ostensible taxes a great deal more than the government gets; because, since all foreign trade is an exchange of commodities, just so far as a protective tariff keeps foreign goods out, it keeps in of necessity domestic goods that would gladly go out, and thus domestic producers lose their best and freely chosen market; because there is no general gain in taking money out of one set of pockets in the mostly vain hope of transferring it to another set of pockets; because, so soon as the system becomes general, even manufacturers, who have to buy "protected" materials, soon have to pay more protection than they get; and because, just so far as the importables are raised in value by protective tariff taxes, the exportables are depressed in value, thus throwing the vast losses of the system upon those who grow the exportables.

No man in his senses can pretend that protective tariff taxes are a direct benefit to farmers, since these taxes cannot increase the number of mouths that eat the farmer's produce, and since we do not import agricultural produce to any great extent to be raised in price by these taxes so that our farmers can sell their produce for more. On the other hand, it is perfectly plain that these taxes cause an enormous loss to farmers, because they grow the exportables that are necessarily depressed in value by just so much as the importables are enhanced in value by these taxes. According to the Bureau of Statistics, this country exported in 1873, $649,132,563. Of this immense sum, $449,328,590, or more than two thirds of the whole, was in strictly agricultural products. What we export buys all that we import; most that we export is farmer's produce; but so far as the imports are burdened with protective taxes, the farmer's exports are lessened in value, that is to say, they will not go so far, they will not buy so much. The farmer has to give more of his grain, his hams, his pork, his lard in order to get what he wants in return. It makes no difference that others come in to help him make his exchange. He is the real exchanger. These middle-men pay him less for his produce than they would otherwise gladly pay him. His exports suffer a loss in price equal to the gain in price of the imports caused by the protective taxes.

Under protection the farmer suffers a double loss. He must submit to pay a great deal more for his supplies, whether these be foreign goods protectively taxed, or domestic goods raised in price by such taxes; and on the other hand, he cannot get nearly so much for what he has to sell. He is smitten on the one cheek, and then told by his masters in Pennsylvania and New England to turn the other also. He sends out more than two thirds of all the exportables of the country, to have them shaved and whittled down in price and value by the artificial obstacles set up in our ports to prevent the return of the things which these exportables went forth to buy. If everything else that I say be forgotten, I beg the farmers of the West to remember, that protection cuts right into the heart of the value of their exportable commodities. Nay more; it sometimes prevents the export of these commodities altogether. The harvest in Europe this season has been unusually good; the European demand for the bread-stuffs and other food products of our country is likely in consequence to be rather slack. Already the price of wheat in New York and Chicago has felt the influence of this in a decline; still, if we were allowed by the tariff to take into this country freely the things which we want, of which foreigners have a surplus to sell, they would take now freely of us our surplus bread-stuffs, and we could afford to let them have them. In one word, we could export more food products at all times, with a greater profit on each transaction provided we could get our return cargoes free of protective taxes. We could sell more when the price was high, and longer after it became lower, than we can possibly do now. A protective tariff tends to stop the exports by making the imports dearer; and as the farmers furnish the bulk of the exports, the principal losses of the tariff fall upon them. As things now are, it is true indeed that the gold price of produce in Liverpool determines the point of profitable export from New York; but a lower gold price in Liverpool would still allow a profitable export from New York, provided the gold price received here would buy more of all the commodities wanted by the farmers. Thus we see that protection is a double foe to the farmers; it causes them to get less for what they raise and to give more for what they buy. Protection in its best estate is a short-sighted, narrow-minded prejudice; whenever it passes beyond that, it becomes a consciously deceitful scheme of plunder, by which a few seek to enrich themselves at the expense of the many. Those many are mainly the farmers. They are abundantly able, numerically and otherwise, if they will only unite to do it, to put down forever this monstrous injustice of legislation. I hope that their rising intelligence and the courage that is born of union, will seize this lying fraud by the throat, and shake the life out of it, as a dog shakes the breath out of a woodchuck!

Poor money and protective tariffs are natural allies; carry on their work of destruction in similar ways; each intensifies the mischief of the other; and both combine their results in hostility to the agricultural interests, since each compels the farmer to give more for his supplies and take less for his produce. On the other hand, hard money and free trade are natural allies also, working in the same harness, defrauding nobody, just to all because natural and free, and enabling the masses of mankind to maintain the advantageous places which the Heavenly Father designed them to hold. To be consistent with himself a hard-money man should be a free trader also; and a man who believes that legislators are wiser than natural laws, should consistently believe both in commercial restriction and in rag-money, since both are artificial creatures of the Legislature. Accordingly, there has been considerable tendency during the last fifty years for men to range themselves in parties on the one side or the other of these two combined questions; but unfortunately they have come to think more of the party name and organization than of the principles on which parties profess to be originally founded; and when the perversion has thoroughly taken place, as it has in this country at this moment, scarcely anything is a greater foe to real progress than this hollow party spirit. What is it to be a Republican to-day? What is it to be a Democrat to-day? No man can possibly answer these questions, because there are no vital and general differences now involved in these names.

Party spirit has been particularly injurious to the farmers of this country, because they have ranged themselves pretty evenly in both of the two political parties, and the two parts have thus completely neutralized each other. The interests of the farmers have had no weight in either of the political parties, simply because the farmers themselves stood over against each other in two opposing camps. Thus the farmers, as such, lost all weight and influence in political affairs. They are to be congratulated and applauded that the mass of them have made up their minds to act no longer with the old political parties, or with any other parties in fact, for the present. Let them adhere to this determination; the country will be all the better for it. Let them avoid entangling alliances, and snap their fingers at the caucus. Let them act as a unit in accordance with their own deliberate conviction of their own interests; for their true interests are also the true interests of the whole country. Let them hold this attitude steadily for five years, and there is not a single point of public policy favorable to themselves that they cannot triumphantly carry. If they come to see eye to eye, as pray God they may, that a labor-wrought dollar, and not a printing-press dollar, is the only dollar fit to be exchanged against their own labor-wrought produce, then they can confer upon themselves and the whole country the inestimable boon of labor-wrought dollars! If they come to see, as please God they will, that what is called "protection" is only another name for spoliation; that what is called "fostering" industry only makes industry to flounder; that tariffs take but never give; that trade is good and gainful; that the world's market, whether to sell in or buy in, is always better than the market of a single country; that natural competition is the life of business and of progress; that restrictive tariffs keep home things in, that want to go out, as well as foreign things out, that want to come in; that exportables are depressed in value in proportion as importables are artificially enhanced in value; and that God Almighty knows better how to adjust all the obstacles to international trafic than any Congress that ever sat, or ever will sit;—then can they easily abolish this antiquated scheme of greed and grab, and open up for themselves and for all their fellow citizens, both to sell in and to buy in, the unrestricted markets of the world!

Comparative Statement of Taxation in State, etc., in U. S.; also total amount of property, population, per capita tax, value to population, etc.

STATES.	Internal Revenue, 1872, by States.	Impost Revenue pro rata. $5 40 per Cap. on $216,000,000 Rev. 1872.	State, County, Town, Munic. taxation, 1872.	Total taxation 10 per cent. added up to 1873.	Tot. act'l val. '70, deducting public debts, and 100 per ct. for priv. debts.	Amt. of taxes per capita. 1870.	Amt. of taxes per capita. 1850.	Valuati'n per capita, 1870.	Rate per ct.	Total population, 1870, by States.	Total State and local debts.
Alabama	$152,493 35	$4,383,756 80	$2,982,932	$6,618,830 96	$177,880,555	$6 75	$293	$117	5.9	996,992	$41,987,643
Arkansas	88,861 02	2,661,251 40	2,866,890	6,117,102 66	96,812,161	12 83	188	179	7.2	484,471	26,761,265
California	2,367,911 07	3,025,333 80	7,817,115	14,320,401 35	602,582,953	25 02	133	1,072	2.3	560,247	18,089,082
Connecticut	813,984 99	2,902,291 60	6,064,843	10,759,230 84	770,653,812	20 00	416	1,453	1.4	537,453	18,086,906
Delaware	429,392 84	617,141 60	418,092	1,610,089 08	96,128,583	12 88	201	469	2.9	125,015	526,125
Florida	158,142 21	1,013,839 20	496,166	1,834,962 15	—1,431,419	9 77	239	less by 7	......	187,748	22,797,537
Georgia	477,559 90	6,394,186 60	2,621,029	10,448,095 25	199,894,207	8 82	366	169	5.2	1,184,109	34,137,500
Illinois	16,493,169 34	13,713,411 40	21,825,108	66,536,747 61	2,037,296,481	21 68	181	802	2.5	2,539,891	42,191,869
Indiana	5,678,052 51	9,075,439 80	10,891,121	27,989,074 64	1,251,544,023	16 66	203	745	2.2	1,680,637	7,818,710
Iowa	1,012,997 29	6,447,708 00	9,655,614	19,266,851 21	701,558,494	16 12	122	616	2.9	1,194,020	8,043,133
Kansas	161,469 76	1,967,754 60	2,693,992	5,304,327 99	76,007,452	14 83	......	209	7.1	364,399	6,442,282
Kentucky	5,456,628 47	7,133,454 40	5,930,118	20,152,220 00	566,411,587	15 26	304	429	3.5	1,321,011	18,953,484
Louisiana	1,339,007 36	3,925,611 00	7,060,7 2	13,558,530 00	216,123,318	18 65	447	298	6.3	726,965	58,501,174
Maine	214,196 26	3,385,441 00	5,348,645	9,843,080 00	314,906,423	15 72	208	502	3.1	626,915	16,624,624
Maryland	2,653,801 83	3,716,827 60	6,632,842	14,303,718 00	585,683,826	18 30	372	750	2.5	780,094	29,032,575
Massachusetts	3,761,004 95	7,869,695 40	24,922,900	40,208,900 00	1,993,725,665	28 28	571	1,038	2.6	1,457,351	69,211,538
Michigan	2,205,720 72	6,393,918 60	5,412,957	15,412,315 00	705,757,656	13 02	148	596	2.2	1,184,059	6,725,231
Minnesota	241,404 94	2,374,412 40	2,648,372	5,730,507 00	223,431,926	13 12	......	418	3.1	439,706	2,788,797
Mississippi	128,079 31	4,570,778 80	3,736,432	9,310,819 00	214,008,479	11 25	374	258	4.0	827,922	2,994,415
Missouri	4,257,320 15	9,294,993 00	13,908,498	30,198,092 00	1,191,031,167	17 60	119	693	2.6	1,721,295	46,909,865
Nebraska	242,962 38	664,162 20	1,027,327	2,127,896 00	65,098,959	17 30	......	520	3.3	122,993	2,089,264
Nevada	72,305 32	229,451 40	820,308	1,240,940 00	27,131,826	29 20	......	638	4.6	42,491	1,986,093
New Hampshire	325,455 36	1,718,820 00	3,225,793	5,786,074 00	230,317,366	18 18	320	764	2.4	318,300	11,153,373
New Jersey	2,567,442 37	4,892,918 40	7,416,724	16,363,737 00	896,268,451	18 05	404	989	1.8	906,096	22,854,304
New York	19,219,504 52	23,666,846 60	48,550,308	100,579,323 00	6,181,224,792	23 18	345	1,414	1.8	4,382,759	159,808,234
North Carolina	1,408,321 72	5,785,349 40	2,352,809	10,501,126 00	168,982,310	9 82	258	152	6.5	1,071,361	45,887,467
Ohio	14,851,309 42	14,392,404 00	23,526,548	58,047,287 00	2,190,946,324	21 80	252	802	2.5	2,665,260	22,241,988
Oregon	73,544 48	490,980 20	580,956	1,458,032 00	51,118,970	16 03	384	562	2.9	90,923	2[illegible]8,486
Pennsylvania	7,826,275 69	19,078,535 40	24,531,397	56,579,717 00	3,630,285,850	16 06	309	1,031	1.5	3,522,521	89,027,131
Rhode Island	324,552 17	1,173,701 20	2,170,152	4,035,245 00	285,088,398	18 56	540	1,312	1.3	217,353	5,938,624
South Carolina	169,213 58	3,811,892 40	2,767,675	7,421,158 00	129,8[illegible]9,151	10 55	427	183	5.6	705,906	39,158,914
Tennessee	644,480 76	6,896,008 00	3,387,579	12,012,273 00	480,583,342	9 04	198	319	1.8	1,258,520	48,827,191
Texas	272,325 77	4,420,326 60	1,129,577	5,812,228 00	109,039,342	7 10	245	131	5.3	818,571	25,006,600
Vermont	75,860 40	1,784,975 40	1,547,128	3,748,759 00	228,160,153	11 34	290	690	1.6	330,551	3,594,700
Virginia	7,343,799 29	6,615,886 20	4,613,798	19,330,831 00	297,745,823	15 77	300	243	6.4	1,225,163	55,921,255
West Virginia	444,661 59	2,386,875 60	1,722,158	5,144,464 00	189,527,957	11 44	......	438	2.8	442,014	561,767
Wisconsin	1,881,820 97	5,675,618 00	7,355,131	15,708,312 00	701,120,265	14 80	156	758	1.9	1,054,670	5,903,532
District of Columbia	133,424 58	700,580 00	1,581,569	2,425,573 00	97,218,700	18 42	268	739	2.5	131,700	14,777,459
Totals	$106,255,637 50	$202,715,421 40	$587,275,842	*$652,528,713 00	$26,802,676,621	$16 00	$301	$595	3.3	38,690,071	$999,385,982

* Average $17,171,809.

CHAPTER XXIX.

BANKS AND MONEY.

"The basis of our currency is not gold, but the nation's honor, guaranteed by the national loyalty and the general interests of its members."—*Hon. M. Anderson.*

Farmers need Cheap Money—Legislation Controlled by Capitalists—Farmers and Lawyers in Congress—Exemption of Bonds from Taxation—Rate of Interest a Test of Prosperity; of Civilization—Banks and Banking—Savings Banks—Paper Promises made Legal Tenders—Prof. Bonamy Price on Crises and Panics—English Co-operative Associations as Financial Successes.

It has been a favorite theory that the farmer should leave the after-management of his products to other classes of society, especially gifted by nature and qualified by special education and opportunities to deal with them to the best advantage for him and for themselves.

We will judge of the correctness of this principle by its results. The British "Fortnightly Review" thus clearly and impressively states the problem, as it looks from that point:

In this complex industrial system, wealth has discovered the machinery by which the principal, in some cases the whole results of common labor become its special perquisites. Ten thousand miners delve and toil, giving their labor, risking their lives; ten masters give their direction, or their capital, oftenest only the latter. And in a generation the ten capitalists are rioting in vast fortunes, and the ten thousand workmen are rotting in their graves or in the workhouse. And yet the ten thousand were at least as necessary to the work as the ten. Yet more, the ten capitalists are practically the law-makers, the magistrates, the government. The educators of youth, the priests of all creeds, are their creatures. Practically they make and interpret the law—the law of the land, the law of opinion, and the law of God. They are masters of the whole of the social forces. A convenient faith has been invented for them by moralists and economists, the only faith which in these days they at all believe in—the faith that the good of mankind is somehow promoted by a persevering course of selfishness; that competition is, in fact, the whole duty of man. And thus it comes that in ten thousand ways the whole social force is directed for the benefit of those who have.

The farmers are by far the largest class of our population, but are they the most prosperous? Is it not well to inquire what it is that retards their prosperity, and prevents them from exercising a proportionate influence over the public policy of the country?

By reference to the table on page 73, it will be seen that nearly one half of our people are agriculturists; and that there were in 1870, 41,106 lawyers in the United States. It is not extravagant to say that the latter have exerted more practical influence in public affairs than the whole body of farmers.

For instance, we have in Congress one hundred and ninety-eight lawyers and thirteen farmers, or one lawyer to about two hundred of that profession, and one farmer to about one hundred and thirty thousand land-owners or independent agriculturists. It is a fearful commentary upon the working of our government, that the great producing arm of the country is so feebly represented; but the fault and the remedy is entirely in themselves. Prof. Perry says, "there is no objection to raise to lawyers; they are a useful class of men; but there *is* a decided objection to allowing a mere handful of them representing another mere handful of powerful clients, to shape and mold the policy of forty millions of people. That is only a republican form of government, in which they who are intrusted with political franchises, exert an influence somewhat proportionate to their numbers."

The producing classes will have little or no ability to turn the current of legislation in their own favor while their representation is so small; and it is not arraying one class against another, to say that this should be changed in order that justice may be done. I believe that what is best for the laboring men of this country, is the best for all classes, and best for the local, state and national governments, as gatherers of taxes.

Now, as the farmer needs to know what he wants, and how to get it by a more adequate representation, so also he needs to know something of the methods of business, in order that he may not be at the mercy of others.

One of the greatest wants of farmers in all portions of the West, as well as the business men, is, more money at low rates of interest. We have seen elsewhere that one of the questions met by our State Grange was a remedy for the high rates on this coast. The legislation of the country has been under the control of the eastern capitalists who have got the lion's share of the present bank circulation. The patriotism which submitted to the payment of six per cent. interest, gold, upon United States bonds, exempt from taxation, *as a war measure*, will not cover the payment of about $800,000,000 premium, in gold, to the holders of those bonds in time of peace.

Language more forcible than elegant, has been used in the meetings of the Western State Agricultural Societies on this subject, and without regard to other burdens of taxation from which the wealth of the country manages to escape. "When the people of the country get to understand how they have been compelled to pay tribute to capitalists, and how the capitalists have controlled the legislation of this country, by bribery and corruption, and by munificent gifts to men whom they expected to work in their interest when in power; the driving out of the ancient money-changers from the Temple will be a mild affair in comparison with the kicks and cuffs they will receive from an outraged people."

A low rate of interest, then, is a gauge of the farmer's prosperity. The "New York Merchant and Banker" acknowledges it to be the test of civilization:

What is the best criterion of the degree of civilization to which a people has attained? Some promptly answer, "The proportion of those who can read and write in the total population;" but this will not serve, for census figures are not always reliable, and literary instruction by no means secures commercial or political intelligence and prosperity. Others will say, "the relative wealth of countries;" but this is very difficult to determine, and if ascertained, the more important inquiry remains—in which countries is that wealth increasing, and where is it growing less? Others still will name the degree of religious devotion, the extent of virtue, the development of learning, the culture of art and science in various lands; but neither of these is practically available as a standard, since before it can be so applied, it must itself be quantitatively determined.

It then states that there is, however, a test quantitative in its nature, self-determining, and for the most part readily ascertained. It is the average rate of interest actually paid for loans on good security. Not, of course, the rate sanctioned by law; for the only relation of this rate to that actually paid, is commonly a tendency to heighten the latter by increasing the risk of the loan. The rate of "pure interest" does not greatly differ in different countries, and is not far from four per cent. The amounts demanded or offered and actually paid for loans above this rate, consist mainly of premiums of insurance on the risk the lender considers himself to take when he puts his property out of his possession. When it is remembered that confidence is a plant of slow growth; that it is developed by long experience, and very quickly and easily destroyed, and that its development to such a point that premiums on risks of loan are nearly nothing, means that commercial practice and legal administration have convinced property-holders by experience that their property is secured to them through business honor or through the aid of law; when these great and grave facts are borne in mind, it is clear that the countries where interest rules lowest are the most civilized. The fall in the rate when a state of thorough security to property, (which means personal liberty, commercial integrity, and honest government,) has been developed, hastened and furthered by the immigration of capital from less civilized countries. To the land where he learns that his property will be secure, the owner in a country where he feels that his tenure of it is unsafe, sends that property for investment; and the monetary centers of such lands overflow with capital seeking investment at rates astonishingly low, for the sake of the security expected. Hence, for all proper enterprises in such a nation, capital is readily obtainable at a price that permits a development of her resources, compared with which the plausible schemes that politicians propose for government to execute, are as puerile as they are futile.

It then argues that there is one important lesson to be deduced from these facts, viz: That every one in the community, and every law-maker especially, can help or hinder among ourselves the development of such a condition. Every man who faithfully pays his debts and lives an honest life, helps to develop a great civilization, and renders real service to his country. Every man who commits fraud or robbery, does more to destroy confidence, to increase the rate of interest, and to retard civilization, than two honest men can do to help it on. Every law that practically protects men in the possession of their own, operates to lower interest and build up civilization; but every law that operates to make it less secure—tariffs, legal-tender acts, etc.—raises the rate of interest, and postpones the advance of civilization.

The application of this test to our civilization does not give a flattering result, and we must look into the reason. Five per cent. is thought by good judges to be all that the producing classes can afford to pay, and is more than they make, on the average, out of their capital invested in farming. "So long as money-lenders receive a larger income on loans than can be realized out of real estate, money cannot be obtained at a reasonable rate of interest. There is surely no good reason why strips of paper, called money, should bring a larger income than the same amount of money will bring when invested in almost any productive industry."

A look into our American banking system will not be unprofitable to the farmers of California; but first let us find out what banks are, and how they originated.

The word bank comes from the Italian for bench; the Lombard Jews of Italy, who were the first money-lenders in Europe, having been accustomed to transact their business on benches in the market places. When one of these men was detected in cheating, the populace broke his benches, from which custom we get the word bankrupt. In modern times the people allow the fraudulent banker to retire to a palace erected out of the profits of their earnings.

In strict terms, the banker is dealing in money, and his profits are perfectly legitimate, being the difference between the terms on which he borrows and lends. The amount of his business determines his gains. In this manner small sums, which would be unproductive in the hands of individuals, are concentrated for use in building up commerce, trade, and manufactures, and are an incalculable blessing; but when the banks themselves enter into competition with these industries, they at once create monopolies, and become a curse.

In California we have no bankers—that is, no dealers in money. Our banking system, or rather want of system, enables a few men with little or no capital to start a bank—that is, a place where those who are so disposed can deposit their money; because the Constitution of the State prohibits the establishment of banks, such as exist in every other State in the American Union, and in every commercial town in Europe.

The effect of our peculiar plan of banking is, that the banker has everything to gain and nothing to lose. It is well known that such is the potency of bank rings, that constitutional provisions for the protection of creditors are practically inadequate; that vast fortunes are amassed at the expense of depositors; that stocks rise and fall irrespective of their values, while industry suffers, and legitimate business is demoralized. The farmers cannot guard their interests too carefully against these evils. The Bank of California is not a dealer in money, but deals in stocks, mines, purchases coal mines, runs quartz and lumber mills, contracts for and controls the supply of quicksilver, silver and gold coin, tonnage and grain, and is directly or indirectly connected with every speculative enterprise in the State.

The savings banks, which control $40,000,000, are not banks at all, but establishments where people place their money on deposit, subject to be withdrawn on specified notice, provided the funds are on hand. Every depositor in a savings bank signs a paper when making his deposit, to the effect that if the bank has not got the money when he demands it, he is content to wait till it obtains it. This provision is a good thing for the banks, but is not quite so good for the depositor. No matter how stringent the money market, or how great the reduction in the value of real estate—which forms the exclusive security for the depositor's money—the bank is not compelled to sacrifice its property to pay the depositor, who has to wait till real estate rises. So long as these savings banks continue to pay liberal dividends, they can swim along smoothly; but suppose the demand for money fails, and interest drops to three per cent. per annum—what then? It often happens that instead of banks being able to furnish money when there is a sudden panic, they have to call in their loans, thus not unfrequently crippling the most important business interest. The farmers often hear of "crises" and panics in the money market, without a very definite idea of what they are, or how they are created.

Again we turn to Mr. Bonamy Price, who will not only give us the needed explanation, but will tell us how the banking business is managed in our chief market, Great Britain:

What are crises? Great disturbances of the money market; difficulty of obtaining advances; high rates of discount; great firms in danger; who is sound and who is unsound unknown; whose money is safe; whose is unsafe a matter of great uncertainty. Just as it was seen in England in 1866, it is a time when those who are the strongest are exposed to the most formidable dangers. There was probably no institution in London more exposed to peril in 1866 then the great London and Westminster Bank, the largest in England and one of the ablest conducted. The cause of the crisis was simply alarm; simply that those vast bodies of people who had intrusted funds to this institution got into what may be called a panic, to use a common word. In that state of wild alarm, all rushed for their money, everybody catching the contagion, which became more catching because it was unreasonable. There is nothing more stirring than alarm which has no definite cause, which does not know what it goes upon, which, therefore, suspects any cause of mischief because it has none that it can put its finger upon. The fathers of the city, the great bankers and wise men, sat in counsel all night and asked each other "What is the cure?" I believe the cause of these panics can be stated, and when you know the danger and the cause likely to disturb you can take proper precautions. Now, it is not the magnitude of the loss alone which constitutes a crisis. Destruction alone is not the cause. A bad harvest in England is a loss of £30,000,000; that is, in such a case you have got to buy or procure £30,000,000 worth of corn twice over. You have sown, you have tilled, you have put the manure on the land, but the August rain comes in, the corn is not matured, and you have got to live, so you must buy in from the stranger. But that produces no panic, no financial agony. It is a dead loss; a calamity, something bigger than a calamity in the money market. But it does not generate a financial storm. Then a bad war. War is the most destructive thing in the world. It is a deliberate work of men to destroy; they destroy food, clothing, iron, ships. Nothing destroys like war. It is the most uneconomical thing on earth. But a war does not necessarily produce a panic. It is this terrifying fear which we know accompanies a hurricane in London. Very well. Again, take a cotton famine in England. It was a terrific loss of money. Wealth in those districts was paralyzed because America had no cotton. The poor men had no wages. All that vast apparatus of capital was earning nothing; consuming, buying, but not selling. But there was no panic. That year is not enumerated as one of storm. Therefore we don't get, by mere destruction alone, into a reign of panic. Then again, another curious thing. The typhoon has this character; that it whips up the water terrifically in a particular spot, but the neighboring waters are dead calm. At the time in '66, in '47, and other times, when money charges were at twenty, when people could not get advances on the best security, when the bank had to say, "I can't," all this time the market for advancing money on agriculture, to squires and county gentlemen, was so that they could get all they wanted at four per cent. That is absolutely historical. Therefore these convulsions have something very peculiar about them. The real fury of the storm, in its national importance in distinction to individuals, is its bearing upon banks, upon discounts. It is not so much on rate per cent., though that is bad enough, but it is the impossibility of discount which constitutes the terrific agitation and the loss to the nation. Modern trade, as you are well aware, is carried on upon a very peculiar method. I have no doubt it is in New York as in England. The characteristic is that it is carried on with other people's capital, not the traders'. The traders are not the people who provide the capital for their business. Some they do provide; the bulk certainly not. The distinctive peculiarity of modern trade is that it is carried on by bills, and bills have to be discounted, because a bill means, "I cannot pay to-day, but I will pay this at three months." The goods are given, the sale is completed, and the man who sells holds in his hand a piece of paper which says that after three months he will have his money, but not before. The man so circumstanced wants to go on with his business, which he cannot do if he has to wait three months for his funds to come in. How are his working-men to be paid or his ship to be sent away? That is done by discounting bills at banks, and the national strain of the crisis is its action upon the general trade of the nation by acting upon the discount market. This discounting takes place in banks, and, therefore, we now see a locality of the storm. It is somehow or other connected with banks.

Banks are peculiar institutions. I know a great many of the eminent bankers of England well. I have asked directors of banks, the governor of the Bank of England, and personages of that kind a very simple question; but I never met only one man, dead and gone now, who could answer me this question: What is a bank? and what does a bank deal in? That lies at the root of the question of crises. I have only met one, Mr. Potter, the founder of the great London Joint Stock Company, who could answer that question. I know what a grocer is. He deals in candles, in tea, in sago. I know what a fruiter is. If I ask such a man what he deals in, he has not the slightest difficulty in answering my question. It is marvelous in this nineteenth century that of such a great profession, such a great branch of human activity, there is no definition, except perhaps in my writings, of what a bank is and what it deals in. But it is essential, in order to understand crises, to understand what banks are, as they are phenomena of banking. They are the Chinese Sea of banking.

I said in "Frazer" a year ago that a banker did not deal in money above one thirtieth of his business. Of course, in order to go on to that computation I must understand what money is. There is another ugly question.

What is money? I gave a lecture before the Chamber of Commerce of Liverpool on that question. I will, in passing, take the word money. It comes from the temple of Juno Moneta, in Rome. It was the mint of Rome; the money was stamped pieces of metal, generally known by the name of coin. Nothing is money but that; and the Romans had no doubt about it, because they had no paper money. I am very willing, however, for this discussion, to include the bank note as money. Why is not a check money? The bank note itself is not money. A promise to give a thing is not the thing itself. Those who call paper money are in this mess; they say that a piece of paper saying, "I will pay you the money when you ask for it," or "when it is convenient for me," as in the case of your currency, is money. Paper of all kinds are merely title deeds, nothing else. Except when you are passing convertible currency laws, pieces of paper are merely written certificates to go to the judge and jury with, and to send a sheriff to you if you don't give the coin which that calls for. They are evidence to produce before a court of law.

What distinguishes the bank note, so that, in the secondary sense, it cannot be called money, from all pieces of paper, such as checks, bills, and other instruments of that kind, which I wholly deny the smallest possibility of giving the title of money to? The anonymous character of the bank note. If I take a man's check for my horse, ordering Jones & Co. to pay Mr. Price £84, he has not got my horse yet. I have got to ask who he is, and the likelihood of his having £84 at Jones & Co.'s. That money does not circulate. That is not money.

The paper promises issued by the Government of the United States that are made legal tenders come under the definition that I have given of money in the secondary sense. They roll about just like coin, and are taken from hand to hand. I was saying that I estimated the money in use by a banker as one thirtieth. A little time after Sir John Lubbock, of Robarts & Co., analyzed the receipts of £19,000,000, of that firm, and found that in that amount £3 in £100 were cash, and ten shillings only were coin. There was only three per cent I said it was one in thirty, and it turned out to be one in thirty-three and one third. So bankers do not deal in money. If that is not their business, what are these ninety-seven things which are their staple? What is a bank? The answer will depend upon these ninety-seven things. They are, one and all, debts to collect; pieces of paper pushed in upon the counter, all implying that John and William and Dick and Harry owe me a lot of things. You go and collect these debts for me. That is a banker's business; to collect pieces of paper embodying debts, and to collect them. The next thing is, what does a banker do? Does he go and get the money which he has a right to on all these pieces of paper? Not a bit. He is not going to be put to that botheration. What he does is this: A cotton man has just thrown down £5,000 worth of bills upon the counter of the bank. A man who is a dealer in silk turns up five minutes after, and says this: "I want to buy silk, but I have not the 'wherewithal.' I will hold you harmless. I have got security, but security not available to-day." What does the banker do? He says: "Give me these securities; you don't want to sell them; a cotton man has just given me £5,000 worth of cotton bills; I know he will not draw any checks upon these for at least a month. Go and buy silk for a month, and I will meet your checks." The banker has debts to collect, and how does he collect them? By creating fresh debts in which he is the lender. That is banking.

A banker is therefore essentially a broker. I define in my book a bank as an institution for the transferring of debts. A better one is, an institution for the transferring of credits, but a still better one is the following, which I prefer: A banker is essentially a broker. That is his true character and nature; an intermediate agent between two principals. Here is his relation to the cotton man: "You have given me £5,000 worth of cotton bills to collect. I understand from your habits of business that these bills will be with me a month. I am responsible to you for this, but I know I shall have it at my hand." To the other man he is a creator of debts, having lent him £5,000. What has he done? The man who sold cotton has purchasing power. He has the power of buying £5,000 worth of goods all over the town. He virtually says to the banker, "I don't want to buy anything for a month, and I shall not ask you for the proceeds of those bills for a month." But he still has the power of buying £5,000 worth, and that power he transfers to the banker, and the banker to the silk merchant to buy silk. The transfer from the banker to the silk merchant is buying power. It consists of the bills of cotton which went from his store, which must be paid for, and are paid for in silk. This is how I get these great conclusions; that a man who sells, by the act of selling can buy, because all trade and all selling is the exchange of equal goods. That is the meaning of the word selling. The banker is enabled to buy by virtue of the cotton bills, and he buys silk; so the silk changes hands by virtue of the cotton. The banker is merely an intermediate agent, a broker. The banker says, "I will find somebody to use your buying power." The cotton buys the silk. There is a tremendous number of conclusions to come out of that. What comes out of this? The explosion of that delusion which infests the city of London and the newspapers of England, that banking is an affair of currency, an affair of money, and that when there are disorders the cure is in currency. In the full light of the nineteenth century, this is believed by every trader in the United Kingdom; and so when the crisis comes they wake the Chancellor of the Exchequer out of his bed and say to him, "For God's sake, let the Bank of England issue more notes, and we shall be saved." Banking has nothing to do with money, except in one single point. I cannot thoroughly explain that now. If you tell a banker to issue notes, he of course sells them to the public. Every note that is issued by the Bank of England, or the United States Government, or by a private individual, is sold. The customers of this banker are the buyers. He collects their bills and he pays them in his bills. To that extent there is a resource in the banker who lends upon discount. That extent we know is limited in many cases. It has disappeared in England from the country banks. In the case of the Bank of England, that power of selling notes to the public is limited to about £15,000,000. By that means it has the power of lending upon discount. But otherwise banking has nothing to do with currency. It is very true that the banker is bound to pay his debts in currency, but so am I. So are Baring Brothers; so is every trader in the kingdom. It is perfectly possible that to-morrow morning at ten o'clock every creditor in the kingdom can ask for gold. He would have to take a bank note, but he can get the money from the Bank of England.

Now, what is the good of all this investigation? What reference has it to crises? This: that, as I said before, as banking is the region for the commercial typhoons and hurricanes, it is essential to see the causes that act upon banking, and it is not from such rubbish as a certain quantity of bank notes, certain things in the £3 in the hundred; it is from these ninety-seven things; and they are goods, are property, are goods sold, parted with, and the contract expressed on pieces of paper to pay money on demand or at the time specified. That is the force of banking, and, therefore, if banking is abundant, it is because many goods have been sold, and the sellers of these goods do not want to buy much. Let me repeat it. Banking is easy, discount is easy, the rate of interest is low, in the proportion that men have given away their goods and are not disposed to buy to a corresponding full extent of other goods. Then bankers have much to lend. But when this is the other way; when the farmer has spent all his capital in caring for his farm, and the bad and naughty weather comes in August, and the corn is spoiled, then the poor farmer is in very different circumstances with his banker. With a good harvest he has plenty of time to wait. When he has no wheat, or little to sell, he goes into town —perhaps has his old horse to replace with a new one—and he puts nothing in his banker's hands, and very possibly he asks him to lend him money. Look at the effect upon the banker. His means are reduced because the farmer deposited nothing, and perhaps wanted money, and to whom he must lend. That is abundant means for banking and poor means for banking.

Now, this making of railroads, warehouses, beautiful towns, etc., are not foolish things, but they are things which destroy and do not replace, and that is poverty. Poverty means that there are no goods to sell, and when there are no goods to sell there are no goods to buy with. The banker's resources fail, therefore. Then come the crises. They are the consequences of the destruction of property which is not replaced. They are the true children of poverty, and that kind of poverty which produces crises is never more fostered than when bankers encourage useful things, things useful twenty years from this day. The railroad does not replace its money for fifty years. If the actual outlay is £10,000,000, this £10,000,000 spent in food, etc., are not replaced for fifty years. The nation is poor for fifty years. Now, go on with that poverty, and the bedevilment of the money market will go on. The broker between the two men finds that his deposits are coming short, which means that there is no longer any sale of goods. Why? Because you have been destroying the wealth of the country in a way which will lose it for fifty years. It is no better, as far as banking is concerned, than if you had chucked it into the sea. The savings of the nation is the excess of the things it makes in comparison with the things it consumes, and that excess, if it employs it wisely, will make the nation richer. But if it "chucks" it into the sea, it will remain stationary. The secret of crises is the building, beyond the savings, of useful and valuable works.

It is claimed that the English Coöperative Associations are the best financial successes in the world. That of Rochdale, in England, was started by twenty-eight men. After a prolonged strike of the flannel manufacturers, which ended in the utter defeat of the working men, a few of them met together, about thirty years ago, and said one to another: "Is it not possible, instead of the constant strife with capital, which is too strong for us, that we can use the capital spent in this way by ourselves, and do something to become our own employers?" That was at the bottom of the idea of starting a coöperative store, and the twenty-eight men then commenced the Rochdale Society, with a capital of £28 ($140), which at the present time numbers 7,000 members, one for each house in town, and now have an accumulated capital of £150,000 ($750,000), and distributes profits among the working men of the town of between $150,000 and $200,000, annually. The educational funds of the society amount to more than $5,000 yearly; and out of the Rochdale store has sprung a cotton mill and flannel manufactory, which employs a capital of $700,000, in addition to its other capital needed in various ways. The Executive Committee of the National Grange have recommended the Rochdale plan of coöperative societies as worthy of imitation by Patrons.

There are at present seven hundred and fifty coöperative societies in England, representing a business capital of not less than $50,000,000, and the profits amount to more than $3,-800,000 annually. Taking the good, bad and indifferent coöperative societies into account, we find that the average expense upon the business is only five per cent., and that amount includes a sum sufficient to pay the interest upon the capital.

In Germany, coöperative banks were established some twenty years ago, which are said to have proved a great blessing to the laboring classes. The capital of these banks consists of funds known as active and reserve. The first is derived from the monthly or annual contributions of members; the latter is made up of admission fees, and from retaining a percentage of the profits in the bank, to be distributed in case of dissolution. Deposits and loans are made, and these, with the active fund, constitute the working capital. No interest is paid on contributions, but members derive a dividend from the general profits, averaging some fifteen per cent. per annum, and are allowed advances at a low rate of interest, to the amount of their stock, and larger sums, by giving security to other members. The aggregate business of these banks in 1867 was $13,000,000, and the proportion of losses was but one quarter of one per cent., which is creditable alike to the administrative ability of the officers, and the honesty and integrity of its members.

Wise men ask, when they see an acorn before them, does it contain an oak? And, judging from the small beginning and successful growth of these societies, one could not but infer that they contain the germ of true prosperity and happiness. The progress has been striking. It took twenty years for coöperative societies to accumulate the first five million, and only five to accumulate the next. The entire capital of England, at the present time, is about $40,000,000,000, and the profits thirty to forty million, while the profits of coöperative societies are nearly four million, or thirty per cent. on the capital employed. The "California Agriculturist" says: "With the glorious success of our mother country before us, it seems that the working men of the west and the farmers might combine, and by putting the shares at $5 to $10 each, so that all could take part, in a short time could have a substantial coöperative store and manufactory in every town of a thousand inhabitants in the west, and by such a course would dispense with the necessity of shipping our produce to eastern consumers, and paying transportation companies three to four times as much for shipping as the producer gets for raising. When such a movement is organized, there will be no more legislation needed on railroads; and they, like all other branches of industry, will have to work for the same that others do, or suspend operations."

CHAPTER XXX.

EXCEPTIONAL CONDITIONS OF THE PACIFIC COAST AFFECTING AGRICULTURAL PROSPERITY.

SUMMARY OF ADVANTAGES: OF DISADVANTAGES---WET AND DRY SEASONS—VARIABILITY OF THE AVERAGE—IRREGULARITY IN EACH YEAR—TABULAR STATEMENT OF EXTREMES OF RAIN-FALL--SEASONS OF DROUGHT—AMOUNT OF RAIN NEEDED TO SECURE A CROP—AMOUNT ACTUALLY DETERMINED—FENCES AND FUEL---FORESTS AND THE RAIN-FALL—FORESTS AND INLAND NAVIGATION.

PATRONS of Husbandry from the older States will naturally seek for reliable information within the Order with regard to the advantages which the Pacific Coast offers to immigration. We shall endeavor to state these with fairness, believing that the presentation of the shady side will yet leave, in the vast area of unoccupied land, in the salubrity of our climate, the range of our productions, and the variety of industries which must necessarily spring from these, conditions of prosperity unequaled on the face of the earth. The early settlers were wont to call this "God's country;" we believe it is most emphatically and peculiarly "man's country," the chosen field of his highest endeavors and accomplishments.

Of the 40,000,000 of acres of tillable land in California alone, there is probably 18,000,000 which can be obtained at a moderate cost and upon favorable terms. Under the Homestead Act the same facilities exist as eastward; but here the farmer is not obliged to house his stock, to build barns, or, in most cases, to clear his land. A chain of valleys, where wheat can be grown without irrigation, extends from Los Angeles northward to the Russian river, with a great number of smaller tributary valleys or offshoots, remarkably adapted to the purposes of diversified farming and stock growing. There are almost as many climates as townships. Directly upon the coast, in the latitude of San Francisco, neither the grape nor semi-tropical fruits will flourish in the open air; yet three miles from Martinez, in the Alhambra vineyards, every desirable variety of the grape, cherry, peach, almond; the orange, lemon and pomegranate, are grown to perfection. These extremes of variability are found within a few miles of each other.

The "tule" lands are estimated to cover 3,000,000 of acres, and contain the richest soils, to reclaim which, capital is now largely directed. The time is not far distant when they will be covered with the most profitable crops, for which there are all the advantages of cheap water transportation.

But the most marked geographical feature of the Pacific Coast is the great valley which has been so fully treated of in our chapters on irrigation, "of 57,200 square miles in extent, equal to Illinois, Wisconsin, or Michigan, or Iowa, or Ohio and half of Indiana combined, or of half the area of all the Middle States."

All this immense area possesses the working man's climate, a climate resembling that of Italy in its general character, though far more bracing and exhilarating in its effect upon man and animals. The following table, from "Hittell's Resources of California," shows the mean temperatures of January and July, and the difference between them in different localities:

PLACE.	JAN.	JULY.	DIFFERENCE.	LATITUDE.
	deg.	deg.	deg.	deg. min.
San Francisco	49	57	8	37 48
Monterey	52	58	6	36 36
Santa Barbara	54	71	17	34 24
Los Angeles	52	75	23	34 04
Jurupa	54	73	19	34 02
San Diego	51	72	21	32 41
San Luis Rey	52	70	18	33 15
Sacramento	45	73	28	38 34
Stockton	49	72	23	37 56
Humboldt Bay	40	58	18	40 44
Sonoma	45	66	21	38 18
St. Helena	42	77	35	38 30
Vallejo	48	67	19	38 05
Antioch	43	70	27	38 03
Millerton	47	90	43	37 00
Fort Jones	34	71	37	41 40
Fort Reading	44	82	38	40 28
Fort Yuma	56	92	36	32 43

The most serious drawback to California as a farming country, is the frequency of droughts. Oregon and Washington have here an advantage, counterbalanced, to some extent, by their frosts and snows, though the latter seldom involves an utter failure of the crop. In portions of California, two rainless seasons in succession destroy not only crops and fields, but stock also; in the summer of 1863–4, more than 800,000 neat cattle and sheep died of starvation. The difference in the rain-fall varies greatly in different parts of the State. We give the following exhaustive paper on the rain-fall, from the report of the Board of Irrigation Commissioners:

The climate of the Pacific coast west of the Sierra Nevada and Cascade mountains is altogether different from that of the Atlantic coast, and differs also from that of the country between the eastern slope of the Rocky mountains and the Sierra Nevada. The ordinary form of rain-fall tables fails to exhibit its characteristic, so that upon this coast tabulated results of precipitation of rain and snow are made out for the rainy season, which extends from about October 15 to April 1. No rain, in the ordinary acceptation of the term, falls during the dry season, between April 1 and October 15, in the latitude of 38°. Northward of that latitude, and especially northward of latitude 40°, there is frequently a small rain-fall during the summer, and a heavy rain-fall during the winter.

Southward of 38° the rainy season is shortened and the dry season lengthened, so that at San Diego, in latitude 32½°, the rain-fall on the immediate coast averaged only 9.2 inches during twenty-three years.

On the coast, about latitude 28°, is the region of the "doldrums," where little rain falls, but where a cloudy region exists. South of that latitude, the seasons are changed, and our rainy season is the dry season of the southern part of Lower California, and our dry season their wet season.

At the extremity of the peninsula of Lower California, only 3½ inches fell last summer. The rain-fall at San Francisco, which may be taken as a type, averages 23.5 annually, distributed as follows:

Month	Inches.	Season	Inches.
June	0.04	Total for the Summer	0.07
July	0.01		
August	0.02		
September	0.10	Total for the Autumn	3.57
October	0.64		
November	2.83		
December	5.42	Total for the Winter	14.32
January	5.30		
February	3.60		
March	3.18	Total for the Spring	5.56
April	1.74		
May	0.64		
Yearly average			23.52

The tabulated results of rain-fall upon the western coast of the United States, from San Diego to Puget Sound, given by the Smithsonian Contributions, confirm this example as a type, having the following characteristics:

"A most decided minimum during the summer months, amount

at some places, to an absence of rain, and a well marked maximum late in December. Range excessive."

Other tables could be produced to illustrate a characteristic in the winter rain-falls, namely, that during the season there is a marked cessation of rain, ranging from one to four weeks.

This cessation does not occur at any regular epoch, so that its effect is not seen in a chart constructed only upon average quantities, but it has occurred nine years out of ten. Very frequently during this cessation of rain, the cold winds from the north, accompanied by a clear sky, blow fiercely, and blast the young growing crops; or when this dry interval is prolonged, even without these cold northers, the weather is usually clear and fine, perhaps hot, and the young grain withers and may be wholly lost, even for fodder, if the last rains of the season come late.

In some years the rains cease suddenly in February, and the crop is lost. This was notably so in the Great Valley in the spring of 1873, where a most promising harvest was blighted by the ceasing of the rains, and only those few fields that were irrigated yielded a crop; those that had been summer-fallowed yielded about half an average crop; the remainder, especially on the southern half of the valley, yielded, probably, an average of six or eight bushels.

Southward of the Great Valley, to the Mexican boundary, the necessity for irrigation increases, and the problem becomes more intricate, because the extensive arable sections have a limited supply of water, and the country is not so easily watered. In the San Diego river no water flowed through its lower parts for about five years, ending November, 1873.

Although the commission has not been required to examine any other than the Great Valley, the foregoing fact is stated in confirmation of the péculiar climatic conditions of the coast.

The orographical features of the Pacific slope are such that were other conditions equal, the uniformity of rain-fall can nowhere take place.

Speaking generally, the Coast Range of mountains and the Sierra Nevada run parallel with the coast line, and the Great Valley lies between them. The Coast Range of mountains maintains an average elevation of over two thousand feet, reaching as much as six thousand two hundred feet a few miles south of Monterey, and three thousand eight hundred feet to the peninsula of San Francisco.

The southerly storms of winter bring up rain north of latitude 28° to 30°, and drive the moisture-laden air against the southwesterly, or seaward-flanks of these mountain ranges, and the precipitation of rain amounts to two and a half times the quantity that falls upon the eastern flanks. This has been established by measurement at the reservoirs of the Spring Valley Water Company, and confirms the reports of the farmers and stockmen.

Nine years observations at Pillarcitos Dam, give an average of 58 inches of rain, while San Francisco, distant only fourteen miles, has 23.5 inches. The same law holds good along the western flank of the Sierra Nevada, which chain averages nine thousand five hundred feet elevation. From several years observations on the line of the Central Pacific railroad, the fall of rain at Summit station is three times that between Rocklin and Auburn, and many times greater than on the eastern flank of the Sierra, where the rain-fall is very limited. The same law is well known along the southermost part of Lower California.

At the head of Sacramento Valley, in latitude 41°, where the Coast Range of mountains crowds upon the Sierra Nevada, the clouds are banked up heavily, and it is safe to say that four times, and in some seasons perhaps ten times as much rain falls at Shasta as in the region of Kern Lake, at the southwestern extremity of the valley. This latter section is the driest region in the whole valley, and probably only half the rain falls there that falls about the vicinity of Bakersfield.

On the Coast Range of mountains, snow very rarely falls, and never lies over twenty-four hours; but on the Sierra Nevada, it falls to a depth of sixty or seventy feet (observations at Summit station, in 1866–'67), and lies throughout the winter with an average depth of fourteen feet. This snow forms a great natural storehouse of water; it supplies the streams throughout the year. If the greater body of it is melted during the winter by warm rains, it causes disastrous floods; but in ordinary seasons the main body of it is melted about June, and causes the summer rise in the rivers.

The law of the greater precipitation of rain upon the western flanks of the mountains is well exhibited in the number, size and volume of the streams which have their sources in these mountain ranges. The streams of the west, or seaward flank of the peninsula of San Francisco and of the Coast Range northward, are greater than those on the eastern flank, and especially marked is this in the case of the Sierra Nevada, where it may be also noted that the streams of the west flank exceed in aggregate volume those of both flanks of the Coast Range.

The figures to establish this well-known law are not produced in this place, as they will be used in the remarks upon the unequal fall of rain over the country.

The average yearly rain-fall over the basin of the Great Valley, is sufficient to insure good crops annually.

This proposition embraces two vital questions: 1st. What amount of rain-fall, if properly distributed, will insure a crop? 2d. What amount of rain-fall is there over the entire basin of the Great Valley? Fortunately, a good practical example is at hand. During the rainy seasons of 1870–71, 1871–72, 1872–73, a record of the rain-fall at Visalia was kept by Dr. James W. Blake, and is both instructive and reliable. In 1870–71, the total rain-fall was about 6.8 inches; in 1871–2, 10.3 inches; in 1872–3, 7.2 inches. In the first and third of these years, the crops were failures; in the second the harvest was an abundant one. In 1872–3, the distribution was very equable and adequate to the end of February; after that, only one quarter of an inch fell upon one day in March and one in April, and the crops were virtually lost. The critical period in the growing crops appears in this, as in other districts, to be about the middle or end of February, when the grain is several inches high, and another rain-fall of one or two inches would give good crops, while a cessation of rain leaves them blighted. The rain-fall at Visalia, 1871–72, when a full crop was secured, was as follows:

1870.	Inches.	1871.	Inches.
November 26	0.50	January 9	1.05
November 27	0.24	February 4	0.30
November 28	0.44	February 5	0.16
December 17	0.10	February 9	0.17
December 18	0.12	February 22	0.45
December 19	0.33	February 23	0.50
December 20	0.06	February 24	0.38
December 21	0.28	February 27	0.40
December 22	0.68	March 28	0.91
December 23	0.15	March 29	0.05
December 27	0.20	April 13	0.08
December 28	0.98	April 16	0.48
December 29	0.62	April 17	0.07
December 31	0.40	April 27	0.13
		April 28	0.11

Making a total of 10.34 inches.

Throughout the southern sections of California, crops have been secured when 12 inches of rain have fallen in the wet season, but the precipitation is not so reliably uniform as farther north. Farmers and stockmen claim good crops with 15 inches. Owing to the excessive heat of summer, the temperature reaching 130° in the sun at Bakersfield, every particle of moisture is evaporated during the dry season, and the land cannot be plowed until considerable rain has fallen.

The average yearly rain-fall over the whole of the Great Basin, from the Sierra Nevada to the crest line of the Coast Range is not less than 20 inches, as is shown by the statistics of the Smithsonian publications, and other evidence.

At Fort Crook, on the upper Sacramento river, at an elevation of three thousand three hundred and ninety feet, in eight years, from January, 1858, to October, 1867, there has been an average of 23.7 inches of rain-fall.

At Fort Reading, on the Sacramento river, near Reading, in three and three quarter years, from April, 1852, to march, 1856, 29.1 inches.

At Clear Lake, head of Cache Creek, in six years, from 1867 to 1873, 34.4 inches.

At Sacramento, in twenty-four years, from September, 1849, to August, 1872, 19.6 inches.

At Benicia, in thirteen and a half years, from November, 1849, to December, 1864, 15.1 inches.

At Stockton, in three and one half years, from January, 1854, to December, 1857, 13.7 inches.

At Millerton, on the San Joaquin river, in six and three quarter years, from July, 1851, to June, 1858, 19 inches.

From the mouth of the Sacramento southward along the west side of the valley, to its extremity, there are no records by which we can approximate the rain-fall. The average yearly rain-fall north of the mouth of the Sacramento river equals 23 inches; south of the same, 16 inches, including that at Fort Tejon, in the mountains. In the southern part of the valley the estimate is that not more than two crops in five years can be raised. Taking all the estimates, there falls on the average, a superabundance of water for maturing the crops.

But the rain-fall in different years is very variable; seasons of drought and great floods occur, and in any one season the rain is very unequally distributed in different sections. A dry spring, as in 1873, cuts off one half the crop through the moister parts of the valley, and totally destroys the crops in the southern part, except where irrigation is practiced. From all these facts it therefore appears to be sufficiently established, that some system of controlling the waters of precipitation is needed, and that with such a system annual crops may be secured.

No other means of equalizing the rain-fall will ever take the place of that which nature has provided in her forests. The relations of forests to the public welfare are too vast and too important to be presented here. The most magnificent schemes of irrigation will prove but temporary measures of relief, unless our existing forests are spared, or an equivalent of their value as condensers and equalizers of moisture obtained by artificial planting.

Another great drawback upon the agriculture of California is the lack of timber for fences and fuel. The former costs from three to six hundred dollars a mile, according to the distance from market and the quality of the fence made; and though comparatively little fuel is needed in this mild climate, the lack of it is a serious item of inconvenience and expense. In the neighborhood of Los Angeles, and upon the tule lands, the willow answers an excellent purpose for hedges, and soon supplies firewood and charcoal; grape cuttings are also extensively used; but no more promising outlay of labor or capital is found in the State, than the artificial production of wood in large quantities. Happily for us, Australia has given us trees, of marvelous strength, size, durability, and rapidity of growth, in the eucalyptus or sweet gum family, of which not less than thirty-five useful and ornamental species are now acclimated. Trees are indispensable to break the force of the northers, those destructive winds which are the dread of farmers in the Great Valley.

We gladly give space to the valuable suggestions of George May Powell, Chairman of the American Institute Committee on Forests and Inland Navigation:

Both ancient and modern history, as well as philosophy, unite in ascribing the depletion and the disappearance of streams to the disforesting of the regions of which they are the arteries. Our own country is not an exception. Streams which the early records of the United States show to have been sufficient to float not only barges with several tons of produce, but vessels of war even, will not now float a skiff at the same seasons of the year. A very little examination will show that in its bearing on the great question of inland navigation we have as a nation many many millions of dollars annually involved in it. This interest is increasing in magnitude no less rapidly than is our material growth. The famous engineer, Brunel, used to say that "God made rivers on purpose to feed canals." Official experiments carried on in this State, during the last year or two, have demonstrated that by the use of steam on our canals, freight can be transported between the seabord and the great lakes in half the time previously required to move it by horse power. We know, too, that eight pounds of traction are required to move a ton of freight on a level by rail, while less than one fourth that traction is required to move a ton afloat in still water. A fair average price of moving freight by rail is $30 per ton, per 1,000 miles. Most of our farmers' boys have enough arithmetic at command to enable them, by use of the above factors and of the census reports, indicating the amount of grain and other products of farms, mines and factories we have to transport, to show that we have an amount here involved annually exceeding the interest on the public debt. There is no doubt that the great body of our freight can and should be floated instead of rolled, leaving the railways still plenty of work in carrying passengers, express and mails. No more silvaculture than is needed for timber, for fuel and manufacturing, and kindred purposes, or that will "pay" as such, will so restore and preserve these streams as to make them available for the grandest system of inland navigation the world ever saw. England has so elaborate a system, that between using the channels of scarce a score of streams—few of which are large enough to be called rivers in America, together with canal connections, that the aggregate length of her inland lines is more than ten times her territorial length.

To secure a system similarly continuous in this country we should require in some cases to construct "slack water" courses, but that in turn would nearly or quite pay for itself in adding to well distributed hydraulic power for manufacturing purposes. Over a large majority of such lines river boats would run, which would move at full treble the speed of steam canal boats, and so be available for passenger travel. Less than fifty years will see not alone the Mississippi, the lakes and the Atlantic connected by ship canals, and the Chesapeake and Ohio united; it will witness the headwaters between the Missouri and the Columbia, and also many of the minor streams tributary to these and to others of the major arteries, so improved by means of combined forest and navigation engineering that the farmers, miners and manufacturers of the next century will have their freight moved at rates fabulously low compared to those now paid. In cases where "summit levels" could not be "locked" over, the transit could be made, as is now done over the Alleghany mountains, by section-boats mounted on rail-cars. We presume it is not necessary to review the ground gone over in previous papers to show that forest care and culture must, in the very nature of the case, have the effect of restoring and of saving the beautiful streams of our country. That it will have such an effect, no truly scientific man will question for a moment. Water enough falls every year to keep our streams alive and strong; but we want the millions of tons of forest leaves and moss, and the millions of acres of soil loosened by the roots of forest trees, to act as the huge sponge, to hold it back from the sudden plunge into the streams, incident to disforested regions. We want the cooling influence of the vast banks of green forest leaves to more frequently contract the water-laden air, so as to give us many minor rain-falls in places of less and less frequent and more and more violent rains, always and necessarily resulting from wholesale slaughter of our forest friends.

CHAPTER XXXI.

AGRICULTURAL COMMUNITIES.

"Agriculture will never be overstocked in America. She says to other countries, bring us your skill and labor; we offer in return competence, homes and schools."

"The gradual development of the principle of equality is a providential fact; universal, durable, it constantly eludes human interference, and all events, as well as men, contribute to its progress."—*De Tocqueville.*

Isolation of Farmers—Decrease of Agricultural Population: Causes—Genesis of the Middle-man: He Devours both Farmer and Mechanic—Better Education the Remedy—Recruits for the Agricultural Army—Immigration Table—Scandinavia in America—Superiority of the Colony System—Vineland, a model Rural Colony—Outlook and Conclusions.

It will not be denied that one of the greatest discouragements to the life of the farmer has been his comparative social isolation; and all the advantages claimed for coöperation in business enterprises are trifling in comparison with the benefits of social coöperation in establishing rural colonies. Especially is this true of California, where the urban is so much more in excess of the rural population than in the older States, and where the census shows the proportionate rate of increase in the latter to be so much smaller. In the older States we find the original farmers' families have disappeared, and new ones of foreign birth are taking their places. The young crowd into the cities, into the mercantile or professional ranks, until the country is depleted of its most energetic and intelligent members, while the overfull city is unable to utilize the labor force which should have been expended upon the land.

Between the years 1850 and 1870, the population of eighteen of our large cities increased one hundred and thirty-one per cent. Deducting the population of these cities from that of their respective States, we have an increase of fifty-nine per cent. in the country, including all the smaller cities, villages and towns. In some States this disproportion is even greater, as in Massachusetts, where such a test would show that the rural population has not increased at all, during two decades. Even in the new States, the town population is greatly in excess of the country, as is shown by the following statistics of Ohio: Total State population—1850, 1,980,329; 1870, 2,665,-260. Urban population—1850, 400,000; 1870, 1,000,000. Agricultural population—1850, 1,580,329; 1870, 1,665,260. Increase—84,931. This gives an increase of 5.4 per cent. in the agricultural, against an increase of 150 per cent. of the urban population. The cause of this most undesirable state of things is due to a low estimate of the farmer's pursuit, and the absence of the facilities afforded for social enjoyments in compact neighborhoods. Human beings degenerate in proportion to their isolation; for man is preëminently a social animal, and he rises in the scale by the addition of other experiences to his own. The growth of his intellect and affections require the presence of various objects upon which they may be exercised.

We often hear it remarked that any man can be a farmer; that bone and muscle are the only requisites for success in that calling. The well-bred girl turns away from the manly farmer's boy, and encourages the city snob, often against the dictates of her better judgment, because she thinks there is no place on the farm for refinements or sociability, or intellectual pleasures. It is these notions of farming which have made that ogre of the farmers, the middle-man. He is usually a spoiled farmer, whose wife was discontented on account of hard work and social privations, and who had found country life, as Gail Hamilton expresses it, "one uninterrupted flat." Gen. Francis A. Walker, Superintendent of the United States Census, the most reliable and unprejudiced of witnesses, tells us that there has been in the last decade a marked falling off in the number of common laborers, and an increase of forty per cent. of the trading class. While the demand for farm labor exceeds the supply, the farmers "are maintaining a body of persons not less numerous than the standing army of the British empire, and with a far greater number of dependents in the way of wives and children than are charged to the officers and soldiers of that army, all in excess of the legitimate demands of trade." The farmer claims that the middle-man carries off all his profits, and in the somewhat intemperate abuse of this very essential member of the social body, has failed to recognize his origin. Only of the excess should he justly complain.

According to the census of 1870, there are in the United States 12,505,000 bread-earners, who give food, shelter and raiment to the 39,000,000 of inhabitants. Every bread-earner has to feed a little over three mouths. Of these, 5,922,000 are engaged in agriculture, strictly; 1,765,000 in other rural trades and callings, such as blacksmithing, carpentering and the like, making, with their food dependents, 23,830,000 souls out of the 39,000,000. The manufacturers, including operatives and servants, earn bread for 1,117,000. Commerce, including merchants, shop-keepers, sailors, clerks, peddlers, bar-keepers, etc., earn bread for 2,256,000. Railroad and expressmen earn bread for 595,000. Miners for 472,000.

So it comes to this: while agriculture and mechanics fill ten times as many mouths as commerce, twenty times as many as manufactures, forty times as many as railroads, and fifty times as many as mining, yet the least of these, by combination, coöperation and management, exercises three times the influence in the country, and thrice the power with the government, simply because the farmers have not learned how to work and pull together; and, until recently, for a lack of knowledge of the true principles of coöperation and organization.

Now, we have in the Grange a safe, practical organization, simple enough in form to unite the youngest and feeblest agricultural colony, and embracing a wide range of benefits not confined to the agricultural class.

Mechanics have suffered quite as much from middle-men as the agriculturists, and for the same cause, viz., a defective education of both employer and employed. Between the master or employer, who has no skill, and the workman, who has skill without education, the middle-man, who has a little of both, is a kind of necessity. Under the present system, Mr. Scott Russell tells us, the employer of a thousand men may pocket, in the shape of profits, one half of the whole earnings of all the men, or a sum equal to the earnings of fifty or a hundred, as the case may be. But put a hundred men together who have enjoyed equality of education, setting aside all inequalities of birth and fortune, and these proportions must change. "I believe," he adds, "that the education of the future will lead to a great reduction of employers' wages or profits; to a fair fixed interest on all the capital invested; to a fair division of the earnings of work among the men who execute it, in some recognized proportion to the contribution which their skill makes to the perfection of their work, and that the scale of every man's life may be one of steady, continual, meritorious rise."

The abolition of the middle-man, therefore, is to be effected by the intellectual advancement of mechanical and agricultural laborers. But to restore the proper equilibrium between the town and country, we must inquire where the agricultural recruits are coming from, since we cannot hope to turn the current of our native population for at least a generation. This brings us to the great question of immigration. The following table, taken from the Agricultural Report of 1873, shows us the sources from which it has mainly been drawn:

ANNUAL IMMIGRATION INTO THE UNITED STATES FROM 1867 TO 1873, INCLUSIVE.

NATIONALITY.	1867.	1868.	1869.	1870.	1871.	1872.	1873.
Great Britain and Ireland	125,520	107,583	147,716	151,089	143,937	157,905	159,355
Germany	133,426	123,070	124,788	91,779	107,201	155,595	133,141
Austro-Hungary	692	395	2,523	5,284	4,889	6,132	7,835
Sweden	5,316	13,958	24,115	12,009	11,659	14,645	11,351
Norway	1,739	6,461	17,718	12,356	11,307	10,348	18,107
Denmark	1,436	2,019	4,282	3,041	2,346	3,758	5,095
Netherlands	2,223	652	1,360	970	1,122	2,006	4,640
Belgium	789	1,578	1,003	1,039	168	964	1,306
Switzerland	4,168	3,261	3,488	2,474	2,824	4,031	3,223
France	5,237	3,936	4,118	3,586	5,780	13,782	10,813
Spain	904	816	1,112	511	618	558	486
Portugal	126	245	265	291	59	370	34
Italy, including Sicily, Sardinia and Malta	1,624	1,408	2,182	2,940	2,948	7,322	7,511
Greece	10	8	17	15	10	18	37
Turkey	26	13	10	13	21	34	78
Russia	205	204	580	766	1,005	1,311	3,490
Poland	310	248	87	424	832	2,606	2,863
Finland	....	....	....	....	24	71	113
Heligoland	....	....	....	....	2	1	1
Gibraltar	....	....	....	1	4	3	8
Corsica	....	....	....	3	....	....	....
Europe (not specified)	....	....	....	1	....	....	....
Atlantic Islands	391	310	452	574	920	1,168	1,478
West India Islands	817	858	3,016	1,109	1,228	1,309	1,974
North America	6,310	11,172	31,300	53,826	40,432	40,903	30,015
South America	224	145	59	84	110	123	168
Asia	3,961	10,701	15,000	12,058	6,070	10,681	18,219
Africa	25	63	31	24	25	40	13
Australia, Pacific and East India Islands	1	1	44	25	1,289	1,920	1,053
Born at sea	1	3	....	10	77	133	138
Not specified (exclusive of Europe)	11,891	23,292	49,923	67,711	50,182	56,290	....
Countries not stated	2,877	8,107	10,656	22,494	20,882	11,752	....
Total aliens	298,358	297,215	395,922	378,796	367,789	449,483	422,545
Less those not intending to remain in the United States	4,757	8,070	10,635	22,493	20,851	11,733	....
Net immigration	293,601	289,145	385,287	356,303	346,938	437,750	422,545
Total for Europe	283,751	265,855	335,364	288,592	296,756	381,400	369,487

The emigration from Scandinavia has been so great for the last twenty-five years, and has added so much to the growth and prosperity of Iowa, Minnesota and Wisconsin, and in a lesser degree to other Western States, that their example in promoting it may profitably be imitated by any State which aims to develop itself socially and industrially, by adding to its numbers a thrifty, home-building population. From the Scandinavian population, also, the suffrages of the whole people are advancing men into public positions. The State University of Wisconsin has its Norwegian Professor, and lest our next President should be descended from Odin's royal line, it behooves us to know how much more or less an American he would be in consequence.

The civil and political history of the Western States illustrates the "tendency to homogeneousness in all the modes of a civilization which moves in an east and west direction, through the same belt of climate." If the problem of Scandinavian influence had not already been solved in the commingling of their blood and spirit into English character, we might still trust that tendency while we watch their conquest of the northern lands by the same resistless energy which made them masters of the northern seas. This tendency doubtless helps greatly in the assimilation of all the European nationalities that come to us, but in the Northmen kindred and family traits identify them at once with us and our institutions. In response to a toast, "To the Norwegian patriot and musician," Ole Bull replied, "When I am in America I am a Norwegian; in Norway I am always an American."

It is not from Germany but from Scandinavia that the English and American people have derived those infusions of strength and enterprise, and that spirit of dominion and colonization which have carried the sentiments of civil, political and religious liberty, the principles of representative legislation, trial by jury, security of property and the freedom of the press, to the remotest parts of the earth.

Throughout Scandinavia, in the earliest times, the peasantry, —*i. e.* the people—constituted the supreme power, and the "All Thing," or Diet, transformed their simple customs into laws. A peasant was not only an agricultor, but the free-born inheritor of rights in the soil, who became eligible through superiority of wisdom or warlike prowess to an election as Chief, Jarl or King.

The Northmen were also distinguished among heathens for their reverence for women, who were "so true to their country, their friends and their home, that Odin sent down to them the gift of healing from his splendid 'Hlidskjalf.'" Of the three branches of the Scandinavian people, the Norwegians have best preserved these characteristics—the spirit of independence and nationality—and becauso they have so little to learn in respect to self-government, they are, of all foreigners, the best prepared for the duties of American citizenship.

Although Norway is attached to the Swedish crown, and is governed as a hereditary constitutional monarchy, it is almost an independent democratic government. It retains its own official language, currency and flag, and the King is required to be crowned in the cathedral at Drontheim, according to the ancient custom.

The democratic legislative assembly is chosen by the popular vote, convenes triennially by its own right, and cannot be dissolved by kingly interference until the constitutional three months' session has expired.

It is the "Storthing" which makes war, peace, laws and treaties, levies taxes, imposts and tariffs, provides for and controls all finances, salaries and pensions. Every male Norwegian twenty-five years of age may vote if he possesses property to the value of one hundred and sixty-eight dollars; every voter may become a representative when thirty years of age, provided he has resided ten years in the country. The Storthing, in reality a single body, divides its functions by electing one fourth of its members into an upper house, called the Odelsthing, and if a bill passes both divisions of this assembly in three successive storthings, it becomes a law of the land without the royal assent, a right which exists under no other constitution in Europe.

The organization of their judiciary and the government of their towns is marked by the same democratic simplicity. A certain number of householders choose arbitrators for the settlement of neighborhood differences for a term of three years. Above this are sixty-four minor courts, distributed throughout the kingdom, and sitting every three months; as a last resort they have the *hoiste ret*, held at Christiana, consisting of a president and eight assessors. The judges are liable to damages for their decisions.

Every Norwegian parish has its court of the higher law, consisting of the pastor and schoolmaster, whose opinions are authoritative on almost all local questions. As the King is so nearly a lay figure in the civil government, he is permitted to act as the head of the established Church in the bestowal of sees and livings under the eye of the Ecclesiastical Minister and Council of State. This council, consisting of eight persons, represents the King in both ecclesiastical and secular affairs.

It is impossible to overrate the influence of the clergy upon the Norwegian people. Generally well educated themselves, they have fostered education; and though intolerant in the extreme toward all other religions than the Lutheran, they have favored public libraries, literary and scientific societies and the freedom of the press. They have impressed a religious character upon the system of popular education; and every schoolmaster, from the itinerant pedagogue who travels from neighborhood to neighborhood in the sparsely settled regions of the far north, imparting what is better than learning, viz., the love of learning, to the highest official, the teacher is a person in authority. Education is compulsory in both Sweden and Norway; there are primary schools in every parish, supported by small contributions from the pupils and a direct tax upon householders. Their secondary schools, which are daily becoming more practical and technical in their character, are found in all the large towns, Sweden having twenty-seven lower agricultural schools, seven of forestry, nine of navigation and two of mining, besides academies of agriculture and other industries.

It is indeed surprising that so much has been accomplished in the wildest and most inhospitable of lands for the best interests of the people. "Economy is their name, and frugality their surname," was said in reply to the question, "who are they?" asked by a Southern gentleman of a citizen of Milwaukee, when a load of Norsk emigrants landed from the steamer.

It is little wonder that the region of the great lakes and the upper Mississippi should have attracted this enterprising and frugal people. Accustomed to the sea, the ocean voyage has no terrors for them; and, as great numbers came through the St. Lawrence, the expense was very light in comparison to the distance. Newspapers were early established at Bergen and Christiana containing glowing accounts from the pioneer emigrants of the rich prairies, better than the best lands at home; of the noble forests on the Eau Claire and St. Croix, to be had almost for the asking. All over Norway and Sweden silver "skillings" began to be hoarded for the land agent. Often the pastor or schoolmaster was sent out to purchase, and make arrangements for the settlement of fifty or a hundred families.

The people of the northwest had learned to appreciate the value of the Scandinavian population in developing the agricultural resources of the country; had made way for them in schools and churches, and in legislative halls; but not until the civil war did we really know them as our fellow countrymen and women. There came a day in that dark year of 1862 when the Scandinavian Regiment, which never had a drafted man, departed to join the Army of the Cumberland. A finer regiment, or one that had a brighter record than the Fifteenth Wisconsin, was never offered. At Island No. 10, Florence, Murfreesboro, Stone River and Kenesaw they rendered noble service. When they entered the service, the society "Nora," at Chicago, presented them a beautiful flag with the motto, "For God and our Country." On one side was the American colors, with gold stars on a blue field, on the other the Lion and Ax of Norway, on a red field, with date and inscription. When this flag, which never was lowered before the enemy, came back to be hung with the other tattered battle-flags in the capitol, only a handful remained of the brave fellows who took it away. Their Colonel, Hans Heg, was placed by General Rosecrans in command of the Third Brigade. He fell in the great battle of Chickamauga; and to General La Grange, who stood beside him and received his last words, said, "I do not regret this. All I ask is that my children receive a good education." After the next day's disastrous conflict, only seventy-five men could be gathered; many of the officers were killed, others captured, and yet, after being joined by two companies who had been left at Island No. 10, consisting of eighty men, they performed some of the hardest service and won some of the brightest laurels of the war. To the honor of Wisconsin be it said that no child of those fallen heroes has failed to receive a good education.

These illustrations of the capacity of the Scandinavian races for complete assimilation with the great body of the American citizens, whether we employ them in the arts of peace or war, are offered in the hope that efforts will be made to attract them to this coast.

The statistics of the nationalities represented in the State prisons of the Northwest show how rarely the dangerous classes of society are recruited from the Northmen; while the statistics of production for the last twenty years prove what enormous additions they have made to the wealth of the country. A few flourishing Norwegian colonies in our lumber counties, or our dairy counties, would give a new aspect to the labor question in this State.

The women, who like out-door work as well as the men, would cover many an acre with trees and vines, and we should find other use for our flax than burning it. The men make excellent sailors. In Europe they are rapidly developing in the direction of the fine arts, especially in landscape painting. The love of music is almost universal with them. One cannot find an emigrant's hut without its cheap edition of their poets.

Distributed by nationalities, the immigration into the States of the interior has been pretty equally divided between the Germans and Scandinavians. But the Germans swell the population of the cities rather than the country. The Irish, to whom we are so much indebted for our internal improvements, and each of the other nationalities, have laid our country under obligations she will repay a hundred fold; and in thus emphasizing the Scandinavian, we would not be understood as depreciating the others. More space than we can here afford would be required to present, even in outline, the features of Germany in America, as has already been done by Frederick Kapp. The average valuation of the Scandinavian emigrants, including the amount of money brought with them, has been estimated at one thousand one hundred dollars each; justifying the policy of establishing State Bureaus of Immigration, whose officers are charged with the duty of faithfully presenting the advantages of different sections through printed information and responsible agents; of securing desirable land for occupation, and guarding settlers from the thousand impositions to which they are otherwise subjected.

Thirty-three per cent. of the population of the entire Pacific

States and Territories are of foreign birth; 47 per cent. born of foreign parents, over one half having foreign father or mother. Of these, California has about 38 per cent. of foreign birth, 52 per cent. born of foreign parents, and 58 per cent. having a foreign father or mother; Nevada, 60 per cent. ditto; Oregon, 22 per cent.; Washington Territory, 36 per cent.; Utah, 70 per cent.; Wisconsin, 71 per cent.; Minnesota, 66 per cent. The wonderful advancement of the latter States, in material wealth and social progress, furnishes conclusive evidence of the value of immigration. The value of immigrants as creators of wealth depends upon their intelligence and skill. In a company of 8,000, from nearly every nationality in the north of Europe, was found 230 farmers, 1,346 laborers, 81 carpenters, 26 joiners, 12 masons, 41 painters, 12 blacksmiths, 10 clergymen, 34 clerks, 8 gas-fitters, 14 plumbers, 10 printers, 120 seamen, 39 shoe-makers, 7 spinners, 8 tailors, 4 teachers, 9 tinsmiths, 16 weavers, 21 seamstresses, 21 dress-makers, 4 tailoresses, 4 nurses and 1 book-binder, besides 480 female servants, with 785 males and 3,000 females without special occupations.

The Pacific coast offers the richest field for the immigrant. It has room for whole colonies in its nooks and corners; while millions of acres wait to be reclaimed and converted into homes for a teeming population. By some coöperative system, immigrants could pay for these lands in labor employed in the construction of levees. The same is true of large tracts of land in the interior and southern portions of the State, where canals and irrigating ditches will be required.

The community and village systems of farming, which is carried out in some of the European States, is likely to be imitated here, as it has already been at Anaheim, in Los Angeles county, and in the older sectarian colonies of Pennsylvania.

All things considered, Vineland is perhaps the most signal success in drawing off the over-crowded population of cities, and setting them at work upon the land; and it is unquestionably the most prosperous community in the United States. The site fixed upon by the projector of Vineland, Mr. C. K. Landis, was a spot about thirty-five miles from Philadelphia, known as the New Jersey Barrens, owned by one of the railroads, and valued at $5 per acre.

It was a rolling sand prairie, so light and thin that without summer rains it would have been blown away centuries ago.

Small scrub pines and oaks covered it; very little of it had ever been cultivated; from its unpastured wastes only checker-berries and bunches of trailing arbutus came into the Philadelphia market in early spring. Now, California cannot outvie in size and quality the fruit shows from Vineland, to be seen daily on Market street, the luscious strawberries, peaches, melons—or the fresh vegetables.

When Mr. Landis bought his 16,000 acres of the railroad company and set himself to laying out a town, the Chester county farmers laughed in their sleeves. The place could be abundantly watered, but "all the manure in the State of Pennsylvania" was apparently necessary to ensure its productiveness. There was much speculation as to whether it was not merely a dodge of the railroad to raise money on worthless land, from people whose eye-teeth had never been cut.

The site of the town was central on the track, thirty-four miles from Philadelphia, and was laid out in lots of from one to four acres. Outside the limits it was divided into plats of from ten to fifty acres, according to the distance. Mr. Landis for years never raised on his original price—$25 per acre. He gave credit for two thirds of the purchase-money—obtained a "no fence law" for the entire domain—made a few excellent roads, and settlers began to appear. The terms of the sale included an agreement to put up a dwelling house within a year, at a certain distance from the street; to plant shade trees on the borders; to clear and put in tillage a certain proportion, and the keeping of a strip of roadside neatly laid down to grass. The streets were thus made boulevards from the beginning, to which each year will give additional beauty. These street improvements were to be perpetually maintained, if neglected by individuals, at the cost of the property owners, and only live fences were used. Speculation in uncultivated lands, which has been the bane of other settlements, never has occurred in Vineland, the advance in value invariably being upon the improvements of actual settlers, whether permanent or otherwise. Four cardinal principles were subscribed to by every purchaser, which Mr. Landis had laid down for his own guidance:

1. No land to be sold to speculators, but to persons agreeing to improve in a certain time and way.

2. No fences to be required.

3. The public sale of intoxicating drinks should be prohibited, by an annual vote of the people.

4. The maintenance of the best schools.

In a speech before the Legislature of New Jersey last year, Mr. Landis says his temperance regulation was made, not from philanthropy, "but simply from the conviction of its importance to the success of the colony. I was not a temperance man myself," he says, "in the total abstinence sense of the term. In conversation with the settlers, I never treated the subject of liquor-selling as a moral question—probably not one tenth of the voters of Vineland are total abstinence men. The law has been practically in operation since 1861, though the Vineland local option law did not pass till 1863. The vote has always stood against license by an overwhelming majority, there being generally from two to nine votes in favor of liquor-selling."

In twelve years there was a population of eleven thousand, mostly from New England. Fourteen thousand, and within the last year, twenty-three thousand acres have been added to the original tract. This colony was started just at the commencement of the civil war, and has paid sixty thousand dollars of the debt, besides sending its quota to the field. It has built one hundred and seventy-eight miles of excellent roads, twenty school-houses, ten churches, four post-offices, fifteen manufacturing establishments, besides shops and stores, such as would be required by a similar population elsewhere. In the importance of its agricultural productions Landis township ranks the fourth in New Jersey. There are seventeen miles of railways on the tract, and six stations.

If any one would know whether temperance and education are sufficient safeguards against crime, let him read the statistics of the police and poor expenses of this settlement for the last six years:

POLICE EXPENSES.		POOR EXPENSES.	
1867	$50	1867	$400
1868	50	1868	425
1869	75	1869	425
1870	75	1870	350
1871	150	1871	400
1872	25	1872	350

The sheriff of Vineland says, the poor-tax in the township

amounts to five cents per annum for each inhabitant, the police expenses to half a cent!

Have we not here a possible solution of the problem which has vexed many a lover of his kind, viz., how to preserve intact the sanctity of the individual home, while securing the fullest advantages of social union?

The Greeley colony in Colorado furnishes another proof of the entire practicability of carrying out the colonial plan without requiring a religious or sectarian qualification for membership.

"The social and political problem is the incorporation of the entire population into society;" it is the mission of the Patrons to aid in this, by creating a true social spirit among the great class of laborers to which they belong. Leaving Roman luxury and Roman licentiousness to nations in their childhood or their dotage, we believe there is a higher relation than that of landlord and tenant, viz., the relation of founder and partner, and that capital and culture, as well as labor, will only reach their highest uses in helping men to live nobly, simply and peacefully with each other.

In the forming of new colonies the last will be first in respect to results, for it can avoid the mistakes and profit by the experiences of the rest. A diversity of employments should be aimed at in the community and for the individual; not for regular business, perhaps, but to multiply resources in case of need, and because this brings out and utilizes all the faculty of the community.

The agricultural communities of the future, whether separately organized or not, will undoubtedly be less sectarian in religion, less partisan in politics, less contracted by traditions and habits of nation or race. An honorable and emulous class interest will be their distinguishing characteristic; they, with all the other great classes of laboring men, will "lay the foundations of an everlasting commonwealth, whose power shall be manhood; whose organization, a model State; whose spirit, religion; whose weapon, suffrage; whose conservatism, education; whose objects are freedom of industry as well as of opinion, order, economy and peace within the State, and an eternal brotherhood with those who are our wider neighbors."

CHAPTER XXXII.

SELECTED POETRY FOR THE GRANGE.

THE GRANGER'S POLITICS.

"Peace on earth, and good will to men."

The word of the Lord by night,
 To the watching pilgrims came,
As they sat by the sea-side,
 And filled their hearts with flame.

God said, I am tired of kings,
 I suffer them no more;
Up to my ear the morning brings
 The outrage of the poor.

Think ye I made this ball
 A field of havoc and war,
Where tyrants great and tyrants small
 Might harry the weak and poor?

My angel, his name is Freedom,
 Choose him to be your king;
He shall cut pathways east and west,
 And fend you with his wing.

Lo! I uncover the land
 Which I hid of old time in the west,
As the sculptor uncovers the statue
 When he has wrought his best.

I will divide my goods;
 Call in the wretch and slave;
None shall rule but the humble,
 And none but toil shall have.

I will have never a noble,
 No lineage counted great;
Fishers and choppers and plowmen
 Shall constitute a State.

Go cut down trees in the forest,
 And trim the straightest boughs;
Cut down trees in the forest,
 And build me a wooden house.

Call the people together;
 The young men and the sires,
The reaper from the harvest field,
 Hireling, and him that hires.

*From the Ode, and Boston Hymn.—*By R. W. Emerson.*

O, North! give him beauty for rags,
  And honor, O, South! for his shame;
Nevada! coin thy silver crags
  With Freedom's image and name.

I cause from every creature
  His proper good to flow;
As much as he is, and doeth,
  So much shall he bestow.

But, laying hands on another,
  To coin his labor and sweat,
He goes in pawn to his victim,
  For eternal years in debt.

And here, in a pine State-house,
  They shall choose men to rule
In every needful faculty,
  In Church, and State, and School.

The men are ripe of Saxon kind
  To build an equal State—
To take the statute from the mind,
  And make of duty, fate.

United States! the ages plead—
  Present and Past in under-song;
Go, put your creed into your deed,
  Nor speak with double tongue.

Be just at home; then write your scroll
  Of honor o'er the sea;
And bid the broad Atlantic roll
  A ferry of the free.

And henceforth there shall be no chain
  Save underneath the sea;
And wires shall murmur through the main
  Sweet songs of LIBERTY.

The conscious stars accord above,
  The waters wild below,
And under, through the cable wove,
  Her fiery errands go.

For He that worketh high and wise,
  Nor pauses in His plan,
Will take the sun out of the skies
  Ere freedom out of man.

THE GRANGER'S RELIGION.

"In essentials, Unity; in non-essentials, Liberty; in all things, Charity."

"Blessed Jesus, give us common sense, and let no man put blinkers on us that we can only see in a certain direction; for we want to look around the horizon; yea, to the highest heavens, and the lowest depths of the ocean."—*Father Taylor's Prayer*.

NO SECT IN HEAVEN.*

Talking of sects till late one eve,
Of the various doctrines the saints believe,
That night I stood in a troubled dream
By the side of a darkly flowing stream.

And a Churchman down to the river came,
When I heard a strange voice call his name:
"Good father, stop; when you cross this tide
You must leave your robes on the other side."

But the aged father did not mind,
And his long gown floated out behind,
As down to the stream his way he took,
His pale hands clasping a gilt-edged book.

"I'm bound for heaven, and when I'm there
I shall want my book of common prayer;
And though I put on my starry crown,
I should feel quite lost without my gown."

Then he fixed his eyes on the shining track,
But his gown was heavy and held him back;
And the poor old father tried in vain
A single step in the flood to gain.

I saw him again on the other side,
And his silk gown floated on the tide;
And no one asked, in that blissful spot,
Whether he belonged to "the church" or not.

Then down to the river a Quaker strayed,
His dress of a sober hue was made.
"My coat and hat must be all of gray;
I cannot go any other way."

* Author unknown.

Then he buttoned his coat straight up to his chin,
And steadily, solemnly waded in;
And his broad-brimmed hat he pulled down tight
Over his forehead, cold and white.

But a strong wind carried away his hat;
A moment he silently sighed over that,
And then, as he gazed to the farther shore,
The coat slipped off, and was seen no more.

As he entered heaven, his suit of gray
Went quietly sailing away, away;
And none of the angels questioned him
About the width of his beaver's brim.

Next came Dr. Watts, with a bundle of psalms
Tied nicely up in his aged arms;
And hymns as many—a very wise thing,
That the people in heaven "all round" might sing

But I thought that he heaved an anxious sigh,
As he saw that the river ran broad and high;
And looked surprised as, one by one,
The psalms and hymns in the waves went down.

And after him, with his MSS.,
Came Wesley, the pattern of godliness—
But he: "dear me, what shall I do?
The water has soaked them through and through.

And then on the river far and wide,
Away they went down the swollen tide,
And the saint, astonished, went through alone,
Without his manuscript, up to the Throne.

Then, gravely walking, two saints by name,
Down to the stream together came;
But as they stopped by the river's brink,
I saw one saint from the other shrink.

"Sprinkled or plunged, may I ask you, friend,
How you attained to life's great end?"
"*Thus*, with a few drops on my brow."
"But I've been dipped, as you see me now;

And I really think, it will hardly do,
As I'm close-communion, to cross with you;
You're bound, I know, to the realms of bliss,
But you must go that way, and I'll go this."

Then straightway plunging with all his might
Away to the left, his friend to the right,
Apart they went from this world of sin,
But at last together they entered in.

And now, when the river was rolling on,
A Presbyterian church went down:
Of women there seemed an innumerable throng,
But the men I could count as they went along.

And concerning the road, they could never agree,
The *old* or the *new* way, which it could be;
Nor ever a moment paused to think,
That both would lead to the river's brink.

And a sound of murmuring, long and loud,
Came ever up from the moving crowd:
"You're in the old way, I'm in the new,
That is the false, and this is the true."

But the *brethren* only seemed to speak,
Modest the sisters walked, and meek;
And if ever one of them chanced to say
What troubles she met with on the way;

How she longed to pass to the other side,
Nor feared to cross o'er the swelling tide,
A voice arose from the brethren then:
"Let no one speak but the 'holy men;'

For have ye not heard the words of Paul?
'Oh! let the women keep silence all.'"
I watched them long in my curious dream,
Till they stood by the borders of the stream;

Then, just as I thought, the two ways met;
But all the brethren were talking yet,
And would talk on till the heaving tide
Carried them over side by side;

Side by side, for the way was one;
The tiresome journey of life was done;
And Priest and Quaker, and all who died,
Came out alike on the other side.

No forms, or crosses, or books had they;
No gowns of silk or suits of gray;
No creeds to guide them, or MSS.,
For all had put on Christ's righteousness.

A CENTENNIAL HYMN.

BY JOHN GREENLEAF WHITTIER.

This day, one hundred years ago,
The wild grape by the river's side,
And tasteless groundnut trailing low,
The table of the woods supplied.

Unknown the apple's red and gold,
The blushing tint of peach and pear;
The mirror of the river told
No tale of orchards ripe and rare.

Wild as the fruits he scorned to till,
These vales the idle Indian trod;
Nor knew the glad, creative skill,—
The joy of him who toils with God.

O! Painter of the fruits and flowers!
We thank Thee for thy wise design
Whereby these human hands of ours
In nature's garden work with thine.

And thanks that from our daily need
The joy of simple faith is born;
That he who smites the summer weed
May trust Thee for the autumn corn.

The fools their gold, and knaves their power;
Let fortune's bubbles rise and fall;
Who sows a field, or trains a flower,
Or plants a tree, is more than all.

For he who blesses most is blest;
And God and man shall own his worth
Who toils to leave, as his bequest,
An added beauty to the earth.

And, soon or late, to all that sow,
The time of harvest shall be given;
The flower shall bloom, the fruit shall grow,
If not on earth, at last in heaven!

THE REAPER'S DREAM; OR, THE CELESTIAL HARVEST FEAST.

BY T. BUCHANAN READ.

The road was lone, the grass was dank
With night dews on the briery bank,
Whereon a weary reaper sank.
His garb was old; his visage tanned;
The rusty sickle in his hand
Could find no work in all the land.

He saw the evening's chilly star
Above his native vale afar;
A moment on the horizon's bar
It hung, then sank, as with a sigh;
And there the crescent moon went by,
An empty sickle down the sky.

To soothe his pain, sleep's tender palm
Laid on his brow its touch of balm;
His brain received the slumberous calm;
And soon that angel without name,
Her robe a dream, her face the same,
The giver of sweet visions, came.

She touched his eyes; no longer sealed,
They saw a troop of reapers wield
Their swift blades in a ripened field.
At each thrust of their snowy sleeves
A thrill ran through the future sheaves,
Rustling like rain on forest leaves.

They were not brawny men who bowed,
With harvest voices, rough and loud,
But spirits, moving as a cloud.
Like little lightnings in their hold,
The silver sickles manifold
Slid musically through the gold.

O, bid the morning stars combine
To match the chorus, clear and fine,
That rippled lightly down the line,—
A cadence of celestial rhyme,
The language of that cloudless clime,
To which their shining hands kept time.

Behind them lay the gleaming rows,
Like those long clouds the sun-set shows
On amber meadows of repose;
But, like a wind, the binders bright
Soon followed in their mirthful might.
And swept them into sheaves of light.

Doubling the splendor of the plain,
There rolled the great celestial wain,
To gather in the fallen grain.
Its frame was built of golden bars;
Its glowing wheels were lit with stars;
The royal harvest's car of cars.

The snowy yoke that drew the load,
On gleaming hoofs of silver trode;
And music was its only goad.
To no command of word or beck
It moved, and felt no other check
Than one white arm laid on the neck,

The neck, whose light was overwound
With bells of lilies, ringing round
Their odors till the air was drowned:
The starry foreheads meekly borne,
With garlands looped from horn to horn,
Shone like the many-colored morn.

The field was cleared. Home went the bands,
Like children, linking happy hands,
While singing through their father's lands;
Or, arm about each other thrown,
With amber tresses backward blown,
They moved as they were music's own.

The vision brightened more and more;
He saw the garner's glowing door,
And sheaves, like sunshine, strew the floor,--
The floor was jasper,—golden flails,
Swift sailing as a whirlwind sails,
Throbbed mellow music down the vales.

He saw the mansion,—all repose,—
Great corridors and porticos,
Propped with the columns, shining rows;
And these—for beauty was the rule—
The polished pavements, hard and cool,
Redoubled, like a crystal pool.

And there the odorous feast was spread·
The fruity fragrance, widely shed,
Seemed to the floating music wed;
Seven angels, like the Pleiad seven,
Their lips to silver clarions given,
Blew welcome round the walls of heaven.

In skyey garments, silky thin,
The clad retainers floated in
A thousand forms, and yet no din:
And from the visage of the Lord,
Like splendor from the Orient poured,
A smile illumined all the board.

Far flew the music's circling sound;
Then floated back, with soft rebound,
To join, not mar, the converse round,—
Sweet notes, that, melting, still increased
Such as ne'er cheered the bridal feast
Of king in the enchanted East.

Did any great door ope or close,
It seemed the birth-time of repose;
The faint sound died where it arose;
And they who passed from door to door,
Their soft feet on the polished floor
Meet their soft shadows,—nothing more.

Then once again the groups were drawn
Through corridors, or down the lawn,
Which bloomed in beauty like a dawn.
Where countless fountains leapt alway,
Veiling their silver heights in spray,
The choral people held their way.

There, midst the brightest, brightly shone
Dear forms he loved in years agone,—
The earliest loved—the earliest flown.
He heard a mother's sainted tongue;
A sister's voice, who vanished young,
While one still dearer sweetly sung.

No further might the scene unfold;
The gazer's voice could not withhold;
The very rapture made him bold;
He cried aloud, with claspéd hands,
"O, happy fields! O, happy bands!
Who reap the never-failing lands.

"Oh! master of these broad estates,
Behold before your very gates
A worn and waiting laborer waits!
Let me but toil amid your grain,
Or be a gleaner on the plain,
So I may leave these fields of pain!

"A gleaner, I will follow far,
With never word or look to mar,
Behind the Harvest's yellow car;
All day my hand shall constant be;
And every happy eve shall see
The precious burden borne to thee!"

At morn some reapers neared the place,
Strong men, whose feet recoiled apace;
Then gathering round the upturned face,
They saw the lines of pain and care,
Yet read in the expression there
The look as of an answered prayer.

THE GRANGER'S DOXOLOGY.

We thank Thee for the men who lead,
  Who fight our cause with tongue and pen,
Whose love to Thee, best shown in deed,
  Breaks forth in ardent love to men.

We thank Thee, that from north to south,
  From east to west the flame has spread,
And that the breathing from thy mouth
  Has kindled unto life the dead.

Lord, make us patient, as Thou art,
  Yet constant to thy great design;
From thoughts of vengeance keep each heart;
  Justice and love are both divine.

More men, more manhood now accord;
  Make us more worthy to be free;
Where dwells the Spirit of the Lord,
  There is the home of liberty.

INDEX.

www.ingramcontent.com/pod-product-compliance
Lightning Source LLC
LaVergne TN
LVHW020931110826
845150LV00004B/831
9781425552800